Inside
Canadian
Politics

Inside
Canadian
Politics

Second Edition

Alex Marland | Jared J. Wesley

OXFORD
UNIVERSITY PRESS

OXFORD
UNIVERSITY PRESS

Oxford University Press is a department of the University of Oxford.
It furthers the University's objective of excellence in research, scholarship,
and education by publishing worldwide. Oxford is a registered trade mark of
Oxford University Press in the UK and in certain other countries.

Published in Canada by
Oxford University Press
8 Sampson Mews, Suite 204,
Don Mills, Ontario M3C 0H5 Canada

www.oupcanada.com

Library and Archives Canada Cataloguing in Publication
Title: Inside Canadian politics / Alex Marland and Jared J. Wesley.
Names: Marland, Alexander J., 1973- author. | Wesley, Jared J., 1980- author.
Description: Second edition. | Includes bibliographical references and index.
Identifiers: Canadiana (print) 20190189932 | Canadiana (ebook) : 20190189940 | ISBN 9780199032624
(softcover) | ISBN 9780199039234 (looseleaf) | ISBN 9780199032679 (EPUB)
Subjects: LCSH: Canada—Politics and government—Textbooks. | LCGFT: Textbooks.
Classification: LCC JL75 .M42 2020 | DDC 320.971—dc23

Cover images: (clockwise from top right) THE CANADIAN PRESS/Andrew Vaughan,
©Marc Bruxelle/Shutterstock, ©Andreas Prott/Shutterstock, George Rose/Getty Images
Cover design: Laurie McGregor
Interior design: Sherill Chapman

Oxford University Press is committed to our environment.
This book is printed on Forest Stewardship Council®
certified paper and comes from responsible sources.

Printed and bound in Canada

1 2 3 4 — 23 22 21 20

Contents at a Glance

Contents

3   Federalism   66

6 The Legislature 165

7 The Justice System 213

8   Public Policy and the Bureaucracy   248

PART II | Politics and Democracy   289

9   Political Parties   290

10   Elections and Voting   329

11   Media and Communication   369

12   Interest Groups and Social Movements   407

13 Diversity and Representation   437

14 Canada in the World   468

Figures and Tables

Figures

Tables

Preface

Why Getting Inside Canadian Politics Matters

Canadian politics is generally peaceful, respectful of order, and characterized by good government. In other parts of the world there are pitched political battles: government corruption, fights over inequality, systemic discrimination, food shortages, human rights abuses, state control of the media, constitutional crises, leadership coups, and civil wars. Canada features its share of political arguments and struggles. However, compared with most countries, politics in this country is one of rhythm and predictability.

Approximately every four years Canadians vote in national elections. Three or more main political parties compete for votes. The parties make campaign promises and, once elected, do relatively little to alter the course of Canadian history. Governing parties seldom garner the support of half of eligible voters, yet few citizens question their full authority to lead, even as some call for democratic reform. Prime ministers wield considerable authority in this system, flanked by supportive ministers and obedient backbench legislators, and a public service that follows a clear chain of command. Senators, opposition members of the legislature, journalists, activists, and especially judges hold them in check from time to time. The expression "peace, order, and good government" describes Canadian political culture for a reason.

This framework allows for the interplay between concepts such as liberalism, regionalism, multiculturalism, feminism, and colonialism. This makes for intriguing inconsistencies and can produce unexpected alliances in Canada. Indigenous leaders might dissuade community members from voting in federal, provincial, and territorial elections. Political elites might struggle to reconcile religious freedoms with individual choice or freedom of expression with the protection of marginalized groups. The Queen's representative might be faced with choosing whether to appoint an opposition leader as first minister or requiring a general election. Age-old conventions such as cabinet solidarity and party discipline compete with the demands of a shortening news cycle and social media firestorms. The federal government somehow surmounts trade obstacles with international partners with much greater ease than lowering barriers among Canadian provinces. With a greater awareness of what happens inside Canadian politics, you begin to appreciate its complexity and delicate nature.

Structure of *Inside Canadian Politics*

This thoroughly updated edition of *Inside Canadian Politics* integrates new information drawn from the period after Justin Trudeau became Canada's twenty-third prime minister. Among our objectives in preparing this second edition was to improve the book's readability. We rewrote anything in the first edition that we believed was unnecessarily complex and sought to present it in a clearer fashion. We gave the book a solid edit to cut down on unnecessary words and slimmed down content and definitions that detract from what students really need to know. The only names, dates, and numerical data that we kept are ones that we believe readers ought to be aware of. We prioritized discussing seminal events over recent minutiae that may no longer be relevant by the time you are reading this book. We expanded concepts and added new ones that deserve more attention. The result, we hope, is an even more engaging read that is filled with enduring insights that you can apply to other courses and current events. We are optimistic that this revised edition will equip you with information about Canadian politics and challenge you to make informed judgements about a variety of topics.

Each chapter begins with some general questions. What are the politics surrounding the Charter of Rights and Freedoms? How do political cultures vary across the country? How are legislatures structured and organized? How do governments pay for public-policy initiatives? What types of political parties exist? What kinds of activities occur during election campaigns? How do social movements impact Canadian politics? How does Canada participate in improving the global community? These are just some of the many topics explored in the book.

The chapters get you started with a set of three maxims to guide your understanding of the topic being explored. You should know, for example, that the average citizen has many opportunities to make a difference in Canadian politics (Chapter 1), that there is much more to the justice system than courtrooms and judges (Chapter 7), that politicians are not required to answer journalists' questions (Chapter 11), and that Canada has more success negotiating free-trade agreements internationally than it does among its own provinces (Chapter 14). These maxims are useful anchors that help you comprehend the subject matter that follows.

Throughout the book you will notice bolded terms. The **bold** typeface signals that we believe a concept is worth knowing. Its definition is found in the page margin and in the glossary of terms at the back of the book. Periodically you will come across Briefing Note boxes that explain concepts in greater detail.

Stories appear in the Inside Canadian Politics boxes. These features outline concepts in action and show how politics works in practice. They present useful case studies.

A new feature in the second edition is a Professor Profile section found toward the end of each chapter. We reached out to a variety of professors across Canada and asked what they remember from their first Canadian political science course. We wanted to know what attracts them to study politics and what study tips they would relay to students. These profiles will introduce you to some of the many people who research and teach about topics that are discussed in this book.

Each chapter concludes with an Up for Debate supplement that outlines a topical controversy and shows how differing approaches can lead to differences of opinion on divisive issues. You will get the most out of the book and your course if you engage with others about what you read. These Up for Debate supplements are intended for in-class discussion and seminar break-outs. We hope you will consider taking the discussion to the coffee shop or bar, raising it at the kitchen table, or possibly engaging about it in an online forum. We preview each debate topic at the start of the chapter so you can keep the question in mind as you read.

Throughout the book we treat Indigenous and non-Indigenous politics as part of a common Canadian political system. We purposely incorporate the discussion of Indigenous politics into the various themes covered in this book. This approach is an unsettled question among Canadian political scientists and therefore we challenge you to think critically about this treatment. The Professor Profile in Chapter 1 and the Up for Debate supplement at the end of Chapter 13 encourage discussion about this issue.

Two resources are presented in the book's final pages. The First Ministers in Canada appendix lists a chronology of prime ministers and premiers so that you can situate which leaders and which parties were in power at a given period. This information can be insightful as you read the book and are trying to understand interparty and federal-provincial-territorial dynamics at the time of a political event. The Glossary is a convenient reference tool that compiles all of the definitions of bolded terms. We encourage you to supplement these resources by consulting the Constitution Act, 1982, and the Charter of Rights and Freedoms, 1982, which are easily found online.

Overview of the Chapters

The core concepts, maxims, stories, and debates will prepare you for delving more deeply inside Canadian politics. The text is complemented by photographs and cartoons, illustrative charts and figures, and innovative infographics, all meant to reinforce and build on themes developed in the main narrative. Here is an overview of what you can expect from each chapter.

Part I focuses on structures of government and governance in Canada. It begins with Chapter 1, which is an overview of Canadian politics. It will introduce you to fundamental concepts such as democracy, politics, power, and government. It then delves into three overarching elements that we believe every student should know about the cleavages, institutions and history of Canadian politics. This includes tracing politics from the mid-1700s to today. Along the way the chapter touches on fundamentals such as left-wing and right-wing politics, the names of major Canadian political parties, and the Charter of Rights and Freedoms.

Chapter 2 takes you inside Canada's constitution, examining the democratic principles and institutional components that lie at its core. You will learn about the intricate compromises and delicate nuances involved in crafting the country's highest law. You will read about the perils of constitutional politics in a country challenged by the often competing demands of federalism and human rights. The chapter concludes with a debate as to whether changes to the Canadian constitution should be easier to make than current amending formulas allow.

Chapter 3 examines the structure of Canadian federalism in greater depth, tracing Canada's evolution from one of the most highly centralized to one of the most highly decentralized systems in the world. The discussion includes the politics of fiscal federalism and the tensions that accompany the distribution of wealth among Canadian governments. This leads to a debate on whether federalism is working.

Chapter 4 applies a sharper geographic lens to our understanding of Canadian politics. With a special focus on Quebec, it compares the main varieties of regionalism in Canada and discusses their impact on the past, present, and future of Canadian unity. It explores the forces of political culture across the country. The chapter ends by asking whether regionalism is pulling Canada apart.

Chapter 5 offers a glimpse inside the seat of power in Canadian politics: the executive. From the Queen and her representatives, to the prime minister and premiers, to the bureaucracy—all elements of Canada's executive branch play leading and interconnected roles. While they provide checks and balances on each other, and while other institutions are designed to hold them democratically accountable, the question at the conclusion of the chapter remains valid: do Canadian prime ministers and premiers have too much power?

Chapter 6 throws open the doors of Canada's legislatures. The discussion goes beyond the process of a bill becoming law to study the dynamics of partisanship on the rules and business surrounding the legislative process. In particular, the topic of debate surrounds the necessity of strict party discipline in Parliament and the provincial/territorial legislatures. This leads to a chapter on the third and final branch of the Canadian political system.

Chapter 7 goes beyond the conventional examination of the judiciary to expose the inner workings of Canada's broader justice system as a whole. After examining the core principles of Canadian justice and the specific, interconnected roles of judges, Crown attorneys, the police, and corrections officials, the chapter concludes with a debate on the effectiveness of mandatory minimum sentences for criminal offenders.

Chapter 8 takes us back inside the world of the bureaucracy to address the state of public policy and public administration in Canada. The conversation ranges from the role of ideology in the development of government programs and services—those that are part of the social safety net—to the specific processes and challenges involved in creating or changing elements of public policy. To this end, the chapter closes by asking whether all government jobs should be based on merit or whether there is room for political patronage.

Chapter 9 opens Part II, on politics and democracy. It kick-starts a series of discussions about electoral politics and representation in Canada, focusing on political parties. The chapter outlines the various types of political parties operating in Canada today and traces each party's roots to the late eighteenth century. Connecting this conversation to broader issues of democratic diversity, the closing debate surrounds the ability of parties to recruit members of underrepresented and marginalized groups.

Chapter 10 builds on this discussion, focusing on the fundamental democratic values, ideals, and rules underpinning Canadian elections. The chapter assesses how well the electoral system, redistricting processes, campaign finance regulations, and other laws align with the often high-minded norms of democracy. It explores the factors that influence how people vote. The chapter describes how local and national election and referendum campaigns are waged, closing with a debate on whether such campaigns even matter to the functioning of Canadian democracy.

Chapter 11 ties these conversations to the nature of media and political communication in Canada. The practices and biases of news construction and media management are exposed. An introduction to access to information is followed by a rare discussion of the strategies and tactics involved in political marketing today. The capstone debate asks whether social media makes Canadian democracy better or worse.

Chapter 12 steps outside the conventional realm of electoral politics to address the function of political activism in Canada. The roles of interest groups and social movements are discussed, with a particular focus on their performance in lobbying governments to effect political change. With this in mind, the chapter asks to what extent spending by interest groups should be regulated.

Chapter 13 provides a high-level assessment of Canada's ability to promote diversity and representation for all its citizens, taking all of the material in the preceding chapters into account. Specifically, it evaluates the state of Canada's democratic deficit against the backdrop of the country's multicultural mosaic and its constitutional commitment to uphold the inherent right to self-government for Indigenous peoples. The concluding debate asks whether Indigenous and non-Indigenous politics belong in the same political system.

Chapter 14 concludes the book by looking at the broadly interconnected themes of political economy, security, and global affairs. The chapter provides useful perspective on how Canada positions itself in the broader global community and offers valuable context for the sorts of divisions that define the country's internal politics. The final debate of the book asks a pressing question that strikes at the heart of Canadian identity: should Canada give more money for foreign aid?

Together these chapters provide a high-level glimpse inside the world of Canadian politics. The journey begins with the structural components—the institutions and other building blocks—of Canadian democracy, gradually working toward the more behavioural aspects of day-to-day Canadian politics. As you begin learning about Canadian politics, try complementing what you read in these pages by drawing on current information from news sources like *The Globe and Mail*, CBC *News*, or perhaps *The Hill Times*. See what's trending at the #cdnpoli Twitter hashtag. Talk with your peers to see if they have the same reactions to Canadian news stories and political debates that you do. Chances are, you will be exposed to different opinions, and you'll be on your way to getting *Inside Canadian Politics*.

A Word of Thanks

A lot of people participate in publishing a textbook like this. We wish to acknowledge the many external referees across Canada who took time to point out ways to improve the previous edition and who identified opportunities to adjust the revised manuscript. We are committed to producing a quality book and acted on every suggestion wherever possible.

We would like to thank all the professors who agreed to be profiled. We have been fortunate to work with many capable professionals at Oxford University Press, including Stephen Kotowych, Leah-Ann Lymer, Emily Kring, and Lisa Ball; Susan Bindernagel, copy editor; and student research assistants Clare Buckley, Hannah Loder, and Rissa Reist.

Finally, we want to thank you for reading. We hope that something in this book will inspire you to get involved in your political community so that you may learn firsthand about the inner workings of Canadian politics.

From the Publisher

Oxford University Press is pleased to bring you the second edition of *Inside Canadian Politics*, a fresh perspective on the institutions and issues at the heart of Canada's political system. Written by scholars with experience working in public administration, the text explores key topics in Canadian politics—from federalism, regionalism, and diversity, to the party system, media and communication, and elections. Along the way, students are encouraged to discuss and debate the effectiveness of government mechanisms in the daily lives of Canadians. This second edition has been fully updated to include the political realities of Canada today, including discussion of fake news, the effects of social media on democracy, and the renegotiation of crucial trade agreements.

sources of confusion. The following pages examine these and other topics in Canadian federalism. When reading this chapter, be sure to keep in mind the following maxims of federalism in Canada.

✔ Federalism encompasses more than the constitution. While providing a necessary legal foundation for Canadian federalism, sections 91 and 92 of the Constitution Act, 1867, do not paint a comprehensive picture of the balance of power today. By virtue of court decisions and major economic and demographic shifts, Canadian federalism has evolved considerably since Confederation, and it continues to evolve with every global crisis, every leadership change, and other major developments.

✔ Federalism involves more than the premiers and prime minister. To the general public, first ministers' conferences offer evidence that the premiers and prime minister are working together, or not. Since the failure of the 1992 Charlottetown Accord, meetings between the prime minister and premiers have been infrequent, and much Canadian federalism now takes place at the bureaucratic level. New actors, including city and Indigenous governments, are pushing the boundaries of federalism, intergovernmental relations, and multi-level governance in Canada.

✔ Federalism is about more than dividing up resources. Canada's provinces are constantly at odds with each other and the federal government over how best to distribute funding across the country. Fiscal arrangements, like equalization and health transfers, tend to dominate debates. Canadian governments have come together to forge an economic union that extends to social and environmental collaboration as well.

UP FOR DEBATE

Is federalism working in Canada?

Keep this question in mind as you read through the chapter. Consult the end-of-chapter debate supplement for more material to help you engage in an informed discussion of the topic.

The Story of Federalism in Canada

Federalism in Context

Canada's system of government is an amalgam of those of the United Kingdom and the United States. When the United States of America was formed, it brought 13 colonies together into a single federation. A national government would be responsible for policy matters that required central coordination, such as military defence, while individual states such as New York and South Carolina would have the authority to respond to local policy concerns. The American constitution ceded a limited number of powers to the central government based in Washington, DC, with state governments retaining the lion's share of sovereignty in the new republic.

This differed from the **unitary system** of government in place in the United Kingdom, where political decisions were foremost made out of London, and where there was no written constitution to devolve powers to local authorities (see Figure 3.1). Over time, Britain

unitary system
A political system featuring a central government that chooses what powers to devolve to regional bodies.

3 Federalism

Inside This Chapter

- What is federalism, and why was it chosen as a foundation of Canadian democracy?
- How does federalism function in Canada, and who are the major actors?
- How has Canadian federalism evolved over time?

Inside Canadian Federalism

Federalism is a system of government. It enables subnational governments to be responsive to local concerns while pooling resources and ceding some autonomy to achieve a set of common, overarching objectives. Federalism helps keep diverse countries like Canada together—despite regular conflict and competitiveness among regions (see Chapter 4). It is one of the defining features of Canadian democracy and can be one of the biggest

A Guided Tour

Contemporary and accessible, *Inside Canadian Politics* delivers a variety of features designed to get students thinking—and talking— about the issues at the heart of Canadian politics.

Up for Debate

Should Indigenous and non-Indigenous politics be considered as part of a common political system?

THE CLAIM: YES, THEY SHOULD!

Both Indigenous and non-Indigenous politics are integral to our understanding of the broader Canadian political system to which they belong.

Yes: Argument Summary

It is time to stop treating Indigenous politics as separate and apart from non-Indigenous politics in Canada. Far from assimilating Indigenous perspectives into the broader Canadian society, considering the two worldviews as part of a common political system helps foster a common understanding among both sides of the conventional cleavage. The segregation of Indigenous and non-Indigenous politics is counterintuitive given the extent to which both worlds have merged in recent decades. It is also politically counterproductive, because it perpetuates an ages-old division in Canadian society.

Yes: Top 5 Considerations

1. Indigenous politics is part of the mainstream discourse and a fundamental component of the institution of Canadian democracy. This is particularly true of the notion of treaty rights and the inherent right to self-government, which are entrenched in common government practice.
2. As evidenced in each chapter of this book, thanks to advances in scholarship and the progress achieved by Indigenous leaders, it is increasingly difficult to discuss the evolution and present state of Canadian politics without explicit and detailed discussion of the influence of Indigenous peoples. To leave Indigenous peoples out of core discussions about the constitution and core values of representation, or public policy and the courts, would be to miss the major trends and challenges that exist in the system as a whole.
3. Segregation risks a settler colonial approach to ghettoizing Indigenous politics by perpetuating a sense of difference or "otherness." Confining Indigenous politics to a separate chapter in a Canadian politics textbook, for instance, isolates the two sides of the traditional divide, thereby missing an opportunity to build conceptual and political bridges between them.
4. A realistic, pragmatic conceptualization of Indigenous self-government in the twenty-first century involves finding creative ways of integrating, not partitioning, Indigenous and non-Indigenous communities. Successes like the Nisga'a land claims settlement and the establishment of Nunavut are testament to this, as are the 94 calls to action by the Truth and Reconciliation Commission that investigated Canada's residential schools system. They are prime examples of how integrated discussions of Indigenous and non-Indigenous politics improve our understandings and expand the evolution of Canadian politics as a whole.
5. Considering Indigenous and non-Indigenous politics as part of the same political system does not have to mean assimilating the former into the latter. Nor does it mean papering over the disparities between Indigenous peoples and settlers. In fact, only by treating the two traditions as commensurable are we able to integrate Indigenous understandings of and approaches to power, sovereignty, territory, fairness, and diversity into the mainstream of Canadian politics.

Yes: Other Considerations

- When it comes to the core issues of democracy and representation, Indigenous and non-Indigenous politics rest on a shared theoretical foundation. This is why people on both sides of the cleavage find common ground on notions like treaty-making and federalism. The latter owes its origins in large part to the Haudenosaunee Confederacy.

The **Up for Debate feature** at the end of each chapter gives students the tools to dissect a key topic related to the chapter. The debate topic is also previewed at the start of the chapter so that students can keep the question in mind as they read.

Inside Canadian Politics boxes present useful case studies to outline concepts being discussed, and show how politics works in practice. The Vox Pop features also challenge students to take stands on key questions and controversies in Canadian politics today.

74　Part I | Government and Governance

Inside Canadian Politics

What Is at Stake in the Great Pipeline Debates?

Western Canadian oil has been fetching relatively low prices because it cannot be sold on the global market. Existing pipelines send the vast majority of oil sands products to the American Midwest, where a supply glut has forced oil sands companies to sell it for less than they could in Southeast Asian markets.

The impact of lower oil prices on Canadian government revenues is significant. Provincial governments get less in terms of resource royalties, and, along with the federal government, they derive less from personal and corporate income taxes. Lower government revenues may result in fewer government programs—including those that combat climate change.

This is why both the federal and Alberta governments support building, converting, or expanding pipelines, including the Trans Mountain pipeline from northern Alberta to the BC coast. Controversies around Trans Mountain and the failure of other pipeline initiatives raise the question: can one government stand in the way of another when it comes to achieving economic or environmental goals?

Provincial governments like those of Alberta and British Columbia may conduct environmental and regulatory assessments of the leg of the pipeline that runs through their respective jurisdictions. At the same time, the federal government is constitutionally responsible for reviewing all such interprovincial projects, following extensive public hearings by arms-length federal agencies.

The federal government's decision to approve the twinning of the Trans Mountain pipeline, with hundreds of environmental conditions, has been challenged in court. Pipeline opponents, including the BC government, support reducing oil sands production and emissions levels, and preventing oil from travelling through Indigenous and ecologically sensitive lands to vulnerable coastal areas. Pipeline opponents have launched a series of court challenges to stall or halt the project. This obstruction strategy worked, in part, as pipeline owner Kinder Morgan suspended non-essential spending on Trans Mountain in 2018. This prompted the federal and Alberta governments to enter into negotiations with the company to purchase the pipeline project, which Ottawa did for $4.5 billion. From an economic perspective, federal cabinet ministers decided the threat to Canada's international reputation outweighed the potential cost of nationalizing the pipeline, which would cost at least $6 billion more to construct. Electorally, the federal government wagered that any loss of support among environmentalists and First Nations in BC would be offset by gains, or continued support, among Canadians who side with their dual focus on economic development and environmental protection.

Even with the federal government's purchase of Trans Mountain and approval of its expansion, questions remain as to whether a provincial government like BC can generate enough political pressure to prevent an interprovincial pipeline being constructed within its borders.

DISCUSSION ITEM

Major national infrastructure projects involve a number of governmental and nongovernmental actors.

VOX POP

Given the tumultuous pipeline debates in the early twenty-first century, how likely do you think it is that another major pipeline project will be proposed in the near future?

138 Part I | Government and Governance

Table 5.1 Structure of the Executive Council in Federal and Provincial Governments

	Federal Government	Provincial Government	Territorial Government
Head of State	**Monarch** (head of the British royal family, determined by line of succession to the throne)		
Head of State's representative	**Governor General** (appointed by the monarch on recommendation of the PM)	**Lieutenant Governor** (appointed by the GG on recommendation of the prime minister)	**Commissioner** (appointed by the GG on recommendation of the prime minister)
Head of Government	**Prime Minister** (leader of the political party that controls the House of Commons)	**Premier** (leader of the political party that controls the provincial legislature)	**Premier** (in Yukon, leader of the political party that controls the legislature; in Nunavut and NWT, leader selected by members of the legislature)
Executive Body	**The Privy Council** (all current and former members of the federal cabinet, and select others)	**The Executive Council** (all current members of the provincial cabinet)	**The Executive Council** (all current members of the territorial cabinet)
Cabinet	**Prime minister + federal ministers** (appointed by the governor general)	**Premier + provincial ministers** (appointed by the lieutenant governor)	**Premier + territorial ministers** (in Yukon, appointed by the commissioner; in Nunavut and NWT, selected by the members of the legislature and appointed by the commissioner, with portfolios assigned by the premier)
Unique cabinet portfolios	Defence, Foreign Affairs, International Trade, Veterans Affairs, etc.	Education, Municipal Affairs, Social Services, etc.	
Common cabinet portfolios	Indigenous Affairs, Environment, Finance, Health, House Leader, Intergovernmental Affairs, Justice, Labour, Natural Resources, Treasury Board, etc.		

Briefing Notes

Who Is "Honourable"?

In the legislature, parliamentarians often refer to each other as honourable members; however, the formal honorific is reserved for members of the Privy Council. An appointment to the Privy Council is a lifetime membership. Its members are permanently referred to as "honourable" and have the honorifics "P.C." (for "Privy Council") after their name. This means federal cabinet ministers, senators, and speakers of the House of Commons and the Senate are known as "honourable," even after retirement. Federal ministers of state are inducted into the Privy Council, but parliamentary secretaries are typically not. As members of the Privy Council, lieutenant governors retain the term "honourable" for life. However, other provincial dignitaries including premiers and ministers are not members of the Privy Council. They are referred to as honourable only during their term in office. From time to time, select premiers may become members of the Privy Council, as occurred around the time of the patriation debates discussed in Chapter 2. Superior Court judges, chief judges of provincial courts, and judges of the federal Tax Court are known as honourable, although they, too, are not members of the Privy Council. A higher honorific is granted to the most senior public officials. Governors general, prime ministers, and chief justices of the Supreme Court are known as "the Right Honourable" for life. While in office, governors general are referred to as "Her Excellency" or "His Excellency."

Briefing Notes boxes bring clarity to concepts and often-misunderstood aspects of Canada's political system.

Chapter 6 | The Legislature 199

Briefing Notes

Provincial Legislatures and Executive Dominance

A lot of practices in the House of Commons are identical in provincial legislatures. However, parliamentary government functions differently in many provinces. The number of sitting days can be much lower and party discipline much higher. In terms of seats, the average provincial legislature is one-fifth the size of the House of Commons. Yet provincial cabinets are about half the size of the federal one. As a result, a high proportion of members of provincial assemblies are part of cabinet or are affiliated with it as a parliamentary secretary, government whip, and so forth. In Prince Edward Island, one of every three MLAs is in cabinet. In some jurisdictions, backbenchers are invited to serve on cabinet committees. The trend of "executive creep" sees the executive branch encroach upon the legislative branch, leaving fewer legislators to hold the government to account, and raising questions about the strength of responsible government in some provinces.[14]

a standing committee deals with matters concerning a particular department, like the standing committee on health, or a body of government, such as the standing committee on procedures and house affairs. By comparison, an **ad hoc committee** is impermanent and has a specific purpose. It is created with a special mandate that may eventually be completed, such as a special committee tasked with drafting or scrutinizing legislation. In

The Chief Electoral Officer of Canada, Stéphane Perrault (left), and the Commissioner of Canada Elections, Yves Côté, appearing as witnesses for a Committee of the Whole regarding Bill C-76 (Elections Modernization Act) in the Senate in November 2018.

Chapter 11 | Media and Communication 389

are sent to supporters and followers, selective information is posted on websites and social media, and a stream of government-produced photos and video present the leader in a positive light. Legislative debates and public remarks, including social media posts, are heavily scripted. Sometimes only photojournalists are permitted to attend events and thus no questions may be asked of politicians. Interviews are occasionally staged with a friendly moderator before an assembled audience to create the illusion that the leader is being scrutinized. Some academics label Canada a publicity state in reference to the government's emphasis on promotion and persuasion rather than information.[24]

The governing party, of course, would say that this criticism is overblown. Governments are far more transparent and information reaches far more citizens more frequently than at any other time in history. Journalists have unrealistic demands for speedy replies to their queries and represent a risk of torquing information. Government officials take longer to scrutinize what is publicly released because of the pressure of mistakes that reverberate around social media. The PMO's distribution of photographs and video of the prime minister responds to public interest. Finally, the media thrive on conflict and drama, so it makes sense for the government to seek to limit opportunities that stir criticism. Better to create the perception of a powerful leader in control than of a weak one presiding over instability, it is reasoned.

A number of public-relations (PR) tools are employed in the political arena. The communication activities of governments and political actors are largely designed to accommodate the media's needs. The media's appetite for fresh and interesting content while operating under tighter financial constraints leads to their accepting what are known as **information subsidies**. Content that is created and delivered by political actors free of charge is more likely to be reproduced. Information subsidies include news releases with prepared quotes, social media posts, and packaged text, still images, audio, and video distributed digitally. News conferences and other staged photo ops are among the other forms. All of these activities are a blurred version of reality. Repeating these pre-packaged messages without a filter can be tempting to media outlets facing time pressures and dwindling resources. The most skilled political communicators are able to design information subsidies that are brief and clear enough that the media will use them unaltered. Customizing information to fit the media's needs helps to ensure that the message gets across as intended.

information subsidy Free packaged content provided to the media in a manner that is designed to meet their needs.

Briefing Notes

The Planning of Social Media Posts

The free-wheeling nature of social media does not align well with the measured and controlled culture of the public sector. Spur-of-the-moment posts from politicians can have unintended impacts on public policy, for instance, and sometimes their remarks have caused offence. That is why the social media posts from government officials and politicians often involve multiple stages of planning. In the Government of Canada, a single tweet can pass through layers of approvals processes and must also be translated so that it is posted in both official languages. The approved content is rolled out on a schedule to align with a larger government communications calendar. Political parties and caucus research staff participate in planning meetings to come up with ideas for infographics and memes that are then circulated to politicians for posting. What appear to be folksy and spontaneous posts by politicians are often well-orchestrated messages drafted by communications professionals and vetted by senior officials.

Chapter 9 | Political Parties 325

Professor Profile

Anna Esselment

Canadian political parties, campaigns and elections, political marketing
Co-editor of *Permanent Campaigning in Canada* (2017)

Anna Esselment's PhD work focused on the role of partisanship in intergovernmental relations in Canada. Her broader areas of research include political parties, campaigns and elections, political marketing, and Canadian institutions. Previously she worked at Queen's Park as a policy advisor to then opposition leader Dalton McGuinty.

Here is what Anna Esselment told us about her career path from when she was an undergraduate student, why she is drawn to her area of specialization, what is challenging about studying Canadian politics, and what advice she has for students.

* * *

I completed my undergraduate degree at McMaster University in Hamilton. I majored in political science, with a focus on Canadian and American politics, and completed an interdisciplinary minor in international justice and human rights. While I had always been interested in Canadian politics, my introduction to the topic occurred in second year. The course was taught by Dr Will Coleman, who later became my colleague at the University of Waterloo. Dr Coleman was an engaging and effective professor, and I distinctly remember him teaching the class about the Canadian bureaucracy by holding up a can of Campbell's soup and pointing out the various government regulations that affected the manufacturing of that one food product. I found it truly fascinating.

I have had a consistent interest in the institutions and processes of government, but I've focused my own research more narrowly on election campaigns. This has much to do with the three years I spent working at Queen's Park in Toronto, before I went back to school to pursue a PhD. My role as a policy analyst meant I did a lot of work on developing the campaign platform for the next election. I've since remained intrigued by how political parties fight elections, especially the strategies and tactics involved in executing a 45-day contest to win the hearts and minds of Canadian voters.

The most challenging part of studying campaigns is that the people you would most like to talk to—the campaign manager, the head of data analytics, the issues manager, the pollster—are all people who are difficult to reach, especially when the election is in full swing. They are kept busy by the demands of the campaign, and have little time to provide a researcher with context and details about their decisions. This is why research about campaigns mostly occurs in its aftermath, when key members of the campaign staff have more time available. But even then, election strategists can be choosy about who they talk to and about how much they are willing to reveal. Getting people to talk remains a perennial problem facing researchers in this field.

What I find most surprising about studying campaigns is that despite all the changes with technology, at their core very little has changed from campaigns that occurred decades ago. Parties still rely on volunteers to make phone calls and canvass neighbourhoods to identify their supporters; candidates still engage in local debates about the issues Canadians care about. Candidates and their teams still stand on street corners and wave to passing cars, hoping for an encouraging "honk." Campaigns still mobilize their vote the old-fashioned way, which is to call on their identified supporters and give them a lift to the polling station. The data science and accompanying algorithms are helpful, but they have not appeared to drastically alter campaign fundamentals.

If you ever get the opportunity, I encourage you to go out and volunteer for a political party during an election. The experience will give you great insight into the workings of Canadian democracy, and will go a long way to enhance your studies of politics in Canada.

New **Professor Profile boxes** contain first-person narratives in which academics across Canada discuss what attracted them to the study of politics, and give their study tips for students.

A Visual Focus.
A dynamic design, carefully chosen photos and captions, and numerous figures and tables make complex information accessible to student readers.

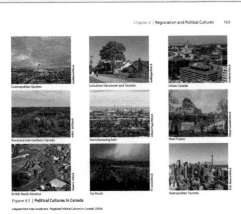

Figure 4.1 | Political Cultures in Canada

Concluding Thoughts

Just about everything that Canadians do is governed by some aspect of public policy. This makes appreciating the scope and complexity of policymaking an integral part of understanding Canadian politics. As discussed in this chapter, problems and solutions are often structured by people selected through a merit-based system that values their ability to formulate recommendations to the government of the day. Yet, elected officials make policy choices based on a host of factors beyond the evidence provided by public servants. Partisanship plays a considerable role in this vein, which is where our attention turns next.

For More Information

Interested in learning more about the nuances of public administration in Canada? Take a look at the many topics covered in *The Handbook of Canadian Public Administration*, 3rd edition, edited by Christopher Dunn (Oxford University Press, 2018).

Want a deeper perspective into how public policy and public administration operate at the provincial level of government? See Michael M. Atkinson and colleagues' *Governance and Public Policy in Canada: A View from the Provinces* (University of Toronto Press, 2013).

Interested in learning about public administration in Indigenous governance? Take a look at Joanne Heritz's article "The Multiplying Nodes of Indigenous Self-Government and Public Administration" (*Canadian Public Administration* 60, no. 2 [2017]: pp. 289–90).

How do government budgets reflect partisan ideology and election promises? François Pétry and Dominic Duval examine two decades' worth of budgets in "Electoral Promises and Single Party Governments: The Role of Party Ideology

Deeper Inside Canadian Politics

1. Some advocacy groups that advance the cause of political minorities receive government funding. However, they are some of the government's biggest critics. Do you agree that some interest groups should be given public funding? If so, how should governments decide which ones to fund?

2. Patronage tends to be decried by the public, attacked by political commentators and the opposition, and derided by editorial cartoonists. Yet no matter what political party

   is in power, it persists. Under what circumstances do you feel that patronage is acceptable and even necessary?

3. Budget deficits and public debt are common because politicians tend to be praised for making spending promises and criticized for spending cutbacks. For this reason, several governments have chosen to break, amend, or repeal balanced budget legislation in place in their jurisdictions. What other policies might be established to prevent governments from spending beyond their means?

Supportive pedagogy includes chapter outlines, key terms defined in the margins and glossary, end-of-chapter discussion questions and lists of additional resources, and an appendix of First Ministers in Canada.

First Ministers of Canada

Prime Ministers since 1867 and Premiers since 1945

CANADA

YEARS	PRIME MINISTER	PARTY*
1867–73, 1878–91	John A. Macdonald	Conservative
1873–8	Alexander Mackenzie	Liberal
1891–2	John Abbott	Conservative
1892–4	John Thompson	Conservative
1894–6	Mackenzie Bowell	Conservative
1896	Charles Tupper	Conservative
1896–1911	Wilfrid Laurier	Liberal
1911–20	Robert Borden	Conservative/Unionist
1920–1, 1926	Arthur Meighen	Unionist/Conservative
1921–6, 1926–30, 1935–48	Mackenzie King	Liberal
1930–5	Richard Bennett	Conservative
1948–57	Louis St Laurent	Liberal
1957–63	John Diefenbaker	Progressive Conservative
1963–8	Lester Pearson	Liberal
1968–79, 1980–4	Pierre Trudeau	Liberal
1979	Joe Clark	Progressive Conservative
1984	John Turner	Liberal
1984–93	Brian Mulroney	Progressive Conservative
1993	Kim Campbell	Progressive Conservative
1993–2003	Jean Chrétien	Liberal
2003–6	Paul Martin, Jr	Liberal
2006–15	Stephen Harper	Conservative
2015–	Justin Trudeau	Liberal

*The federal Conservative party has experienced name changes over time; see Chapter 9.

Ancillary Resource Center

Additional Resources for Students and Instructors

Inside Canadian Politics is supported by a range of ancillary products designed to enhance the learning experience inside and outside the classroom; all are available in the book's Ancillary Resource Centre (ARC) at www.oup.com/he/Marland-Wesley2e.

For Instructors

- An **Instructor's Manual** provides chapter summaries, learning objectives, suggested chapter outlines, and suggested discussion topics and exam questions.
- **PowerPoint** slides provide lecture outlines for each chapter.
- A **Test Bank** provides multiple-choice, true-or-false, short answer, and essay questions for each chapter.

For Students

- A **Student Study Guide** provides key terms, discussion and review questions, lists of further resources, a video guide containing links to videos and related questions, and self-grading quizzes.
- An **Image Bank** provides digital files of photos, figures, and tables from the text.
- **Flashcards** of all key terms and definitions from the text help students with their studying.

Reviewers

Oxford University Press would like to thank the following reviewers and anonymous reviewers whose thoughtful comments and suggestions helped to guide the development of the two editions of this textbook:

Christopher Anderson, Wilfrid Laurier University

Yale Belanger, University of Lethbridge

Mark Blythe, University of Alberta/ MacEwan University

Mona Brash, Camosun College

Louise Carbert, Dalhousie University

Adrienne Davidson, Queen's University

Linda Elmose, Okanagan College

Marcella Firmini, Dalhousie University

Jay Haaland, Kwantlen Polytechnic University

Andrew Heard, Simon Fraser University

Stewart Hyson, University of New Brunswick

John Kennair, Red Deer College

James Lawson, University of Victoria

Tom McIntosh, University of Regina

Antonia Maioni, McGill University

Nanita Mohan, University of Guelph

Nisha Nath, Athabasca University

Stephen Phillips, Langara College

Dennis Pilon, York University

Daniel Reeve, Camosun College

Ivan Savic, Memorial University of Newfoundland, Grenfell Campus

John Soroski, MacEwan University

Erin Tolley, University of Toronto

Nadia Verrelli, Laurentian University

Leslie Wee, George Brown College

Nelson Wiseman, University of Toronto

1

Overview
of Canadian Politics

Inside This Chapter

- What is politics? What is democracy?
- What are the main cleavages in Canadian politics?
- What have been the major issues in Canadian political history?

Inside Canadian Politics

This introductory chapter is intended as a general overview of Canadian politics to set the groundwork for deeper examination. It contains information that may be familiar to some readers and new to others. In many cases, a short explanation is provided and you can spot a definition in the margin of the page. Alternatively you can turn to the glossary on pages 511 to 517 to locate a definition. Major concepts and terminology are discussed in further detail later in the book. At this point, the purpose of the chapter is to simply encourage you to be aware of the Canadian political context. Here are three things that all readers ought to be familiar with from the start of a course in Canadian politics.

✔ **Canadian politics has changed considerably since 1867.** While Canada's constitutional structure has changed remarkably little since Confederation, the political system has undergone significant shifts.
✔ **There are many different ideas and ideologies at play in Canadian politics.** The values and beliefs that divide citizens and their leaders, as we shall see in this chapter, are a major cleavage shaping the dynamics of Canadian politics.
✔ **The average citizen has many opportunities to make a difference in Canadian politics.** There are abundant ways to become involved in politics and government in a variety of paid and volunteer positions. Throughout this book we'll present examples of the kinds of opportunities open to anyone with an interest in, and understanding of, Canadian politics.

The Politics of Representation

To the majority of citizens who do not follow developments that closely, and at times even to those who do, the landscape of Canadian politics can seem confusing. Consider the nature of representation in Canada, for instance. At any given time, a Canadian is represented by a member of the provincial or territorial legislature, by a member of Parliament, and by a senator—all three of whom may be from different political parties. That citizen is also represented by the individual's mayor, reeve, councillor, school board trustee, and many other official representatives at the local level. What if those representatives are affiliated with a political party you don't support, or if they do not look like you? Deciding exactly whom to approach for help with a particular government service or program, or whom to hold to account at the ballot box, can be challenging given these different layers of political representation.

At a broader level, Canadians are represented by heads of government. Each province and territory is led by a premier. The country is headed by a prime minister. As powerful as they are, and although Canada is a **democracy**, none of these highest-ranking leaders is directly elected by the citizens they represent. Rather, the premier and prime minister are chosen by representatives of the Queen of Canada who are appointed to their positions, rather than elected. Is this an effective means of representation? What are the advantages and disadvantages compared with other systems? These are among the many questions that you will be better able to answer after reading this book.

Core Concepts

What is politics? The practice of **politics** has been around since the dawn of human civilization. People, groups, and organizations argue over common priorities and endeavours. These debates tend to centre on who gets what, and when, in terms of a community's shared resources. Discussion involves a competition among individuals and groups for control over the decision-making process. The pursuit of **power** is a cornerstone of politics in Canada today.

The characteristics of democracy are discussed on pages 32–4 in Chapter 2, on the constitution.

democracy
A system of government featuring primary decision-makers chosen by citizens through free and fair elections.

politics
Activities involving the pursuit and exercise of decision-making over the collectivity.

power
The ability to control or influence other members of a political community.

In Canada as elsewhere, the most prominent power struggles occur at the **state** level. Many states exist as countries, like Sweden, Turkey, Vietnam, Peru, Mozambique, Japan, and the United Kingdom. Political authority within these unitary states is concentrated in a single, country-wide government. Other countries consist of several orders of government, with power divided among central and regional authorities. As we will see in Chapter 3, federations like Canada, Argentina, Germany, Ethiopia, India, Australia, and the United States consist of multiple orders of government. Each government within the federation has ultimate authority, or sovereignty, over different areas of **jurisdiction**.

state
A structured political community with a single source of ultimate authority over its territory.

jurisdiction
The ultimate authority to make legal decisions, or the seat of power for such decision-making.

Table 1.1   Chapter Guide to Core Institutional Features of Canadian Politics in This Book

Core Institutional Feature	Chapter
Canada is governed by the rule of law, meaning that all Canadians are subject to the same legal treatment regardless of their status.	The rule of law is discussed in Chapter 7.
Canada is a constitutional monarchy, meaning that sovereignty (or ultimate power) is vested in the Crown, the reigning king or queen. The Queen is Canada's head of state and has representatives based in Canada's capital city (the governor general in Ottawa) and in the 10 provincial capitals (lieutenant governors).	Sovereignty and the Crown are explored in Chapter 2.
The constitution divides jurisdictional powers between a federal government and 10 provincial governments.	Federalism is explored in Chapter 3.
The head of the federal government (the prime minister) is the leader of the political party that has the confidence of the legislature in Ottawa. The head of a provincial government (a premier) has the confidence of their respective provincial legislature. Within Quebec, the premier is called the "premier ministre."	First ministers are a topic of Chapter 5.
The prime minister or premier and their ministers together dominate the political executive. They are known as the cabinet. They are in charge of making government decisions, thereby exercising power delegated by the Crown at the federal or provincial level.	Cabinet is explained in Chapter 5.
In Ottawa, the federal Parliament is composed of the Crown and two legislative bodies: a popularly elected lower house (the House of Commons) and an appointed upper house (the Senate). To become a federal law, a bill must be approved by both houses of Parliament and the governor general. In the provinces, legislatures consist of only one house or chamber; there are no provincial senates. The provincial assembly and the lieutenant governor must approve a bill before it becomes a provincial law.	Legislative assemblies are examined in Chapter 6.
Under the principle of responsible government, the cabinet must maintain the confidence of the elected legislature in order to remain in power. One of the ways a loss of confidence in the government is signified is when a motion is defeated in a critical legislative vote, such as a budget bill.	Responsible government is a subject found in Chapter 2.
Canada is a representative democracy, with members of federal and provincial legislative assemblies elected using single-member plurality electoral systems. Whichever candidate gets the most votes is elected to represent citizens in that electoral district.	Elections and electoral systems are the topics of Chapter 10.
Most Canadian systems are characterized by strong party discipline, meaning that members of Parliament are likely to side with the leader of their party on most legislative votes.	Party discipline is featured in Chapter 9.
Governments are supported by a non-partisan, independent civil service, which helps to develop and implement policy on their behalf.	The civil service is profiled in Chapter 8.

Note: Canada's three territories generally follow similar institutional principles, except that Nunavut and the Northwest Territories operate under consensus government (without political parties).

> > > > > > > > > > > > > > >
See pages 67–8 in
Chapter 3 for the
differences between
federal and unitary
systems of government.

government
The people and systems
that govern a society by
designing, overseeing, and
implementing laws and
public policy. Can refer to the
cabinet and/or the broader
public sector.

citizen
A member of a state who
is under the authority
and protection of its
government.

Indigenous people
First Nations, Métis, and Inuit
living in Canada.

First Nations
Indigenous groups
descended from a variety of
historical Indigenous nations;
collectively, the earliest
inhabitants of North America
and their descendants, other
than Métis and Inuit.

In this sense, the Canadian federation consists of 11 sovereign governments: one at the country-wide level, and 10 at the provincial level. The central (federal) government based in Ottawa has jurisdiction over the Armed Forces and defence, citizenship, and other areas of national jurisdiction. The provinces maintain authority over healthcare, education, municipalities, and other local matters. In practical terms, Canada's three territories have many of the same powers as provinces. The territories' autonomy is limited by the fact that the federal government holds full sovereignty over their jurisdiction.

State decisions are made by **governments**. In democratic states like Canada, most members of government are elected to their positions on a regular basis. Thus, **citizens** play a more active role in democratic states than do subjects in autocracies. Citizenship involves a combination of rights and responsibilities that are not enjoyed by people living in many other parts of the world.

To summarize, politics in the Canadian federation involves the pursuit of political power through democratic means. Individuals and groups compete to control the levers of decision-making found in a national government and in subnational governments. This competition takes place on many levels (locally, regionally, nationally, globally), in many dimensions (cultural, territorial, intergovernmental, ideological, partisan), in many venues (boardrooms, campaign trails, courtrooms), on many issues (healthcare, education, national defence), involving many players (politicians, judges, citizens). The chapters that follow dig deeper inside Canadian politics to explain how this process unfolds. Table 1.1, on page 3, outlines some of the core institutional features of Canadian politics that the book delves into.

Indigenous Peoples

The special rights of **Indigenous peoples** often rest uneasily with the core concepts just discussed. Indigenous peoples' rights reflect their ties to the land, their legal and political rights as original occupants of present-day Canada, and their cultural distinctiveness from the dominant groups that have often marginalized Indigenous peoples' political influence through colonialism. Indigenous societies were divided along tribal lines centuries before the first contact with European settlers. They likewise failed to prevent the sort of internecine warfare that defined cultures throughout the rest of the world. Nevertheless, Indigenous political institutions—like the brand of federalism developed by the Haudenosaunee (Iroquois)—served as models to settlers when it came to advancing cultural accommodation and collaboration among disparate groups.

Between the seventeenth and nineteenth centuries, European settlers began arriving in greater numbers. They did not extend appropriate respect in incorporating Indigenous peoples into the original institutions of the Canadian state. The Crown signed treaties with many **First Nations** that established nation-to-nation relationships between Indigenous peoples and the British and (future) Canadian governments. These arrangements were often cast aside in the name of political expediency or settler colonialism. As a result, for centuries, Indigenous peoples have been treated as responsibilities, even wards, of the state. This contributed to measures like the Indian Act, the reserve system, and forced relocation. For instance, the Canadian state separated thousands of Indigenous children from their families and placed them in residential schools from the 1880s to the 1990s. They were subjected to what the Truth and Reconciliation Commission (TRC) later labelled "cultural genocide." During the Sixties Scoop that began in the 1960s, many

Justice Murray Sinclair (centre) and Commissioners Chief Wilton Littlechild and Marie Wilson pull back a blanket to unveil the final report of the Truth and Reconciliation Commission of Canada in Ottawa in December 15, 2015. The TRC's final report includes a list of 94 calls to action. Consult the report, which is widely available online. Which of the recommendations do you feel are the most difficult to implement? Have you seen any visible progress toward meeting them? Are there additional ways to promote reconciliation among Indigenous and non-Indigenous peoples in Canada?

Indigenous peoples, often children, were forcibly removed from their homes. The government deliberately attempted to isolate them from the cultural influences of their communities. The government's policy was to assimilate Indigenous peoples into mainstream Canadian society through adoption into settler families. Intergenerational trauma means the legacy of this **settler colonialism** persists to this day. An attempt at reconciliation among Indigenous and non-Indigenous peoples is among the most pressing challenges facing Canadians and their political leaders.

settler colonialism
Belief in the supremacy of European settler institutions over those of Indigenous groups, and policies and practices that impose this belief.

See Inside Canadian Politics: How Is the Federal Government Approaching Reconciliation? on page 24 later in this chapter.

Three Elements of Canadian Politics

At this point, we offer three ideas that we feel every student or observer of Canadian politics should bear in mind. The following three statements serve as common threads for the discussions found later in this book:

1. Canadian politics is defined by the CLEAVAGES of geography, demography, and ideology.
2. The INSTITUTIONS of Canadian democracy are Anglo-American hybrids.
3. Understanding Canadian politics requires some awareness of Canadian HISTORY.

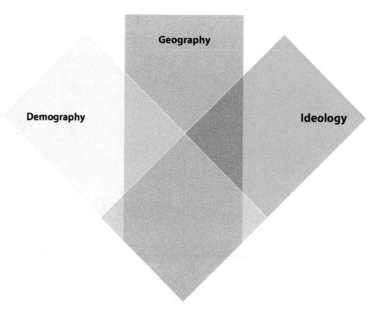

Figure 1.1 | **Mutually Reinforcing Cleavages in Canadian Politics**

1. Core Cleavages

cleavage
A division that separates opposing political communities.

institution
A structure that defines, constrains, or encourages behaviour within a political system.

Every country has its own political fault lines. The **cleavages** that are mostly responsible for shaping the dynamics of Canadian politics today are geography, demography, and ideology. These cleavages are deeply engrained in the country's political psyche. All of Canada's major political **institutions**—its constitution, legislature, courts, laws, political parties, and more—are shaped by these cleavages. Major debates are staged along matters of territory, race, and core beliefs about the role of the state in society and the economy. Discussed below, these various factors are mutually reinforcing: certain ethnic communities tend to be concentrated in select parts of Canada, while different regions and cultural communities tend to adhere to unique sets of ideological beliefs (Figure 1.1). Other cleavages are certainly present in Canadian politics. Gender, language, class, religion, and other divisions continue to animate debates in various parts of the country at different times.

The cleavages of geography, demography, and ideology leave little room for additional forms of political expression and debate. The structure of Canada's political institutions means that other lines of division, such as settler colonialism, gender, and class, often fail to achieve long-term salience. As a result, issues like reconciliation, gender equality, or income inequality, and proposed solutions like self-government, affirmative action, or the redistribution of wealth, tend to be overshadowed. This may be changing, given that Justin Trudeau's Liberal government has made reconciliation, feminism, and the middle class part of its core focus. Nevertheless, historically, discussions about linguistic accommodation or the proper distribution of federal transfer funds to the provinces tend to dominate. In this sense, Canadian politics is as much about what interests are organized into the system as what is organized out of it.

THE CANADIAN PRESS/Jonathan Hayward

Gas prices vary widely across Canada. The overall cost to consumers depends less on where the gasoline is sourced and more on how governments choose to tax it at the pump. In addition to the federal tax, provincial and municipal governments levy sales, gasoline, carbon, transit, and other taxes designed to generate government revenue and, in some cases, discourage consumption. Do you think the price of gasoline is fair where you live? Should there be a limit on the extent that gas prices should be allowed to vary?

a) Geography

Canadian democracy has always been conducted along geographic lines. The notion of who controls which territory was fundamental to Canadian politics even prior to the country's founding in 1867. Treaties and other political agreements were reached with First Nations to decide issues over land. British colonial leaders banded together under a power-sharing deal that divided sovereignty among themselves and, despite treaties to the contrary, stripped First Nations communities of their land and autonomy. To this day, federal elections are waged in each of over 300 separate districts across Canada, where constituents elect their own member of Parliament to represent the community. Similarly, each province is allotted a certain number of senators and is often represented in the federal cabinet and on the Supreme Court of Canada. Likewise, Indigenous governance has been focused around territory. The federal government relegates First Nations authority to Band Councils housed on reserves across the country. Indigenous communities assert their inherent right to self-government through land claims, among other means. These rules and approaches help to embed regional representation within the central institutions of the Canadian state. This perpetuates the power of geography in influencing Canadian politics.

It should come as little surprise that Canada's geography defines its politics. Canada is next only to Russia as the world's largest country in terms of land mass. The distances that divide Canadians on the West Coast of British Columbia from those on the East Coast of

Figure 1.2 | Canada: An Infographic

Drawing heavily on stereotypes, this illustration captures some of the cultural features unique to different parts of the country. How do you think these cultural characteristics inform the political culture of each region? How would your political outlook be influenced by, for instance, "cowboys," "smog," or "diamonds" and "people who talk funny" in your home province?

Source: © 2012 by Kirstin Hallett, Jacaranda Marketing + Design

Newfoundland, or that separate people from the northern reaches of Nunavut from those at the southern tip of Ontario, can be measured as much by kilometres as by their distinct political perspectives. People in different parts of Canada have different interests, priorities, and viewpoints based on the unique shared experiences within their communities. Growing up in a rural or remote environment shapes one's political perspective differently than growing up in a well-to-do suburb, or living in a big city. Being endowed with a wealth of natural resources like oil and gas informs a community's economy and outlook, often putting it at odds with neighbours with fewer natural advantages. All told, attitudes toward authority, community, distribution of wealth, mutual obligations, and other political beliefs vary depending on where a person lives. If you know someone from a different part of Canada, or even a different part of your province, chances are that person's political attitudes will vary from your own.

Political scientists refer to these geographically defined communities as having unique political cultures that distinguish them from their neighbours. Observers often divide Canada into several regional political cultures, as discussed in Chapter 4. Some see clear divisions between westerners, easterners, northerners, and central Canadians. Others see unique political cultures within these regions, such as within the Prairies or in the Atlantic region. Given the federal nature of power sharing in Canada, leaders of

Protesters hold up signs during a demonstration in 2019 against Quebec's secularism legislation (Bill 21). The Quebec government's approach to banning religious symbols is less popular in other parts of the country. How do you think geography, demography, and ideology align in Canada?

these provincial communities have had the opportunity to build their own "small worlds" within the confines of the Canadian state.[1]

Indeed, provinces are playing a greater role than ever before. Provincial power is related to the steady growth of government programming and Canada's emergence as an economy based on natural resources (like oil, gas, agriculture, timber, and fish) and the knowledge sector (rooted in universities and colleges). Federal and provincial governments collaborate on several areas of common interest. Yet, the provinces are autonomous when it comes to defining their own priorities and direction. As a result, no two provinces have the same set of political priorities and processes. This helps to ensure that Canadian politics remains defined by geography. Each province consists of its own unique political world. These differences can be overstated at times. Some Canadians share more in common with their counterparts in other parts of the country than they do with their neighbours. This said, geography remains deeply embedded in Canada's system of government and politics.

b) Demography

Demography is a second dominant cleavage in Canadian politics. Canadians may be divided into many categories according to gender, age, class, education level, and so on. Many of these divisions remain below the surface of mainstream political debate. Others figure prominently in legislative debates, court cases, election campaigns, and other political arenas.

Consider ethnicity. Corresponding with its self-image as a multicultural **mosaic**, Canada is divided into many ethnic communities, each with its own political outlook.

mosaic
A metaphor used to depict Canada's multicultural character, which features many distinct yet interdependent ethnocultural communities.

The evolution of Canada's political institutions attests to the depth and persistence of cultural differences between its French- and English-speaking communities, for instance. Where they exist in large numbers, like Filipinos in north Winnipeg or Sikhs in Surrey, ethnic groups may exert significant influence on the political system. This includes electing candidates to Parliament, the provincial legislature, or city council. Groups that are geographically dispersed, like many Muslims and other religious minorities, face steeper challenges when it comes to representation in Canada's political system, defined as it is along territorial lines. The fact that Canadian elections are fought in geographic districts helps to suppress the influence of other demographic communities, as well. Discussed in Chapter 13, women face significant obstacles when it comes to equal representation in Canadian politics. So, too, do members of sexual minority communities, lower-income households, and other traditionally marginalized groups.

c) Ideology

The third major cleavage in Canadian politics surrounds **ideology**. An ideology is the core political belief system that a group of citizens holds about the way power should be distributed or exercised. It is sometimes argued that Canadian politics is relatively devoid of ideological debate or conflict. That is, there is more philosophical agreement than discord in Canada. There are, however, many nuances that help to distinguish the different ideological camps in this country.

Left-Wing and Right-Wing

In politics, ideology is often imagined as a spectrum of views ranging from left to centre to right. We explain the differences between left-wing and right-wing below and again in Chapter 9.

Left-wing thinkers value policies that achieve equality for all Canadians. They tend to focus their attention on improving the lives of society's most disadvantaged. Left-wingers want government to be active in promoting the public good, trust experts in the bureaucracy to administer programs that will improve society, and resist business-style thinking. They are often regarded by critics as idealists with a romantic view of the potential and role of government to improve society at home and promote peace abroad. Left-wing thinkers tend to value socio-cultural inclusion over conformity. They support group rights, including those of Indigenous peoples and members of traditionally marginalized communities. Left-leaning Canadians believe that unjust social forces may be responsible when people find themselves in a disadvantaged situation. Thus they believe in the rehabilitation of criminals and a strong welfare state.

Among the many ideologies that are foremost associated with the left wing is **feminism**. Feminists promote equality of the sexes. Men have occupied elite positions of power, which has contributed to their privilege. By comparison, women are professionally and privately disadvantaged in the economy, politics, and society. Many feminists push for women's rights, equal treatment, and the reduction if not elimination of gendered roles and norms. Feminism transcends left-wing thinking, however. Some people on the political right support feminist values and principles of fair treatment of women as individuals.

>>>>>>>>>>>>>>>>>>
Attempts to bridge the divide between Canada's French and English populations are discussed in Chapter 2, on the constitution.

ideology
A set of ideas that form a coherent political belief system.

left-wing
A political tendency that promotes a bigger role for government and proactive measures to achieve social and economic equality.

feminism
A political ideology and social movement that seeks to advance women's rights and achieve gender equality.

Right-wing thinkers tend to favour approaches that promote equal treatment and traditional values. In other words, right-wingers believe that all Canadians should be accorded the same rights and privileges and that all Canadians should live according to the same set of basic rules. They feel that the economic system rewards those who are industrious and work hard. **Right-wing** Canadians are concerned about government inefficiencies and believe businesses and charities are often better at delivering services to citizens. Those on the political right tend to view society as a collection of equal individuals, and question the extension of special programs, services, and rights to particular groups, like Indigenous peoples. Right-wing people typically are less accepting of untested reforms; they seek to preserve the status quo or, in some cases, revert to more traditional practices. In this sense, people on the right often promote a more limited and possibly negative view of the role of government, particularly when it comes to redistributing wealth or promoting group rights over individual freedoms. Many right wingers find value in government intervention on social and moral issues, however. Right-wing individuals are often pro-police and pro-military, for example, or seek to use state levers to ensure conformity on matters of conscience and traditional values. They tend to advocate for tougher sentencing of criminals and a more proactive role for Canada in armed conflicts overseas. On feminism, they believe that women should be treated equally to men as individuals, and are opposed to special treatment that discriminates against others.

Overall, the following dimensions separate the left and right in Canada:

- Fiscally, left-wing people favour government spending on social programs, while those on the right favour lower taxes and debt reduction.
- Institutionally, the left favours reform of democratic structures, while the right favours tradition.
- Socially, the left promotes inclusion, while the right promotes conformity.
- Legally, the left tends to want restrictions on law enforcement and military action, while the right tends to be more assertive and punitive.

Throughout this book you will learn more about political ideologies and their connections with political parties. At this stage, it is useful to be familiar with the three main political parties in Canada, and to impress that the name of a political party does not necessarily signify its political ideology (see Briefing Note).

The **Liberal Party** of Canada has been in power in Ottawa more than any other party. Its ideology straddles the political centre. Sometimes it is positioned centre-left, as it is under Justin Trudeau, and other times centre-right as it was in the 1990s. There are Liberal parties in the provinces that vary from centre-left to centre-right. The party's origins are in the liberal philosophy that balances equality of result and equality of right.

The **Conservative Party** of Canada has alternated forming government in Ottawa with the Liberals. Its ideology ranges from the centre-right to the right. The party's name has changed over the years and it does not currently have any official ties with provincial parties. Similar provincial parties include the Progressive Conservatives, which operates in many, but not all, provinces. The party's origins are in the conservative philosophy that balances various strands of fiscal libertarianism and social traditionalism.

The **New Democratic Party (NDP)** of Canada has never formed a federal government. Its ideology spans the centre-left to the left. It was formed through a formal partnership

right-wing
A political tendency that promotes a smaller role for government and a greater emphasis on individual responsibility and market-based competition.

Liberal Party
A party that straddles the political centre and has governed Canada at the federal level longer than any other major party.

Conservative Party
A centre-right major party that has periodically formed the Government of Canada.

New Democratic Party (NDP)
A left-wing major party that has formal ties with organized labour.

Briefing Note

Big-L, Small-l Liberalism and Big-C, Small-c Conservatism

Canadian political scientists often differentiate certain overlapping political ideologies and political party names by referring to whether the first letter is capitalized or not. In short:

- big-L Liberal refers to the Liberal Party or someone who identifies as a Liberal partisan;
- small-l liberal refers to the ideology of liberalism, which generally is a belief system that promotes equality of opportunity;
- big-C Conservative refers to the Conservative Party, sometimes the Progressive Conservative Party, or someone who identifies as a Conservative partisan; and
- small-c conservative refers to the ideology of conservatism, which generally speaking is a belief system that combines worldviews of individualism and traditionalism.

The reason that big-L, small-l, big-C, and small-c nuances are used is to avoid confusion when speaking about these parties and ideologies. If you say the following sentence out loud, you can imagine how different people might interpret what you are saying differently, which the use of capitalization would disentangle: "The Conservatives often attract conservatives and liberals who do not support the Liberals." That sentence is written appropriately for an essay or textbook. But hearing someone say it is confusing. To avoid confusion you would speak in the following manner: "The Conservative Party often attracts small-c conservatives and small-l liberals who do not support the Liberal Party." These nuances are further explained in Chapter 9.

with Canada's largest trade union. There are party affiliates in most provinces that have close ties with the national party and that sometimes form provincial governments. The party's origins are in a democratic socialist movement dating back to the 1930s that promoted the interests of workers and farmers.

2. Key Institutions

A second maxim underpinning Canadian politics concerns its unique combination of British and American traditions. With its colonial origins as British North America, Canada's institutions and practices are drawn from both sides of the Atlantic Ocean.

Canada inherited its common-law and Westminster parliamentary traditions from Britain. The countries both have the same monarch. The constitutional laws governing Canadian democracy are replete with age-old British statutes and conventions. Moreover, Canadian politics owes its ideological foundations to the British model. Discussed above, the contours of the left–right spectrum draw heavily on the British example.

From the United States, Canada borrows the federal principle that involves dividing power among a common central government and a series of regional ones. As in the US, this balance between shared and local rule has been precarious from the start, shifting continuously over time. On one side stand the forces of centralization. These forces ensure that the federal government has the authority to devise and impose common standards for essential programs like healthcare; to promote harmonization of laws and policies from province to province in order to reduce barriers to trade and mobility; to cultivate a strong, shared identity among Canadians; and so forth. On the other side stand the forces of decentralization. Decentralization aims to preserve provincial autonomy as a venue for the definition of local priorities, the expression of local interests, and the achievement of local objectives; as a means of fostering policy experimentation and learning among provinces; and as a bulwark against the breakdown of local communities. Canada is the only country in the Western world without a national Department of Education, for instance. Policies about curriculum, teaching standards, and so on are the responsibility of each provincial and territorial government. Canadians consistently list medicare as among the most important elements of the country's political culture and identity. Yet there are at least 14 healthcare systems in Canada: one for each province and territory and one at the federal level. All of this illustrates the ways that power is devolved to provinces.

The American influence is felt elsewhere throughout Canadian politics. To many observers, the Charter of Rights and Freedoms, established in 1982, imported elements of the American Bill of Rights. It brought a US style of litigiousness and judicial lawmaking that, until the 1980s, was rare in Canadian politics. In a similar vein, Canadian political strategists borrow heavily from American-style campaign strategies, including many innovative political marketing techniques. It is easy to overstate the so-called Americanization of Canadian politics, particularly given Canadians' exposure to US popular culture and the integration of the North American economy. Some critics cite the increased level of negative advertising, the president-like concentration of power in the prime minister's office, and other developments as evidence that Canadian politics is heavily influenced by American politics.

Over time, Canadian politics has been shifting out of the British orbit and into the American one. Generally speaking, Canadian economic, institutional, and ideological underpinnings are becoming more American and less British. Nestled in between are the remnants of the political influence of France, namely the civil law system that is found in Quebec and the policy of official bilingualism that requires that all federal government services be available in English and French. In other ways, Canada exhibits its own national character, including the gradual adoption of Indigenous principles and approaches, as this book shows.

3. Historical Evolution

This introductory chapter illustrates that Canadian politics is shaped by centuries of history. Shifting balances of power, the emergence of new policy areas, and various external forces have all contributed to political change in Canada. Even in elements that appear relatively stable, like the persistence of age-old cleavages and institutions, subtle developments have sent Canadian politics in new directions.

A brief tour of the three centuries offers perspective on the evolution of Canadian politics, in other words: of how we got to here. In general, modern Canadian political history can be divided into three main eras since 1867, as outlined in Table 1.2.

The Road to Confederation (Pre-1867)

European settlers first built lasting settlements in what they called the Americas in the seventeenth century. This occurred thousands of years after Indigenous peoples first populated what many referred to as Turtle Island. In a history too detailed to be covered

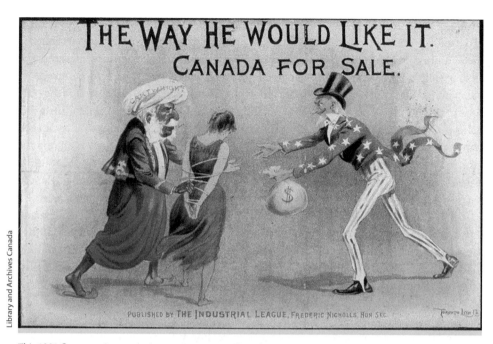

Library and Archives Canada

This 1891 Conservative campaign poster portrays Canada as a young woman the Liberals were prepared to sell into servitude to Uncle Sam. In what ways is Canada's political culture influenced by American politics? What might a feminist say about the poster?

here, the ensuing two centuries saw a series of military and economic alliances form among Indigenous, British, French, and Spanish peoples as European states sought to control the continent. In the process, Europeans brought disease and settler colonial practices that decimated the Indigenous presence in what is now North America.

The Seven Years' War (1756–63) involved territorial battles by European powers across five continents. The war featured fierce battles, including the Battle of the Plains of Abraham outside Quebec City in 1759, and the Conquest of 1760 when French forces surrendered in Montreal. In 1763, Britain defeated France to end the war. Britain gained jurisdiction over New France, an area of North America colonized by French settlers. Different Indigenous communities fought on each side of these battles, drawn into the conflict as part of their alliances with British and French forces.

A key turning point in modern Canadian political history came with the signing of the Royal Proclamation of 1763, the foundation of Canada's constitutional order. The Royal Proclamation was issued by the King of Great Britain. The document recognized the self-governing status of Indigenous peoples in North America. It established a nation-to-nation relationship between them and the British Crown. Yet, the Proclamation declared British sovereignty over most lands in what is now Eastern Canada and United States, including those populated by Indigenous peoples.[2] A so-called Indian reserve was set up east of the Appalachian Mountains, ostensibly to discourage skirmishes between European settlers and Indigenous peoples. The buffer zone created by this reserve satisfied no one and failed to serve its purpose. Indigenous peoples gradually had their lands taken by settlers bent on Western expansion.

Colonists viewed the buffer zone as an intrusion on their democratic rights and a pretext for the American Revolution. As well, the Royal Proclamation sought to impose

Table 1.2   Three Eras of Canadian Politics (1867-present)

	First Era (1867 to early 20th c.)	Second Era (mid- to late 20th c.)	Third Era (late 20th to early 21st c.)
Central political issues	• federal union • westward expansion • settler colonialism • free trade	• national identity and unity • constitutional amendment • free trade	• fiscal matters • healthcare • terrorism • climate change • reconciliation
Deepest cleavages	• East/West • male/female • French Canada/English Canada	• Quebec/rest of Canada	• West/East • rural/urban/suburban • Indigenous/non-Indigenous
Principal sites for political conflict	• Parliament/legislatures • courts	• Parliament/legislatures • intergovernmental conferences • broadcast media	• courts • broadcast media • social media
Dominant political parties (federal level)	• Liberals • Conservatives	• Liberals • Progressive Conservatives • Cooperative Commonwealth Federation/ New Democrats	• Liberals • Conservatives (and predecessors) • New Democrats • Bloc Québécois
Key events and developments	• Confederation (1867) • Northwest Uprisings (1870, 1885) • World War I (1914–19) • Great Depression (1930s) • World War II (1939–45)	• Quiet Revolution (1960s) • Centennial (1967) • White Paper on Indian Policy (1969) • patriation of the constitution, Charter of Rights and Freedoms (1982) • megaconstitutional negotiations (Meech Lake and Charlottetown Accords) • Quebec referendums (1980, 1995) • Free Trade Agreement (FTA) (1987) and North American Free Trade Agreement (NAFTA) (1994)	• 11 September (2001) • Afghanistan War (2001–11) • Great Recession (2008–9) • Truth and Reconciliation Commission (2008–15) • Canada-European Union Comprehensive Economic and Trade Agreement (CETA) (2017) • Canada-United States–Mexico Agreement (CUSMA)

British institutions and laws on Quebec, which was not well received by the French residents. The backlash ultimately led to the Quebec Act, 1774, which recognized French civil law, extended Quebec's boundaries, and granted religious freedom. The Quebec Act was one of several acts passed by the British Parliament that agitated American patriots. The resulting Revolutionary War (1775–83) divided the 13 colonies from their British North American counterparts in what is now Central and Atlantic Canada. Many Loyalists to the British Crown moved north to what is now Canada, both during and after the conflict. Those arriving in Nova Scotia and Prince Edward Island joined colonies where legislative assemblies had already been elected. The system of representative government followed soon afterwards in New Brunswick, Upper Canada, and Lower Canada.

Peace between the Americans and British was uneasy and short-lived. Conflict erupted again when the US declared war over infringements on shipping goods to Europe during the Napoleonic Wars. As part of the British Empire, Canadian colonists were drawn into the War of 1812, as were many Indigenous allies on both sides. To the surprise of their American counterparts, the Canadian colonists proved their mettle on the battlefield and resisted their overtures to throw off the yoke of British control. They neither declared their own independence nor joined the United States. Following the famous incident in which British soldiers torched the US capital, forcing the Americans to reconstruct and whitewash the Presidential Mansion (making it the White House), peace was once again restored.

Meanwhile, the British colonies were travelling a democratic path as they progressed from representative government. Up to this point, representatives were elected to participate in approving laws and debating issues of the day. The evolution to **responsible government** meant that the executives overseeing the government must maintain the confidence of the people's elected representatives. Nova Scotia became the first British colony in the world to achieve responsible government, doing so in 1848. The system of government soon followed in Prince Edward Island, New Brunswick and Newfoundland. However, conflict in the south was about to leave its mark on Canadian history.

Amid the American Civil War (1861–65), colonial leaders from Nova Scotia, New Brunswick, Prince Edward Island, and the Province of Canada (which would become Quebec and Ontario) gathered in high-level conferences to discuss the value and viability of joining together in a new commercial and military union. Newfoundland sent observers, but did not participate. These meetings culminated in a deal known as **Confederation**, embodied in the British North America Act, 1867.

First Era of Canadian Politics (1867–early 1900s)

When the British Parliament passed the BNA Act, 1867, on 1 July 1867, the legislation became Canada's central constitutional document. It established the institutional foundations for the new country. The Act fell short of establishing complete sovereignty for Canada, however, as the drafters failed to incorporate a formula to change the constitution. For over a century any changes to Canada's written constitution would require the approval of the British government. The BNA Act papered over a key element of the Royal Proclamation of 1763. Drafters attempted to extinguish the Indigenous right to self-government by declaring "Indians and Lands Reserved for the Indians"—as worded in section 91(24)—to fall under the jurisdiction of the Canadian state.

Throughout this early period, Canadian settlers and their politicians were challenged with how to expand the new country's reach into the vast lands known as Rupert's Land and the North-Western Territory. Initially, the Canadian federation consisted of just four provinces: Ontario, Quebec, New Brunswick, and Nova Scotia. The constitutional family grew steadily over the course of the next half-century, with Manitoba (1870), British Columbia (1871), Prince Edward Island (1873), Alberta (1905), and Saskatchewan (1905) entering the union. All the while, Canadian politics was dominated by the issue of how to assume and maintain control over the vast lands in their half of the continent.

It was an era marked by Canada as a British society prevailing over French traditions and Indigenous peoples. All British laws were in force in Canada until 1931 when the **Statute of Westminster** was passed. Canada did not exercise military independence

responsible government
The constitutional principle whereby the executive (cabinet) must be supported by a majority of elected members of the legislature.

Confederation
The federal union of provinces and territories forming Canada, originally comprised of Ontario, Quebec, New Brunswick, and Nova Scotia.

Statute of Westminster
A British law that permitted its Dominions to opt out of future legislation passed by the British Parliament.

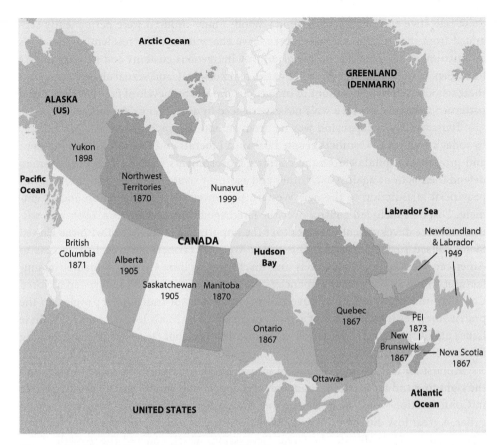

Figure 1.3 | Map of Canada's Provinces and Territories

The borders of the various provinces and territories changed many times during the years of Canada's formation, and eventually settled into the ones that we know today, as pictured above. Dates indicate time of entry into Confederation.

until the Second World War. Prior to that, Britain spoke for Canada in international forums, and Canadians initially served under British military units. Citizens of Canada were considered a subset of British subjects until the Canadian Citizenship Act came into force in 1947. The British-based Judicial Committee of the Privy Council (JCPC) was the country's highest court until it relinquished that authority in 1949 to the Supreme Court of Canada.

Expansionism would involve negotiating independence from Britain, establishing a police presence, devolving powers to new provincial governments, and protecting Western areas against potential takeover by the United States. It involved colonizing these territories, displacing Indigenous peoples, and accelerating a process of assimilation that some have associated with cultural genocide. The passage of the federal Indian Act in 1876 further entrenched the Canadian state's approach to Indigenous peoples. It labelled them as an area of policy responsibility, marginalized them with the establishment of reserves, and rejected their inherent rights to self-governance with the founding of the Band system.

Perhaps no institution is more emblematic of Canada's paternalistic approach to Indigenous peoples than the **residential schools system**, which attempted to assimilate Indigenous children by forcibly removing them from their communities and placing

residential schools system
A program of state- and church-run schools designed to assimilate Indigenous children into whitestream Canadian society.

them into state and religious boarding schools. Many children were permanently separated from their families. Some experts have characterized the residential schools as an instrument of cultural genocide given that Indigenous customs and languages were forbidden. In addition, widespread physical, psychological, and sexual abuse occurred at these schools, setting generations of Indigenous peoples on a cycle of family violence and patterned substance use on a scale not experienced by any other group in Canada.

Thus, westward expansion was far from smooth or uncontroversial, particularly by today's standards. Conflicts erupted between Liberals and Conservatives in Ottawa and provincial capitals across the country. Governments were pushed into court to defend their actions against each other and against private interests. The denial of full provincial jurisdiction to the new Western provinces sparked alienation and resentment. Disputes included control over the language of instruction in schools and natural resource development. Debates over the importance of free trade with the United States caused further division. This pitted Western farmers seeking freer access to American markets for their goods and machinery against Central Canadian manufacturers, railway barons, and financiers seeking to keep their advantages in a closed Canadian market. The federal government's treatment of Indigenous peoples on the prairies even resulted in a pair of armed conflicts, led by Métis leader Louis Riel. These issues and developments deepened the ethnic and regional cleavages that marked the first era of Canadian politics.

Amidst all this, women struggled to gain property rights, the right to vote, and the right to stand for election. Francophones sought assurances that their dualist role in Confederation would be protected and not pushed aside by Anglophones. Canada suffered great loss during the World Wars, which was a formative period for nationalism, and hardship during the Great Depression, which spurred the growth of the welfare state.

Second Era of Canadian Politics (mid-1900s–late 1900s)

The two World Wars and the Great Depression marked a long transition period between the first and second eras of modern Canadian politics. If its first 50 years could be considered its infancy as a country, throughout the ensuing three decades, Canada came of age as a society, as a political culture, and as a democracy. Canadians assumed leadership and an independent stature on the international stage thanks to their participation in the global conflicts. The Depression had a huge effect on the country's internal political attitudes, as the Co-operative Commonwealth Federation, later transformed into the NDP, emerged as a competitive third political party. Change to political institutions occurred, as governments collaborated and competed in building one of the world's most comprehensive social-welfare states. These calamities—the World Wars and the Depression—forged a sense of common purpose among many Canadians, but not all. Indigenous peoples remained marginalized in Canadian democracy. Regional, ethnic, and ideological divisions separated Canadians who supported the war efforts (primarily in English Canada) from those who did not (primarily in Quebec), and those who supported the expansion of the state (liberals and socialists) from those who did not (conservatives).

As Canada entered the post-war period, its politics turned toward questions of national identity and unity. Unlike the first era, the epicentre for these debates was not the West but rather Quebec. For decades, Quebecers had railed against the consensus surrounding Canada's involvement in the World Wars. Yet as a voice of the province of Quebec and francophones generally, the Quebec government had taken an inward-looking approach. It seldom engaged meaningfully with the federal and provincial governments on the Canadian stage. At the same time, the ultra-conservative Union Nationale government in Quebec City played only a small role in the everyday lives of Quebecers. Other provincial governments were working with Ottawa to build more expansive health, education, and social programs. But in Quebec, these services continued to be directed largely by the Catholic Church. By the end of the 1950s, Quebec was an outlier—a predominantly rural, conservative province in a quickly modernizing Canadian society.

This changed rapidly in the decades that followed, as the provincial Liberal Party in Quebec led what became known as the Quiet Revolution. In short order, the Quebec government displaced the Catholic Church as the central institution in Quebec society, building some of Canada's most progressive social programs in the process. The Quebec government began asserting itself at meetings with the federal government and other provinces, hosting the first Annual Premiers' Conference in 1960. The Quiet Revolution built on, and reinforced, a growing nationalism movement in Quebec—one that, to this day, continues to wax and wane, vacillating between building a stronger province within Canada and establishing an independent Quebec state. Regardless of the status of the nationalist movement, the Quiet Revolution helped to establish Quebec's claim to special status within the Canadian federation. This informed a national unity discourse that dominated the second era of Canadian politics.

See Regionalism in Quebec, beginning on page 109 in Chapter 4, for a discussion of the Quiet Revolution and Quebec nationalism.

The developments in Quebec coincided with a parallel identity-building exercise in English Canada. In the early 1960s, the country went through a divisive public discussion about national identity as the federal government sought to create a Canadian flag, culminating in the adoption of the maple leaf in 1965 (see Inside Canadian Politics: How Did Canada Choose the Maple Leaf as the Country's Flag?). In 1967, monuments were erected and historical celebrations were held to commemorate Confederation. Expo '67, the world fair held in Montreal, promised to give Canada and other members of the global community a glimpse at tomorrow. Coming together to celebrate these events was a Canadian population that was undergoing a dramatic transition. In addition to the advent of the civil rights movement, which saw advances for women and other groups that were traditionally marginalized, the post-war period saw a massive increase in immigration to Canada from Europe and the developing world. The face of Canada literally and figuratively changed in a few short decades. What was once a largely French-Catholic and English-Protestant mainstream was becoming increasingly multicultural. Immigrant and visible-minority communities began asserting themselves in the political arena.

Paradoxically, Indigenous Canadians experienced more marginalization just as Canada's multicultural mosaic was taking shape. The federal government's White Paper on Indian Policy (1969) signalled its intention to dismantle the Indian Act in an effort to assimilate First Nations people into the broader, predominantly European society. The ensuing debate mobilized Indigenous peoples on a regional and national level. Prime Minister Pierre Trudeau and his minister of Indian affairs, Jean Chrétien, based the policy prescription on the principle of equality, arguing that converting reserve land to private property, settling outstanding land claims and extinguishing treaties, and devolving responsibility over "Indian affairs" to the provinces would result in fairer treatment of

Indigenous people. Indigenous groups were quick to condemn the government's proposals. During the consultations prior to the white paper's release, many Indigenous groups asked the government to amend (not abolish) the Indian Act: they wanted to see Indigenous rights enhanced, not extinguished; Indigenous representation in federal decision-making increased, not submerged; and federal fiduciary responsibility for Indian affairs increased, not merely handed off to the provinces. Facing vocal opposition across the country, the federal government abandoned the white paper soon after it was released.

These identity-building processes collided amid the constitutional negotiations of the 1970s and 1980s. Politicians sought to bring the Canadian constitution under full domestic control, a move requiring the incorporation of the elusive amending formula so that the document could be changed without the approval of British Parliament. The patriation process included discussion about the entrenchment of a new **Charter of Rights and Freedoms**. Both the constitutional amending formula and the Charter proved points of contention among the federal and provincial governments. At several points, governments found themselves arguing before the Supreme Court of Canada, which insisted that any constitutional consensus must involve substantial provincial consent. In the end, the new constitution—complete with a complex amending formula and somewhat watered-down Charter—received support from nearly all governments before Queen Elizabeth II gave assent in 1982. It contained a new section recognizing Indigenous treaty rights, providing the first, albeit limited, constitutional acknowledgment of Indigenous peoples' inherent right to self-government in over two centuries.

Charter of Rights and Freedoms
A portion of the Constitution Act, 1982, enshrining Canadians' core liberties and entitlements vis-à-vis their governments.

Inside Canadian Politics

How Did Canada Choose the Maple Leaf as the Country's Flag?

For many Canadians, it is difficult to picture a union jack or red ensign flying on Parliament Hill, or to imagine a time when the maple leaf did not represent Canada on flagstaffs around the world. The adoption of the Canadian flag in 1965 symbolized the evolution of both the Canadian state and its people. To many at the time, the new maple leaf flag became the embodiment of Canada's new place within the Commonwealth of Nations, within North America, and within the world as a whole. The flag also announced the birth of a new cultural dynamic.

In 1867, as a British dominion, Canada's national flag was the Union Jack. This was unsuitable in war because of the need to distinguish military units. A modified version of the Union Jack, known as the Red Ensign, became Canada's unofficial flag. In the early 1960s, following a national design contest, Liberal prime minister

Lester Pearson unveiled the so-called "Pearson pennant" with three red maple leaves on a white backdrop with vertical blue bars on each of the left and right sides. The maple leaf was a political symbol that had been used for years in songs and in the uniforms of Canadian sports teams. World War I soldier patches marked one of the first uses of the maple leaf as a means of differentiating Canadians from the British. The idea was dismissed as an affront to Canada's British heritage by the Progressive Conservative Party. War veterans preferred the Red Ensign. Some thought combining the ensign with another cultural symbol, like the fleur-de-lis, would help provide balance.

A national debate ensued. Conversations in public places, in classrooms, and around the dinner table contributed to the evolution of a more modern and

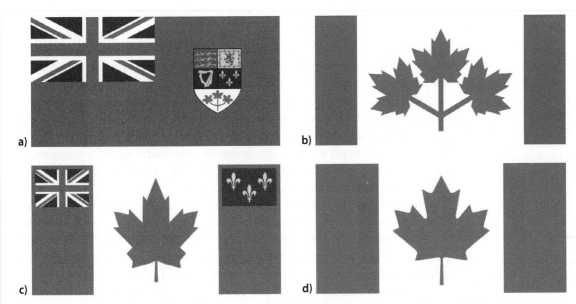

Figure 1.4 | Variations on the Canadian Flag: (a) the Red Ensign; (b) the Pearson Pennant; (c) the Diefenbaker Proposal; (d) the Canadian Flag

independent Canada. An all-party parliamentary committee reviewed approximately 6000 design submissions. It settled on the red-and-white maple leaf design that we know today—the same motif that appeared in a 1903 Quebec political cartoon.[3]

The flag debate was divided largely along regional lines and reinforced by political parties' support bases. Progressive Conservative leader and former prime minister John Diefenbaker argued that a Canadian flag should reflect the contributions of the county's two founding settler groups—the French and the English—by incorporating the fleur-de-lis and the union jack. The Conservatives wanted to modify the red ensign, Canada's national flag since its sanction by Mackenzie King in 1945, by placing the fleur-de-lis in a more prominent position and adding a single green maple leaf. Members

of Parliament from Quebec advocated a new flag with no emblems to tie it to foreign nations. They argued it ought to symbolize the future of the Canadian nation and the unity of its peoples. Prime Minister Pearson countered that the design ought to contain a central symbol which would "divide us the least."

After a rancorous discussion in the House of Commons, and amid minority government conditions, the Flag Act, 1965, was passed, and the maple leaf became Canada's national emblem. Thus, on the eve of the centennial of Confederation, Canada adopted a new national symbol that helped sever symbolic ties to its British heritage. The road to patriation was even longer: it would take another two decades to achieve consensus on the amending formula necessary to bring the constitution home to Canada.

DISCUSSION ITEM

Establishing new national symbols often entails divisive political debate.

VOX POP

What do you think of the Canadian flag? How do you think it has influenced Canada's sense of nationalism?

distinct society
A proposed designation
for the province of Quebec,
recognizing that it features
a French-speaking majority,
a unique culture, and a
civil-law tradition.

Crucially, the new constitution did not receive support from the government of Quebec, whose opposition prolonged the high-stakes negotiations for another decade. In 1980, amid the patriation discussions, Quebec held a referendum on separation from Canada. The separatists lost the vote and the event provided a sense of urgency to address Quebec's concerns. Among the province's subsequent suggested changes to the constitution was the formal recognition of Quebec as a **distinct society**. Governments from across Canada initially agreed on two complete constitutional reform packages, neither of which was implemented. The lack of change produced a new wave of separatist sentiment in Quebec, and in 1995, the newly elected Parti Québécois convened a second sovereignty referendum. This time, the margin of victory for the "non" side was much slimmer: just 50.6 per cent of Quebecers voted to remain in Canada.

The Quebec referendum brought a tumultuous close to the second era of modern Canadian politics. Questions of national identity and unity, and constitutional preoccupations, overshadowed many other pressing issues. In particular, they distracted many governments and Canadians from the significant economic challenges facing the country, as federal and provincial budgets continued to fall further into deficit while public debts mounted. Much maligned at the time, the introduction of the Goods and Services Tax (GST) and the passage of the North American Free Trade Agreement (NAFTA) were among the few notable achievements in this area. The political turmoil contributed to fracturing of political parties along geographic lines. The Bloc Québécois separatist party emerged in Quebec and the conservative Reform Party, later succeeded by the Canadian Alliance, grew in the West. This helped set the stage for a new era of Canadian politics.

Third Era of Canadian Politics (late 1900s–early 2000s)

After the national unity drama climaxed in the mid-1990s, governments across Canada turned their attention away from the constitution, focusing more on their own ballooning budgets and slow economic growth. The country went through one of its most comprehensive rounds of fiscal restructuring since the Second World War, reversing many earlier approaches and policies in the growth of Canada's welfare state. The federal government launched a series of strict spending cuts, most notably to the transfers it provided to provincial governments for programs and services like healthcare, education, and social assistance. Many provinces cut spending in these areas as well, resulting in a noticeable retrenchment in the area of social policy across Canada. By the turn of the century, these reductions placed nearly all federal and provincial governments on firmer fiscal ground, with most posting budgets that did not rely on borrowing more money. In the meantime, the spending cuts hit Canada's universal healthcare system particularly hard, prompting Canadians to identify healthcare as their most important political concern in public-opinion polls. This pushed governments to re-invest in the health sector, while seeking to improve the quality of healthcare through collaborative efforts and the sharing of best practices.

This firm fiscal focus was disrupted, at least momentarily, by the events of 11 September 2001. The 9/11 terrorist attacks in New York City, Washington, and Pennsylvania reverberated throughout the world. Canada and the US enacted sweeping new anti-terrorism legislation that redefined the balance between public safety and civil liberties. The immediate response to the 11 September attacks demonstrated the close relationship between Canada and the United States. Its aftermath illustrated the extent to which each government maintained its independence in the area of foreign policy. When Canada rejected the Americans' invitation to join coalition forces in Operation Iraqi Freedom, it became the latest in a series of high-profile differences of opinion over military policy that began, in modern times, with the war in Vietnam. Overall, leaders of the two countries seem better aligned when they share a common ideological outlook. Canada contributed to the American-led war on terror by sending troops to Afghanistan and participating in active combat. Canadian society's views of its military shifted from an image of under-funded peacekeepers to armed soldiers on the front lines.

Fiscal tensions re-emerged in 2008. A major economic recession, triggered by the collapse of the poorly regulated American housing market, affected markets around the world. As witnessed countless times before, the close integration of the US and Canadian economies exposed Canada to a significant shock, although firmer banking regulations north of the border blunted the blow. The Government of Canada's response to the recession was a massive, cost-shared stimulus package involving significant, one-time investment in infrastructure across Canada. The joint commitment challenged all Canadian governments to maintain their budget balances, and pushed all but a few into significant and long-term deficits.

The recession accelerated and highlighted a long-term power shift in Canadian politics. Strong petroleum-based economies in the West weathered the economic storm much better than their neighbours in Central and Eastern Canada. British Columbia, Alberta, and Saskatchewan are serving as Canada's economic engine in the twenty-first century. For the first time in Canadian history, the economy of Ontario—home to Canada's largest population and its manufacturing hub—performed below the national average, with the provincial government receiving **equalization** payments from Ottawa. The shift of economic and political influence from east to west occurred against a backdrop of greater economic co-operation. Canadian governments negotiated a free-trade deal with the European Union, worked to reduce inter-provincial trade barriers, and present a united front in the face of American demands to renegotiate the North American Free Trade Agreement.

equalization
A federal transfer program that is designed to lessen the fiscal disparities among provinces.

Canadian politics recently experienced significant social change as well. Court decisions enforcing the Charter of Rights and Freedoms facilitated societal change faster than many governments were willing to advance, in areas such as same-sex marriage, prostitution, and physician-assisted death. Other areas of social change have been initiated by politicians, notably the legalization of cannabis. Environmentalism and concern about climate change has risen as a sustained area of public concern. The leader of the Green Party of Canada participated in party leader election debates and became the first member of the Greens to be elected to the House of Commons.

Free trade, including the Canada-United States-Mexico Agreement, is discussed on pages 471–81 in Chapter 14, on international trade, security and global affairs.

This era gives rise to a new set of geographic divisions and salience to an ages-old ethnic cleavage. The alienation of Western Canadians reached another crescendo, as the federal government moved to place a price on carbon. Divisions within the region emerged amid attempts by oil companies to build and expand pipelines across the Alberta/British Columbia border. These regional tensions notwithstanding, political scientists have discovered that, more than ever before, Canadians' political attitudes depend on the size of community in which they live. The gradual urbanization of Canadian society has continued over the past century, reinforcing a longstanding political cleavage: rural Canadians are among the most conservative in their outlook on most issues, and urban Canadians more progressive. This division manifests itself in the success of the federal Conservatives, provincial Progressive Conservatives (or equivalents—not all provinces have PC parties), and other right-leaning parties in rural areas throughout the country, and the success of Liberals, New Democrats, and other left-leaning parties in most cities. In recent decades, suburbanites have emerged as a separate category, motivated by a blend of conservative approaches to fiscal issues and left-wing approaches to social and moral ones. Parties across the spectrum at both the federal and provincial levels have taken note, particularly since suburban areas have become true battlegrounds in most elections. This is manifested in their policies, communications, outreach, and fundraising.

Beyond the politics of rural, urban, and suburban regions is the vast socioeconomic and cultural divide between Indigenous peoples and other people in Canada. It has only recently reached a relatively sustained level of political salience, thanks in large part to decades of pressure and advocacy by Indigenous leaders. This newfound mobilization is facilitated, in part, by the ability of social media to connect a geographically disparate political group, epitomized by the Idle No More movement founded in 2012. More than ever before, issues like land claims negotiations, environmental sustainability, economic development, First Nations education, water quality, violence against Indigenous women and girls, and Indigenous child welfare are now treated as leading news stories, as topics trending on Twitter, in major party platforms, and as full agenda items for federal–provincial–territorial intergovernmental conferences. The work of the Truth and Reconciliation Commission brought historical injustices to light, and encouraged governments and citizens to address the intergenerational effects of residential schools on Indigenous peoples and Canadian society. To what extent this increased attention will result in concrete action remains to be seen.

Inside Canadian Politics

How Is the Federal Government Approaching Reconciliation?

In 2007, the federal government took the first real step toward recognizing and resolving the legacy of Canada's Indian residential schools with the signing of the Indian Residential Schools Settlement Agreement. It provided for compensation payments to the estimated 110,000 residential school survivors, and also included support and treatment programs and commemorative activities. In 2008, with leaders of all National Indigenous Organizations and dozens of residential school survivors in attendance in the House of Commons, Prime Minister Stephen Harper offered an apology for the Government of Canada's role in the program.

The Truth and Reconciliation Commission was established to explore the impact of the schools and to educate all Canadians about this history and its ongoing effects on all parts of society. Reconciliation involves establishing a respectful relationship between Indigenous and non-Indigenous peoples in Canada. The commission's final report was released in December 2015. Prime Minister Justin Trudeau's government committed to addressing all 94 of the Truth and Reconciliation Commission's calls to action. This commitment included disbanding the Department of Indian and Northern Affairs in favour of two new government departments: Crown-Indigenous Relations and Northern Affairs, and Indigenous Services. The former was charged with leading the government's effort to dismantle the paternalistic Indian Act system and replace it with a series of new nation-to-nation relationships with Indigenous peoples. The government also committed to reviewing all federal laws and polices related to Indigenous peoples, and confirming a new set of principles and an implementation framework for engaging Indigenous peoples in government work.

In its throne speech to open the 43rd Parliament, the Trudeau government further committed to introduce new legislation to implement the United Nations Declaration on the Rights of Indigenous Peoples. Among other promises, the government also pledged to co-develop approaches to address problems with safe drinking water on reserves and close the gap in terms of healthcare outcomes between Indigenous and non-Indigenous peoples. "The path to reconciliation is long," stated the throne speech. "But in its actions and interactions the Government will continue to walk it with First Nations, Inuit, and Métis peoples."

DISCUSSION ITEM

It will take a significant amount of sustained political will to remove the remnants of settler colonialism from the institutions of the Canadian state.

VOX POP

Do you think the federal government's actions to date represent an appropriate and sufficient response to launch the process of reconciliation? Why or why not?

Situating Indigenous Politics

This raises a key consideration when studying Canadian politics: should Indigenous and non-Indigenous politics be treated separately, or is it more appropriate to treat them as common elements of the same political system? This is a crucial question, which is why discussion of Indigenous and non-Indigenous politics is woven throughout this book, culminating in a penultimate Up for Debate section at the end of Chapter 13.

It used to be commonplace to treat Indigenous politics as a distinct, often subordinate element of Canadian politics. This tends to de-emphasize the parallels between Indigenous and non-Indigenous politics, particularly on fundamental issues like diversity, representation, activism, and governance. Treating the two sides separately draws much-needed attention to the deep disparities and divisions between them. However, differentiation limits our ability to draw connections and lessons that are common and valuable to our understanding of Canadian politics as a whole. In this textbook, based on the trajectory of Indigenous politics, discussion is integrated throughout the various themes. Readers are encouraged to think critically about this approach when engaging in the debate found at the end of Chapter 13.

Concluding Thoughts

Politics remains what Professor Harold Lasswell deemed it over a century ago: the struggle to determine who gets what, when, and how.[4] This involves mobilizing different groups of people to help set priorities and establish agendas for government action. While the major issues have shifted somewhat over the course of Canadian history, the same basic organizing principles have prevailed. This has meant the same sorts of geographic, demographic, and ideological groups have dominated Canadian politics, to the exclusion of traditionally marginalized communities. In the remainder of this book, we discuss the impact of these structures and dynamics on the quality of Canadian democracy.

For More Information

How Canadians Govern Themselves is a freely available booklet that provides a tour of the Canadian political system. It was written by Eugene Forsey, a former Senator. It is available online through the Library of Parliament.

Essential Readings in Canadian Government and Politics (2nd edition) is a collection of key readings used in Canadian political science. It is edited by Peter Russell, François Rocher, Debra Thompson and Amanda Bittner and published by Emond Montgomery Publications.

The Public Servant's Guide to Government in Canada (published by University of Toronto Press) is a short, user-friendly introduction to working in the public service in Canada. It is peppered with practical tips and was written by the authors of *Inside Canadian Politics*.

Deeper Inside Canadian Politics

1. Canadian politics has been described as a hybrid of the United Kingdom and the United States. What are the two most obvious impacts of British influence on Canadian politics? What are the two clearest signs of Americanization?

2. Canada's three main political cleavages overlap to a considerable extent. Describe two ways in which geography, demography, and ideology intersect with one another to explain a political phenomenon in Canada. For instance, how do the three cleavages help us to understand recent election outcomes or challenges related to certain areas of public policy?

3. Why do you suppose it took 150 years for Canadian governments to pursue meaningful reconciliation with Indigenous peoples? What key developments contributed to the opening of this dialogue?

4. There have been a lot of critical junctures throughout Canadian history. If you could go back in time to revisit one episode or event to change the course of Canada's political evolution for the better, which turning point would you choose and why?

Professor Profile

Gina Starblanket

Indigenous politics, politics of decolonization in Canada
Star Blanket Cree Nation, Treaty 4 territory

Courtesy Gina Starblanket

Gina Starblanket studies the contemporary politics of treaty implementation in Canada. Her work centres on Indigenous political theories and practices, with specific focus on issues related to gender, feminism, identity, colonization, Indigenous resurgence, and relationality. She is interested in advancing critical analyses of ongoing conditions of colonialism in Canada, and in challenging the ways in which colonial logics are reproduced within the discipline of political science and its canons.

Here is what Gina Starblanket told us about her career path from when she was an undergraduate student, why she is drawn to her area of specialization, what is challenging about studying Canadian politics, and what advice she has for students.

* * *

I completed my undergraduate degree at the University of Regina with an honours in political science. My first introduction to a Canadian politics course was one of the first classes I ever took. I was 17, and it was very early in the morning. At the time, my major was human justice (I switched in my second year), so I had very little interest in Canadian politics and didn't see the relevance to my life or the life of others.

I began my post-secondary education interested in the problematic of how to bring forward healthy modes of co-existence between living beings in shared spaces. Over the years, I have sought to take up this problematic in a number of different ways. I initially looked at questions of identity and human rights, reflecting on the possibilities for justice that Indigenous peoples might find through appeals to universal rights frameworks, both domestic and internationally. Over time, I began to recognize the forms of oppression and violence that Indigenous peoples face as fundamentally related to issues of land appropriation, labour, race, and gender and coercive social, economic, and political assimilation. I found that political science allowed me to undertake a greater breadth of inquiry into these interconnected issues. As I studied these questions, I also became increasingly interested in the internal politics within Indigenous communities as we work toward decolonization and resurgence.

The most challenging part about studying Indigenous politics within the field of political science is that the field has not always been receptive to Indigenous peoples' own framings and challenges to the problematic of settler colonialism. Like many Indigenous scholars, I have often found myself carving out space within the discipline to ground my theoretical approach and analyses in Indigenous knowledge, philosophies, and methodologies. I knew early on that I wanted to do research and teach in Indigenous politics, so I always had to create space within the traditional disciplinary subfields and schools of thought. Because I'm particularly interested in the political issues impacting Indigenous women, I've often found my research crisscrossing with other disciplines as well and so I've also had to explain and account for the interdisciplinary nature of my work (which is really characteristic of the interconnected nature of Indigenous knowledge). What surprises me is how much of a desire there still is among students and other scholars to proliferate simplistic understandings of Indigenous politics. Some audiences have incredible difficulty recognizing the nuances, variations, and even contradictions in the political landscape between and within Indigenous communities, as if this diversity doesn't also exist in other political formations as well. Yet this attention to difference is vital to anticolonial efforts, as it allows us to strengthen our own political theories and ideas, while presenting challenges to colonial structures from a variety of angles.

A tip I would provide for students studying Canadian politics is to constantly interrogate and challenge the very constitution of Canada—its supposed foundations, narratives, mythologies, virtues, and values. These all contribute to the ongoing denial of Indigenous political life, but when one contemplates Indigenous understandings of the terms upon which we agreed to share the land with newcomers, the legitimacy of the current configurations of power falls apart very quickly.

Up for Debate

Get ready to strike up a conversation! Look for debates at the end of each chapter throughout *Inside Canadian Politics*. Ideally, instructors will provide class time for students to chat with each other about provocative issues, or provide virtual spaces like course blogs. Each Up for Debate provides information on both sides of the argument and is followed by resources for further reading. As you read on, you'll get a chance to contemplate answers to the following questions:

- Should it be easier to amend the Canadian constitution? (Chapter 2)
- Is federalism working in Canada? (Chapter 3)
- Is regionalism pulling Canada apart? (Chapter 4)
- Do Canadian prime ministers and premiers have too much power? (Chapter 5)
- Is strict party discipline necessary in Canadian legislatures? (Chapter 6)
- Do mandatory minimum prison sentences go too far? (Chapter 7)
- Should all government jobs be awarded based on merit? (Chapter 8)
- Should party leaders take bold steps to increase the presence of women and other Canadians underrepresented in legislatures? (Chapter 9)
- Are election and referendum campaigns mostly a waste of time? (Chapter 10)
- Does social media make Canadian democracy better or worse? (Chapter 11)
- Should spending by interest groups be regulated in Canada? (Chapter 12)
- Should Indigenous and non-Indigenous politics be considered as part of a common political system? (Chapter 13)
- Should Canada give more money for foreign aid? (Chapter 14)

PART I
Government and Governance

2

The Constitution

Inside This Chapter

- What are the key democratic principles underpinning Canada's constitution?
- What are the core components of Canada's constitutional order?
- How has the Canadian constitution evolved over time?
- What are the politics surrounding the Charter of Rights and Freedoms?

Inside the Constitution

This chapter traces the history of Canadian politics through the lens of its constitutional order. Some of the material may be a refresher from Canadian history or other social-science courses. Much of the content is explored in greater detail in subsequent chapters. For the time being, the chapter provides a high-level overview of the key documents, conventions, and principles that underpin the country's politics and democracy. When reading, keep in mind the following maxims about the constitution.

✔ **The constitution consists of both written and unwritten rules.** We sometimes refer to the constitution as though it were a single document in which all of Canada's governing principles are neatly set down in writing. Many political conventions and court decisions underpin the constitutional order. You will need far more than a copy of the Constitution Act, 1982, to navigate Canadian politics and democracy.

✔ **Minor adjustments are as difficult as major ones.** It is natural to think that smaller aspects of the constitution could be changed without much difficulty. However, it is better to think of the Canadian constitution as a package of age-old compromises. Tweaking one element means altering a whole series of historical trade-offs—something prime ministers and premiers have come to know all too well throughout Canadian history.

✔ **The constitution is more than just a government document.** Many people believe the constitution to be a body of laws and principles that are of practical importance only to people actively involved in running the country. This was perhaps true at Confederation in 1867, when constitutions were all about dividing powers and defining jurisdictions. Today, Canadians have a personal stake in the content of their constitution, and judges have become increasingly important political players, with the embedding of the Charter of Rights and Freedoms in 1982.

UP FOR DEBATE

Should it be easier to amend the Canadian constitution?

Keep this question in mind as you read through the chapter. Consult the end-of-chapter debate supplement for more material to help you engage in an informed discussion of the topic.

Key Constitutional Principles

Canada's constitution is the supreme law of the land, meaning all other laws must be consistent with its principles. These provisions distribute power and constrain the authority of any one politician or institution. Lying at the heart of the constitution are three key principles, the combination of which makes Canada unique: parliamentary democracy, federalism, and Indigenous and treaty rights. In the sections that follow, we devote more space to the discussion of Indigenous rights than the other two principles. This is due in part to the fact that they are unfamiliar to many students of Canadian politics, and due in part to the fact that parliamentary democracy (Chapters 5 and 6) and federalism (Chapter 3) are covered in greater detail later in this text.

Parliamentary Democracy

Canada is a **parliamentary democracy**, a form of government in which a group of elected representatives commanding a majority of votes in the legislature approves of political decisions on behalf of the entire population. This is also known as the Westminster

parliamentary democracy A democratic system in which government executives must be supported by a majority of elected representatives in a legislature.

parliamentary system, after the Palace of Westminster, the seat of power in the United Kingdom. Canada's system of government features:

- a government led by a prime minister and cabinet, supported by a majority of elected legislators, and a constitutional requirement for an election at least every five years;
- an opposition consisting of members outside the governing party;
- a permanent public service, separate from and at the service of the government; and
- a judiciary independent from government influence.

While it has evolved considerably over time, parliamentary democracy in Canada today is best understood as a combination of four different facets:

1. liberal democracy,
2. representative democracy,
3. constitutional monarchy, and
4. responsible government (see Table 2.1).

1. Liberal Democracy

liberal democracy
A system in which equality, rights, and freedoms are preserved through public debate and free and fair elections.

Canada is a **liberal democracy**. Unlike people living under authoritarian regimes, Canadians have the opportunity to choose officials to represent them in government and the freedom to live without fear of arbitrary treatment by those in positions of power. This liberal democratic label distinguishes today's Canada from its more elitist origins in the nineteenth century, when citizens enjoyed fewer safeguards against government intrusion. Gradually, governments across the country have established more legal protections for Canadians, a process that culminated in the Charter of Rights and Freedoms being enshrined in the Constitution Act, 1982. A liberal democracy should not be confused with the Liberal Party, a political organization that we examine in Chapter 9.

rule of law
The principle that no one is above the law, and that any powers granted to elected or non-elected officials must be conferred by legislation.

Grounded in the **rule of law**, the Canadian constitution preserves equality, rights, and freedoms, including individual and group rights, the protection of minority interests, and the sanctity of the private sphere. These rights and freedoms have been protected over time by a combination of parliamentary action and judicial rulings. They have been the subject of great debate over the course of Canadian history. Some view these freedoms in terms of positive rights that are extended to individuals and groups by the state. Others view them in terms of negative liberties that hold Canadians' lives must be kept safe from intrusion by the state. Similar tensions surround the precise definition of equality. Some feel that Canadians should be treated in precisely the same manner under the law, while others feel equality requires that certain types of people be afforded differential treatment.

Table 2.1	Characteristics of Westminster Parliamentary Democracy		
Liberal Democracy	**Representative Democracy**	**Constitutional Monarchy**	**Responsible Government**
• rule of law • rights, freedoms • equality	• mostly elected legislators	• sovereignty rests with the Crown • Crown acts on advice of political executive	• fusion of powers • confidence principle • cabinet solidarity • ministerial responsibility

The fact that the precise definitions of rights, freedoms, and equality are ambiguous is perhaps as much a product of the openness of Canada's democratic debate as it is a reflection of the depth of disagreement among its citizens.[1] These debates came to a head with the development of the Charter of Rights and Freedoms (1982), discussed later in this chapter.

2. Representative Democracy

Second, Canada is a **representative democracy**. Most policy decisions are made by politicians elected by citizens to represent their interests. This is an indirect form of democracy, in that a group of elected officials determines the public will. These elected representatives retain political authority even when initiatives, plebiscites, referendums, and other forms of **direct democracy** are used in Canada. Even when citizens vote on a specific policy issue, elected officials make the ultimate decision as to whether or not to follow the public's lead.

Depicted in Figure 2.1, Canada's system of representative democracy is shaped by territory, meaning that officials are elected to represent specific geographic constituencies. This differs from forms of democracy where representatives are accountable to groups that are not defined by territory—for instance, representing women, Indigenous peoples, ethnic groups, unions, classes, or specific occupational groups. Populist parties in the early twentieth century held this form of representation in high regard, even reforming electoral systems in some provinces for a short period, to reduce the role of territory in defining representation. These experiments were short-lived, however.

With the exception of Northwest Territories and Nunavut, which operate based on a consensus (or non-partisan) form of government, Canada's form of representative democracy has evolved along partisan lines. The role of political parties in Canadian democracy is discussed in Chapter 9.

3. Constitutional Monarchy

Furthermore, Canada is a **constitutional monarchy**, which distinguishes it from republican and presidential systems like the United States. Ultimate sovereignty in Canada rests with the **Crown**, not the people's representatives or any single politician. The Crown is a timeless concept, embodied in the monarch, whose representatives must approve all government actions before they come into effect.

representative democracy
A system in which citizens elect officials to make political decisions on their behalf.

direct democracy
A system in which citizens make political decisions by voting on individual issues, such as through a referendum.

The national referendum on the Charlottetown Accord, the province of Quebec's referendums, and other instances of direct democracy in Canada are detailed in Chapter 10, on democracy and elections.

constitutional monarchy
A system in which the sovereignty of the Crown is maintained, but exercised by elected officials according to prescribed rules.

Crown
The legal concept dictating the supremacy of the monarch over the executive, legislative, and judicial branches of government.

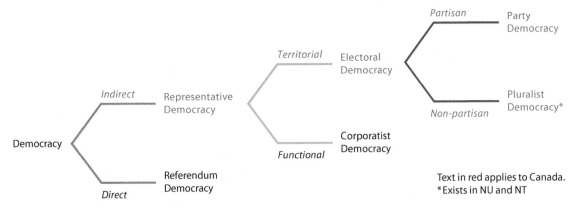

Figure 2.1 | Variants of Representative Democracy

Source: Adapted from Kaare Strom (2000), "Parties at the Core of Government," in Russell J. Dalton and Martin P. Wattenberg (eds.), *Parties without Partisans* (Oxford: Oxford University Press): p. 184.

This makes the reigning king or queen Canada's head of state. Queen Elizabeth II is represented federally by the governor general and by various lieutenant governors at the provincial level. By constitutional convention, the Crown almost always acts only on the advice of cabinet, formally known as the political executive. The cabinet, in turn, must act with the full confidence of the legislature, whose members are elected by Canadians. In practice, Canada's monarch and her representatives serve primarily as symbolic representatives of Canadians. Yet they wield substantive authority when it comes to authorizing government actions. This includes assenting to bills and dissolving legislatures, as well as appointing high-level officials, such as cabinet ministers, senators, and judges. In the words of political scientist David E. Smith, the authority of the Crown is a relatively "invisible" but powerful organizing principle of Canadian democracy.[2] In these ways, Canada's constitutional monarchy is distinct from absolute monarchies, where kings, queens, princes, or other unelected officials preside over their countries as dictators.

4. Responsible Government

responsible government
The constitutional principle whereby the executive (cabinet) must be supported by a majority of elected members of the legislature.

The fourth and final pillar of Canada's system of parliamentary democracy is the principle of **responsible government**. This concept requires that a first minister and the cabinet maintain the confidence of the lower house, lest they be stripped of government powers.[3] That is, on major votes, a majority of the people's elected representatives present in the legislature must support the government. Otherwise, the reins of power must be handed over to another group that has the support of a majority of those elected representatives, or else the legislature must be dissolved and a general election held. At the federal level, the government has lost the confidence of the legislature six times in Canadian history. Most often, the federal government has been defeated on budget votes (1926, 1963, 1974, and 1979), but in recent times governments have fallen after the opposition introduced motions of non-confidence (2005 and 2011).

Federalism

federalism
A constitution-based division of powers between two or more orders of government.

Federalism divides political powers between the central (federal) and multiple subnational (provincial) governments. Unlike unitary governments where power is concentrated in a single order of government and delegated to subordinate ones, federations like Canada feature power-sharing arrangements that allow regional governments considerably more autonomy. We devote a sizeable portion of our historical account below, and all of Chapter 3, to the concept and inner workings of federalism in Canada. For now, suffice it to say that this combination of shared and self-rule is among the defining features of Canada's constitution, alongside Canada's status as a parliamentary democracy and its provisions for Indigenous and treaty rights.

Indigenous and Treaty Rights

Until recently, most discussions of Canada's constitutional order would have ended with these two constitutional principles, parliamentary democracy and federalism. The resulting outlook was colonial, reflecting a prevailing belief that Canadian politics and constitutionalism began with the establishment of European institutions. Increased scholarly scrutiny and the political success of Indigenous peoples in Canada in asserting their rights are challenging this belief.

Decolonizing Canadian politics takes time, and **reconciliation** with Indigenous peoples starts with a better appreciation of how deeply embedded colonialism is in our society and political institutions. It involves appreciation for the inter-generational legacy of historical injustices and an understanding that things were not always this way. At the same time, there is no consensus on how to resolve matters such as Indigenous self-government, including within Indigenous communities, which have a diversity of views.

Indigenous peoples developed a nation-to-nation relationship with European settlers at first contact in the seventeenth century. This mutual respect was codified in the British **Royal Proclamation of 1763**. That Proclamation recognized that Indigenous peoples had title to lands in North America unless and until that title is ceded to the Crown through formal treaties or purchase. Over time, First Nations signed several treaty agreements with the British and Canadian Crown, beginning with the Treaty of Niagara 1764. Post-confederation, these treaties, numbered from Treaty 1 in 1871 to Treaty 11 in 1921, established mutual duties and obligations between the Crown and Indigenous peoples. This gradually opened up land to new colonial settlement in what is now Western Canada. In return, Indigenous communities were given small tracts of land (reserves), annual payments, food aid, and other forms of government assistance including healthcare and education. Indigenous peoples retained the right to hunt, trap, and fish on their original lands in perpetuity. Similar arrangements were made outside the formal treaty process in other parts of the country. This makes it more challenging for Indigenous peoples to assert their rights and claims to land.

Historians and Indigenous studies scholars dispute the terms and nature of these treaties. Many argue that the deals were coerced, negotiated in bad faith, poorly recorded, or struck without respect for traditional forms of Indigenous leadership (e.g., without approval of hereditary chiefs or the input of women). Many point to the fact that the treaties never involved ceding sovereignty to the British or Canadian state. While living under the protection of the Crown, as did French and British subjects, Indigenous peoples retained their autonomy and never agreed to be subjects of either monarch. They did not consent to the purported sale of Rupert's Land by the Hudson's Bay Company to the Canadian government in 1869. The company had trading rights, not title, over the land in question. Nor do many Indigenous people acknowledge the federal government's subsequent transfer of control over these lands and resources to provincial governments in 1930.

Rather, many Indigenous peoples point to the **two-row wampum**, which is said to have commemorated a treaty between the Mohawk and the Dutch in 1613, as emblematic of the relationship that was forged through treaties. The belt features two rows of purple beads, one representing the First Nations people and one, the European settlers. The two rows run like parallel streams, just as the two peoples were expected to live their lives: together, but in their own respective boats, each with their own laws and customs. Three cross-cutting beads of respect, peace, and friendship bind the two streams together to form an inter-cultural commitment to working together. Over time, the two-row wampum and other symbols like the shaking-hands image found on treaty medallions have come to symbolize Indigenous peoples' understanding of their relationship with the Crown: while Canadian and Indigenous societies coexist in peace and friendship, each should respect the right of the other to **self-government**.

reconciliation
The process of establishing respectful relationships among Indigenous people and non-Indigenous people.

Royal Proclamation of 1763
A British document setting out the terms of European settlement in North America following the Seven Years' War.

two-row wampum
A ceremonial beaded belt symbolizing the parallel paths and equal-order relationship between the Crown and First Nations people.

self-government
The inherent right of a people to sovereignty (or self-determination) over their own affairs.

Paul Morigi/AP Images for The Smithsonian's National Museum of the American Indian

The concept underlying the two-row wampum continues to animate self-government claims among Indigenous peoples across North America. Haudenosaunee tradition records the 1613 treaty with the Dutch as follows: "As long as the Sun shines upon this Earth, that is how long OUR Agreement will stand; Second, as long as the Water still flows; and Third, as long as the Grass Grows Green at a certain time of the year. Now we have Symbolized this Agreement and it shall be binding forever as long as Mother Earth is still in motion."[4] In what ways are unwritten agreements like two-row wampum preferable to written ones?

See Indigenous Representation in Canada, beginning on page 457 of Chapter 13, for a discussion of the barriers to Indigenous self-government in Canada.

Discussed later in this chapter, respect for the idea of Indigenous self-government faded quickly among federal, provincial, and territorial governments. It was replaced by settler colonialism that subjects Indigenous peoples to the full, and often differential, authority of the Canadian state. More than a century into Confederation, a consensus among federal, provincial, and territorial governments about narrower concepts of Indigenous and treaty rights led to their enshrinement in Section 35 of the Constitution Act, 1982. The refusal by federal and provincial governments to include "inherent rights" in the constitution resulted in "existing rights" being incorporated instead. In 1995, the federal government established a policy recognizing the deeper concept of inherent rights as the foundation of its self-government negotiations with First Nations. In sum, Indigenous and treaty rights have become a defining feature of Canada's constitution—albeit more in theory and political rhetoric than in policy or practice. Even when these rights have been recognized by federal, provincial, and territorial governments, implementation has been slow and uneven.

Core Components of the Constitutional Order

constitutional order
The body of written and unwritten rules that govern all laws in Canada.

Together, the principles of parliamentary democracy, federalism, and Indigenous and treaty rights are enshrined in various parts of Canada's **constitutional order**. We use the term order because not all of Canada's constitution is recorded in a single piece of text. Indeed, much of the constitution is not even recorded on paper: the supreme body of rules governing Canada's entire political system is not written down in a single document. These rules are neither recorded nor easily referenced, and, as a result, are often debated among people with different perspectives on the principles that underlie them. This sort of ambiguity can frustrate students and practitioners of Canadian politics, but as we will discuss, it may be partly responsible for the survival of Canadian democracy.

Constitutional Laws and Amendments

When most Canadians think of the Canadian constitution, their minds turn to the document negotiated by John A. Macdonald and the Fathers of Confederation in the 1860s. Others may think of the document signed by Queen Elizabeth II in Ottawa in 1982. In reality, several pieces of legislation are considered part of the canon of entrenched constitutional law in Canada. Some of these are listed in Table 2.2, although many scholars contend the list is much lengthier. In the following sections, we detail the substance and relevance of these various written laws.

From time to time, these laws have been amended and replaced, thus changing Canada's constitutional order. In the early years of Confederation, formal constitutional reform was relatively rare and incremental, proceeding through three main means:

1. through formal constitutional amendments to the British North America Act, made by the British Parliament at the request of Canadian governments,
2. through the passage of other laws in Canada and Britain, and
3. through court decisions.

Between 1867 and 1982, the British Parliament made 19 formal changes to the BNA Act at the request of the Government of Canada. These constitutional amendments ranged from strengthening the system of federal–provincial transfer payments to adding new provinces.

Table 2.2   Key Milestones in Canada's Constitutional Evolution

Legislation	Major Impacts on the Constitutional Order
Royal Proclamation of 1763	• lays the groundwork to recognize existing Indigenous rights and title, including the right to self-government
Quebec Act of 1774	• establishes religious, linguistic, legal, and political rights of citizens of the Province of Quebec
Constitutional Act of 1791	• establishes representative government in Upper and Lower Canada (latter-day Ontario and Quebec)
Act of Union, 1840	• reunites Upper and Lower Canada under a common legislature, and temporarily abolishes special rights for French Canadians
British North America Act, 1867 (in 1982 it was renamed the Constitution Act, 1867*)	• establishes the Confederation of New Brunswick, Nova Scotia, Ontario, and Quebec
Statute of Westminster, 1931	• establishes the equality of British and Canadian parliaments
Canada Act, 1982	• patriates the Canadian constitution
Constitution Act, 1982*	• establishes a domestic amending formula, entrenches the Charter of Rights and Freedoms, gives constitutional recognition to Indigenous rights

*Canadian legislation; all other laws passed by the British Parliament

Another change came via the Supreme Court Act, 1875. This legislation created a domestic high court for the young dominion, yet the Supreme Court of Canada would remain subordinate to the British Judicial Committee of the Privy Council (JCPC) until 1949. Other federal laws, like the Bill of Rights, the Indian Act, and the Canada Elections Act, form part of the constitutional order, as they directly impact core institutions and principles of Canadian democracy.

Many of these laws were passed prior to the establishment of the **amending formula** in 1982. The formula set thresholds of government support required to revise the various elements of Canada's constitution. While often referred to as a single formula, there are actually five separate amending rules requiring at least the consent of the jurisdictions affected and at most the consent of Parliament and all 10 provincial legislatures (see Table 2.3). The complexity of amending the Canadian constitution reflects the intensity of the negotiations surrounding it.

amending formula
A set of rules governing how the constitution can be changed.

Constitutional Conventions

As mentioned, not everything in the Canadian constitution is recorded in legislation. A number of entrenched practices that evolved over time are so fundamental to how the Canadian system of government operates that they are treated as part of the constitution. Canada operates on a series of these **constitutional conventions** that, together, form an unwritten foundation for all other laws and behaviours.

Constitutional conventions vary in definition, importance, acceptance, and inviolability.[5] The most fundamental conventions govern the core facets of Canadian democracy. As such they command the utmost respect and attention. Clear rules like responsible government, ministerial responsibility, cabinet solidarity, and judicial independence must be

constitutional convention
An unwritten rule that binds political actors to adhere to the traditions of the constitutional order.

Table 2.3 The Amending Formula

Formula	Consent Required	Matters Covered by the Formula
Unanimity formula (section 41)	Parliament plus all 10 provincial legislatures	• the office of the Queen and her representatives • the minimum number of senators per province • the use of French and English • the composition of the Supreme Court • the amending formula itself
General formula (section 38)	Parliament plus the legislatures of at least 7 provinces comprising at least 50 per cent of the population of the provinces combined (the "7/50" formula)	• the principle of representation by population in the House of Commons • the number and residency requirements of senators for each province • the powers of the Senate and method of selecting senators • the Supreme Court of Canada in general • the creation of new provinces or extension of provinces into existing territories
Parliament-only formula (section 44)	Parliament alone	• any matters not outlined in sections 41 and 42 that address the federal legislative and executive branches
Province-only formula (section 45)	Provincial legislature affected	• any matters confined to the province's own constitution (e.g., the Manitoba Act, 1870)
Province-specific formula (section 43)	Parliament plus the legislature(s) of the province(s) to which the amendment applies	• changes to provincial boundaries and the use of English and French

strictly observed, as breaches would be tantamount to tearing the very fabric of Canada's constitutional order.[6] Other conventions are equally relevant to the functioning of Canadian democracy, but the way these are defined and applied is more flexible or ambiguous. For instance, the term prime minister did not appear in the BNA Act, and was only added as part of the Constitution Act, 1982. The word "premier" remains absent to this day. Nevertheless, the rules establishing their powers over things like appointments are just as constitutional and real as if they had been set down in writing.

Conventions are the most stringent form of unwritten rules that underpin Canada's constitutional order. They define what shall be done in a particular set of circumstances. Other types of rules provide guidelines with varying degrees of flexibility. They are not enforceable in court. Rather, political actors are duty-bound to follow them by a combination of habit and political or moral suasion. These range from customs (long-time traditions or rituals), to practices (common ways of doing things), to norms (standards of behaviour). Breaking these rules usually brings consternation from other political actors, criticism by the media, and occasionally rebuke from voters. Nonetheless, politicians are known to test the limits of these rules, whether out of ignorance or to provoke conflict. The distinctions between the various terms are captured in Table 2.4.

The process for judicial appointments is explained on pages 232–6 of Chapter 7, on the justice system.

The issue of regional representation and regional ministers is discussed on page 144 of Chapter 5, on the executive.

Judicial Opinions

On occasion, courts are asked to weigh in on matters of constitutional importance. Judicial decisions may become part of the Canadian constitutional order, as well. In a process known as judicial review, courts are often asked to rule on the constitutionality of particular pieces of government legislation. This allows citizens, corporations, interest groups, and other Canadian governments to challenge the authority of government decisions.

Reference cases and judicial review are also discussed on page 221 of Chapter 7, on the justice system.

The list of pivotal legal decisions is too lengthy to itemize here. Suffice it to say that the judiciary's opinions on matters like workers' rights (the Labour Conventions case), the welfare state (the Employment Insurance Act reference), the environment (the Crown Zellerbach case), and the economy (the Securities Act reference) created important precedents and rules for Canadian federalism. Other court cases define the scope and character of human rights in Canada. The judiciary makes up somewhat for the lack of representation among women, Indigenous peoples, people of colour, persons with disabilities, and other traditionally marginalized groups around the constitutional negotiating tables.

Table 2.4 Types of Constitutional Rules

Constitutional Rule	Summary	Description	Example
Conventions	What we must do	Constitutionally binding rules, supported by a reason, precedents, and agreement	The Crown dissolves the legislature upon request from the first minister.
Customs	What we've usually done	Traditions that are binding by the force of habit	The Crown doesn't enter the lower house of the federal Parliament.
Practices	What we're doing these days	Things we've been trying out, subject to change when necessary or expedient	These days, the House of Commons is usually asked to vote on combat missions.
Norms	What we should do	Moral rules that we're honour-bound to follow	The Crown's powers shouldn't be abused for partisan ends.

Source: Philippe Lagassé (September 14, 2018, @PhilippeLagassé). Reprinted with permission.

A formative ruling was the Persons case (1929). The Supreme Court, which at the time was not the final court of appeal in Canada, had ruled that only men could be senators because that court interpreted the word "persons" as it was used in the constitution to mean "men." This judgement was overturned upon appeal to Britain's top court, the JCPC. That court decreed that women are eligible for appointment to the Senate of Canada on the same basis as men. This meant that Canadian women are legally "persons" under the British North America Act, 1867. After this ruling, non-Indigenous women were entitled to stand for public office, to vote, and to exercise many other democratic rights and privileges on the same terms as men. There was no further sex-based discrimination based in law. Similarly, the courts have helped to define and enforce Indigenous title and treaty rights, through rulings including R v. Sparrow (1990), R. v. Marshall (1999), Daniels v. Canada (2016), and the Tsilhqot'in Nation case (2014); and the rights of LGBTQ2+ (lesbian, gay, bisexual, transgender, queer, two-spirited) Canadians, through cases like Vriend v. Alberta (1998) and the Same-Sex Marriage reference (2004).

Once court rulings and opinions are released, and pending further legislative or judicial responses, they join formal laws and conventions as part of the Canadian constitutional order. It was the court that defined Canada's constitution as "a living tree capable of growth and expansion within its natural limits."[7] That turn of phrase captures the widely held view that the Canadian constitution must constantly evolve to meet the need of an ever-changing Canadian society. Rather than being grounded in nineteenth-century values, or interpreted word-for-word as an ordinary statute, the constitution must grow and adapt to the times.

The Evolution of the "Living Tree"

The following sections tell the story of the Canadian constitution as a living tree over the country's first century-and-a-half. It is a tale of leaders struggling to come to terms with how to balance the main elements of the constitutional order: liberal democracy, representative democracy, constitutional monarchy, responsible government, federalism, and Indigenous and treaty rights. Notable developments are noted in the margins, to draw your attention to the key moments in Canada's constitutional evolution.

The Road to Confederation (pre-1867)

As mentioned earlier, Canada's constitution traces its roots long before 1867. The Royal Proclamation of 1763 laid the foundation for the Crown's obligations to respect Indigenous rights, including the right to self-government, and to treat Indigenous peoples as equal nations or orders of government. These rights would be ignored and eroded.

The British government's Quebec Act of 1774 placed a considerable amount of this reserved land under the control of the new Province of Quebec. It granted government officials in Quebec the right to openly practise their Catholic faith and employ French legal traditions in civil matters. These entitlements made them unique among British colonists, and contributed to the resentment driving American colonists to fight for independence. The Constitutional Act of 1791 preserved these rights for French-speaking colonists after the war. One set of laws applied in French Canada and another in English Canada. It divided the vast Quebec territory into two halves: Upper Canada, which eventually became Ontario, and Lower Canada, which became latter-day Quebec. Both colonies were granted representative government. Colonists gained increased democratic control over their public affairs.

This division fostered some peace among French- and English-speaking Canadians. Yet the lack of autonomy bred resentment in both colonies. Following a pair of brief but jarring armed rebellions, the British government dispatched Lord Durham to investigate ways of meeting the colonists' demands for fully responsible government (as opposed to being ruled by an unelected British appointee). In his 1839 report to Britain, Durham described the tension between English and French settlers in Lower Canada as that of "two nations warring within the bosom of a single state." The symbolism of this phrase continues to resonate centuries later.

Upon Durham's recommendation, the British Parliament passed the Act of Union, 1840. That legislation reunited Upper Canada and Lower Canada under a common legislature and eventually, in 1848, provided the inhabitants with full-fledged responsible government. Seats in the new Province of Canada legislature were divided evenly between Canada West, whose 450,000 residents were predominantly English-speaking Protestants, and Canada East, whose 650,000 inhabitants were largely French-speaking Catholics. At the time, this division was viewed as a means of assimilating Quebecers and limiting their political influence in North America. French was temporarily banned as an official language of government and French-Canadian educational and civil law institutions were abolished. Deadlock gripped the legislature. Coalitions were led by premiers from each section and major legislation required the support of majorities in both Canada West and Canada East. Rapid British immigration soon reversed the population balance between the two sections. By the 1860s, politicians in Canada West were clamouring for increased influence.

It was at this point that delegates from the various British North American colonies began serious talks about union. In 1848, the colony of Nova Scotia became the first member of the British Empire outside of the United Kingdom to negotiate responsible government. That form of government was subsequently won by reformers in New Brunswick and Prince Edward Island. The three Maritime colonies considered unifying under a common political system. They did so without the enthusiasm of their Newfoundland neighbours. Leaders in Canada East and Canada West more or less invited themselves to these discussions, which evolved into negotiations of a broader political union.

Indigenous peoples were excluded from the constitutional negotiations because colonial leaders treated the deal as one among heads of their own governments. Treaties between the Crown and First Nations were pushed aside in favour of a *terra nullius* (literally, "nobody's land"; a legal concept meaning unoccupied or uninhabited according to colonizers) view of Indigenous lands and the treatment of Indigenous peoples as inferior to Europeans. Assimilation and cultural genocide ensued, as recently affirmed by the Truth and Reconciliation Commission's 2015 report.

Likewise, women were excluded from the negotiation of Canada's first written constitution. Rooted in British colonial traditions, this exclusion became a longstanding trend, as men of British and French descent played a dominant role in shaping the country's constitutional landscape for its first 125 years.

As it was, most colonial delegates realized the economic and military benefits of union. Most held a healthy reverence for British parliamentary traditions. United under a common central government, the separate colonies could create a larger common market and begin building a secure economy and society. Central Canadian manufacturing interests would secure captive markets in the Maritimes. In turn, all residents would gain rail access to the frontier of the new country. There was great anticipation of settling the vast Western lands and reaping their natural wealth, particularly given the military and economic threats posed by American encroachment from the south, and in ignorance or purposeful disrespect of Indigenous rights. Most colonial leaders looked forward to the prospect of creating a central government to handle areas of common interest like banking, currency, and national defence, while retaining control over their own local and cultural matters. Leaders from the various colonies differed on the means of achieving this union and on how government powers would be divided.

The most populous region, Canada West, wanted a strong central government—one whose powers would displace those of the British Parliament, and one whose seats would be distributed among the new provinces according to population. Leaders from other regions were less enthusiastic about empowering a national government over which they held relatively little control. While supportive of union, delegates from Canada East sought the sort of cultural protections that they enjoyed under previous constitutional settlements, namely the preservation of the French language, civil law, and Catholic education. The Maritime colonies pushed for a similar level of local autonomy. This would be manifest in a decentralized division of powers, a robust set of subsidies and debt payments, and regional representation in the institutions of the central government, including the Upper House of Parliament.

Canadian Confederation (1867)

See pages 71–2 of Chapter 3, on federalism, for a discussion of six aspects of the BNA Act—including POGG and the powers of disallowance and reservation—designed to ensure that the federal government would have more power than provincial governments.

Given these divergent interests, delegates to the first confederation negotiations were drawn to the balance provided by a federal system of government. At the insistence of Canada West, they opted for a highly centralized form of federalism, one in which the central government obtained overwhelming authority. The form of government initially intended was so centralized that some historians doubt Canada's status as a true federation in 1867. It more closely resembled a unitary state like the United Kingdom, where all power is vested in a central government. The newly created federal government was granted:

- the dual powers of disallowance and reservation, which offered it a virtual veto over provincial legislation;
- the levers of "peace, order, and good government" (POGG) and the declaratory power that provided the authority to act in the entire nation's interests; and
- residual powers over any policy area not explicitly enumerated as falling under provincial jurisdiction.

These centralizing measures were intended to prevent the type of divisive conflict that erupted in the United States, where strong states drew the country into civil war on the eve of Canadian Confederation.

Thus, British parliamentary traditions were melded with a more centralized form of American-style federalism.[8] According to the Westminster model, sovereignty in the new country would remain vested in the Crown, concentrated in political executives held to account by legislative assemblies, and exercised through the conventions of responsible government. Sovereignty would be divided between the federal and the provincial orders, albeit unevenly and in favour of the federal government. Regional representation would be built into the upper house, with an equal number of Senate seats awarded to each of the new provinces of Quebec and Ontario, and divided

Few Canadian politicians have been as controversial and constitutionally impactful as Louis Riel (centre). In leading an armed insurrection against the nascent federal government, establishing a provisional government (shown in this photo taken in December 1869), and enshrining French and Catholic rights in the new provincial constitution, Riel is considered a formative figure in the establishment of Métis rights and a founder of Manitoba. Yet, at the time these events took place, he was variously considered to be a patriot and traitor. Riel remains a symbol of the broader struggle for Métis rights against cultural assimilation. Why do you think attitudes towards him have evolved over time?

between New Brunswick and Nova Scotia. These components were incorporated into the British North America Act (1867) passed by the British Parliament and given royal assent by Queen Victoria on 29 March of that year. The new Dominion of Canada would be created as of 1 July 1867.

> **KEY DATE: 1867**
>
> The British government passes the British North America Act, establishing Canada's first modern, written constitution.

Not all British North Americans favoured Confederation. Opponents in Canada West thought the deal gave too much power to commercial and political interests in Montreal. Critics in Canada East feared the new constitution would consign French Canadians to being a permanent minority in the new Canada. Provincial autonomists in the Maritimes thought Confederation ceded too much authority to the larger and more economically powerful provinces of Ontario and Quebec. This was a major reason that leaders from PEI and Newfoundland refused to join Confederation in 1867, along with the lack of promise a continental railroad would have for their island-based populations. Republicans across the new country expressed disappointment at a lost opportunity to shed ties to the British Empire and join a new North American union with the United States. The voices of these opponents were drowned out at the Confederation conferences, however.

The Path to Patriating the Constitution (1867–1982)

The BNA Act, 1867, was passed by and remained under the ultimate control of the British Parliament. This meant that if Canadians wanted to revise the terms of Confederation, any changes to the text required approval by the British government, and would be passed only upon the "request and consent" of Canada. Whenever the composition of Canada's

Library and Archives Canada, PA-012854

House of Commons or Senate was altered, if a new province was created, or if there was a shift in the jurisdictional responsibilities between the federal and provincial orders, Canadian officials would have to approach the British government to pass a new BNA Act.

Seeking British approval persisted throughout much of the twentieth century. The heads of government across Canada failed to reach agreement on an appropriate amending formula that would allow them to take complete control over this core constitutional document. For its part, the British government showed little interest in maintaining authority over Canada's constitutional affairs. The British Parliament passed the Statute of Westminster, 1931, which affirmed that the legislatures of the various former British colonies were of equal status to the British Parliament and could pass their own laws independent of British government oversight. The various BNA Acts were explicitly excluded from the Statute of Westminster, however, as the federal and provincial governments continued to disagree on how to make future changes to the constitutional order.

The search for an amending formula intensified around Canada's centennial in 1967. Many politicians argued that Canada should enter its second century as a fully sovereign country. Put simply, in the absence of the British Parliament as an arbiter and in order to bring the constitution under home rule in Canada, first ministers would have to agree among themselves how future changes to the document would be approved. Several amending formulas were developed over the course of the twentieth century. All failed to receive the endorsement of Quebec. Premiers of that province insisted on a Quebec veto and severe limits on the federal government's ability to intrude on provincial jurisdiction as part of a new constitutional package. Indeed, over the course of the next three decades, Quebec politicians and the interests they championed featured prominently on the national stage.

The election of René Lévesque's Parti Québécois (PQ) in Quebec in 1976 made the prospects of agreement on an amending formula even less likely. A separatist party, the PQ was more committed to negotiating a new **sovereignty-association** with the rest of Canada than it was concerned with formalizing Quebec's place within Confederation. The PQ resolved to fulfill its promise to hold a province-wide referendum on whether or not to separate from Canada. This was a significant concern to all federalists. Prime Minister Pierre Trudeau, a Quebecer and staunch defender of federalism, staked his political career on formalizing home rule over the constitution and entrenching in it a new charter of rights.

There were many other points of contention beyond the elusive amending formula and Quebec's place in Confederation. Heated negotiations surrounded the establishment of constitutional protection of rights and freedoms, and the balance of power between the federal and provincial governments. Among the most significant was the constitutional status of Indigenous peoples. As noted earlier in the chapter, Indigenous peoples' inherent right to self-government was constitutionally recognized as early as the Royal Proclamation of 1763. This right was all but ignored by the Crown in the intervening centuries as British, colonial, and Canadian governments seized control of Indigenous lands. Within a decade of the BNA Act, the federal government passed the Indian Act (1876), which further institutionalized the subordination of First Nations to the Canadian state by defining how they should govern themselves, and even who constituted "Indians." After nearly a century, the federal government's 1969 White Paper ("Statement of the Government of Canada on Indian Policy") proposed dismantling the Indian Act altogether. Instead of returning to the nation-to-nation framework that preceded Confederation, Ottawa aimed

KEY DATE: 1976

René Lévesque's separatist Parti Québécois forms a provincial government for the first time.

sovereignty-association
A legal arrangement whereby Quebec would be politically independent but maintain economic ties with Canada.

to assimilate Indigenous peoples into Canadian society, abolishing treaty rights and completing the process of subordinating First Nations, Métis, and Inuit peoples to the Canadian state.

In the lead-up to the patriation of the constitution, Indigenous leaders placed public and legal pressure on the federal government to rectify this treatment of nations and people as wards of the state. Their efforts culminated in section 35 of the Constitution Act, 1982, which recognizes and affirms existing Indigenous and treaty rights as enjoyed by all First Nations ("Indian"), Inuit, and Métis peoples. Many critics felt that section 35 fell short of protecting Indigenous rights in Canada. Few participants or observers saw Indigenous rights as the focal point of constitutional negotiations at the time, a period dominated by political tensions between Canadian federalists and Quebec separatists.

In 1980, nearing the end of its tenure, the Lévesque government followed through on its promise to hold a referendum on Quebec sovereignty. The referendum campaign was tumultuous, with strategists on both sides aiming to capture the hearts and minds of Quebecers. During the campaign, Prime Minister Pierre Trudeau promised a renewed form of federalism as part of his patriation package. His pledge appealed to many Quebecers, 60 per cent of whom voted "non" in the referendum.

Trudeau had grown impatient over the provinces' lack of agreement with his **patriation** plans, however. In 1978, his government issued a report entitled *A Time for Action*, outlining Ottawa's intention to proceed with patriation with or without the support of the provincial governments. The move prompted opposition across the country. The governments of Manitoba, Quebec, and Newfoundland referred the federal plans to their respective provincial courts of appeal for judicial review. These cases eventually made their way to the Supreme Court of Canada in the form of the *Patriation Reference*. In it, the Court ruled that the federal government was required to consult meaningfully with the provinces and obtain their substantial consent before patriating the constitution. This ruling forced the federal government back to the negotiating table.

Emboldened, premiers from all provinces except Ontario and New Brunswick formed the so-called Gang of Eight to deal with the federal government. Those premiers had a hardline stance on a **7/50 amending formula**, under which ordinary changes to the constitution could only be made with agreement of Parliament, plus two-thirds of provincial legislatures representing 50 per cent of Canadians. Furthermore, they resisted the proposed **Charter of Rights and Freedoms**, which they viewed as encroaching on the ability of provincial governments to define the scope of liberty and equality within their own jurisdictions. Their stances produced a deadlock that was broken only through a creative compromise known as the "Kitchen Accord" (see the Inside Canadian Politics: Why Was the 1981 Kitchen Accord So Significant? on page 47). The deal granted the federal government the Charter. This came with a notwithstanding clause (discussed later in this chapter) that addressed the eight premiers' concerns about provincial governments and legislatures needing to retain the power to have the final say over human rights. The Gang of Eight received their 7/50 general amending formula, although significant areas of the constitution remained under the exclusive purview of the federal government.[9]

Quebec was not part of this backroom deal. On the evening of 4 November 1981, the prime minister and the other nine premiers reached an agreement to patriate the constitution, without Quebec's approval. In its aftermath, the Lévesque government expressed public consternation over what it called the **Night of the Long Knives**, an event that some Quebeckers today cite as evidence that the constitution was forced on Quebec.

KEY DATE: 1978

The Pierre Trudeau government proposes to patriate the constitution unilaterally, prompting court action by several provinces.

KEY DATE: 1980

The PQ government holds Quebec's first sovereignty referendum, resulting in a 20-point victory for the "non" side.

KEY DATE: 1981

The Supreme Court of Canada releases its opinion in the *Patriation Reference*, deciding that fundamental constitutional changes require a substantial degree of provincial consent.

patriation
The process through which Canadian governments gained the authority to amend the country's main constitutional documents.

7/50 amending formula
A rule for passing most amendments to the constitution, requiring the consent of Parliament and the legislatures of seven provinces representing 50 per cent of Canada's population.

Charter of Rights and Freedoms
A portion of the Constitution Act, 1982, enshrining Canadians' core liberties and entitlements vis-à-vis their governments.

It took until April 1982 for the Canadian governments to finalize, and for Queen Elizabeth II to sign, the Constitution Act, 1982. Quebec appealed to the courts to have the laws overturned, arguing that by convention the province held a veto over constitutional amendments. The Supreme Court rejected this argument. The new constitution remained intact. The British North America Act, 1867, was officially renamed the Constitution Act, 1867, thereby commemorating the document's transition from British to Canadian law.

The Mega-constitutional Period (1982–1995)

Patriation was an uncertain victory for the first ministers involved in the deal. Several constitutional shortcomings soon became apparent, most notably the failure to address Indigenous peoples' inherent right to self-government, to incorporate Quebec's interests into the new constitutional framework, and to account for the timelines imposed by the new amending formula.

As part of the Constitution Act, 1982, first ministers agreed to hold a series of constitutional conferences with Indigenous groups to discuss the appropriateness of further amendments to address their concerns. These conferences received less fanfare than those surrounding Quebec's status in Confederation. Nevertheless, the conferences did generate some notable results. Reforms were made to section 35 to clarify that the term "treaty rights" encompasses those rights that exist through land claims agreements as well as rights that may be acquired in the future. As a result of pressure from the Native Women's Association of Canada, treaty rights were guaranteed for both men and women. This

KEY DATE: 1981

On 4 November, a deal is reached to patriate the constitution. Quebec officials are not present, and not supportive.

Night of the Long Knives An incident in November 1981 in which the federal government and 9 of 10 provincial governments reached a deal to patriate the constitution, without the presence of Quebec government officials.

KEY DATE: 1982

In April, the Canadian constitution is patriated.

See Up for Debate: Should it be easier to amend the Canadian constitution? on page 63 of this chapter for a debate supplement that guides a discussion around this unsettled topic.

THE CANADIAN PRESS/Ron Poling

On Parliament Hill in Ottawa, 17 April 1982, Queen Elizabeth signed the Proclamation of the Constitution Act, 1982 as Prime Minister Pierre Trudeau (seated) looked on. The patriation of the constitution meant that henceforth Canada would no longer need to seek approval from Britain to amend its own constitution. As well, the Charter of Rights and Freedoms enshrined the legal protection of human rights in Canada. Why do you think some Canadians are proud of their constitution, including the Charter of Rights and Freedoms, while others might not be?

Inside Canadian Politics

Why Was the 1981 Kitchen Accord So Significant?

Debates over the amending formula hinged on the level of federal–provincial agreement required to make changes to the various parts of the Canadian constitution. Throughout history, would-be reformers proposed a variety of rules, such as the 1927 Lapointe formula, the 1965 Fulton-Favreau formula, and the Victoria Charter of 1971. None of these formulas achieved consensus across Canada.

Agreement proved possible only when the amending formula was packaged with a unique combination of other constitutional compromises. This became known as the "Kitchen Accord"—so named because it was reportedly negotiated by three justice ministers in the kitchen of the Government Conference Centre in Ottawa, late in the evening on 4 November 1981. Through it, all jurisdictions except Quebec agreed to entrench a new Charter of Rights and Freedoms in the constitution, including a notwithstanding clause that would allow legislators to override certain provisions; and to incorporate the 7/50 amending formula. This general amending formula would apply to most parts of the constitution. More fundamental changes to the constitution would require unanimity among Parliament and provincial legislatures. Remaining amendments could be made by Parliament alone, or by Parliament and the province(s) directly affected by the proposed changes.

DISCUSSION ITEM

Significant breakthroughs in constitutional negotiations are often achieved among a smaller group of government representatives, away from the media spotlight.

VOX POP

Why do you think it was so difficult for Canada's first ministers to reach an agreement on an amending formula? Why do you think the governments involved felt they should proceed without Quebec?

ended discrimination against women who married someone who was non-status. Aside from these amendments, the 1983–4 constitutional conferences set a precedent for future rounds of negotiation. Henceforth Indigenous peoples, represented by national Indigenous organizations, would need to be involved in any new mega-constitutional deals.

Changes in government marked the beginning of a new era, with Progressive Conservative Prime Minister Brian Mulroney and Liberal Premier Robert Bourassa coming to power in Ottawa (1984) and Quebec City (1985), respectively. Both governments were committed to bringing Quebec back into the constitutional family. Premier Bourassa made the first move in 1986, releasing five conditions for Quebec to agree to engage in amendment negotiations:

KEY DATE: 1986

Quebec Liberal premier Robert Bourassa releases five conditions for Quebec to engage in constitutional negotiations.

1. constitutional recognition of Quebec as a "distinct society";
2. a Quebec veto over all constitutional amendments;
3. total control for Quebec over immigration to the province;

4.   Quebec input into Supreme Court appointments and a guaranteed three seats on the nine-person bench; and,

5.   strict limits on the federal spending power, achieved by allowing provinces to opt out of national programs with full compensation.

The five conditions were built on the notion that Canada consisted of two founding nations: French Canada, represented by the Government of Quebec, and English Canada, represented by the federal and other provincial and territorial governments. This conceptualization did not align with that of Indigenous peoples in Canada or of those who viewed Canada as comprising 10 equal provinces. Furthermore, it conflicted with visions of Canada as one country governed by a strong central government. Nonetheless, seizing the opportunity to negotiate with a non-separatist government in Quebec, other first ministers pulled onside with this vision of federalism. So began the intense bargaining surrounding the so-called "Quebec Round" of constitutional negotiations.

In 1987, the first ministers met at Meech Lake, Quebec. They reached an agreement in principle that would become known as the **Meech Lake Accord**. The package addressed all five of Quebec's conditions. Most of the requests for Quebec autonomy were broadened to apply to all provinces who wished to exert those powers. Quebec's request for input into Supreme Court of Canada appointments, for example, was extended to include provincial input in general. In addition, the Meech Lake Accord promised to establish annual first ministers' meetings among the prime minister and premiers. Given that several of these proposed reforms would fundamentally alter the constitutional order, the package triggered the unanimity provisions of the amending formula. This meant Parliament and the legislatures of all provinces would have to pass the Accord.

After a marathon negotiating session, all 10 provincial premiers and the prime minister signed the Meech Lake Accord in June 1987. The Quebec National Assembly became the first legislature to pass the Accord later that month. The other first ministers committed to having their respective legislatures approve the deal before the constitution's three-year amendment deadline expired. In just over a year, the Accord passed in Parliament and all but the legislatures of New Brunswick, Newfoundland, and Manitoba.

That is when the amendment process stalled, amid developments far removed from the closed-door negotiation rooms in Ottawa and Meech Lake. Opposition mounted over the awarding of federal contracts to Quebec and the Quebec government's passage of restrictive new language laws favouring French. Critics worried that adding a new "distinct society" clause to the constitution would provide Quebec with too much autonomy. They feared that this status would marginalize linguistic minorities in the province and francophones throughout the rest of Canada. Others saw emboldening provincial governments as limiting the development of strong national programs. They fretted about the increased use of provincial vetoes as preventing any hope of future constitutional amendments. Indigenous groups opposed the exclusion of more comprehensive self-government reforms from the constitutional package. As in 1982, they were told to wait until future rounds of negotiation.

Above all else, opposition to the Meech Lake Accord centred on the process by which it was reached: through a series of backroom negotiations by, as it became known, "11 white men in suits" (i.e., the prime minister and the 10 provincial premiers), involving little to no public input. These developments, the emergence of two new federal political parties (the separatist Bloc Québécois and the Western-based Reform Party), and changes

Meech Lake Accord
A failed constitutional amendment package in the late 1980s that would have recognized Quebec as a distinct society.

KEY DATE: 1987

On 3 June, all first ministers sign the Meech Lake Accord, an amendment package designed to bring Quebec fully into the constitutional family.

in government in Manitoba and Newfoundland forced first ministers back to the negotiating table in an effort to save the deal.

The last-ditch efforts came to naught. A companion deal was struck to address New Brunswick's concerns over language issues, but the ratification process remained at a standstill in the remaining two holdout provinces. Procedural rules in Manitoba required unanimous support of all members of the legislative assembly to fast-track passage of the Accord before the three-year deadline expired. Manitoba MLA Elijah Harper, a member of the Oji-Cree community of Red Sucker Lake, refused to support the Accord, citing its failure to accommodate Indigenous concerns. Meanwhile, Clyde Wells, a vocal critic of the Accord, was elected premier of Newfoundland. After revoking his government's approval of the Accord, he refused to convene the province's House of Assembly for another vote. To the chagrin of the other governments, the Meech Lake Accord officially died in June 1990.[10]

> **KEY DATE: 1990**
>
> The Meech Lake Accord expires, having failed to pass in the legislatures of Manitoba and Newfoundland.

The Quebec government responded swiftly, introducing a bill establishing that Quebecers would hold a referendum in late 1992. It would be up to the rest of Canada to decide whether the referendum would be about Quebec separating from Canada or a referendum on a new constitutional amendment package. In other words, unlike the previous "Quebec Round" of negotiations, the prime minister and premiers in the rest of the country would have to initiate the "Canada Round" and entice Quebec to the bargaining table with the opening offer.

The other governments proceeded to build a new constitutional amendment proposal based on the foundations of the Meech Lake Accord. This included familiar terms regarding provincial input on federal appointments, limits on federal spending, and more provincial control over constitutional amendments. The English-Canadian proposal included a series of new provisions raised by other provinces and groups.

Chief among these innovations was the entrenchment of a "Canada clause" at the beginning of the Constitution Act, 1982, which would define the fundamental qualities of Canadian democracy. These terms included Quebec's status as a "distinct society" as well as commitments to parliamentary democracy, the equality of peoples and provinces, and Indigenous rights. The new constitutional package recognized the inherent right of self-government for Indigenous peoples. It proposed to create a third constitutional order for Indigenous peoples, autonomous from the federal and provincial governments. The new package provided for the creation of a new "triple-E" Senate, requiring that senators be elected, not appointed; that the Senate seats be divided equally among provinces, not among regions; and that the Senate's powers be effective, not ornamental. The new deal would extend exclusive provincial jurisdiction over natural resources (forestry and mining), culture (tourism and recreation), and urban affairs (including housing). Lastly, the accord included a social charter, committing governments to pursue common objectives in healthcare, education, environmental protection, and other policy areas, as well as a commitment to enhancing internal trade. In short, the scope of proposed changes dwarfed those involved in the Meech Lake and the patriation deals, fundamentally changing all three pillars of the Canadian constitutional order. The new accord promised to reshape parliamentary democracy, federalism, and Indigenous self-government in Canada.

The new amendment package was dubbed the **Charlottetown Accord** in recognition of Charlottetown, PEI, being the site of a climax of negotiations. All first ministers and leaders of major Indigenous organizations signed the new accord by August. As before, the deal required the unanimous support of all provincial legislatures and Parliament.

> **Charlottetown Accord**
> An accord in the early 1990s that proposed to renew the constitution, but was defeated in a national referendum in 1992.

This time, by virtue of Quebec's promise to put the deal to its residents, the accord would have to pass a nationwide series of provincial referendums scheduled for 26 October 1992. This was a crucial difference between the Meech Lake and Charlottetown processes, as the Meech Lake pact was never put directly to the public for a vote. The results of these referendums were not constitutionally binding on the various governments. Nevertheless, politically it would be very challenging for first ministers to introduce and pass the Accord in their home legislatures if the majority of their constituents were opposed.[11] The decision to hold nationwide referendums would add a layer of complexity to any future attempts at constitutional amendment. Now that Canadians had been directly consulted, it would be difficult to justify changing the constitution in legislatures alone.

In an unusual show of unity, the three largest federal political parties, all provincial premiers, and many First Nations and business leaders campaigned in favour of the Accord. In an odd twist, Quebec sovereignists, alienated Western Canadians, and supporters of former prime minister Pierre Trudeau and his original constitutional vision joined forces to oppose the Accord.

In the end, the Charlottetown Accord was defeated by a margin of 55 per cent to 45 per cent Canada-wide, and failed to achieve majority support in six provinces.[12] The only provinces where it passed were Ontario, New Brunswick, Newfoundland, and PEI; it also passed in Northwest Territories. Research suggests that Canadians found a variety of flaws in the accord, viewing it as too generous to others and not generous enough to themselves. Many associated the accord with its principal architect—Prime Minister Mulroney—whose popularity had plummeted following a series of unpopular political initiatives. This included his government's establishment of the Goods and Services Tax and the Free Trade Agreement with the United States.

The public's rejection of the Charlottetown Accord marked the beginning of the end of the mega-constitutional period. The failure of the two constitutional accords aggravated regional grievances. Canadians had become disdainful of political elites. Changes in government in Ottawa and in Quebec once again reduced appetites for further negotiations. Premiers and Canadians across the country appeared fatigued and discouraged at the prospects of achieving comprehensive constitutional reform.

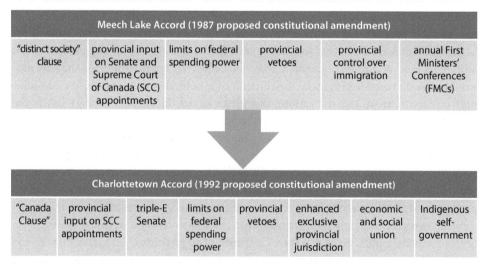

Figure 2.2 | Comparing the Proposed Meech Lake and Charlottetown Accords

Jilted after two failed attempts to bring them into the constitutional family, Quebecers participated in a second referendum on sovereignty in 1995. Barely half (50.6 per cent) voted to stay in Confederation. The 1995 Quebec referendum was a tumultuous, emotional event. It substantiated that many Quebecers were frustrated with their status in Canada and, for some, registered their passionate desire for Quebec to become an independent country (see Chapter 4 for more on this). The vote ushered in a new era of non-constitutional renewal of the Canadian federation. Few Canadians or politicians are interested in engaging in the sort of heightened debates that tore at the threads of national unity for almost three decades.

> **KEY DATE: 1995**
>
> The "non" side wins the second Quebec sovereignty referendum, this time by just over 50,000 votes.

The Post-constitutional Period (1995–present)

After the 1995 Quebec referendum, Canadians politicians and senior-level officials declared the constitution off limits. Other major issues had fallen down the political agenda for over two decades. The economy and healthcare were showing signs of neglect.

Yet first ministers could not entirely ignore the constitutional fissures. Rather than reopen formal amendment discussions, they proceeded through non-constitutional, incremental reforms. When taken as a whole, these measures went some distance toward addressing many of the grievances that led to the divisive debates in the first place.

> **KEY DATE: 1996**
>
> The federal government passes a regional veto law, placing constraints on its own ability to amend the constitution.

Most of these reforms were designed in a symmetrical way, extending new authority to all provinces equally, and not to Quebec alone. In 1996, the federal government passed An Act Respecting Constitutional Amendments, which gave Quebec, Ontario, BC, and Alberta effective vetoes over future changes to the constitution. The act established regional vetoes by stipulating that Parliament would not endorse constitutional amendments unless they had the support of a majority of provinces. Specifically, Parliament would require the support of each of Quebec, Ontario, and British Columbia, as well as at least two Atlantic provinces (totalling more than 50 per cent of the region's population), and a minimum of two Prairie provinces (totalling more than 50 per cent of the region's population).

In the midst of the Charlottetown round of constitutional negotiations, the federal government launched a **Royal Commission on Indigenous Peoples** (RCAP). The 1996 RCAP report People to People, Nation to Nation sought to sow the seeds of reconciliation between Indigenous and non-Indigenous peoples in Canada. The Royal Commission concluded that: "The main policy direction, pursued for more than 150 years, first by colonial then by Canadian governments, has been wrong." Assimilationist policies like the

BUT IF MEECH WAS AS IMPORTANT TO CANADA AS YOU'VE ALWAYS SAID IT WAS, WHY DIDN'T YOU LET CANADIANS VOTE ON THE MATTER?

BECAUSE CLYDE IT WAS FAR TOO IMPORTANT.

© McCord Museum

With legislation in several provinces requiring governments to consult the people prior to passing a constitutional amendment in their legislatures, and with a precedent set by the Charlottetown Accord, future changes to much of the constitution will likely involve a nationwide referendum. Are referendums the most effective way of generating the necessary level of agreement across Canada? Or is approval by elected representatives the best means of handling constitutional questions?

Royal Commission on Indigenous Peoples (RCAP) An investigation launched to study the relationship between Indigenous and non-Indigenous peoples in Canada.

residential schools system and Sixties Scoop that aimed to assimilate Indigenous communities and forge equality between Indigenous and non-Indigenous Canadians had done more damage than good.

To remedy the situation, the RCAP report outlined the premises for Indigenous self-government in Canada, as follows:

- For many Indigenous peoples, the right to be self-governing is derived from the Creator, who gave each nation responsibility for caring for the land and each other.
- Indigenous self-government is protected through international law, which states that all peoples have the right to "self-determination," including the freedom to choose their own forms of government.
- Indigenous self-government was recognized by the first European settlers, and was never ceded by Indigenous peoples (through conquest, treaty, or otherwise).
- Indigenous self-government is enshrined in the Canadian constitution, which acknowledges that it predated Confederation and was a key element of the bargain that allowed non-Indigenous peoples to found this country.

Among the responses to the RCAP report was the idea of a nation-to-nation paradigm. Within this concept, Indigenous peoples constitute autonomous government units, albeit highly interdependent with those of the Canadian state. **Treaty federalism** is among the most widely accepted models under this approach. It adds a layer of representation to the traditional concept of Canadian federalism.[13] It acknowledges that sovereignty in Canada is not simply divided between the federal and provincial orders of government. As well, treaty federalism is invested in Indigenous peoples through the inherent right to self-government.

treaty federalism A system of governance recognizing the equal-order relationship between First Nations and the Crown.

This has given rise to the notion that Indigenous peoples constitute a third order of government in Canada. Contrary to the traditional interpretation of the Canadian constitution, Indigenous affairs would no longer be an area of federal jurisdiction, and the federal government would not hold sovereign authority over Indigenous people. Just as provincial powers are not delegated to provincial governments by the federal order, neither would Indigenous rights and authority be delegated by provincial or federal governments.

RCAP's harshest critics sit at the opposite pole of perspectives on the future of Indigenous self-government. Many opponents of the parallelism approach argue against establishing separate institutions or systems of rights for Indigenous peoples, viewing such provisions as placing group rights over the individual rights shared equally among all Canadians. Critics suggest that fostering further separation between Indigenous and non-Indigenous modes of governance would only exacerbate the socioeconomic gaps that exist between the two communities. Political scientist Tom Flanagan maintains that:

> In order to become self-supporting and get beyond the social pathologies that are ruining their communities, Aboriginal people need to acquire the skills and attitudes that bring success in a liberal society, political democracy, and market economy. Call it assimilation, call it integration, call it adaptation, call it whatever you want: it has to happen.[14]

citizens plus The notion that Indigenous peoples (ought to) hold a special set of rights in addition to those conferred by Canadian citizenship.

Another model is known as **citizens plus**. According to political scientist Alan Cairns, Indigenous peoples retain all of the rights accorded to all Canadians (including those contained in the Charter of Rights and Freedoms) plus a set of rights unique to Indigenous peoples (including those embodied in the Royal Proclamation of 1763, treaties, and government legislation). According to this view, Indigenous self-government should be considered within the confines of the Canadian state and citizenship, without the formal establishment of independent, sovereign nation-states, and without subsuming it under the current constitutional order. The citizens-plus approach emphasizes the commonalities and shared interests between the Indigenous and non-Indigenous communities in Canada, and acknowledges that—like many non-Indigenous people—Indigenous peoples often hold multiple identities. These differences and similarities should be recognized, while forging a common, pan-Canadian set of interests and political community.

Debates between these three worldviews have been fought not just in the public and political spheres but also in the courts. In the Calder (1973) and Guerin (1984) decisions, the Supreme Court ruled that Indigenous title to land could pre-date white settlement. In the Sparrow (1990), Van der Peet (1996), and Marshall (1999, 2007) cases, the court held that Indigenous hunting and fishing rights are "evolving" and constitutionally protected against provincial regulation. Through the Delgamuukw (1997) and Haida Nation (2004) cases, the court established that the Crown has the duty to consult Indigenous groups prior to developing lands to which they could stake claims. And in Tsilhqot'in Nation (2014), the Supreme Court of Canada ruled that, while underlying control over the land rests with the Crown, Indigenous peoples with valid title claims must be consulted and accommodated before any decisions are made with regard to the use and management of the land, including its natural resources.

As not all lands in what is now Canada were formally ceded to the British or Canadian Crown, Indigenous peoples continue to stake **land claims**. In light of this fact, the British Columbia and federal governments continue to negotiate land claims settlements in the province, the most comprehensive of which was the Nisga'a Treaty. The 1999 agreement provided for a form of self-government for the 5500 Nisga'a peoples living in the Nass River Valley of BC. The Nisga'a government has legislative authority over some land and resources management issues, taxation, citizenship, language, and culture. These laws exist in parallel with federal and provincial laws, and are subject to the Canadian constitution, including the Charter of Rights and Freedoms. The Nisga'a government may also make laws in areas like health and social services, environmental protection, and transportation, although federal or provincial laws continue to hold primacy. In addition to recognizing these powers, the treaty and related agreements transferred nearly $250 million to the Nisga'a, provided ongoing (but gradually tapering) federal and provincial transfers for the delivery of health, education, and social services by the Nisga'a government, and recognized over 2000 square kilometers of land as Nisga'a territory. In these ways, the Nisga'a treaty came closest to establishing what RCAP labelled the "Nation Government" model of self-government.

At the same time, the federal government was also negotiating the Nunavut Land Claims Agreement, which culminated in the creation of a new, Inuit-majority Northern territory in 1999. Nunavut's territory was carved out of the eastern portion of Northwest Territories, and is the largest subnational unit in North America, with also the lowest number of inhabitants. The creation of Nunavut took a substantial amount of direct democracy to achieve. In an initial territory-wide plebiscite in 1982, 56 per cent of Northwest Territories voters agreed that the territory should be divided. In a second plebiscite, held a decade later, the proposed border between NWT and Nunavut was endorsed by 54 per cent of

land claims
Statements of Indigenous entitlement to territory within Canada.

voters. A third vote, in November 1992, saw the Nunavut Land Claims Agreement and the establishment of the new territory endorsed by 85 per cent of NWT residents who voted. The Nunavut territorial government retained the same constitutional status as the governments of Northwest Territories and Yukon, with jurisdiction over land use management, economic and resource development, and property taxation remaining subject to federal oversight. As in the Northwest Territories, Nunavut's legislative assembly operates a form of consensus government, with no political parties. In these ways, Nunavut approaches what RCAP referred to as the "public government" model of Indigenous self-government.

The Charter of Rights and Freedoms

The Charter of Rights and Freedoms was the catalyst of the patriation deal. Prime Minister Pierre Trudeau made it his personal mission to bring the British North America Act fully under Canadian control and to entrench certain fundamental liberties in an expanded constitution.

As discussed at the outset of this chapter, Canada is a liberal democracy in which individual and group rights are protected by law and under the constitution. Not all rights receive government protection and none come without important limits. There is a thin line between rights and freedoms, on one hand, and needs and desires, on the other. What is a fundamental liberty to one person may be a luxury or privilege to another.

rights
Legal claims or entitlements to have something or to act in a particular manner.

In general, **rights** may be divided into two kinds. There are some granted to individuals, like the right to vote, and those belonging to groups, like the rights of francophones to receive education and government services in French. Similarly, **freedoms** come in one of two forms. Freedoms may be negative liberties, which protect people from interference by government or other people, like the freedom of religion. Other freedoms are positive entitlements, which empower people to exercise their autonomy, like the freedom to move freely throughout the country. Taken together, rights and freedoms come in a wide variety of forms, from Indigenous and cultural, to political and legal, to moral and rational, to economic and social.

freedoms
The autonomy to live and act without external restraint.

Some, but not all, of these rights and freedoms are found in the predecessor to the Canadian Charter, the Canadian **Bill of Rights, 1960**. At the time the Bill of Rights was passed in 1960, Canadians were both witnesses to and active participants in a global human rights movement. Their constitution had been founded on the liberal-democratic principles of equality and protection of minorities. These notions were broadened and elevated to greater salience amid civil rights campaigns elsewhere in the world, most notably in the United States. These events coincided with the centennial of Confederation, prompting many leaders to re-envision Canadian citizenship.

Bill of Rights, 1960
A federal law detailing Canadians' rights and freedoms vis-à-vis the federal government.

Given these developments, Canadians and their leaders were primed for a debate over whether to entrench a more comprehensive set of rights and freedoms in the constitution. Constitutionalizing these rights would mean affording the judiciary a greater role in defining and protecting them. The courts would be asked to adjudicate between varying views of entitlements and liberties if they were entrenched in the constitution. This prospect did not sit well with supporters of **parliamentary supremacy**, particularly those in provincial governments. Discussed earlier in the context of patriation, they feared a new federally defined charter interpreted by federally appointed judges would disturb provincial governments' jurisdiction over human rights in Canada.

parliamentary supremacy
A doctrine under which legislatures and executives, not courts, define key elements of public policy.

Critics of this model pointed to a plethora of human rights abuses by Canadian governments acting under the guise of parliamentary supremacy. The forced displacement and oppression of Indigenous peoples, the residential schools system, the sterilization of mentally disabled people, the lack of the universal right to vote, the suppression of the press, and the internment of Japanese Canadians during World War II are among many high-profile cases. Furthermore, the centrepiece of the Canadian human rights regime, the Bill of Rights, lacked the necessary scope or force to prevent future abuses from occurring. It did not apply to governments beyond the federal level. It did not hold primacy (or precedence) over other federal laws. It contained no prescribed remedies in the event it was violated. Its rights remained defined as they were at the time of passage. Moreover, as an ordinary federal law, it could be amended at the sole discretion of the federal government.

In the end, those wanting to entrench rights in the written constitution and those wanting to preserve the power of legislatures reached a compromise. They sought to embed a set of rights and freedoms in the newly patriated constitution while allowing legislatures to override certain provisions under specific conditions. The **notwithstanding clause**, as it came to be known, was a key component in the Kitchen Accord, and came with a strict set of rules for its use. Federal, provincial, and territorial governments could pass laws that violated a particular set of rights and freedoms in the Charter (those in section 2 or sections 7–15). Such rights included "fundamental freedoms" like freedom of conscience and association, legal rights, and equality rights. Democratic rights, mobility rights, and language rights were excluded from the scope of the notwithstanding clause, meaning that no legislature could pass laws contravening them. The same was true of other core rights found elsewhere in the constitution, like Aboriginal treaty rights in section 35.

If a government chose to pass a law that violated certain rights, it would have to publicly declare this by inserting a clause in the act stating that the law exists "notwithstanding" the Charter. Such laws would expire after five years. If a government wished to maintain the new law, it would have to re-enact the legislation once every election cycle, which would allow the public an opportunity to evaluate the government's choice.

Charter advocates believed that the notwithstanding clause marked a major deficiency in the new constitution. It created a hierarchy of rights, some of which were violable by government and others that were not, and it allowed for the development of different regimes in various provinces across the country. To Charter critics, the notwithstanding clause did not go far enough to protect the concept of parliamentary supremacy. They felt the entire scope of the Charter of Rights and Freedoms should be subject to its provisions, and felt that the five-year sunset requirement placed undue burdens on duly elected legislators. In the end, the compromise satisfied neither side entirely.

notwithstanding clause
Section 33 of the Constitution Act, 1982, which permits legislatures to pass laws that breach certain rights and freedoms.

The Canadian Press Images/Edmonton Journal

From 1928 to 1972, over 4000 vulnerable Albertans were forcibly sterilized by the Alberta government under the auspices of eugenics. Among them, Leilani Muir (pictured above) was forced to have her fallopian tubes destroyed at the age of 15 during what doctors told her was an appendectomy. Muir went on to successfully sue the Alberta government, prompting it to introduce legislation in 1998 to compensate sterilization victims and prevent them from suing for additional compensation. They sought to limit victims' legal rights by adding the notwithstanding clause. Within a day, public pressure forced the government to withdraw the bill. In your opinion, under what circumstances is the notwithstanding clause a necessary safeguard for Canadians' rights and freedoms?

The notwithstanding clause was not the only limitation placed on the rights and freedoms in the Charter. Section 1 establishes that these terms are guaranteed "subject only to such reasonable limits prescribed by law as can be demonstrably justified in a free and democratic society." In other words, governments may be justified in limiting certain Charter rights in exceptional cases. The courts use this **reasonable limits clause** as a filter when deciding cases involving alleged violations of Charter rights. Indeed, section 1 forms a key element of the Supreme Court's **Oakes test**, named after a defendant whose narcotics conviction was overturned in 1986 because his right to be presumed innocent was violated without due cause. Judges apply the Oakes test to determine whether the purported democratic objectives of the law outweigh the negative impacts it would have on Canadians' rights and freedoms (see Figure 2.3). If the court determines that a law violates a Charter right, the judges consider whether the overall objective of the law is sufficiently important—that is, whether it addresses problems that are so pressing—as to justify that breach. If the answer is yes, the court asks whether the measures the law takes are suitable and proportionate to achieve those objectives and, ultimately, whether the means justify the ends.

As entrenched in the Constitution Act, 1982, the Charter contained a defined set of rights and freedoms, but these were not set in stone. Indeed, the list of rights and freedoms is continually revisited, and occasionally revised, through court interpretations. At the time it was established, the Charter protected:

- fundamental freedoms, including those of conscience, religion, thought, belief, opinion, expression, the press, peaceful assembly, and association;
- democratic freedoms, including the right to vote, to hold office, and to participate in elections at least once every five years;

reasonable limits clause
Section 1 of the Charter, which allows governments to pass laws that would otherwise contravene rights and freedoms but that are deemed necessary to protect other democratic norms.

Oakes test
A model employed by the court to weigh the democratic benefits and assess the constitutionality of a law that breaches certain Charter rights.

SECTION 1 CHARTER OF RIGHTS AND FREEDOMS

The *Canadian Charter of Rights and Freedoms* guarantees the rights and freedoms set out in it subject only to such reasonable limits prescribed by law as can be demonstrably justified in a free and democratic society.

Legal Importance

| Is the objective of the law "sufficiently important to warrant overriding a constitutionally protected right or freedom"? | Does the law "relate to societal concerns which are pressing and substantial in a free and democratic society"? |

if yes

Balance and Proportionality of the Law Being Tested

| Are the measures "carefully designed to achieve the objective"? | Do the measures "impair as little as possible the right in question"? | Does the importance of the objective outweigh the harmful effect? |

Figure 2.3 | The Oakes Test

The Oakes test was established by the Supreme Court of Canada in the case of R v. Oakes (1986). The test is used to assess the constitutionality of a law that breaches Charter rights.

- mobility rights, to move and pursue a livelihood in any province;
- legal rights, namely to life, liberty, security of the person, access to timely justice, and freedom from unreasonable search and seizure (habeas corpus);
- equality rights, such as the rule of law and freedom from discrimination;
- language rights when interacting with governments; and
- minority language education rights.

This list of rights was not exhaustive. The Charter did not set out social rights, such as rights to education, housing, or healthcare. It did not protect economic rights, like rights to employment or private property, or the right to strike. The Charter did not include

Inside Canadian Politics

How Did Signage Become a Charter of Rights Issue?

The Ford case (1988) provides a good example of the notwithstanding clause and the Oakes test in practice. A group of Montreal merchants took the Government of Quebec to court over the province's language laws, which at the time prohibited the use of English-only signs in their businesses. Lower courts in Quebec found in favour of the merchants, declaring the law unconstitutional. The Quebec government appealed the case to the Supreme Court of Canada. In its ruling, the Supreme Court found in favour of the business owners, deciding that the part of Quebec's language law prohibiting English-only signage contravened Quebecers' constitutional right to freedom of expression. While deciding that the purpose behind the sign law met the importance standard in its goal to preserve French language and culture, the justices found that the precise means through which the Quebec government went about achieving that objective were too heavy-handed. The Court struck down the law as unconstitutional.

The Quebec government responded by making very minor changes to the law in 1989, and invoked the notwithstanding clause to protect it from further judicial scrutiny. It was able to do so as all governments are permitted to violate Canadians' freedom of expression, provided they explicitly invoke the notwithstanding clause. Four years later, the Quebec government made the necessary changes to comply with the Supreme Court opinion, amending the law to include a more proportionate means of meeting its objective. In this case, it required that French be the predominant, but not exclusive, language on all signage in the province. The notwithstanding clause was not invoked on this new law.

DISCUSSION ITEM

Canadian governments are permitted to violate certain rights and freedoms, but such decisions are subject to judicial review.

VOX POP

Sections 1 and 33 establish real limits on rights and freedoms found in the Charter. How effective and justified are these limits? Who should have the final say on the limits of rights and freedoms in the Charter: appointed judges or elected politicians?

Indigenous rights, although some of these are entrenched elsewhere in the constitution (including Section 35). Nor did the written document enumerate constitutional protections for Canadians on the basis of their sexual orientation; this was later read into the document by the courts. Moreover, the Charter applies only to Canadian governments, not to private disputes involving individual Canadians, businesses, and other organizations; those rights issues remain under the purview of provincial human rights legislation. This said, the advent of the Charter of Rights and Freedoms marked a remarkable innovation in Canada's constitutional order—one that established Canada as a constitutional model for other common-law countries.[15]

>>>>>>>>>>>>>>>>>
The individual rights of Canadians are discussed in Chapter 7, on the justice system.

Charter Politics

As discussed, the Charter changed the way Canadians saw their rights and freedoms, and transformed the way governments sought to define, promote, preserve, and contest them. The courts played a relatively passive role vis-à-vis federal and provincial governments prior to 1982. The new regime assigned the judiciary a role to interpret human rights and freedoms in Canada as well as to define them.

As with other parts of the constitution, judges are empowered to use the Charter to strike down (or nullify) laws that contravene it. The Supreme Court struck down a ban on tobacco advertising, for example, as the prohibition ran contrary to the freedom of expression (the 1995 RJR-MacDonald case). Alternatively, judges may strike down parts of a law, grant an exemption to particular groups or individuals, or postpone the nullification until the government is able to respond. This was the case in the 2013 Bedford decision, where the Supreme Court served the federal government one year's notice that major elements of its prostitution laws were unconstitutional. Furthermore, judges are permitted to "read in" new rights, supplementing those that were originally included in the Charter. The Supreme Court did this when extending equality rights to homosexuals in several landmark cases, culminating in the Same-Sex Marriage reference.

These instances of judicial review may make it appear, and even make it more likely, that judges have the final say when it comes to the rights and freedoms Canadians enjoy. This is not necessarily the case. According to the **dialogue model**, judicial review is only one side of the democratic conversation. The other half is spoken by governments, who have the opportunity to respond to judicial rulings by amending or abandoning legislation. If the rights in question fall under sections 2 or 7–15 of the Charter, governments may opt to re-pass the law by invoking the notwithstanding clause, as discussed earlier.

dialogue model
The notion that the definition of rights and freedoms is reached through the interaction of judges, legislatures, and executives.

As of 2019, the only effective use of the notwithstanding clause has occurred in Quebec. As a signal of the provincial government's opposition to patriation, Premier Lévesque inserted a notwithstanding clause in each and every statute passed by the Quebec National Assembly from 1982 to 1985, a practice that ended when his government left office. Lévesque attempted to extend this principle retroactively, passing a law stating that all Quebec statutes passed before 1982 existed notwithstanding the Charter. In the Ford case, the Supreme Court later ruled that this blanket, retroactive exemption of Quebec laws from the Charter was invalid (*Ford v. A.G. Quebec*, [1988] 2 S.C.R. 712). Premier Bourassa subsequently used the notwithstanding clause to briefly shield Quebec's sign law from being struck down by the courts, as noted in Inside Canadian Politics: How

Did Signage Become a Charter of Rights Issue? on page 57. Decades later, the Legault government invoked the notwithstanding clause in passing its law barring Quebec public servants from wearing religious symbols (see Chapter 13).

Several other provincial and territorial governments have threatened to invoke the notwithstanding clause. Some have even passed legislation doing so. Yet none of those laws came into effect. For its part, the federal government has never attempted to invoke the notwithstanding clause.

Observers interpret this dearth of section 33 activity in a number of ways. Parliamentary supremacists view it as the result of the chill being placed on legislative responses to court decisions. Legislators, they argue, are wary of invoking the clause for fear of public backlash, given the results of opinion research that indicates Canadians trust judges and courts more than they trust politicians and legislators. From the opposite side, judicial supremacists view this as evidence of the success of the Charter, as it demonstrates the important check-and-balance served by the courts in protecting Canadians' rights and freedoms from government overreach.

All told, we can group proponents and opponents of the post-1982 Canadian rights regime into two camps.[16] **Charterphiles** value the fact that the system offers a new access point for Canadians seeking to defend or expand rights protections. Rather than having to lobby governments or field candidates for office, which can be difficult for minority or traditionally disadvantaged Canadians, rights-based interest groups make use of the alternative route provided by the courts. In this sense, Charterphiles view judges as independent, objective, expert arbiters of human rights issues, more distanced from the ideological, partisan, and majoritarian world of traditional electoral politics.

In the other camp are **Charterphobes**. They disagree with the direction in which the Charter steers rights-based discourse in Canada. Many view the rise of judicial supremacy and litigiousness (or jurocracy) as an unfortunate departure from Canada's parliamentary traditions. Charterphobes lament the fact that, rather than having duly elected officials defining and adjudicating rights disputes, it is appointed and unaccountable judges who now appear to have the greatest lawmaking powers. To them, this judicial power undermines fundamental principles of democracy.

Contrary to popular conceptions and general patterns, not all Charterphiles sit on the left side of the political spectrum, and not all Charterphobes are conservative. Consider several high-profile Charter cases. Left-leaning proponents of the Charter system were pleased with the outcome of the Keegstra case, where a high school teacher was found guilty of inciting hatred against Jewish Canadians by teaching anti-Semitic lessons in his high school classroom. The ruling placed limits on freedom of expression in the interests of preventing hate speech against identifiable groups in Canada. Yet other cases can shake progressives' faith in the judicial process, particularly when judges reject positive rights claims—as occurred when the right to strike was denied in the Alberta Labour reference—or provide Canadians with certain negative liberties. The latter resulted from the Chaoulli decision, when the Court established that the right to security of person could extend to the freedom to seek private healthcare alternatives if the public system did not meet certain standards.

The same type of moral conflict occurs on the other side of the spectrum from time to time. The Supreme Court striking down prostitution laws (the Bedford decision) and

Charterphiles
Supporters of the enhanced role of judges in the Canadian rights regime.

Charterphobes
Opponents and skeptics of the enhanced role of judges in the Canadian rights regime.

For a discussion of diversity and the courts, see pages 454–6 of Chapter 13, on diversity and representation.

permitting physician-assisted death (the Carter decision) drew the ire of right-wing Charterphobes, who viewed these as judicial overreach. Yet decisions like Chaoulli and the Alberta Labour reference can turn otherwise staunch opponents of the judiciary into proponents of the judges' decisions.

Concluding Thoughts

Understanding Canadian politics requires a deep appreciation for its constitutional history. Politicians cannot dabble in ignoring or changing the constitution. They cannot simply propose formal amendments or establish laws that tinker around the edges. Doing so raises real opposition from governments, interest groups, businesses, and citizens whose rights and powers may be threatened. Indeed, notwithstanding the advent of the Charter in 1982 (pun intended) and recognition of Indigenous rights to self-government, Canada's constitutional order has remained relatively constant over the past two centuries. The country's supreme law remains rooted in the same principles of federalism, dynamics of regionalism, and institutions of parliamentary democracy that predated Confederation. Those subjects form the basis of the next four chapters.

For More Information

Wonder which values underlie the Canadian constitutional order? So did Janet Ajzenstat and Peter Smith in their edited volume *Canada's Origins: Liberal, Tory or Republican?* (Carleton University Press, 1995). Indigenous rights and the Canadian constitution are examined by Dimitrios Panagos in *Uncertain Accommodation: Aboriginal Identity and Group Rights in the Supreme Court of Canada* (UBC Press, 2016).

Looking for the cornerstones of Canada's parliamentary democracy? David E. Smith writes about the Crown, Senate, and Commons in *The Constitution in a Hall of Mirrors: Canada at 150* (University of Toronto Press, 2017).

Want to learn more about the role of Indigenous people in shaping the constitution? Directed by Maurice Bulbulian, the documentary *Dancing around the Table* is available on the National Film Board website.

Just how difficult is it to amend the constitution in the twenty-first century? Ask Emmett Macfarlane and his contributors to *Constitutional Amendment in Canada* (University of Toronto Press, 2016).

Considering ways of overcoming these challenges and reforming the constitutional order? You're not alone: Peter Aucoin, Mark Jarvis, and Lori Turnbull contemplate constitutional reform in *Democratizing the Constitution: Reforming Responsible Government* (Emond Montgomery, 2011).

Want to learn more about the inner workings of Westminster traditions in Canada? Read insights in *Responsible Government: Clarifying Essentials, Dispelling Myths and Exploring Change*, by Peter Aucoin, Jennifer Smith, and Geoff Dinsdale (Canadian Centre for Management Development, 2004).

Ever consider what role bureaucrats play in responsible government? Donald Savoie examines the relationship between the political executive and the public service in *Breaking the Bargain: Public Servants, Ministers and Parliament* (University of Toronto Press, 2003).

Want to read the actual words of the Fathers of Confederation, and learn more about how they reached the deal? Consult *Canada's Founding Debates* (Janet Ajzenstat et al.; University of Toronto Press, 1999) and *1867: How the Fathers Made a Deal* (Christopher Moore; McClelland and Stewart, 1997).

Want first-hand accounts of what really happened behind the scenes of the various rounds of mega-constitutional negotiations? See *And No One Cheered: Federalism, Democracy and the Constitution Act* (Keith Banting and Richard

Simeon, eds.; Methuen, 1983); *Meech Lake: The Inside Story* (Patrick Monahan; University of Toronto Press, 1991); and *The Charlottetown Accord, the Referendum, and the Future of Canada* (Kenneth McRoberts and Patrick Monahan, eds.; University of Toronto Press, 1993).

Curious about the democratic trajectory of Canada's constitutional evolution? Peter Russell examines the issue in *Canada's Odyssey: A Country Based on Incomplete Conquests* (University of Toronto Press, 2017).

Ever thought that first ministers ought to just leave the constitution alone? Read David Thomas's *Whistling Past the Graveyard: Constitutional Abeyances, Quebec, and the Future of Canada* (Oxford University Press, 1997).

Skeptical of dialogue theory and the impact of judges in Canada's constitutional order? Read Dennis Baker's *Not Quite Supreme: The Courts and Coordinate Constitutional Interpretation* (McGill-Queen's University Press, 2010).

Want access to all of the key constitutional documents? Canadiana.ca has assembled an annotated constitutional history. Go to www.canadiana.ca, or search: Canada in the Making constitution.

Looking to view behind-the-scenes footage of the mega-constitutional era? The CBC has ample news coverage in its online archives: www.cbc.ca/archives.

Want to learn more about how the extension of rights to some Canadians can be perceived as a restriction on others' freedoms? For a case study, review Brenda Cossman's research on "Gender Identity, Gender Pronouns, and Freedom of Expression: Bill C-16 and the Traction of Specious Legal Claims" (*University of Toronto Law Journal*, 2018).

Deeper Inside Canadian Politics

1. Is the Canadian system of governance more or less democratic than the American system of governance? In your answer, provide a concrete definition of the term "democracy," and present substantial evidence to support your position. Your response should address potential criticism from the opposing side of the debate.

2. Identify the three most important ways in which Canada's system of parliamentary democracy ought to be reformed. In your answer, clearly state the problem(s) with the way parliamentary democracy functions in Canada, and the specific means by which you would address these shortcomings. In defending your choices, address why you rejected other leading problems and solutions.

Professor Profile

Lori Turnbull

Canadian parliamentary governance, political ethics, public engagement
Co-author of *Democratizing the Constitution: Reforming Responsible Government* (2011)

Lori Turnbull's research and teaching focus on parliamentary democracy and governance, public sector ethics, and democratic reform. She has held policy advisor roles in the Privy Council Office and has worked as a policy researcher for a federal commission of inquiry. Her award-winning book *Democratizing the Constitution: Reforming Responsible Government*, co-authored with Peter Aucoin and Mark Jarvis, argues that the Canadian constitution and its unwritten conventions fail to place sufficient constraints on prime ministerial power.

Here is what Lori Turnbull told us about her career path from when she was an undergraduate student, why she is drawn to her area of specialization, what is challenging about studying Canadian politics, and what advice she has for students.

* * *

I completed my undergraduate degree in political science at Acadia University. My intro to political science class was taught by a brilliant, creative, conscientious professor named Greg Pyrcz who loved political philosophy. I remember the course as a challenging one that taught me to question my assumptions and to be conscious of the fact that the institutions that govern our society are rarely just, fair, or equal in their treatment of people. Power is present in all of our social interactions and structures; it is the responsibility of political scientists to study and understand power dynamics using critical lenses.

My research focuses on parliamentary governance in Canada and other Westminster countries. I love this subject because it is ever-changing and inherently political.

Parliamentary systems create a lot of space for negotiation between political actors, the outcomes of which are not always predictable. Parliamentary systems are intended to be adaptable to new events and circumstances and, for this reason, our constitution has both written and unwritten components. The unwritten conventions are what give the constitution its flexibility. However, the fact that they are unwritten makes them harder to define and understand. In the absence of a consensus around how the constitution works, enforceability is compromised and the integrity of the system becomes vulnerable.

There is a surprising degree of variation between Westminster systems in terms of their approaches to managing this common challenge. For example, the United Kingdom relies on a cabinet manual to develop a consensus around how governance is practised; this helps to mitigate the uncertainty and confusion around constitutional rules but, because it is not binding, it preserves the flexibility that defines Westminster systems. Canada has had a cabinet manual of sorts but it does not provide this function, and so Canada lags behind other Westminster countries in its development of the Westminster model.

If I could offer one tip to political science students studying Canada, it would be to study what you are passionate about—even if others are not as swept away by the subject matter as you are. You'll make your greatest and most creative contribution in the area that truly drives you.

Up for Debate

Should it be easier to amend the Canadian constitution?

THE CLAIM: YES, IT SHOULD!

Constitutional amendment is too difficult to achieve in Canada, to the detriment of meaningful and necessary democratic reform.

Yes: Argument Summary

The amending formula places the Canadian constitution in concrete shoes. The level of elite accommodation required to reach the necessary federal–provincial agreement sets a high bar. Add to that the necessity of engaging special interest groups and securing the support of the judiciary and the public, and the threshold is nearly insurmountable. As a result, the Canadian constitution remains mired in the regional and governmental conflicts of the nineteenth century, and Canadians remain stuck with many of the same institutions they had in that era.

Yes: Top 5 Considerations

1. The rigidity of the amending formula leaves several fundamental issues unresolved. For instance, full incorporation of Indigenous rights remains elusive. The appointed Senate is a relic of the Victorian era that is misaligned with Canada's democratic values.

2. Leaving certain constitutional questions unaddressed for generations results in pent-up frustrations, which boil over from time to time in full-blown national unity crises. The 1995 Quebec referendum demonstrates how the failure to achieve constitutional reform can have the perverse effect of destroying the constitutional order entirely.

3. The nature and history of constitutional reform in Canada make piecemeal reforms nearly impossible. Achieving consensus around any one area of the constitution cannot be accomplished without making trade-offs involving other parts of the constitution. This time-consuming process of linkage and packaging pushes negotiations behind closed doors, waters down any attempts at meaningful reform, and draws attention and political capital away from other important areas of public policy like healthcare or the economy.

4. Constitutional deals almost inevitably end up before two courts: the judiciary, and the court of public opinion. The former is an independent, but ultimately unaccountable, arbiter. The latter has demonstrated little appreciation for the nuanced value of grand constitutional compromises that may appear to favour "them" over "us."

5. The original amending formula made constitutional reform arduous enough. The precedent of holding referendums and federal regional veto law (An Act Respecting Constitutional Amendments, 1996) adds extra layers of difficulty.

Yes: Other Considerations

- The strict nature of the amending formula provides governments with incentives to push the envelope when attempting democratic reform. Pierre Trudeau's plans to unilaterally patriate the constitution and impose a Charter of Rights and Freedoms, and the Stephen Harper government's abortive attempts to effect Senate reform without the input or consent of provincial governments, amounted to playing politics with the supreme law of the land.

- The political fallout stemming from the failure of the Meech Lake and Charlottetown Accords has become a warning to future prime ministers: re-open the constitutional debate at your peril.

- Proposing any fundamental change to the constitution prompts other political interests to lobby against that change unless their concerns are addressed. This results in unnecessarily divisive political debates, often to the detriment of national unity.

THE COUNTERCLAIM: NO, IT SHOULDN'T!

The amending formula is appropriately rigid, protecting the core elements of Canadian democracy from whimsical change.

No: Argument Summary

Constitutional reform should not be easy. As the supreme law of the country, the constitution forms the foundation of Canadian democracy, and it should not be uprooted casually. The amending formula is built on the premise that fundamental changes to the constitution require the substantial consent of the partners of Confederation. Law and practice now dictate that governments should act only with a popular mandate expressed through referendum. Building this level of consensus takes time and effort, as it should. The deals struck in 1867 and 1982 involved a highly complex series of trade-offs and compromises. These bargains did not coalesce overnight, and they should not be altered or broken without a similar level of consideration.

No: Top 5 Considerations

1. Plenty of flexibility exists in the Canadian constitutional order to allow for Canadian democracy to evolve with the times. Look no further than the expansion of the right to vote and other rights and freedoms that took place throughout the twentieth century, and the continued extension of rights that persists to this day.
2. Not all constitutional change occurs through formal amendments to the Constitution acts. A combination of conventions and judicial review keep Canada's constitution in line with evolving democratic norms.

3. In particular, the emerging convention that the public must be consulted prior to any fundamental constitutional change should not be seen as a weakness. It is a strength of Canadian democracy, and a sign that Canadians view the Constitution Act as the people's document—not simply one that belongs to governments and political elites.
4. The high threshold set by the amending formula forces governments to consider alternative means of democratic reform, through non-constitutional channels. This results in fruitful experimentation, like the advent of Senate nominee elections in Alberta, or Justin Trudeau's appointment of so-called independents rather than partisans.
5. The tendency for amendment negotiations to result in mega-constitutional accords reflects the highly complex, interconnected nature of the grand bargains that emerged in 1867 and 1982. Altering the terms of Confederation should be just as complicated, considering changes to any one element of those original deals amounts to reneging on the bottom-line terms of some partners.

No: Other Considerations

- Whether by convention, by law, or by common practice, many of Premier Bourassa's five conditions for Quebec have become widely accepted as facts of Canadian political life. The closed-door, closed-off nature of executive federalism has given way to a more transparent brand of intergovernmental relations.
- Decades of constitutional strife contributed to placing Canada in a perpetual state of crisis. By refraining from re-opening constitutional debates, successive prime ministers have avoided aggravating regional and other political tensions.

Discussion Questions

- There are serious flaws with the design of the Canadian constitution; conversely, changing the constitution risks splitting the country apart. Do you think it is better to put up with the constitution the way it is, or is it time to start a new round of constitutional negotiations? Why?
- In your opinion, what is the best way to engage Canadians in a debate about how to reform the constitution?

- To what extent is it a problem that the Government of Quebec did not support the passage of the Constitution Act, 1982? Is obtaining Quebec's formal endorsement of the constitution viable, necessary, or desirable?
- Considering the thresholds imposed by the amending formula, combined with the emergence of regional vetoes and referendums, how likely is the constitution to be amended in your lifetime? What would it take?

Where to Learn More about the Canadian Constitution

Peter Aucoin, Mark Jarvis, and Lori Turnbull, *Democratizing the Constitution: Reforming Responsible Government* (Toronto: Emond Montgomery, 2011).

Adam Dodek, *The Canadian Constitution* (Toronto: Dundurn, 2013).

Janet Ajzenstat, *The Canadian Founding: John Locke and Parliament* (Montreal-Kingston: McGill-Queen's University Press, 2007).

Andrew Heard, *Canadian Constitutional Conventions: The Marriage of Law and Politics*, 2nd ed. (Don Mills ON: Oxford University Press, 2014).

Peter Hogg, *Constitutional Law of Canada* (Toronto: Carswell, 2013).

Christopher Manfredi, *Judicial Power and the Charter: Canada and the Paradox of Liberal Constitutionalism* (Toronto: McClelland & Stewart, 1993).

Peter Russell, *Constitutional Odyssey: Can Canadians Become a Sovereign People?* (Toronto: University of Toronto Press, 1993).

David E. Smith, *Federalism and the Constitution of Canada* (Toronto: University of Toronto Press, 2010).

David E. Smith, *The Invisible Crown: The First Principle of Canadian Government* (Toronto: University of Toronto Press, 2013).

David E. Smith, *The Constitution in a Hall of Mirrors: Canada at 150* (Toronto: University of Toronto Press, 2017).

David Thomas, *Whistling Past the Graveyard: Constitutional Abeyances, Quebec, and the Future of Canada* (Toronto: Oxford University Press, 1997).

James Tully, *Strange Multiplicity: Constitutionalism in an Age of Diversity* (Cambridge: Cambridge University Press, 1995).

3

Federalism

Inside This Chapter

- What is federalism, and why was it chosen as a foundation of Canadian democracy?
- How does federalism function in Canada, and who are the major actors?
- How has Canadian federalism evolved over time?

Inside Canadian Federalism

Federalism is a system of government. It enables subnational governments to be responsive to local concerns while pooling resources and ceding some autonomy to achieve a set of common, overarching objectives. Federalism helps keep diverse countries like Canada together—despite regular conflict and competitiveness among regions (see Chapter 4). It is one of the defining features of Canadian democracy and can be one of the biggest sources of confusion. The following pages examine these and other topics in Canadian federalism. When reading this chapter, be sure to keep in mind the following maxims of federalism in Canada.

✔ **Federalism encompasses more than the constitution.** While providing a necessary legal foundation for Canadian federalism, sections 91 and 92 of the Constitution Act, 1867, do not paint a comprehensive picture of the balance of power today. By virtue of court decisions and major economic and demographic shifts, Canadian federalism has evolved considerably since Confederation, and it continues to evolve with every global crisis, every leadership change, and other major developments.

✔ **Federalism involves more than the premiers and prime minister.** To the general public, first ministers' conferences offer evidence that the premiers and prime minister are working together, or not. Since the failure of the 1992 Charlottetown Accord, meetings between the prime minister and premiers have been infrequent, and much Canadian federalism now takes place at the bureaucratic level. New actors, including city and Indigenous governments, are pushing the boundaries of federalism, intergovernmental relations, and multi-level governance in Canada.

✔ **Federalism is about more than dividing up resources.** Canada's provinces are constantly at odds with each other and the federal government over how best to distribute funding across the country. Fiscal arrangements, like equalization and health transfers, tend to dominate debates. Canadian governments have come together to forge an economic union that extends to social and environmental collaboration as well.

UP FOR DEBATE

Is federalism working in Canada?

Keep this question in mind as you read through the chapter. Consult the end-of-chapter debate supplement for more material to help you engage in an informed discussion of the topic.

The Story of Federalism in Canada

Federalism in Context

Canada's system of government is an amalgam of those of the United Kingdom and the United States. When the United States of America was formed, it brought 13 colonies together into a single federation. A national government would be responsible for policy matters that required central coordination, such as military defence, while individual states such as New York and South Carolina would have the authority to respond to local policy concerns. The American constitution ceded a limited number of powers to the central government based in Washington, DC, with state governments retaining the lion's share of sovereignty in the new republic.

This differed from the **unitary system** of government in place in the United Kingdom, where political decisions were foremost made out of London, and where there was no written constitution to devolve powers to local authorities (see Figure 3.1). Over time, Britain

unitary system
A political system featuring a central government that chooses what powers to devolve to regional bodies.

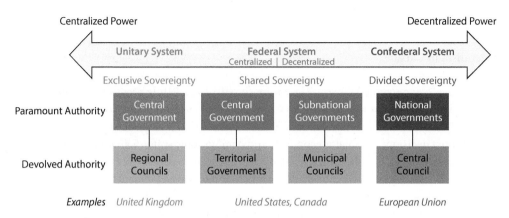

Figure 3.1 | Unitary, Federal, and Confederal Systems

has confronted serious regional tensions in Northern Ireland, Wales, and Scotland, which have led to the gradual **devolution** of central authority. Governments in the US and Canada have brokered such regional tensions under relatively stable systems of federal government, America's Civil War and Quebec's sovereignist referendums notwithstanding.

In formal terms, **federalism** is a system of governance featuring at least two orders of government. Each of these types of government derives

- its authority from a distinct electorate;
- its sovereignty from a separate basis; and
- its jurisdiction from a common constitution.

In true federations, regional governments retain **sovereignty** in some areas while surrendering some independence to a central government to act on behalf of all members. Each order of government has the legal authority to govern and to control state resources over geographical areas and topics outlined in the constitution. In confederations like the European Union, member states retain full sovereignty, though they may delegate some decision-making to a central institution. Just as central governments in unitary states may remove any powers they delegate to regional governments, so, too, may member states in a confederation withdraw their support from common decisions made by a central authority. By contrast, in federations like Canada, powers cannot be altered or revoked by either order without permission of the other.

devolution
The act of transferring (devolving) powers from a central government to regional or local governments that remain under its constitutional purview.

federalism
A constitution-based division of powers between two or more orders of government.

sovereignty
The power to exercise government authority over a polity within a defined geographical area.

Briefing Notes

Confederation

The terms "federation" and "confederation" have different meanings. When the original colonies came together to form the Dominion of Canada, they labelled their union Confederation. Their choice of terms is misleading today. Political scientists distinguish between federations like Canada, on one hand, and confederations like the European Union, on the other.

The Origins of Canadian Federalism

Every federation has its own unique origin story, drawing on a particular set of philosophical principles, catalytic events, and constitutional models. The conventional view of Canadian history holds that the Canadian constitutional drafters drew their greatest inspiration from the United States—the Western world's first modern federation. Contemporary scholarship challenges this historical understanding.[1] Evidence suggests the American constitutional architecture is, itself, based partly on the Six Nations (Iroquois) Confederacy, which is a form of governance developed by the Haudenosaunee. Evidence of the Haudenosaunee's direct influence on Canadian drafters of the constitution has yet to be established. Nevertheless, the presence of a federation of First Nations in such close proximity to the British North American colonies suggests that there was at least some familiarity with that form of governance among the settler political elite. In opting for federalism, geography became the primary mode of democratic representation in Canada, reinforcing the colonial power structures in place prior to Confederation.

Numerous factors supported the choice of a federal system of government for the Dominion of Canada. Militarily, the mighty Union Army was wrapping up an ultimately successful campaign against the Southern Confederacy. Many Canadian colonists feared that these American troops, already mobilized, would turn northward in pursuit of more territory. The nineteenth-century American belief system known as "manifest destiny" held that the United States was destined to rule the entire continent of North America. The possibility of American expansion made some form of central military force very attractive in the Northern British colonies.

The colonies saw great value in economic and monetary union. The ramping down of favourable British import policies and the end of reciprocity (i.e., free trade) with the United States persuaded the British North Americans to forge a common market. Looking westward, Canadian leaders saw the potential benefit in admitting new territories—and, eventually, provinces—as the circumstances allowed. Combined with provincial control over language, education, and other cultural issues, the federal option appeared to strike a suitable balance between areas of shared rule and self-rule.

Domestically, federation helped to break the sort of deadlocks experienced by the joint legislature in the United Canadian legislature, comprised of what is now Ontario and Quebec. A bicameral Parliament would offset representation by population in the lower house, which became the House of Commons, with regional representation in the upper house, which became the Senate of Canada. For economic and military reasons, federalism was preferred to a looser confederal alliance; for democratic and political ones, they favoured federalism to a unitary form of government.

Distinguishing Features of Canadian Federalism

Federalism within a Constitutional Monarchy

A distinguishing feature of Canadian federalism is that it operates within a constitutional monarchy, as we saw in the previous chapter. In Commonwealth federations like Canada and Australia, separate orders of government share their monarch, in a situation known as a **divided Crown**. In Canada, sovereignty is divided between the federal and provincial orders of government. Their powers are derived from the authority of the Crown.

divided Crown
A monarchy whose sovereignty is split among different orders of government.

There is theoretically no hierarchy in Canadian federalism today. While it is common to refer to different levels of government, neither provincial nor federal order is subordinate to the other when it comes to discharging its constitutional obligations. This relationship was unclear in the early years of Confederation until the Judicial Committee of the Privy Council (JCPC) ruled in 1892 that "a Lieutenant-Governor . . . is as much a representative of Her Majesty for all purposes of provincial government as the Governor General himself is, for all purposes of Dominion government."[2] This does not mean that each has an equal amount of responsibility, nor does it mean that each has an equal ability to fulfill its obligations. As we shall see, these constitutional provisions are only one element of the federal model in Canada. Governments have a host of political and fiscal tools at their disposal to stall or thwart their counterparts across the country. Federalism simply means that each order of government is equally authoritative in the exercise of its sovereignty.

This division of powers is constitutionally entrenched, primarily in sections 91 and 92 of the Constitution Act, 1867. Matters of common, national interest are reserved for the federal government, while matters of a more local or regionally sensitive nature fall under provincial jurisdiction (see Table 3.1). Among the constitutional responsibilities of the federal government are banking, money, and trade; international and Indigenous treaties; most taxation; the postal service; the census; military defence; penitentiaries; offshore fisheries; interprovincial ferries; and employment insurance. Provincial governments exercise authority over local matters including hospitals, education, municipalities, licences (e.g., shops, bars, auctions, marriage), some taxation (e.g. property), and natural resources. The constitution defines areas of concurrent (or shared) jurisdiction, including agriculture and immigration. Federal laws are authoritative if federal and provincial laws conflict in these areas. This reflects the original intent of the Canadian constitution, which sought to provide a strong central government. Over time, however, areas of provincial jurisdiction have increased in public importance and cost.

The three Northern territories and the thousands of municipalities across Canada do not have the constitutional status that is accorded to provinces. In many ways, governments in Yukon, Northwest Territories, and Nunavut govern in the same manner as provinces. They have control over their own healthcare and education systems, and they are gaining increased control over their natural resources. Ultimately, their authority is

Table 3.1 Federal and Provincial Powers in Canada

Federal Jurisdiction	Provincial Jurisdiction	Concurrent Jurisdiction
• any mode of taxation	• administration of justice	• agriculture
• census and statistics	• direct taxation	• immigration
• criminal law	• education	
• currency and banking	• hospitals	
• fisheries	• incorporations and	
• Indians and Indian lands*	commercial licensing	
• marriage and divorce	• local works	
• military and defence	• municipalities	
• navigation and shipping	• natural resources	
• postal service	• property and civil rights	
• trade and commerce	• public lands	
• treaties	• solemnization of marriage	
• weights and measures		

* The use of the term "Indian" here for First Nations people preserves the language used in the relevant legislation.

devolved from the federal government; it can be rescinded or altered at any time without the permission of the territorial governments.

A similar power relationship exists between municipalities (i.e., cities, towns) and provincial governments. Municipalities are to provinces as territories are to the federal government. Most municipal governments have the ability to levy property taxes, carry out infrastructure projects, and establish bylaws to govern citizens' behaviour. Yet, their powers and revenues exist at the discretion of their respective provincial governments.

Centralization and Decentralization

Canada is among the world's most **decentralized** federations. Collectively, Canadian provinces have more revenue-generating capacity and a greater scope of responsibility than constituent units in other federations, such as the United States and Switzerland. This is different than the original intentions of Confederation. John A. Macdonald and his fellow constitutional framers wished to create a highly **centralized** version of federalism. In fact, so many elements of centralization were incorporated into the British North America Act that many political scientists and historians question Canada's status as a true federation, at least in the beginning. In six specific ways, the BNA Act makes it clear that the intent was to treat the federal government, rather than the provinces, as the primary decision-maker:

1. Section 55 of the Act identifies the power of **reservation**. This allows a province's lieutenant governor to set aside a piece of provincial legislation for review by the governor general. As the governor general acts only on the advice of the prime minister and the cabinet, effectively, reservation means the federal government can prevent a bill passed by a provincial legislature from becoming law. The federal government has not exercised its power of reservation since 1961, when the lieutenant governor of Saskatchewan withheld passage of legislation concerning a corporation's access to minerals.

2. Section 56 gives the federal government the power of **disallowance**, which permits it to nullify any provincial statute within one year of passage. Disallowance was used in the nineteenth century to protect the federal government's commercial interests, such as ensuring the development of the Canadian Pacific Railway, but it has not been used since 1943. In that case, during World War II, the government of Alberta attempted to introduce legislation that would make it illegal to sell land to a Hutterite, or to any "enemy alien." The federal government disallowed the law, deeming that it extended beyond provincial authority because provinces do not have the power to identify military enemies.

3. The "peace, order, and good government" (**POGG**) clause in section 91 of the constitution states that "It shall be lawful for the Queen, by and with the advice and consent of the Senate and House of Commons, to make laws for the peace, order, and good Government of Canada." The POGG clause establishes the principles on which the country is founded, and over time has been used to establish that the interests of federal institutions shall preside over provincial or local arms of government. To proponents of centralization, the POGG clause gives the federal government overwhelming authority in defining the national interest, and extraordinary powers in times of national emergency.

decentralized federalism A federal system of government where the regional units have considerable power.

centralized federalism A federal system of government where the national government has considerable power.

reservation The constitutional power of the federal government to withhold the passage of provincial legislation, so as to cause short-term or permanent delay.

See Constitutional Monarchy on page 33 of Chapter 2 for an explanation of the Crown's role in Canadian politics.

disallowance The constitutional power of the federal government to veto provincial legislation and cause its termination.

POGG The acronym for the constitutional objective of "peace, order, and good government."

4. Section 92, which enumerates most of the powers accorded to provincial governments, mentions **declaratory power**: the federal government's ability to control any public works or undertakings deemed to be in the best interests of Canada or at least two provinces. Recently, the use of the declaratory power has been considered in the building of national infrastructure projects, including pipelines. This pits national priorities and federal government prerogatives against local interests and provincial preferences.

5. Some sections of the constitution stipulate that federal laws prevail in the event of conflict with provincial laws. This is known as federal paramountcy. For instance, section 92A grants authority over non-renewable natural resources to the provinces, but with the caveat that if "such a law of Parliament and a law of a province conflict, the law of Parliament prevails to the extent of the conflict." Another example is section 95, which allows provinces to make laws regarding agriculture and immigration, "as long and as far only as it is not repugnant to any Act of the Parliament of Canada."

6. The constitution gives the federal government all **residual powers**, that is, those powers not explicitly outlined in the constitution. This means that any policy area developed subsequent to 1867—for instance, aviation or telecommunications—falls under federal jurisdiction. This is the opposite of the United States.

THE CANADIAN PRESS/Darryl Dyck

Some municipal, environmental, and Indigenous groups in British Columbia have called on their provincial government to oppose the building of more pipelines across the province from Alberta's oil sands. Depicted above, proponents from Alberta and BC emphasize the potential economic gains from pipeline expansion. The federal government favours pipeline construction for economic reasons, and can invoke its declaratory power to approve new projects in spite of any objections that might be raised by the BC government. Is using the declaratory power a practical means of settling disputes between provinces, or does it give the federal government too much power? See Inside Canadian Politics: What Is at Stake in the Great Pipeline Debates for more on this topic.

Canadians, including newly elected politicians, are often surprised to learn that the federal government can overturn a law passed by a provincial legislature. Enshrined in the British North America Act, 1867, the powers of reservation and disallowance establish a hierarchical relationship between Ottawa and the provincial capitals. In the early years of Confederation, the federal minister of justice reviewed provincial laws to determine whether they were in the best interests of the young country.[3] Lieutenant governors reserved 69 provincial bills in Canada's first century, and the federal government disallowed 112 provincial acts over the same period. The federal government justified its actions on a host of grounds, deeming the provincial legislation to be contrary to the constitution, the federal government's priorities, the national interest, or fundamental standards of justice. While the federal government reserved or disallowed acts from all provincial legislatures except Newfoundland, which did not join Canada until 1949, the vast majority of cases involved the Western provinces. Some provincial governments deliberately provoked the federal response, including feigned attempts by Alberta to legislate monetary policy and currency, both areas of federal jurisdiction. The effect of the federal government's actions was to foster a heightened sense of Western alienation (see Chapter 4). The Constitution Act, 1982, preserved the federal government's supremacy. However, invoking either reservation or disallowance would put the prime minister in political peril. In recent decades, the only serious mention of disallowance and reservation has concerned the federal government's ability to prevent a province's unilateral secession from Canada. Many experts agree that the two powers are no longer operative, having fallen into disuse.

At times, having constitutional authority to decide a political debate places federal leaders in a quagmire. As described in Chapter 12, on interest groups and social movements, the provision in section 93(4) for the federal cabinet to "make remedial laws" on matters of education presented a serious problem for five Conservative prime ministers during the Manitoba schools crisis in the late 1880s and early 1890s.

The Tools of Federal Power

In addition to these constitutional provisions, the Government of Canada has historically exercised its clout through its **federal spending power**. This power is not specifically enumerated in the constitution. Through it, the federal government has gained the ability to spend in any area where it has seen fit to do so. It furnishes the Government of Canada with the means to develop policy in areas under exclusive provincial jurisdiction. By spending federal funds directly on Canadians, their businesses, or their local institutions, the federal government can set the terms determining how those monies can be spent, thereby establishing national standards. Quebec in particular has pushed back, demanding that it alone should decide how best to respond to local needs. Other provinces, such as those in Atlantic Canada, have tended to tacitly endorse the use of federal spending power because they recognize that their citizens will benefit from funds designed to raise services to national standards. Nevertheless, the federal spending power is a bone of contention between Ottawa and the provinces.

A further means by which federal politicians are able to exercise their influence is through the **appointment power**. This refers to the authority of the first minister to fill senior government jobs. For example, the positions of governor general and lieutenant governor are filled upon a recommendation from the prime minister. The federal government has exclusive jurisdiction over the selection of regional representatives to national

federal spending power
The capacity of the federal government to spend its available funds, even on areas that fall outside its constitutional jurisdiction.

appointment power
The authority to decide who should be selected to fill a government position.

Inside Canadian Politics

What Is at Stake in the Great Pipeline Debates?

Western Canadian oil has been fetching relatively low prices because it cannot be sold on the global market. Existing pipelines send the vast majority of oil sands products to the American Midwest, where a supply glut has forced oil sands companies to sell it for less than they could in Southeast Asian markets.

The impact of lower oil prices on Canadian government revenues is significant. Provincial governments get less in terms of resource royalties, and, along with the federal government, they derive less from personal and corporate income taxes. Lower government revenues may result in fewer government programs—including those that combat climate change.

This is why both the federal and Alberta governments support building, converting, or expanding pipelines, including the Trans Mountain pipeline from northern Alberta to the BC coast. Controversies around Trans Mountain and the failure of other pipeline initiatives raise the question: can one government stand in the way of another when it comes to achieving economic or environmental goals?

Provincial governments like those of Alberta and British Columbia may conduct environmental and regulatory assessments of the leg of the pipeline that runs through their respective jurisdictions. At the same time, the federal government is constitutionally responsible for reviewing all such interprovincial projects, following extensive public hearings by arms-length federal agencies.

The federal government's decision to approve the twinning of the Trans Mountain pipeline, with hundreds of environmental conditions, has been challenged in court. Pipeline opponents, including the BC government, support reducing oil sands production and emissions levels, and preventing oil from travelling through Indigenous and ecologically sensitive lands to vulnerable coastal areas. Pipeline opponents have launched a series of court challenges to stall or halt the project. This obstruction strategy worked, in part, as pipeline owner Kinder Morgan suspended non-essential spending on Trans Mountain in 2018. This prompted the federal and Alberta governments to enter into negotiations with the company to purchase the pipeline project, which Ottawa did for $4.5 billion. From an economic perspective, federal cabinet ministers decided the threat to Canada's international reputation outweighed the potential cost of nationalizing the pipeline, which would cost at least $6 billion more to construct. Electorally, the federal government wagered that any loss of support among environmentalists and First Nations in BC would be offset by gains, or continued support, among Canadians who side with their dual focus on economic development and environmental protection.

Even with the federal government's purchase of Trans Mountain and approval of its expansion, questions remain as to whether a provincial government like BC can generate enough political pressure to prevent an interprovincial pipeline being constructed within its borders.

DISCUSSION ITEM

Major national infrastructure projects involve a number of governmental and nongovernmental actors.

VOX POP

Given the tumultuous pipeline debates in the early twenty-first century, how likely do you think it is that another major pipeline project will be proposed in the near future?

institutions, including senators. Members of the federal cabinet, including regional ministers, are selected by, and are loyal to, the prime minister. Less noticeably, the federal government appoints the members of the boards of directors of a considerable number of federal bodies. These range from organizations that have a significant national presence, such as VIA Rail, to those with a focused local role, such as the Jacques Cartier and Champlain Bridges agency.

The Limits of Federal Dominance

Together, these powers were intended to produce a highly centralized federation in Canada. The evolution of Canadian federalism has revealed the fragility of even the best-laid constitutional plans. The federal powers of disallowance and reservation fell into disuse—a status that, according to convention, limits the federal government's ability to invoke them in the future. Constitutionally, both are considered lapsed powers, despite being retained in the text of the Constitution Act, 1982. Politically, the use of either power rests on the willingness of the federal government to disrupt the activities of a democratically elected provincial legislature.

Over time the courts have placed strict limits on Parliament's ability to legislate in the interests of "peace, order, and good government." This leaves the federal government with authority to make laws only in emergencies, in cases of provincial inability or incapacity, and in areas of national concern. Since the late 1960s, some provinces have attempted to place restrictions on the declaratory and federal spending powers. As we saw in the last chapter, efforts at amending the constitution to this effect during the patriation, Meech Lake, and Charlottetown rounds of negotiation were unsuccessful. Federal governments have made a political commitment to consult provinces in advance of introducing any new national programs involving provincial jurisdiction.

The federal spending power is a leading irritant among provinces. Tensions surface whenever Ottawa threatens to enforce federal standards through legislation. Examples include the Canada Health Act, which ties federal funding to five conditions defined by Parliament; new national programs such as the Millennium Scholarship Fund, which funded post-secondary students according to federal stipulations; and the Canada Job Grant, which aimed to better align Canadian skills with labour market needs. For the most part, the federal government defends its use of the federal spending power as a necessary element in forging Canada's social union. Without the ability to spend in areas of provincial jurisdiction, Ottawa and its (left-leaning) ideological and (less-affluent) provincial compatriots fear the loss of national standards in social programs, resulting in an uneven patchwork of provincial services.

Some provinces, particularly Quebec and Alberta, have sought to limit Ottawa's ability to spend in areas of provincial jurisdiction. They cite the value and constitutionality of having governments that are more sensitive to local needs determining the proper policy direction in matters like education and healthcare. They insist on the ability to opt out of any federal initiatives with full compensation so that they can initiate their own comparable programs and services. Historically, there have been several compromises negotiated on the use of the federal spending power, beginning with the ill-fated Victoria Charter in 1971, the Meech Lake and Charlottetown Accords, through the Social Union Framework Agreement in 1999. Comprehensive, constitutional agreement on the federal spending power eludes Canadian governments.

Interpretations of Canadian Federalism

Major Models of Federalism

As we mentioned in the introduction to this chapter, where you stand on Canadian federalism depends on where you sit. The definition, nature, merits, and even the terms of Confederation differ widely across the country (see Table 3.2).

Federalism can be interpreted as a system in which the roles and responsibilities of each order of government are clearly delineated. According to this **classical federalism** perspective, the Canadian constitution created a series of impermeable "watertight compartments." This view of federalism maintains that the jurisdiction of the provinces is distinct and protected from that of the federal government, and vice-versa. In other words, each level of government minds its own affairs. This characterized Canadian politics roughly from when Wilfrid Laurier became prime minister in 1896 to the onset of World War I. In modern times, the compartment model is espoused by those who wish to disentangle federal and provincial jurisdictions by having Ottawa withdraw from matters of provincial responsibility, including healthcare and social programs.

The reverse of classical federalism is **co-operative federalism**. This is where federal and provincial governments operate in partnership to solve policy challenges through consensus. The golden era of co-operative federalism occurred after World War II, when Ottawa sought to finance the expansion of the welfare state. Federal governments sponsored the growth of social programming that adhered to national standards. The provinces were willing to accept federal funds, even though strings were attached to ensure the monies were spent in ways that aligned with Ottawa's priorities. This spirit of co-operative federalism is responsible for the establishment of a variety of cost-shared programs, including medicare, which is discussed later in this chapter.

classical federalism
A model of federalism in which federal and provincial governments operate independently of each other in their own respective areas of jurisdiction.

co-operative federalism
A model of federalism in which federal and provincial governments work together to solve public-policy problems.

Table 3.2	Models of Federalism in Canada	
Federalism	**Defining Characteristic**	**Example**
Classical	Federal and provincial governments look after their separate jurisdictions.	The federal government does not meddle in healthcare or education.
Co-operative	Federal government leads, working with provincial governments.	The federal government creates national programs supported by the provinces.
Collaborative	Provincial and territorial governments collaborate to provide leadership.	The Council of the Federation, created in 2003, provides a forum for premiers and various working groups to collaborate with each other.
Emergency	The federal government takes the lead in a national crisis.	The federal government initiates spending programs to stimulate the economy after the global recession.
Symmetrical	All provinces are treated equally.	All provinces have equal powers when it comes to designing and implementing their respective healthcare systems.
Asymmetrical	Some provinces receive special powers, especially with respect to Quebec.	Quebec is granted unprecedented jurisdiction over immigration.
Treaty	First Nations enjoy equal status with the federal and provincial governments representing the Canadian Crown.	First Nations maintain sovereignty over education.

The co-operative model differs from the province-driven model of **collaborative federalism**. Coined by political scientists David Cameron and Richard Simeon, the term reflects the realities of governance in a globalized and interconnected modern society.[4] The role that provincial and territorial governments play in public life means that they no longer can risk being dependent on the federal government, especially with the threat of cuts to fiscal transfers. Rather, they may proceed to seek to resolve policy issues amongst themselves. The **Council of the Federation** was formed in 2003 with this objective in mind. It supports regular meetings among provincial and territorial leaders and has spawned working groups to pursue common goals in the economic, health, energy, seniors, and Indigenous affairs sectors. National-level policy no longer needs to be championed by the federal government, nor does it need to depend on the federal spending power, because when the provinces and territories work together, they can advance a common agenda.

In times of calamity, all of the approaches mentioned so far give way to **emergency federalism**. In periods of war, terrorism, natural disaster, pandemics, national unity crises, or global economic strife, all eyes turn to the Government of Canada to take the lead. The federal government's constitutional powers ensure that it is the primary political actor on matters of national importance. Furthermore, it can invoke emergency powers, engage the country in national endeavours, and negotiate with leaders of other countries.

There are other ways to categorize Canadian federalism. One perspective involves assessing the balance of power among the members of Confederation. We spoke earlier about centralized versus decentralized forms of federalism, which depend on which order of government (federal or provincial) holds sway. Another viewpoint considers the balance of power among the provinces themselves. In this vein, some observers see Canada's federation

collaborative federalism
A model of federalism in which provincial governments take the lead to solve common public-policy problems together.

Council of the Federation
An organization that supports regular meetings among provincial and territorial premiers.

emergency federalism
A model of federalism in which the federal government assumes control in a national crisis.

THE CANADIAN PRESS/Adrian Wyld

Co-operative federalism periodically plays out on the international stage. In 2015, Prime Minister Justin Trudeau invited premiers to attend the United Nations COP21 climate change conference in Paris. Participating premiers (pictured here) contributed to negotiations that culminated in the Paris Agreement. Since then, as discussed in Chapter 14, federal-provincial harmony has eroded over how best to achieve Canada's carbon-reduction targets. Once agreed to, do international commitments make it easier or more challenging to develop intergovernmental consensus here at home?

as consisting of a compact of 10 equal units. All came together as equal partners to form a common union; therefore, each province is deserving of the same powers and authorities under the constitution. All jurisdictions should have the same autonomy when it comes to establishing their healthcare and education systems, for instance. This sets up a form of **symmetrical federalism**, wherein the powers granted to one province must be available to all provinces. The symmetrical perspective treats all provinces as equals, irrespective of their geographic size, population, economic capacity, history, or political identity.

Others view Canada from a two-nations perspective, also known as the concept of deux nations. This view considers Confederation as an agreement between French Canada (represented by Quebec) and English Canada (represented by Ottawa and/or all other provinces). Two-nations proponents view Quebec as possessing a unique constitutional status among all provinces (see Chapter 4). They advocate an **asymmetrical** distribution of powers that favours La Belle Province. Quebec has more control over immigration than any other province, for instance. The province enjoys enhanced powers to select and integrate newcomers compared to other jurisdictions. Typically, then, an asymmetrical style of federalism refers to Canada treating Quebec as a founding partner, rather than just one of 10 equal provinces. More broadly, this approach to federalism suggests that some provinces in some situations deserve unique treatment or status. Indeed, provinces other than Quebec at times argue that their own situation is unique and that a particular policy matter warrants special treatment. This produces a competitive dynamic and inevitable conflict as other provinces jostle for more power and resources.[5]

Others reject both the symmetrical and two-nations views, preferring to recognize the sovereignty of Indigenous peoples. Known as **treaty federalism**, this model treats Indigenous sovereignty on par with the Canadian Crown, such that there are not simply two orders of government in Canada (federal and provincial), but three. This approach corresponds with the principles embodied in the two-row wampum model and the Royal Proclamation of 1763, discussed in Chapter 2. It is also part of a growing literature on multilevel governance in settler colonial states like Canada. Just as federal and provincial governments continue to negotiate the terms of self-rule and shared rule, so, too, do Indigenous governments engage with their federal and provincial counterparts to honour the terms of historical treaties. They seek to establish new systems of governance that respect Indigenous peoples' inherent right to self-government.

As we observed in Chapter 2, the ambiguities of the constitution allow all of these views to co-exist in Canada. Indeed, somewhat ironically, the strength of the federal culture in Canada may contribute to the development of these diverging perspectives.

The Politics of Fiscal Federalism

The regional tensions mentioned in the last section are acute when it comes to funding government programs and services. The importance that Canadians attach to social-welfare programs means that provincial governments are more powerful than Confederation anticipated. This growth is largely attributable to the lead role that provincial governments play in maintaining Canada's **social safety net**. The term "social safety net" suggests that the government will catch people before they fall on hard times, through publicly funded programs that help those in need and improve society. Government is able to encourage citizens to take the risks necessary to advance their well-being and that of their community without fear of becoming destitute, such as taking family leave, going back to

symmetrical federalism
A model of federalism in which provincial governments are entitled to equal powers.

asymmetrical federalism
A model of federalism in which jurisdictional powers are distributed unequally among provinces.

treaty federalism
A system of governance recognizing the equal-order relationship between First Nations and the Crown.

social safety net
Government-funded social-welfare programs designed to assist citizens in their time of need.

school, or starting a small business. Of the various support networks the social safety net comprises, some are exclusively the federal government's responsibility (e.g., employment insurance, old age security, family allowance), some are exclusively the provincial government's domain (e.g., healthcare, childcare services, social assistance), and some are intergovernmental (e.g., pensions).

The federal government helps to finance some of these provincial programs and services, such as health insurance, student loans, social assistance, and housing subsidies. There are financing agreements in place between federal, provincial, and municipal levels of government, as well as not-for-profit organizations, to provide services such as food banks and emergency shelters. Establishing which level of government should pay and be accountable for what type of service is a constant source of dispute.

Gaps in the System

The constitutional division of powers is only one component of Canadian federalism. Fiscal resources are just as relevant in determining the shape of Canadian politics. **Fiscal federalism** refers to the system of funding transfers that redistribute revenue between the two orders of government and reduce disparities among jurisdictions. Normally this involves the federal government distributing funds to provincial and territorial governments. It may include federal–municipal or federal–citizen grants as well. Fiscal transfers are designed to balance the capacities of the various governments to deliver programs and services to all Canadians, regardless of where they live. In this vein, federalism has two dimensions: one horizontal (among provinces) and one vertical (between the federal and provincial orders).

Every federation has fiscal gaps among their various governments. That is, some governments have more revenue at their disposal than others do. Horizontal fiscal gaps exist when certain regional governments enjoy greater revenue-generating capacities than others. In Canada, regional disparities stem almost entirely from differential access to natural resources like oil and gas. Those provinces that enjoy bountiful resource bases—like BC, Alberta, Saskatchewan, and Newfoundland and Labrador—are deemed to be more affluent than their counterparts in other parts of the country. This fiscal calculation is problematic when we consider that the economic value of natural resources is subject to profound fluctuation.

In and of themselves, these horizontal fiscal gaps do not automatically create problems in Confederation. If the distribution of population aligned with these revenues—such that provinces with greater wealth also had larger populations, and those provinces with less wealth faced fewer demands in terms of spending—there would be little cause for concern. Likewise, there would be few to no gaps if programs and services cost the same amount to deliver in all parts of the country, and if average incomes and business performance was uniform from province to province. This ideal alignment does not exist, however. Instead, Canada has a **horizontal fiscal imbalance**, whereby provinces have varying abilities to raise revenues, affecting their ability to deliver comparable public services. Take, for example, Alberta compared with Newfoundland and Labrador. Alberta is home to over 4.3 million residents; Newfoundland and Labrador's population is approximately 525,000. Alberta's oil and gas wealth spans decades, such that the province was debt-free from 2004 to 2013, and it consistently spent more per capita on programs and services while maintaining Canada's lowest rates of taxation. Conversely, Newfoundland and Labrador has accumulated substantial debt, reflecting the fact the province has some of Canada's highest rates of unemployment and underemployment, some of the country's

fiscal federalism
The manner in which revenues and responsibilities are distributed among various orders and governments.

horizontal fiscal imbalance
A situation in which some provinces have greater capacity to fund their constitutional responsibilities than others.

lowest income levels, and significant reliance on government assistance. Its offshore oil and gas revenues are a recent phenomenon. Governments in both of those provinces enjoy a windfall of revenues that are envied by others, but they must respond to different local circumstances. The value of these resources is subject to the ups and downs of prices set on international commodity markets. Once these natural resources are exhausted, the non-renewable revenue streams will dry up without considerable investment in other sectors. Indeed, faced with massive revenue declines due to the low price of oil, both provinces have been grappling with spending restraint and have registered significant budget shortfalls. Thus, even provinces with generous resource bases have dissimilar policy priorities and spending pressures.

At the same time, vertical fiscal gaps exist wherever the revenue-generating abilities of the central government are different from the (collective) fiscal capacities of the regional governments. In other words, one order of government is able to generate more revenue than another. We might assume that the federal government is at a significant fiscal advantage because of the federal spending power. However, Canada is the only federation in the world in which the vertical fiscal gap favours the provinces. That is, as a group, the provincial governments enjoy more "own-source" revenue than the federal government. This gap exists even before federal transfers are counted, and is once again attributable to the fact that the provinces have exclusive access to natural resource revenues.

At first blush, this vertical fiscal gap suggests the Canadian provinces should be contributing money to the federal government, and not vice versa. Revenues are only one half of the fiscal equation. On the expenditure side, provinces are collectively responsible for a larger proportion of public programs and services than the federal government—and increasingly so. Since the advent of the modern welfare state in the aftermath of World War II, the provinces have inherited responsibility for the fastest-growing areas of government spending, most notably healthcare and education. Under these circumstances, the provinces may enjoy a higher level of revenue, collectively, than the federal government, yet they remain challenged to provide the scope and quality of public services that Canadians demand. This gives rise to the **vertical fiscal imbalance**—a situation in which the federal government has more revenue than it can spend in its own areas of jurisdiction, while the provincial governments have more constitutional responsibilities than they can afford. In many instances, the vertical fiscal imbalance forces provincial governments to raise taxes, cut services, and/or run budget deficits and accumulate debt (see Chapter 8).

vertical fiscal imbalance The federal government has an excess of revenue, and the provinces an excess of responsibilities, with respect to their constitutional obligations and fiscal capacities.

Addressing Imbalances

Different federal transfer programs exist to address the horizontal and vertical imbalances in Canada's system of fiscal federalism. Three of these deserve the bulk of attention, as they are by far the largest and most contested: equalization, the Canada Health Transfer (CHT), and the Canada Social Transfer (CST).

Equalization

equalization A federal transfer program that is designed to lessen the fiscal disparities among provinces.

Equalization is the primary transfer program designed to address the horizontal imbalance in Canada. It operates alongside regional development initiatives and differential formulas built into other federal programs, like employment insurance. The equalization program was established in 1957 as a mechanism of distributing federal funds to those provinces deemed to be in greatest need. The program's principles were enshrined in section 36(2) of the Constitution Act, 1982, to ensure that "provincial governments have sufficient revenues to provide reasonably comparable levels of public services at reasonably comparable levels of taxation." This means full elimination of the program would require a formal constitutional amendment, including Parliament and the legislatures of several recipient provinces. Equalization payments are paid to the most disadvantaged provinces out of the federal government's general revenues, and the formula by which the funds are distributed has varied over time. The most recent set of changes to the equalization formula came between 2007 and 2009, when the federal government moved to simplify and, at least initially, enrich the size of the program. A separate program, Territorial Formula Financing, sends annual unconditional transfers from the federal government to the three territorial governments to ensure they are in a position to offer Northern residents comparable services at comparable rates of taxation to their provincial neighbours.

The federal government typically consults with provinces every five years regarding the funding formula for the program. The distribution of equalization funds is determined by Ottawa and, as the Trudeau government demonstrated in 2018, they are under no obligation to negotiate with provincial governments when it comes to renewing or revising the formula. Since 2007, the equalization formula has been based on a 10-province standard, meaning that all jurisdictions are included in the calculation of the country's average revenue-generating capacity. Provinces that fall below the national average receive equalization payments based on their population size, while those above that average do not. Not all revenue sources are included in this calculation. Four tax-base indicators are incorporated—personal income taxes, corporate taxes, sales taxes, and property taxes—and provinces are assessed according to how much they could generate if all provinces had the same tax rate. A fifth indicator—50 per cent of natural resource revenues—is included in the calculation of each province's fiscal capacity.

Some premiers attempt to use media pressure to persuade the federal government to devise a formula that will benefit their province the most.[6] This can lead to divisive politicking, pitting so-called "have" provinces (the wealthier provinces who are ineligible for equalization) against so-called "have-not" provinces (those whose financial capacity is below the national average, qualifying them for equalization), or fomenting dissent among recipients over who receives how much. The term "have-not" is so pejorative in Canadian politics that some now use the nomenclature "have-less" and "have-more" to distinguish the provinces that do and do not receive equalization funding.

There are a number of persistent myths about Canada's equalization program. For instance, there are no perennial "takers" and "makers" in Canada. It is sometimes believed that certain provinces are always dependent on transfers from Ottawa while others never benefit. In fact, every province has received equalization at one point or another in Canadian history. Alberta was among the first set of "have-not" or "have-less" provinces, even though it has not received payments from the program since 1962. Ontario received equalization payments for the first time in 2009, the same year that Newfoundland and Labrador moved into the "have" or "have-more" category for the first time. Quebec and the three Maritime provinces have received equalization payments for decades, while other provinces, notably BC and Saskatchewan, have rotated in and out of the "have-more" category several times.

Another misunderstanding is that equalization payments do not flow directly from have-more provinces to have-less provinces. Critics promote a misconception that equalization funds flow from more affluent to less affluent provinces. Rather, the transfers flow from the general revenues of the federal government to provincial governments with lower-than-average fiscal capacities. That said, compared to their counterparts in have-less provinces, individuals and corporations in Canada's richer provinces contribute more to the federal government in terms of tax dollars than their provinces receive in federal transfers or program spending.

It is not possible to trace, and judge, how provinces spend equalization funds. Some critics of the equalization program argue that recipient provinces squander their transfers, using their equalization funds to lower taxes, depress electricity prices, or create lavish public-service programs. Such judgements are speculation. Equalization is an unconditional transfer that flows into the general revenues of each recipient province. It exists alongside own-source revenues like personal and corporate income taxes, rates for which tend to be higher among have-less governments. As such, it is not possible to determine how each province spends its equalization allotment. Determining whether seemingly generous government programs in have-less provinces are due to equalization or higher taxes is futile.

Vertical Transfers: The CHT and CST

In contrast to equalization, the other two major funding mechanisms—the Canada Health Transfer (CHT) and Canada Social Transfer (CST)—serve to diminish the vertical fiscal imbalance. As its name suggests, the CHT flows from Ottawa to all provinces to help cover the costs of healthcare. Conversely, the CST is intended to assist with the costs of maintaining a host of other social programs, ranging from education to welfare. All provinces receive both the CHT and CST, with each transfer being distributed based on each province's population (per capita).

Initially, Ottawa transferred funds to the provinces on a shared-cost basis for health, post-secondary education, and welfare programs (Figure 3.3). In some instances, Ottawa provided matching funds as a means of facilitating the growth of provincial welfare states.

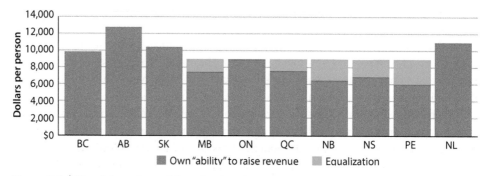

Figure 3.2 | Fiscal Capacity and Equalization, by Province (Fiscal Year 2018–19)

Federal equalization payments bring have-less provinces up to the national average in terms of revenue-generating capacity. But have-more provinces still generate far more revenue per capita, due largely to health natural resource endowments that translate into greater government revenues (royalties and personal and corporate income taxes).

Note: Displays each province's own fiscal capacity, the equalization payment required to bring it up to an "average" level, and the "adjustment payment" to fix the pool of equalization paid. In 2018/19, adjustments totalled $1.76 billion.

Source: Federal Equalization Workbooks, Table 1, Graph by Trevor©trevortombe

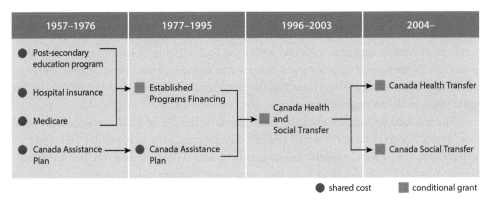

1957–1976	1977–1995	1996–2003	2004–
● Post-secondary education program			
● Hospital insurance	▪ Established Programs Financing	Canada Health and Social Transfer	▪ Canada Health Transfer
● Medicare			
● Canada Assistance Plan	● Canada Assistance Plan		▪ Canada Social Transfer

● shared cost   ▪ conditional grant

Figure 3.3 | The Evolution of Vertical Transfers

These came to be known as "50-cent dollars" because they came with the stipulation that a province must pay half. Popular if not sustainable in the immediate post-war period, these shared-cost models strained federal and provincial budgets.

In the late 1970s, the federal government began transitioning from the use of unconditional (or block) transfers toward an increased reliance on **conditional grants**. If a province accepted these funds, it was obliged to spend them as per the conditions set by the federal government. For example, the Canada Health and Social Transfer (CHST), in place from 1996 until 2003, prohibited provinces from imposing residency requirements on Canadians receiving welfare services. This meant that a provincial government could not turn away clients based on the fact they had lived outside the province for a specified period of time, ensuring that all Canadians had access to services across the country. It forced provinces to abide by the five conditions of the **Canada Health Act**, namely that provincial health services be:

1. publicly administered,
2. portable across the country,
3. comprehensive in terms of medically necessary services,
4. universally available, and
5. accessible to all.

Provinces that failed to live up to these five conditions—for instance, by allowing certain types of private health services for insurance—were subject to reductions in federal transfers. These mobility conditions continue to apply to the CST and CHT, just as the Canada Health Act continues to apply to the latter. Ottawa imposes similar conditions on dozens of other federal–provincial transfer programs related to justice, infrastructure, labour market development, immigration, environmental sustainability, cultural development, and many other sectors.

Recent developments have challenged the foundations of Canada's system of federal–provincial fiscal transfers. As of 2014, both the CHT and CST involve **per capita transfers**. This means that these federal funds are distributed to provinces based on the size of their populations rather than on needs-based factors, as they had been previously. In an effort to prevent less affluent provinces from losing out as a result of this shift to per capita funding, the federal government promised that no province would lose CHT or CST

conditional grants
Federal transfers to the provinces that may only be used for a specific purpose, and are subject to federal government restrictions or standards.

Canada Health Act
Federal legislation imposing conditions on provincial governments for the expenditure of funds from health transfers.

For more on medicare and the Canada Health Act see pages 278–9 of Chapter 8.

per capita transfers
Federal funds distributed to provinces based on how many people live in their jurisdictions.

funding year-over-year. In establishing a series of so-called "escalators," Ottawa guaranteed that all three major transfers would grow at a predictable rate, eventually in line with the growth in Canada's gross domestic product (GDP) or three per cent, whichever is higher. These federal reforms were designed to encourage provincial governments to rationalize their spending over time, but they may result in adverse policy implications for areas with declining populations.

The sudden, unforeseen economic downturn in the fall of 2008 prompted a second look at this fiscal framework. While retaining its commitment to move the CHT and CST to per capita formulas, the federal government placed a ceiling on the growth of the equalization program. The so-called "GDP cap" made any increase in Ottawa's contribution to equalization contingent upon Canada's economic growth. Critics in have-less provinces claimed the federal government reneged on the earlier CHT/CST/equalization deal, eroding the principles of adequacy, stability, and predictability upon which it was based. The change came at an inopportune time, pushing equalization-receiving provinces into even more difficult fiscal positions during an economic recession.

Making matters worse, for the first time in history, the recession pushed Ontario into have-less status. Canada's largest province drawing funds from equalization left less revenue for the remaining recipients, further challenging them to provide comparable services at comparable rates of taxation. While Ontario became a have-more province in 2018, future federal governments will continue to face pressure to reform the equalization formula and perhaps the entire interconnected transfer system.

Other Transfers

In addition to the big three (equalization, CHT, and CST), the federal government provides a series of other transfers to the provinces. Among them are the following:

- infrastructure funds (to build roads and bridges, for example);
- devolved services agreements (e.g., to provide services on behalf of the federal government, such as education or policing services in First Nations communities);
- one-off grants to provincially run universities and hospitals;
- shared-cost programs like legal aid; and
- fiscal stabilization and disaster financial assistance funds to cushion provincial governments against sudden, drastic drops in revenue and increases in expenditures.

Every year, the federal government enters into hundreds of these sorts of fiscal arrangements with each province. Federal funding to the three territorial governments is covered under an entirely separate set of arrangements, with the block Territorial Formula Financing grants making up a large proportion of each territory's budget.

Fiscal Federalism: Is It Working?

Critics of Canada's system of fiscal federalism allege that it disrupts market forces. They argue that it keeps weaker provincial economies alive, provides incentives for Canadians to remain in slow-growth regions, dampens inter-provincial economic competition, and fosters a sense of dependency on federal funding. This prompts calls for the reform, if not abolition, of the equalization program in particular. Some disparage vertical transfers like the CST and CHT for blurring the lines of democratic accountability: with federal dollars flowing into provincial programs and services, critics find it challenging to assign credit or blame for policy outcomes.

Others see advantages in Canada's system of fiscal federalism. Some view equalization as akin to a national system of revenue sharing, not unlike models in use in professional sports leagues. For instance, the National Hockey League redistributes some of its revenues to the smallest markets for the good of the league as a whole. Wealthy teams that contribute the most to the league's success, like the Toronto Maple Leafs, do not qualify for revenue sharing. Less profitable teams operating in small markets receive funds. The analogy points to the advantages of creating a stronger national economy (or league) by contributing to the growth of smaller provincial economies (or teams). Just as sports leagues generate more revenue and build their market shares by building their brand in smaller markets, federations, too, are stronger when their weaker members are more economically viable. This economic union is stronger both internally by creating domestic markets for Canadian goods and services and externally in the eyes of international investors.

Proponents of Canada's fiscal federalism look at the equalization program as a sort of governmental safety net, allowing provinces to take risks in developing their own-source revenue streams without fear of insolvency. As evidence of this success, they point to the experience of formerly have-less provinces that became have-more, notably Saskatchewan, which achieved marked success in developing its potash industry. Proponents argue that the equalization program and CST/CHT strengthen Canada's social union by fostering the equality of all Canadians regardless of where they live, and by helping long-term communities of interest to survive and thrive.

executive federalism
A system in which the elected leaders of federal and provincial governments make public-policy decisions.

THE CANADIAN PRESS/Jonathan Hayward

The development of offshore oil and gas reserves moved Newfoundland and Labrador into have-more status. But the province still struggles to balance its budget due to turbulent resource prices, persistently high unemployment, and the relatively high costs of delivering programs and services to its aging and rural and remote residents. What can be done to prevent the province from slipping back into have-less status?

Inter-state and Intra-state Federalism in Canada

When it comes to negotiations over Canada's social and economic union, Canadian politics has been dominated by **executive federalism**. The term refers to instances where intergovernmental bargaining, deal-brokering, and policy decisions take place among leaders of the various federal, provincial, and territorial governments. Executive federalism was prevalent during the so-called mega-constitutional period discussed in Chapter 2.

This elite-driven set of negotiations produced a series of real and tentative constitutional accords. However, the outcomes were widely panned for reflecting the aims of 11 white men in suits who negotiated behind closed doors, and for not sufficiently reflecting the priorities of the broader public and special interests. Executive federalism persists today through meetings of premiers and ministers, and private one-on-one meetings between the prime minister and first minister colleagues.

While the summit-style meetings that characterize executive federalism garner more media attention, the day-to-day relationships among Canadian governments are maintained at the bureaucratic level in what is known as **functional federalism**. In the most active and expansive sectors, like health and social services, provincial and territorial civil servants hold weekly teleconferences to collaborate on matters of mutual interest. This sort of intergovernmental dialogue occurs behind the scenes and is crucial to maintaining Canada's social and economic union. In the aftermath of the mega-constitutional era, first ministers and citizens alike become wary of grand political negotiations and summits. In this atmosphere of constitutional fatigue, most activity in Canadian federalism shifted away from the high-stakes political level.

There are two main sets of actors in Canadian federalism: those who work in inter-state institutions, like the Council of the Federation, and those who work within intra-state institutions, like the Canadian Senate. As its name suggests, **inter-state federalism** takes place among governments, their leaders, and their officials. Meetings among prime ministers, premiers, and various ministers are by far the most visible forms of inter-state federalism. They are by no means the most frequent. In fact, **first ministers' meetings** among the prime minister and all 13 provincial and territorial premiers are far rarer since the mega-constitutional period. In power for nearly a decade, Prime Minister Harper convened only two first ministers' meetings, both taking place in a brief two-month period amid the Great Recession. Prime Minister Justin Trudeau has hosted at least one a year. Nevertheless the practice remains more ad hoc and less frequent than in the late twentieth century.

Meetings among premiers, without the prime minister, are far more frequent. Since being created in 2003 to replace the Annual Premiers Conference, the Council of the Federation brings together all 13 premiers, face to face, at least twice per year. They also engage in periodic conference calls and gather each summer in regional forums like the Western Premiers' Conference, the Council of Atlantic Premiers, and the Northern Premiers' Forum. They join their American counterparts around tables like the National Governors Association, Western Governors Association, and New England Governors meetings. While generally productive, these meetings rarely garner the same level of media attention paid to a full forum comprising all first ministers.

Provincial ministers meet on an annual basis, too. Justice ministers gather once per year to discuss common challenges, just as ministers of finance, health, culture, infrastructure, agriculture, energy, and other sectors do. Some of these meetings feature federal, provincial, and territorial representatives, while others are composed exclusively of provincial or provincial and territorial members. Some are regional and some are national in scope.

In contrast to inter-state federalism, **intra-state federalism** takes place within the bounds of the central government. In Canada, regional and provincial interests are built into several federal government institutions. A prime example is the Senate, where seats are distributed on a regional basis (see Chapter 6). Compared to other federations, like

functional federalism
A system in which civil servants conduct the bulk of intergovernmental activity.

inter-state federalism
A system of formal interactions among government officials and leaders.

first ministers' meetings
Formal gatherings of the premiers, sometimes hosted by the prime minister.

intra-state federalism
A system in which regional interests are represented within the institutions of the central government.

the United States, Canada's intra-state institutions are far weaker than its inter-state ones are. Whereas federal US senators tend to wield more power in relation to state governors when it comes to national policymaking, Canadian senators are dwarfed by provincial/territorial premiers.

Yet regional representation is found in other institutions. The federal cabinet typically contains ministers from each province, with lead ministers from each jurisdiction referred by some as lieutenants or regional ministers. Federal political parties are structured around regional lines, with provincial executives and campaign managers (see Chapter 9). Justices of the Supreme Court are selected from various provinces; Quebec perennially receives three seats on the bench, and the other six spots are distributed among the remaining provinces on a rotating, regional basis. At the functional level, the federal government maintains offices in various regions of the country. Combined, these intra-state institutions are designed to integrate regional interests within the confines of the central government.

The distribution of Supreme Court judges is explained on page 231 of Chapter 7, on the judiciary.

The Evolution of Canadian Federalism

We have maintained from the outset of this chapter that one's view of Canadian federalism depends on where one sits. It depends, too, on what period one is considering. The following brief history (supported by Figure 3.4) summarizes the lessons from this chapter while giving structure to the evolution of Canadian federalism:

- Confederation sought to create a highly centralized form of government in Canada, one in which power tipped largely in favour of Ottawa and away from the provincial capitals. However, a series of factors coincided to decentralize the Canadian federation.
- A strong provincial rights movement—led initially by Ontario premier Oliver Mowat, his Maritime colleagues, and his partners in the corporate sector—helped to shift the balance of power through a combination of politics, lobbying, and court action. The last of these approaches, litigation, found supporters in London, where the Judicial Committee of the Privy Council released several province-friendly rulings that helped weaken section 91 (federal powers) and bolster section 92 (provincial powers) of the BNA Act.
- A combination of war and economic calamity led to a period of emergency federalism, which shifted power back to Ottawa once more, as provincial governments welcomed—even insisted upon—federal intervention in the interests of national security.
- Struck by the federal government in 1937, the Rowell-Sirois Commission released its report amid this tumultuous period. Among other findings, the Commissioners recommended that the federal government assume control over unemployment insurance and pensions, and establish a more robust system of federal-provincial transfers, including equalization. Governments heeded this advice in the decades to come.
- The beginning of Quebec's Quiet Revolution in the 1960s, and the election of the Parti Québécois government in 1976, accelerated the post-war decentralization of Canadian federalism (see Chapter 4). Quebec's push for more autonomy resulted in more authority for provincial governments and placed brakes on the federal government's centralizing ambitions for Canadian federalism.

- The Pierre Trudeau government's introduction of the controversial National Energy Program galvanized decentralist sentiments in Western Canada. Governments and citizens railed against the federal Liberal government's attempts to redistribute the natural resource wealth of the Western provinces (particularly Alberta) to the weaker economies in Central and Eastern Canada. Western Canadians saw the federal program as an intrusion in areas of provincial jurisdiction (see Chapter 4).
- Together with the 1980 Quebec referendum, the events listed above set the stage for the mega-constitutional period of Canadian federalism: an era in which first ministers would come to agreement on no fewer than three constitutional reform packages.
- The failure to satisfy the Quebec government during the patriation of the constitution and the failure of provincial legislatures to ratify the Meech Lake and Charlottetown Accords paved the way to Quebec's second referendum on sovereignty in 1995 (Chapters 2 and 4).
- In the aftermath of that vote, the federal government took several steps to assuage those who wanted to see a more decentralized Canadian federation. The Clarity Act, through which Parliament gave itself the authority to determine what constitutes a clear question and clear majority upon which to negotiate any potential secession following a referendum on provincial sovereignty, was not among them. Ottawa would grant the provinces increased control over immigration and labour market development and place certain limits on the federal spending power. These moves did not go as far as many provincial governments liked and did not resolve the growing vertical fiscal imbalance since the 1995–6 federal budget. Combined with a reinvestment in fiscal transfers, the federal government's approach served to decentralize control over health and social programs in Canada.
- This process was complemented by the formation of the Council of the Federation in 2003, through which provincial and territorial premiers have asserted their authority

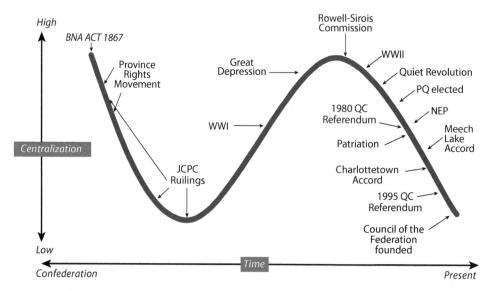

Figure 3.4 | The Centralization and Decentralization of the Canadian Federation

Source: Adapted from Robert J. Jackson and Doreen Jackson, *Politics in Canada: Culture, Behaviour and Public Policy*, 7th edn (Toronto: Pearson Education, 2009): p. 202.

and prominence in national policymaking in Canada. This reach has extended to the international realm, with federal governments inviting premiers to negotiate trade agreements and climate accords.

- The federal Liberals' return to power did not reverse this decentralization. The Justin Trudeau government's attempts to establish a national climate change strategy and interprovincial pipeline projects encountered strong opposition from certain premiers who openly campaign and litigate against these attempts to centralize power.

Concluding Thoughts

Federalism is one of the most fundamental, yet most contested, elements of Canadian democracy. There are those who yearn for the days of classical federalism, when for a very brief period areas of federal and provincial jurisdiction were contained in watertight compartments. Others see Canadian federalism in terms more of interlocking compartments, espousing a view that recognizes the importance of governments working together to address national policy issues. Some seek a more centralized form of federalism, while others see virtue in enhancing provincial powers. Some view Canadian federalism in symmetrical terms, with all provinces entitled to the same powers, while others see certain provinces as exercising and/or deserving different sets of powers because of their unique status. All of these views have been accommodated to a greater or lesser extent at different points in the history of Canadian federalism.

Beyond dispute, however, federalism helps structure Canadian politics along territorial lines. This can lead to tensions among communities in different parts of the country, as we will see in the next chapter, on regionalism.

For More Information

How democratic is Canadian federalism? Jennifer Smith assesses this as part of the Democratic Audit series in her book *Federalism* (UBC Press, 2004), as do Herman Bakvis and Grace Skogstad in *Canadian Federalism: Performance, Effectiveness and Legitimacy* (Oxford University Press, 2012).

How does inter-state federalism really work in Canada? Bakvis, Baier, and Brown take us inside the world of intergovernmental relations in *Contested Federalism: Certainty and Ambiguity in the Canadian Federation* (Oxford University Press, 2019).

What did the Fathers of Confederation really think about federalism? Return to the foundations of our democracy with *Canada's Founding Debates*, edited by Janet Ajzenstat et al. (University of Toronto Press, 1999) and Christopher Moore's *1867: How the Fathers Made a Deal* (McClelland and Stewart, 1997).

What role have the courts played in the evolution of Canadian federalism? John T. Saywell examines this in *The Lawmakers: Judicial Power and the Shaping of Canadian Federalism* (University of Toronto Press, 2002), as does Alan Cairns in "The Judicial Committee and Its Critics" (*Canadian Journal of Political Science*, 1971).

How does "functional federalism" really function? Gregory Inwood, Carolyn Johns, and Patricia L. O'Reilly take us *Inside the Worlds of Finance, Environment, Trade, and Health* to examine *Intergovernmental Policy Capacity in Canada* (McGill–Queen's University Press, 2011).

How does Canadian federalism compare to other forms of federalism? The former president of the Forum of Federations, George Anderson, has written a pair of concise primers that introduce students to the world of federalism: *Federalism: An Introduction* (Oxford University Press, 2007) and _al Federalism: A Comparative Introduction_ (Oxford University Press, 2009).

What are the normative underpinnings of Canadian federalism? Samuel V. LaSelva has written the seminal account in _The Moral Foundations of Canadian Federalism: Paradoxes, Achievements, and Tragedies of Nationhood_ (McGill–Queen's University Press, 1996).

What are the prospects for future constitutional amendments to redefine Canadian federalism? Ask David Thomas, whose book _Whistling Past the Graveyard: Constitutional Abeyances, Quebec, and the Future of Canada_ (Oxford University Press, 1997) addresses many of the implications.

Which came first: Canada's federal institutions or our federal society? Alan Cairns was the first political scientist to tackle this question, in his seminal piece "The Governments and Societies of Canadian Federalism" (_Canadian Journal of Political Science_, 1977).

How does federalism affect the development of public policy in Canada? Kathryn Harrison critically examines this question in her book _Passing the Buck: Federalism and Environmental Policy_ (UBC Press, 1997).

How well does Indigenous self-government fit with notions of federalism? Martin Papillon addresses this in "Adapting Federalism: Indigenous Multilevel Governance in Canada and the United States" (_Publius: The Journal of Federalism_, 2011).

Want to see what happens at intergovernmental meetings? The Canadian Intergovernmental Conference Secretariat has been supporting and documenting meetings of various federal, provincial, and territorial officials since 1973. To view press releases from these hundreds of meetings, visit: www.scics.ca.

Need more information on how federal-provincial transfers are distributed in Canada? The federal Department of Finance maintains an updated database here: http://tinyurl.com/fedprov.

Looking for academic literature on Canadian federalism? The Institute of Intergovernmental Relations is a prime resource: www.queensu.ca/iigr.

Deeper Inside Canadian Politics

1. Criticisms of the federal form of governance have evolved throughout Canadian history. Compare and contrast the opposition to Confederation in the 1860s with the criticisms of mega-constitutionalism a century later. What are the similarities between these two sets of critiques? What are the differences?

2. Identify three elements that distinguish Canadian federalism from federalism in other countries. For each element, discuss whether it represents an advantage or a disadvantage over other forms of federalism.

Professor Profile

Loleen Berdahl

Canadian federalism, regionalism, public policy

Co-author of *Looking West: Regional Transformations and the Future of Canada* (2014)

Courtesy Loleen Berdahl

Loleen Berdahl's research enhances our understanding of how institutions, cultures, and politicking impact the way Canadians perceive the political world around them. Her insights on Western Canada, in particular, inform a deep grasp of Canadian federalism and regionalism. Drawing on her interest in teaching and educational leadership, her work also considers career mentorship, as evidenced in her co-authored book *Work Your Career: Get What You Want from Your Social Sciences or Humanities PhD* (2018). Previously she worked for 10 years in the non-profit sector.

Here is what Loleen Berdahl told us about her career path from when she was an undergraduate student, why she is drawn to her area of specialization, what is challenging about studying Canadian politics, and what advice she has for students.

* * *

I never set out to be a political scientist, or to be an academic. I started my undergraduate studies at the University of Saskatchewan as a biology major, with every intention of becoming a physician. I quickly found that university-level science did not interest me. I spent a year or so taking different classes, mentally trying on various majors, including English and religious studies, and somehow political science ending up fitting my interests and talents best. Looking back, this is a surprise: at the time, Canadian political science was focused on mega-constitutional debates, with groups of men negotiating the terms of our country behind closed doors, and it seemed rather far away from my life. Perhaps that is what drew me in: a sense that important decisions were so divorced from the real world, or at least my experience of the real world.

After I finished my PhD at the University of Calgary I worked at a think tank for 10 years. There I researched Western Canadian public policy, considering the role of the four Western provinces within Canada and how these provinces could work together to advance their shared interests. This work meant that I was often studying federal relationships with provincial and/or municipal governments. I found the intergovernmental dynamics quite interesting: the concerns about jurisdiction, the questions about funding arrangements, and above all the importance of interpersonal dynamics.

When I became a faculty member at the University of Saskatchewan I continued to study these topics. Over time I became particularly interested in the relationships among provincial and territorial governments, and substate intergovernmental relations became a bit of a focus for me. This can be a challenging area to study in that much of the information I would like to have is not publicly accessible, and officials are understandably cautious in what they are willing to share.

The advice I like to give to students is to identify your strengths, those activities that come naturally to you, such as critical thinking or writing or leading groups, and develop these further. Focus on your career competencies and skills rather than preparing for a single particular career. Looking back on my experience, I can see that a lot of my path has been simply following what interested me, and letting things unfold. I am glad I gave myself the space as an undergraduate student to experiment with different areas of study, and I continue to do this with my research and my career.

Up for Debate

Is federalism working in Canada?

THE CLAIM: YES, IT IS!

The concentration of power in Canada's political system strikes just the right balance between the federal and provincial orders of government.

Yes: Argument Summary

Canada has become one of the world's most decentralized federations. It is true that the Fathers of Confederation dreamed of a much stronger federal government, assigning glorified municipal powers to the provinces in 1867. The federation has evolved considerably since then, adapting to the new and increasing demands that Canadians have placed on their governments. Most of these new responsibilities have fallen to the provinces and territories and, with notable financial assistance from the federal government, they have built and maintained some of the strongest health, education, and welfare systems in the world. Canadian federalism has become a model for other countries, allowing the provinces to wield an effective amount of authority over matters of regional importance, and the federal government to retain a considerable amount of power to govern on behalf of all Canadians.

Yes: Top 5 Considerations

1. Canadian federalism must be sufficiently flexible to accommodate the country's varying political cultures and regional characteristics. Policy designed in government offices in Ottawa may not be suitable for implementation across the country, where there are varying socioeconomic and socio-political considerations. Regional federal ministers, premiers, and provincial ministers are the conduits for local perspectives that national policymakers may otherwise overlook.

2. No less of a centralist than Pierre Trudeau once referred to the provinces as laboratories of social experimentation. Indeed, federalism has allowed provinces and territories to experiment with different models of public policy and service delivery, then share best practices to spread innovations across the country. Universal healthcare, which began in Saskatchewan, is a prime example.

3. Federalism fosters healthy competition among provincial governments, while providing for a minimum standard of performance. For instance, while provinces and regions continually compete to create the most attractive climate for business investment, federal transfers ensure that every government is able to deliver comparable levels of social services at comparable rates of taxation.

4. The federal government is not nearly as weak as centralists would have you believe. Above all, Ottawa wields the federal spending power, which allows it to fund (and thereby shape) activities that fall within provincial jurisdiction. If Ottawa chooses not to implement national standards or schemes, that is their choice; they are free to do so, but are often reluctant for fear of disrupting effective, and popular, provincial programs and services.

5. The persistence of the vertical fiscal imbalance ensures that the federal government will always hold the purse strings in Confederation. This means they will continue to set the overall economic and social agenda in Canada, funding (or defunding) programs that meet Ottawa's objectives and thereby influencing provincial governments' own priorities.

Yes: Other Considerations

- Centralists may criticize Canada's patchwork of social programs, but such critiques overlook the reality that federalism responds effectively to the unique needs and tastes found among people of different regions. Just as not everyone loves plaid, not everyone loves private automobile insurance, and some prefer a government-run insurance program.
- Where provinces feel that the federation is too decentralized, they have bound together in national or regional alliances. Consider the Council of the Federation's energy strategy and healthcare innovation working groups, joint cabinet meetings in Western and Central Canada, or harmonization in Atlantic Canada.

THE COUNTERCLAIM: NO, IT ISN'T!

Provincial governments have far too much power and their quest for local control is watering down what it means to be Canadian.

No: Argument Summary

John A. Macdonald and his colonial counterparts had it right when they designed a centralized form of federalism for Canada. Over a century-and-a-half later, their best-laid plans have gone to waste. To compete in a global economy, and to protect the integrity of Canada's economic, social, and environmental union, requires strong central influence. Empowered parochial provincial premiers stand in the way of this unity, hampering Canada's competiveness on the world stage and threatening the quality of Canadians from coast to coast to coast.

No: Top 5 Considerations

1. When the BNA Act came into force in 1867, it was not possible to predict the pervasiveness of the modern welfare state. The provincial governments' authority over healthcare and education are two constitutional responsibilities that warrant significant national standards. While the federal government has used its spending power to promote common healthcare standards, there is no such national standard for education; there isn't even a federal Department of Education, limiting our ability to develop and train Canadians to compete in the international economy.

2. Strong provincial governments stand in the way of national projects for which the federal government has constitutional authority to pursue. Building pipelines to tidewater is only the most recent in a long list of national initiatives stalled and even halted by intransigent provincial governments bent on satisfying their parochial interests over the national public good.

3. The special status accorded to Quebec has driven the decentralization process, particularly over the past five decades. By demanding autonomy over policy areas like immigration, pensions, and federal appointments, Quebec has encouraged other provinces to follow suit. This type of policy distinctiveness only serves to aggravate regional tensions, to treat people differently, and to blur what it means to be Canadian.

4. When premiers are successful in securing special treatment for their provinces in Confederation, this only motivates other premiers to table their own list of grievances. Continual spats over the perceived unfairness of the equalization formula (e.g., pundits asserting that Alberta is subsidizing Quebec) are an example of a recurring source of controversy that pits provinces against each other.

5. Provincial politicians' appetite for more power can never be satisfied. Their bickering and grandstanding is so upsetting to the national fabric that prime ministers dare not reopen constitutional debates. As a result, Canada has a constitution that is deeply flawed and inequitable, yet consensus on even minor constitutional changes remains elusive.

No: Other Considerations

- Provincial government services play an integral role in the lives of Canadians. However, the unicameral legislature, unbridled authority of the premier's office, the often limited resources of opposition parties, and the smaller news bureaus of local media mean that provincial government decisions are not subject to sufficient scrutiny.

- Premiers may resort to extreme measures to pressure federal politicians to meet their demands. The well-known examples of Quebec sovereignty referendums are interspersed with more episodic events such as Newfoundland Premier Danny Williams ordering all Canadian flags removed from provincial government buildings in 2004, Quebec Premier Pauline Marois's challenging of federal Senate reform legislation and Supreme Court appointments, and pipeline pouting by BC Premiers Christy Clark and John Horgan.

Discussion Questions

- Do you believe that Canada should have a strong national government, or that powers should be devolved to the provincial and territorial governments? Why?

- At various points in time Canadians have the opportunity to elect a member of Parliament, a provincial representative (MLA, MPP, MNA, or MHA), and municipal representatives. They also have an appointed representative in the Senate. Does federalism mean that we have too many politicians?

- In your opinion, does federalism keep this country together because it allows provincial governments to respond to the varied policy preferences of Canadians, or does it result in stronger regional tensions?

- Does federalism give too much power to large provinces at the cost of small provinces, or do small provinces receive more than their fair share?

- Does it make sense that Canadian social programs (such as medicare and employment insurance) follow some common principles, but nevertheless Canadians receive different types of service depending on where they live? Or should service be identical across the country?

Where to Learn More about Federalism in Canada

Keith Banting. *The Welfare State and Canadian Federalism* (Montreal and Kingston: McGill-Queen's University Press, 1982).

Daniel Béland, André Lecours, Gregory P. Marchildon, Haizhen Mou, and M. Rose Olfert, *Fiscal Federalism and Equalization Policy in Canada: Political and Economic Dimensions* (Toronto: University of Toronto Press, 2017).

Loleen Berdahl, "(Sub)national Economic Union: Institutions, Ideas, and Internal Trade Policy in Canada," *Publius: The Journal of Federalism* 43, no. 2 (2013): pp. 275–96.

Alain-G. Gagnon, ed. *Contemporary Canadian Federalism: Foundations, Traditions, Institutions* (Toronto: University of Toronto Press, 2009).

John Kincaid and Richard L. Cole, "Citizen Attitudes toward Issues of Federalism in Canada, Mexico, and the United States," *Publius: The Journal of Federalism* 41, no. 1 (2011): pp. 53–75.

Richard Simeon, *Federal-Provincial Minister Diplomacy* (Toronto: University of Toronto Press, 1972).

Donald V. Smiley, *The Federal Condition in Canada* (Toronto: McGraw-Hill Ryerson, 1987).

Hamish Telford, "The Federal Spending Power in Canada: Nation-Building or Nation Destroying?" *Publius: The Journal of Federalism* 33, no. 1 (2003): pp. 23–44.

Robert C. Vipond, *Liberty and Community: Canadian Federalism and the Failure of the Constitution* (Albany: State University of New York Press, 1991).

Linda A. White, "Federalism and Equality Rights Implementation in Canada," *Publius: The Journal of Federalism* 44, no. 1 (2014): pp. 157–82.

4

Regionalism and Political Cultures

Inside This Chapter

- What is regionalism, and why is it so strong in Canada?
- What are the three main varieties of regionalism in Canada?
- What are the sources and consequences of regionalism in Canadian politics?
- What is political culture? How do political cultures vary across Canada?

Inside Regionalism in Canada

It is natural in a country as vast as Canada that many political discussions devolve into debates around land and territory. Indigenous people organized themselves geographically long before colonial settlement. Their kinship ties, alliances, and trade networks connected and divided communities across a large landmass. Colonial leaders drew arbitrary, constantly shifting, borders to distinguish between French and English territories, often disregarding the terms of treaties with Indigenous people. Over time, these lines morphed into the provincial borders we see today. Combined with internal divisions between north and south, urban and rural, these geographic divisions fostered the growth of different political communities across Canada. Each has its own view of itself and its neighbours. Be mindful of the following maxims as you read through the chapter.

✔ **Regionalism means different things to Canadians across the country.** People in all parts of the country identify with the culture, history, geography, and political interests of their local communities. These attachments vary in degree and kind. Different brands of regionalism focus on achieving different levels and sorts of autonomy compared to others.

✔ **Regionalism can be a unifying force.** Regionalism is often portrayed as a threat to national unity. When managed effectively, however, it can act as a safety valve of sorts, helping to preserve union through diversity. In fact, some types of regionalism involve bringing communities into the Canadian political order, not out of it.

✔ **Regionalism is far from mystical.** Some believe that differences along regional lines are inevitable in a country the size of Canada. In reality, no invisible forces sustain regionalism in Canada. Rather, a combination of socioeconomic and historical factors are at play in our schools, laws, and election campaigns.

UP FOR DEBATE

Is regionalism pulling Canada apart?

Keep this question in mind as you read through the chapter. Consult the end-of-chapter debate supplement for more material to help you engage in an informed discussion of the topic.

Regionalism and National Identity in Canada

Canada is a country comprised of nations, regions, and political cultures. These political constructs are enshrined in law, institutions, and ways of life. These concepts are disputed by some citizens and groups. For instance, **Turtle Island** is a name used by many Indigenous communities to describe the landmass of North America. It is based on stories of creation that depict the land as a living being. Using the term helps Canadians who identify as settlers to reframe their role in Canada's colonial present. It serves as a reminder that the land was not empty when the first settlers arrived. It situates the Indigenous people as the original inhabitants of the land. Moreover, it challenges notions that the land should be divided along political boundaries like provincial borders.

A region is a territory with its own unique political characteristics. At its core, **regionalism** is a form of geographic identity and a psychological connection to that territory—an identification with it, and a commitment to it.[1] In other words, if a region is a matter of geography, regionalism is a state of mind. It is a shared sense of purpose and identity among people within a particular territory. The outlooks in different regions of

Turtle Island
The name used by many Indigenous communities for what is now called North America.

regionalism
An allegiance or psychological connection to a territory with its own unique political characteristics.

Canada are reflected in distinct political cultures within the country's main regions. These main regions are normally considered to be Atlantic Canada, Quebec, Ontario, the West, and the North. Another common way of looking at these variances is to divide Canada along provincial or territorial lines. Regions span a geographic area that develop their own names. Regions within Canada may comprise multiple provinces, such as the **Prairies** or the **Maritimes**; the 10 provinces and three territories; areas within a province, such as Cape Breton Island in Nova Scotia or The 6 (Toronto) in Ontario; and sometimes interprovincial, such as Mantario (the Manitoba/Ontario region between Kenora and Winnipeg) or the National Capital Region that comprises Ottawa, Gatineau, and the surrounding area.

Regionalism is as much an inward expression of group cohesion as an outward expression of identity, frustration with the national political system, and demands for improvements. Behind the regional grievances in Canada are ideological clashes, class and identity struggles, and the geographic imbalance of power in the Government of Canada.[2] These regional tensions periodically challenge national unity. In the late twentieth century, as part of the Canadian National Election Study, researchers posed the following statement to respondents:

> People often think of Canada as being divided into regions, but they don't always agree on what the appropriate regional divisions are. We would like to know if you think of Canada as being divided into regions.[3]

The vast majority that answered that, yes, they did think of Canada as being divided into regions. They were then asked to identify which region they lived in, and what the other regions in Canada were. In total, respondents gave over 3000 unique responses. Replies ranged from the West and the East to the country and the city; from the forgotten region and the most powerful region to the industrial heartland and the grain belt; from the Canadian Shield and the Arctic to Atlantic Canada and the Pacific Coast; and so on. Researchers also asked participants to engage in the following exercise:

> Here is a blank map of Canada. It has no writing on it at all. We would like you to write in five words or phrases that you think best describe politics in Canada. You can put down anything you want and write anywhere on the map, but you can only put down five things.[4]

This time, respondents offered more than 2000 different responses, many involving personal judgements about the rest of the country. Some labelled Central Canada as privileged, favoured, having lower taxes, and having better roads. Others drew borders along linguistic and ethnic lines, or made reference to dominant parties and personalities. Still others labelled certain regions as parochial, self-centred, arrogant, inward-looking, or a number of other pejorative terms. In short, Canadians had little trouble looking at politics through a regional lens, although they disagreed when it came to naming or defining the borders around Canada's various regions.

Approaches to the Study of Regionalism

Regionalism continues to be a fundamental element of Canadian politics decades later. It remains one of the most contested subjects of political science research. Just like their survey respondents, Canadian political scientists are far from reaching a consensus when

Prairies
The provinces of Alberta, Saskatchewan, and Manitoba.

Maritimes
The provinces of New Brunswick, Prince Edward Island, and Nova Scotia. When Newfoundland and Labrador is added, the four provinces constitute the Atlantic region.

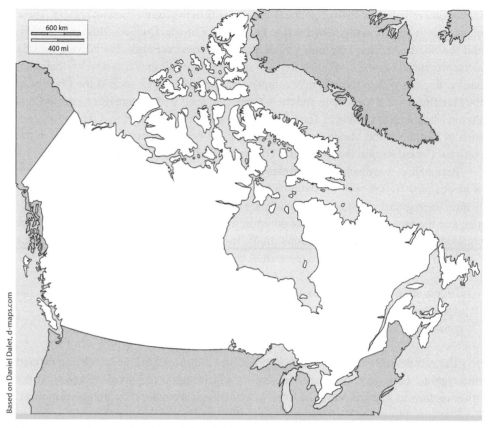

Based on Daniel Dalet, d-maps.com

How would you draw a regional map of Canada? Complete the exercise described above by writing in five words or phrases you think best describe politics in Canada. Put down anything you want and write anywhere on the map.

it comes to defining the terms "region" and "regionalism." In essence, a region is primarily defined by territory. This distinguishes it from other forms of community rooted in gender, ethnicity, language, or other non-geographic variables. As well, a region is innate, meaning it is not artificially constructed by politicians or map-makers, but grounded in an almost primal set of common values and mutual needs. From this perspective, regions are a combination of geography and community—"the product of historical experience, human organization, and social interaction," in political scientist Janine Brodie's words.[5] Regions are not artificial constructs according to this view, but rather natural elements of political reality.

Others, like Richard Simeon, consider regions as "simply containers. . . . How we draw the boundaries around them depends entirely on what our purposes are."[6] In this worldview, regions are artificial devices—frames applied by academics to make sense of patterns of political attitudes and behaviour, or by governments seeking to organize the political world. Regional lines could be drawn around political borders (creating 10 provincial and three territorial areas), topographic regions (the Maritimes, the Prairies), historical regions (Old Canada in the east and New Canada to the west), or transprovincial regions (the West, the North, Central Canada, Atlantic Canada), or even within individual provinces (Eastern, Northern, Southern Ontario).

In other words, where naturalists like Brodie see regional boundaries as inherent parts of the political environment (to be discovered, not imposed), positivists like Simeon view regional boundaries as flexible and contingent on the purposes of the observer.

Regional Political Cultures

Whether organic or imposed, regional divisions are among the deepest, most enduring political cleavages in Canada. Canadians living in a geographic area tend to share common expectations of government. Collectively these expectations are slightly different from the views of Canadians residing in other areas of the country.

In this sense, much is often made of the distinct **political cultures** that exist across the country. These common sets of values underpin each political system and distinguish it from its neighbours. Often stereotypical and unstated, each political community has its own, unique political culture—a guiding ethos, a constellation of political values that is bound up in its symbols and reflected in the attitudes of its mainstream members. For instance, why is it that the residents of St John's identify so passionately with the seal hunt, but their neighbours in Halifax are less enthusiastic and Torontonians are vehemently opposed, even though few residents in any of these capital cities have participated in the annual hunt? Why is Canada Day such an enormous national celebration in some areas of the country—but to others 1 July is a solemn day to remember World War I (in Newfoundland), is marked as "Fête du déménagement" because apartment leases expire (in Quebec), a day to question what Canada is (for those grappling with reconciliation), or merely a day off work? How does the celebration within Quebec of French and Québécois culture on Saint-Jean-Baptiste Day (24 June), also known as the Fête Nationale du Québec, compare with how communities across the country recognize Canada Day? These are a few of the countless ways that political culture varies within Canada.

Many scholars treat Canada as comprising multiple political cultures, as much as a single, overarching political culture. Western Canadians are often viewed as being more populist, individualist, and right-wing than their Eastern neighbours, for instance. Alberta is often portrayed as the cradle of Canadian conservatism. It is home to the country's lowest taxes and labour standards, and highest support for traditional marriage and the federal Conservative Party. Conversely, politics in Atlantic Canada reserves greater space for government intervention in the economy. There, government is largely seen as being responsible for creating jobs. For many, social assistance and regional development programs are favoured over the

political culture
A society's innate political characteristics, embodied in the structure of its institutions and the beliefs of its members.

THE CANADIAN PRESS/Jeff McIntosh

Supporters wave signs at an anti-carbon tax rally in Calgary in 2018. The introduction of a price or tax on carbon has been controversial in Canada. It sparked protests and a constitutional challenge in Saskatchewan; the governments of Prince Edward Island and Manitoba rejected the idea; a provincial levy contributed to changes in government in Ontario and Alberta. Meanwhile, the BC government barely raised an eyebrow when it established Canada's first carbon tax back in 2008. What explains these regional variances?

laissez-faire, small-government ethos that is more prevalent in the West. Quebec maintains a polarized political culture unto itself, defined at times by a left–right ideological divide and a cleavage between federalist and nationalist forces. Meanwhile, Central Canada—Ontario and, at times, Manitoba—maintains its own middling political culture, a microcosm of the broader Canadian ethos described above. Canadian provinces have sufficiently diverse attributes that each has its own political culture and yet shares commonalities with other provinces (see Table 4.1).

While it is tempting to simplify regional politics using these stereotypes, Canada's various political cultures are far from monolithic. Not all Quebeckers believe the province has a distinct status within Confederation, just as not all central Canadians are moderates.

Table 4.1   The Varied Characteristics of Canadian Provinces and Territories

Region	Characteristics
West Coast region	
British Columbia 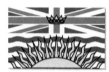	British Columbia is Canada's westernmost province, and Vancouver is Canada's gateway to the Asia–Pacific. About one-half of all the goods produced in BC are forestry products; it is also known for mining, fishing, and agriculture. The province's large East and South Asian communities have made Cantonese, Mandarin, and Punjabi the most spoken languages in its cities after English. The capital, Victoria, is a tourist centre and headquarters of the navy's Pacific fleet. Political culture: a "frontier-orientation" and "self-image of splendid isolation in paradise"[7] Year of entry into Confederation: 1871 Percentage of Canada's population: 13.5% (5,034,500) Seats in the federal Parliament in Ottawa: 48 (42 MPs, 6 senators) Seats in the provincial Legislative Assembly in Victoria: 85 MLAs
Prairie region	
Alberta 	Alberta is the most populous Prairie province. It is Canada's largest producer of oil and gas, and the oil sands in the province's north are being developed as a major energy source. Alberta is also renowned for agriculture, especially for its vast cattle ranches. Political culture: shaped by "struggles with the federal government, a tendency toward populist politics, and the power of symbolic conservatism"[8] Year of entry into Confederation: 1905 Percentage of Canada's population: 11.7% (4,362,500) Seats in the federal Parliament in Ottawa: 40 (34 MPs, 6 senators) Seats in the provincial Legislative Assembly in Edmonton: 87 MLAs
Saskatchewan 	Saskatchewan is the country's largest producer of grains and oilseeds. It also boasts the world's richest deposits of uranium and potash, used in fertilizer, and produces oil and natural gas. Regina is home to the training academy of the Royal Canadian Mounted Police, while Saskatoon, the largest city, is the headquarters of the provincial mining industry. Political culture: "moderate conservatism based on a wellspring of optimism, confidence, and a sense that the future is now"[9] Year of entry into Confederation: 1905 Percentage of Canada's population: 3.1% (1,169,100) Seats in the federal Parliament in Ottawa: 20 (14 MPs, 6 senators) Seats in the provincial Legislative Assembly in Regina: 58 MLAs
Manitoba 	Manitoba's economy is based on agriculture, mining, and hydroelectric power generation. The province's most populous city is Winnipeg, which is home to Western Canada's largest francophone community. Manitoba is also an important centre of Ukrainian culture and has the largest proportion of Indigenous people of any province. Political culture: "centrist tendencies grounded in the very concepts of modesty and moderation that make up its popular 'middleman' image"[10] Year of entry into Confederation: 1870 Percentage of Canada's population: 3.6% (1,362,800) Seats in the federal Parliament in Ottawa: 20 (14 MPs, 6 senators) Seats in the provincial Legislative Assembly in Winnipeg: 57 MLAs

Ontario region

Ontario

More than one-third of Canadians live in Ontario. Toronto is Canada's largest city and its main financial centre. Many Ontarians work in the service, manufacturing, or agriculture industries. Founded by United Empire Loyalists, Ontario also has the largest French-speaking population outside of Quebec.

Political culture: the pursuit of economic success, the recognition of Ontario's pre-eminence within Canada, managerial efficiency within government, and a respect for diversity of interests[11]

Year of entry into Confederation: 1867

Percentage of Canada's population: 38.7% (14,490,200)

Seats in the federal Parliament in Ottawa: 145 (121 MPs, 24 senators)

Seats in the provincial Legislative Assembly in Toronto: 107 MPPs

Quebec region

Quebec

More than three-quarters of Quebecers speak French as their first language. Quebec industries include forestry, energy, and mining, as well as cutting-edge industries such as pharmaceuticals and aeronautics. Quebec films, music, literary works, and cuisine have international stature. Montreal, Canada's second-largest city, has considerable cultural diversity.

Political culture: "significant provincial government involvement in Quebec's economy and society have resulted in protectionist and interventionist political culture and public policies"[12]

Year of entry into Confederation: 1867

Percentage of Canada's population: 22.6% (8,462,200)

Seats in the federal Parliament in Ottawa: 102 (78 MPs, 24 senators)

Seats in the provincial National Assembly in Quebec City: 125 MNAs

Atlantic Canada region

New Brunswick

New Brunswick was founded by the United Empire Loyalists and has a vibrant French cultural heritage. It is the only officially bilingual province. Forestry, agriculture, fisheries, mining, food processing, and tourism are the principal industries.

Political culture: "In some ways, it is a static, parochial, traditional, . . . province. Yet, given the occasional appearance of protest parties, a more nuanced interpretation is required."[13]

Year of entry into Confederation: 1867

Percentage of Canada's population: 2.1% (773,000)

Seats in the federal Parliament in Ottawa: 20 (10 MPs, 10 senators)

Seats in the provincial Legislative Assembly in Fredericton: 49 MLAs

Nova Scotia

Nova Scotia's identity is linked to its Celtic and Gaelic traditions. Its economy features shipbuilding, fisheries, and shipping, as well as offshore oil and gas exploration, and has a history of coal mining, forestry, and agriculture. The capital of Halifax has played an important role in Atlantic trade and defence, and is home to Canada's largest naval base.

Political culture: "Quite independently of any measurable factual basis, the idea of a traditionalist political culture continues to feature prominently in public discourse in the province, especially in regard to government's role in the economy."[14]

Year of entry into Confederation: 1867

Percentage of Canada's population: 2.6% (966,900)

Seats in the federal Parliament in Ottawa: 21 (11 MPs, 10 senators)

Seats in the provincial House of Assembly in Halifax: 51 MLAs

Prince Edward Island

Prince Edward Island is the smallest province, known for its beaches, red soil, tourism, and agriculture, especially potatoes. It is connected to mainland Canada by the Confederation Bridge. The provincial capital is Charlottetown, where parts of the 1867 British North America Act and the 1992 Charlottetown Accord were negotiated.

Political culture: "self-consciously traditional, with a strong and enduring attachment to local identity"[15]

Year of entry into Confederation: 1873

Percentage of Canada's population: 0.4% (155,300)

Seats in the federal Parliament in Ottawa: 8 (4 MPs, 4 senators)

Seats in the provincial Legislative Assembly in Charlottetown: 27 MLAs

Newfoundland and Labrador

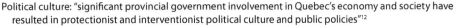

Newfoundland and Labrador is the oldest colony of the British Empire and is known for its fisheries, coastal fishing villages, and distinct culture. Today, offshore oil and gas extraction contributes a substantial part of the provincial economy, as do the immense hydroelectric resources in Labrador.

Political culture: "Whatever their differences . . ., Newfoundlanders collectively share a political identity distinct from that of Canadian mainlanders, particularly when latent nationalism is activated by premiers who have allegedly been wronged by outsiders."[16]

Continued

Year of entry into Confederation: 1949
Percentage of Canada's population: 1.4% (522,500)
Seats in the federal Parliament in Ottawa: 13 (7 MPs, 6 senators)
Seats in the provincial House of Assembly in St John's: 40 MHAs

The North	Political culture: "Although some in Southern Canada may see the North as a single, undifferentiated mass, each territory has distinctive elements in its political cultures—note the plural, for in each territory a variety of political subcultures exist."[17]

Yukon

Mining has been a significant part of the Yukon economy ever since thousands of miners arrived during the Gold Rush of the 1890s. Yukon holds the record for the coldest temperature ever recorded in Canada (−63°C). It is the only territory to use a political party system.
Year of entry into Confederation: 1898
Percentage of Canada's population: 0.1% (40,200)
Seats in the federal Parliament in Ottawa: 2 (1 MP, 1 senator)
Seats in the territorial Legislative Assembly in Whitehorse: 19 MLAs

Northwest Territories

The capital of Northwest Territories, Yellowknife, is called the "diamond capital of North America." More than half the population is Indigenous (Dene, Inuit, and Métis).
Year of entry into Confederation: 1870
Percentage of Canada's population: 0.1% (44,400)
Seats in the federal Parliament in Ottawa: 2 (1 MP, 1 senator)
Seats in the territorial Legislative Assembly in Yellowknife: 19 MLAs

Nunavut

Nunavut was established in 1999 from the eastern part of Northwest Territories. The population is about 85 per cent Inuit, and Inuktitut is an official language and the first language in schools.
Year of entry into Confederation: 1999
Percentage of Canada's population: 0.1% (39,170)
Seats in the federal Parliament in Ottawa: 2 (1 MP, 1 senator)
Seats in the territorial Legislative Assembly in Iqaluit: 19 MLAs

Source: Modified from: Government of Canada. "Discover Canada: The Rights and Responsibilities of Citizenship" (2013), www.cic.gc.ca/english/resources/publications/discover/section-13.asp. Flags: © iStock/mstay.

Note: 2019 population estimates (Statistics Canada, rounded data)

Sub-cultures exist in each region, some of which challenge the dominant political values of their society. There are free-market conservatives in Atlantic Canada just as there are socialists in Alberta. These anomalies prove the rule, however. The fact we label them as sub-cultures or counter-cultures acknowledges the existence of a broader, more mainstream set of political values.

These regional images are grounded in our historical view. The differences among them are starker in stereotype than in reality. When political scientists remove the regional lens from their analyses, and if they examine Canadians without first dividing them by province of residence, other patterns emerge. Ailsa Henderson's study found that when it comes to their attitudes, voting behaviour, party preferences, political activity, and ideology, Canadians live in nine distinct communities (see Figure 4.1). Many of these communities defy our traditional conception of regions as contiguous and provincially defined. According to her research, people in each of those nine groups have more in common with each other than with members of the other eight communities.

In particular, regionalism in Canada is increasingly being viewed through an urban-suburban-rural lens. Canadians in major cities across Canada tend to have more in common with each other, demographically and ideologically, than they do with their neighbours in rural and remote communities within their own provinces. Right-wing parties tend to fare better in areas outside these metropolitan areas, where communities are often older, less diverse, and more conservative. City dwellers tend to elect more left-wing representatives, while suburbs have proven to be the battlegrounds between parties on both ends of the spectrum. If socio-demographic trends continue, these divisions could become further exacerbated.

Cosmopolitan Quebec

Suburban Vancouver and Toronto

Urban Canada

Rural and mid-northern Canada

Manufacturing belt

New France

British North America

Far North

Metropolitan Toronto

Figure 4.1 | Political Cultures in Canada

Adapted from Ailsa Henderson, "Regional Political Cultures in Canada" (2004)

Federal political parties are similarly moving away from approaching Canada as a collection of regions. Instead, the development of campaign promises and political communication is treating voters on the basis of whether they live in a city, in the suburbs, or in a rural area. Historically, portfolios in the federal cabinet have formally recognized a variety of regions. At various points, a number of federal ministers have responsibility for regions of the country in their formal titles. For instance, there might be a minister of the Economic Development Agency of Canada for the regions of Quebec; the minister of the Canadian Northern Economic Development Agency; and the minister for the Arctic Council. There are ministers tasked with overseeing the Atlantic Canada Opportunities Agency, the Federal Economic Development Initiative for Northern Ontario, the Federal Economic Development Agency for Southern Ontario, and Western Economic Diversification. All such categorizations may be commonplace for federal politicians, public administration, and political science. Their regional meanings are likely familiar to most Canadians.

The federal government does not use a single definition of the make-up of Canadian regions. The federal public service routinely groups provinces together to assist with service delivery, policymaking, and resource distribution. Historically, the Government of Canada was guided by the constitution's model of allocating seats in the Senate. That organized provinces into four regions: the West, Ontario, Quebec, and the Maritimes. The last of these regions became known as Atlantic Canada when Newfoundland joined

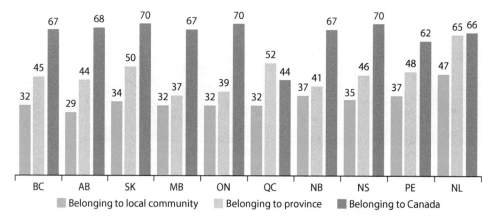

Figure 4.2 | Percentage of People Who Describe Their Sense of Belonging as Being Very Strong, by Province

Source: Data from Statistics Canada, General Social Survey 2013; graphic created by Jonathan Rivait/National Post.

Canada in 1949. Over time, the growth of British Columbia gave many an impression that it deserved to be distinguished from the Prairies and not lumped into a monolithic Western Canada. This crystalized in the mid-1990s, when the federal government committed to veto any proposed constitutional amendment that lacks the support of each of five regions in Canada, namely British Columbia, the Prairies, Ontario, Quebec, and the Atlantic region. The three territories are alternately grouped together as the North or else clustered with the region that is situated closest to them. For instance, BC and Yukon are sometimes known as the Pacific region.

Most Canadians identify most closely with their home community, in whatever manner they choose to define home. For some, it is their hometown; for others, wherever they currently live. For still others, home is their province, or perhaps Canada as a whole. According to survey evidence, a majority of Canadians think of themselves foremost as Canadian, or else identify with Canada and their province (see Figure 4.2). Few citizens identify exclusively with their province; most feel an equal or stronger attachment to the country as a whole. Nevertheless, a sizeable number of Quebecers define themselves only with their province, or first with Quebec and second with Canada. This contrasts sharply with neighbouring Ontario, where a majority of respondents identify as a Canadian only, or as Canadian first. And Atlantic Canada is not a monolith, given that the strength of regional attachment fluctuates between and within provinces. To be certain, identification with one's region does not preclude identification with one's country, just as having many regional political cultures does not necessarily detract from Canada's broader political culture.

The targeting of electors based on shared interests that transcend regional boundaries is discussed on page 295 of Chapter 9, on Canadian political parties.

Types of Canadian Regionalism

Sectionalism, Nationalism, and Secessionism

Regional leaders seek to gain greater influence over their own political affairs by dismantling or reforming institutions that subject them to rule by leaders from other parts of the country. It is common for regional leaders to demand more political power and resources, either in an effort to protect what they already have, or in an attempt to enhance their clout. Politicians often tap into citizens' feelings of economic and political inferiority

Table 4.2 Strains of Canadian Regionalism

Type of Regionalism	Political Grievances	Objectives
Western Canada		
Western alienation (sectionalism)	• restricted control over natural resources • lack of free trade • preferential treatment of "Old Canada" • low representation in Parliament	• symmetrical federalism • Senate reform • free trade (internal and international)
Ontario		
sectionalism	• federal–provincial transfers • shift of influence to Western Canada	• reforms to equalization • per capita transfer formulas • representation by population in national institutions
Quebec		
autonomism, federalism (sectionalism, nationalism)	• centralization of the federation • federal unilateralism • vertical fiscal imbalance • dominance of English Canada	• decentralization • asymmetrical federalism • "distinct society" status
separatism (nationalism, secessionism)	• lack of self-determination • lack of constitutional status for Quebec nation • federal unilateralism	• sovereignty–association • secession from Canada
Atlantic Canada		
sectionalism	• representation by population in national institutions • marginalization	• constitutional protections • harmonization
Newfoundland nationalism (nationalism, sectionalism)	• loss of distinctiveness in Confederation • lack of control over off-shore oil resources	• Atlantic Accord
The North		
sectionalism	• lack of political and economic control • marginalization • lack of national urgency on climate change	• equal political status with provinces • devolution • creation of Nunavut

when they attempt to mobilize these regional grievances. They may also appeal to populist tendencies when challenging elites from outside the region. Whenever one region advances an argument for favoured status, other regions are prompted to respond with their own demands, which strains national unity.

Many shades of regionalism have existed throughout Canadian history. These variants range from general forms of geographic solidarity to militant independence movements. The latter have been relatively rare and short-lived, including nineteenth-century movements like the Métis resistance in Manitoba and Saskatchewan, and radical twentieth-century terrorist organizations like the Front de Libération du Québec (FLQ). Today, mainstream Canadian regionalism comes in three general strains, namely sectionalism, nationalism, and secessionism (Table 4.2).

Sectionalism

The first strain of regionalism is **sectionalism**. It involves a strong sense of territorial cohesion combined with a significant feeling of alienation from the rest of the country and/or the central government. Sectionalism often manifests itself in a desire for increased

sectionalism
An emotional connection with one's regional homeland, more than with one's country.

input into national policymaking processes, for local autonomy, or for both. It may be inward-looking and defensive, or outward-looking and proactive. Over time, sectionalism has taken different forms in different parts of the country.

Sectionalism is especially prominent when the general public rallies behind a populist leader who champions the cause. Canada is prone to periodic pulses of **populism**, a phenomenon that transcends the political spectrum, and that is concerned for the average person over the privilege of political and economic elites. Populism is a grassroots political movement that aims to wrest power from the establishment and bring it closer to the people.[18] Followers put enormous trust in populist leaders who use rhetoric to stir sectionalist or nationalist sentiments, and advocate radical change in order to protect regional values. Populists typically promote nostalgia, criticize the system that keeps their "people" on the political periphery, and pledge an end to corruption among the political elites they seek to unseat. Left-wing populists push for measures like proportional representation and affirmative action to open up the political establishment to new voices. Right-wing populists ally with libertarians to take power away from government and put it in the hands of individual citizens. Some of Canada's more prominent premiers have been populists who fiercely defended provincial interests, such as Alberta's Ralph Klein, Newfoundland's Danny Williams, and Saskatchewan's Brad Wall. Ontario Premier Doug Ford is another populist leader.

Sectionalism tends to be strongest in the West. **Western alienation** traces its roots to the nineteenth century, driven by a persistent sense of economic and political marginalization. One prominent economic dispute erupted over John A. Macdonald's National Policy (1879), and the corresponding protectionist measures that erected tariffs and imposed higher business costs on Western farmers. Another dispute arose over the National Energy Program (1980), which proposed to redistribute oil revenues from Alberta to the federal government and Eastern provinces. Such policies reflect a Central Canadian perception of what constitutes the Canadian interest, and inform Westerners' frustrations with the federal system.

Periodically, Westerners respond to such grievances by rejecting traditional parties. Federal–provincial disputes spawned Western-based protest parties like the Progressives, Social Credit, and the Co-operative Commonwealth Federation (CCF) in the early twentieth century. A more recent political movement led to the formation of the Reform Party of Canada in 1987. Under the slogan "The West wants in," Reformers opposed unique treatment for any regions or provinces, and pushed for Senate reform and other changes to ensure Western voices are more adequately represented in Ottawa. In an effort to broaden its appeal beyond its Western base and form an alternative government, the party rebranded itself as the Canadian Alliance before eventually merging with the PC Party in 2003 to form the Conservative Party of Canada. Among its lasting successes, Reform pressured the federal government to get deficit spending under control, and remodelled Canadian conservative politics. Most significantly, Stephen Harper, one of Reform's original senior members, went on to lead the new Conservative Party to government in 2006.

The West is not uniformly or permanently disaffected, of course. The Reform Party was more popular in Alberta and BC than it was in Saskatchewan and Manitoba, and Western alienation waned during the Harper years. The return of the Liberals to power in Ottawa under Justin Trudeau reignited the flames of Western alienation, particularly in Alberta and Saskatchewan. Prime Minister Trudeau is a champion of carbon pricing and progressive social policies. His father was the architect of the notorious National Energy

populism
A political movement that seeks to reduce elite authority over ordinary people, and that is often led by a charismatic figure.

Western alienation
Political discontent in areas west of Ontario, normally encompassing frustration with perceived political favouritism to areas east of Manitoba.

Chapter 9 provides a summary of Western protest parties. See especially page 313.

Program. These ideologies draw the ire of conservatives in those resource-based economies.

Alienation exists outside the West. In Quebec, federalists have pushed for more autonomy and special status for the province within Confederation. Atlantic Canadians have long advocated for protections to ensure that, despite their declining share of the national population, they remain well represented in federal institutions. This includes constitutionally entrenching the so-called Senate floor rule, which ensures each province has no fewer MPs than it has senators, and the grandparenting clause, which guarantees each province no fewer seats than it had in 1985. Atlantic Canadian sectionalism manifests itself, periodically, in calls for a formal Maritime Union—the kind originally contemplated when Confederation was negotiated. Formal merger of the three Maritime (or the four Atlantic) provinces is little more than an idea given the political obstacles involved. For instance, it is unclear where the capital city would be located, and how provincial governments would retain autonomy over local matters like education and healthcare. Yet, through cooperation at the Council of Atlantic Premiers, the governments of New Brunswick, Nova Scotia, PEI, and Newfoundland and Labrador have taken significant steps toward harmonizing areas of public policy, such as apprenticeship training and cannabis regulation. By combining forces, governments aim to remain economically competitive in the face of steep competition from neighbouring regions in Canada and the United States.

Meanwhile, for decades, northerners pressured Ottawa for increased control over their own political and economic affairs. Their efforts culminated in the creation of Nunavut in 1999 and the transference of province-like powers through devolution. Yukon subsequently became the first Northern territory to gain greater control over lands and resource management. A similar agreement-in-principle was later signed between Ottawa and Northwest Territories. Long-term negotiations are underway in Nunavut.

A form of sectionalism exists in Ontario, as political leaders there dispute the province's unequal treatment in Confederation, particularly in terms of federal–provincial fiscal transfers. Historically, Ontario-based regionalism is the weakest in Canada, with most Ontarians identifying with the broader Canadian community. This is understandable, considering the province's dominant position in Confederation. Its industries are integral to Canada's overall economic performance; its population dwarfs all others; and its political influence in Ottawa is unparalleled. This sentiment changed with the economic recession that began in 2008. The province began a slight but perceptible economic, demographic, and political decline vis-à-vis Western Canada. That year, the Ontario premier promoted a so-called "fairness campaign" in an effort to focus the federal government's attention on Ontario's economic interests. A decade later, populist PC leader Doug Ford rode to power on a platform of restoring the province to its prior place of prominence and resisting federal intrusion in areas of provincial jurisdiction, such as a carbon tax.

Grain Growers Guide, December 1915

Bob Chambers, *The Halifax Herald*, 19 February 1968

For much of the twentieth century, regionalism was symbolized in political cartoons by the milch cow. The first cartoon is from 1915 (top), and the second is from 1968 (bottom). Former Saskatchewan premier and federal NDP leader Tommy Douglas is famously purported to have said, "Canada is like an old cow. The West feeds it. Ontario and Quebec milk it. And you can well imagine what it's doing in the Maritimes." Does this imagery still hold true today?

Nationalism

Nationalism constitutes a second type of regionalism in Canada. It is a highly politicized identity, often grounded in a romanticized ideal community. Citizens' nationalist sentiments are based on a regional grievance, and a powerful connection with their homeland. These emotions are hardened by exposure to media and through personal experiences, and can be exploited by politicians. People identifying with a nation share a sense of political culture that is developed and reinforced through an often selective recall of history. This myth-building means that nationalism tends to involve invented traditions, exaggerated grievances, and an ignorance of self-culpabilities. It can exacerbate feelings of economic oppression and may identify scapegoats who are to blame for holding the nation back from reaching its full potential. This can lead to in-group and out-group dynamics, where those belonging to the nation share a sense of togetherness and unity against a common foe. The cause of nationalism is often championed by charismatic leaders whom citizens feel epitomize their identity and concerns. This sense of pride can motivate the oppressed to rise up and achieve political gains. However, public emotions can be manipulated through propaganda, leading to an exaggerated sense of victimhood, irrational anger, and civic unrest.

The presidency of Donald Trump in the United States spawns comparisons with populist movements in Canada. While by no means mainstream, hats displaying slogans like "Make Ontario Great Again" and "Make Alberta Great Again" have turned up at conservative rallies in different parts of the country. In part, these sentiments tap into a sense of regional alienation or perceived inferiority. If a province can be portrayed to have fallen behind others—or, at least, not experienced the same gains as its neighbours—populist leaders may draw on these feelings to generate support for their cause. Making a province great again means restoring its prominent place in Confederation, usually through a province-first set of policies that prize local economic development and autonomy over national unity. To critics, these demands accompany calls to restore the pre-eminent position of previously dominant groups, like white men. What common

Briefing Notes

Nationalism in Canada

It is easy to conflate the terms "nation" and "country," or "nationality" and "citizenship," when it comes to describing Canadian politics. Globally, most nations are nation-states, with the dominant ethnic community commanding sovereignty over its own territory. Even in multi-cultural countries like Germany, France, and Spain, political power is wielded by a single, predominant ethnic group (Germans, the French, and Spaniards,

respectively). By contrast, Canada is both a multi-cultural and a multi-national state. This means there is no countrywide form of nationalism. Rather, there are several different forms of nationalism within a single state. Nations in Canada refer to select groups of regional factions, chiefly in Quebec and Indigenous communities. The appropriate term for pride in being Canadian is "patriotism."

elements of populism, regionalism, and conservatism make them such a potent political force when combined?

Nationalism involves a unique combination of group characteristics compared to other forms of regionalism. The members of a nation are considered to share a common ethnic background, to have ties to an ancestral homeland, and to possess a strong sense of self-determination. Civic nationalists may work together to achieve more political autonomy and even outright independence. Economic nationalists support policies that place their own community's prosperity ahead of all others. Ethnic nationalists preserve and promote their community's cultural heritage.

While, by definition, nationalism requires a homeland, its reach is not necessarily confined to a specific geographic area. First Nations members reside throughout the country, which is one of the reasons they have experienced difficulties mobilizing. Members of the Métis Nation are likewise spread throughout the West. Similarly, Quebecers or Newfoundlanders who leave their home provinces often still self-identify as such. Residents within those provinces may claim that such labels are reserved for those who are born on provincial soil and embody a political culture that can only be inherited, not learned.[19] This sense of ethnic nationalism can marginalize outsiders, reinforced with mildly derogatory terms such as "Anglos," "mainlanders," or "come from away."

Secessionism

The third form of Canadian regionalism is **secessionism**. As its name suggests, the concept entails a desire to secede, or separate, from Canada entirely. Separatist political parties include the Parti Québécois and the Wexit Party, In Quebec, separatists may be motivated by a combination of civic, economic, or ethnic nationalist arguments. In the West, support for separatism trends along with economic fortunes and the partisanship of the federal government. These forces collided in 2019, pushing separatist sentiments in Alberta and Saskatchewan above those found in Quebec. Secessionism tends to flare up when there is a regional grievance that is interpreted as an affront to a regional identity. It rises in response to other provinces gaining more power, often under the direction of a populist leader.

secessionism
A widely held sentiment that a province or territory should leave the Canadian federation.

Regionalism in Quebec

Some observers equate regionalism in Quebec with nationalism. In reality, all three forms of Canadian regionalism—sectionalism, nationalism, and secessionism—interact with one another in Quebec. The province's history illustrates the tensions that develop between provincial and federal governments when it comes to defining and meeting the demands of regionalists across the country.

The Growth of Quebec Nationalism from Confederation to the Quiet Revolution

Quebec has a distinct character within Canada. Since Quebec's earliest days as a French colony, its politics have featured a unique legal structure, the Code Civil as opposed to English common law. Its dominant linguistic and cultural community stands in sharp contrast to the mainstream Canadian society outside the province. Indeed, the differences between Lower Canada (now Quebec) and Upper Canada (now Ontario) were so stark that institutions were developed to accommodate the diversity, including divided legislatures and special majority voting rules. This approach to treating Canada as being formed by two founding nations is often resurrected as a basis for giving Quebec unique treatment within Confederation.

Throughout most of the first century of Confederation, Quebec's distinct nature manifested itself in an inward-looking, protectionist brand of sectionalism. The conservative Union Nationale provincial governments of Maurice Duplessis (1936–9, 1944–59) embodied this image. Premier Duplessis sought to protect Quebec's autonomy and that of the Catholic Church from encroachment by Ottawa and the rest of Canada. Like most of his predecessors, Duplessis was a champion of the province's autonomy within Confederation, and he had little interest in expanding Quebec's influence on the broader Canadian stage. However, it soon became obvious that a province could not insulate itself from global economic and cultural forces. Evidence that French culture needed protection from English continentalism began to mount.

Amid the global nation-building era immediately following World War II, some francophones in Quebec began adopting the term "Québécois" to express their unique cultural and political position—not just within Canada, but on the world stage. By the 1960s, the movement was known as the **Quiet Revolution** (*Revolution tranquille*). Quebec nationalists elevated the newly named National Assembly above the traditionally dominant Catholic Church as the primary source of power and influence within the province. Until that time, Quebec's identity struggle was defensive and protectionist, and coloured by the conservative nature of the Church. The Quiet Revolution marked the dawn of a new era of Quebec's taking active measures to strengthen its identity and position within Confederation. Quebec politicians began demanding more local political and economic control over government affairs so that Quebec could become *maîtres chez nous*, "masters of our own house." Secessionist-minded nationalists united under a common "sovereignist" (or separatist) banner, seeking to establish an autonomous state for Quebec outside of Canada. The separatist movement was marred by the radicalism of the Front de Libération du Québec (FLQ), which mounted a campaign of terror in Quebec in the 1960s, culminating in the October Crisis of 1970 that featured bombings and the assassination of a Quebec politician.

See page 215 of Chapter 7, about Canada's justice system, for a description of the October Crisis.

Quiet Revolution
An early 1960s modernizing movement in Quebec, geared toward a stronger provincial government and outward nationalism.

<<<<<<<<<<<<<<<<<<<<<
Quebec's use of the notwithstanding clause to protect its French-only signage law is discussed in the Inside Canadian Politics box on page 57 of Chapter 2, on the constitution.

Briefing Notes

Quebecers and the Québécois

Residents of Quebec go by different labels. "Quebecer" describes a resident of the province, regardless of the individual's language of choice. French-speaking residents of Quebec are often referred to as Québécois or Québécoise, depending on their gender. Francophones who can trace their ancestry within the province are often referred to as *pure laine* Québécois or Québécoise. When used collectively, the term "Québécois" refers to the cultural nation of self-identifying individuals based in Quebec.

Thus, two branches of the nationalist movement evolved in Quebec. Federalists seek greater autonomy for the provincial government within Confederation. Sovereignists are bent on achieving independence from Canada. The Parti Québécois emerged as the most successful champion of the sovereignist cause. They first formed the provincial government in 1976 under René Lévesque (see Figure 4.3).

Among the legacies of the Lévesque government was the passage of Bill 101, the Charter of the French Language. It details how the Quebec government will use its resources to protect and promote the French language in the province. This includes enforcing French as the normal language of instruction in schools, commerce, and government. For instance, the Quebec government reminds businesses that it is their responsibility to ensure that workers in the service industry greet customers in French, not English. Bill 101 is controversial. Court challenges regarding the portion of the law prohibiting English-only signs contributed to the use of the notwithstanding clause and, in part, to the failure of the Meech Lake Accord. Since that time, businesses using English names are required to comply with the revised legislation, such as the international restaurant chain McDonald's removing the apostrophe from its signage in Quebec.

Federalists and Sovereignists during the Mega-constitutional Era

Parti Québécois governments held two referendums in Quebec. The divisive campaigns pitted federalists against separatists. The first Quebec referendum, held in 1980, sought a mandate to negotiate **sovereignty-association** with Canada. This concept fell short of full and immediate independence from Canada. If the referendum passed, the Quebec government would work out the terms of an economic and monetary

The transformation of Quebec from an insular, agrarian society into an outward-facing, industrial economy hinged on its ability to develop its natural resources. Its energy sector was pivotal, as depicted in this 1962 Liberal Party of Quebec campaign poster. In 1963, the provincial government nationalized electricity production in Quebec, consolidating all private companies under a new crown corporation, Hydro-Québec. This economic nationalism had social and cultural effects, as increased government revenues were used to fund a growing welfare state and as Hydro-Québec staff were now free to work in French. Its success made Hydro-Québec a symbol of the new Quebec nationalism emerging at the time.

sovereignty-association
A legal arrangement whereby Quebec would be politically independent but maintain economic ties with Canada.

Briefing Notes

Soft and Hard Nationalism

Commentators often refer to two types of nationalists in Quebec. Hard nationalists are more commonly known as sovereignists or separatists. They are disenchanted by efforts to secure more autonomy within Confederation. Hard nationalists view full independence from Canada as the only means of advancing the interests of the Quebec nation. Those who support more autonomy for Quebec, but who shy away from full independence if it threatens the economic and social stability of the community, are known as soft nationalists. Some of them side with federalists on matters of national unity. Other soft nationalists vote with their sovereignist counterparts as a means of strengthening the Quebec's leverage in matters of federal-provincial relations or constitutional reform.

union with Canada, and subject that agreement to a second referendum. The proposed economic association would involve a common currency, free trade, and other economic matters. This two-step process was designed to gain support from Quebecers who might not outright support Quebec becoming an independent country. During the 1980 referendum campaign, Prime Minister Pierre Trudeau promised soft nationalists a renewed place for Quebec in Confederation as part of the ongoing constitutional negotiations, provided they voted against the referendum's proposal. The pledge proved to be part of a victory for the "non" side, as 59.6 per cent of Quebecers voted against the notion of sovereignty-association. This win was tainted by four in ten Quebecers voting to take steps toward withdrawing from Confederation. Moreover, the prime minister's promise set up expectations for changing the constitution to grant Quebec special treatment.

Few hard or soft nationalists supported the outcome of the ensuing constitutional negotiations. The inclusion of language rights in the new Charter of Rights and Freedoms two years after the referendum diluted the distinctiveness of the Quebec nation and the provincial government's status as Francophone Canadians' only legitimate representative. As Prime Minister Trudeau put it, "Quebec cannot say it alone speaks for French Canadians. . . . Nobody will be able to say, 'I need more power because I speak for the French-Canadian nation.'"[20]

Premier Lévesque objected to the final terms of the constitutional bargain. As noted in Chapter 2, the patriation deal was forged without his input or consent in what became known as the Night of the Long Knives. Despite Quebec's disapproval, the Constitution Act, 1982, was given Royal Assent. The Supreme Court ruled that the constitutional settlement was valid and applied to Quebec.

General elections brought new governments in Ottawa and in Quebec City within a few years of the constitution's patriation. Progressive Conservative Prime Minister Brian Mulroney and Liberal Premier Robert Bourassa found common ground in seeking to keep Quebec's soft nationalists within the federalist camp. Together, they set about crafting a constitutional amendment package that culminated in the **Meech Lake Accord**. As detailed in Chapter 2, the Accord was signed by the prime minister and all provincial premiers in 1987, and was approved by the Quebec National Assembly in June of that year. It proposed to constitutionally recognize Quebec as a "distinct society," while securing for all provinces greater autonomy and input into federal appointments. The amendment process foundered, however. The legal fuzziness of those two polarizing words—"distinct society"—became both a compelling reason for Quebec nationalists to support the Accord, and ultimately its undoing in other parts of Canada where it was viewed as conferring too much power and status.

Prominent Quebec nationalists interpreted the failure of the Meech Lake Accord as a sign of English Canada's rejection of Quebec's distinct status within Confederation. Popular support for Premier Bourassa's government waned in the province. At the federal level, disaffected nationalist MPs crossed the floor to form their own party, the Bloc Québécois.

These events, plus the rise of the Reform Party in Western Canada, created a sense of urgency around a second constitutional reform package, the **Charlottetown Accord**. As with the Meech Lake Accord, it would have recognized Quebec's distinctiveness. However, it did not use the same distinct society language. The provision was couched in a broader framework that included a variety of other democratic principles, among them gender equality and Indigenous self-government. Once again, the first ministers

The Night of the Long Knives is discussed on page 46 of Chapter 2, on the Constitution.

Meech Lake Accord
A failed constitutional amendment package in the late 1980s that would have recognized Quebec as a distinct society.

Charlottetown Accord
A failed accord that proposed to renew the constitution, but was defeated in a national referendum in 1992.

Key Federal Prime Ministers		Major Events		Key Quebec Premiers	
1968	Trudeau (Lib)				
		1970	October Crisis		
				1976	Lévesque (PQ)
1980	Trudeau (Lib)	1980	Sovereignty Referendum		
1984	Mulroney (PC)	1982	Patriation		
		1987–90	Meech Lake Accord Negotiations	1985	Bourassa (Lib)
		1992	Charlottetown Accord Referendum		
1993	Chrétien (Lib)			1994	Parizeau (PQ)
		1995	Sovereignty Referendum	1996	Bouchard (PQ)
		1998	Secession Reference		
		2000	Clarity Act		

Figure 4.3 | **Events and Leaders in Quebec Nationalism, 1968–95**

endorsed the accord, and many members of the corporate and social elite voiced support for it. Yet the Charlottetown Accord failed to receive a majority of popular support in a Canada-wide referendum in 1992. Voters in only five provinces and territories (New Brunswick, Newfoundland, Ontario, PEI, and Northwest Territories) supported it. More than half (57 per cent) of Quebecers voted against the Charlottetown Accord and it was likewise rejected in all four Western provinces. This second failed attempt was interpreted as a continued affront to Quebec's place in Canada.

The Bloc Québécois is discussed in the context of protest parties, on page 313 of Chapter 9.

Changes in government once again ensued within a couple of years. General elections propelled the federal Liberals to power in Ottawa and the Parti Québécois to government in Quebec. New premier Jacques Parizeau moved swiftly to hold Quebec's second sovereignty referendum, in October 1995. Prime Minister Jean Chrétien, himself a Quebecker, decided to avoid being drawn into the debate, out of fear of stirring anger in the province about federalist intervention in localized matters. Early polls demonstrated a substantial lead for the federalist side. Momentum gradually shifted toward the sovereignists as the "oui" campaign progressed. Some federalists worried that the PQ government was intentionally using a murky question that mentioned an offer "for a new economic and political partnership" with Canada. Quebecers worrying about the implications of an independent Quebec were assured by some on the "oui" side that they would continue to have a Canadian passport, use Canadian currency, and be protected by the Canadian military. Opinion polls revealed a slim lead for the sovereignists in the closing days of the referendum campaign. The federal government decided to get involved and an estimated 100,000 Canadians from outside Quebec converged on Montreal to take part in a unity rally. The "non" side prevailed by just over 50,000 votes, with 50.6 per cent voting against sovereignty, but with 49.4 per cent voting "oui."

After the Referendums: Quebec Nationalism since 1995

In the aftermath of the second referendum vote, Premier Parizeau blamed illegal financial contributions to the "non" campaign and "the ethnic vote" for the referendum's defeat. He accused federal politicians of spending vast amounts of money in contravention of the province's campaign finance rules. He portrayed what many federalists and soft nationalists saw as the ugly side of Quebec nationalism. By targeting immigrants and people of colour, he exhibited the xenophobia and racism that exists among some ethnic nationalists.

Bouchard resigned his seat as a Bloc Québécois MP to become the leader of the Parti Québécois (PQ) and premier of Quebec. The PQ won the subsequent provincial election; however, support for sovereignty waned, and the party avoided holding another referendum. Hard nationalists continued to push for a third referendum. Federalists argued that Quebecers were tired of the secession question. Both continued to joust for the hearts and minds of the soft nationalists who felt that Quebec deserved unique status.

In Ottawa, the federal government pursued a two-pronged, non-constitutional response to the 1995 referendum results. The two responses were dubbed Plan A (a friendly approach) and Plan B (a firm approach).

Plan A involved reaching out to Quebecers in an attempt to convince them that Canada is stronger with Quebec and vice versa. This included providing Quebec with a veto over future constitutional amendments and self-imposed limits on the use of the federal spending power. It also involved the creation of the sponsorship program, an advertising campaign designed to increase the salience and popularity of the federal government in Quebec. This would ultimately lead to the sponsorship scandal, a topic discussed in Chapter 11.

Plan B raised the bar for Quebec sovereignists to achieve independence. Throughout the 1995 referendum campaign, debate swirled around the process required for a province to leave Confederation, such as the wording of a referendum question. The wording of the 1980 and 1995 referendum questions is a source of debate because they were arguably designed to distort a voter's response.

1980 Quebec Referendum Question

The Government of Quebec has made public its proposal to negotiate a new agreement with the rest of Canada, based on the equality of nations; this agreement would enable Quebec to acquire the exclusive power to make its laws, levy its taxes and establish relations abroad—in other words, sovereignty—and at the same time to maintain with Canada an economic association including a common currency; any change in political status resulting from these negotiations will only be implemented with popular approval through another referendum; on these terms, do you give the Government of Quebec the mandate to negotiate the proposed agreement between Quebec and Canada?

1995 Quebec Referendum Question

Do you agree that Quebec should become sovereign after having made a formal offer to Canada for a new economic and political partnership within the scope of the bill respecting the future of Quebec and of the agreement signed on June 12, 1995?

Many people believe that the questions were not sufficiently clear to allow Quebecers to make an informed choice between the status quo and a new state of affairs.

Following the 1995 referendum the federal government sought to clarify those terms and conditions. The federal government asked the Supreme Court for an opinion on the issue. In the Secession reference (1998), the Court concluded that provinces cannot uni-laterally secede under Canadian or international law, and that Parliament has the power to determine what constitutes a clear referendum question. The Court found that the Government of Canada would be obligated to enter into negotiations with any province if a clear majority of that province's electorate were to vote in favour of independence. The federal government proceeded to pass the **Clarity Act**. The legislation grants the Parliament of Canada the authority to determine what constitutes a clear majority of votes and what is a clear question in any secession referendum. Furthermore, the Clarity Act empowers Parliament to vote on whether the wording of a referendum question is sufficiently clear before the referendum vote is held. All of this reduces the potential for secessionists in any area of Canada to manipulate an independence referendum that they initiate. Building on the Canadian experience, the referendum question later put before Scottish voters in 2014 simply asked: "Should Scotland be an independent country?"

The Government of Quebec responded with its own legislation. The province's leg-islature passed Bill 99, An Act Respecting the Exercise of the Fundamental Rights and Prerogatives of the Québec People and the Québec State. Its terms proclaimed Quebec's right to declare self-determination, stating that "No other parliament or government may reduce the powers, authority, sovereignty or legitimacy of the National Assembly, or impose constraint on the democratic will of the Quebec people to determine its own future." As mentioned, the Clarity Act authorizes the House of Commons to decide what constitutes a sufficient majority of Quebecers voting to support a sovereignty proposal. By comparison, Bill 99 states that a majority vote of "fifty per cent of the valid votes cast plus one" in a referendum is sufficient to identify which side is the winner. Thus, Quebec legislation establishes that a referendum can be won by a single vote, whereas Canadian legislation states that it is not up to Quebec alone to decide what constitutes sufficient support for separation.

The next significant flash of Quebec nationalism ignited under Prime Minister Harper's Conservative government. In 2006 the Bloc Québécois took steps to present a motion in the House of Commons recognizing "Quebecers as a nation." The Bloc resolu-tion would likely have been largely symbolic with no legal force. The move was designed to provoke federalist parties to vote against it. This would give sovereignists a reason to reignite their calls for independence. Federalist parties were put in a difficult position, as voting in favour of the motion could spark regionalist reactions in the rest of the country, while voting against it could be viewed as yet another rejection of Quebec's unique status in Confederation. As a pre-emptive measure, Prime Minister Harper introduced his own motion before the Bloc resolution reached the floor, calling upon the House of Commons to recognize "that the Québécois form a nation within a united Canada." The **Quebec nation motion** passed with the unanimous support of Conservative, Bloc Québécois, and NDP members in attendance. The Conservative intergovernmental affairs minister resigned on the principle of cabinet solidarity, explaining that while he favoured civic nationalism, he opposed pandering to ethnic nationalism.[21] Liberal MPs were divided on the motion. The political symbolism of recognizing the Québécois as a nation in this man-ner has muted calls for unique status.

Clarity Act
Federal legislation passed in 2000 that sets out the terms for the federal government to deal with a province proposing to secede.

Quebec nation motion
A non-binding federal motion passed in 2006 that recognized the unique character of the Québécois.

Since reaching 49 per cent in 1995, and 55 per cent in the early 2000s, support for Quebec sovereignty has remained below 40 per cent, dipping into the teens throughout Justin Trudeau's first term as prime minister. The Parti Québécois and Bloc Québécois plummeted in the polls and their numbers dwindled so considerably that both lost official party status in the National Assembly and House of Commons. Despite the BQ's resurgence in the 2019 federal election, the party avoids talk about sovereignty on the campaign trail. This reflects a new reality that public-opinion polls show that more than four in five Quebecers believe that Quebec should remain in Canada. Nearly three-quarters of Quebec francophones feel this way and nearly two-thirds of them think that the issue of Quebec sovereignty is settled.[22] It is unclear whether Quebec separatism is vanishing or is simply dormant.

Institutions emerged to solidify the unique status of Quebec within Confederation over the course of these tumultuous decades. At the same time, consensus grew across Canada that Quebec warrants some form of special treatment. Although not enshrined in the constitution, and while falling short of some nationalists' ambitions, a number of advancements were made on all five demands articulated by Premier Bourassa in the period leading up to the Meech Lake Accord (see Table 4.3).

Many of these advancements were made in a symmetrical fashion. Guarantees to Quebec being extended to other provinces was criticized by Quebec nationalists who sought asymmetrical treatment of Quebec as a unique province (and nation) within Confederation (see Chapter 3). This final point illustrates the tensions that often develop between competing types of regionalism in Canada: whereas nationalists may seek a unique status for their province or region within Canada, sectionalists may rally against such treatment, evoking principles of provincial equality.

There are other forms of nationalism at play in Quebec. Underlying Parizeau's "ethnic vote" comment, the composition of the Quebec population is changing through

Table 4.3 Progress on Quebec's Five Demands for Constitutional Renewal

Bourassa's Five Demands (1985)	Advancements Since 1985
Recognition of Quebec as a distinct society	• 1997 – All premiers outside Quebec endorse the Calgary Declaration, a non-binding accord recognizing that "the unique character of Quebec society, including its French-speaking majority, its culture and its tradition of civil law, is fundamental to the well-being of Canada. Consequently, the legislature and Government of Quebec have a role to protect and develop the unique character of Quebec society within Canada." • 2006 – The House of Commons votes overwhelmingly in favour of a motion recognizing "that the Québécois form a nation within a united Canada."
Right of veto for Quebec over constitutional amendments	• 1996 – The federal government passes An Act Respecting Constitutional Amendments, giving Quebec (and other regions) vetoes over most changes to the Canadian constitution.
Limits on the federal spending power	• 1999 – The federal government signs on to the Social Union Framework Agreement, which, with other provisions, places limits on the use of the federal spending power.
Quebec input into appointing senators and Supreme Court justices	• 2015 – The federal government's processes for selecting senators and Supreme Court justices involve explicit input—though not approval—of provincial governments where vacancies occur. • 2019 – A formal agreement allows the Quebec government to select two members of the advisory board to fill Supreme Court vacancies from Quebec.
Increased provincial powers over immigration	• 1991 – The Canada–Quebec Accord enhances the Quebec government's control over immigration to the province.

globalization. Today, four-fifths of Quebecers speak French as a first language, but the focus of the national identity debate has shifted. **Allophones** (Canadians who speak neither official language) comprise a growing proportion of the Canadian population, including Quebec's. Canada's constitutional protections and multiculturalism policies are designed to afford these political minorities the freedom to maintain their own ethnic and political cultures. Allophones are changing the fabric of Canadian and Quebec society. Ethnic nationalist responses to these changes appear popular in Quebec. Conservative policies on immigration and conformity to so-called "Quebec values" received support among provincial voters in recent campaigns. Civic nationalism may be declining just as ethnic nationalism is becoming more prominent.

THE CANADIAN PRESS/Ryan Remiorz

For decades, research revealed a series of cross-cutting cleavages in Canada—overlapping political divisions like region, religion, race, language, political economies, and ideology that tended to reinforce one another. In the early twentieth century, Francophone Canadians tended to be rural, Catholic, white, conservative, and live in Quebec. These features combined to distinguish them from counterparts in the rest of Canada. The Quiet Revolution, globalization, immigration, and the decline of separatism diminished some of these differences, exposing Quebec society to many of the debates that other Canadians confronted earlier. Do you think Quebec society is better or more weakly positioned to engage in debates over multiculturalism than the rest of Canada?

The Evolution of Regionalism in Canada

Understanding regionalism in Canada requires an in-depth understanding of the country's history. The roots of regionalism run deep. Structural factors combine with the actions of key political actors and patterns of behaviour. Geography is, obviously, one of the structural factors contributing to regionalism. The placement of a particular region at the core or periphery of the country may explain a lot in terms of its level of integration or alienation. So, too, might its endowment with either abundant or scarce natural resources. Demography is another factor in determining the shape of regionalism in Canada. Each region features its own ethnic makeup and has Indigenous, immigrant, senior, or youth constituencies. This diversity helps define the level of internal unity and external uniqueness among Canada's various regions. Formal political institutions like federalism, the constitution, the first-past-the-post electoral system, premiers' forums, and so on provide structural foundations. Patterns of socialization, political competition, and elite accommodation all contribute to the intensity and longevity of regionalism. In this vein, the forces that contributed to the origins of regionalism in Canada (see Figure 4.4) are distinct from the forces that have helped to sustain it over the past century-and-a-half.

Regionalism suppresses other forms of political conflict. Regional frustrations tend to get on the national agenda more frequently than the politics of class, gender, Indigenous rights, LGBTQ2+ equality, and other concerns that transcend geography. Critics of regionalized politics allege that Canadian political elites conspire to marginalize disadvantaged groups in favour of regionally based ethnic and linguistic communities.

allophones
Canadians whose dominant language is neither French nor English.

> > > > > > > > > > > > > >
Quebec's intercultural debates are discussed in Chapter 13, on diversity and representation. See especially page 452.

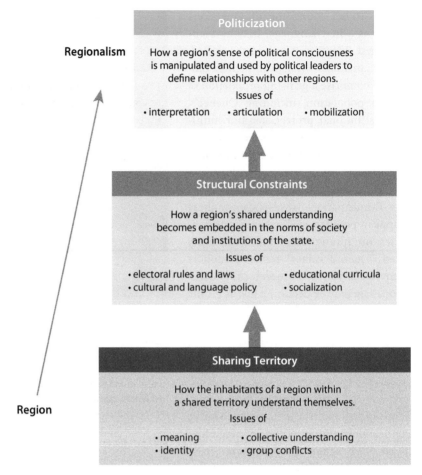

Figure 4.4 | The Origins of Regionalism

Source: Adapted from Figure 2.1 in Harry Hiller, "Region as a Social Construction," in *Regionalism and Party Politics in Canada*, ed. Lisa Young and Keith Archer (Don Mills, ON: Oxford University Press, 2002), 36.

Origins of Regionalism

Political scientist Nelson Wiseman (2007) points to settlement patterns, formative events, and economic staples as interrelated factors that laid the foundations of regionalism in Canada.

Each region in Canada is shaped by its own unique pattern of immigration. Earlier settlers had a strong impact on the political cultures of their new communities. They are fragments of their native countries, bringing with them the ideologies and institutions of their old homelands. The first immigrant wave, from France until 1760, helped establish an agrarian, conservative culture in Quebec and Acadia. Decades later, United Empire Loyalists from the United States arrived in the Maritimes and Ontario, cementing the regions' penchant for British political institutions and outlook. British immigration continued throughout the next two centuries, imprinting Ontario and the Maritimes with a liberal-tory bent, then fostering labour–socialist leanings on the Prairies. Western

American settlers pushed northward in the early twentieth century. Liberal–populists became a founding fragment of Alberta's early population.

Each region has undergone its own formative and transformative events. The American Revolution was a formative moment for Maritimers and Ontarians alike. It sparked a massive migration of United Empire Loyalists that gave the liberal democracies of these two regions a so-called "tory touch" not found elsewhere in Canada. This toryism features a more collectivist vision of conservatism, and a corresponding reverence for law and order, the social fabric, and the monarchy. The Riel resistance had a comparable impact on Prairie political culture, burying the roots of Indigenous and Western alienation in the region's political soil. The arrival of the Canadian Pacific Railway to British Columbia sealed the terms of the province's entry into Confederation and opened BC as the gateway to Canada's West. In Newfoundland debates about entering Confederation reflect and shape the province's relationship with the rest of Canada. Newfoundlanders' and Labradorians' entry into Canada in 1949, a few generations after their Maritime neighbours joined, sets their province apart.

See the discussion of ideology on page 300 of Chapter 9 for an explanation of toryism.

Each of Canada's regions features a unique endowment of natural resources, or staples.[23] According to staples theory, regions whose economies thrive on boom-and-bust commodities, like oil and gas, develop more capitalist cultures compared to regions whose economies are built on less lucrative and more vulnerable resources, like wheat or fish. Regions that rely on less valuable resources tend to develop a higher level of expectation for government intervention in the economy. To them, government is often seen as one of the few sources of economic security. Historically, the Atlantic Canadian economy has been based on fishing and agriculture; Central Canada on manufacturing; that of the Prairies, on agriculture and energy; and that of BC, on forests and minerals.[24] The recent rise and fall of offshore oil and gas revenues in Newfoundland and Labrador, and to a lesser extent in Nova Scotia, will test the lasting impact of the region's historically insecure staples on its regional culture. To date, spending demands by residents have outstripped the revenues generated from those non-renewable resources.

Persistence of Regionalism

These historical factors go only so far in explaining the persistence of regionalism in Canada. Regions do not freeze into place following settlement. How is it that events, institutions, and economics that originated with settlers more than a century ago continue to exert influence on Canadian politics? How does regionalism continue to define Canadian politics, given that innovations in transportation and communication have broken down many of the geographical barriers that separate Canadians? How can regionalism be so intense if most citizens today were either not born or not living in this country when these original forces were at play? The reason for the persistence lies in a combination of socialization, institutionalization, and politicization.

Socialization

Regionalism is passed down from generation to generation and from residents to newcomers through a process known as socialization. A host of actors—from families, churches, schools, and peer groups to artists, academics, bureaucrats, and the media—play leading roles in instilling foundational beliefs. Most experts on socialization agree that the process is cumulative, so that things we are taught to believe early on tend to act as a filter for later learning.[25] Many Canadian children are exposed to politics in the home. Parents often act as role models in this regard and participate in passing regional views from generation to generation.[26] Peers have a similar impact. Schools are venues for socialization. Teachers and textbooks relay selective information about the myths of the past, today's political realities, and projections of the future.[27] Likewise, academic discourses help to reinforce existing political cultures by sanctifying certain historical narratives. The artistic community and the media play similar roles in popularizing views about regional cultures in Canada.

Political scientist Barry Cooper's (2002) observations regarding the impact of the **Laurentian thesis** are particularly insightful. According to this view, Quebec and Ontario were granted pre-eminent status among all provinces at the time of Confederation and in the century that followed. The Laurentian thesis holds that their dominance was enshrined in the constitution, granting them full regional status, including 24 Senate seats each. The outlying jurisdictions were considered subordinate, particularly as new provinces were added in the West. The two founding Maritime provinces were granted 10 senators each and full control over their natural resources. By comparison, the Western provinces were granted six Senate seats each and lacked jurisdiction over resources until 1930. This differential treatment contributed to the development of Western alienation.

The persistence of the Laurentian thesis has been challenged. *The Globe and Mail* columnist John Ibbitson and pollster Darrell Bricker expose the myth in their book *The Big Shift* (2013). They argue that immigration patterns are transforming Canadian society such that political power is shifting westward and toward electoral districts that are populated predominantly by allophones. The worldview of Canada as a fragile state that needs the federal government to bind Canadians through a nationwide welfare state and through special favours for Quebec no longer holds, they argue.

Laurentian thesis
A theory that historic perceptions of Central-Canadian dominance have spawned regionalist resentment in peripheral parts of the country.

Institutionalization

In addition to these forces of socialization, regional divisions become institutionalized. Federal economic development programs, organizations, structures, laws, and other systems develop in ways that further entrench geographic differences in Canada. Federalism is the most pertinent of these institutions. As discussed in Chapter 3, federalism was selected as a means of forging a pan-Canadian union that respected regional differences. The institutions of federalism—the division of powers, intra-state bodies like the Senate, inter-state bodies like first ministers' meetings, and so on—did not predate the existence of Canada's regional communities. Yet federalism reinforces those differences. It empowers provincial governments to legislate in a wide range of areas and emboldens premiers to act as spokespeople for and defenders of provincial interests.

Federalism allows provincial governments to establish systems of taxation, healthcare, social services, and education that meet the needs of their residents and align with their own political cultures. Quebec has Canada's most comprehensive public daycare system, for example. The province's extensive government programs and relatively high rates of taxation align well with its social-democratic political culture, just as Crown corporations may be attributed to, and contribute to, that province's social-democratic tradition. The same is true, to a lesser degree, in Manitoba and the Atlantic provinces. Alberta's low-tax environment—a luxury derived from its endowment of natural resources—both matches and strengthens its laissez-faire conservative political culture. To a lesser extent, the same pattern occurs in Saskatchewan and British Columbia. Federalism encourages diversity in public policy and reinforces regional cleavages in Canada.

To appreciate the power and nature of socialization, consider the following popular story, based loosely on the research of primatologist G.R. Stephenson:

Five monkeys were placed in the centre of a cage, along with a ladder at the top of which sat a banana. Every time a monkey started up the ladder, scientists would douse the entire cage with cold water. After a few times, the monkeys began threatening those who would approach the ladder, such that no monkey dared consider capturing the banana. Once this context had been established, scientists began replacing each of the monkeys in the cage, one by one. Not having witnessed the cold-water implications of climbing the ladder, each new monkey was tempted to go after the banana. But, one by one, each was dissuaded by the other monkeys in the cage. By the end of the experiment, none of the five original monkeys was left in the cage. And, yet, none of the new monkeys would attempt to climb the ladder.

Some psychologists and business scholars use this research as evidence of how culture is passed to newcomers. The culture persists even when the initial conditions and actors that fostered the culture no longer exist. The same process is at play in transmitting political culture. Few Canadians today personally experienced events like the Great Depression or governance under the Union Nationale. Today's youth and recent immigrants were not present during the Quebec referendums or the controversy surrounding the National Energy Program. Yet these events continue to shape politics. Socializing forces are at play in transmitting the political culture of the region in which all Canadians live, transmitted from generation to generation, and from longtime residents to newcomers.

As a function of these cleavages, it is unsurprising that debates periodically erupt over the distribution of wealth from one region to another. Regional divisions are laid bare in news stories and at major intergovernmental meetings. The constitutional conferences that brought together the prime minister and all premiers used to provide a national forum for premiers to bargain and, in some cases, grandstand. Since then, full first ministers' meetings involving the prime minister and premiers have become less frequent. Instead, premiers gather on their own through institutions like the Council of Atlantic Premiers, the Western Premiers' Conference, the New West Partnership, and the Northern Premiers' Forum (see Table 4.4). These meetings strengthen regional tendencies and deepen regional cleavages. Premiers meet on a regional basis several times per year, often in advance of summer meetings of the Council of the Federation. They use these meetings as opportunities to build regional consensus, advance joint priorities, explore opportunities for collaboration, and promote common positions on the national and international stage.

See the discussion of inter-state federalism in Chapter 3 for more on first ministers' meetings.

Table 4.4   Major Provincial and Territorial Meetings

Institution (year established)	Members	Meeting Dates
Northern Premiers' Forum (2003)	Yukon, Northwest Territories, Nunavut	April/May
New West Partnership (2010)	British Columbia, Alberta, Saskatchewan	variable
Western Premiers' Conference (1973)	British Columbia, Alberta, Saskatchewan, Manitoba, Yukon, Northwest Territories, Nunavut	early June
Council of Maritime Premiers (1972)	New Brunswick, Nova Scotia, Prince Edward Island	variable
Council of Atlantic Premiers (2000)	New Brunswick, Nova Scotia, Prince Edward Island, Newfoundland & Labrador	early June
Council of the Federation (2003)	All provinces and territories	late July and January

To that end, premiers often travel together abroad and work with their counterparts in other countries. Premiers from the Atlantic provinces and Quebec have met with New England governors on an almost annual basis since 1973. Western premiers have met with Western US governors since 1990. These meetings foster transnational regions that are held together by coalitions of subnational governments.

Politicization

Lastly, regionalism persists in Canada because it is continually politicized by politicians. For regional consciousness to enter and remain a part of the political discourse, it must be interpreted, articulated, and mobilized by political elites.[28] Successful politicians take advantage of code politics, campaigning on the core beliefs that prevail within their province or region, and that reinforce a sense of otherness in comparison with the rest of Canada. At times, these codes cultivate a type of siege mentality, presenting a leader as the great guardian of the province or region against outside influence. Often the outsider they seek protection from is the federal government. This type of rhetoric is especially evident in peripheral regions like the West and Atlantic Canada. Yet throughout history it can be found in the campaign platforms of leaders across the country.[29]

Canada's political system is rife with incentives that encourage politicians to engage in regionalized politics. Premiers and senators represent their respective provinces on the national stage. The single-member constituencies in Canada's electoral system, discussed in Chapter 10, are organized along geographic lines. Members of Parliament and members of subnational legislatures represent their own territorial districts. While party discipline remains strong in Canada, and while advances in communication and transportation allow for nationwide campaigns, these constituency boundaries exert a powerful influence on the structure of Canadian elections. Each general election consists of candidates who appeal to local interests and issues in their electoral districts. National leaders are encouraged to appeal to the same dynamics. Historically, specific platforms or agendas are released for each region. Provincial or regional lieutenants are appointed to oversee the campaign in different parts of the country. In some federal elections, a party's chief lieutenant in a province is the premier—or, alternatively, a premier may be its greatest local adversary.

Briefing Notes

Regional Tensions between Quebec and Newfoundland and Labrador

Rivalries periodically develop between regions. The feud between Newfoundland and Quebec is a case in point. Bad blood between them stems from territorial disputes over Labrador's boundary that should have ended with a 1927 decision of the Judicial Committee of the Privy Council that ruled in favour of Newfoundland. The two provinces' animosity increased with a 1969 agreement that allows Quebec to acquire power from the Churchill Falls hydroelectricity station at cut-rate prices. Attempts by Newfoundland to reopen the lopsided deal, including through court action, have failed and the province is obligated to continue to sell power to Quebec at well under market value through 2041.[30] So sour is the relationship that, as Newfoundland develops new hydro projects, the two provinces cannot come to terms on an agreement to route energy exports through Quebec to the United States. Moreover, Quebec challenges any federal government investment in Newfoundland hydro as preferential treatment. Regional aggravation persists through media coverage of tussles over the official Labrador boundary line. The government of Quebec requires its public institutions to use maps that include a portion of southern Labrador within Quebec.[31]

Regionalism and National Unity

What holds Canadians together? Regional conflicts result in instability and even civil war in other countries. Yet, regionalism has been thriving within the bosom of the Canadian state for over 150 years. What makes Canada so unique in this regard?

Part of the answer can be found in the structure of Canada's political institutions. These institutions both allow and actively promote unity through diversity. Federalism and our electoral system act as safety valves by allowing for the legitimate expression of regional differences within the boundaries of Canadian democracy. The Canadian constitution entrenches regional protections. Minority rights are provincially guarded and nationally guaranteed against both global forces and domestic governments. Residents of all provinces, large and small, are represented in Parliament. A combination of custom and necessity ensure that all regions have influence during election campaigns and national policymaking.

Moreover, regional and pan-Canadian institutions like premiers' conferences have become more powerful and institutionalized. This occurred despite the propensity of premiers to act in their jurisdictions' self-interest. The quest for collective provincial clout has fostered broader consensus among provinces and territories. In the face of globalization, instead of championing protectionism, provincial and territorial governments are working together to promote common interests on the domestic and international stage.

Indeed, most forms of Canadian regionalism are of the sectionalist variety. This means that their adherents are looking for a better deal within Canada, not outside it. No country is forever safe from secessionism. Nonetheless, Canadians seem to view regionalism as a fact of life, not a threat to it.

Concluding Thoughts

While often viewed as divisive, regionalism may be seen as a unifying force that brings together people who share political concerns. Put simply, people in various parts of Canada approach politics differently. In the previous chapter, we discussed how federalism empowers these regional communities to govern their own affairs while remaining contributing members of the broader Canadian federation. In the chapters that follow, you will gain a better sense of how other political institutions—beginning with executives (Chapter 5) and legislatures (Chapter 6)—both reinforce and keep these regional dynamics in check.

For More Information

Are there really regional cleavages in Canadian public opinion? Yes and no. Christopher Cochrane and Andrea Perrella suggest there is some evidence in their 2012 *Canadian Journal of Political Science* article "Regions, Regionalism and Regional Differences in Canada" (45: 829–53). By contrast, Ailsa Henderson takes a revolutionary view of "Regional Political Cultures in Canada" in her 2004 article found in the same journal (37: 595–615). Her findings are mirrored in Maxime Héroux-Legault's 2016 study of "Substate Variations in Political Values in Canada" (26: 171–97), which finds that other ideological lines of division cut across regional boundaries.

How do newcomers adapt to regionalism in Canada? In a 2010 article, Antoine Bilodeau and colleagues analyze "The Development of Dual Loyalties: Immigrants' Integration to Regional Canadian Dynamics" (*Canadian Journal of Political Science* 43: 515–44).

What are the historical foundations of Canadian regionalism? David Bell traced *The Roots of Disunity* in 1992 (Oxford University Press), while Nelson Wiseman went *In Search of Canadian Political Culture* in 2007 (UBC Press). Mildred A. Schwartz wrote the seminal work on the topic in her 1974 book *Politics and Territory: The Sociology of Regional Persistence in Canada* (McGill–Queen's University Press).

How do regional premiers' conferences work? J. Peter Meekison, Hamish Telford, and Harvey Lazar edited the volume *Reconsidering the Institutions of Canadian Federalism* as part of the annual "Canada: The State of the Federation" series (McGill–Queen's University Press, 2004).

How does the federal party system affect regionalism in Canada? Lisa Young and Keith Archer and their contributors present a series of responses in *Regionalism and Party Politics in Canada* (Oxford University Press, 2001).

How have successful federal politicians built regional coalitions in Canada? John Duffy explores over a century of electioneering in *Fights of Our Lives: Elections, Leadership, and the Making of Canada* (Harper Collins, 2002).

How have provincial politicians constructed unique political cultures? Jared Wesley explores the development of *Code Politics: Campaigns and Cultures on the Canadian Prairies* (UBC Press, 2011).

What is the state of Western alienation in the twenty-first century? Roger Gibbins and Loleen Berdahl offer a retrospective and prospective look at regionalism in *New West, New Canada* (University of Toronto Press, 2014).

What was the atmosphere really like around the 1995 Quebec referendum? *CBC News* produced a three-hour documentary, "Breaking Point" to commemorate the tenth anniversary of the campaign, interviewing all of the key players. It is now available on YouTube.

Are Métis people an ethnic group or a nation? Chris Andersen argues firmly in favour of the latter in *Métis: Race, Recognition, and the Struggle for Indigenous Peoplehood* (UBC Press, 2015).

Deeper Inside Canadian Politics

1. There are a lot of ghosts in the graveyard of Canadian regionalism. Examine one of the following issues and explain how it continues to influence politics in Canada:
   a) the National Energy Program
   b) distinct society
   c) the Atlantic accords
   d) the changes to the equalization formula
2. Premiers meet several times each year on a regional and national basis. Drawing on the communiqués (press releases) from the most recent meetings of the Western, Atlantic, and Northern premiers' forums, describe the sorts of activities that governments commit to undertaking on a regional basis. Is there any correlation with the outcomes of Council of the Federation meetings?
3. In the past, there have been heated debates concerning the abolition of the Canadian Senate. How would abolishing the Senate affect regionalism in Canada?
4. According to Roger Gibbins, senior fellow at the Canada West Foundation:

Regional differences and hence regional conflict are inevitable in a country of Canada's size and complexity. The regions—be they provinces, the northern territories, or more abstract amalgamations such as the West and Atlantic Canada—differ substantially in their economic foundations, socio-demographic composition, and political cultures. Therefore regionalism—the intrusion of territorially based interests, values, and identities into national public life—is unavoidable. . . . However, we can and should ask to what extent our political institutions moderate or exacerbate regional conflict and regional alienation.[32]

Has Canadian federalism been successful in handling and containing regional conflict? Or have its institutions and practices intensified such conflict? In short, when it comes to regionalism in Canada, has federalism been part of the solution or part of the problem?

Professor Profile

David McGrane

Regionalism, provincial politics, Canadian political parties, social democracy
Author of *The New NDP: Moderation, Modernization and Political Marketing* (2019)

Courtesy David McGrane

David McGrane straddles two political worlds. As a professor, he has written books about public policy in Saskatchewan, and journal articles on such topics as multiculturalism in Western Canada, provincial voting behaviour, and childcare in Atlantic Canada. As a member of the Saskatoon community, he is involved with environmental activism, organized labour, and diverse social democratic causes.

Here is what David McGrane told us about his career path from when he was an undergraduate student, why he is drawn to his area of specialization, what is challenging about studying Canadian politics, and what advice he has for students.

* * *

I was born and raised in Moose Jaw, Saskatchewan. As soon as I graduated from high school, I went to nearby University of Regina to study political science. Besides what I heard my family discuss at Christmastime, I had very limited knowledge about federal and provincial politics when I first stepped into my introduction to Canadian politics class in my second year of university. Looking back over 20 years later, it is clear that this class ended up being a turning point in my life that shaped my political and academic career. It was the first time that I read the Regina Manifesto, the founding document of the CCF-NDP, and the first time that I read Seymour Lipset's classic book on Saskatchewan politics entitled *Agrarian Socialism*. The paper that I wrote for that class about the ideological evolution of the CCF-NDP, particularly its Saskatchewan section, was a very early version of the ideas that I eventually developed when I wrote my doctoral thesis and published my first book: *Remaining Loyal: Social Democracy in Quebec and Saskatchewan* (McGill-Queen's Press, 2014). Thinking about social democracy in the Canadian context also motivated me to join the Saskatchewan NDP. Two decades later I became president of the party!

A focus of my research throughout my career has been the role of regionalism in Canada and Canadian provincial politics. I was drawn to studying this area because, despite provincial governments having significant power over the important programs like healthcare, education, and social assistance, there is very little research on provincial politics. Once I began to be interested in the study of provincial politics, it was a short journey towards looking at how regionalism influences the politics of Canada. I ended up researching the fiscal relations between provincial governments and the federal government, differences between regional and provincial political culture, and voter behaviour in provincial elections. What animates much of this research is the conviction that provinces matter and the operation of provincial governments creates powerful forces of regionalism in Canada that shape our national politics. While it may not seem as glamorous as what goes on in Ottawa, Washington, or New York at the United Nations, what goes in provincial capitals in Canada affects our lives in numerous ways and impacts our friends, families, and neighbours.

What always surprises me about studying provincial politics is how provinces can be so similar and so unique at the same time. Every province has its own distinctive political traditions and institutions, but there are always fascinating commonalities among provinces. Examining provinces in comparison to each other consistently yields interesting findings and allows us to understand each individual case much better. As such, I always encourage students to employ a comparative lens when researching political events and political practices. You will learn much more by comparing two or more cases to one another as opposed to just looking at one case in isolation.

Up for Debate

Is regionalism pulling Canada apart?

THE CLAIM: YES, IT IS!

Regionalism is a negative force and threatens national unity.

Yes: Argument Summary

Geography is a primary lens through which citizens and politicians view Canadian democracy. Canadians choose a representative of their local geographic community when they vote in provincial and federal elections. In Ottawa, those MPs are expected to keep the interests of their constituents in mind when engaging in caucus and committee work. When first ministers select certain representatives to become minsters, they pay attention to geography, ensuring that the various regions have at least one representative in cabinet. When prime ministers select appointees to the Senate and Supreme Court, by law they must do so on a regional basis. In all of these instances, region serves as a filter for representation. This pushes other cleavages aside, papering over disparities when it comes to the representation of Indigenous people, women, people of colour, and other traditionally marginalized groups. It sidelines ideological debates over the future of Canadian society, locking the system in a primitive struggle over turf as opposed to principle.

Yes: Top 5 Considerations

1. Canada's first-past-the-post electoral system is firmly rooted in territorial representation. At the federal level, this means election campaigns featuring over 300 local contests, many fought over regional interests. National party organizations employ provincial directors to orchestrate regional campaigns. All of this reinforces the importance of region as a political and policy consideration during elections.

2. The federal government continues to operate on a regional basis, appointing regional ministers (e.g., a Quebec lieutenant) and staffing regional offices in major departments (like Indigenous affairs). Provincial cabinets and governments are constructed in a similar manner.

3. The regions themselves are morphing in response to new policy challenges and political debates. For instance, two previously united provinces have clashed over the construction and expansion of Trans-Mountain pipelines from Alberta to BC's West Coast.

4. Recent populist movements in Ontario and Alberta tapped into a perceived sense of status loss among members of each region. This alienation is motivated, in large part, by the sense that each province is being left behind economically and mistreated by the federal government.

5. Regionalism crowds out discourse about settler colonialism, individual equality, group rights, national economic development, and many other significant public-policy issues. These problems fester, placing further strain on the political system.

Yes: Other Considerations

- The ebbs and flows of Western alienation and support for Quebec sovereignty do not signal a permanent decline in regionalism. Changes in government leadership in Ottawa and the provinces have a major impact on regional tensions. Discussion about Alberta separation perculated in the aftermath of the 2019 federal election and, without any Liberal MPs from Alberta or Saskatchewan, the Trudeau government lacked representation from those Prairie provinces.

- The Quebec government has launched constitutional challenges to the federal government's authority to unilaterally reform the Canadian Senate, change the rules of royal secession in Canada, and appoint a justice to the Supreme Court. Conservative forces in Alberta, Saskatchewan, and Ontario challenged the federal government's authority to establish a national price on carbon. Moves like these prevent nationwide policymaking.

- There is a constant battle for regional power. Toronto politicians sometimes talk about the city separating from Ontario. Labradorians have their own unofficial flag and get frustrated that the island of Newfoundland benefits from Labrador resources. Some residents of Cape Breton Island push for it to become a province separate from Nova Scotia. Political parties have advanced the interests of Acadians in New Brunswick and the frustrations of disaffected Albertans. During the Quebec sovereignty debates, the question of whether Quebec itself is divisible arose. These are just some of many examples of region-based grievances within the Canadian federation.

- Regional economic blocks are expanding and strengthening. The New West Partnership Trade Agreement improved credential recognition across the four westernmost provinces; Atlantic harmonization projects such as the Atlantic Workforce Partnership and the Atlantic Procurement Partnership streamlined transportation systems in the region; and the Pan-Territorial Adaptation Strategy helps Nunavut, Northwest Territories, and Yukon to coordinate their actions on climate change. These moves weaken Canada's economic and environmental union.

THE COUNTERCLAIM: NO, IT ISN'T!

Regionalism has been dying in Canada ever since the sovereignists were defeated in the 1995 Quebec referendum.

No: Argument Summary

The divisive tone of Canadian politics that characterizes much of its history climaxed with the 1995 Quebec sovereignty referendum. Since then, the federal government has taken several important steps to address Quebec's grievances, as well as those of the West and Atlantic Canada. In doing so, Ottawa strengthened the powers of all provinces and stepped out of areas of provincial jurisdiction, allowing each province more autonomy over its own affairs. This has muted the age-old grievances based on Ottawa's overreaching.

No: Top 5 Considerations

1. The resounding defeat of the Parti Québécois in the 2014 and 2018 provincial elections signalled Quebecers' loss of appetite for civic nationalism. During the 2019 federal election campaign, the leader of the Bloc Québécois avoided invoking separatism. While soft nationalism persists in Quebec, separatism has reached sustained lows in terms of popular support. The new generation of Quebec voters, in particular, considers the separatism question to be settled. The federal government has taken meaningful action to address age-old grievances of Quebec nationalists. The certainty provided by the Clarity Act sets a very high bar for future referendums.

2. The Western-based Reform Party rebranded itself twice before merging with the PCs to become the Conservative Party of Canada. With the election of one of Reform's former top officials, Stephen Harper, to the prime minister's office, the West officially was "in." The return of the Liberal Party to power did not diminish the West's influence to a great degree. Over one-third (35%) of the members of Harper's final cabinet were from the West. Given that the four Western provinces make up 31.5 per cent of the national population, Justin Trudeau's first cabinet was relatively well-balanced, with 25 per cent of its ministers hailing from the West. This number decreased following the 2019 federal election, but Trudeau has found other ways of incorporating Western voices in decision-making, including the use of special advisors.

3. Atlantic Canadians' concerns over health and social transfers, equalization, and off-shore oil development were largely assuaged through reforms in the 2008 to 2014 period. While critics continue to hold that federal transfer payments to their region could be higher, they are at their highest point in history, and growing.

4. Periodic, populist displays of regionalism are more theatrical than real. When provinces threaten to boycott each other's exports or to block shipments of goods across their borders, it amounts to grandstanding. The same goes for municipal politicians who threaten to secede from their provinces.

5. Different brands of regionalism tend to feed off one another. When Quebec nationalism and calls to establish a distinct society surged in the 1990s, it prompted a response from Western Canada for equal treatment. This spiralled into the divisive debates over the Meech Lake and Charlottetown accords.

No: Other Considerations

- Regional concerns are no longer top of mind for most Canadians. For a number of years, healthcare and the economy—not national unity—have topped the list of concerns among Canadians, even those within Quebec. The perpetual state of political crisis that characterized the late twentieth century is unrecognizable for new Canadians and Canadian youth.
- Western alienation is based on a myth. The West is well-represented within the federal government. Its economy has long outperformed its counterparts in the rest of Canada. Saying the West is alienated neglects the privileged status the region attained in recent decades. What grievances exist are primarily partisan and ideological, rather than regional.
- Canada's major political parties engage in regional brokerage—bringing together communities and interests across geographic divides using modern campaign technology and new strategies that target non-geographic constituencies based on age, gender, ethnicity, and other factors. There is no longer enough regional disenchantment to spur a regional party to assemble enough support to remake the Canadian party system.

Discussion Questions

- Do you identify most with your home community, your province, or your country? How does this compare with other people you know?
- How can Canadians amend their constitution without aggravating regional identities and straining national unity? Is it better just to put up with the status quo?
- In an increasingly globalized world, does it make sense for provincial governments to protect their turf, or should they be finding ways to co-operate with each other? What explains their current political stances?
- Do you think a province will ever separate from Canada? Why or why not?
- To what extent do you think that the growing number of allophones in Canada, particularly in urban centres, is causing politicians to think in multicultural terms rather than regional terms?

Where to Learn More about Regionalism in Canadian Politics

David Cameron and Richard Simeon, "Intergovernmental Relations in Canada: The Emergence of Collaborative Federalism," *Publius: The Journal of Federalism* 32, no. 2 (2002): pp. 49–72.

Christopher Cochrane and Andrea Perrella, "Regions, Regionalism and Regional Differences in Canada," *Canadian Journal of Political Science* 45, no. 4 (2012): pp. 829–53.

Charles Conteh, *Policy Governance in Multi-Level Systems: Economic Development and Policy Implementation in Canada* (Montreal and Kingston: McGill–Queen's University Press, 2013).

David McGrane and Loleen Berdahl, "'Small Worlds' No More: Reconsidering Provincial Political Cultures in Canada," *Regional & Federal Studies* 23, no. 4 (2013): pp. 479–93.

Éric Monpetit, Erick Lachapelle and Simon Kiss, "Does Canadian Federalism Amplify Policy Disagreements? Values, Regions and Policy Preferences," *IRPP Study* 65 (2017): 1–27.

Michael D. Ornstein, H. Michael Stevenson, and A. Paul Williams, "Region, Class and Political Culture in Canada," *Canadian Journal of Political Science* 13, no. 2 (1980): pp. 227–71.

Denis Savoie, "All Things Canadian Are Now Regional," *Journal of Canadian Studies* 35, no. 1 (2000): pp. 203–17.

R.A. Young, Philippe Faucher, and André Blais, "The Concept of Province-Building: A Critique," *Canadian Journal of Political Science* 17, no. 4 (1984): pp. 783–818.

5

The Executive

Inside This Chapter

- What are the main components of the executive branch in Canada?
- How does the political executive function?
- How are political executives held accountable to the legislature and to Canadians?

Inside the Executive

Power concentrates at the top of Canadian governments. Sovereignty is vested in the Crown. In Chapter 2, we saw that Westminster parliamentary traditions, including the principle of responsible government, place great powers in the hands of premiers, prime ministers, and their cabinets. Those traditions also impose accountability on these executives, because many of their actions are subject to the endorsement of the legislature, the

Crown, or both. In addressing the following maxims, this chapter pulls back the curtain on the formal and political executive, revealing the institutions, actors, and relationships that drive governments in Canada.

✔ **The executive branch of government is large.** The formal executive comprises the Crown and its representatives, while the political executive encompasses the prime minister and cabinet, or the various provincial and territorial premiers and their ministers. They work in tandem with the upper levels of the public service and senior political staff.
✔ **The prime minister does not wield absolute control over Canadian politics.** Popular accounts treat the prime minister's role as akin to that of an autocrat who single-handedly directs policy while crafting and controlling the political message. This alarmism misjudges the many constraints on the Canadian prime minister's power.
✔ **Executives have always had a lot of power.** The belief in growing executive power assumes there was once a time when Canadian legislators enjoyed a golden age of influence over their counterparts in the executive. In fact, remarkably little has changed by way of the formal rules of parliamentary democracy in Canada. The strengthening of party discipline is arguably offset by other constraints that have developed to keep executives accountable to their respective legislatures.

UP FOR DEBATE

Do Canadian prime ministers and premiers have too much power?

Keep this question in mind as you read through the chapter. Consult the end-of-chapter debate supplement for more material to help you engage in an informed discussion of the topic.

The Executive Branch

Atop the Canadian political system sits the executive: the decision-makers and their staff who preside over the direction of their respective governments. The executive branch is, most often, the strongest of three interconnected branches of government in Canada, with the others being the legislative branch (Chapter 6) and the judicial branch (Chapter 7).

Executives are the leaders who have authority and responsibility for decision-making in their organizations. Just as the chief executive officer of a corporation is its most senior manager, in politics there are presiding officers who head up various aspects of government, and who are the chief decision-makers. Depicted in Figure 5.1, there are two types of government executives overtop the public service:

1. the formal executive, comprising the figureheads who hold ceremonial, mostly symbolic positions of authority; and
2. the political executive, made up of the elected power brokers who make the broad policy decisions.

The political executive works with public-service managers, encompassing the appointed senior bureaucrats who advise the cabinet and who oversee the bureaucracy

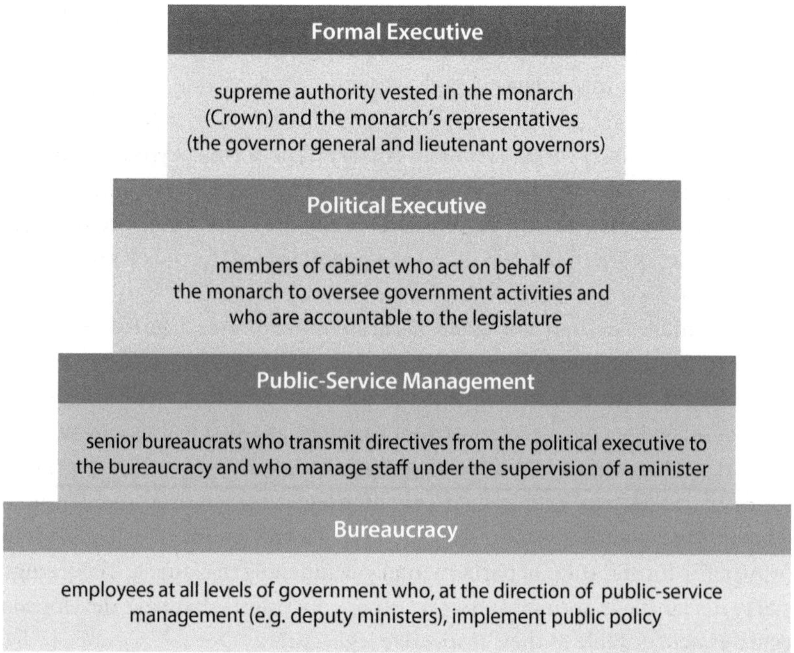

Formal Executive

supreme authority vested in the monarch
(Crown) and the monarch's representatives
(the governor general and lieutenant governors)

Political Executive

members of cabinet who act on behalf of
the monarch to oversee government activities and
who are accountable to the legislature

Public-Service Management

senior bureaucrats who transmit directives from the political executive to
the bureaucracy and who manage staff under the supervision of a minister

Bureaucracy

employees at all levels of government who, at the direction of public-service
management (e.g. deputy ministers), implement public policy

Figure 5.1 | Layers of the Executive in Canada

as it implements those policy decisions. The concentration of power in the centre of government is sometimes criticized. The broad authority of a small group of political elites appears to be at odds with grassroots notions of democracy. On the other hand, the Canadian executive has the ability to be decisive and affords senior politicians the benefit of a strong network of expertise when formulating and implementing policy. Generally speaking, the interaction between the different layers of the executive normally, but not always, produces a smooth system of governance.

The Formal Executive

head of state
The highest-ranking figure in a sovereign state, serving as its foremost ceremonial representative.

monarch
The absolute head of a monarchy, whose power is typically derived by birth.

The figurehead with supreme power in a political system is known as the **head of state**. In the United States, the president is both the head of state and the head of government. In the United Kingdom, the head of state is a king or queen whose powers have been reduced to ceremonial duties. The head of state has enormous executive authority that may or may not be exercised, depending on the political system.

Canada's head of state is the king or queen holding the hereditary position of **monarch**. Since 1952, the monarch has been Queen Elizabeth II. In all likelihood, the position will one day be assumed by her first-born child, Charles, just as Elizabeth II was the heir to the throne under her father, King George VI. Unless circumstances change, Charles will become King of Canada; his first-born child, Prince William, will eventually inherit the crown; and one day, Prince George of Cambridge, the first-born child of Prince William and Princess Kate, will become King. Thus, for over six decades, Commonwealth countries including Canada have been presided over by a queen, but future generations seem destined to be ruled by kings.

The supreme authority of the monarch is stated in the Canadian constitution. Article III of the Constitution Act, 1867, frames the organization of the formal and political executive in Canada. It declares that "The Executive Government and Authority of and over Canada is hereby declared to continue and be vested in the Queen." The monarch technically has supreme power. In practice the position involves ceremonial duties as the face of the **Crown** in Canada. The Crown and its representative, the monarch, are non-partisan symbols of all government institutions. This is one of the reasons Queen Elizabeth II appears on Canadian currency, for example. Ceremonial duties include touring, attending special events, being a patron of select charities, granting honours, and sending anniversary messages as well as words of condolence. The monarch is the symbolic head of the Canadian military, by virtue of section 15 of the Constitution Act, 1867. That section states "The Command-in-Chief of the Land and Naval Militia, and of all Naval and Military Forces, of and in Canada, is hereby declared to continue to be vested in the Queen."

Crown
The legal concept dictating the supremacy of the monarch over the executive, legislative, and judicial branches of government.

The constitutional monarch who presides over the United Kingdom is jointly the monarch for 15 other Commonwealth realms around the world, including Australia, Barbados, Canada, Jamaica, and New Zealand. Each of these countries affirms the monarch's status as its head of state through its own domestic laws. Queen Elizabeth II maintains several official residences in the UK, including Windsor Castle and Buckingham Palace in South-eastern England. Since she does not reside in Canada, her executive authority is delegated to a local resident, as per section 10 of the Constitution Act, 1867.

The **governor general** (GG) carries out tasks on behalf of the monarch and is likewise responsible for the constitutional operations of the Canadian state. Governors general are selected by the monarch on the advice of the Canadian prime minister. They typically serve for a term of five years, or longer if their term is extended. The primary responsibility is to ensure that Canada has a functioning, constitutional government. This begins with appointing a prime minister as head of the government and following that person's advice to appoint and swear in key government officials, including cabinet ministers, senators, and justices of the Supreme Court. Among the governor general's formal duties are reading the Speech from the Throne, opening and closing Parliament, signing bills into law to grant royal assent, and proclaiming that writs of election be issued. The governor general is responsible for traditional ceremonial work, such as presenting honours and awards on behalf of all Canadians, representing Canada abroad,

governor general
The monarch's representative at the federal level in Canada.

Briefing Notes

Heads of State and Heads of Government

In many presidential systems—like that of the United States—the head of government is simultaneously the head of state. These two roles are separated in constitutional monarchies like Canada. The Canadian head of state is the monarch (a king or queen), who is represented by the governor general at the federal level and by a lieutenant governor in each province. First ministers serve as the heads of government—the prime minister at the federal level and premiers at the provincial level.

THE CANADIAN PRESS/Adrian Wyld

A governor general must be careful to stay out of the political arena. Julie Payette gave a speech championing the role of science in society a month after she was appointed Canada's twenty-ninth governor general. In it, Her Excellency disparaged people who question climate change, who believe in creationism, who follow horoscopes, and who practise alternative medicine. Some scientists and politicians cheered her on social media. However, critics pointed out that the monarch's representative should be apolitical, and avoid judging the personal and political beliefs held by citizens. Do you think Payette's remarks were appropriate?

and promoting national unity and identity. Furthermore, they undertake promotional duties in support of special causes such as philanthropy and volunteerism, learning, and innovation.

Increasingly, GGs are selected from a broader cross-section of Canadian society, with appointments alternating between anglophones and francophones since the 1950s. In recent years, members of socio-demographic groups that rarely if ever are first ministers have been appointed to the positions of governor general (based in Ottawa) and lieutenant governor (based in provincial capitals), including women, Indigenous peoples, members of visible minority communities, and persons with disabilities.

As discussed in Chapter 3, the Crown is divided in Canada, meaning that the monarch is represented in Ottawa by the governor general and in the provinces by **lieutenant governors** (LGs). The LGs perform similar duties with respect to provincial matters. Each lieutenant governor is appointed by the governor general on the advice of the prime minister and serves for an average of five years. There is no requirement for the GG or the PM to consult the premier in appointing an LG. Similar positions, called commissioners, exist in the three territories. Each commissioner serves as a representative of the federal government, not of the monarch.

As representatives of the head of state, the governor general and lieutenant governors have a variety of formal executive powers, which in practice are likely to be used only upon

lieutenant governor
The monarch's representative in each province.

the direction of the prime minister. The most significant is **prerogative authority**, which grants final say to the head of state on any matter not explicitly addressed in the constitution, such as proroguing Parliament, approving orders-in-council, appointments to Royal Commissions, or declaring war.

prerogative authority
Powers that are not explicitly granted to the political executives, and that remain vested in the Crown.

In 1947, the Letters Patent Constituting the Office of the Governor General and Commander-in-Chief of Canada were passed. The Letters Patent granted the governor general considerable authority to act on behalf of the monarch, such as appointing the cabinet, granting royal assent, and appointing judges. Over time, the scope of this prerogative authority has narrowed, as legislatures assume increasing responsibility and demand more accountability from the Crown. Today, the GG and LGs behave almost exclusively in a ceremonial manner. On rare occasions, the prime minister seeks approval directly from the monarch, such as a recommendation for a new Governor General.

Owing to the supremacy of the Crown, the governor general or lieutenant governor can exercise reserve powers that act as a safeguard. The vice-regal representatives can opt to ignore requests from a first minister, ranging from a request to appoint a senior official to the very matter of governing. Among them are the power of disallowance, which means to prevent a bill passed by a legislature from becoming law. These reserve powers are set aside for extraordinary circumstances and rarely, if ever, used. They offer an assurance that a first minister's conduct will stay within constitutional boundaries.

Only twice at the federal level has the governor general unilaterally switched which party holds power without requiring a general election. The first time surrounded the Pacific Scandal of the 1870s, discussed in Chapter 8. The next time was during the infamous **King–Byng affair**. At the conclusion of the 1925 federal election, the Conservative Party had 115 seats, the Liberals 100, and the Progressive Party 22 seats. We might therefore assume that the leader of the Conservatives, Arthur Meighen, would be appointed prime minister. Not so. Liberal Prime Minister Mackenzie King, who had requested the election, could remain in the role as long as he could demonstrate that he still controlled a majority of votes in the House of Commons. Senior Liberals negotiated with the Progressives and secured their support. King now controlled 122 seats to Meighen's 115. There was no longer a need for the governor general to intervene. A year later, having lost the support of Progressive MPs, Prime Minister King again asked Governor General Viscount Byng to dissolve Parliament and call an election. In an unusual move, Byng refused, on the basis that Canadians had recently gone to the polls. Instead, he invited Meighen to form a government, because the Conservatives held the most seats and had not yet been asked. Prime Minister Meighen and the Conservatives assumed control of the government. Just two months later the Conservative government fell, and a general election was called. During the ensuing 1926 election campaign, King made an issue out of the matter, and his Liberal Party was returned to power. The King–Byng affair remains a warning that a Canadian head of government must not assume that an executive request will be approved by the Crown's representative. The role of the vice-regal representative as an umpire when there is political controversy surrounding a change of government was resurrected nationally during the coalition crisis of 2008 (see Chapter 6) and provincially after the 2017 British Columbia election.

King–Byng affair
A 1926 constitutional crisis when the governor general refused the prime minister's request for a general election.

There is varying consternation in Canada about the relevance of the monarchy and its representatives. The topic galvanizes tories and members of the Conservative Party, who tend to revere the monarchy, its stability, and its traditions. Conversely, progressives and members of the New Democratic Party are prone to view the monarchy as anti-democratic and too expensive. Neither group of partisans places high priority on raising the matter.

Abolishing the monarchy has not been a serious topic of constitutional debate since the 1840s—before Canada was formed.

Public-opinion surveys in Canada tend to show divided support for remaining a constitutional monarchy or becoming a **republic** with an elected head of state. Support for becoming a republic is most pronounced in Quebec.[1] There, the monarchy is seen as a symbol of colonial dominance, particularly among francophones. In 2009, for instance, some Quebec nationalists threw eggs at Prince Charles when he visited Montreal, claiming a cultural genocide had been committed and waving signs that said, "Majesty go home!"

The idea of Canada's becoming a sovereign republic like the United States does not tend to be part of the political discourse. Nonetheless, the symbols of the monarchy are emphasized to varying degrees by governments of different stripes. Under the federal Liberals, in 1968 the word "royal" was removed from branches of the Canadian military, and two paintings by Quebec artist Alfred Pellan were displayed in the lobby of the foreign affairs national headquarters in Ottawa. In 2011, Conservative Prime Minister Stephen Harper's government changed the name of the Maritime Command back to the Royal Canadian Navy, and the Air Command back to the Royal Canadian Air Force. The Pellan paintings were replaced with a portrait of Queen Elizabeth II. Four years later, among the first actions by Liberal Prime Minister Justin Trudeau's government were to put the Pellan paintings back up and remove the Queen's portrait.[2]

The Political Executive

In practice, Canada's monarch reigns but does not rule, while **first ministers** rule but do not reign. Put another way, power formally resides with the monarch, but it is exercised by politicians. This transfer of executive authority from the head of state's representative to the **heads of government** sees the governor general or lieutenant governors routinely act on the advice of the prime minister or premier. However, the GG or LG always reserves the right to refuse a first minister's advice. In this way, the monarch reflects the concerns of subjects while upholding the Canadian constitution. Thus, the monarch, governor general, and lieutenant governors are expected to rise above political debate and behave as constitutional custodians. These relationships are depicted in Figure 5.2.

Interestingly, the original Canadian constitution made no explicit mention of a prime minister or premier. Rather, section 11 of the BNA Act, 1867, stated:

> There shall be a Council to aid and advise in the Government of Canada, to be styled the Queen's Privy Council for Canada; and the Persons who are to be Members of that Council shall be from Time to Time chosen and summoned by the Governor General and sworn in as Privy Councillors, and Members thereof may be from Time to Time removed by the Governor General.

This provision stipulates that members of an executive body known as the **Privy Council** serve at the pleasure of the governor general. The governor general appoints members on advice of the prime minister. The appointment is for life. Privy councillors are responsible for the daily management of the federal government although, in practice, this power is exercised by the cabinet. Chief justices, retired governors general, and anyone who was ever appointed to the federal cabinet are all permanent members of the Privy Council. The term "privy" means "private," signifying the Privy Council's origins as a formal body of the monarch's closest advisers. To be granted access to top-secret information,

republic
A system of government in which sovereignty is vested in the people, not the Crown.

first ministers
The heads of government in Canada, namely the prime minister and the premiers.

head of government
The highest-ranking elected official in a jurisdiction, namely the prime minister or premier who is appointed by the Crown to lead the executive.

Privy Council
The formal body of prominent federal politicians and officials that typically advise the governor general. Not to be confused with the Privy Council Office (PCO).

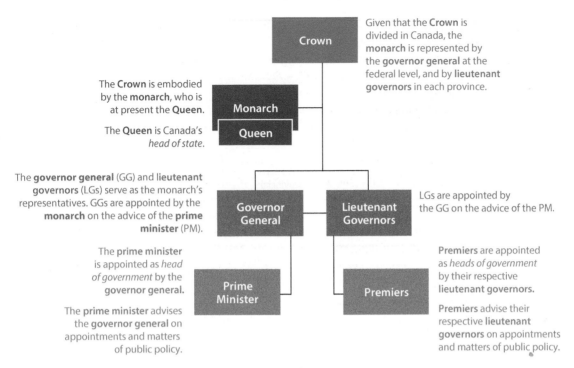

The **Crown** is embodied by the **monarch**, who is at present the **Queen**.

The **Queen** is Canada's *head of state*.

Given that the **Crown** is divided in Canada, the **monarch** is represented by the **governor general** at the federal level, and by **lieutenant governors** in each province.

The **governor general** (GG) and **lieutenant governors** (LGs) serve as the monarch's representatives. GGs are appointed by the **monarch** on the advice of the **prime minister** (PM).

LGs are appointed by the GG on the advice of the PM.

The **prime minister** is appointed as *head of government* by the governor general.

The **prime minister** advises the **governor general** on appointments and matters of public policy.

Premiers are appointed as *heads of government* by their respective lieutenant governors.

Premiers advise their respective **lieutenant governors** on appointments and matters of public policy.

Figure 5.2 | The Formal and Political Executive in Canada

members of the Security Intelligence Review Committee are appointed to the Privy Council, as are leaders of opposition parties when they need to be briefed on matters that cannot be publicly revealed, such as security threats. Thus, the Privy Council is a formal body of current high-ranking political actors and is simultaneously an extended ceremonial group of people who are privy councillors for life.

Historically, the Privy Council was created to guide the decisions of the head of state. In practice, the full Privy Council seldom meets, nor does it advise the GG or LGs. Instead, executive powers are conferred upon only those members of the Privy Council who are current members of the government **cabinet**, which is headed by the current prime minister or premier (see Table 5.1). Since the heads of government and members of cabinet ordinarily have seats in the legislature, whereas the majority of Privy Council members do not, this arrangement ensures greater accountability to the electorate. We discuss the cabinet throughout this chapter.

Thus, at the federal, provincial, or territorial level, the political executive consists of the first minister and the cabinet. At all times there are 14 cabinets operating in Canada. Each citizen is governed by the decisions of the federal cabinet and, depending on where that individual lives, the applicable provincial or territorial cabinet. The political executive is responsible for ensuring that the government functions effectively within the jurisdiction, by:

- maintaining solidarity and secrecy;
- organizing legislative votes;
- advising the heads of state on key appointments;
- controlling the public purse by initiating all money bills;
- initiating legislation and regulations; and
- executing intergovernmental and international agreements.

The functions of the Security Intelligence Review Committee are discussed on page 487 of Chapter 14, on Canada in the world.

cabinet
The leaders of the political executive, consisting of the sitting prime minister and federal ministers, or the premier and provincial ministers.

Table 5.1   Structure of the Executive Council in Federal and Provincial Governments

	Federal Government	Provincial Government	Territorial Government
Head of State	Monarch (head of the British royal family, determined by line of succession to the throne)		
Head of State's representative	Governor General (appointed by the monarch on recommendation of the PM)	Lieutenant Governor (appointed by the GG on recommendation of the prime minister)	Commissioner (appointed by the GG on recommendation of the prime minister)
Head of Government	Prime Minister (leader of the political party that controls the House of Commons)	Premier (leader of the political party that controls the provincial legislature)	Premier (in Yukon, leader of the political party that controls the legislature; in Nunavut and NWT, leader selected by members of the legislature)
Executive Body	The Privy Council (all current and former members of the federal cabinet, and select others)	The Executive Council (all current members of the provincial cabinet)	The Executive Council (all current members of the territorial cabinet)
Cabinet	Prime minister + federal ministers (appointed by the governor general)	Premier + provincial ministers (appointed by the lieutenant governor)	Premier + territorial ministers (in Yukon, appointed by the commissioner; in Nunavut and NWT, selected by the members of the legislature and appointed by the commissioner, with portfolios assigned by the premier)
Unique cabinet portfolios	Defence, Foreign Affairs, International Trade, Veterans Affairs, etc.	Education, Municipal Affairs, Social Services, etc.	
Common cabinet portfolios	Indigenous Affairs, Environment, Finance, Health, House Leader, Intergovernmental Affairs, Justice, Labour, Natural Resources, Treasury Board, etc.		

Briefing Notes

Who Is "Honourable"?

In the legislature, parliamentarians often refer to each other as honourable members; however, the formal honorific is reserved for members of the Privy Council. An appointment to the Privy Council is a lifetime membership. Its members are permanently referred to as "honourable" and have the honorifics "P.C." (for "Privy Council") after their name. This means federal cabinet ministers, senators, and speakers of the House of Commons and the Senate are known as "honourable," even after retirement. Federal ministers of state are inducted into the Privy Council, but parliamentary secretaries are typically not. As members of the Privy Council, lieutenant governors retain the term "honourable" for life. However, other provincial dignitaries including premiers and ministers are not members of the Privy Council. They are referred to as honourable only during their term in office. From time to time, select premiers may become members of the Privy Council, as occurred around the time of the patriation debates discussed in Chapter 2. Superior Court judges, chief judges of provincial courts, and judges of the federal Tax Court are known as honourable, although they, too, are not members of the Privy Council. A higher honorific is granted to the most senior public officials. Governors general, prime ministers, and chief justices of the Supreme Court are known as "the Right Honourable" for life. While in office, governors general are referred to as "Her Excellency" or "His Excellency."

Heads of Government

In Canada, the head of government, unlike the head of state, is a politician. The **prime minister (PM)** is the leader of the party that has control over the House of Commons. The PM is indirectly elected as the federal head of government—meaning that the choice of who should be prime minister is not identified on election ballots. On Election Day, Canadians elect their respective members of Parliament (MPs), and the party with the most MPs is typically asked by the governor general to form a government. The leader of that group becomes prime minister.

The same dynamic exists in the provinces. A **premier** is the head of the political party that holds the most power in the provincial legislature and is appointed by a lieutenant governor. The premier is the chief executive who presides over the administration of the provincial government. Heads of territorial governments are likewise called premiers. In Nunavut and Northwest Territories, which do not have political parties, the premier is chosen by a vote of the legislature and is appointed by the commissioner.

Canadians who are not a member of a legislative assembly are sometimes appointed as prime minister or premier. In a number of provincial elections (Alberta 1989, BC 2013, Quebec 1985, Newfoundland 1989) and one federal election (1925), the leader of the party that won enough seats to form government failed to win the race in his own constituency. Each of these men was appointed head of government. Soon afterward, each won a seat in a by-election and joined his government colleagues in the legislature. As well, a governing party may select a new leader who does not hold a seat in the legislature. Such was the case when lawyer John Turner was appointed prime minister of Canada in 1984. Turner requested a general election just nine days after being sworn in, but his party was swept out of power and he was not elected as an MP.

Canadian heads of government wield considerable executive power. The prime minister and premiers decide how their governments should be structured, how to deal with policy issues, and what legislation to introduce. A first minister is the face of the government, commanding media attention at home and representing constituents internationally. The routine responsibilities of a first minister include managing cabinet, making policy decisions, publicly explaining the government's positions, and attending public events. The head of government meets with international and domestic counterparts in private and during summits. When the legislature is in session, there is the added duty of leading legislative business and fielding inquiries during Question Period. A first minister can advise the GG or LG on whether to call an end to a legislative session or when to call an election. During an election campaign, these responsibilities are replaced with visiting communities, participating in leaders' debates, and posing for photo-ops.

One of the allures of office is the ability to dispense public resources. As heads of government, first ministers wield an appointment power that involves advising the monarch's representative on who should hold key public positions. This includes identifying who gets to be a member of cabinet, who should preside over courts, who heads government departments, and which individuals should fill other public posts, ranging from members of boards to heads of agencies. The prime minister, unlike a premier, has the added perk of advising who should be appointed to the Senate and to diplomatic positions abroad. These powers encourage would-be appointees to do the bidding of the leader. Politicians and others are mindful that one day they might be rewarded for their loyalty.

prime minister (PM)
The head of government at the federal level.

premier
The head of government in a provincial or territorial government.

In Northwest Territories and Nunavut, the premier and cabinet ministers are selected by members of the legislature. In 2018, a majority of Nunavut MLAs voted to replace the premier with another member from the legislature. The MLAs avoided publicly explaining their rationale. In what ways might this approach to selecting the political executive be superior to the process used at the federal level and the provinces? How might it be less democratic?

patronage
The awarding of government jobs, contracts, and/or other financial benefits to friends of the government party.

Prime Minister's Office (PMO)
Partisan staff who advance the political interests of the federal cabinet, in particular those of the prime minister.

premier's office
Partisan staff appointed who advance the political interests of the provincial cabinet, in particular those of the premier.

There is a gradual movement toward reducing the first ministers' appointment power. Some **patronage** positions are becoming elected posts, are being opened to public competition, or are being eliminated altogether. For instance, seats in the Senate of Canada are historically reserved for party loyalists. As discussed in Chapter 6, Canadians can now apply to the Independent Advisory Board for Senate Appointments and be considered for a Senate appointment. No prior political connections are required. However, the prime minister will only appoint those whose political values align with those of the governing party.

All significant decisions in the federal government flow through the **Prime Minister's Office (PMO)**. The PMO encompasses the prime minister's chief of staff, principal secretary, director of communications, press secretary, caucus adviser, an issues management team, and other advisers and support personnel. The PMO is an integral part of the political executive. It works in tandem with the Privy Council Office (discussed later, under public-service management), which is the bureaucratic arm of the PMO.

The PMO employs the government's most powerful political staff. Between 70 and 90 people work in the PMO, all of them loyal to the governing political party and its leader. They offer strategic advice, recommend people for some patronage positions, and coordinate the PM's busy schedule. PMO staff handle media relations, speechwriting, and most of the prime minister's social-media posts. They provide logistical support for communication events, such as news conferences, public speaking engagements, and tours. These high-ranking political staff play an active role in ensuring that the policy initiatives prioritized by the PM are implemented by ministers and officials throughout the government. In the provinces, **premiers' offices** are similarly the focal point for government decision-making and communications coordination.

The preeminent PMO employee is the **chief of staff**. That individual is in charge of PMO employees and is in daily contact with the prime minister. The chief of staff is the one who helps to ensure that the PM's requests are acted upon by coordinating PMO staff, ministers, and their senior staff. A chief of staff tends to act discreetly, despite having considerable authority and political clout. The position involves a combination of political smarts and human resource skills, a willingness to be on call 24/7, and an ability to deal with the unexpected in a high-stakes work environment. A chief of staff to Prime Minister Jean Chrétien once quipped, "I tell people I don't need a degree in political science to do this job—I need one in marriage counselling"[3] while Katie Telford, chief of staff to Prime Minister Justin Trudeau, remarks: "you have to wake up every morning prepared . . . to deal with anything."[4] Chiefs of staff work closely with the government whip (discussed in Chapter 6) to ensure that elected members of the prime minister's party remain aligned with the government's priorities. Each premier's office similarly employs a chief of staff who is in constant contact with the premier and senior political staff across government.

The media and political scientists routinely raise concerns that first ministers, acting through the PMO or premiers' offices, wield too much power. Their political staffers are unelected, removing the ability of Canadians to hold them to account. One *Globe and Mail* columnist dubbed Jean Chrétien the "friendly dictator" and another chronicled Stephen Harper's despotic reign over "Harperland."[5] While campaigning to become prime minister, Justin Trudeau pledged to reduce the concentration of power in the PMO, intending on reversing a trend that began during his father's tenure as the head of government. Critics point out that PMO staff continue to be redeployed to other areas of government so that the central agency has a firm grip on departmental business.[6] Political science, while taking a more measured approach to studying these themes, likewise argues that Canadians should be concerned that too much power is concentrated in what is sometimes called "the centre" of government.[7] This reflects perceptions that a head of government has significant control with few constraints.

The first minister's political clout is formidable. Members of the governing party, including ministers, routinely support their leader. The presence of cabinet members in a parliamentary legislature inhibits the checks and balances found in presidential systems of government.[8] Conventions surrounding cabinet responsibility mean that ministers must support the agenda of their government. In Canada, the head of government has access to considerable central agency resources, including policy expertise, budgetary resources, and information control—none of which are available to the government's opposition. As political scientist Donald Savoie observed two decades ago, "The prime minister, much more often than not, now embodies political authority within the federal government rather than cabinet or individual cabinet ministers."[9] The problem of concentrated authority is even more pronounced in the provinces where there are fewer constraints on a premier and premier's office staff. Pressure from opposition parties, interest groups, and the media tend to be less intense at the provincial level. This gives premiers even more power relative to their federal counterpart.

chief of staff
The most senior, non-elected partisan employee in the government.

VOX POP

Thinking about current media characterizations of the prime minister, to what extent does Savoie's remark hold true today? How would you refine it to reflect the situation in your province's or territory's government?

When considering the source of first ministers' power in Canada, remember the so-called "five Ps":

1. prerogative, meaning they possess significant decision-making authority when advising the Crown on matters including the opening and closing of the legislature and who sits in cabinet;
2. Parliament, in that first ministers have control over the legislative process and agenda, including the ability to summon parliamentarians to meet and ask the monarch's representative to end a session (prorogation) or dissolve it to initiate a general election;
3. party, as they sit atop their political party apparatus, and have authority over election strategy, campaign slates, and election platforms;
4. patronage, because they control access to plum political appointments and may direct government resources toward favoured projects and initiatives; and
5. the press, as first ministers are focal points of most media attention.

Together, these sources of power grant first ministers a sizeable political advantage over their fellow legislators, cabinet members, opposition leaders, and opponents.

presidentialization
The concentration of executive power in the office of the prime minister or premier, at the expense of broader cabinet authority.

The centralization of power in the PMO and premiers' offices gives rise to the notion of the **presidentialization** of politics in Canada. The concept implies that Canada's heads of government are becoming akin to presidents with fewer constraints.[10] Among the many ways this appears is when a minister is designated as deputy prime minister or deputy premier, similar to a vice-president. In Canada, the symbolic title has no force of law and it is not always conferred. Nevertheless, it signifies that there is a second-in-command to a supreme leader in the style of a president. Other features of a presidentialized parliamentary system are processes that run through the first minister's office, diminished input from cabinet ministers on major government decisions, increased party discipline, and voters who prioritize the leader above all else.[11]

The power of Canadian first ministers does face some limits. The Constitution places significant constraints on the prime minister and premiers, vesting all sovereignty in the Crown. Party leaders may face internal pressure as others manoeuvre for their job. They must balance preferences within their party, caucus, and cabinet with those of their own constituents and the broader public. Powerful organized interests can mobilize against them; key allies can talk about switching sides; and supporters can threaten to withhold donations. In several jurisdictions the first minister is bound by legislation, like reform acts, balanced budget laws, or fixed election dates. The media and public opinion can limit a first minister's power, particularly when opposing interest groups are at their most effective. A modern head of government is faced with a deluge of complaints and conflicts with limited options for moving forward.

First ministers also act as checks on each other. Observers often remark that the most effective brake on the prime minister's authority lies in premiers' offices across the country. Premiers have, both individually and as a group, halted or altered federal plans for cross-country initiatives, including Senate reform, international trade agreements, cannabis legalization, and climate-change initiatives. Premiers can stymie their counterparts' political agendas—just ask any premier with economic development plans, including interprovincial pipelines and cross-border alcohol sales. A prime minister can likewise thwart premiers. The term **first minister diplomacy** was coined by political scientist Richard Simeon to describe intergovernmental relations in Canada. It recognizes that prime ministers and premiers are the chief executives of their governments. Both tact and skill are necessary to achieve consensus on major policy initiatives.

Cabinets

As explained at the outset of this chapter, the government is run by a committee of active members of the political executive, known as the cabinet. They develop government policies and oversee day-to-day administrative matters. The cabinet is typically made up of select members of the legislature belonging to the governing party. Its composition is at the discretion of the first minister who advises the monarch's representative on which members to appoint. Thus, the prime minister recommends to the governor general who should be in the federal cabinet, and premiers provide a list of names to lieutenant governors for appointment to provincial cabinets. **Ministers of the Crown** occupy most of the cabinet positions. They are often joined by the government House leader and some so-called junior ministers. At the federal level, a government representative in the Senate traditionally belongs to cabinet; under Prime Minister Justin Trudeau, a senator attends select cabinet committee meetings. These members are collectively accountable to the monarch's representative and, in particular, to the legislature.

At the federal level, cabinet typically consists of between 35 and 40 members, whereas provincial cabinets tend to operate with roughly half as many people. In rare circumstances, an individual without a seat in the legislature is appointed to cabinet, normally to fill a gap in representation. For instance, a prime minister might want a senator from a province that did not elect anyone from the governing party, or a person with specialized expertise who promises to run for office at the next opportunity.

Members of cabinet meet frequently to make government policy decisions, address issues of the day, and review proposed legislation. Almost without exception, cabinet meetings take place behind closed doors, and deal with top-secret business. There are rare instances of transparency, such as British Columbia holding portions of the meetings in public. Details are treated as cabinet confidences, meaning that information is not made public about who was present, what background materials were prepared, what issues were on the agenda, and who said what. Meetings are chaired by the first minister, whose style may range from command and control to collegial and collaborative. Some political staff may attend, notably the chief of staff. Normally, the only public servant present is the government's top civil servant (the clerk or chief deputy minister) who is on hand to offer information and to subsequently ensure that the public service navigates the implementation of cabinet directives.

Most members of cabinet become ministers of the Crown. Ministers are assigned different **portfolios**. These sets of responsibilities typically deal with a specific policy area, like education, health, or social services. They might also cover functional responsibilities, such as Indigenous relations, intergovernmental affairs, or finance. Ministers are held accountable for the performance of their portfolios by fielding questions in the legislature, from journalists, and increasingly on social media. The minister is in regular contact with senior public servants who relay directions to other bureaucrats, provide the minister with information, and present recommendations.

first minister diplomacy
The characterization of Canadian premiers and prime ministers as the primary spokesperson of their government's interests.

minister of the Crown
The political head of a government ministry, responsible for directing and overseeing the activities of its departments and agencies, boards, and commissions.

portfolio
An office or area of responsibility for a minister of the Crown.

Sometimes ministers are assigned additional duties over and above their portfolios. They may serve as regional representatives, lead in specific priority areas, or perform double duty by acting as minister for another portfolio when that position is temporarily vacant. When a newly elected party replaces an existing government, it is common for the size of cabinet to be reduced in number and for ministers to have multiple responsibilities. When Justin Trudeau became prime minister, he was jointly the minister responsible for youth, a largely symbolic move given it is a portfolio without a department of public servants to support it. At the provincial level, many premiers assume responsibilities as ministers responsible for Indigenous, intergovernmental, or international relations.

Regional ministers are designated as cabinet representatives of large geographic regions. Whether or not the designation is formal and publicly stated, the duties of a regional minister entail being the government's go-to person for a large city or for an area within a province. At the federal level, a regional minster may become responsible for an entire province. Typically, all political decisions affecting a given region must flow through the regional minister's office, which increases that minister's clout.[12] Beyond the symbolism of such representation, there is the practical need to direct the flow of information and communication. For instance, a regional minister can be delegated duties to be the prime minister's chief liaison with a premier, with mayors, and with other regional political actors. That individual may have special influence over the party's election strategy. Prime Minister Justin Trudeau did away with the formal title of regional ministers. Specific ministers are instructed to meet with provincial premiers to conduct intergovernmental relations.

Occasionally an experienced, high-profile minister who wins the trust of the prime minister or premier will rise to become the de facto head of government, assuming greater control of key government decisions. The situation develops over time, as the minister's capable handling of important portfolios, sage advice at the cabinet table, and influence among other ministers are noticed. As sensitive issues emerge, the minister may be asked to lead the file; as other ministers exit cabinet, the minister may assume their portfolios in an acting capacity. Eventually, the minister may be asked to head up a "super ministry" of combined departments. Perhaps the most powerful minister in Canadian history was C.D. Howe, a politician with an autocratic style who managed multiple ministries, and who accumulated power under successive Liberal prime ministers (see Inside Canadian Politics on the following page).

Ensuring that all regions are represented in cabinet is so important that first ministers will sometimes get creative to guarantee proper geographic representation. For instance, at times the federal Conservative government of Stephen Harper was without an MP from Vancouver, Montreal, Prince Edward Island, and Newfoundland and Labrador. Prime Minister Harper ensured those regions had cabinet representation by encouraging a Vancouver-area Liberal MP to cross the floor to take up a Tory cabinet position; appointing a Montreal-based party fundraiser as a Quebec senator, who was then brought into cabinet; and tapping a Nova Scotia minister to assume responsibility for PEI and, later, Newfoundland and Labrador. Prime Minister Justin Trudeau similarly required creativity after the 2019 election. Without any Liberal MPs in Alberta or Saskatchewan, we would normally expect that senators from those provinces would be appointed to the cabinet. However, Trudeau's determination to remove political partisanship from the Senate meant that option was unfeasible. Instead, he appointed an MP from Winnipeg to serve as his special representative for the Prairie region, and welcomed

regional minister
A minister whose portfolio includes additional responsibility for government in a broad geographic area.

Inside Canadian Politics

How Did Opposition Parties Use Parliament to Hold the "Minister of Everything" to Account?

The most powerful minister was surely C.D. Howe, a member of the federal cabinet for 22 consecutive years under Liberal prime ministers Mackenzie King (1935–48) and Louis St Laurent (1948–57). Howe was minister of munitions and supply during World War II. During the post-war years, he was minister of reconstruction, and then minister of trade and commerce. His autocratic style of decision-making, combined with the fact he held the confidence of the prime minister, ensured that the policy goals that he championed were achieved.

Howe's impatience with parliamentary procedure contributed to his political downfall during the pipeline debate of 1956. Minister Howe wanted the government to fund a pipeline that would transport natural gas from Alberta to Central Canada. The pipeline was to be built by an American company. To expedite approval of the pipeline and limit criticism from the opposition parties, the Liberals invoked closure to cut off parliamentary debate, a procedure that is often portrayed as anti-democratic. The boldness of the procedural move attracted the censure of political critics, who saw the government as taking the legislature for granted after nearly two consecutive decades in power. Following a month of heated exchanges, the pipeline bill was approved, but within a year the Liberal Party's reign, and Howe's political career, would be over. Decades later, the lessons about concentrating power in a single minister remain relevant, and Howe remains one of the most powerful ministerial figures in Canadian history.

DISCUSSION ITEM

A minister who gains the trust of the premier or prime minister can wield considerable power within cabinet, at times rivalling the authority of the first minister.

VOX POP

What are the benefits and dangers of having a "minister of everything" in cabinet?

a former federal minister and deputy prime minister from Alberta to serve as an unpaid advisor on Western Canada.

Ministers carry out their work with the support of political staff. Like the PMO or premier's office, but on a much smaller scale, ministerial teams include a chief of staff, an executive assistant, legislative assistants, and constituency assistants. In smaller provinces and territories there are fewer political staff than this, perhaps just an executive assistant and a constituency assistant. The chief of staff and executive assistant handle government business for the minister. They provide issues management support, interact with central agencies, and communicate political decisions to public servants. Legislative assistants participate in the drafting of bills. Constituency assistants attend to inquiries from citizens in the minister's electoral district. These partisans may have been involved in the governing party's election campaign, may have personal ties with the minister, or may have been hired at the prerogative of the first minister's office. In addition, ministers are supported by communications personnel, who in some jurisdictions are political staff whereas in others they are nonpartisan public servants. These types of positions are often filled by young people, except the chief of staff position, which requires broader experience.

The political executive sometimes includes ministers of state (sometimes known as associate ministers) who are junior members of cabinet. They may act on behalf of ministers by responding to questions in the legislature, serving on committees, and meeting with stakeholders in their particular areas of responsibility. Ministers of state have narrow policy responsibilities, are supported by a small staff, and typically report to a specific minister of the Crown. They do not oversee a department. There is rarely a responsibility to advance files or deal with issues that require cabinet's attention. A minister of state may have no designated area of responsibility whatsoever. A person in this position used to be known as a minister without portfolio, whose presence in cabinet usually involved some symbolic, representational, or partisan objective.

Parliamentary secretaries (sometimes known as parliamentary assistants or secretaries of state) are not normally part of the cabinet. They perform duties on behalf of a minister of the Crown, such as delivering speeches, giving interviews, and attending special events. They lack significant power or decision-making authority and not formally a part of their respective ministries. They do not have policymaking or leadership authority, do not introduce their own bills or motions, do not have automatic or full membership in cabinet committees, and do not have control over departmental resources. Rather than providing policy leadership, a parliamentary secretary's primary role is to link the minister to the legislative branch. This means serving as a liaison between the minister and colleagues in the legislature, committees, and caucus, ensuring that the minister's legislative agenda is communicated, understood, and supported. Parliamentary secretaries may respond on behalf of ministers to policy-related questions during Question Period by drawing on information provided to them by the ministry.

Parliamentary secretaries are generally considered patronage positions. They are used as signals to sometimes restless **backbenchers** (discussed in Chapter 6) that they are on track to become a minister. Ultimately, ministers of the Crown are responsible for everything that happens under their portfolio, including the actions of ministers of state and parliamentary secretaries. Thus, a criticism of these partisan appointments is that they are largely toothless and an unnecessary public expense. They are foremost a tool for the first minister to keep members of the governing party happy who might otherwise be disgruntled. This must be balanced against their function as a valuable training ground for a cabinet appointment and as a support for busy ministers.

The governing party assembles a cabinet to develop policy initiatives and oversee the day-to-day administration of government. Likewise, each opposition party maintains its own **shadow cabinet**. It consists of **critics** assigned to each of the major government portfolios. A shadow cabinet is not part of the political executive and thus has no authority over the public service. Its role is to hold the government to account by posing questions of its ministers. As their title suggests, opposition critics are responsible for scrutinizing the work of their assigned minister of the Crown, acting as the chief party spokesperson in the legislature, committees, and the media. They lead their party's own policy development in that subject area. Thus, when a minister makes a policy announcement, the

backbencher
A rank-and-file member of the legislative assembly without cabinet responsibilities or other special legislative titles or duties.

shadow cabinet
A group of opposition party members responsible for holding ministers of the Crown to account for their actions.

critic
An opposition party member assigned to scrutinize the activities of a particular minister of the Crown.

media invariably seeks a quote from the applicable opposition critics, who tend to flag problems with what the government is doing. On occasion, a critic praises the government, perhaps because the cabinet decided to act in a manner that the critic was publicly demanding.

Deciding whom to appoint to cabinet is a complex proposition for a number of reasons.[13] Prime ministers and premiers are generally confined to selecting from the candidates who won seats in the general election. It is possible to appoint a member of cabinet who does not serve in the legislature; however, this is seen as undemocratic, and therefore is conducted in rare circumstances. Next, there is an imperative to balance geography and socio-demographic considerations. As mentioned, region is a priority, and increasingly so is gender balance. There are other factors to consider, such as a member's diverse skills and experience, loyalty to the leader, and prospects for re-election. The cabinet appointment process has been described by political scientist Matthew Kerby as a "witch's cauldron" due to the many personal and political factors at play.[14] He found that a member of a governing party stands the greatest chance of being recommended for appointment to cabinet if the member has past experience as a minister and/or was a legitimate challenger for the party leadership. Women, lawyers, and regional representatives are more likely to be appointed—provided, of course, they are present in the government's caucus in the first place. Like Sylvia Bashevkin before them, political scientists Linda Trimble and Manon Tremblay refer to the "higher the fewer" principle: compared with men and once elected, female politicians have as good, or better, chances of making it to cabinet.[15] Women are more likely to be appointed as ministers of social matters such as education, environment, and health, whereas men are more likely to be appointed to economic portfolios such as finance, treasury board, and natural resources. Nevertheless, in recent years, the presence of women at the cabinet table has increased. Since 2008, women have chaired cabinet as premier of Nunavut, Newfoundland and Labrador, British Columbia, Alberta, Quebec, and Ontario. Cabinets in the governments of Canada, Alberta, and Quebec have featured an equal number of men and women. First ministers who want to practise gender parity in cabinet must prioritize getting more women elected.

The membership of cabinet changes over time and between elections. **Cabinet shuffles** range from innocuous role changes to major events. The biggest cabinet turnover occurs after a general election, because ministers who did not seek re-election or were defeated must be replaced, and potentially a different party forms the government. Major change occurs when the ruling party selects a new leader, who often decides to use a shuffle to reward supporters and demote detractors, and to steer the government in a new direction.

Cabinet shuffles are a routine occurrence. Politically, shuffles are used to refresh portfolios that acquired bad reputations, to remind ministers that they serve at the pleasure of a higher authority, and to suppress grumbling among backbenchers who hope one day to be appointed. Shuffles demote or remove weak performers who are a source of public controversy. The government avoids admitting fault by simultaneously promoting or transferring accomplished ministers, thereby celebrating the accomplishments of other ministers, and signalling the policy files that are of growing importance. Shuffled ministers are exempt from answering questions about previous ministries they headed. Aside from the first minister, only the current minister or designate can speak officially on behalf of a government department, which is a key element of ministerial responsibility. Administratively, many shuffles involve the creation of new ministries and departments, or a redefinition of portfolios depending upon the government's priorities of the day. As an

Women who have cracked glass ceilings in Canadian politics are discussed on pages 438 to 439 of Chapter 13, on diversity and representation.

cabinet shuffle
A change in the composition of a government's political executive between elections.

THE CANADIAN PRESS/Mark Blinch

Changes in government mean changes in priorities and the make-up of cabinet. When Doug Ford became Progressive Conservative premier of Ontario he reduced the size of cabinet by a third. He brought his main leadership rivals, many people with private-sector experience, and those from previously unrepresented regions into the political executive. Unlike his predecessor, whose cabinet was balanced between men and women and contained many members from visible minority communities, Ford's first cabinet consisted of two-thirds men and one non-white member. On what criteria should first ministers be judged when it comes to the composition of their cabinets?

election campaign approaches, any ministers who are not seeking re-election are likely to be shuffled out, and members of the legislature in competitive ridings might be shuffled in.

Being part of cabinet does not necessarily mean that power is distributed equally. The head of government is meant to be *primus inter pares* (Latin for "first among equals"), meaning that ministers are led by one of their own, and are generally left to lead their portfolios. In reality, by virtue of their position, prime ministers and premiers are superiors among their hand-picked followers. Some ministers are part of the **inner cabinet**, which is an unofficial term to describe the handful of members of cabinet who are closest to the head of government. Members of the inner cabinet typically hold the most powerful cabinet portfolios, tend to be regional ministers, and are often members if not chairs of the most influential cabinet committees. These ministers hold the most sway around the cabinet table and often have a high public profile. It is difficult to know who they are because cabinet is conducted in secret and the informal descriptor is used only by those who follow politics.

A first minister considers the opinions of a small number of advisors who supplement guidance from the inner cabinet. The unofficial term for them is a kitchen cabinet. We know very little about these people. To varying degrees a first minister consults with select senior public servants, top party personnel, a cluster of political staff (especially the chief of staff), and political consultants. Advice is considered from long-time friends, and certain family members, including a spouse. A small number of ministers in the inner cabinet are likely part of the kitchen cabinet. Given the (unknown) influence of such people,

inner cabinet
Members of the political executive who hold its most important portfolios, including finance, treasury board, and justice (among others).

In 2013, 6 of the 13 premiers attending the Council of the Federation meeting were women. Near the close of the decade, however, all first minister positions were once again held exclusively by men (pictured above in Saskatoon in July 2019). Why do you think Canadian heads of government are more likely to be men?

most of whom are not accountable to the legislature, some critics view them as potential cause for concern, while others see them merely as trusted sources of advice. Identifying the members of a kitchen cabinet can help you figure out who are the real powerbrokers in a government.

Canadian cabinets have some characteristics that differentiate them from political executives in other countries around the world. In Canada, cabinets tend to be unusually large for the size of their electorates, given the need to accommodate a more diverse constituent base. They are highly institutionalized, meaning that ministers have access to a larger amount of resources and are bound by a more complex series of rules, checks, and balances. Canadian cabinets almost always consist of members from only one political party. They feature more democratically selected members and exercise greater authority over the legislative branch.

Cabinet Processes

Ministers receive an abundance of information to help them prepare for cabinet meetings. This includes memorandums to cabinet authored by public servants and brought forward by a minister seeking a decision on a particular matter. Political staff ensure that the memo reflects political realities. The size of cabinet membership, considerable time constraints, and the volume of government issues mean that it is impossible for every matter to be examined in detail in full cabinet meetings. Cabinet therefore makes considerable use of **cabinet committees**. These small subgroups of ministers hold closed-door meetings to examine issues and report back in private to the full cabinet for a government decision. At the federal level, some major cabinet committees have become institutionalized (see Table 5.2), complemented by a handful of other committees that are subject to change depending on the prime minister's policy priorities.

cabinet committee
A subgroup of cabinet members assigned to scrutinize a particular set of executive actions.

At the federal level, the most powerful cabinet committee is Agenda, Results and Communications. Members on that committee rank among the government's most capable and trusted ministers. It is chaired by the prime minister and meets to strategize longer-term issues, to develop and maintain a consistent government narrative and message, and to review cabinet recommendations. The Operations Committee (previously known as Open Transparent Government and Parliament) deals with shorter-term issues management, including the government's legislative agenda, as well as reforming democratic processes. The Treasury Board Committee is the nucleus of fiscal decisions, particularly those dealing with the budget. Various cabinet committee structures exist at the provincial level of government. Treasury Board is a constant across governments over time.

Other cabinet committees reflect priorities of the government of the day. For instance, in 2019, Prime Minister Justin Trudeau created a total of seven cabinet committees. These included those listed in Table 5.2, plus Economy and Environment, Reconciliation, Health and Social Affairs, and Global Affairs and Public Security. Some of these resembled those in the 42nd Parliament, while others were new.

Ministers seek approval from cabinet for specific courses of action. Often the minister's request is referred to the relevant cabinet committee for discussion and review. A decision made by the full cabinet is based on all available information and is recorded as a Minute of Council. At the federal level, this written decision is understood to reflect the views of the full Privy Council, including those who are not members of cabinet, and is submitted to the monarch's representative. A Minute of Council either directs whether information, such as a government report, should be shared with the governor general (or lieutenant governor) or it seeks authorization for a course of action, such as appointing someone to a government board.

Not all matters requiring the signature of the GG or LG need to be vetted by cabinet. A minister may submit a routine request directly to the monarch's representative in the form of a Governor in Council (GIC) submission. It is prepared by public servants and signed by the minister. Drafts of a GIC are vetted by analysts in the Treasury Board Secretariat, Department of Justice, and the Privy Council Office before the minister signs. To authorize the government to act on the cabinet's request, whether communicated in the

Table 5.2   Main Cabinet Committees, Government of Canada*

Committee Name	Number of Ministers (approximate)	Committee Priorities
Agenda, Results and Communications	prime minister (chair) + 8 members	• national unity • strategic agenda of government • strategic communications
Treasury Board	president of the Treasury Board (chair) + 5 members	• oversight of government's spending and human resources • approves regulations and most orders-in-council
Operations	president of the Queen's Privy Council for Canada (chair) + 6 members	• day-to-day parliamentary planning and coordinating cabinet committee business • urgent and emerging issues

*2019 data. All cabinet committees are supported by staff in the PMO and PCO. The Treasury Board receives further assistance from staff in the Treasury Board Secretariat.

Source: Prime Minister of Canada, "Cabinet committee mandate and membership" (2019), www.pm.gc.ca.

form of a Minute of Council or Governor in Council, the governor general or lieutenant governor signs an Order in Council. An Order in Council has the force of law, and permits the political executive and the public service to proceed with implementation.

Executive Accountability

Holding the executive branch accountable is a common challenge facing all democracies. In Canada, the government (cabinet) is held to account through the principle of responsible government. As discussed in Chapter 2, this concept holds that those appointed to govern must be supported by the people's elected representatives, which in the Westminster system means the political executive must maintain the confidence of the legislature. Individual legislators are also held to account by their constituents in elections. This means the government is indirectly accountable to the public. The cabinet is directly accountable to the legislature which, in turn, is accountable to Canadians. The entire legislature must face the Canadian electorate at least once every five years. An election ensures that the government reflects the public will by allowing voters to render a decision about who should form the next government.

The legislature holds the executive to account through the **confidence convention** (also known as a confidence vote). This principle ensures that all major cabinet decisions receive the support of at least half of those legislators present to vote. If a majority votes against the cabinet, then the legislature is deemed to have lost confidence in the government and the government must resign. A general election must then be held or, under extremely rare circumstances, the monarch's representative may call on an opposition party leader to form government. As mentioned, a change of government without an election occurred after the Pacific scandal and after the King–Byng affair, and in both cases a general election followed soon afterward. As discussed below, there have been several more recent scenarios at the provincial level.

confidence convention
The practice under which a government must relinquish power when it loses a critical legislative vote.

Matters of confidence vary. By convention, they include votes on the budget and on the government's reply to the Speech from the Throne, which sets out the government's legislative agenda. Opposition parties may put forward motions of non-confidence or attach amendments to any piece of legislation to that effect. Governments themselves may declare any vote a matter of confidence. This can elevate minor matters to become critical to the government's survival. Not all legislature votes are measures of confidence in the government. The government may lose many minor motions and parliamentary issues without fear of losing power.

Most governments fall of their own volition. The first minister typically asks the GG or LG to dissolve the legislature and call an election. Alternatively, the first minister orchestrates the government's defeat on a confidence vote. It is rare for governments to be defeated on matters of confidence. It is even rarer that they fall on a confidence motion advanced by an opposition party. But it does happen, particularly when the governing party has fewer than half the seats in the legislature, and rarely when there is a majority government. In the ensuing election, the governing party may be defeated at the polls in favour of a new government, or the governing party might be returned to office with a larger number of seats than before.

Consider the following recent examples. Just 50 days after the 2017 BC provincial election, the minority Liberal government lost a confidence motion. The premier (Christy Clark) approached the lieutenant governor to request a dissolution of the legislature and thus a new election. The LG rejected the premier's advice and appointed the Leader of the Official Opposition (John Horgan of the NDP) to lead a minority government. Supported by the third party (the Greens), the new NDP government passed its first Speech from the Throne and budget, maintaining the confidence of the legislature. A year later, another lieutenant governor played a central role in determining who should govern. The 2018 New Brunswick provincial election resulted in a hung parliament, with the official opposition obtaining one more seat than the governing Liberals. The premier (Brian Gallant) asked the LG to allow him to stay on as head of government. The LG agreed so that the premier might test the confidence of the new legislature. The government fell soon after, and the LG appointed the official opposition leader (Blaine Higgs of the Progressive Conservatives) to form a new government.

Beyond the confidence convention, two conventions of accountability apply to cabinet ministers. The first is **cabinet solidarity**, which holds that, as a group, cabinet ministers are accountable for all government decisions. Even if a minister privately disagrees with a course of action or played no direct role in it whatsoever, the minister must not disagree in public. Cabinet solidarity encompasses legislative votes and public statements. Cabinet ministers must vote in unity and the public comments of one minister must reflect the public position of cabinet as a whole. Ministers take a lifetime oath of secrecy and therefore do not speak about cabinet debates even after they have left office. On rare occasions, governments relax the rules surrounding cabinet solidarity, as sometimes occurs when it announces a free vote on a hot-button issue.

cabinet solidarity
The understanding that members of the executive remain cohesive and jointly responsible for the government's undertakings.

THE CANADIAN PRESS/Chad Hipolito

Lieutenant Governor Judith Guichon (left) and BC premier Christy Clark (right) at Clark's swearing-in ceremony in June 2017. Clark's minority government lost a confidence vote about a month later, which ultimately resulted in the LG inviting the Leader of the Official Opposition (John Horgan of the NDP) to lead a minority government. Do you think the LG fulfills a valuable role in the government-formation process? Or should premiers have the unfettered authority to call elections?

A minister who disagrees with a cabinet decision must accept it or resign. Solidarity promotes strength, trust-building, and efficiency. Constituents can be frustrated when their member of the legislature supports a policy decision that will have negative implications in their riding. By extension, cabinet solidarity in Ottawa can upset premiers who decry that a federal minister's position is at odds with provincial interests, even though premiers themselves command unwavering solidarity from their own cabinets. Such conflicts are fodder for political media, which reports on the drama and division. It raises an interesting question: does a minister exist foremost to promote the government's position to constituents or to promote constituents' position to the government? The latter does occur, but typically behind closed cabinet meeting doors.

Cabinet is collectively responsible for government actions, but ministers remain individually accountable to the legislature. The principle of **ministerial responsibility** holds that a minister is directly accountable for decisions taken in her or his portfolio. This practice means that a minister takes questions about decisions made by the public servants who work under the minister's direction. Furthermore, the minister speaks for decisions undertaken by previous ministers in that portfolio. As the public face of a ministry, it is the minister who accepts credit for good news and policy initiatives. Equally, the minister must shoulder the blame in the event of problems—even if the minister had no knowledge of what transpired until after the fact. Thus, ministers are responsible for their own actions, for ministry policies, for misspending, and for bureaucratic errors. This accountability measure typically involves providing responses during Question Period or in various legislative and cabinet committees, as well as to the media.

ministerial responsibility The understanding that ministers remain individually responsible for the activities of staff in their respective departments.

A minister who fails to follow the principle of cabinet solidarity or ministerial responsibility may cease to be part of the political executive. Controversy can potentially trigger a cabinet shuffle or, at the extreme, the minister's resignation from cabinet entirely. Ministers may choose to resign if they feel unable to support a cabinet decision or if they take responsibility for gross mishandling of affairs in their ministry. If a head of government is planning on sacking a cabinet minister, a senior political staffer will likely inform the minister that there is a window of opportunity to resign before being fired. These kinds of executive-level conflicts are rare in Canada, although it is not unusual for ministers to resign their cabinet positions in times of government unpopularity. Removal from cabinet involves the same process as appointment: the monarch's representative acts on the advice of the first minister.

The concentration of power at the top of the government hierarchy raises concerns about the limited role of backbenchers. Stifling party discipline, feelings of disempowerment among legislators, and the politicization of legislative committees contribute to perceptions of a democratic deficit in Canada. The notion of a democratic deficit refers to a disconnect between people's expectations of how democratic institutions should function and the actual performance of those institutions. In a major speech delivered by Liberal MP Paul Martin in 2002, the former finance minister lamented that average MPs do not have enough power, and that what matters most to having any policy influence is "who do you know in the PMO."[16] He advocated ways to address the democratic deficit. Martin argued for loosening party discipline. He proposed to consult MPs after first reading of a bill, to provide them with more opportunities to introduce bills, and to give standing legislative committees more autonomy. As well, he believed that MPs ought to have the opportunity to review partisan appointments. Martin became prime minister soon

For more about democratic deficit see pages 445–8 of Chapter 14.

afterwards. Yet many years later reforms he proposed still do not exist and MPs are arguably more marginalized than ever.

In 2015, Conservative MP Michael Chong surprised many when his private member's bill, designed to put more power in the hands of MPs, became law. Bill C-586, commonly known as the Reform Act, amended the Elections Act and the Parliament Act. The legislation shifted responsibility for approving candidate nominations away from party leaders to designated individuals other than the leader. In theory, this reduces the power of the leader to threaten a candidate or MP that they cannot represent the party in an election. In practice, party structures require that all candidates and MPs support

Inside Canadian Politics

Is It True That Ministers Must Resign in the Face of Controversy?

Ministerial responsibility is sometimes misunderstood as requiring cabinet ministers to resign for the misconduct or poor performance of their employees. This is not a convention of responsible government. Only two federal cabinet ministers have ever resigned over issues of individual ministerial responsibility, which is to say that they accepted accountability for ill administration of their ministries.[17] Henry Stevens, federal minister of trade and commerce, resigned in 1934 after being publicly rebuked by Conservative prime minister R.B. Bennett for shaming the business community through his chairmanship of a royal commission examining corruption. Stevens went on to form his own (short-lived) political party before returning to the Conservative caucus. Half a century later, John Fraser, as minister of fisheries and oceans in the Mulroney government, resigned from cabinet. He had intervened to approve the release of tuna that his department

officials deemed unfit for human consumption. A far greater number of ministers have resigned over refusal to support cabinet decisions.

Ministerial responsibility does not shield civil servants from accountability for their actions. Non-partisan deputy ministers are accountable to their ministers. All department staff are accountable to their deputies for the performance of their duties. Ministers and deputies who discover malfeasance in their departments are often swift to discipline individual staff. In recent years, bureaucrats have been called to appear before parliamentary committees examining their decisions and performance. Several federal civil servants were called before the Public Accounts Committee, for example, to testify about the sponsorship scandal. The Privy Council Office explained this as maintaining the accountability of bureaucrats to their respective ministers, while allowing them to be accountable to Parliament.

DISCUSSION ITEM

Being accountable to Parliament for mistakes made within your ministry does not mean having to resign from cabinet.

VOX POP

Do you think ministers should take more responsibility for the actions of their staff, resigning when major problems occur under their watch? Or should unelected public servants themselves be more accountable?

the party's principles and the leader. As well, the law requires each party's newly elected caucus to vote on whether they will follow the new rules during the life of that Parliament. Should the party leader decide to remove an MP from the caucus, or to recruit an MP from another party, caucuses that opted in are given the chance to vote on the move. Party caucuses opting in have the power to decide when a party leader should be replaced. They can also decide whether to remove the caucus chair. These moves can be initiated by a written request that must be signed by at least 20 per cent of the party's MPs, followed by an internal secret ballot vote that must receive the support of a majority of the party's MPs. All of this is designed to empower backbenchers and reduce the authority of the party minister.

The Trudeau Liberals subsequently sought to introduce some reforms to reduce the power of the political executive. Among the notable changes was increasing the transparency of government appointments and committing to a schedule of days that the legislature will be open. As is common, opposition parties make promises about democratic reform that once in government are not implemented. For instance, the Justin Trudeau government experimented with a special "Prime Minister's Question Period," but soon abandoned the idea. The SNC-Lavalin controversy that erupted in 2019 (see pages 222–3) revealed the considerable power concentrated in the centre of the Trudeau government, particularly PMO staff.

Public-Service Management

The formal and political executives sit at the apex of Canada's democratic system, as Figure 5.1 showed. They are dwarfed in size and complexity by the bureaucratic structure supporting them. **Public-service management** encompasses non-partisan government employees holding a wide variety of high-level positions in the government. Otherwise known as public civil-service executives, they are considered permanent because, unlike their formal political counterparts, they typically remain in place regardless of the election cycle.

Cabinet is supported by the **Privy Council Office (PCO)**, the most senior body of public servants. The PCO's policy expertise complements the political advice provided by partisans in the PMO. The central functions of the PCO are to act on the wishes of cabinet, to assist in coordinating cabinet submissions and cross-ministry initiatives, to provide impartial advice to the political executive, and to ensure the government's directives are understood by senior public servants across government. Specifically, the primary tasks of the PCO are to:

- provide unbiased advice to the prime minister, cabinet, and cabinet committees on matters of national and international importance;
- ensure the smooth functioning of the cabinet decision-making process and facilitate the implementation of the government's agenda; and
- foster a high-performing and accountable public service.[18]

At the provincial and territorial level, similar roles are filled by public servants in the Executive Council Office.

public-service management Non-partisan bureaucratic officials serving at the pleasure of the Crown and the first minister.

Privy Council Office (PCO) The central agency responsible for coordinating the federal government's overall implementation of policy. The PCO is not to be confused with the Privy Council.

Public servants in the Privy Council Office are nonpartisan professionals. Yet they are politically astute and among the most influential public servants in the system. They must coordinate communications among government departments. They act as a bridge between the nonpartisan and partisan sides of government. For instance, drafting a speech for the prime minister requires integrating the policy priorities and key messages favoured by the current party in power. A PCO speechwriter will compile information from the public service, may consult with political staff in minister's offices, and then turn the speech over to PMO staff for revision and approval. Among the many employees in the PCO are:

- a national security adviser, who briefs the prime minister about security intelligence;
- an associate secretary to cabinet, who acts on behalf of the clerk where necessary and who is deputy minister of intergovernmental affairs;
- assistant deputy ministers, who deal with intergovernmental policy and federal, provincial, and territorial (FPT) relations;
- deputy and assistant secretaries to cabinet, who coordinate policy among departments and manage issues;
- various directors, who assist with the preparation of cabinet documents, communications, and intergovernmental matters; and
- staff who assist cabinet committees.

PCO positions can be created to deal with special topics, such as the deputy minister who led a 26-member Afghanistan task force to advise Prime Minister Harper about Canada's evolving military presence in that country, or the team created to advise the Justin Trudeau government about Canada–US relations during Donald Trump's presidency. The prime minister's chief of staff interacts regularly with the PCO and normally attends the weekly meetings of its senior staff. In the provinces, PCO functions are typically performed by office staff of the Executive Council.

clerk of the Privy (or Executive) Council
The highest-ranking public servant in the federal (or provincial/territorial) bureaucracy.

The most senior federal bureaucrat is the **clerk of the Privy Council**. In the provinces and territories, the position is filled by the clerk of the Executive Council. Just as the first minister's chief of staff is head of political staff, the clerk is the head of the public service, and both positions are in regular contact with the head of government. The clerk is secretary to cabinet and often the only public servant to attend cabinet meetings. The clerk is on hand to clarify questions about government process and to ensure that cabinet receives information. As deputy minister to the prime minister (or premier), and the most senior public servant, the clerk oversees the implementation of cabinet's directives by the public service. The role includes responsibility for managing the Privy (or Executive) Council Office. As well the clerk works with leaders of the public-service commission to encourage the professional development of the public service.

deputy minister
Reporting to the minister, the highest-ranking public servant in a given government department.

Deputy ministers (DMs) are bureaucrats who occupy a key role within the senior ranks of the non-partisan public service. Typically selected by the clerk, formally appointed by cabinet, and serving at the pleasure of the first minister, the DM is the top public servant and functional head of a department. Under the minister's instruction, a deputy minister manages departmental business, including the budget. The DM also follows directives received from the clerk. DMs are non-partisan appointees who may have worked their way up through the public service. Some are recruited from the outside. Some of them may have ties to the governing party in their background. They provide policy advice to the minister, ensure that the minister's directives are implemented, and occasionally perform duties on behalf of the minister, such as meeting with stakeholders. A deputy minister is a public servant and not a politician (see Figure 5.3).

There may be multiple deputy ministers within a minister's portfolio. Departments are administrative units of public servants. They are organized in a relatively similar manner across government. This improves the efficiency of public administration as ministers, political staff, and public servants communicate with their counterparts in other departments. The public servants are typically assigned to a deputy minister who reports to a minister responsible for that policy area. For example, the deputy minister of education heads the Department of Education, and reports to the minister of education for the administration of all public servants who work in the department.

Ministries are broader units assigned to a minister. Ministries include departments and any parliamentary secretaries, as well as agencies, boards, and commissions (ABCs) that fall under that minister's authority. Unlike departments, ABCs typically report directly to the minister, and are not accountable to any department or deputy. In this sense, ministers may be responsible for more than one department, oversee several ABCs, and have more than one deputy minister or executive officer reporting to them. For example, provincial ministers of health often have separate deputy ministers devoted to acute care (hospitals and clinics) and wellness (health promotion and prevention), in addition to chief executive officers who report to them on the operations of individual regional health authorities. Similarly, ministers responsible for post-secondary education may have separate departments devoted to universities and colleges as well as labour market development.

Governing increasingly requires teamwork across departments. As the integration between departments and central agencies grows, so do the interactions between DMs

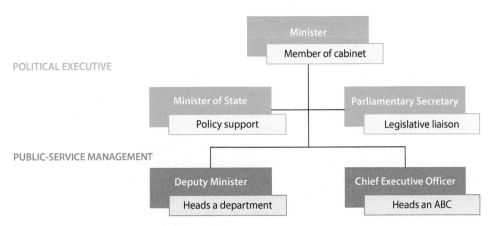

Figure 5.3 | Elements of a Ministerial Portfolio

and deputy minister equivalents, like presidents of key government agencies and Crown corporations. They regularly consult with each other on policy issues and participate on interdepartmental committees. At the federal level they attend weekly deputy minister breakfast meetings chaired by the clerk. Each department employs several assistant or associate deputy ministers (ADMs), who work under the direction of the deputy. An ADM often has specialized knowledge or skills, and oversees staff in a division of the department.

In general, the public service consists of central agencies, line departments, and ABCs. Central agencies such as the Privy Council Office coordinate policy across government. Line departments such as departments of health focus on program and service delivery under specific policy portfolios. Agencies, boards, and commissions such as the Canadian Human Rights Commission provide programs and services at arm's length from government. While their names may vary, all three types of bodies exist in federal, provincial, and territorial governments. Central agencies are briefly discussed below; line departments and ABCs are examined in Chapter 8.

> The functions of the public service are discussed throughout Chapter 8, on public policy and the bureaucracy.

Central Agencies

central agencies
Coordinating bodies that steer government business across all departments.

Generally speaking, the main **central agencies** in the federal government are the Prime Minister's Office, the Privy Council Office, and the Treasury Board Secretariat. Two departments that tend to behave as central agencies are finance and justice. Only the PMO, described earlier in the chapter, employs exclusively political staff; the other central agencies are staffed by non-partisan public servants. The PCO, also described earlier, is the bureaucratic cousin of the PMO. Dispensing both political and policy advice was part of the mandate of the PCO for the first century of Confederation. Premiers' offices often contained a combination of political and policy staff as well, prior to the emergence of non-partisan Executive Council Offices. In both cases, this concentration of power across central agencies is, as mentioned, dubbed simply "the centre."[19]

Treasury Board Secretariat (TBS)
The central agency responsible for coordinating government spending, as well as human and technical resources.

The **Treasury Board Secretariat (TBS)** employs public servants to support the management work of the Treasury Board cabinet committee. This includes providing information and advice based on scrutiny of existing and proposed government spending. The TBS enforces policies and guidelines with an eye to cost efficiencies and standardization across government. As a central agency, the TBS has responsibility for encouraging effective management of a variety of government-wide activities. It oversees the Treasury Board's standards for information management and technology, the management and accountability of deputy ministers, risk management, and human resources. The latter includes remuneration, pensions, and benefits.

Within the federal TBS is the Office of the Comptroller General of Canada. The Comptroller General provides internal government advice on financial accounting such as audits, contracting, and property management.

Department of Finance
The central agency responsible for setting and monitoring the government's fiscal and economic policy, including overseeing the budget process.

A fourth central agency is the **Department of Finance**. Its primary coordination role is the preparation of the government's annual budget and any related economic updates or reports. The Department of Finance is responsible for articulating taxation, borrowing, and tariff policies, as well as fiscal transfers to the provinces and territories. At the federal level, the department has jurisdiction over financial institutions such as the banking industry. Its staffing follows the normal model for a department, in that the minister is supported by a management team comprising a DM and ADMs, as well as possibly a parliamentary secretary. The finance department has a smaller complement of staff than many line departments involved in the delivery of public programs and services.

Concluding Thoughts

Responsible government provides the foundation for an effective and accountable executive branch. Cabinet is accountable to the legislature through the confidence convention. In turn, individual legislators are accountable to voters in their constituencies. This makes the government indirectly accountable to Canadians. Despite these checks, Canada's parliamentary system appears hardwired to concentrate power in the hands of each first minister and/or in the central agencies of government. In the next chapter, we explore the role of the legislative branch in holding the executive to account.

For More Information

How is power concentrated in the centre of government? Donald Savoie examines the evolution of the prime minister's office in his seminal book *Governing from the Centre: The Concentration of Power in Canadian Politics* (University of Toronto Press, 1999). JP Lewis tests the Savoie thesis by asking federal and provincial cabinet ministers. His results are presented in "Elite Attitudes on the Centralization of Power in Canadian Political Executives: A Survey of Former Canadian Provincial and Federal Cabinet Ministers, 2000–2010," *Canadian Journal of Political Science* 46 (December 2013): pp. 799–819.

How do first ministers interact? Richard Simeon explains the intricate processes involved in *First Minister Diplomacy: The Making of Recent Policy in Canada* (University of Toronto Press, 2006).

What about cabinets? Loleen Berdahl explores the emergence of a new brand of executive federalism in "Region-building: Western Canadian Joint Cabinet Meetings in the 21st Century," *Canadian Public Administration* 54 (June 2011): pp. 255–75.

What do political staff do? Jonathan Craft examines the role of partisan advisors in *Backrooms and Beyond: Partisan Advisors and the Politics of Policy Work in Canada* (University of Toronto Press, 2016).

How democratic are Canada's political executives? Graham White examines the power of prime ministers, premiers and ministers in his book *Cabinets and First Ministers* (UBC Press, 2005).

Just how malevolent can Canada's political executive be? Lawrence Martin peers behind the prime ministerial curtain in *Harperland: The Politics of Control* (Viking Canada, 2010).

Is the power of the prime minister exaggerated? Former Harper chief of staff Ian Brodie draws on his experiences to argue that a prime minister faces considerable constraints on power. Read about it in *At the Centre of Power: The Prime Minister and the Limits on Political Power* (McGill-Queens University Press, 2018).

Where is authority truly concentrated in democracies like Canada's? Donald Savoie expands his scope beyond *Governing from the Centre* (University of Toronto Press, 1999) to ask *Power: Where Is It?* (McGill–Queen's University Press, 2010).

How have provincial executives evolved over time? Christopher Dunn explains the development of *The Institutionalized Cabinet: Governing in the Western Provinces* (McGill–Queen's University Press, 1995).

Want to see what the governor general does day to day? Subscribe to the GG's YouTube channel: www.youtube.com/user/CanadaGG/.

Want the Web's most vigorous defence of the monarchy in Canada? Visit the Monarchist League's website: www.monarchist.ca/.

Looking to track the popularity of first ministers? Angus Reid conducts quarterly public-opinion polls on the topic. Visit their website (http://angusreid.org/) and search: premiers approval. For a historical look on the prime minister's approval rating, visit: www.queensu.ca/cora/_trends/PM_Approve.htm.

Deeper Inside Canadian Politics

1. Critics argue that the monarchy has outlived its usefulness in Canadian democracy. What are the arguments for and against change? What sorts of changes would be required to abolish the monarchy in Canada?

2. Who do you think wields more power relative to the rest of the actors in their political system: a premier or a prime minister? Why?

3. In response to a reporter's question as to why he placed so much emphasis on gender parity in his first cabinet, Prime Minister Justin Trudeau replied, "Because it's 2015." Why do you suppose it took so long to achieve this milestone at the federal level? Why do most provinces fail to reach gender parity in cabinet?

Professor Profile

Donald Savoie

Canadian public administration, public politics, economic development

Author of *Governing from the Centre: The Concentration of Power in Canadian Politics* (1999)

Courtesy Donald Savoie

Donald Savoie is perhaps Canada's most eminent scholar of the study of government. He has published over 40 books and authored dozens of reports commissioned by governments. He has won numerous prizes and awards for his work. He is particularly well known for his argument that power is concentrated in the centre of government.

Here is what Donald Savoie told us about his career path from when he was an undergraduate student, why he is drawn to his area of specialization, what is challenging about studying Canadian politics, and what advice he has for students.

* * *

I did my undergraduate degree where I now teach—Université de Moncton. I took a double-major in political science and economics. My first introduction to Canadian politics course was Canadian Politics 101. I was torn, initially, between pursuing my studies in political science and economics. I soon discovered that political science held more promise to gain insights about how my country works and how government decides. I was hooked and there has been no turning back. The political science field holds special appeal because it is all encompassing—it speaks to the interests of individuals, communities, nation states, and the international setting, to voting behaviour, to the study of constitutions and our political and administrative institutions.

I wanted to study Canadian politics because I saw government as a powerful force in my community and in the broader Canadian society. I wanted to go inside the plumbing room of governments to see how policies and decisions are actually struck and how policymakers deal with various political and economic forces. I saw my own community and my region grow in part because of government decisions and I wanted a better understanding of both the why and the how.

I soon discovered that to understand how government decides, one cannot simply rely on government press releases, ministerial speeches, or annual reports. They can never tell the whole story. I decided to go inside government and interview politicians and public servants to understand how things work. A culture of secrecy is deeply ingrained in government and one needs to knock on the doors of policy- and decision-makers to see how government decides. The views of practitioners have had a profound impact on my work.

In my experience, the image that many Canadians have of politicians and public servants as misguided and self-serving does not reflect reality. The great majority of politicians and public servants I met are highly dedicated Canadians dealing with wicked problems that cannot be solved, only managed. Working in government is now only for the brave and we should be grateful to those who are willing to serve. Imagine for a moment a country without a government or with political and administrative institutions too weak to provide the most basic of public services—chaos, corruption, and the inability to grow an economy would be sure to follow.

Political science, more than any other discipline, equips you to challenge falsehoods and unrelenting attacks on institutions. You will have the knowledge, through your political science studies, to identify the weaknesses in our political institutions, to help improve their performance, and to come to their defence when needed. Robertson Davies once argued that "Canada is not a country you love. It is a country you worry about." Political and administrative institutions are, by definition, works in progress that must always be attended to. Political science provides a road map on how to get involved and how to contribute to the public interest. I urge you to do so because our Canada is well worth worrying about.

Up for Debate

Do Canadian prime ministers and premiers have too much power?

THE CLAIM: YES, THEY DO!

Prime ministers and premiers are too powerful in Canadian politics.

Yes: Argument Summary

There is good reason for the conventional wisdom that Canada's prime ministers and premiers are too powerful. Never before has a leader's public persona been as important as it is today. Canada's first ministers are the focus of a permanent, tightly controlled marketing campaign, making their names synonymous with not just the parties but the governments they represent. Simultaneously, the need for government departments to operate in unison increases the authority of political staff and central agencies, which assume greater coordination and direction roles. The presidentialization and centralization of Canadian government is an unrelenting reality that the parliamentary system of government was not designed to handle. As a result, the power and autonomy of the legislative branch and most parliamentarians is declining, and the ability of anyone other than the courts to hold first ministers to account is sometimes suspect. This is especially evident in provinces, particularly if the premier is a populist or nationalist who faces a weak opposition.

Yes: Top 5 Considerations

1. The power of the Canadian first minister is increasing, in a trend that has been described as the "presidentialization" of the parliamentary system. Yet Canadians do not directly elect prime ministers or premiers, and the system is not designed to hold the head of government directly accountable. In the presidential system, the executive branch is separate from a more independent legislative branch, providing an effective check on executive authority. In the parliamentary system, the first minister exercises control over both branches.

2. Governments worldwide are becoming centralized, regardless of which political party is in power. In Canada the increasing clout of central agencies—namely, the prime minister's office or premier's office, the Privy Council Office or Executive Council, the Department of Finance, and the Treasury Board—is reducing ministerial and departmental autonomy.

3. The first minister enjoys a number of advantages of office that can be used to solidify a grip on government. This includes the power to appoint people to government positions, to chair cabinet and key cabinet committees, and to steer government policy.

4. The power of a Canadian first minister over the governing party is significant, particularly if the position was earned by securing the broad support needed to win a leadership campaign.

5. Premiers are especially powerful due to the smaller nature of provincial politics, the propensity for weak opposition, and reduced media scrutiny. The power of a populist or nationalist who epitomizes a political community and who pursues politics that disrupt national unity is particularly worrisome.

Yes: Other Considerations

- First ministers who have a majority of seats in the legislature wield even more power than those who govern with a minority.

- The strength of party discipline in Canada augments the clout of a first minister.

- Political parties routinely emphasize leadership, as do the media. This results in portrayals of the Canadian system of government being a "friendly dictatorship," as *The Globe and Mail*'s Jeffrey Simpson put it in a book of that title.

- The power of a first minister is such that unelected political staffers working in the prime minister's office or the premier's office issue instructions to members of cabinet and especially to backbenchers.

THE COUNTERCLAIM: NO, THEY DON'T!

The amount of power that prime ministers and premiers have is exaggerated.

No: Argument Summary

Canada's parliamentary system is designed to concentrate power in the hands of the few. Someone has to lead in any organization, democratic or not. The system ensures there is balance between giving leaders the latitude they need to carry out their constitutional responsibilities, and the constraints needed to prevent abuse. First ministers exercise their power responsibly and according to constitutional standards. Alarmist statements to the contrary (e.g., that they are dictators) are hyperbole and lack an understanding of the horrible alternatives to democracy. Premiers and prime ministers are formally accountable to their respective legislatures and cabinets, and ultimately answerable to the electorate. They also place checks on each other. Moreover, there are a growing number of watchdogs, both inside and outside government, that place brakes on first ministers' authority. Finally, there is an expanding network of rules that constrain power, and a trend toward transparency.

No: Top 5 Considerations

1. Critics hold misconceptions about Canada's system of government, basing their views on a populist style of democracy that has never existed in this country. The Westminster system is designed to vest ultimate sovereignty in the Crown, and to concentrate power in an accountable political executive. Logic suggests that power within that legislature and cabinet will be concentrated in one form or another. In Canada, this concentration is guided by the constitution, traditions, and our political culture.

2. First ministers' authority is waning. They are taking it upon themselves to place constraints on their own power. Nearly all have supported fixed-election-date legislation to limit their ability to manipulate the parliamentary life cycle; many have backed balanced-budget legislation to bind themselves to fiscal discipline; they have created a plethora of arm's-length watchdogs; and they have institutionalized the appointments process to provide transparency and democratic input.

3. The exercise of power by first ministers has never been more transparent. Their day-to-day business is in public view thanks to the 24/7 news cycle, access to information legislation, and party members' access to social media.

4. Federalism plus responsible government equals executive federalism. To the outsider, this system of first-minister diplomacy appears to grant unlimited powers to each head of government. In reality, each first minister acts as a check on the others thanks to the institutionalization of provincial–territorial relations, the rules spelled out in our constitution, and the guidelines established through successive court rulings.

5. Most formal studies of the concentration of power are based on evidence and anecdotes collected from people on the periphery. This includes bureaucrats in line departments, disgruntled backbenchers, jaded journalists, and the like. This is akin to asking an accountant whether she feels the CEO has too much control over the company, or an intern whether he feels powerless in an international NGO.

No: Other Considerations

- Members of a governing party who hold a seat in the legislature almost always publicly support their prime minister or premier. When a parliamentarian openly criticizes the leader, or votes against the government on a major issue, it is a sign of individualized disgruntlement. It is rare for multiple parliamentarians on the government benches to behave in such a manner.

- Citizens who complain about the concentration of power in the PMO or premier's office should job shadow a central agency official for a week. They would gain an appreciation for just how difficult it is to coordinate, let alone steer, counterparts in different line departments.

- First ministers are not predominant in their own spheres of authority. Alberta premiers have publicly battled with British Columbia premiers over access to oil markets. Quebec premiers have been frustrated by the prime minister's role in sovereignty referendums. Premiers have thwarted, stalled, derailed, and hijacked various prime ministers' efforts to renew the constitution.

Discussion Questions

- To what extent should we be concerned that the current prime minister has too much power? What about the current premier of your province?

- First ministers portrayed in some media circles as authoritarian are viewed in others as delivering strong leadership; those who change their minds in response to political pressure are portrayed by the media as more democratic but weak. If you were a prime minister or premier, which public image would you prefer?

- What does the term "presidentialization" imply? Can it accurately be applied to parliamentary government? If yes, is the presidentialization of the parliamentary system of government a positive or negative development? Why?

- Is it possible that the concentration of decision-making leads to better government? How?

- Suppose there is a very unpopular prime minister or premier. What options do Canadians have if they feel that the first minister should be removed from office before the next scheduled general election?

Where to Learn More about Executive Power in Canadian Politics

Stephen Azzi and Norman Hillmer, "Evaluating Prime Ministerial Leadership in Canada: The Results of an Expert Survey," *Canadian Political Science Review* 7, no. 1 (2013): pp. 13–23.

Herman Bakvis and Steven B. Wolinetz, "Canada: Executive Dominance and Presidentialization," in *The Presidentialization of Politics: A Comparative Study of Modern Democracies*, ed. Thomas Poguntke and Paul Webb (Oxford: Oxford University Press, 2005).

Luc Bernier, Keith Brownsey, and Michael Hollett, eds., *Executive Styles in Canada: Cabinet Structures and Leadership Practices in Canadian Government* (Toronto: University of Toronto Press, 2005).

Patrice Dutil, *Prime Ministerial Power in Canada: Its Origins under Macdonald, Laurier, and Borden* (UBC Press, 2017).

Matthew Kerby, "Ministerial Careers," in *The Selection of Ministers Around the World*, ed. Keith Dowding and Patrick Dumont (New York: Routledge, 2014).

Jonathan Malloy, "The Executive and Parliament in Canada," *The Journal of Legislative Studies* 10, no. 2 (2004): pp. 206–17.

Donald J. Savoie, *Governing from the Centre: The Concentration of Power in Canadian Politics* (Toronto: University of Toronto Press, 1999).

Richard Simeon, *Federal–Provincial Diplomacy: The Making of Recent Policy in Canada* (Toronto: University of Toronto Press, 2006).

Jeffrey Simpson, *The Friendly Dictatorship* (Toronto: McClelland and Stewart, 2001).

Paul G. Thomas, "Governing from the Centre," *Policy Options* (December 2003): pp. 79–85.

Linda Trimble and Manon Tremblay, "Representation of Canadian Women at the Cabinet Table," *Atlantis* 30, no. 1 (2005): 31–45.

Graham White, "The 'Centre' of the Democratic Deficit: Power and Influence in Canadian Political Executives," in *Imperfect Democracies: The Democratic Deficit in Canada and the United States*, ed. Patti Tamara Lenard and Richard Simeon (Vancouver: UBC Press, 2012).

6

The Legislature

Inside This Chapter

- How are legislatures structured and organized in Canada?
- How do legislatures conduct routine business?
- How do legislatures differ across Canada?

Inside the Legislature

Many Canadians' exposure to the legislative process is what makes the news: raucous exchanges between the opposition and government, loud heckling and sarcastic cat-calls, chaotic yet somehow scripted post-session scrums. This chapter throws open the doors of Canada's legislatures to demonstrate how governments are held to account and

Canadians are represented in the twenty-first century. Peering inside the legislature means moving beyond surface observations and recognizing certain maxims about legislative politics.

✔ **Media coverage of Question Period is theatre rather than the essence of the legislative process.** Elected officials do much more than participate in Question Period. The vast majority of legislators' work takes place outside the legislative chamber, whether in committees, in meetings, on the phone, or at home in their constituencies.

✔ **There is more to legislative activity in Canada than what goes on in Ottawa.** An increasing amount of public policy—particularly on matters of highest priority to Canadians, like healthcare and education—takes place in provincial and territorial capitals across the country. Understanding the legislative branch means examining these 13 assemblies as well as Parliament.

✔ **Legislatures are the primary mechanism for ensuring that a prime minister or premier does not have too much power.** Many people believe that government stalls or stops unless there is a majority government with a strong leader who commands the confidence of the legislature. They feel that legislatures hold little value in terms of the policymaking process, as power remains concentrated in the hands of the first minister and cabinet. In fact, minority governments are common, and individual legislators play a more significant role than conventional wisdom suggests.

UP FOR DEBATE

Is strict party discipline necessary in Canadian legislatures?

Keep this question in mind as you read through the chapter. Consult the end-of-chapter debate supplement for more material to help you engage in an informed discussion of the topic.

The Structure of Legislatures

Canada has a total of 14 legislatures, including the federal Parliament in Ottawa. Each of the provinces and territories has a legislature, located in its capital city, whose practices generally follow those of the federal House of Commons. In addition, there are a variety of other forums for elected officials, such as Indigenous assemblies and municipal councils. However, only the federal and provincial legislatures receive specific mention in the Canadian constitution.

It is worthwhile reviewing some of the key concepts raised in earlier chapters before delving more deeply into the inner workings of Canadian legislatures. Canada is a parliamentary democracy based on the federal model. This means that Canada is a liberal democracy (built on a system of rights, preserved by free and fair elections), a representative democracy (in which elected officials make decisions on behalf of the citizenry), a constitutional monarchy (rooted in Westminster parliamentary traditions), and a federation (with a divided Crown whose sovereignty rests with both the federal and the provincial orders of government). Perhaps most relevant to our discussion here, Canada operates on the principles of responsible government, which require political executives to maintain the confidence of their respective assemblies in order to continue governing. This constitutional framework establishes the role of Canadian legislatures.

As Canada is a representative democracy, citizens have the opportunity to elect members of a national legislative assembly and a provincial or territorial legislative assembly the constitution specifies that these separate elections must occur at least once every five years. Elections enable voters to authorize the government's agenda and hold their representatives accountable for their actions. In practice, elections occur more frequently than every five years, particularly in minority government circumstances, and in jurisdictions with **fixed-date election laws** defining the election cycle as four years. Even where a fixed-date election exists, there can be ways to hold an early election or delay until the constitutional maximum. There can also be a snap general election, as when the governor general or lieutenant governor agrees with the first minister's request to dissolve the legislature, or when a majority of elected representatives no longer supports the government. A **by-election** may need to be held in an electoral district between general elections if an elected representative resigns or dies while in office.

The **confidence convention** gives the legislative branch power over the government of the day. The principle of responsible government requires that the first minister and the cabinet resign if a majority of members of the legislature explicitly vote to withhold confidence from the political executive. This ensures that executives who have the power to make government decisions have the support of at least half of all elected representatives on the most significant matters. The confidence convention applies to voting on the budget, the throne speech, motions of non-confidence, and anything that the government declares in advance will be a confidence matter. The government falls if the governing party does not carry a majority of legislators' support on these votes. This is typically followed by a general election allowing citizens to render their own judgement. On rare occasions, the monarch's representative may appoint the leader of the Official Opposition to form a government without calling an election (see Chapter 5 for the King–Byng affair). Governments can and do lose votes on minor matters without significant consequence, such as a non-binding motion advanced by one of their non-cabinet members.

At the federal level, Parliament is a **bicameral legislature**, meaning that it consists of two separate houses: the House of Commons and the Senate. Two legislative chambers provide more scrutiny of government business and proposals. By contrast, provincial and territorial legislatures are **unicameral**, many having abolished their upper houses decades ago in favour of a single chamber of elected officials. Operating just one elected assembly means that government bills move more efficiently through the review process, with less scrutiny.

The House of Commons and the Senate

There are three components of the Parliament of Canada: the Crown, the House of Commons, and the Senate. In Chapter 5 we discussed the Crown, represented by the monarch and governor general. The other two components of the legislature are the lower and upper chambers which are located in Ottawa, the capital city of Canada. Their permanent location is within the Parliament building complex, on Parliament Hill. The nineteenth-century buildings are currently undergoing a major renovation to preserve the exterior stonework and ironwork and modernize the internal office spaces. The nature of the work means that the chambers will be temporarily relocated within the Parliament Hill precinct until approximately 2028.

fixed-date election law
Legislation prescribing that general elections be held on a particular date, or range of dates, typically every four years.

by-election
A district-level election held between general elections.

By-elections are discussed in greater detail on page 357 of Chapter 10.

confidence convention
The practice under which a government must relinquish power when it loses a critical legislative vote.

bicameral legislature
A legislative body consisting of two chambers (or "houses").

unicameral legislature
A legislative body consisting of one chamber (or "house").

House of Commons
The lower house of the Canadian Parliament, consisting of elected members from across the country.

The more significant of the two federal legislative chambers is the **House of Commons**. As its name suggests, the House is meant to represent the interests of the common people— the citizens of Canada. It is responsible for:

- supervising, authorizing, and otherwise holding to account the executive;
- debating bills and passing them to become laws;
- authorizing the spending and raising of money; and
- representing Canadians when debating the pressing political issues of the day.

Provincial and territorial legislatures perform the same functions within their respective jurisdictions.

The House of Commons has more power than the Senate because of its public legitimacy and ability to introduce bills that involve spending money. As well, by convention, the House is where the prime minister and almost all cabinet ministers hold their seats. In contrast with senators, representatives in the House of Commons are elected, and their party affiliation has significant bearing on the operations of the assembly. **Members of Parliament (MPs)** are elected to represent one of 338 electoral districts across Canada. Their work has evolved from being foremost concerned with legislative affairs to constituency casework. In Ottawa, they attend debates and votes in the House of Commons, participate in legislative committees and attend weekly **party caucus** meetings. In their constituency, they tour the area to make public appearances and maintain visibility. They are assisted by staff based in a parliamentary office who foremost attend to legislative work and by staff in constituency offices who help citizens with issues. When the House is sitting, MPs tend to be in Ottawa Monday through Thursday, and in their constituency Friday through Sunday. We discuss the role of backbench MPs later in the chapter.

member of Parliament (MP)
One of the 338 representatives elected by Canadians to serve in the House of Commons.

party caucus
All the members of a political party who hold a seat in the legislature.

Unicameral legislatures are found in each province and territory. Members are tasked with monitoring the work of the respective provincial or territorial government. These representatives are known as members of the Legislative Assembly (MLAs), except in Newfoundland and Labrador, Quebec, and Ontario, where slightly different titles are used (see Figure 6.1). The operations of these unicameral legislatures are relatively comparable to those of the House of Commons. The political interests of every Canadian are therefore represented by a number of appointed senators, one elected MP, one elected provincial or territorial politician, and, usually, at least one municipal councillor and perhaps a school board trustee. As discussed in Chapter 13, Indigenous people in Canada are represented by a variety of other hereditary, appointed, and elected officials.

VOX POP

It may seem as though Canadians have a lot of elected political representation, until you consider that in the United States, many citizens elect all manner of public officials, from judges to senators to dog catchers. What would be the advantages and disadvantages of electing judges in Canada? What about senators? How about dog catchers?

Senate
The upper house of the Canadian Parliament, consisting of members chosen by the executive.

The one assembly in Canada whose members are appointed and who can keep their seat for up to 45 years without contesting an election is the **Senate** of Canada. Like its prototype, the British House of Lords, it was intended as a venue for "sober second thought." The Senate was originally designed as a counterweight to the Commons by assuring

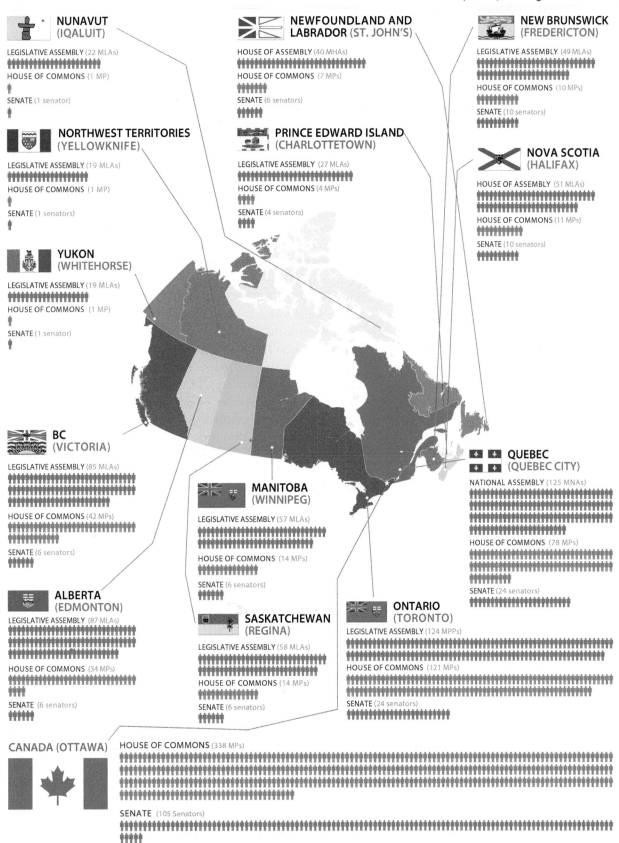

Figure 6.1 | Characteristics of Federal, Provincial, and Territorial Legislatures

Source: Composite by Laurie McGregor; Map: © iStock/Diane Labombarbe; People icon: © iStock/MrsWilkins; Flags: © iStock/mstay.

representation in Parliament for the elite members of Canadian society. This is among the reasons that all members of the Senate must be at least 30 years old and own property in the area that they represent. As an unelected body, it is equipped to raise difficult questions about proposed laws and public policy. However, it is subject to criticism as a remnant of a less democratic era.

Senators are summoned to their positions by the governor general, on advice of the prime minister of the day. This makes Canada's upper house one of the few remaining non-elected legislative bodies in Western democracy. Senators may retain their seats without facing election until they turn 75 years of age, at which point they are required to retire. Conscientious senators who ignore the pressures of public opinion can take a longer-term view on public policy than their elected counterparts. Their experience affords them a perspective that is less common among elected representatives, who spend far fewer years in Parliament and are often concerned with re-election.

Among the Senate's main functions is to provide representation of regions in Parliament. Seats in the Commons are distributed based on population, so larger provinces receive greater representation, and small provinces have fewer representatives. Senate seats are allocated on a regional formula. Consequently, some smaller provinces are granted a relatively louder voice in the Upper House than their population size would otherwise allow. A senator is viewed as representing the entire province, except in Quebec, the only province where senators are assigned to specific geographic districts.

Politicians and pundits alike constantly say that the Canadian Senate needs to be fundamentally changed, or even abolished. Since Confederation, would-be reformers have focused on improving the Canadian Senate through its composition and its powers, and through the selection and the tenure of its members. The main issues of contention and proposed reforms are as follows.

- Composition: Senate seats are distributed on a regional basis, meaning that some provinces receive a complement of 24 senators, while others receive just 6 each. One way to address this discrepancy would be to divide seats equally among all provinces, regardless of the province's size.
- Powers: A more effective Senate would possess new tools that empower senators to conduct more than routine legislative business. Suggestions include providing the Senate with veto powers over federal appointments, language legislation, international agreements, and other matters. Any new powers would need to be balanced against the possibility of deadlock with the House of Commons. An elected body must have supremacy over an appointed one. Most proposals give the House of Commons primacy in case of conflict (e.g., by making any Senate vetoes temporary).
- Selection or Election: The process of appointment could be replaced with a system of direct or indirect elections. Others suggest supplementing the appointment process. Elections would help make senators democratically accountable to Canadians.
- Tenure: Senators were appointed for life prior to a 1965 constitutional amendment. Since then, senators are eligible to serve until a mandatory retirement age of 75. Viewing this as virtually a lifetime appointment, reformers seek fixed terms, on a renewable or non-renewable basis.

During the mega-constitutional period and driven by the Alberta government and federal Reform Party, all four of these elements were incorporated into a series of proposed constitutional amendment packages, most notably in the Charlottetown Accord. As

Between 1989 and 2012, the Alberta government held a series of four Senate nominee elections, so that voters could select whom they felt the federal government should appoint to fill senate vacancies from their province. The Mulroney government chose Stan Waters from this list in 1990, and the Harper government chose four more, including Bert Brown (pictured above with Stephen Harper). Why do you think the Alberta government adopted this practice, and why did they abandon it? Why did federal Conservative prime ministers opt to fill vacancies using the Alberta nominee list, while Liberal prime ministers did not?

discussed in Chapter 2, that constitutional package was defeated in a national referendum in 1992. Since then there have been varied attempts at reforming the Senate.

In the twenty-first century, Senate reform efforts have been gradual. The Harper government introduced seven pieces of Senate reform legislation dealing with the selection and tenure of senators. None passed Parliament. The process for developing these proposed reforms avoided engaging the provinces in full-blown constitutional negotiations. Instead, some of the discussion played out in the courts. The courts looked unfavourably on the Harper government's attempts at Senate reform. In 2012, the Quebec government challenged Ottawa's plans by referring one of the federal bills to its provincial Court of Appeal. Quebec argued that the proposed reforms involved fundamental changes to the constitution and, as such, required the involvement of the provinces. The Court of Appeal agreed. For its part, the federal government referred a series of questions to the Supreme Court of Canada. These asked for the Court's opinion on the constitutional approach required to effect changes to the tenure, selection, and property qualifications of senators, as well as the process required to abolish the Senate entirely. The Supreme Court responded that all significant reforms would require meaningful consent from the provinces. The ruling ended the federal government's plans to modernize the institution unilaterally. No first minister appeared interested in re-opening constitutional negotiations.

The Senate Reform reference came at the height of scandals surrounding the expense reports of several senators. The Senate suspended three of its members without pay and forced them out of the Upper House for the remainder of the parliamentary session. While in opposition, Liberal leader Justin Trudeau took the unprecedented step of expelling all Liberal senators from his party caucus. Supporters praised the move as a means of distancing elected representatives from unelected officials. Once in government, Prime Minister Trudeau continued to keep senators out of the Liberal fold.

VOX POP

In what ways should the Senate be reformed? Why is change so difficult?

Prime ministers are careful about the strategic calculations of making appointments because Senate appointments tend to attract negative media coverage. Historically, prime ministers tended to reward party loyalists with Senate seats. Pessimists suggest the Senate merely employs party fundraisers and a party's election campaign organizers. At times, it is a job given to candidates who failed to win a seat in the House of Commons in an election, and has been a position given to former ministers. Optimists remark that high-profile Canadians are sometimes appointed, such as athletes and journalists, as well as community activists. On rare occasions, the prime minister has recommended that the governor general appoint a supporter of a different political party. Prime Minister Harper's approach to the Senate was unusual in that he went extended periods without filling seats. There were so many vacancies that the Senate experienced difficulty operating. When he resigned as prime minister, Harper left vacant 23 seats, inadvertently giving the next government an opportunity to transform the Senate membership using a novel process.

The Trudeau government's consultative process for the appointment of senators aims to "restore public trust in the Senate and move towards a less partisan and more independent Senate."[1] Canadians are now required to submit an online application if they wish to be considered for appointment to the Senate. Applications are reviewed by an Independent Advisory Board for Senate Appointments, an arm's-length body that provides a shortlist of five prospective appointees to the prime minister for each vacancy that arises. The board consists of three permanent federal appointees and two members nominated by the provincial or territorial government where the vacancy is to be filled. They assess the applicants' eligibility and evaluate their suitability based on several merit-based criteria. These criteria include non-partisanship, knowledge of the legislative process and constitution, personal integrity, experience in public and community service, and leadership. According to the board's guidelines, applicants are "considered with a view to achieving gender balance in the Senate. Priority consideration will be given to applicants who represent Indigenous peoples and linguistic, minority and ethnic communities, with a view to ensuring representation of those communities in the Senate." This signals Prime Minister Trudeau's interest in using Senate appointments to increase socio-demographic diversity in Parliament. Newly appointed senators sit under the label of independent. This reduces, but does not eliminate, the criticism that the Senate is little more than a way for the prime minister to reward supporters with lucrative patronage appointments.

The appointment process is only one of many complaints about the Senate. The institution's image problem is closely related to the near-lifetime tenure of its members.

It is exceptionally difficult to oust senators who do not carry out their duties or break the rules. There was once a senator who moved to Mexico and over a period of seven years attended a total of two weeks of meetings in Ottawa. Then there was the afore-mentioned controversy over the three senators who were embroiled in an expense-claims scandal. These may be extremes, but the inability to expel wrongdoers leads to public consternation, thereby damaging the reputation of the legislative assembly as a whole and its most upstanding members. Even if senators are sanctioned by losing their party affiliation, they can continue to sit, and even if they resign they still receive a generous pension.

The lack of public accountability results in calls for significant reforms or for the Senate's outright abolition. Complaints from opposition parties like the New Democratic Party and the former Reform Party of Canada have tapped into Western Canadian pop-ulist sentiments. The Reform Party emerged in the West as Canada's political leaders debated constitutional amendments in the late 1980s and early 1990s. The party advocated for "triple-E" Senate reform, which would provide each province with an equal number of seats, make senators' work more effective, and require that senators be elected. Pro-posals to change the Senate were included with the failed Meech Lake and Charlottetown Accords constitutional amendments.[2]

Even so, a fascinating experiment is under way with the Senate. Senators appointed since 2015, coupled with some Conservative and Liberal senators who decided to abandon their party affiliation, are non-affiliated. Some of them sit together under the banner In-dependent Senators Group (ISG). This group now outnumbers senators sitting as Conser-vatives, Liberals, or non-affiliated. An optimistic view sees this as evidence that the Senate is transforming into a non-partisan chamber whose members studiously examine bills passed in the House of Commons without interference from a party leader. A pessimistic view is that the ISG is merely a political ploy given that its members are mostly people who subscribe to the Liberal Party's core values. Moreover, a lack of partisanship in the Senate can rob the government of key allies to pass legislation in a timely fashion.

Briefing Notes

The Independent Senators Group

The Independent Senators Group has a charter outlining the tenets that unite its members. Senators in the ISG may not be directly involved with a political party, the speaker of the Senate, or the government representative. The char-ter identifies the purpose of the ISG formation, which is to participate in the coordination of activities in the Senate chamber and committees; to share information; to coordi-nate collective action about Senate administrative matters; to respect the freedom of ISG senators to express their opin-ions; and to build on Prime Minister Trudeau's efforts to modernize the Senate. The charter establishes that the ISG observes the core principles of integrity, equality, indepen-dence, freedom of conscience, transparency, and efficacy. The group meets weekly to discuss legislation and holds a second weekly meeting for more in-depth discussion.

Number of Seats in the Parliament of Canada

As Table 6.1 shows, the biggest challenge in designing a legislature concerns how seats are distributed. The rule of thumb is that representation in the Senate is based on geography and fixed, whereas representation in the House is based on population, and is constantly growing.

Seats in the House of Commons are allocated by considering each province's population. The formula then makes some adjustments, following the "Senate floor" rule that a province cannot have fewer MPs than it has senators, and a grandparenting clause stipulating that no province can have fewer MPs than it had when the Representation Act was first passed in 1985. As well, the geographic areas that MPs represent shift as the boundaries of electoral districts are adjusted to reflect population movement. The result is that Quebec and Ontario have the most seats in the House of Commons. Representation from the West has been growing and the presence of the Atlantic region in the elected chamber has been proportionately shrinking.

The composition of the Senate is organized around regions of the country. The formula allocates 24 senators among the three Maritime provinces, 24 to Quebec, 24 to Ontario, and another 24 among the four Western provinces. The seat allocation is rounded out by the addition of the territories (1 senator each) and, in 1949, of Newfoundland (6 senators). This formula disproportionately rewards the four original signatories of Confederation and creates odd dynamics that tend to disadvantage the Western region in particular. Quebec and Ontario each have four times as many Senate seats as any Western province; even Atlantic Canada collectively has more seats than the West.

The last time the Senate membership increased was in 1999 when Nunavut was allocated a seat upon its creation. The total of 105 senators could nevertheless change quickly.

Table 6.1   Distribution of Canadian Senators and Members of Parliament

Region	Population*	Land Area (km²)	Senators	MPs	Average # of Constituents per MP
British Columbia	4,817,000	925,186	6	42	114,690
Alberta	4,286,000	642,317	6	34	126,058
Saskatchewan	1,164,000	591,670	6	14	83,143
Manitoba	1,338,000	553,556	6	14	95,571
Ontario	14,193,000	917,741	24	121	117,298
Quebec	8,394,000	1,365,128	24	78	107,615
New Brunswick	760,000	71,450	10	10	76,000
Nova Scotia	954,000	53,338	10	11	86,727
Prince Edward Island	152,000	5,660	4	4	38,000
Newfoundland & Labrador	529,000	373,872	6	7	75,571
Yukon	38,000	474,391	1	1	38,000
Northwest Territories	45,000	1,183,085	1	1	45,000
Nunavut	38,000	1,936,113	1	1	38,000
Canada (total)	36,708,000	9,093,507	105	338	108,604

*2017 population statistics. Rounded figures.

Sections 26 to 28 of the Constitution Act allow for the special appointment of one or two senators for each of the four regions. If this provision were triggered, the total number of Senate seats would increase to either 109 or 113—the maximum allowed—and would return to 105 as senators retired.

This obscure provision is intended to ensure that the unelected upper house does not block the business of the elected lower house. A prime minister can ask the governor general to summon more senators to break any deadlocks. This provision was last used in 1990. Prime Minister Brian Mulroney and his Progressive Conservative party had a majority of seats in the House of Commons. The Liberals held a majority of seats in the Senate. The Liberal senators vowed to vote down the PC government's bill that proposed to create a goods and services tax (GST). The governor general approved Prime Minister Mulroney's request to invoke the constitutional clause. Eight Conservative senators (two per region) were appointed to ensure the bill's passage. The will of the elected representatives triumphed over that of appointed members. Therefore, the Senate may stall debate over a particular government bill, but the prime minister has the ability to override most obstruction.

The Partisan Composition of Elected Assemblies

The partisan composition of the legislature is largely determined by the outcome of the previous election. Most candidates campaign on behalf of a political party. Those who are elected assume their seats in the assembly according to party. Party standings can fluctuate between general elections as by-elections are held and members leave a party caucus to sit as an independent.

Occasionally, a member of a legislature leaves one party to join another, an act known as **crossing the floor**. Floor crossing refers to the idea that the seat of a member on one side of the chamber is literally moved to another area of the chamber. Changing parties while in office is controversial because the reasons for the change may be unclear; the member's constituents may not support the move and voters normally have to wait until the next election to hold the member to account.

crossing the floor
A situation in which a member of the legislature leaves one political party to join another party.

When a member of the legislature crosses the floor there is dramatic media coverage. There is speculation about whether the member had a private disagreement with the party leader or was motivated by inducements offered by the other party. Public attention is especially warranted when control over the government is at stake. There have been some high-profile cases of floor crossing in the twenty-first century. At the federal level, a Conservative MP joined Paul Martin's Liberal cabinet, potentially saving it from defeat on a budget vote. Less than a year later, one of Martin's ministers was re-elected in a general election won by Stephen Harper's Conservative party, but immediately left the Liberals to sit in the Conservative cabinet. On the provincial scene a monumental event occurred in 2014. An astounding nine opposition members of the Alberta legislative assembly, including the leader of the official opposition, crossed the floor to join the government caucus. In the ensuing provincial election just six months later, not a single one of the floor-crossing MLAs was elected to serve in the legislature. Some chose not to run, some lost a nomination race to be the candidate for their new party, while others were defeated in the general election.

Generally speaking, there are two main ways the membership of a legislature may be organized. A majority government is formed when more than half of the members are affiliated with the same political party. Or, if no party has more than half the seats, then a minority government is the typical outcome. Coalition governments have occurred a handful of times in Canadian politics. However it is common to distinguish between majority government and minority government (see Figure 6.2).

Majority Governments

Majority governments exist wherever one political party holds more than 50 per cent of the seats in the legislature. In the case of the federal government, this means a majority of seats in the House of Commons, so at least 170 of the 338 MPs. Elsewhere, the minimum threshold is as low as 10 in the Yukon Legislative Assembly which has 19 seats, to a high of 63 members needed for majority in the National Assembly of Quebec which has 125 seats.

In majority government situations, the business of the assembly is reasonably efficient and predictable, as a political agenda can be spread over a number of years. The opposition parties do not have enough members to explicitly obstruct or otherwise impede the government's plans. Thus, any vote will result in a win for the government—provided enough members of the governing party are present for the vote, and provided all of them vote along party lines. Under these circumstances, the prime minister or premier can be confident that their bills and motions will be carried. A majority government thus provides reasonable assurances that the party's election promises will be implemented. It offers stability and provides the governing party with the opportunity to make difficult decisions. However, because a majority government is not compelled to act on the wishes of its opponents, legislation may be rushed through without considering an array of perspectives. This can result in one-sided policy that disadvantages certain segments of society or that lacks the benefit of deeper scrutiny. This is particularly likely at the provincial level, where majority governments are more common and more lopsided.[3] A situation where one party has most of the seats and the opposition parties lack enough members to appropriately scrutinize the government is rare at the federal level. There is so much diversity across Canada, and so many more seats in Parliament, that the prime minister typically faces a more vibrant opposition.

Majority governments are seldom built on the support of half of the voting population. Because of the vagaries of the first-past-the-post electoral system and the presence of many competitive parties across the country, the party that wins the most district races need not win a majority of votes across the country. Winning more than 50 per cent of the popular vote—the total of all votes cast—is exceptionally rare in federal politics. Indeed, there have been only three so-called **earned majorities** since World War I: the Mackenzie King government of 1940 when the Liberals received 51 per cent of the popular vote; John Diefenbaker's Progressive Conservative government of 1958 whose candidates were supported on nearly 54 per cent of ballots cast; and the Mulroney PC government of 1984 that obtained 50 per cent of votes. The Mulroney case is the only time a governing party received a majority of the popular vote in every single province. Landslide victories and earned majorities are far more common at the provincial level, as Table 6.2 shows.

At the federal level, the electoral system and multi-party environment combine to produce more **manufactured majorities** than earned majorities. Manufactured majority governments are those in which the governing party has more than half of the seats in the legislature, but obtained less than half of the popular vote in the preceding election. For instance, in the 2015 federal election the Trudeau Liberals received less than

majority government
A government in which the governing party controls more than half of the seats in the legislature.

earned majority
A majority government in which the governing party's share of the popular vote is at least 50 per cent.

manufactured majority
A majority government in which the governing party's share of the popular vote is less than 50 per cent.

	Table 6.2	Composition of Federal and Provincial Governments, 1965–2019			
Jurisdiction	**Earned Majority Governments**	**Manufactured Majority Governments**	**Minority Governments**	**Coalition Governments**
Federal	1	10	7	
BC	1	11	1	
AB	7	7		
SK	6	7	1	1
MB	1	13	1	
ON		11	4	
QC	2	10	2	
NB	4	9	1	
PE	12	2	1	
NS	2	9	4	
NL	10	5	1	

Earned and manufactured majorities are discussed again on page 341 of Chapter 10, in the context of Canada's single-member plurality (or first-past-the-post) electoral system.

40 per cent of the votes, and yet 54 per cent of the seats. The inflation of seats for the winning party is commonplace in Canadian politics. Sometimes, the electoral system may even produce a so-called wrong winner. In those rare circumstances, the most seats belong to a party whose candidates received fewer votes, overall, than one of its opponents. An example of a wrong winner occurred in the 2019 Canadian federal election. The Liberals obtained 33.1 per cent of the votes compared with the 34.4 per cent cast for the Conservatives. Yet, because the Liberal Party's votes were more efficiently distributed across the country, that party won 157 seats compared with 121 for the Conservatives.

Minority Governments and Coalitions

Other times, no party wins a majority of seats in an election. This results in a hung parliament, a term used in the British Westminster system but infrequently used in Canada. It refers to the fact that the electorate, like a hung jury, failed to produce a decisive verdict on which party should control the legislature. Logic dictates that hung parliaments are more likely to occur in party systems with more than two strong contenders. This is because a majority government is all but assured when there is no third party to draw support away from the top two parties. In a hung parliament, the party with the most seats usually, but not necessarily, forms government. The governing party's grip on power is more tenuous than in a majority situation. Under the principle of responsible government, the executive is required to maintain the confidence of the legislature. In a hung parliament, the legislature's support is far from guaranteed. Hung parliaments usually last about half the duration of majority governments for this reason.

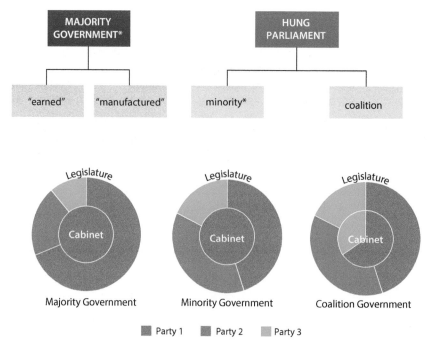

Figure 6.2 | **Majority, Minority, and Coalition Governments**

* Majority government and minority government are the terms most commonly used to describe the organization of Canadian legislatures.

There are two types of hung parliaments. The difference depends upon how cabinet is structured. In Canada, governing parties with less than half the seats are most likely to form a **minority government**. Some governing parties, such as the Trudeau Liberals after the 2019 federal election, take their chances that opposition members in the legislature will support their initiatives on a vote-by-vote basis. The opposition parties might want to avoid a snap election and vote with the government to avoid its defeat on a confidence matter. Later on, the opposition parties might move a motion of non-confidence and defeat the government, provided that the first minister has not already sought a snap election.

Alternatively, the governing party can negotiate the temporary support of another party through a formal agreement. This is what the British Columbia NDP did after the tight 2017 provincial election. The Green Party pledged not to withdraw their confidence in the government in return for the NDP's commitment to pursue electoral reform and to oppose the construction of a new pipeline to the West Coast. Similar arrangements propped up minority governments in Manitoba and Ontario in the 1980s.

Minority governments typically ensure that competing perspectives are considered by political elites. A minority scenario reduces the power of the political executive, and it increases the relevance of backbench representatives from all parties, whose votes now matter in terms of supporting or toppling a government.[4] Successful minority governments demand collaboration between parties on both sides of the aisle, forcing compromises and accommodation, and producing some of the most dynamic environments for public-policy innovation. Some of Canada's more significant policy milestones were developed in minority government situations:

- King's Liberal governments (1925–6, 1926–30), supported by the Progressives, increased immigration, developed Canada's first pension plan, and transferred control over natural resources to the Western provinces.

minority government
A government in which the governing party controls less than half of the seats in the legislature.

- Supported by the CCF/NDP, Diefenbaker's PC government (1957–8) and Pearson's Liberal governments (1963–8) forged Canada's country-wide system of universal healthcare.
- A Pearson minority government was responsible for adopting a new Canadian flag.
- Pierre Trudeau's minority government (1972–4), supported by the NDP, revamped Canada's social security, election financing, and foreign investment systems.
- Harper's minority governments (2006–11), supported at times by various parties, established a new accountability regime; declared Quebec a nation within Canada; and apologized for, and launched a commission of inquiry into, the treatment of Indigenous people in residential schools.
- Justin Trudeau's minority government (2019–) is poised to take action on a number of issues related to reconciliation and climate change, supported by the NDP in particular.

Critics may question the ability of Canadians to hold their representatives accountable for joint decisions made by multiple parties. Moreover, a minority government can produce high-stakes brinksmanship, overspending, an aversion to long-term planning, and steeped partisanship.[5] As a result, minority governments often feature some of the tensest times in the life of a legislature. Perhaps fortunately, these periods tend to be short-lived, lasting on average half the length of a majority government.

A second form of hung parliament is less common in Canada than in other parts of the world. **Coalition governments** occur when two or more political parties collectively have enough seats to form a government, and they are willing to share power. Instead of the strongest party forming a minority government on its own, its leader invites legislators from another party to join them in the executive. Coalition governments are rare. The aforementioned British Columbia situation is a good example. It informs us that party leaders who reach an agreement with another party to prop up the government are seldom willing to appoint that party's members to cabinet. Intense competition between political parties means that the idea of collaborative politics including coalition government is an aberration.

Coalition government has only occurred once at the federal level in Canada. During World War I, Prime Minister Borden formed the so-called Union Government. At the time, the conscription issue (i.e., mandatory military service) divided the Liberal and Conservative parties, and Liberals in Western Canada joined with like-minded Conservatives to form a pro-conscription coalition government following the 1917 election. The cabinet contained 12 Conservatives including Prime Minister Borden, 9 Liberals, and 1 member of the Labour Party. To this day, that Labour member is the only minister at the federal level in Canada not affiliated with either the Conservative or Liberal parties. The Union Government was short-lived, with Borden retiring three years later.

There have been three coalition governments at the provincial level in Canada. Two of them took place during World War II. A wartime cabinet in Manitoba at one point contained members from six different parties. Another saw Liberal–Progressive Conservative coalitions in British Columbia. The third occurred in Saskatchewan from 1999 to 2000, when NDP premier Roy Romanow welcomed two dissident Liberals into cabinet.

Legislative Institutions

The federal and provincial legislatures share a number of common features. These commonalities exist irrespective of which political parties hold seats or who is first minister.

The events that led to the adoption of the Canadian flag are chronicled in Chapter 1, on page 20 (Inside Canadian Politics: How Did Canada Choose the Maple Leaf as the Country's Flag?).

coalition government
A hung parliament in which the cabinet consists of members from more than one political party, a rarity in Canada.

Inside Canadian Politics

What Happened with the Coalition Crisis of 2008?

The plausibility of coalition government rocketed to Canadians' attention after the 2008 federal election. The result returned the Conservative Party to office with a second consecutive minority government. With 143 of 308 seats, the Conservatives would have to rely on support from at least one of the Liberals (77 MPs), the Bloc Québécois (49 MPs), or the NDP (37 MPs) to survive votes of confidence. The legislature was so divided that Parliament's two independent MPs had the potential to hold the balance of power on some votes. The Conservatives took a bold approach by issuing a fiscal update that dared the opposition parties to defeat them on a vote of confidence. There was no new government spending to stimulate economic growth (a Liberal demand) and there was a pledge to restrain the ability of civil servants to strike (an NDP no-go). Within the update was a plan to wind down the government's per-vote funding subsidy provided to political parties.[6] The opposition parties would be forced to lay off party staff, cut down on public outreach and travel, and likely reduce their communication and research budgets.

The developments led to the "coalition crisis." To everyone's surprise, on 1 December 2008, the leaders of the Liberal Party and the NDP signed a formal agreement to form a coalition government. The deal would have seen Liberal leader Stéphane Dion preside over a cabinet of Liberals and some New Democrats. A side deal stipulated that the Bloc Québécois would support the coalition in the legislature. The Bloc's support was necessary lest the proposed coalition government, which would have fewer seats than the Conservatives, lose the confidence of the house. The three parties maintained that together they had a majority of seats (163 to the Conservatives' 143) and that a majority

of Canadians had voted for them (54 per cent, compared with 37.7 per cent who voted Conservative). Prime Minister Harper denounced the opposition leaders' plans as an undemocratic plot by "socialists and separatists." The coalition moved forward even when the Conservative government announced that it would remove the party financing element from the fiscal update and backed down on the right-to-strike provisions.

The day after the coalition's news conference, it became known that the prime minister was planning to ask the governor general to prorogue Parliament to prevent a vote of non-confidence. Rallies were organized across Canada. The Green Party leader announced her support for the coalition; Conservatives alleged her allegiance was purchased with the promise of a Senate seat. The leader of the provincial Parti Québécois used the turmoil as proof that Canadian democracy was dysfunctional and as grounds for Quebec separation. Prime Minister Harper claimed that the opposition leaders had refused to display a Canadian flag at their signing ceremony, despite photographs and video proving otherwise. The media reported that later the Conservative caucus was heard singing O Canada, which fed a growing image in English Canada that patriots were defending the government from a separatist takeover. Public-opinion polls found that a majority of Quebecers and supporters of the three opposition parties were in favour of the coalition, but that a majority of Canadians outside of Quebec were opposed, as were almost all Conservative supporters.[7]

On 3 December, Harper delivered a rare, pre-recorded, prime-time televised address, once again deploring the notion of a coalition government as undemocratic. Dion's taped address followed and left many unimpressed by the

The Chamber

The chamber of the legislature is the forum where elected officials convene to discuss the issues of the day, to debate motions, and to vote. Generally speaking, members of the government party caucus sit together on one side of the chamber, and opposition members sit on the other side. This seating arrangement reflects centuries of Westminster parliamentary tradition in which the best public policy is seen to derive from adversarial debate

production quality, if not the content. Scathing reviews observed that the video appeared to have been filmed on a camera phone and judged that it lacked the strength and substance required of a prime-minister-in-waiting.[8] The next day, a number of prominent Liberals publicly called for Dion to immediately step down as leader. The communication stumble effectively marked the end of the coalition project.

The governor general returned from an international trip to weigh options. Should she agree to Prime Minister Harper's pending request to prorogue Parliament for several months? Or should she let the government fall even though an election was just held? If the government were defeated on a non-confidence motion, should the governor general call a new election, or should power be handed over to the leader of the official opposition to form a coalition government?

On 4 December, the prime minister met with the governor general to make his formal request that she prorogue Parliament. She assented, thereby ending the first session of the 40th Parliament. Within days, Dion announced his resignation as Liberal leader. In the New Year, the second session opened with the government's throne speech, which introduced a budget that contained stimulus spending provisions and left untouched the per-vote subsidies. The Liberals supported the budget, thus assuring the continuity of the government.

The coalition case is evidence that Canada's adherence to Westminster parliamentary traditions helps to maintain order in times of high tension, preventing constitutional crises and ensuring the continuity of power. It also prompts conversation about Canada's electoral system and its aversion to coalition government, despite the long history of coalition government in Europe.[9]

THE CANADIAN PRESS/Sean Kilpatrick

Protesters on Parliament Hill express their opposition to the proposed Liberal–NDP–Bloc coalition. Rallies were held in favour of the coalition. Read some media commentary from the time of the crisis: why was the proposed coalition so polarizing? What do you think was the biggest reason?

DISCUSSION ITEM

The term "coalition" carries a negative tone in Canada, thanks largely to a political culture that conditions Canadians to prize party competition over collaboration.

VOX POP

Do you think the governor general was correct to approve the prime minister's request to prorogue Parliament? Why do you think political parties working together is considered abnormal in Canada?

between the government of the day and Her Majesty's Loyal Opposition. Seating parliamentarians on opposite sides of the chamber forces the government to face its opponents. High drama occurs when exchanges become shouting matches across the aisle.

Some legislative assemblies in Canada are arranged differently. Depending on the size of each party caucus, it may be necessary to physically seat opposition party members or independents on the government side, or vice versa. The Manitoba Legislature is configured in a horseshoe shape. Assemblies in Northwest Territories and Nunavut are arranged in a circle. Many municipal and city councils arrange their members in this circular pattern by virtue of a similar lack of political parties and a conscientious desire to avoid adversarial dynamics. A notable feature is that these assemblies are much smaller than the House of Commons—seating 338 MPs in any configuration would not enable the type of discussion that is possible with a small group.

In the middle of a chamber floor sits a table where legislative staff are ready to provide advice on parliamentary rules and procedures. A ceremonial mace sits on or near the table when the legislature is meeting as a symbol of the supremacy of the Crown. The Speaker's chair is positioned in front of the table and serves as a reminder of the moderator's authority. The public gallery is found above the chamber. A press gallery reserves seats for accredited journalists.

The consensus government of Northwest Territories and Nunavut is explained later in this chapter, on page 205.

Roles in the Legislature

speaker
The member of the legislature responsible for presiding over its rules and general decorum.

Legislative proceedings are overseen by a moderator known as the **speaker**. That individual is the only party-affiliated member of a legislature who is expected to behave in a non-partisan manner. Dressed in traditional black-and-white robes and seated in a ceremonial chair at the front of a chamber, the speaker is the designated moderator of legislative debate, and is responsible for overseeing the legislature's operations. The position entails enforcing rules, monitoring votes, and following established customs. This includes limiting the time that members can speak, ordering that so-called "strangers" (non-members watching from the public galleries) be removed from time to time, and ensuring that there are no disturbances during voting. The speaker does not take part in debate and only casts a vote in the event of a tie. The speaker is responsible for adjourning each sitting of the legislature. Rulings by the speaker cannot be appealed.

The speaker is selected for the position in a secret ballot by other members. This is the first order of business after a general election. Typically, the choice is based on the candidate's parliamentary experience, fair-mindedness, and appreciation for the rules of parliamentary procedure. The speaker continues to represent constituents, and is typically affiliated with a political party, but must be careful to put party affiliation on hold. By tradition, the speaker is literally dragged into the designated position at the front of a chamber by the first minister and leader of the opposition. The ancient custom evokes the history of the position in Britain where speakers who delivered bad news to the monarch risked being executed.

Maintaining decorum in a highly charged atmosphere is a difficult proposition for most speakers. Partisan rancour often results in loud heckling that can drown out debate. Emotional exchanges are a natural aspect of any democratic forum. Incivility is particularly acute when a controversial issue is being debated and there is animosity between politicians. Conversely, sometimes all members of the legislature exhibit a respectful and even sombre tone.

parliamentary privilege
The extraordinary rights and immunities enjoyed by members of a legislature to ensure they can carry out their duties without interference from the executive or the courts.

The speaker is responsible for ruling on the protection of free speech. Members of Canadian federal, provincial, and territorial legislatures enjoy an exceptional status of protection known as **parliamentary privilege**. They are constitutionally immune from being sued for defamation or other libel because of something they say in the legislature. This is why members often dare opponents to repeat their remarks outside of the chamber, where normal free-speech limitations exist. Other rights related to parliamentary privilege

THE CANADIAN PRESS/Sean Kilpatrick

As part of parliamentary tradition, each newly selected speaker is escorted to the chair by the first minister and leader of the official opposition. The speaker is expected to feign reluctance and be "dragged" up the aisle—a custom dating back to the early days of the position in Britain, when speakers who ruled against the Crown were subject to punishment by the monarch. In 2019, Liberal MP Anthony Rota (pictured above with Andrew Scheer and Justin Trudeau) was elected speaker by secret ballot of members of the forty-third Parliament. What qualities do you think MPs look for when choosing a speaker? Why do you think that in a majority government a speaker is rarely drawn from the opposition benches?

include freedom from intimidation and from being arrested in a civil action. This does not extend to immunity from criminal proceedings. Members are not summoned to serve on a jury. Collectively, the members of a legislature are the ones who regulate their own activities, such as determining how to discipline someone who breached parliamentary privileges or controlling which outsiders may enter the legislative precinct.

There can be sanctions when incivility and obstruction escalate. The speaker threatens to "name" the member when a member behaves poorly. This means temporarily expelling that person from the legislature. Legislatures may suspend their own members for set periods of time. Such escalations are unusual. At an extreme, an individual member or a government as a whole can be found to be in **contempt**. This formal censure declares that some action has occurred that is an affront to the legislature, such as disobeying accepted practices, ignoring a ruling of the speaker, or obstructing the business of the legislative assembly.

Being held in contempt is a significant parliamentary event and yet most citizens are likely disinterested. In 2011, a House of Commons committee recommended that the governing Conservatives be found in contempt of Parliament. The minority government had refused to provide MPs on that committee with requested information about government spending. The leader of the official opposition introduced a motion of non-confidence, which passed in the House of Commons, and the Conservative government fell. The principle of responsible government dictated that Prime Minister Harper ask the governor

contempt
A formal denunciation of a member's or government's unparliamentary behaviour by the speaker.

general to dissolve the legislature and sign a writ of election. The opposition parties raised the contempt matter during the election campaign. Nevertheless, on Election Day the Conservative Party increased its seat count and formed a majority government. Meanwhile, the Liberal Party relinquished its status as official opposition by placing third, and two of the three opposition party leaders lost their own seats. Consequently the government strengthened its position despite being brought down by the opposition parties just five weeks earlier for being in contempt of Parliament. The election results are a sharp reminder that activities in the legislature that matter a great deal to parliamentarians do not necessarily matter to Canadians at the ballot box.

There are other positions affiliated with the speaker's office. The deputy speaker serves when the speaker is unavailable and bears the title Chair of Committees of the Whole. At the federal level, the deputy speaker must be fluent in the official language that is not ordinarily used by the speaker (i.e., French, if the speaker's first language is English). The speaker's office employs public servants who assist with coordinating documents, managing members' expense claims, and overseeing the production of video proceedings. Some positions, such as the sergeant-at-arms and the usher of the black rod, are largely ceremonial. The clerk of the legislature and other staff provide essential support, such as advising on rules of order. Among the services rendered is transcribing debate into the official record of proceedings, known as Hansard. The financial affairs of the House of Commons are monitored by the all-party Board of Internal Economy.

A number of other members of a legislature have extra duties. In recognition of their special status, these members occupy the front benches, which is to say the chairs in the front rows. Chief among these is the prime minister (or premier) and cabinet. For the purposes of organizing activity in the legislature, the most important position is that of the **house leaders**. Ordinarily an expert in parliamentary procedure, this person maintains timetables of events, prepares a list of members who will speak on an issue, and rises on points of order. At the federal level, most parties appoint key individuals to fulfill similar roles in the Senate. These positions are so integral to the government's agenda that the prime minister usually appoints House and Senate leaders to cabinet. Under Justin Trudeau's approach, a member of the Independent Senators Group has the title government representative in the Senate, and is responsible for coordinating the passage of government legislation.

Opposition parties similarly assign a variety of duties to their members. The Official Opposition, in particular, must project an image of being ready to assume power as the government in waiting. Chief among them is the **leader of the official opposition (OLO)**. The leader of the OLO is typically the head of the party with the second-highest number of seats in the legislature. That individual leads off Question Period. Collectively, non-government party leaders are known as opposition leaders. Discussed in Chapter 5, opposition leaders create shadow cabinets consisting of critics. Critics in small parties must scrutinize multiple portfolios due to their caucus size. This is particularly true in the provinces, though the situation occurs in the House of Commons.

The Rank and File: Backbenchers

Most elected representatives in a legislature are known as private members. They do not have extra powers or responsibilities beyond representing their constituents. Most of them are commonly called **backbenchers** because they are assigned chairs located in the back of the

---

house leader
A member of the legislature responsible for the overall performance of a political party in the legislative process.

leader of the official opposition
Typically, the leader of the party with the second-most seats in the legislature.

backbencher
A rank-and-file member of the legislative assembly without cabinet responsibilities or other special legislative titles or duties.

Briefing Notes

Her Majesty's Loyal Opposition

Westminster parliamentary democracy assigns adversarial roles to the government and Her Majesty's Loyal Opposition. The system is designed to balance rigorous debate while maintaining allegiance to Canada's system of parliamentary democracy. Not all leading opposition leaders have accepted this dual responsibility. The Progressives declined to serve as the official opposition when they formed the second-largest party in the House of Commons following the 1921 election. They objected to the old-style, adversarial partisan politics that the role implied. In that case, the third-ranked Conservatives assumed the mantle as Her Majesty's Loyal Opposition. Conversely, when the separatist Bloc Québécois elected enough members to sit as the second-largest caucus in Parliament following the 1993 federal election, the party chose to serve as official opposition. This established an ironic situation. A party dedicated to removing Quebec from Confederation, that was critical of the monarchy, and that wanted to dissolve the Canadian state was officially labelled as "Her Majesty's Loyal Opposition."

legislative chamber. Their focus tends to be on assisting constituents with obtaining government services. A backbencher and support staff may work on behalf of a constituent to solve problems dealing with government service and policy. They encourage constituents to contact the MP's office for information about Government of Canada services including social security programs, citizenship inquiries, Canadian passports, immigration matters, business opportunities, grants and funding, student loans, and taxation issues. Backbenchers routinely attend community events ranging from official openings to funerals; send congratulatory messages to constituents to mark a notable achievement ranging from wedding anniversaries to winning a talent competition; and deliver petitions in the legislature. They and their staff use a mixture of communications tools to share information with their constituents. While these are the sorts of activities undertaken by all elected officials, including cabinet ministers, backbenchers have more time to attend to constituency matters.

In *Representation in Action: Canadian MPs in the Constituencies*, political scientists Royce Koop, Heather Bastedo, and Kelly Blidook provide a fascinating account of life as a member of Parliament.[10] They job shadowed MPs in different electoral districts across Canada to identify representational styles. The book is filled with stories of MPs trying to build a personal connection with constituents, whether by defending the government at public meetings or by stopping into convenience stores throughout a rural riding to buy confectionary items as an excuse to say hello to the shopkeeper. Some MPs are eager to knock on doors between elections to talk with constituents; others are introverts who prefer to focus on public policy. All of them find some way to work within the strict confines of partisanship to represent their constituencies in the manner that best suits their own individual personalities.

Behind the scenes, the work of elected officials is supported by political staff, including constituency assistants who busily manage phone calls, emails, letters, and office visits from citizens, politicians, reporters, interest group leaders, party officials, and others. Staff are often, though not always, the ones posting to social media accounts under a politician's name. MPs place a high priority on addressing the demands of their constituents.

Another set of political staff provide caucus-wide support services, such as research and communications. These positions are funded by the House of Commons and engage in partisan work. They report to the party leader and promote the interests of the prime minister's office, official leader of the opposition, and so forth. They distribute party talking points, social media shareables, formatted speeches, and newsletter templates. Some MP s welcome the support of these party officials because it saves them time and helps them stay on message. Others chafe at the party leader exerting authority over the independence of the people's representatives. Similar support services exist at the provincial and territorial levels.

Maintaining Party Discipline

party discipline
Legislators' strict adherence to the directives of their party leadership.

This brings us to one of the most contested elements of Canadian politics: the role of **party discipline**. Elected officials are expected to vote as the party leader instructs. For instance, in the first year of the Justin Trudeau government, Liberal MPs were unanimous on 79 per cent of votes, Conservatives on 87 per cent, NDP MPs on 95 per cent, and the Bloc Québécois on 98 per cent of votes.[11] Most MPs therefore almost always vote the party line. Unanimity can be even more common in the provinces.

In public, party members are instructed to stay on message, especially with respect to any policy matters outlined in the party platform. The stakes are highest for the governing party, which has an agenda to fulfill and cannot risk losing a major vote in the legislature. Yet, even opposition party leaders lean on their caucus members to prevent off-message flare-ups from distracting from their efforts to unseat the government. Whether in government or opposition, publicly challenging the party line is risky, and presenting a united front is the norm.

Party discipline allows the party leader to:

- choose which parliamentarians may ask questions in the legislature;
- appoint parliamentarians to legislative committees and indicate what strategy they should deploy;
- promote members of the parliamentary wing of the party through the assignment of official positions, seating arrangements in the chamber, and extra privileges;
- instruct parliamentarians how to vote in the legislature and in committees, regardless of their constituents' wishes or their personal preference;
- sanction, demote, or eject a caucus member from the party;
- choose whether to deploy party resources to a candidate's riding during an election campaign; and
- refuse to approve a candidate's nomination to represent the party in an election.

Party discipline helps strengthen the leader's authority over the legislative process. Parties evolved as a solution to the so-called "loose fish" problem: in the absence of parties, government leaders were challenged to marshal votes in favour of their legislative initiatives. The actions and demands of backbenchers are less predictable without party discipline; party discipline creates a more orderly, albeit hierarchical, means of structuring parliamentary votes. When functioning well, party discipline inhibits instability and infighting. The practice increases cabinet's ability to accomplish its agenda and become more attractive to voters. We return to party discipline in the Up for Debate discussion at the end of the chapter.

To ensure control, each party designates one of its members as a **party whip**. The whip's primary responsibility is to inform fellow members of their tasks and to ensure unison. Most of the role involves human resources management and internal communications. On rare occasions, the whip must work with the leader to sanction or even remove an elected representative from caucus. The whip works with the caucus chair, a backbencher who manages caucus meetings and coordinates social events. In some small provinces, the party whip and caucus chair positions are held by a single backbencher.

Party coordination and control can make some backbenchers feel like they lack free will. They are criticized for behaving like trained seals in the legislature and as parrots who repeat their party's key messages. They may feel as though they sit between a rock—their party leadership's position on a particular issue—and a hard place—their constituents' opposing views. From this perspective, party discipline conflicts with the principle that members of a legislature are meant to represent the views of the people who elected them. On the other hand, operating as a team forces members to pick their battles, to lobby for change in closed-door caucus meetings, and to achieve compromise. By uniting parties behind a common set of policy positions, party discipline allows voters to judge their performance and hold them accountable.

Party discipline is strong but not insurmountable. A leader's power over caucus is limited by several factors. The leader must maintain the respect and loyalty of fellow party members, for instance. On certain controversial, divisive issues, the leader may allow a **free vote**. Temporarily relaxing party discipline permits members to vote their conscience, without penalty, regardless of the party's official position. When used judiciously and without pretense, free votes may allow a party to promote a democratic image, and help the leader to avoid a caucus revolt.

Justin Trudeau's Liberals promised more free votes for their members. The party has three core requirements that all of its candidates are obliged to agree with before being allowed to run under the Liberal banner. A Liberal MP is expected to vote with the party on confidence matters, on issues involving the implementation of the party platform, and on any topic related to upholding the Charter of Rights and Freedoms. The small number of Liberal MPs who breach these guidelines are sanctioned. They are permitted to vote as they wish on other issues.

Offices of the Legislature

The operations of the legislature are supported by a unique group of public servants. They are accountable to the assembly, itself, rather than the government or any one ministry.

The highest-profile officer of the legislature is the **auditor general**, whose office employs accountants tasked with examining public-sector spending. Auditors question the value for money and accounting practices of government departments. They carry out financial audits, performance audits, and special examinations. The auditor general issues reports about government misspending and offers recommendations for improvement. These reports can attract considerable media attention and prompt a government response.

The auditor general does not pass judgement on the government's budget. In Ottawa, the Office of the Parliamentary Budget Officer independently analyzes budget figures and estimates. It looks into other financial matters at the request of a legislative committee or parliamentarian. In the period leading up to an election campaign, it responds to requests

party whip
Individual member of the legislature responsible for ensuring that caucus members toe the party line.

The delegate view of representation, also known as substantive representation, is described on page 442 of Chapter 13.

free vote
A bill or motion in the legislature on which party members, except members of cabinet, are allowed to vote however they choose without sanction.

auditor general
An independent officer responsible for auditing and reporting to the legislature regarding a government's spending and operations.

from political parties seeking cost estimates of financial proposals. The position was created, in part, as a countermeasure to governments that fudge budget projections for political gain.

Another prominent officer of the legislature is the Chief Electoral Officer. At the federal level, the Office of the Chief Electoral Officer is commonly known as Elections Canada. The non-partisan agency is responsible for the administration of free and fair elections. It coordinates polling stations, organizes communications campaigns to raise awareness, manages election workers, monitors election activities to ensure compliance with regulations, and files post-election reports. Elections Canada is discussed in Chapter 10.

A growing number of other offices of the legislature have emerged across Canada. The list also includes the privacy commissioner, who advocates for the privacy rights of Canadians, and the access-to-information commissioner, who assists citizens with concerns about the government's freedom-of-information practices. Positions that are unique to the House of Commons include the commissioner of official languages and the commissioner of lobbying. Other legislatures may use different titles, may combine titles, or may have other offices that do not exist at the federal level. For instance, in Ottawa there is a conflict of interest and ethics commissioner as well as a public sector integrity commissioner; in Quebec there is simply an ethics commissioner; and in Ontario the position is known as the Office of the Integrity Commissioner. Whereas at the federal level there is a privacy commissioner and an information commissioner, at the provincial level these positions are fused into a single office, such as BC's Office of the Information and Privacy Commissioner. As well, some provincial legislatures have different offices entirely, such as an ombudsperson or a child and youth advocate. Few Canadians directly avail these services, though many may indirectly benefit from the efforts of these government watchdogs.

Inside Canadian Politics

How Were Free Votes Used to Deal with the Legalization of Same-Sex Marriage?

Moral issues are some of the most challenging for political parties to navigate. They deal with personal beliefs and can be highly divisive, both in the electorate and within parties' own caucuses. This was the case with legalizing same-sex marriage. For centuries, marriage laws permitted the legal union of heterosexual couples only. Most political parties avoided discussing any reforms to these laws. This changed when a 2004 Supreme Court reference declared the traditional definition of marriage unconstitutional. Existing laws discriminated against LGBTQ2+ people and would need to be amended.

In response, federal party leaders used a combination of free votes and party discipline to navigate a change to marriage laws that would legalize same-sex unions. They did so amid a minority government situation. Prime Minister Martin's cabinet would be required to support the new legislation, Bill 3, by virtue of cabinet solidarity. The prime minister allowed Liberal backbenchers a free vote on the issue, however. So, too, did the leaders of the Conservative Party and Bloc Québécois. The leader of the NDP chose to whip his caucus, obliging New Democrats to vote in favour of legalizing same-sex marriage.

The Liberal cabinet voted nearly unanimously in support of Bill C-38; none opposed, and one member abstained. The Liberal backbench was divided. While 59 Liberal backbenchers voted in favour of the bill, 32 opposed, with 3 abstaining. Most Bloc MPs voted in favour and most Conservatives voted against. Despite the requirements of party discipline imposed on the NDP, one New Democrat voted against the motion, citing personal religious convictions. She was removed from the NDP shadow cabinet, lost a subsequent nomination race to run as a party candidate in the next election, and ultimately resigned from the NDP caucus to sit as an independent. She ran, but finished third, in the subsequent federal election. Bill 38 passed in the House of Commons by a final tally of 158 to 133, with 15 MPs not voting. It then passed with 47 in favour, 21 opposed, and 3 abstentions in the Senate. The Civil Marriage Act received Royal Assent on 20 July 2005.

DISCUSSION ITEM

Leaders may publicly release their members from the constraints of party discipline, yet the results of free votes nevertheless often break down along traditional party lines.

VOX POP

Why do you suppose that members of the legislature tend to support their party leader's position during free votes? Why do you suppose some members abstain from voting?

Legislator Remuneration

A source of constant debate is how much the people's representatives should be paid for their work. The concept of parliamentary indemnity holds that there must be an attractive pay package to attract top-quality representatives. Otherwise, relatively well-paid professionals will not put their careers on hold to enter the political realm. Moreover, if representatives are poorly paid, they are more susceptible to accepting bribes from people who want political favours. A further consideration is that being a public figure, especially a member of cabinet, is a stressful and demanding job that can involve long hours when the legislature is sitting. Members spend a lot of time travelling and may have to live in the capital city away from family, attend community events on the weekends, and be on call. In the legislature, a member is prone to be subjected to heckling, heated exchanges, negativity, and character attacks. This treatment often extends beyond their day jobs. Members of the government who make unpopular decisions are criticized in the media and berated by constituents on social media, through contact with the member's office, and in person. Even backbenchers forgo their ability to venture into public places for fear of being intercepted by citizens anxious to chat, banter, and complain. The worst aspect of life for a public official may be the teasing or bullying a member's children are subjected to at school because of the parent's political career, a cruelty for which higher pay is seldom seen as an appropriate form of compensation. The volume and intensity of criticism directed at public officials is especially harsh on social media. Women and people of colour can be particularly susceptible to critique. This includes ad hominem remarks, which are criticisms of the individual instead of the issue.

For these reasons, the remuneration and perks afforded to elected officials are relatively generous. There are extra stipends for supplementary duties ranging from being a member of cabinet to being the deputy chair of a legislative committee. Table 6.3 illustrates the range of additional funds for extra positions, using British Columbia as the example. Salaries for public officials are subject to frequent review, increasing over time and periodically decreasing when a government cuts its operating budget. In addition to their salary, members of legislative assemblies participate in generous pension and supplementary health plans that are well above the private-sector standard, and that are often more lucrative than public-service plans. Other perks of office include all-expenses-paid trips on parliamentary junkets, sometimes to foreign countries. Parliamentarians submit claims for travel, food, accommodations, and office expenses that sometimes become a source of controversy due to their extravagance or embellishment. They have access to support staff in their office and they are invited to innumerable social events. If they are defeated in an election, they receive a substantial severance package. When they retire, most enjoy supplementary pension and health benefits, which might begin well before reaching the age of 65. Furthermore, members of the legislature receive non-monetary incentives. This includes the psychological benefits of influencing public policy and the

Table 6.3	Additional Remuneration for Extra Positions, Legislative Assembly of British Columbia, 2018
Position	**% of Basic Compensation**
MLA's regular salary	100 ($108,000)
Premier	+90 extra
Minister	+50 extra
Minister of State	+35 extra
Speaker	+50 extra
Deputy Speaker	+35 extra
Government Whip	+20 extra
Deputy Government Whip	+15 extra
Government Caucus Chair	+20 extra
Deputy Chair, Committee of the Whole	+20 extra
Parliamentary Secretary	+15 extra
Leader of the Official Opposition	+50 extra
Official Opposition House Leader	+20 extra
Official Opposition Whip	+20 extra
Official Opposition Deputy Whip	+15 extra
Official Opposition Caucus Chair	+20 extra
Leader of the Third Party	+25 extra
Third Party House Leader	+10 extra
Third Party Whip	+10 extra
Third Party Caucus Chair	+10 extra
Chair, Select Standing or Special Committee	+15 extra
Deputy Chair, Select Standing or Special Committee	+10 extra

Source: http://members.leg.bc.ca/mla-remuneration/salaries-allowances.htm

ego boost of being in the public eye and a public figure. Nevertheless, for some citizens, these financial incentives do not offset the considerable demands of running for office and serving as a member of a legislature.

Even with the stresses of office, there are good reasons to be critical of the extravagance of these rewards. Despite the fact that many jurisdictions assign the review of legislators' pay to committees or commissions, members are collectively responsible for setting their own remuneration schemes. In particular, their pension plan may be viewed as unjustifiably rich, with some long-time MPs eligible to be well-paid when they retire from politics. That pension may be on top of any other pension(s) that they earned in a career outside of politics. There are instances of retiring MPs receiving multiple publicly funded pensions. For instance, a former parliamentarian might qualify for a House of Commons pension, and a pension from the provincial assembly where they previously served. That parliamentarian might further qualify for a third public-sector pension if that individual worked as a teacher, nurse, bureaucrat, or in some other public-sector position before entering politics.

Given the rewards and benefits of public life, it's a wonder some elected and appointed officials see the need to take advantage of the system. Yet there have been numerous scandals about unethical and/or illegal spending behaviour. Cases include a Nova Scotia MLA being reimbursed for a generator stored in his garage, members in various legislatures claiming tens of thousands of dollars in housing allowances by lying about the location of their primary residence, and an Alberta MLA using Airbnb to rent out his publicly funded apartment. Increasingly there is public scrutiny of such behaviour and auditors general and ethics commissioners are granted permission to review expense claims. Moreover, a growing trend is to proactively post online the expense claims of ministers and members of legislative assemblies. The combination of transparency and scrutiny reduces the potential for questionable behaviour.

As the attentive public becomes more aware of the perks of public office, it is prone to contrast this with the declining number of sitting days of most legislatures. Citizens may conclude that politicians are working less than they should. A legislature tends to sit roughly at the same times of year when children are in school and adjourns for lengthy breaks around Thanksgiving, Remembrance Day, Christmas, Easter, and for the summer. The number of sitting days varies depending on the jurisdiction. Most are moving toward fixed calendars that identify when the legislature is in session. Legislatures are closed for long stretches, and some members, particularly provincial backbenchers, may see little need to come into the office every day. The competitiveness of the party system, the proximity to an election, the presence of a majority versus a minority government, the activist nature of a government's agenda, the level of public unrest—these are all things that can increase or reduce how often members assemble. The higher number of sitting days in Parliament reflects the diversity of competing perspectives, the volume of bills, the vitality of the committee system, and the extra-parliamentary scrutiny from the media and elsewhere.

Generally speaking, across Canada the number of sitting days used to be higher than it is today. The 1970s and 1980s featured deep constitutional discussions and debate. Technological innovations sped up transportation, communication, and research, enabling members to make decisions and carry out business outside the chamber. The working hours of most members have expanded in concert with the public's increasing expectations of prompt service, even as the public assumes that their representatives are working less because the assembly meets less often.[12]

VOX POP

Why would a lawyer, businessperson, union leader, physician, or anyone else earning a high salary take a pay cut to enter the rough-and-tumble world of politics?

Briefing Notes

The #MeToo Movement and Canadian Legislators

Politics involves lots of social mingling and power relationships. Consequently there are elected officials and especially political staff who are vulnerable to harassment. In 2015, the House of Commons introduced the world's first MP-to-MP code of conduct on sexual harassment, with mandated periodic reviews. The global #MeToo movement subsequently brought to the fore a large number of high-profile sexual harassment complaints and abuses of power. Canadian politics was rocked as allegations—mostly from women against male politicians—brought down a number of political careers. Parliamentarians across the country undergo training about workplace harassment.

The Life of the Legislature

All legislatures in Canada follow a common rhythm. Each session of each legislature begins with a throne speech, includes a presentation of the budget and the budget estimates, and ends with prorogation or dissolution (see Figure 6.3). Other business is conducted in the interim, such as the government party advancing legislation, the opposition attempting its own initiatives, and private members introducing motions.

The lifespan of the legislature is like that of a hockey season. Each hockey season consists of individual games, which consist of periods separated by intermissions. Likewise each Parliament (or legislature or assembly) has individual sessions, which consist of sittings separated by times of recess. A Parliament usually lasts four years. The typical session lasts one to three years, and can contain hundreds of individual sittings. Starting a new session in between elections is a way for the government to reset its agenda.

Every Parliament, legislature, or assembly is named chronologically, and—except in cases of resignations and by-elections—contains a relatively static group of legislators. For instance, the federal election of 2019 was the forty-third in Canadian history. That September, Prime Minister Trudeau asked the governor general to dissolve the forty-second Parliament, setting in motion a general election whereby all 338 electoral districts simultaneously held elections of candidates to become a member of Parliament for each riding. When Canadians voted in October 2019, they elected 338 MPs who formed a new Parliament, and only the voters of the Montreal district of Papineau were able to directly vote for Justin Trudeau. Each legislator was officially sworn in, with oaths administered by the governor general. When the House of Commons convened it was the first session of the forty-third Parliament. A similar process occurs in the provinces and territories.

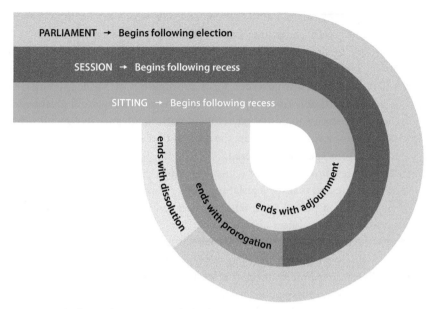

Figure 6.3 | The Parliamentary Life Cycle

Most parliaments consist of two to five legislative sessions, which are numbered. Each session begins with the swearing in of all members of the legislature, and the selection of the speaker. The first major event involves the **speech from the throne**. The event offers the governing party, via the monarch's representative, an opportunity to outline its legislative agenda for the life of that session. The contents of the speech typically contain items drawn from the party's most recent election platform. The red carpet is rolled out for the monarch's representative, who arrives at the legislature to great fanfare. The pageantry and formal rituals are reminders of the supreme executive authority of the Crown in Canada's parliamentary system of government. When a throne speech is delivered in Ottawa, the governor general sits in the speaker's chair in the Senate and is flanked by the prime minister. Supreme Court justices, parliamentarians, and other distinguished guests fill the Senate chamber to listen to the monarch's representative formally enunciate the government's priorities and planned initiatives. The speech is written by partisans in the prime minister's office who integrate election campaign commitments, input from government departments, and recent events that are deemed to warrant government attention. By repeatedly saying, "My government will . . ." the governor general gives public notice from the Crown what initiatives the appointed cabinet intends to pursue. The same custom is carried out in provincial and territorial legislatures, with the corresponding roles being filled by the lieutenant governor or commissioner, the premier, provincial justices, and staff in the premier's office.

Once read, the speech from the throne is put to a vote in the legislature. Members have an opportunity to debate, and in rare cases reject, the government's legislative agenda. If the speech is rejected, the government is denied the confidence of the house and must resign.

Each session consists of hundreds of sittings. Meetings of the legislature are scheduled to coincide with the legislative agenda and seasonal calendar. At the conclusion of a sitting, the speaker announces that the legislature is closed for the day, which is known as

speech from the throne Document read by the governor general, lieutenant governor, or commissioner officially opening a new session of the legislature and detailing the government's plans.

adjournment
The temporary suspension of a legislative sitting until it reconvenes.

prorogation
The process by which a legislative session is closed in anticipation of a new speech from the throne being delivered.

dissolution
The process by which a Parliament or legislature is closed, resulting in a general election of new members.

budget
A document containing the government's projected revenue, expenditures, and economic forecasts.

Budgets are discussed in the section on financial administration in Chapter 8, on public policy.

adjournment. Business is put on hold until the next meeting, which can begin as early as the next morning or many weeks later, after a scheduled break, called a recess.

The business of the legislature grinds to a halt when a session comes to an end. In an effort to reset the legislative agenda, every year to three years the first minister approaches the governor general or lieutenant governor for a **prorogation** of the legislature. All work, including legislation, that is currently before the legislature ceases and must be re-introduced in the next session should the government wish to advance it. Any bills that are close to being ready for a vote must restart the process of review. When the legislature is reconvened, a new throne speech is delivered.

First ministers request prorogation for a host of reasons. Some decide that their legislative agenda is complete and that the legislature needs a fresh start. Others seek prorogation to begin a cooling-off period amid tense parliamentary debates or even scandal. Historically, these requests are almost always granted. On rare occasions, authorizing a prorogation request is controversial, as with the coalition crisis in 2008 (see page 180).

Eventually, the composition of the legislature needs to be renewed via a general election. Constitutionally, this renewal must occur at least every five years, except in the event of "real or apprehended war, invasion, or insurrection." In such cases, an election could be postponed, as long as no more than a third of members are opposed. The only time the federal Parliament exercised this constitutional clause was during Borden's Conservative government during World War I. A one-year extension was granted in 1916, allowing the twelfth Parliament to sit for a total of six years.

On a more practical level, government agendas tend to run their course over the life of a Parliament, and animosity among legislators may grow. Moreover, the governing party may lack public legitimacy to take bold action or remain in office. Political parties, even the governing party, may have a new leader who has not yet faced the electorate in that capacity. In any of these cases, the first minister may wish to seek a new batch of legislators and renewed support from the electorate before proceeding with new legislation. To renew the composition of the assembly membership, the first minister must request **dissolution** of the legislature, which brings that numbered Parliament to an end. If the governor general agrees with the request, writs are signed for a new general election. The same procedure for dissolution applies at the provincial/territorial level with the lieutenant governor or commissioner.

In the past, the prime minister or premier tended to request dissolution when the chances of winning an election were greatest. Electoral fortunes are brightest when the governing party enjoys a high public approval rating or when the opposition parties are especially weak or disorganized. Nowadays, all jurisdictions except Nova Scotia and Yukon have fixed-date election legislation stipulating when the next election is to be held. Regardless of these laws, and particularly in minority government situations, a government may lose the confidence of the House, triggering dissolution before the end of the parliamentary term. Moreover, the possibility remains that the first minister will seek to time the election call to the governing party's advantage.

Another key element of the parliamentary life cycle is the annual government **budget**. Each year, typically after the Christmas break, the government introduces its fiscal plans. In essence, the budget proposes how the government intends to raise and spend money, and includes its forecast for how the economy will fare in the year ahead.

After the finance minister delivers the budget in the legislature, the budget is debated, usually for a period of four days. At this time, a formal vote is held to determine whether or not a majority of the members in the legislature approve of the government's broad fiscal plans. This is a central tenet of responsible government, wherein the political executive must have the confidence of the people's elected representatives. If a political party controls a majority of the seats, the budget vote is a foregone conclusion, and the budget will pass. However, in a minority-government situation, there is considerable drama. If the governing party does not persuade members of another party to vote in favour of the budget, then the government falls and there is usually an election.

The budget debate is followed by **budget estimates**. The estimates process ensures that members of the legislature from different parties have an opportunity to scrutinize line-by-line spending plans for the upcoming fiscal year (1 April to 31 March). Typically, representatives from the department concerned, namely the minister and deputy minister, are expected to answer committee members' questions about the estimates. Issues that emerge can inform future lines of government critique for the opposition and areas of inquiry for journalists.

budget estimates
The detailed, line-by-line statements of how each department will treat revenues and expenditures.

Daily Business

The daily business of a legislature likewise ranges from events that command the general public's attention to minutiae that only interests policy wonks.

The routine business of the legislature is governed by **standing orders**. These formal rules differ from legislature to legislature. The standing orders are non-partisan but nevertheless favour the government party over the opposition. The procedures specify the length of time a member may speak or a motion may be debated. They stipulate the need for members to address each other by titles as opposed to their given names. Standing orders prescribe the meeting times for each sitting, which for the House of Commons are presented in Figure 6.4. These adjournment times are subject to change if a motion is passed to continue the sitting so that some specific business can carry on without interruption. There is a general trend toward making legislatures more family-friendly. Some standing orders allow breastfeeding in the legislative chamber. In Manitoba, the standing orders allow MLAs to spend time with their families in the evening. The various activities identified in the standing orders of the House of Commons are identified in Table 6.4.

standing orders
The body of rules governing the conduct of the legislature.

In preparation for proceedings, the government house leader identifies a priority list of items that the governing party wishes to advance. The order paper is presented at the start of each day to members for their collective approval. Once it is approved, it guides the day's business, and staff in the speaker's office proceed with preparing support materials, such as the circulation of photocopied documents.

The daily activity that attracts the most attention is oral questions, commonly known as **Question Period**, or QP. This is the scheduled time for opposition members to question the head of government and cabinet members. On the opposition side, preparation involves researching, drafting, and rehearsing questions, as well as jostling for who gets to speak. On the government side, ministers attempt to anticipate what questions will be lobbed their way, and review the briefing notes prepared by public servants in their department. Bureaucrats prepare lengthy briefing binders for their respective ministers' use and are on call in the event that the opposition raises an issue with which the minister is unfamiliar. Internally, the various parties identify key message themes that they want to repeat so that their main points are consistent and conveyed to onlookers in the press gallery. Time may be spent rehearsing.

Question Period
The time allotted for members to ask oral questions of the government in the legislature.

Hours	Monday	Tuesday	Wednesday	Thursday	Friday	Hours
10:00–11:00					Government Orders	10:00–11:00
11:00–11:15	Private Members' Business	Routine Proceedings .... Government Orders		Routine Proceedings .... Government Orders	Statements by Members	11:00–11:15
11:15–12:00					Oral Questions	11:15–12:00
12:00–1:00	Government Orders		Review of Delegated Legislation*		Routine Proceedings .... Government Orders	12:00–1:00
1:00–1:30						1:00–1:30
1:30–2:00						1:30–2:00
2:00–2:15	Statements by Members	Statements by Members	Statements by Members	Statements by Members	Private Members' Business	2:00–2:15
2:15–2:30	Oral Questions	Oral Questions	Oral Questions	Oral Questions		2:15–2:30
2:30–3:00						2:30–3:00
3:00–5:30	Routine Proceedings .... Government Orders	Government Orders	Routine Proceedings .... Notices of Motions for the Production of Papers .... Government Orders	Government Orders		3:00–5:30
5:30–6:30		Private Members' Business	Private Members' Business	Private Members' Business		5:30–6:30
6:30–7:00	Adjournment Proceedings	Adjournment Proceedings	Adjournment Proceedings	Adjournment Proceedings		6:30–7:00

Figure 6.4 | Weekly House of Commons Timetable

Note: If required, House to sit at 1:00 p.m. for the review of Delegated Legislation pursuant to Standing Order 128(1).

Source: Reproduced with permission from the Parliament of Canada.

Question Period is an integral part of Canada's system of responsible government. It allows opposition and government backbenchers to hold the political executive to account. This is done in the public eye. Citizens may view legislative proceedings in person from the public gallery; journalists live tweet from the press gallery and file news stories; most legislatures broadcast QP on television and/or online; and official records are transcribed and recorded in Hansard. The event is a spectacle that combines information and entertainment.

Critics point out that Question Period is seldom answer period, in that participants do not reasonably expect to secure information from the government, nor do ministers intend to offer it. Rather, the opposition often uses QP to embarrass the government and draw public attention to an issue. Cabinet members attempt to respond earnestly while also deflecting criticism. This conditions members to focus on witty remarks, sharp questions, and theatrics in an attempt to secure the short sound bites that make the news and are easily shared on social media. Consider the following QP exchange from June 2018 on the final day before the House of Commons adjourned for summer recess.

Table 6.4   Summary of Routine Events in the House of Commons

Event	What Is It?
Private members' business	Members are given a 60-second opportunity to share uplifting news, such as an accomplishment by a constituent. Motions concerning government policy can be raised.
Public bills, private bills, notices of motions	Notice is given for future discussion about proposed legislation (i.e., the motion to introduce a bill, known as "first reading").
Government orders	Time is allotted for any business that was proposed by a minister for discussion, such as debate on a bill. This makes up a considerable amount of daily activity.
Tabling of documents	Reports and other papers are formally presented to the House, ranging from annual reports to special requests for written information.
Statements by ministers	Short information or policy announcements are made by ministers, with opportunities for the opposition to briefly respond.
Oral questions	A period of time is given to backbenchers to ask questions of government members.
Presentation of reports from interparliamentary delegations	The head of a group that has included at least one member of the legislature and that has recently returned to Canada reports on its activities.
Presentation of reports from committees	A designated member gives a brief summary of a committee's report.
First reading of Senate public bills	A bill approved by the Senate is introduced for review in the House of Commons.
Motions	As most motions are dealt with in other orders of business, this has become a catch-all for remaining motions, such as seeking approval of a committee report or a motion concerning house proceedings/sittings.
Presenting petitions	A member presents a list of constituent signatures in support of a plea for government action. These must have been inspected in advance by the clerk of petitions. No debate in the House ensues after a petition's presentation, and the matter is referred to the relevant ministry for a written response.
Questions on the order paper	A member can submit a written question about public affairs to a minister for response.

Source: Adapted from the Parliament of Canada, Standing Orders of the House of Commons (2013). Not intended to be an exhaustive list.

It is one of countless similar examples of the back-and-forth that occurs in Question Period, wherein the opposition tries to embarrass the political executive, and the government's representative tries to turn the tables by repeating key messages about the government's accomplishments:

Hon. Andrew Scheer (Leader of the Opposition, Conservative): Mr Speaker, the prime minister is incapable of managing taxpayers' money responsibly. More than $8 million on a temporary skating rink, $215,000 for an illegal vacation on a private island, at least $1.5 million for a disastrous trip to India, and tens of thousands of dollars on non-essential items to renovate the prime minister's cottage in Harrington Lake. Why does the prime minister keep spending so recklessly and sending the bill to the next generation?

Right Hon. Justin Trudeau (Prime Minister, Liberal): Mr Speaker, we promised Canadians that we would invest in the middle class and those working hard to join it. That is exactly what we have done with historic investments in infrastructure and with the Canada child benefit, which is helping nine out of 10 families and will lift 300,000 children out of poverty. We lowered taxes for the middle class and increased them for the well-off. Not only are we investing for the benefit of Canadians, but we also secured the strongest growth in the G7 last year. We are creating the growth that Canadians need.[13]

At the federal level, the parliamentary calendar stipulates that 20 days be allocated to the opposition parties so that they have time for debate about their own motions. These opposition days, also known as supply days, are opportunities for non-government parties to advance their own agendas. This includes debate about new policy ideas and is an opportunity to critique the government. Scheduled **opposition days** take on greater significance in a minority-government situation because they can be used to introduce a motion of non-confidence. Depending on the standing orders governing a particular legislature, the government may have more or less control over the scheduling of opposition days.

Legislative Committees

Question period gets all of the attention, but the real business of the legislature tends to occur in **legislative committees**. These are small groups of members of the legislature, belonging to different political parties, who meet to discuss government activities and call expert witnesses to testify. These are distinct from the cabinet committees discussed in Chapter 5 whose deliberations are secret. The membership of those committees is decided by the first minister and is comprised entirely of members of cabinet. By comparison, legislative committees are multiparty forums whose membership is decided by each party leader, and includes backbenchers. Committee members gain experience and knowledge. They have an opportunity to influence government policy. The post offers a bit of prestige and is a stepping stone in their political career. Members of cabinet do not necessarily belong to legislative committees and may be precluded from participating. It might be inappropriate for ministers to attend even unofficially. This is because committee members need freedom to constructively examine the government's policies and plans.

Legislative committees are tasked with subjecting a bill or an issue to scrutiny. They do so before it is voted on by the entire legislature. This work takes time and slows down the passage of proposed legislation. Their meetings are typically open to public viewing and might be televised and/or broadcast online. Sometimes a parliamentary secretary is assigned to represent the minister's interests. This can upset members when the committee is supposed to be arm's-length from the political executive. Legislative committees are most active at the federal level where there are more members and more resources. For some backbenchers, committee work can involve considerable work while the legislature is in session. For instance, in Ottawa a backbencher on the standing committee on foreign affairs and international development is engaged in numerous files of global significance, and travels to exotic locales. The workload contrasts with that of members of the standing joint committee on the Library of Parliament.

Chairs of legislative committees moderate discussions and fulfill similar duties as the deputy speaker. The chairs are selected according to rules that vary from legislature to legislature. In the House of Commons, committee members have the power to select their own chairs, meaning that, particularly in minority governments, it is possible for opposition parties to chair committees. In other jurisdictions, chairs are selected by party leadership. Committee chairs exercise power over the group's agenda and decorum.

Legislative committees differ in their membership, focus, and duration. The main point of distinction is between standing and ad hoc committees. A **standing committee** is permanent. It is designated in the standing orders as playing such an essential role in the business of the legislature that it must operate regardless of the party in power. Typically,

opposition days
Time allotted to opposition parties to raise their own motions and legislation.

legislative committee
A small group of legislators assigned to deliberate and report back to the legislature.

standing committee
Also known as a permanent legislative committee, whose existence is defined by standing orders.

Briefing Notes

Provincial Legislatures and Executive Dominance

A lot of practices in the House of Commons are identical in provincial legislatures. However, parliamentary government functions differently in many provinces. The number of sitting days can be much lower and party discipline much higher. In terms of seats, the average provincial legislature is one-fifth the size of the House of Commons. Yet provincial cabinets are about half the size of the federal one. As a result, a high proportion of members of provincial assemblies are part of cabinet or are affiliated with it as a parliamentary secretary, government whip, and so forth. In Prince Edward Island, one of every three MLAs is in cabinet. In some jurisdictions, backbenchers are invited to serve on cabinet committees. The trend of "executive creep" sees the executive branch encroach upon the legislative branch, leaving fewer legislators to hold the government to account, and raising questions about the strength of responsible government in some provinces.[14]

a standing committee deals with matters concerning a particular department, like the standing committee on health, or a body of government, such as the standing committee on procedures and house affairs. By comparison, an **ad hoc committee** is impermanent and has a specific purpose. It is created with a special mandate that may eventually be completed, such as a special committee tasked with drafting or scrutinizing legislation. In

THE CANADIAN PRESS/Sean Kilpatrick

The Chief Electoral Officer of Canada, Stéphane Perrault (left), and the Commissioner of Canada Elections, Yves Côté, appearing as witnesses for a Committee of the Whole regarding Bill C-76 (Elections Modernization Act) in the Senate in November 2018.

Ottawa, where there are two legislative chambers, many standing and ad hoc committees are made up of members exclusively from either the House of Commons or the Senate. However, some joint committees feature representation from MPs and senators, such as the standing joint committee on the Library of Parliament.

Instead of a standing or ad hoc committees, an issue may be referred to **committee of the whole** for deliberation. This is a committee meeting open to the full membership of the legislature, including the political executive and the minister responsible for proposed legislation. The speaker is not present and a designate presides, normally the deputy speaker. Committee review is an opportunity to identify potential amendments and lines of argument. The smaller number of members in provincial and territorial legislatures may allow for efficient work by the committee of the whole—which is problematic when it replaces review that should be performed by a more specialized legislative committee, without ministers present. In all jurisdictions, the committee of the whole provides an opportunity for special debate.

The Legislative Process

Laws are created, changed, and repealed after public debate and scrutiny. They begin as ideas, perhaps based on a political ideology, due to pressure from special interests, and/or as a response to an emerging situation. Often, but not always, these ideas are included in a political party's election platform, are mentioned in the throne speech, and/or appear in ministerial mandate letters. Some ideas for laws are fast-tracked, whereas others linger for years. For instance, the 11 September terrorist attacks in the United States caused governments worldwide to urgently revise laws designed to ensure domestic security. Conversely, legislating action to protect the natural environment might languish.

An idea for a law is formalized when it is written out as a **bill**. A bill is draft legislation that must be submitted to, debated among, and supported by members of a legislative assembly before it can become law. Most bills are drafted by the public service at the direction of a member of the political executive and are endorsed by cabinet before being presented to the legislature. Other times bills may be prepared by members of the legislature themselves, including by backbenchers. Once passed, a bill may be called a law, an act, or a statute.

There are several types of bills. They are distinguished by their targets, sponsors, and structure. The first type divides private bills, which deal with matters that apply to a small subset of the Canadian population, and public bills, which apply to society as a whole. A classic example of a private bill existed prior to 1968. Couples seeking a divorce were required to petition Parliament, which prompted an investigation and a vote in the Senate. Private bills are uncommon today, but they are used to guide the activities of corporate entities governed by Parliament such as Scouts Canada. Public bills are far more common. They may be divided into two main categories: government bills and private members' bills.

Government bills are introduced by cabinet. A government bill is proposed legislation that has been endorsed by the governing party. Only a minister can move for its introduction to the assembly. Government bills either involve spending and revenue (money bills) or they do not. Money bills cannot be introduced by private members or senators. Only cabinet members may introduce legislation to that effect.

Private members' bills (PMBs) are introduced by backbenchers of any party and are not to be confused with the private bills noted earlier. A private member's bill is a proposal

committee of the whole
Another name for the body of all legislators meeting as a committee, minus the speaker.

Agenda-setting is discussed in the section on the public-policy cycle on page 255 in Chapter 8.

bill
A piece of draft legislation tabled in the legislature.

from a member who is not part of cabinet. The practice raises awareness on matters of concern to a member's constituents or draws focus to issues not on the government's agenda. PMBs are rarely passed.

Lastly, bills are either stand-alone legislation that address one particular area of public policy, or are grouped into an **omnibus bill**, which addresses a wide range of issues. For example, a bill on cyber-crime may be considered stand-alone in that it focuses solely on one topic. By contrast, budget implementation bills, passed shortly after the budget is approved, are often omnibus bills. They contain amendments to a host of existing laws adjusted by the new fiscal plan. Likewise, treaty implementation bills are typically omnibus pieces of legislation, like the ones that federal, provincial, and territorial governments passed following the establishment of the United States-Mexico-Canada Agreement. Opposition parties often criticize governments for using omnibus bills as a means of obscuring issues. It is a tactic that groups together a variety of issues into a single bill and complicates debate on topics that warrant individual attention. The Trudeau Liberals amended the rules of the House of Commons so that the Speaker has the power to split a bill up when there is a lack of common elements. Nevertheless, the Liberals still used the tactic to avoid debating a series of stand-alone bills, and the Speaker did not intervene.

omnibus bills
Bills or laws that address a wide variety of public-policy issues in a single document.

The process for passing a government bill into law varies somewhat among jurisdictions. It normally begins with a policy idea being pitched by a minister in cabinet. In Ottawa, this requires a formal policy proposal that is drafted by departmental staff so that it can be referred to an applicable cabinet committee for review. To prepare a proposal, public servants research the subject matter, review legislation in other jurisdictions, revise multiple drafts, and consult with other departments. They potentially seek input from stakeholders and partners, namely other orders of government, Indigenous communities, interest groups, industry, or the public. Staff in the minister's department begin to draft legislation if the cabinet committee endorses the proposal. The staff submit this to the Department of Justice, where government lawyers scrutinize and tweak the draft bill. That draft is submitted back to a cabinet committee for review, and if it approves the draft, then the document is submitted to the full cabinet for approval. If cabinet consents, the bill is signed by the first minister or the house leader for its presentation to the legislature.

A government bill is introduced to the legislature by the sponsoring minister. This verbal introduction is known as first reading. This permits the legislature's staff to circulate printed copies to other members. The bill is scheduled for debate through its inclusion on the order paper. First reading therefore serves to give advance notice of an upcoming discussion about a bill. Each bill is numbered sequentially depending on the order in which it is introduced. At the federal level, the numbers and letters have special meaning. Bills initiated in the House of Commons are given names beginning with "C" and bills originating in the Senate are labelled with an "S." Thus the label Bill C-7 denotes a government bill introduced by a minister in the House of Commons whereas Bill S-306 would signify a public bill introduced by a member of the Senate.

A little-known tradition in the Parliament of Canada is the pro forma nature of the first bill introduced in both chambers at the start of a session after a throne speech. Each initial bill follows a tradition of presenting standard, incomplete legislation that is only given first reading and is not voted upon. The practice originated in the mid-sixteenth century in Britain. In Ottawa, Bill C-1 and Bill S-1 use old titles dating back decades, and always involve reading the same text. The purpose is to formally establish the legislature's ability to choose which items to implement from the throne speech and in which order.

It is a mechanism to assert the autonomy of the legislature over the Crown. Thus, the first bill moved by Prime Minister Justin Trudeau at the opening of Parliament was worded as follows, as it was for previous prime ministers and will be for his successors:

42:1 Hansard (2015/12/04)
[Bill C-1. Introduction and first reading]
An act respecting the administration of oaths of office

Whereas the introduction of a pro forma bill in the House of Commons before the consideration of the Speech from the Throne demonstrates the right of the elected representatives of the people to act without the leave of the Crown;

Whereas that custom, which can be traced to 1558 in the Parliament at Westminster, is practised in a number of jurisdictions having a parliamentary form of government;

And whereas it is desirable to explain and record the constitutional relationship represented by that custom;

Now, therefore, Her Majesty, by and with the advice and consent of the Senate and House of Commons of Canada, enacts as follows:

1. This bill asserts the right of the House of Commons to give precedence to matters not addressed in the Speech from the Throne.

A bill introduced by a minister stands a good chance of being passed, particularly during a majority government. By comparison, a bill introduced by an opposition MP or a private member is likely to be defeated. The best chance of success for such a bill is if it is sponsored by a member of the governing party and/or if it is presented during a minority government.

Sometime later, the schedule of events identified on the order paper indicates that it is time to debate the bill. The minister motions that debate may begin, which is known as second reading. At this stage the government outlines the purpose behind the legislation. Members debate the draft bill, and in most but not all Canadian legislatures, the bill is referred to the appropriate legislative committee for clause-by-clause scrutiny and possible amendments. This may take time, particularly if expert witnesses are called.

Once amendments are accepted, the bill moves to third reading, which is a vote on the amended bill by the entire legislature. The speaker asks members to rise to indicate if they support the bill and wish to have their vote of assent ("yea") recorded, or if they are opposed and wish to have their vote against ("nay") documented. Members can abstain, in which case they are treated as though they were not present to vote. There are various reasons for abstaining. It is a common way to unofficially register disagreement with the official party line about how to vote. In instances where the member of one party is absent due to illness, personal emergency, or travel, a pairing convention exists whereby a member of the opposing party agrees to refrain from casting a vote. Pairing is typically arranged by party whips on a case-by-case basis, and becomes particularly important in minority government situations when a single vote can topple a government.

In the Canadian Parliament, where there are two chambers, a bill that passes through either the House of Commons or the Senate must then pass through the other chamber via the same process. Bills may be introduced in either chamber, except those involving government spending, which must be initiated in the House of Commons by a member of cabinet. A bill that does not make it through both chambers during a legislative session because the legislature is prorogued or dissolved is said to "die on the order paper" and must be re-started from the beginning in a future session.

Several steps remain after a bill is supported by a majority of members who are present for third reading. The endorsed bill must be signed into law by the GG (federal bills), LG (provincial bills) or commissioner (territorial bills). The signing is called **royal assent** and affirms the consent of Canada's formal executive, where sovereignty ultimately rests. Bills that are sent for royal assent typically contain a proclamation date indicating when their provisions come into force. This allows governments to delay the implementation of an act to permit Canadians time to adjust. Lastly, cabinet or individual ministers may be called upon to pass **regulations** to implement the terms of the legislation. Often, the substance of a law is found in how it is to be administered, making regulations that are published in the *Gazette* an important source of information for those affected. The *Gazette* is the official journal listing government appointments, changes to laws and regulations, and other notices.

Legislators have many additional tasks. They often vote on **motions** seeking to bind Parliament to a particular course of action. Among other things, motions may be used to censor, suspend, or even expel members; to officially support or condemn the actions of other governments; or to apologize on behalf of the government. Motions can enable non-ministers to have some success, even if their bill is defeated. An example is the private member's bill initiated by a New Democrat MP in the thirty-eighth Parliament and twice by another NDP MP in the forty-first Parliament. They sought to eliminate the GST on menstrual products, arguing that these essential items should not be subject to the sales tax. The topic attracted the government's attention in 2015 when activists got involved to urge Canadians to write to MPs, to sign petitions, to participate in protests and join the conversation on Twitter under the hashtag #NoTaxOnTampons. The NDP member used an opposition day to introduce a motion, worded as follows: "That, in the opinion of the House, the government should remove the GST from feminine hygiene products." The motion passed unanimously, with 258 yeas and 0 nays. Soon afterward, on 1 July 2015, the Conservative government announced that the GST henceforth no longer applies on pads, tampons and other menstrual products sold in Canada. The tax might still apply if it were not for the PMB initiated by an opposition backbencher.

This legislative process sounds orderly and straightforward. However, both the government party and the opposition deploy tactics in a bid to achieve their objectives. The governing party has the most tools available. It can stipulate a maximum length of time a bill can be debated. It can invoke **closure** on a bill, which cuts off debate and permits one day to complete that stage of the three-reading process. But the opposition has its own repertoire of strategic manoeuvres. Chief among these is the **filibuster**, which is a coordinated effort among non-government members to protest a bill by delaying its passage. In a filibuster, members take turns speaking over and over again, sometimes about nonsense, purely to avoid ceding the floor to the government. During a filibuster, members may talk all through the night and may schedule rotations so that members can take naps in their offices before returning to the chamber. As with any activity in the legislature, filibusters are governed by different rules in different jurisdictions.

royal assent
The final stage of legislation being approved, involving the monarch's representative signing the bill into law.

regulation
A directive passed by the executive specifying how the primary legislation is to be administered.

motion
A proposed parliamentary action.

closure
A procedure requiring that debate conclude so that the question may be addressed by the end of the sitting.

filibuster
The extension of parliamentary debate, typically by opposition members, to delay the passage of a bill.

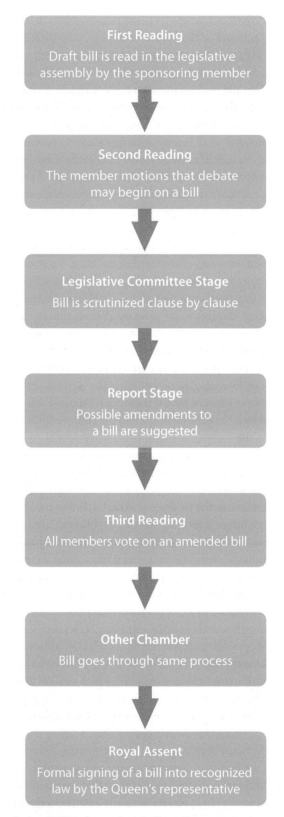

First Reading

Draft bill is read in the legislative assembly by the sponsoring member

Second Reading

The member motions that debate may begin on a bill

Legislative Committee Stage

Bill is scrutinized clause by clause

Report Stage

Possible amendments to a bill are suggested

Third Reading

All members vote on an amended bill

Other Chamber

Bill goes through same process

Royal Assent

Formal signing of a bill into recognized law by the Queen's representative

Figure 6.5 | How a Federal Bill Becomes Law in Canada

Territorial Legislatures

So far, our discussion focuses on how legislatures operate at the federal and provincial level. The territories were granted responsible government amid the patriation debates of the late 1970s. Until then, federally appointed commissioners served as heads of government; today, premiers do. Most of the content up to this point applies to Yukon, the only one of the three territories whose legislature has political parties. Legislatures in Northwest Territories and Nunavut operate on the same Westminster parliamentary traditions as those in other jurisdictions. They contain executives that are accountable to the legislature, and non-cabinet members who hold governments to account; decisions are made based on majority rules (not unanimity); and the principles of ministerial responsibility and cabinet solidarity apply. However, there are differences because those two territories operate **consensus government** systems without political parties.

In the absence of political parties, executives in NWT and Nunavut are chosen by the committee of the whole, which is to say by a vote of all members of their respective territorial assemblies. Territorial representatives select the speaker, premier, and members of the cabinet by means of secret ballot. Afterward, the premier assigns portfolios to individual ministers.[15] Members of the legislature who are not part of cabinet serve as critics of the government. Their role as critics is less adversarial and less coordinated than is found among provincial opposition party members.

Consensus government has roots in Indigenous principles of governance. It is grounded in the notion that community decisions should be made through listening and a collaborative search for solutions. Consensus government is more of a process or culture than a decision-making formula. As noted earlier, the NWT and Nunavut legislative chambers have seats arranged in a circular pattern, reflecting the Indigenous traditions of collaboration over conflict. Despite its name, consensus government does not involve the absence of opposition, conflict, or debate.

The simplest way to conceive of this form of government is to consider how Canadian legislatures operated before the advent of the modern political parties. Northwest Territories and Nunavut encounter many of the challenges that led to the development of political parties elsewhere in Canada. They neither enjoy the benefits nor suffer the downsides of party discipline. As with any political system, consensus government has its share of advantages and disadvantages, such as changing a premier without much public explanation.

Political parties are not formally banned from practising in those territories. Doing so would constitute a breach of the Charter right to assembly, mentioned in Chapter 2. Rather, the political culture in these jurisdictions, grounded in Indigenous traditions, militates against the development of political parties. Those candidates who do appear aligned with parties, or who appear to be forming them, face stiff resistance. This said, the member of Parliament for each territory is affiliated with a federal party, and federal cabinets often feature at least one member from these electoral districts.

consensus government
A system of governance that operates without political parties.

Concluding Thoughts

Compared to an idyllic view of democracy, the role of Canadian legislators may appear far less glamourous. Most of the time, legislative debates are routine matters of business rather than high-minded debates over ideology and public policy. The outcome of most votes is a foregone conclusion, and rarely does the fate of a law or government hang in the balance. In general, party discipline has strengthened, and legislative institutions operate according to many of the same broad principles and general rules that they did in the nineteenth century. This level of predictability provides important stability to the system. Governments in Canada remain accountable to their respective legislatures, regardless of the level of drama involved in their day-to-day functioning. Discussed in the next chapter, both the executive and legislature have important relationships with the third branch of Canadian government: the judiciary.

For More Information

How democratic are Canadian legislatures, really? David Docherty audits the various federal, provincial, and territorial assemblies in *Legislatures* (UBC Press, 2004).

Are hung parliaments underappreciated in Canada? Peter Russell lays out his case in *Two Cheers for Minority Government: The Evolution of Canadian Democracy* (Emond Montgomery, 2008).

What can be done about political parties preparing scripts for MPs who parrot the party line? The Samara Centre for Democracy explores this in "Flip the Script: Reclaiming the Legislature to Reinvigorate Representative Democracy" (2018). Find out more at www.samaracanada.com.

What do MPs do outside Ottawa? Royce Koop, Heather Bastedo, and Kelly Blidook examine *Representation in Action: Canadian MPs in the Constituencies* (UBC Press, 2018).

How does the size of the executive affect the ability of the legislature to hold government accountable? Paul E.J. Thomas and J.P. Lewis explore "Executive Creep in Canadian Legislatures" (*Canadian Journal of Political Science*, 2018).

Is it possible to renew the Senate of Canada? Contributors to Jennifer Smith's *The Democratic Dilemma: Reforming the Canadian Senate* (McGill–Queen's University Press, 2009) identify the obstacles and opportunities facing would-be reformers.

How does the Senate compare to similar upper houses elsewhere? David E. Smith examines *The Canadian Senate in Bicameral Perspective* (University of Toronto Press, 2006). Also consider a report authored by the government representative in the Senate, Peter Harder, titled "Complementarity: The Constitutional Role of the Senate of Canada" (2018).

How does consensus government work in the North? Ailsa Henderson "Rethinks Political Culture" in her book *Nunavut* (UBC Press, 2007).

Want to review throne speeches and budget speeches, and even compare them to political party platforms? The Poltext Project compiles hundreds of these documents: http://poltext.org.

Looking for a law? The Canadian Legal Information Institute (CanLII) maintains a database of all existing and inactive legislation from all orders of government: www.canlii.org.

Want to read bills currently before a legislature, or what is said during the debates? The Bora Laskin Law Library at the University of Toronto has created a portal for access to all bills, statutes, debates, and regulations across Canada. Search online: Current Canadian legislation Bora Laskin Law Library.

Does the House of Commons code of conduct on sexual harassment go far enough? Read a feminist perspective authored by Cheryl N. Collier and Tracey Raney in "Canada's Member-to-Member Code of Conduct on Sexual Harassment in the House of Commons: Progress or Regress?" *Canadian Journal of Political Science* (2018).

Deeper Inside Canadian Politics

1. There are plenty of ways for people to learn more about the business of a legislature:

   - Canadian legislatures offer guided tours of the building and the floor of the assembly.
   - When the legislature is sitting, the proceedings are usually broadcast on television and online, and the public is allowed to sit in the gallery to watch in person. Committee meetings are somewhat less accessible but, depending on the situation, may be open to the public.
   - Senators and elected representatives may be available to meet with constituents.
   - A popular job for many students is as a legislative page. A page is hired by the office of the speaker to provide assistance with proceedings, such as distributing official documents to members, filling water glasses, and attending to special requests.
   - Students are often hired to act as tour guides, particularly on Parliament Hill.
   - Finally, across Canada there are many Model Parliament organizations, where students get the opportunity to role-play in the legislature.

2. Some people argue that backbenchers have more power in minority government situations than in majority governments. Do you agree? Why or why not?

3. Is there a role for appointed senators in a twenty-first-century Canadian Senate? If so, what is it?

Professor Profile

Jonathan Malloy

Parliament, political institutions, Ontario politics
Past president of the Canadian Study of Parliament Group

Jonathan Malloy

Jonathan Malloy has been studying Canadian parliamentary institutions for more than a quarter century. He researches prime ministerial leadership and the interplay of political institutions with Canadian society. He is a keen observer of Ontario politics and was an intern at Queen's Park in Toronto.

Here is what Jonathan Malloy told us about his career path from when he was an undergraduate student, why he is drawn to his area of specialization, what is challenging about studying Canadian politics, and what advice he has for students.

* * *

As a high school student I was fascinated by politics and was sure I would study political science at university, although I wasn't really sure what the difference was. In my first year at the University of Waterloo, I took a public-policy course with Professor Sandra Burt. I remember my delight in how she encouraged us to step back and really analyze the different sides and factors affecting a public issue (a core aspect of political science), and not just argue for a particular solution (the essence of politics). My later first true course on Canadian politics was with Peter Woolstencroft, who further forced me to rigorously evaluate all sides and defend my analysis. An Albertan by background, he also injected a huge understanding of Western Canada into this Ontario kid.

At the end of my BA, I applied for the Ontario Legislative Internship Program (OLIP), as I was still drawn to the idea of politics and action. Being an OLIP intern set the direction of my career. I learned I did not have the quick instincts to be a political staffer. But I was fascinated by the ambiguity of legislatures and the conflicting understandings and expectations of them. For example, should rep-

resentatives vote on the basis of their own views, the views of their constituency, or the views of the party on whose label they were elected? Each can be correct. This question of institutional ambiguity—the multiple and conflicting expectations placed on public institutions—has been the most defining aspect of my research ever since.

The most challenging aspect of studying legislatures is their black-box nature. While they operate in the public spotlight, legislators' real power and influence is subtle and often behind the scenes. It's there, but can be difficult to trace and pinpoint, and good research needs to avoid quick assumptions and narrow conclusions about what's really going on.

The most surprising aspect of studying legislatures is the cyclical nature of the debates. People have been complaining for a very long time about the decline of Parliament. But the exact reasons keep shifting; solutions lead to new problems; and what were once seen as bad times may be later selectively viewed as a golden age. Legislatures are paradoxes and puzzles, which make them intellectually fascinating. But what goes around usually comes around again.

My advice for students studying Canadian politics—and anything else for that matter—is the importance of developing a balance of normative and empirical analytical ability. The capacity to passionately and rigorously argue for something, and yet also to be able to step outside and look at your own ideas externally with a critical eye, and to appreciate and understand why others hold different views, is a valuable skill often in short supply, and badly needed in public and political life in Canada and elsewhere.

Up for Debate

Is strict party discipline necessary in Canadian legislatures?

THE CLAIM: YES, IT IS!

Party discipline is a necessary element of a healthy democracy in Canada.

Yes: Argument Summary

Party discipline has a poor reputation because it is misunderstood. Romanticists who espouse a greater role for backbenchers are blind to the repercussions of an undisciplined political party. Ensuring that parliamentarians vote as a cohesive group, deliver the same public messages, and support each other are among the many benefits of party discipline. In particular, the practice ensures stability in government and removes the opportunity for critics to attack the government over petty internal differences. Moreover, it forces members of each caucus to reach compromises on political issues. In the end, like all forms of democratic authority, party discipline carries with it as many benefits as burdens.

Yes: Top 5 Considerations

1. Party discipline emerged as the cure for the so-called "loose fish" syndrome that characterizes most non-partisan legislatures. By providing order and predictability to voting, the mechanisms of party discipline prevent the legislative process from devolving into a series of inefficient, one-off negotiations on every bill or motion. It allows the monarch's representative to select a viable, stable political executive to lead the country. In a parliamentary system of government, being assured of how a parliamentarian will vote is crucial for the government party and ministers' bills because they risk defeat if the confidence of the legislature is not maintained.

2. Party discipline provides accountability. Canadians know what they're voting for in an election, and can hold all members of that party to account for their performance toward meeting the objectives stated in their platforms. In the absence of parties, representatives would have very narrow and often conflicting mandates, making it difficult to make gains on behalf of their constituents, let alone achieve consensus on issues of importance to all citizens.

3. By concentrating power in the party leadership, party discipline prevents manipulation of the legislative process by small groups of legislators or influential outsiders. Campaign finance rules place the heaviest responsibility and restrictions on party leaders. Discipline inhibits legislator-level manipulation of the system by lobbyists and special interests.

4. Most Canadians will never get inside the closed doors of caucus meetings. This is often where the real conflict in Canadian democracy takes place. When the legislature sits, party leaders and/or ministers meet with caucus to discuss their plans. If the pitch falls flat, the idea is unlikely to proceed. Competing ideas are negotiated, with the resulting policy or decision reflecting a broad consensus among the party's elected representatives.

5. Leaders can be overthrown by rank-and-file party members through a formal leadership review if that individual's actions are viewed as draconian or against the best interests of their followers. Caucuses can force the resignation of party leaders, including first ministers. These incidents are rare, perhaps because the fear of revolt deters leaders from overexerting their power.

Yes: Other Considerations

- Simply because members emerge united from cabinet, caucus, or constituency meetings doesn't mean that they didn't disagree vehemently behind closed doors.

- Publicizing internal grievances provides opposition parties, pundits, and the media with ammunition to critique the party, its members, and its ideals. History shows that only political parties that demonstrate strength and stability through unity are trusted by Canadians to form and manage government.
- Party discipline is the antidote to chaos, inefficiency, and narrow-mindedness in Canadian legislatures. It prevents the type of grandstanding and brinksmanship found in systems like the United States, where weak party discipline empowers individual representatives to hold major initiatives hostage for personal gain.
- Party discipline is not a straitjacket. Politicians have more freedom to speak freely than media portrayals suggest. They leave caucus voluntarily almost as frequently as they are expelled, and many cases of expulsion result from a conscious choice on the part of the member. When they leave, these politicians serve or even campaign as independents. Some are successful in these roles, wielding the balance of power in the legislature and successfully defending their seats.
- Sitting premiers (e.g., Ralph Klein in Alberta) and prime ministers (e.g., Jean Chrétien) have stepped down from office amid pressure from their membership and/or caucus. And they led some of the most stable, popular governments in Canadian history!

THE COUNTERCLAIM: NO, IT ISN'T!

Party discipline is a significant impediment to rigorous political debate in Canada.

No: Argument Summary

Members of Canadian legislatures almost always vote with their party. They are unlikely to speak out against the party's position or leader. They invariably vote in favour of motions that are in the best interests of the party, even if that harms the interests of their constituents. The power of party officials to control perks such as whether a member can speak in the legislature means that parliamentarians are incentivized to follow the instructions of the party whip or risk being sanctioned. The idealized notion of free speech and pluralistic debate in a democracy is therefore contravened by Canada's rigid party discipline. Conformity, command, and control are prized above openness, transparency, and accountability—all to the detriment of constructive democratic debate.

No: Top 5 Considerations

1. Strong party discipline undermines the principles of responsible government, which state that the political executive must maintain the confidence of a majority of members of the legislature. Party discipline makes government members accountable to the premier or prime minister, not vice versa.
2. Every party designates a parliamentarian as a party whip, tasked with ensuring that members fall in line with what the party leadership decrees. In Britain, there are different types of whip votes to signify to parliamentarians the degree of freedom to break ranks, but in Canada even insignificant votes matter. Those who behave independently are sanctioned in ways that include being socially ostracized, having perks removed or withheld, and potentially being pushed out of the party.
3. Those who hold senior positions within a political party, such as the party leader and the house leader, decide which members of their party should be authorized to speak in the legislature and which ones should be appointed to parliamentary committees. One consequence is that the legislative branch is more likely to descend into partisan theatrics at the cost of honest debate.
4. Party discipline stifles democratic debate, or—at the very least—pushes it behind closed caucus and cabinet doors. This is contrary to the principle of transparency, and prevents Canadians from holding their duly elected representatives to account for their actions.
5. There are means of relaxing party discipline without abolishing it entirely. Elsewhere and at earlier points in Canadian history, caucuses held greater control over the selection and removal of leaders, and parliamentarians were allowed to speak their conscience through a greater number of free votes.

No: Other Considerations

- In the Westminster system, political parties are incentivized to promote cohesion so that they alone can control the government. Elected representatives are discouraged by their parties from speaking off-message for fear of creating controversy and losing public favour. The centralization of power in the leader's office means that communication is scripted and parliamentarians are rarely able to pass private members' bills.
- Party discipline can be so stifling that sometimes parliamentarians exit their parties to sit as independents, or they cross the floor to join another party. This is anti-democratic because there is no requirement for a by-election to provide constituents with an opportunity to have their say. The person who was elected on the basis of affiliation with a party may end up working to oppose it.
- Partisan identities and party loyalties run so deep that coalition governments are exceptionally rare in Canada. Revolts against the leader of a Canadian political party are uncommon.
- Party discipline means that there is less likelihood of holding the government to account. Questions asked in the legislature are scripted and are likewise met with responses that stick to party messaging.
- Strong party discipline is not necessary for a fully functioning democracy. Discipline is weaker in the United States and United Kingdom—two of the most stable and effective democracies in the world. Party discipline does not exist at all in Northwest Territories, Nunavut, and the vast majority of municipalities across Canada.

Discussion Questions

- Why do you think party discipline is so strong in Canada compared with other countries that use the parliamentary system of government?
- To what extent is party discipline anti-democratic?
- Suppose that you were a member of Parliament, and an issue that you had passionately supported since childhood arose in the House of Commons. Now suppose that your political party as well as the majority of your constituents were strongly opposed to that very issue. What do you do?
- What kinds of reforms could solve the alleged problem of strict party discipline?
- Under what circumstances would you be inclined to vote for an independent candidate over one running with a major political party?
- What are the strengths and weaknesses of a consensus style of government compared with one using party discipline?

Where to Learn More about Legislative Party Discipline in Canada

Sylvia B. Bashevkin, *Toeing the Lines: Women and Party Politics in English Canada*, 2nd edn (Oxford University Press, 2003).

Kenneth R. Carty, William Cross, and Lisa Young, *Rebuilding Canadian Party Politics* (UBC Press, 2000).

David Docherty, *Legislatures* (UBC Press, 2005).

Paul Geisler, "Will the Reform Act, 2014, Alter the Canadian Phenomenon of Party Discipline?" *Manitoba Law Journal* 38, no. 2 (2015): pp. 17–43.

Monique Guay, "Party Discipline, Representation of Voters and Personal Beliefs," *Canadian Parliamentary Review* 25, no. 2 (2002): pp. 7–9.

Christopher J. Kam, *Party Discipline and Parliamentary Politics* (Cambridge University Press, 2009).

Matthew Kerby and Kelly Blidook, "It's Not You, It's Me: Determinants of Voluntary Legislative Turnover in Canada," *Legislative Studies Quarterly* 36, no. 4 (2011): pp. 621–43.

Anthony Kevins and Stuart N. Soroka, "Growing Apart? Partisan Sorting in Canada, 1992–2015," *Canadian Journal of Political Science* 51, no. 1 (2018): pp. 103–33.

Jonathan Lemco, "The Fusion of Powers, Party Discipline, and the Canadian Parliament: A Critical Assessment," *Presidential Studies Quarterly* 18, no. 2 (1988): pp. 283–302.

Jonathan Malloy, "High Discipline, Low Cohesion? The Uncertain Patterns of Canadian Parliamentary Party Groups," *Journal of Legislative Studies* 9, no. 4 (2003): pp. 116–29.

L. Marvin Overby, Christopher Raymond, and Zeynep Taydas, "Free Votes, MPs, and Constituents: The Case of Same-Sex Marriage in Canada," *American Review of Canadian Studies* 41, no. 4 (2011): pp. 465–78.

Parliament of Canada, *House of Commons Procedure and Practice*, 2nd edn. (2009), www.parl.gc.ca.

Ian Stewart, *Just One Vote: From Jim Walding's Nomination to Constitutional Defeat* (University of Manitoba Press 2009).

7

The Justice System

Inside This Chapter

- What are Canada's legal foundations?
- Who plays the various roles in Canada's justice system?
- How is the justice system structured in Canada?

Inside the Justice System

Most examinations of Canadian democracy separate governance into three distinct branches: the executive, the legislature, and the judiciary. Discussion of the judiciary is about more than the laws, judges, and the courts over which they preside. Canadian justice is an expansive patchwork of provincial, territorial, and federal institutions. Among the many actors are judges and lawyers, ministers and bureaucrats, police and corrections officers. Peering inside the Canadian justice system reveals a few key maxims to consider while reading this chapter.

✔ **Blurry lines separate the political and judicial realms.** Canada's judges are protected by the principle of judicial independence. This prevents politicians from blatantly interfering with the affairs of the courts. Nevertheless, the line becomes blurry considering the politicized nature of judicial appointments and the increasing role of judges in crafting public policy.

✔ **There is more to the justice system than courtrooms and judges.** When you think of the justice system, your first thoughts may evoke judges presiding over courtrooms, where witnesses are called and cross-examined, and decisions are handed down. In fact, the vast majority of activity in the Canadian justice system takes place outside the courtroom. Ministers of justice, Crown attorneys, clerks, magistrates, police officers, prison guards, lawyers, bar associations, public servants, and many other actors support judges in upholding Canadian justice and maintaining law and order.

✔ **Constitutional responsibility for justice is shared—and the federal government does not always hold the upper hand.** The Canadian justice system is complex, with many parts falling under federal, provincial/territorial, or municipal authority. Yet it is highly integrated, meaning that if one order has jurisdiction over a particular area it needs to work closely with its partners to ensure consistency and effectiveness.

UP FOR DEBATE

Do mandatory minimum prison sentences go too far?

Keep this question in mind as you read through the chapter. Consult the end-of-chapter debate supplement for more material to help you engage in an informed discussion of the topic.

Principles of Canadian Justice

Laws are best understood as a set of legal rights and responsibilities. They permit Canadians to live in a free and fair society—provided they live up to certain obligations to the state and to each other. Laws are established by various governments. The responsibility for determining how laws should be interpreted, applied, and enforced falls to the judiciary and the broader justice system. People employed throughout Canada's justice system are subject to some core principles:

1. the rule of law;
2. the rule of judicial impartiality; and
3. the rule of judicial independence.

rule of law
The principle that no one is above the law, and that any powers granted to elected or non-elected officials must be conferred by legislation.

The first of these core principles applies to all Canadians, whether or not they are employed in the justice system. To say that Canadians are protected by the **rule of law** means that all citizens are subject to the same treatment under the justice system regardless of their status or position in society. Everyone is governed by the same set of laws.

People are not subject to arbitrary treatment by those in positions of power. No one in Canada wields any special powers unless conferred on them by law. This principle helps to establish a sense of accountability and orderliness by ensuring that all government actions must be authorized by democratic processes.

The rule of law has been enshrined in English democracy since King John signed the Magna Carta in 1215. It is so fundamental to Canadian justice that it is entrenched in the preamble of the Charter of Rights and Freedoms. Over time, the principle has come to embody the notion that all laws be made transparently and publicly accessible, that they be applied consistently and without discrimination, and that they provide affordable access to justice for all Canadians.

Several rights flow from the rule of law. This includes the right not to be unlawfully detained, otherwise known as **habeas corpus**. A writ (court order) of habeas corpus requires the government to bring a prisoner before the court to determine whether the individual is being detained constitutionally. Without it, Canadians and foreign nationals on Canadian soil could be detained indefinitely without cause. This right forms a core element of the British common-law traditions inherited by Canada, and is entrenched in section 10(c) of the Charter of Rights and Freedoms, which states: "Everyone has the right on arrest or detention . . . to have the validity of the detention determined by way of habeas corpus and to be released if the detention is not lawful."

> **habeas corpus**
> The right not to be detained without cause or due process.

Prior to the introduction of the Charter in 1982, the federal government suspended Canadians' habeas corpus rights on three occasions under the War Measures Act. During World War I, Ukrainian Canadians, suspected communists, and other so-called enemy aliens were detained. During World War II, Canadians of Japanese heritage were removed from their homes and placed in internment camps; smaller in number, those of German ethnicity, Italian ethnicity, and those suspected of having fascist or communist sympathies were also detained. During the October Crisis of 1970, those suspected of domestic terrorism were arrested and held without cause or due process.

The October Crisis remains the only occasion on which Canadians' habeas corpus rights were suspended in peacetime. The event prompted much reflection by Canadians and their leaders on the rule of law. In 1988, the federal government repealed the War Measures Act, replacing it with a new Emergencies Act. The new legislation subjected cabinet's authority to declare an emergency to parliamentary review. Moreover, it ensured that any temporary laws put in place must respect the Charter of Rights and Freedoms. These new protections remain subject to the notwithstanding clause and the reasonable limits clause, meaning that governments can still suspend such rights under extraordinary circumstances.

Two other core principles of Canada's justice system concern the role of judges. Under the rule of **judicial impartiality**, protected by section 11(d) of the Charter, judges are expected to preside over courts to ensure Canadians are "presumed innocent until proven guilty according to law in a fair and public hearing by an independent and impartial tribunal." This means that each side in a court dispute has the opportunity to present evidence. The case must be based solely on that evidence and neither side must have an inherent advantage over the other. Judicial impartiality means that judges must leave their personal opinions and values aside when presiding over these cases. Their decisions must be based on the laws in question and the facts presented. To guard against the possibility of unfair treatment, Canadians are afforded the right to appeal lower-court judgements, provided they have reasonable grounds to believe that the judge acted in a biased fashion or if new evidence can be presented. Judges are barred from engaging in public debate about any

> **judicial impartiality**
> The principle by which judges decide cases based on evidence and an objective interpretation of the law.

THE CANADIAN PRESS/Chuck Mitchell

Wayne Cuddington/Postmedia News

Since the October Crisis (left), Canadians' habeas corpus rights have not been suspended, even during the 2014 attack on Parliament Hill (right). Under what circumstances might it be reasonable for the government to suspend Canadians' habeas corpus rights? What are the dangers of taking such a step?

Inside Canadian Politics

Did Pierre Trudeau Go Too Far During the October Crisis?

In Chapter 4 we touched on the terrorism of the Front de Libération du Québec (FLQ). During the 1960s, that Quebec-based organization committed over 150 violent crimes, including bank robberies, the detonation of hidden bombs, and an explosion at the Montreal Stock Exchange. At least five people died and dozens more were injured. In October 1970, an FLQ cell kidnapped the British trade commissioner, and a second cell kidnapped Quebec's minister of labour. Prime Minister Pierre Trudeau's

government ordered the army to guard Parliament Hill. A famous television interview occurred on the steps of the Parliament building the next day when CBC journalist Tim Ralfe questioned Trudeau about the guards.

> **Journalist (Tim Ralfe, CBC):** . . . what you're talking about to me is choices, and my choice is to live in a society that is free and democratic, which means that you don't have people with guns running around in it.

Prime Minister Pierre Trudeau: Correct.

Journalist: And one of the things I have to give up for that choice is the fact that people like you may be kidnapped.

P. Trudeau: Sure, but this isn't my choice, obviously. You know I think it is more important to get rid of those who are committing violence against the total society and those who are trying to run the government through a parallel power by establishing their authority by kidnapping and blackmail. And I think it is our duty as a government to protect government officials and important people in our society against being used as tools in this blackmail. Now, you don't agree to this, but I am sure that once again with hindsight, you would probably have found it preferable if [the British trade commissioner and the Quebec minister of labour] had been protected from kidnapping, which they weren't because these steps we're taking now weren't taken. But even with your hindsight I don't see how you can deny that.

Journalist: No, I still go back to the choice that you have to make in the kind of society that you live in.

P. Trudeau: Well, there are a lot of bleeding hearts around who just don't like to see people with helmets and guns. All I can say is, go on and bleed, but it is more important to keep law and order in this society than to be worried about weak-kneed people who don't like the looks of a soldier's helmet.

Journalist: At any cost? How far would you go with that? How far would you extend that?

P. Trudeau: Well, just watch me.

Journalist: At reducing civil liberties? To that extent? . . . [Does] this include wire-tapping, reducing other civil liberties in some way?

P. Trudeau: Yes, I think the society must take every means at its disposal to defend itself against the emergence of a parallel power which defies the elected power in this country and I think that goes to any distance. So long as there is a power in here which is challenging the elected representative of the people I think that power must be stopped and I think it's only, I repeat, weak-kneed bleeding hearts who are afraid to take these measures.[1]

Within a matter of days after this interview, the Quebec premier requested deployment of the Canadian army in that province, the federal government invoked the War Measures Act to temporarily suspend civil liberties in Quebec, and the Quebec minister's dead body was discovered in the trunk of a car.

DISCUSSION ITEM

As political leaders, even avowed champions of human rights may be forced to reconcile those interests with the need to maintain national security and public safety.

VOX POP

Do you think the circumstances of the October Crisis warranted the suspension of habeas corpus rights? Why or why not? Do you find it surprising that the only prime minister to suspend habeas corpus rights in peacetime is also the one responsible for later introducing Canada's Charter of Rights and Freedoms? What does it tell you about the perceived gravity of the situation that Pierre Trudeau was willing to take such a measure?

ongoing or previous cases, expressing any political opinions that could lead Canadians to view their decisions as biased, or undertaking business outside of their judicial duties.

Under the final principle, that of **judicial independence**, judges are free from the influence of the legislative and executive branches. Judges have the ability to decide cases without fear of intrusion or retribution by governments. They are afforded political immunity, which includes guaranteed tenure and salaries that are not directly determined by government. They have control over the administration of their courts, which allows judges to decide which cases to hear and how to manage them at trial. Politicians are barred both from interfering in judicial appointments and from publicly commenting on, or privately intervening in, cases before the courts. Without these safeguards, judges could become beholden to political masters, who could withhold or reduce judges' livelihoods if they disagreed with the outcome of a particular case, or micro-manage judges' dockets and procedures. In this sense, judicial independence is key to maintaining the rule of law and preserving judicial impartiality.

The Foundations of Canadian Law

All laws in Canada fall into two general categories (see Table 7.1). **Public laws** are legal rules that impact society as a whole. They define the legal relationships among citizens and organizations, and between citizens and their governments. Criminal, constitutional, and administrative laws all fall under the public category. **Private laws** concern the narrower relationships among individuals and organizations. To illustrate, if someone commits murder, we might at first assume that it would be dealt with under private law because it involved two individuals. However, murder is a punishable crime that is an affront to society at large, and so it is dealt with under public law. Conversely, if two people are in a dispute and no laws that concern the state are broken, then this falls under private law. A disagreement between a landlord and a tenant that escalates to small-claims court is an example.

Private law—again, law that governs the relationships among individuals and organizations in matters that do not have broader public concern—is built on two distinct legal systems in Canada. The first is the British-style **common-law system**, which applies throughout the nine English-speaking provinces and the three territories. It is grounded in the rulings passed down over centuries of court decisions known as case law. Common law is based on the notion that judicial decisions represent the common customs of the community. Hence, certain unwritten rules exist without having been recorded in statutes, like those concerning common-law marriage. In common-law systems, judges are bound to consider previous court rulings as authoritative, using them as precedents on which to base their own decisions. This principle is known as stare decisis, according to which similar cases are treated consistently. Judges may set new precedents in cases involving novel circumstances. Governments may pass laws to overrule these precedents or to codify them. In some cases, governments respond to a court decision striking down a law by doing nothing.

The second form of private law is based on Roman traditions, and applies in Quebec. Legal traditions in the **civil-law system** are grounded in a written civil code. This code serves as a foundation for all other laws concerning non-criminal matters. The preservation of Quebec's civil-law system has been a point of contention since the French relinquished control over their North American colonies in the eighteenth century. Quebec's

judicial independence
The principle by which judges are free from political interference when deciding cases.

public laws
Rules governing individuals' relationships to the state and society.

private laws
Rules governing the relationships among citizens and organizations.

common-law system
A legal order based on customs, usage, and precedent.

civil-law system
A legal order used in Quebec that is based on a written code.

Table 7.1	Public Law and Private Law			
Type of Law	**Aims to Protect**	**Parties Involved**	**Examples of Penalties**	**Sub-types**
Public	Public interests	State + others	Incarceration, community service, fines	Constitutional, criminal, administrative
Private	Private interests	Non-state actors	Loss of custody, compensation, restitution	Family, contract, tort

civil code traces its roots to the 1804 Napoleonic Code and has undergone several rounds of revision. Since 1994, it has contained 10 books relating to areas including basic individual rights; family law; wills and estates; property rights; contract law; mortgages; and legal rights.

Many of these elements align with common-law traditions in the rest of Canada. Yet the uniqueness of the Quebec code requires that lawyers and judges be versed in the civil-law tradition before engaging in cases involving it. For this reason, the Supreme Court of Canada has at least three justices from Quebec, all of whom must have experience with civil law in the province.

While Quebec and the rest of Canada have distinct legal systems governing private laws, all public laws—including criminal, constitutional, and administrative laws—apply throughout the country. All public law in Canada is rooted in the common-law system. Consequently, the province of Quebec has a bijuridical system. Its private laws are based on the civil code and its public laws are based on common law.

Broadly speaking, the federal government has authority over the definition of criminal law, while civil law and the administration of justice are matters of provincial jurisdiction. All other public law matters, including constitutional law and administrative law, are shared between the two orders. More detail on these various branches of public law is provided below.

Functions and Roles in the Justice System

A basic objective of the Canadian justice system is to foster safe and secure communities. It does this by administering a fair and independent process to decide disputes among citizens, their governments, and their various organizations. A number of different actors from a variety of governments must work together to achieve this goal, including cabinet ministers, judges, lawyers, law enforcement officers, and correctional services workers.

Ministers of Justice and Public Safety

Political responsibility for the Canadian justice system is spread across the country. Duties and obligations typically fall under two separate categories. The justice portfolio includes the court system while the public safety portfolio involves all matters of community security. At the federal level, these portfolios are usually assigned to two separate ministers— the minister of justice and the minister of public safety. In most provinces and territories, these responsibilities are divided into separate departments but fall under the minister of justice (see Figure 7.1).

The **minister of justice** is one of the highest-ranking members of a provincial/territorial or federal cabinet. As the title suggests, that minister is responsible for overseeing

minister of justice
The member of the government responsible for the administration of the justice system within a given jurisdiction.

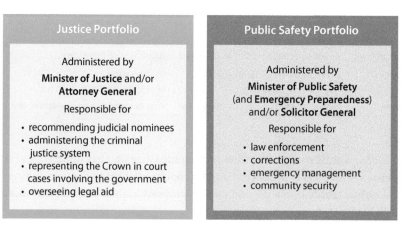

Justice Portfolio	Public Safety Portfolio
Administered by **Minister of Justice** and/or **Attorney General** Responsible for • recommending judicial nominees • administering the criminal justice system • representing the Crown in court cases involving the government • overseeing legal aid	Administered by **Minister of Public Safety** (and **Emergency Preparedness**) and/or **Solicitor General** Responsible for • law enforcement • corrections • emergency management • community security

Figure 7.1 | **Federal Justice and Public Safety Portfolios**

the justice department. Like their cabinet colleagues, justice ministers are subject to the same sort of political influences in making policy decisions involving their portfolio, which for a federal minister includes pressure from the prime minister and the PMO.

attorney general
A cabinet member and the highest-ranking elected legal officer in a jurisdiction.

Most ministers of justice also serve as their jurisdiction's **attorney general**. The role of an attorney general includes recommending judicial nominees to cabinet, administering the criminal justice system, representing the Crown in civil-law matters involving the government, providing legal advice to the rest of the government, and overseeing Canada's systems of legal aid. For this reason, an attorney general is normally expected to be a lawyer. In fulfilling this role, an attorney general is supposed to be protected from political interference. The constitutional principle of prosecutorial independence helps safeguard the rule of law, preventing people from using political leverage to secure harsher or more lenient treatment for certain individuals and organizations. The dual role of a minister of justice and attorney general can create internal tensions. As discussed in Inside Canadian Politics: Should the Roles of Minister of Justice and Attorney General Be Held by Different People? there can be blurred lines between policy and politics, on one hand, and prosecutorial independence, on the other.

solicitor general
A cabinet member typically responsible for the penal and policing aspects of the justice system.

While attorneys general are responsible for the administration of justice, **solicitors general** carry out duties related to public safety. This includes law enforcement, corrections, emergency management, and overall community security. As of 2005, the federal government no longer has a solicitor general, with those duties passing to the minister of public safety and emergency preparedness. Most provinces and territories have solicitors general, although the same person may also be the attorney general and minister of justice.

Ministers responsible for justice and public safety meet face to face at least once a year to discuss areas of shared concern. They gather to discuss access to justice, crime prevention, rehabilitation, and justice system efficiencies. The structured nature of these meetings reflect the highly integrated nature of the Canadian justice system.

The Judiciary

The judiciary serves as an umpire of sorts with respect to interpreting and applying the laws passed by governments across the country. Judges are called upon to decide winners and losers in disagreements over property, disputes over constitutional jurisdiction, conflicts over rights and freedoms, and criminal charges laid by governments against people and organizations.

The judiciary encompasses the entire system of courts across Canada. Generally speaking, the judiciary interprets and applies laws developed by the executive and passed by the legislature. Canadian courts also maintain considerable authority to shape and re-shape the legal landscape. This authority is particularly evident through opinions related to the constitution.

The courts fulfill the following major functions:

- guardianship over the legal system through judicial review;
- adjudication of disputes between Canadians, their governments, their businesses, and other organizations through court cases; and
- guidance of Canada's democratic system through commissions of inquiry.

Guardianship

Among its primary responsibilities, the judiciary is charged with upholding the supreme law of the land, the Canadian constitution. Through a process known as **judicial review**, the courts assess the actions and laws of Canadian governments to ensure they are consistent with the constitution. Thus, the Canadian judicial system is structured on the ability of appointed judges to interpret the constitution and to exercise the power to overrule laws passed by the legislators who were elected by the people.

judicial review
The authority of the courts to adjudicate matters of constitutional law.

These **constitutional law** cases typically involve deciding whether Canadians' rights and freedoms were breached by government, or whether a federal or provincial government has jurisdiction over a particular policy area. The advent of the Charter of Rights and Freedoms in 1982 elevated the role of the courts in deciding the scope of civil rights and liberties in Canada (see Chapter 2). Courts like the Justice Committee of the Privy Council and Supreme Court of Canada have played pivotal roles in deciding the balance of power between provincial and federal governments over time.

constitutional law
The branch of public law dealing with the authority of the state.

Most constitutional law cases arrive in court when citizens and governments challenge each other through criminal or civil court action. In a non-traditional route, cases are referred to the courts by the governments themselves. Such instances are known as **reference cases**. Governments may ask the court to rule whether their own law or that of another Canadian government is constitutional, or they may send the court a series of specific legal questions they would like answered. Governments may refer cases only to the highest court in their respective jurisdictions. This means that the federal government may refer questions, bills, or laws to the Supreme Court of Canada. Provincial and territorial governments cannot. Rather, subnational governments may refer cases only to their respective courts of appeal. Governments are not limited to referring their own laws for judicial review; they may choose to refer laws of other governments, as well.

reference cases
Proceedings initiated by governments asking for the court's opinion on the constitutionality of legislation.

The federal government has referred 16 sets of questions since the Supreme Court became Canada's top court in 1949. Many of the reference cases focused on constitutional matters, including clarifying the process required to reform or abolish the Senate (Reference re Senate Reform, 2014 and Reference re Authority of Parliament in Relation to the Upper House, 1980) and for a province to leave Confederation (Reference re Secession of Quebec, 1998). One reference case challenged a province's unilingual status (Reference re

Inside Canadian Politics

Should the Roles of Minister of Justice and Attorney General Be Held by Different People?

The dual roles of minister of justice and attorney general have co-existed without much public controversy over the course of Canadian history. The minister of justice is a member of cabinet who oversees the Department of Justice and need not be a lawyer. The attorney general is the government's most senior legal advisor. Usually the roles are held by the same minister.

Tensions between the two offices arose in 2019. Federal Minister of Justice and Attorney General Jody Wilson-Raybould, a Liberal MP, had faced pressure from the Trudeau government to strike a deal so that the Quebec-based company SNC-Lavalin could avoid criminal prosecution over foreign bribery. At issue: to what extent should a prime minister and political staff exert influence on an attorney general in the course of handling legal cases?

In 2015, the RCMP brought charges against SNC-Lavalin for fraud and corruption in their dealings with the Government of Libya. If convicted, the company would be ineligible to bid on Canadian government contracts for up to 10 years, severely affecting their business and potentially leading to job losses. In 2018, the Justin Trudeau government amended the Criminal Code to allow for the signing of deferred prosecution agreements (DPA) with those accused of certain offences. These agreements allow criminal charges to be dropped if specific conditions are met. A deferred prosecution agreement is an alternative sentencing procedure

Former Minister of Justice and Attorney General Jody Wilson-Raybould prepares to give testimony about the SNC-Lavalin affair before a House of Commons justice committee hearing on Parliament Hill in February 2019.

that allows companies and their representatives to accept responsibility for wrongdoing. It minimizes the impact a criminal conviction would have on employees, pensioners, and shareholders uninvolved in the offence.

SNC-Lavalin mounted a sustained lobbying campaign to secure a DPA. The Prime Minister's Office and Privy Council Office held numerous conversations with the attorney general to encourage her to overrule the Public Prosecution Service of Canada's refusal to negotiate an agreement. Concern that potential job losses could hurt the Liberal party's election

Manitoba Language Rights). Others focused on matters of public policy (Reference re Same-Sex Marriage) or cases involving the state's involvement with individual people (Reference re David Milgaard Conviction, 1992 and Reference re Ng Extradition, 1991).

Eleven reference cases initiated by provincial governments reached the Supreme Court of Canada. This occurs after those governments refer cases to their respective superior courts, and then the Supreme Court agrees to hear an appeal of the initial decision. Most appeals involved challenges to the scope of the federal government's authority. For example, a series of provincial reference questions coalesced into the Patriation Reference (1981), which established the federal government's inability to seek major constitutional amendments without substantial provincial consent. The Quebec Veto Reference

chances in Quebec was raised. Minister Wilson-Raybould repeatedly refused to entertain the idea of a DPA and warned that efforts to pressure her constituted political interference.

In the ensuing months, Wilson-Raybould was shuffled out of her position, briefly serving as minister of veterans affairs before resigning from cabinet. The episode prompted the resignation of the prime minister's principal secretary; the president of the Treasury Board; and the clerk of the privy council. As well, another Liberal minister resigned from cabinet in solidarity with Wilson-Raybould. The House of Commons Justice Committee held public hearings, during which Wilson-Raybould testified. The prime minister subsequently expelled both former ministers from the Liberal caucus and they sat as Independent MPs.

The ethics commissioner later concluded that the prime minister and his staff acted unethically in their handling of the SNC-Lavalin affair. He concluded that the prime minister contravened the Conflict of Interest Act and breached the principle of prosecutorial independence. Opposition parties called for an RCMP investigation into the matter, and even the resignation of the prime minister. For his part, Prime Minister Trudeau tasked a former minister of justice and attorney general to study the benefits of separating the two roles, as is done in the United Kingdom. The ensuing report concluded that the benefits of having the attorney general in cabinet outweighed the risks to prosecutorial independence. Rather than splitting the roles, the report recommended that stricter protocols are required to guide interactions between the attorney general and other ministers, and that political staff should not engage in such conversations.

In 2019, Wilson-Raybould became the first woman elected as an Independent MP since party labels were added to the ballot in the early 1970s. The re-election of the Liberal government, combined with the Bloc Québécois holding the third-most seats in the House of Commons, raised the possibility that the new attorney general might authorize a DPA for SNC-Lavalin. However, in a minority government situation the opposition parties have a greater opportunity to hold the government and attorney general to account. The Conservatives in particular were adamantly opposed to a negotiated agreement to drop criminal charges against the Quebec-based company.

DISCUSSION ITEM

As members of government, attorneys general may be subject to political pressure.

VOX POP

What are your thoughts about the SNC-Lavalin affair? To what extent would separating the roles of the minister of justice and attorney general help shield the latter from political interference? Do the potential benefits of fusing the two roles outweigh the potential costs?

established that this consent did not have to be unanimous (Reference re Amendment to the Canadian Constitution, 1982). The Quebec government successfully challenged parts of federal legislation regarding assisted human reproduction as being beyond Parliament's authority (Reference re Assisted Human Reproduction Act, 2009). A similar challenge by the Alberta government regarding the registering of firearms was rejected by the Court (Reference re Firearms Act, 2000). Another reference case in Saskatchewan helped establish the definition of effective representation when it comes to designing electoral maps (Reference re Provincial Electoral Boundaries, 1991). The relative paucity of reference cases illustrates that politicians and governments rarely refer questions or legislation to the courts for judicial review.

Even so, the courts have played a major role in the evolution of Canadian federalism. Their decisions have served to bolster central government authority in certain areas and at particular points in time; in others, judges have contributed to the decentralization of Canadian federalism discussed at length in Chapter 3. Overall, the courts minimized the powers granted to the federal government by offering a limited interpretation of the "peace, order, and good government" (POGG) clause in the constitution. This restricted the federal government's authority over the economy to international and interprovincial matters. The provinces' consent would be required before signing a treaty impacting their areas of jurisdiction. The JCPC expanded the provinces' purview over property and civil rights. They gained authority over large policy areas like liquor control and labour. While the Supreme Court offered a more balanced view of Canadian federalism after World War II, the early JCPC rulings helped Canada evolve into a highly decentralized federation, aside from the temporary wartime solidarity and enhanced federal powers that came with it.

Adjudication

The courts fulfill a broader adjudication role. They ensure that private disputes over property and contracts are settled in a fair and just manner, and that charges, regulatory decisions, or other disputes between citizens and their government are resolved. Adjudication involves either criminal or civil law.

criminal law
Body of legal rules governing misconduct affecting both victims and society as a whole.

Criminal law involves activities that, while often harming individuals, have a broader effect on society as a whole. Criminal law thus falls within the realm of public law. When someone acts violently toward another person—for example, committing assault or robbery—this is seen as both an offence against the victim and as a crime against the community. Such crimes offend society's core values of civility and violate everyone's sense of security. Section 91 of the Constitution Act, 1867, establishes that the power to define crimes is a federal responsibility. The Criminal Code of Canada contains hundreds of criminal offences. It lists the range of penalties that judges may impose, including jail time, probation, community service, fines, and other sanctions. The federal Youth Criminal Justice Act contains a similar catalogue of offences and sentences for individuals aged 12 to 17. Citizens accused of a crime that is punishable by at least five years' imprisonment have the right to choose trial by jury or trial by judge alone. Judges or juries in criminal cases must render verdicts based on proof beyond a reasonable doubt. The burden of proof falls to the Crown, as accused persons are considered innocent until proven guilty.

Criminal laws apply to private parties in Canada. This extends beyond individual citizens to businesses, unions, interest groups, and other organizations. The federal criminal law power includes areas such as environmental protection, for instance, meaning that companies can be charged for polluting. Criminal law in Canada is part of a broader category of penal laws that make certain acts or behaviours illegal. Provincial/territorial laws and municipal bylaws may impose penalties, including fines for speeding and public intoxication.

Governments have alternative dispute-resolution processes to help settle cases outside the traditional courtroom. Out-of-court negotiation, mediation, and arbitration can avoid the adversarial, costly nature of court cases while reducing the demands on an overburdened court system. Indigenous justice initiatives exist in several provinces and territories. These approaches aim to establish culturally sensitive alternatives and supplements

Inside Canadian Politics

How Has the Death of Colten Boushie Shaped Views of the Justice System?

The justice system is imbued with many of the same controversies found elsewhere in Canadian democracy. Consider the 2018 trial of a 56-year-old white man, Gerald Stanley, who was charged with the murder of a 22-year-old Cree man, Colten Boushie.[2] Two years earlier in rural Saskatchewan, five Indigenous persons were travelling in an SUV that got a flat tire. One of them tried to break into a truck on a ranch. They then drove the SUV to Stanley's farmstead. One of them got onto an all-terrain vehicle and tried to start it, prompting Stanley's son to yell. Boushie and two of his friends remained in the SUV. Stanley kicked the SUV and his son broke the windshield with a hammer. Accounts of what happened next differ considerably—but the inescapable fact is that during the altercation Stanley shot and killed Boushie with a handgun. Stanley was charged with murder. During the trial he maintained that his gun went off by accident. Stanley was acquitted by what appeared to be an all-white jury. After the verdict, members of Boushie's family and Indigenous leaders called for

Participants in a vigil in Montreal show support for Colten Boushie's family following the acquittal of the Saskatchewan farmer Gerald Stanley, who had been charged in connection with Boushie's death.

THE CANADIAN PRESS/Ryan Remiorz

changes to the justice system. The federal minister of justice and attorney general was among a number of politicians who tweeted that Canada's justice system needs to be improved.

DISCUSSION ITEM

The Canadian justice system is subject to political and colonial controversies that confront other government institutions.

VOX POP

Was justice served in this case? What is the likelihood that the verdict would be different if the Indigenous status of those involved were different? Was it appropriate for federal officials to comment on the verdict? Are justice system reforms necessary and, if so, what sorts of changes are required?

to the criminal justice system. Sentencing circles are one such innovation, with judges inviting the offender, victims, elders, social services, lawyers, family, and supporters to discuss possible sentencing outcomes. While the judge is not bound by the circle's recommendations, this style of **restorative justice** focuses on rehabilitation and reconciliation with the victims, and allows for community input into the decision.

restorative justice
Drawn from Indigenous traditions, a set of principles that emphasizes repairing relationships among criminal offenders, their victims, and the community.

administrative law
The branch of public law involving the review of government decisions and disputes between citizens and state agencies.

administrative tribunals
Quasi-judicial bodies empowered to decide administrative law cases, and whose decisions may be appealed to the court system.

civil law
The body of rules governing disputes between or among private parties.

Courts may also be called upon to adjudicate cases based on **administrative law**. This involves determining whether government actors perform their duties in an authorized and fair manner. Typically, administrative law cases require adjudicators to decide whether a government official or body acted within its statutory authority, or whether it applied legal rules in an unbiased manner. Most administrative law cases are heard by **administrative tribunals**. Consequently, a number of disputes are resolved without resorting to the courts. Administrative tribunals hear disputes over the application of regulations concerning property, human rights, and government benefits, among other topics. These tribunals operate parallel to the court system. Their decisions may be reviewed by superior or federal courts.

Civil law deals with issues of a more private nature. This is why civil law is synonymous with private law, discussed above. Civil law involves harm to individuals but not necessarily to the broader community. An individual who feels wronged may launch a lawsuit asking the court to adjudicate a dispute over contracts, property sales, child support, negligence, or other matters. The government has no role in civil proceedings unless the state is the plaintiff (the suing party) or the defendant (the respondent), or its officials are called to testify. The court must decide whether the case has merit and, if so, what sort of corrective action is required of the losing party. Corrective action typically involves paying restitution to cover damages. Judges and juries decide civil-law cases on a balance of probabilities. They must weigh whether it is more or less likely that the defendant caused harm to the plaintiff. This standard of proof is considerably lower than that required for a finding of guilt in criminal proceedings, which is guilt beyond a reasonable doubt.

Guidance

The judiciary may be called upon to lead task forces, inquests, and commissions of inquiry into matters of public-policy or public-sector misconduct. Government initiates these fact-gathering missions when they sense that an issue of public importance was mishandled. Generally speaking, a task force is comprised of a group of people who examine a topic related to their specific expertise. For instance, a task force of experts might be struck to investigate how the government should help workers transition out of a sector of the economy that is being phased out, such as coal mining. Alternatively, public inquests are led by subject-matter experts who examine the circumstances around someone's death. A coroner could lead an inquest to examine whether personnel who responded to a 911 call could have saved someone from dying if first responders had handled the emergency differently.

A **commission of inquiry** is a broader undertaking. It has the power to formally call witnesses to testify under oath and invite written submissions from the public. The topics that commissions of inquiry investigate are wide-ranging. Examples include a forensic audit of government spending, examining botched testing in the healthcare system, establishing why fisheries are in decline, analyzing the failings of a megaproject, and so forth. All of these types of panels collect evidence to inform a final report to the government. Depending on the mandate given to them by the government, these commissions may consult broadly and offer a set of wide-ranging recommendations, or report back on a narrower set of questions.

Judges are often trusted to investigate controversial issues confronting governments or communities. This is because they are highly respected for their independence, fairness,

commission of inquiry
An independent body of experts created by a government to investigate an issue of great importance.

Royal commissions are discussed on page 261 of Chapter 8, on the public policy and the bureaucracy.

and skills in inquisition. For instance, a judge led the Royal Commission on Equality in Employment. Another led a series of commissions into a variety of matters including child and family law, the construction of the Mackenzie Valley Pipeline, Indigenous healthcare, and electoral reform in Vancouver. Other commissions of inquiry are led by academics, former politicians, or other experts.

The highest-profile commissions of inquiry typically focus on government scandals. For example, the Government of Quebec appointed a Superior Court justice to investigate corruption in the province's construction industry. Another inquiry looked into allegations that a former Canadian prime minister secretly accepted thousands of dollars from a businessman involved with negotiating the purchase of government aircraft. Discussed in Chapter 8, Justice John Gomery oversaw the Commission of Inquiry into the Sponsorship Program and Advertising Activities. Many justices play such prominent roles in the proceedings that their names become synonymous with their investigations (e.g., the Gomery Commission).

All told, judges have led hundreds of independent inquiries in Canadian history. Commissioners' reports are not binding on the government of the day. Nevertheless, their recommendations often influence public opinion and form the basis of policy debate. There is considerable media attention when a high-profile task force, inquest, or commission of inquiry publicly releases its final report. A member of cabinet will announce what the government intends to do about the recommendations. The government's response can range from a vague promise to consider the report to a firm commitment to implement all recommendations as written. For instance, when the Truth and Reconciliation Commission made 94 calls to action, governments and many public bodies across Canada committed to respond to them.

Peace Officers

Canada's police and prison systems are under civilian control. Law enforcement and incarceration are not responsibilities of the military nor are they delegated to private security firms. They are matters of public administration, like those discussed in Chapter 8. Yet they are also integral to our understanding of how the justice system functions. In Canada, most **peace officers**—police, sheriffs, customs officers, corrections officers, parole officers, conservation officers, and so on—are specially trained government employees. They are responsible for enforcing a host of laws within their respective authorities. The laws that they administer range from those found in the federal Criminal Code to those in provincial/territorial statutes. This means that provincial peace officers are empowered to enforce many federal and provincial/territorial laws. Peace officers in Canada are separate and apart from special constables, who are employed by universities, transit authorities, and other public bodies, and private security personnel, who patrol businesses including retail stores. Special constables do not have the authority to enforce provincial/territorial or federal laws and are highly regulated by Canadian governments.

peace officer
A specially trained individual granted government authority to enforce laws.

Crown Attorneys

Peace officers who uncover evidence of a crime turn over this information to other officials in the justice system. In criminal cases, **Crown attorneys** decide whether to prosecute alleged offenders on behalf of the victim and community as a whole. Such crimes are

Crown attorney
A lawyer who acts on behalf of the government when deciding how to pursue criminal cases.

Inside Canadian Politics

How Was the Missing and Murdered Indigenous Women and Girls Inquiry Conducted?

Prime Minister Justin Trudeau announced the formation of a National Inquiry into Missing and Murdered Indigenous Women and Girls in 2015. The Inquiry's mandate was to "look into and report on the systemic causes of all forms of violence against Indigenous women and girls, including sexual violence," as well as "the underlying social, economic, cultural, institutional, and historical causes that contribute to ongoing violence . . ." The work included reviewing police files, meeting with survivors and victims' families, and providing recommendations to governments. The federal government chose Marion Buller to be chief commissioner. Buller is a member of the Mistawasis First Nation and the first Indigenous woman appointed as a Provincial Court Judge in British Columbia. The investigation was officially supported by provincial and territorial governments across the country, which passed legislation empowering commissioners to examine all areas of jurisdiction.

THE CANADIAN PRESS/Adrian Wyld

From left to right, Chief Commissioner Marion Buller and Commissioners Brian Eyolfson, Qajaq Robinson, and Michèle Audette prepare the final report of the National Inquiry into Missing and Murdered Indigenous Women and Girls to give to the federal government at the closing ceremony in Gatineau in June 2019.

considered in terms of their impact on society. Victims are not required to press charges. This said, Crown attorneys work with victims and police to determine whether criminal cases proceed to court. They determine the specific charges and proposed penalties. Crown attorneys are appointed and directed by attorneys general across Canada and fall under their direction. Consequently, provincial governments may enforce the same federal laws in different ways. This illustrates the complexities of Canada's justice system. Authority over the definition and administration of criminal law is divided between the federal and provincial orders, respectively.

The Structure of the Justice System

As discussed above and illustrated in Figure 7.1, Canada's justice system is divided into two main portfolios, with the courts on one side and public safety on the other. Each component divides responsibilities among the federal and provincial orders, with provincial governments devolving a number of duties to their respective municipalities. In this sense, the Canadian justice system is highly integrated. It requires federal–provincial/territorial coordination to ensure an appropriate level of consistency across the country.

The Commission faced logistical challenges due to the many different sets of laws governing public inquiries—federal law, ten provincial sets of laws, and laws in the three territories. Privacy legislation made it difficult to obtain contact information from families and survivors. Federal government policies related to hiring and the procurement of office space imposed long delays. These challenges were complicated by the resignations and firings of several high-ranking support staff and one of the other commissioners.

Criticism ensued that the Commission was taking too long and failing to meaningfully support Indigenous families. The Assembly of First Nations called for Chief Commissioner

Buller's resignation. Buller defended the need to proceed deliberatively, examining all police files and all related issues, human trafficking, sexual exploitation, and substance dependence. The National Inquiry delivered its final report in June 2019. It made 231 recommendations couched within what it deemed a "genocide" due to the colonial systems and actions that led to harms against Indigenous women and girls. The recommendations included calls to improve social, economic, cultural and political circumstances; to create new bodies, such as a national Indigenous and human rights ombudsman; and for governments in Canada to collaborate with Indigenous peoples on a national action plan.

DISCUSSION ITEM

Governments often appoint justices with particular skill sets and backgrounds to lead public inquiries.

VOX POP

Why do you think governments chose a national inquiry as a means of addressing the challenges around missing and murdered Indigenous women and girls? Were critics right to call for the resignation of the Chief Commissioner for the perceived shortcomings of the inquiry? Would a non-judge have been a better choice to lead this Inquiry? Why or why not?

The Courts

Canada's system of courts is both hierarchical and integrated. It is hierarchical in that it allows more serious cases, and appeals from lower levels, to proceed to higher courts. It is integrated in terms of its division of jurisdiction and responsibilities between the two orders of government. The federal and provincial governments are responsible for appointing judges to different courts. Certain courts hear cases related exclusively to areas of federal jurisdiction, as with the Tax Court of Canada and the military courts. Other courts hear cases involving provincial/territorial legislation such as family or traffic courts. Table 7.2 lists the functions of these various bodies. An illustration of the hierarchical organization of the Canadian court system is provided in Figure 7.2.

In each province and territory, except Nunavut, there are two levels of courts. The first consists of provincial and territorial courts. They are typically referred to as section 92 courts because they were created under the provincial powers portion of the Constitution Act, 1867. These courts hear cases on a wide variety of subjects in both public and private law. Referred to as lower courts, they are the true workhorses of the Canadian justice system as they handle the vast majority of cases. To deal more efficiently with caseloads, most jurisdictions have specialized court streams to deal with particular areas of the law, routing cases through small claims, criminal, family, and youth divisions. Municipal bylaw courts deal with matters like traffic violations. The judges of provincial and territorial courts are chosen by the applicable provincial/territorial justice minister or attorney general, and appointed by the lieutenant governor or territorial commissioner on the advice of cabinet. These judges are otherwise known as magistrates.

The second of these two levels are superior courts, whose specific names vary across the country. They are known as section 96 courts because they fall under the federal powers listed in the Constitution Act, 1867. Superior courts have inherent jurisdiction, which means that they are empowered to hear any case that is brought before them, unless that authority is granted to another court explicitly by legislation. Superior courts typically deal with the most serious criminal and civil cases, preside over divorce proceedings, and hear appeals from provincial or territorial courts. Furthermore they review decisions of some provincial agencies, boards, and commissions (ABCs), including administrative tribunals. The judges on superior courts are appointed by the federal justice minister, but they are funded by provincial and territorial governments.

Courts of appeal exist in every jurisdiction as well. As the name suggests, they review decisions from lower courts at both the provincial and the superior level. They hear constitutional cases referred to them by their respective provincial and territorial governments. Unlike lower courts, appeals courts typically feature panels of three judges who, together, preside over cases. As in superior courts, appeals court judges are appointed by the federal government. The operations of the courts themselves are administered and paid for by the provincial and territorial governments.

Table 7.2   Courts of Law in Canada

Court	Judicial Appointments	Court Administration	Areas of Jurisdiction
Provincial/Territorial Courts	Province/Territory	Province/Territory	• matters specifically designated by the province/territory
Superior Courts*	Federal	Province/Territory	• all matters not specifically assigned to other courts • serious cases • divorce • appeals from lower courts • review of decisions made by provincial ABCs and tribunals
Courts of Appeal	Federal	Province/Territory	• appeals arising from provincial/territorial and superior courts • references from provincial/territorial governments
Federal Courts	Federal	Federal	• matters specifically designated by the federal government • review of decisions made by federal ABCs and tribunals
Tax Court of Canada	Federal	Federal	• matters relating to federal tax laws
Federal Court of Appeal	Federal	Federal	• matters of constitutional and administrative law • appeals arising from the Federal Court and Tax Court of Canada
Military Courts	Federal	Federal	• matters relating to military justice (including those under the National Defence Act and Code of Service Discipline)
Court Martial Appeal Court	Federal	Federal	• appeals arising from military courts
Supreme Court of Canada	Federal	Federal	• appeals arising from lower courts • reference cases from the federal government

*Known as Court of Queen's Bench (AB, SK, MB, NB); Provincial Supreme Court (BC, NS, NL, PE, YT, NWT); Superior Court (ON, QC); or Court of Justice (NU).

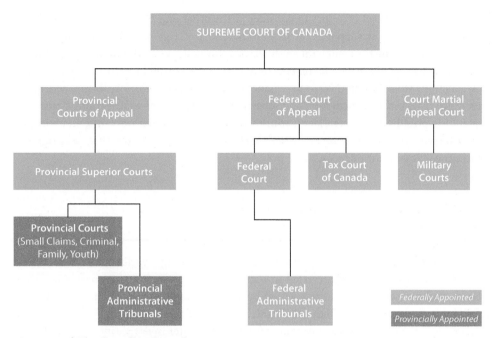

Figure 7.2 | The Canadian Court System

Note: While similar to provincial courts, territorial courts are distinct in ways not represented in this figure.

Federal courts deal with matters involving federal law, such as citizenship and immigration. This may include reviewing the decisions of federal ABCs and tribunals. They may hold hearings across the country. Some federal courts exist to deal with specialized matters. Appeals about taxes are heard by the federal court of appeal and appeals about military justice are heard by the court martial appeal court. Judges for all of these federal courts are appointed by the federal government.

The **Supreme Court of Canada** holds jurisdiction over all laws in Canada and is the country's final court of appeal. Established by the federal government in 1875, it did not assume its status as the highest judicial authority in Canada until 1949, when it displaced the British-based Judicial Committee of the Privy Council (JCPC). The Supreme Court of Canada consists of eight justices and one chief justice. No fewer than five justices may review a particular case, which number 100 per year, on average.

Supreme Court of Canada Canada's final court of appeal.

Whenever someone asserts, "We're going to appeal this all the way to the Supreme Court!" they presume that Canada's top court has the time and interest to consider the appeal. This is not always possible. For the most part, the Supreme Court selects which cases it will hear, and prioritizes matters that are in the national interest. It may choose to hear cases from appellants who have exhausted all levels of appeal in lower courts. Priority is given to cases on a matter of public importance and/or cases that warrant reconsideration by the highest court on a question of law or fact. Other cases proceed directly to the Supreme Court as appeals of right. This includes criminal cases where one of the appeals court judges dissents on a point of law. The Supreme Court hears reference cases submitted to it by the federal government. It may grant leave to hear appeals of provincial/territorial references once they have been adjudicated by courts of appeal.

There is a final set of actors to consider at the other end of the judicial system. The Canadian judiciary is supported at its foundation by a large number of **justices of the peace**. Appointed by the lieutenant governor or commissioner on the advice of provincial/territorial cabinet, these judicial officers have varying responsibilities from jurisdiction to jurisdiction. Most are empowered to conduct hearings outside or before formal court proceedings. This includes mediation and settlement conferences as well as routine business, including presiding over marriages, administering oaths, issuing warrants, and witnessing affidavits. In larger provinces, justices of the peace may preside over bail hearings and cases involving minor offences.

The Judicial Appointment Process

Provincial, Territorial, and Federal Court Appointments

The appointment process for provincial/territorial court judges varies across the country. For the most part, lawyers interested in becoming a judge apply for appointment to the bench and have their applications vetted by a judicial appointments council. In British Columbia, for example, the Judicial Council consists of three judges and a justice of the peace, two lawyers, and three members of the public. After investigating each applicant, the council compiles a list of suitable judges for consideration by the provincial attorney general, who then forwards the selection to the provincial cabinet for approval. If the candidate is endorsed, the premier advances the person's name to the lieutenant governor, who makes the final appointment on the advice of the government.

One level up, the federal government appoints superior court judges through a similar application and vetting process. To be eligible for appointment, candidates must have at least 10 years' experience practising law in the jurisdiction for which they are being appointed, and must meet qualifications listed in section 3 of the Judges Act. Judicial advisory committees are empanelled in each jurisdiction, comprising a representative selected by the provincial/territorial government, lawyers from the Canadian Bar Association and provincial/territorial law society, a senior judge, and members of the public and law enforcement community as selected by the federal government. These committees investigate the candidate's personal and professional history. They render an opinion about whether or not the candidate should be recommended for appointment. The federal attorney general reviews the list of recommended applicants and presents a nominee to the federal cabinet for approval. The prime minister advances the nominee's name to the federal cabinet for consideration when someone is being considered for the chief justice position in a given province or territory. If approved, the prime minister offers this advice to the governor general, who makes the formal appointment on behalf of the Crown.

Judges who were elevated from lower courts do not have to undergo the first part of this screening process. The attorney general may conduct the investigation before submitting the nominee for cabinet consideration. A similar process exists for all federal courts, as well, with a single judicial advisory committee serving the entire country.

Supreme Court Appointments

Appointments to the Supreme Court of Canada follow a unique process that has become more transparent over time. It continues to evolve in the absence of any legislated or

Briefing Notes

The Bar and the Bench

Lawyers are called to the bar before they may practise as barristers in court. In figurative terms, the bar is used to refer to all lawyers who passed their bar examination, who are deemed qualified to represent others in court, and who are members of their provincial/territorial law society. In literal terms, the bar is the barrier that separates the public area at the rear of a courtroom from the front area where the judge, lawyers, parties, and court workers sit. Lawyers selected to serve as judges are summoned to the bench—the raised platform and desk from behind which they will hear cases.

codified rules. Processes not only change from government to government, but individual prime ministers have employed different procedures for different appointments over the course of their terms. The flexibility of the system makes a definitive checklist or process map elusive, although a general flow chart is provided in Figure 7.3.

According to the Supreme Court Act, at least three of the nine justices must be appointed from the province of Quebec. This provision ensures that the court has enough justices who are qualified to preside over cases involving Quebec's civil code. The Quebec government has a unique amount of input in the selection of these justices. It is the only province that is permitted to appoint members to the advisory board that makes recommendations to the prime minister on Supreme Court appointments.

By convention, the remaining six seats on the bench are distributed among the Western provinces (two), Ontario (three), and the Atlantic provinces (one). By custom, one of

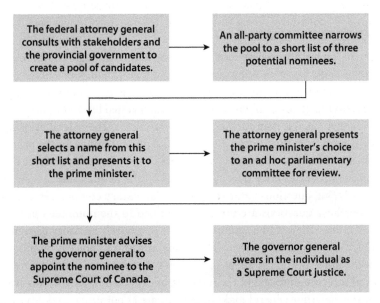

Figure 7.3 | Standard Supreme Court Appointment Process

THE CANADIAN PRESS/Fred Chartrand

Justices of the Supreme Court of Canada pose for a group photo in February 2018. The court is regionally balanced and reflects a diversity of genders, religious beliefs, and English and French backgrounds. What, if anything, does the socio-cultural background of a judge tell us about the individual's ability to serve? Should special measures be taken to ensure that a wider range of socio-economic factors are taken under consideration when selecting justices? To what extent does this matter?

the justices is selected directly from among lawyers, while the remainder are elevated from other judicial positions. A candidate for the Supreme Court must have been a member of that individual's respective provincial/territorial law society for at least 10 years or have served as a superior court judge. From time to time, federal court judges are elevated to the Supreme Court.

In general, the federal attorney general consults widely in the legal community when creating a pool of candidates for a Supreme Court appointment. Consultations occur with senior members of the judicial, legal, and law-enforcement communities, as well as the appropriate provincial government. This pool is then vetted by an all-party selection panel, which narrows the list even further, typically to three. The federal attorney general selects one person from this short list, recommending a nominee for the prime minister's consideration. Most nominees for the Supreme Court of Canada undergo a variety of public screening processes once they are selected by the prime minister. Sometimes this includes answering questions before ad hoc parliamentary committees and in televised interviews. These questions are normally confined to the nominee's professional career and credentials. These ad hoc committees act in a purely advisory capacity; they do not have the power to confirm or veto the prime minister's choice of nominees, but they do promote public awareness about the process. At times, the federal government forgoes this final screening process in the interests of expediency. As with other federal appointments, the governor general makes the ultimate appointment, on advice of the prime minister.

Criticisms of the Appointment Process

At all levels of the judiciary, these screening and vetting procedures are designed to select the most competent judges to serve on Canada's courts. Nevertheless, the processes and their outcomes are subject to steady criticism.

Critics note that the screening and vetting procedures have not ensured gender balance on the bench. Women make up roughly one-third of all federally appointed judges on the Supreme Court, the Federal Court of Appeal, the Federal Court, the Tax Court, various provincial courts of appeal, and superior courts.[3] This disparity persists despite the fact that women make up the majority of law students and nearly 4 in 10 lawyers in Canada. Explanations for the lack of gender balance range from the lack of women applicants to judicial positions to discrimination in the appointments process.

Screening procedures are designed to prevent flagrant patronage appointments to the bench and to protect judges' political independence. Gradually, processes have become more transparent, amid accusations that provincial and federal governments were selecting candidates with close party ties. Some critics argue that this vetting process falls short of placing any sort of constraint on governments. Initial pools and short lists are ultimately determined by attorneys general and their officials. The final recommendation to the Crown lies solely with the first minister and cabinet. Those candidates who are thought to share political values with the governing party may have an edge over those who do not.

Other critics feel that the public screening process for Supreme Court justices is too politicized. Subjecting judicial nominees to public screening disturbs the independence of the judiciary and gives Parliament undue influence over the composition of the Supreme Court. The Canadian judicial appointments system is a far cry from the American one, where nominees for the US Supreme Court are subject to a more highly politicized confirmation process. As discussed, judges in Canada are appointed by governments, not elected by voters. So, too, are the Crown attorneys that prosecute crimes on behalf of the government. Appointing people to legal roles helps to distinguish the Canadian system from the American one, where many judges and prosecutors are elected. The American system holds judges and prosecutors accountable to the public for their decisions. The Canadian system—modelled on British tradition—maintains the judiciary's distance from public opinion. Once appointed, judges serve until a mandatory retirement age, which is age 75 for federal appointees and age 70 for some provincial/territorial judges. They are immune from the possibility of dismissal for any reason short of gross personal or professional misconduct.

There are ways to hold Canadian judges accountable for their actions. A federally appointed judge's decision can be appealed to a higher court. Furthermore, Canadians and governments may lodge a formal complaint with the Canadian Judicial Council about a judge's conduct in presiding over their case. The council consists of a panel of 39 high-ranking judges, who, after investigating the complaint, may recommend to the government that one of their peers be removed from the bench. This decision would be based on the judge's failure to live up to the expected ethical standards. Those standards include being diligent, independent, and impartial, while respecting the importance of integrity and equality in decision-making. Similar judicial councils exist for judges appointed by provincial and territorial governments.

Judicial investigations are exceedingly rare. When they occur, they typically result in the resignation of the accused judge. Removal of a federally appointed judge would require a joint resolution by the House of Commons and the Senate—something that has never occurred. In other words, judges enjoy tremendous security of tenure and remain in their positions regardless of whether the government of the day disagrees with their decisions. Through retirement or resignation, they leave the bench of their own accord.

Law Enforcement

Federal Law Enforcement Agencies and the RCMP

Law enforcement in Canada is another complex component of the justice system. Various orders of government establish police services to oversee compliance with their own legislation and regulations. All told, policing costs governments over $14 billion per year,[4] and encompasses nearly 70,000 officers across Canada. These figures may sound enormous, yet Canada's police force is smaller per capita than those of many other Western democracies, including the United States.

Constitutionally, most policing falls under provincial responsibility in Canada. Provinces are responsible for establishing police forces and setting policing standards within their borders. In practical terms, most provinces devolve authority over city policing to municipal governments, allowing city councils to hire and maintain their own forces. At the same time, most provinces contract the federal government to provide rural and remote police services through the **Royal Canadian Mounted Police** (RCMP). The RCMP was originally founded as the North-West Mounted Police in 1873. The establishment of a federal police presence in the northwestern regions of the continent militated against the lawlessness of the American Wild West. This national police force fulfilled the principle of "peace, order, and good government" found in section 91 of the Canadian constitution. Since that time, the RCMP has evolved to play a significant role in policing the country, and the Canadian Mountie has become one of the most recognizable articles of Canadiana.

The RCMP falls under the direction of the federal minister of public safety and emergency preparedness. It operates through local detachments located throughout Canada. The RCMP provides a variety of services to other police forces across Canada. These are either offered free of charge or through cost-sharing or cost-recovery arrangements with provincial and territorial governments. For instance, to assist police in conducting investigations, the RCMP provides the National Police Services which offers forensics, intelligence, and training. The force maintains several national databases, including the National DNA Data Bank and the Canadian Police Information Centre.

The RCMP enforces federal laws through different sections:

1. commercial crime, including so-called white-collar crimes involving fraud and counterfeiting;
2. criminal intelligence, particularly concerning organized crime like gangs;
3. customs and excise, including smuggling;
4. drugs, including domestic and international trafficking;
5. immigration and passports; and
6. federal law enforcement, including consumer and environmental protection.

The RCMP is responsible for the country's protective policing service. It provides security details for the prime minister, governor general, visiting dignitaries, parliamentarians, federal judges, Supreme Court justices, and others designated by the minister of public safety. As discussed in Chapter 14, the RCMP works in close connection with other federal security agencies to preserve national security.

RCMP
Royal Canadian Mounted Police; pan-Canadian police force commissioned by the federal government.

The principle of peace, order and good government is discussed in Chapter 2, on the constitution.

Inside Canadian Politics

What Is Next for Legalized Cannabis?

In the 2015 federal election, the Liberal Party of Canada committed to "legalize, regulate, and restrict access to marijuana." The pledge included a promise to "keep marijuana out of the hands of children and profits out of the hands of criminals." The choice to decriminalize cannabis (marijuana) use was the federal government's to make by virtue of its jurisdiction over criminal law and the definition and production of illicit drugs. The federal government set the high-level policy direction for legalization. This left many of the strategic and operational decisions to provincial and territorial governments because they control how cannabis is distributed, sold, and consumed within their respective communities. These decisions included setting the legal age of possession, whether to allow private businesses to sell recreational cannabis, and the locations where it can be consumed. All told, hundreds of laws and regulations needed to be adapted in a short period to legalize recreational cannabis in Canada.

In 2018, Canada became the second country in the world to legalize the recreational use of cannabis on the national level. The new system of legalized cannabis use amounts to a patchwork of different approaches from jurisdiction to jurisdiction. Tight timelines prevented meaningful intergovernmental collaboration. Provincial and territorial governments chose to replicate their approaches to alcohol and tobacco regulation, which were already distinct across the country. Canadians are permitted to grow, buy, sell,

Customers wait in the pouring rain to purchase cannabis from a Cannabis NB store in Saint John, New Brunswick on the first day of legalization in Canada in October 2018. How might the federal government have ensured a more integrated system of cannabis legalization across Canada? Is there a better approach to preserve public safety and promote public health in different parts of the country?

and consume cannabis according to rules that differ depending on where they live.

The Trudeau government created a new system to grant pardons to those convicted of cannabis possession, although they stopped short of fully expunging their records. Governments were relatively silent about addressing the legacy of cannabis prohibition on Indigenous and racialized communities, both of whom were disproportionately impacted by prohibition. Advocates continued to pressure governments after legalization of the drug.

DISCUSSION ITEM

Removing criminal penalties was only the first, small step in the legalization of recreational cannabis in Canada.

VOX POP

Do you think specific measures should be taken to address the historical legacy of the prohibition of cannabis? If so, what policies would you prioritize?

In addition to the RCMP, the federal government maintains law enforcement agencies to police its borders, prisons, parks, and oceans. It employs compliance officers, inspectors, investigators, and other peace officers to protect its staff and enforce its laws. These organizations and individuals operate in areas such as the military, the environment, health, food inspection, railways, consumer protection, national buildings (including Parliament), and the postal service.

Law Enforcement in the Provinces and Territories

Provinces have jurisdiction over most areas of law enforcement within their borders. Seven provinces and all three territories sign contracts with the federal government making the RCMP their official provincial police force. Ontario maintains its own province-wide police force, known as the Ontario Provincial Police. Likewise, the Sûreté du Québec polices the province of Quebec. In Canada's easternmost province, the Royal Newfoundland Constabulary operates in the most populous regions, whereas the policing of rural and remote parts of Newfoundland and Labrador are contracted to the RCMP.

Provincial and territorial police—whether the RCMP, on contract, or one of the three stand-alone police forces—are responsible for many forms of law enforcement. Their duties encompass everything from highway traffic enforcement and maintaining provincial firearms registries to conducting province-wide criminal investigations and assisting in inter-provincial cases. Depending on the matter under investigation, provincial and territorial police officers may be empowered to arrest and charge a suspect, or turn the accused and any evidence over to the federal government.

Local law-enforcement duties are typically devolved from the province to its larger municipalities. This includes crime prevention, apprehending suspects, providing victim services, executing warrants, participating in prosecutions of offenders, and otherwise enforcing municipal bylaws to preserve the peace of the community. These larger communities maintain city police forces, like the Brandon Police Service or the Halifax Regional Police. Smaller municipalities unable to afford their own police forces rely on the provincial or territorial government to provide law enforcement through either the provincial police force or the RCMP. Each province and territory employs sheriffs, bailiffs, wardens, and other peace officers. Sheriffs may handle security for the premier and lieutenant governor or commissioner, transfer prisoners, issue subpoenas, and oversee traffic enforcement. Bailiffs often deal with courtroom security, repossessions, and evictions. Wardens are responsible for patrolling parks and jails.

Since the 1970s, the federal government has reached a number of tripartite agreements with First Nations bands and provincial governments to empower First Nations police officers to deliver services on reserve. These officers may act as part of a stand-alone Indigenous police force or as dedicated personnel within existing provincial or federal forces.

Looking at how law-enforcement agencies operate in Alberta offers a good illustration of the varied nature of policing in Canada. Ten police services operate in that province. In its largest communities, the Alberta government devolves law-enforcement powers to municipal governments including Calgary, Edmonton, Lethbridge, Medicine Hat, Taber, and Lacombe. Other provinces do likewise, permitting city and town governments to set up their own local police forces, which operate under provincial authority and according to provincial standards. For rural policing, the Alberta government signed a Provincial Police Services Agreement with the federal government. This agreement contracts the RCMP to enforce laws in towns, villages, Métis settlements, and other municipal districts with fewer than 5000 residents. The RCMP has separate contracts with larger municipalities to provide policing services in their communities. The Alberta government pays 70 per cent of the costs associated with this rural and remote policing; the federal government pays the remaining 30 per cent. Again, similar arrangements exist in all other provinces except Ontario and Quebec, where provincial governments operate their own provincial police services and do not contract the RCMP.

The Alberta and federal governments signed a series of tripartite agreements with some of the largest Indigenous communities in the province. These agreements establish independent First Nations police services operating exclusively on those reserves. The policing services are funded jointly by the federal and provincial governments. For example, on the Blood Indian Reserve, the First Nation manages its own police service in accordance with provincial legislation and regulations. In other First Nations in the province, RCMP members provide law-enforcement services through a series of cost-sharing arrangements with the Alberta government. Similar tripartite arrangements exist throughout Canada as part of the federal First Nations Policing Program.

In addition to these police forces, and like all other provinces, Alberta has corps of conservation officers and investigators, as well as a provincial sheriff's department. The "K" Division of the RCMP maintains over 100 detachments throughout Alberta. These detachments employ more than 2500 officers. Over 2000 of them are on contract to the province and municipalities. The remaining 500 work collaboratively with other police forces in the province to suppress organized crime, halt the drug trade, address terrorist threats, combat economic crimes, protect VIPs travelling throughout the province, and protect Canada's border with the United States. Lastly, law enforcement officers and provincial justice officials work in close co-operation with the RCMP and CSIS to monitor and address any threats to critical infrastructure and public security in the province.

The Correctional System

Much like its court and law enforcement systems, Canada's **correctional system** is highly integrated, with responsibilities divided between the two orders of government. The largest part of Canada's correctional system is run by provincial governments through their solicitors general. Those individuals are responsible for overseeing the detainment of people awaiting trial and those found guilty of minor offences. They oversee the administration of youth detention centres and the conduct of those serving community-based sentences. The federal ministry of public safety operates federal prisons to house Canada's most serious offenders. A limited number of federal institutions house people who have broken federal laws. This includes those awaiting deportation for immigration offences.

Canada's correctional system has institutions to hold people in custody. This includes remand centres, provincial jails, federal penitentiaries, and other facilities. Community supervision programs exist for people on parole, on probation, in community service, or

correctional system
The network of community-based and institutional programs designed to detain, rehabilitate, and deter those involved in illegal activity.

facing fines. Approximately three-quarters of the correctional population is under community supervision. The remainder is incarcerated in institutional settings. This balance reflects the overall priority of the correctional system in Canada. The intent is to reform or rehabilitate offenders as opposed to simply punish or detain them. Striking a balance between these two approaches remains a perennial challenge for all actors in Canada's justice system.

Canada operates a separate system of justice for youth aged 12 to 17. The Youth Criminal Justice Act and similar federal and provincial statutes treat young offenders differently from adults. Young people in this age group are subjected to lesser sentences. Young offenders are incarcerated in youth detention centres run by provincial and territorial governments.

remand
Court-ordered, temporary detention for accused offenders awaiting trial.

Canada's adult prison population is divided roughly equally among those temporarily detained awaiting trial and those sentenced to serve time in provincial and federal facilities. Accused offenders awaiting trial are held in **remand**. Most of the time they are temporarily held in provincial/territorial remand facilities or jails. Offenders sentenced to serve time are incarcerated in either provincial/territorial jails (for sentences of less than two years) or federal penitentiaries (for sentences of two years or more).

The number of Canadian offenders has been proportionately declining. For every 1000 Canadians, roughly 6 are under some sort of state supervision in Canada, whether in institutional facilities or in the community. The high point was 7 of every 1000 in the 1990s. The decline is driven mostly by a decrease in the number of Canadians on probation, on parole, or under other forms of community supervision. The rate of adults in custody has risen slightly over time, owing mostly to an increase in the number of people in remand—that is, detained while awaiting trial.

This increase in Canada's remand population is reason for concern. There is overcrowding as well as a high volume and slow pace of cases proceeding through the courts. The situation prompted the Supreme Court of Canada to set aside one man's drug

Briefing Notes

Prisons in Canada

There are four main types of correctional facilities in Canada:

- provincial remand centres;
- provincial youth detention centres;
- provincial jails; and
- federal penitentiaries.

Territorial governments run facilities similar to those in the provinces. Note the terminology: there are no federal jails or provincial penitentiaries. The distinction between provincial and federal prisons depends on the length of the sentence. Canadian prisons are not organized around the jurisdiction responsible for the law that was broken or necessarily where the offence was committed. Adults sentenced for more than two years serve time in federal prisons. All others are sent to provincial correctional facilities. Federal penitentiaries come in a variety of forms, including minimum-, medium-, and maximum-security prisons.

convictions due to unreasonable delays in his case. In R v Jordan (2016), the Supreme Court established maximum periods between a person's charges and trial—18 months for cases in provincial court, and 30 months for others. Beyond these limits, the Court ruled it was a violation of a person's right "to be tried within a reasonable time" (Section 11(b) of the Charter of Rights and Freedoms). Hundreds of cases were stayed or charges dropped in the aftermath of the Jordan decision. Federal, provincial, and territorial justice departments are challenged to find ways to reduce the backlog of cases in the court system.

The problem of releasing accused offenders due to systemic delays is being addressed by hiring more Crown attorneys and court staff, streamlining court processes, developing alternative routes to justice (including drug treatment courts), and finding other efficiencies in the justice system. A further policy change is discontinuing the so-called two-for-one credit for time served in remand. That policy granted offenders in remand who were awaiting trial two years credit on their sentences for every one year spent in pre-trial detention. The two-for-one credit was an incentive for offenders to seek ways to delay proceedings because doing so meant they would serve less time in prison.

Critics warn that stricter **mandatory minimum sentences** may lead to more legal appeals and delays. Criminals are required to be sentenced to minimum time periods for some of the worse forms of crime, such as murder, sexual assault, drug trafficking, firearms offences, and so forth. In 1982, when the Charter of Rights and Freedoms was introduced, there were six mandatory minimums in the Criminal Code. Today there are approximately 100 of them when minimums in the Controlled Drugs and Substances Act are included. Judges no longer have discretion to divert certain criminals out of the institutional setting. Some judges are refusing to implement minimum sentences because they believe the sentencing is unreasonable. The judges' rulings are resulting in sentencing inconsistencies across the country.[6]

Rates of adult incarceration vary across Canada and are among the lowest in the Western world. Quebec has the country's lowest rate of incarceration. Manitoba, Saskatchewan, and the three territories feature the highest. At just over 1 in 1000, the number of adults in state custody in Canada is seven times lower than in the United States, and half of what it is in Mexico,[7] but higher than many European countries. The entire correctional system costs Canadians over $4 billion per year. It costs almost twice as much to incarcerate an individual in a federal penitentiary as in a provincial or territorial jail. This is because of the higher level of security and more specialized forms of rehabilitative programming.

mandatory minimum sentence
The shortest allowable prison term a judge may impose upon a person convicted of certain crimes, such as firearms and drug offences, or under certain conditions (e.g., a repeat offence).

Concluding Thoughts

Canada's complex justice system divides responsibility over the creation, interpretation, and enforcement of Canada's laws among a variety of political actors. This division of power helps to distribute an immense amount of labour and resources. It also prevents any single authority from exerting complete control over law and order. The rule of law ensures all of the actors in Canada's justice system are subject to a core set of democratic principles. As a result, Canadians, regardless of where they live, are subject to roughly the same treatment. At the same time, Canada's justice system is relatively decentralized, meaning that provincial governments maintain control over the administration of justice within their respective jurisdictions. All told, the organization of the justice system creates many challenges in terms of coordination. Yet there are opportunities to tailor justice to local customs and needs and to share best practices developed in certain jurisdictions.

For More Information

Want an insider's look into Canadian policing? Long-serving officer Robert Chrismas shares his views on the fast-paced evolution of *Canadian Policing in the Twenty-First Century* (McGill–Queen's University Press, 2013).

Seeking to delve more deeply into the correctional system in Canada? Curt Griffiths explores *Canadian Corrections* (Nelson, 2010) and the critical issues facing the system today.

Eager to peer behind the bench? Using interviews with current and former Supreme Court justices and their staff, Emmett Macfarlane delves into the role of the court in Canadian democracy, as well as the norms that guide its justices, in *Governing from the Bench: The Supreme Court of Canada and the Judicial Role* (UBC Press, 2012).

Interested in how Supreme Court justice appointment hearings proceed? Erin Crandall and Andrea Lawlor examine the process in their 2015 article "Questioning Judges with a Questionable Process: An Analysis of Committee Appearances by Canadian Supreme Court Candidates" (*Canadian Journal of Political Science* 48, no. 4 [2015]: pp. 863–83).

Want to explore the realities and possibilities of Indigenous justice in Canada? See David Milward's *Aboriginal Justice and the Charter: Realizing a Culturally Sensitive Interpretation of Legal Rights* (UBC Press, 2013).

Curious about the role of race in Canada's criminal justice system? Editors Wendy Chan and Kiran Mirchandani explore the intersection of ethnicity and justice in *Crimes of Colour: Racialization and the Criminal Justice System in Canada* (University of Toronto Press, 2001).

Interested in how mental health is an issue in the criminal justice system? See Joseph H. Michalski's 2017 article "Mental Health Issues and the Canadian Criminal Justice System" (*Contemporary Justice Review* 20, no. 1: 1–24).

Wonder about how parole works? In *Parole in Canada: Gender and Diversity in the Federal System* (UBC Press, 2017), Sarah Turnbull examines how the parole system reinforces gendered, racial, and settler colonial norms in Canadian criminal justice.

Worried about the implications of biology casework for your civil liberties? Neil Gerlach explores the practice of biological testing and banking in *The Genetic Imaginary: DNA and the Canadian Criminal Justice System* (University of Toronto Press, 2004).

Looking for a primer on Canadian law and politics? F.L. Morton and Dave Snow are the editors of *Law, Politics, and the Judicial Process in Canada*, 4th edn (University of Calgary Press, 2018).

Want to learn more about youth justice in Canada? See John A. Winterdyk and Russell Smandych's edited collection, *Youth at Risk and Youth Justice: A Canadian Overview*, 2nd edn (Oxford University Press, 2016).

Want to examine the full text of any Canadian law or judicial ruling? The Canadian Legal Information Institute (CanLII) maintains a comprehensive, fully-searchable database. Go to: www.canlii.org.

Seeking the basics on the rule of law and other core concepts in Canadian jurisprudence? The Centre for Public Legal Education in Alberta has put together several online presentations as part of their LawCentral Schools project. Search: "The Law That Rules."

Deeper Inside Canadian Politics

1. Recreational cannabis was partially legalized in 2018, but governments acknowledged that many policy issues would need to be addressed and revisited in the months and years to come. How well has legalization progressed in terms of meeting the dual goals of enhancing public health and bolstering public safety? What evidence can you provide to support this assessment? Given your view, do you think a similar approach toward legalizing illicit drugs, in general, would help or hinder public health and safety in Canada?

2. Research the transfer of Omar Khadr from US custody in Guantanamo Bay to Canadian custody. Given the nature of his offences and the age at which he committed them, was he transferred to the appropriate facilities in Canada? Why or why not?

3. In your opinion, does Canada treat criminals too harshly or too softly? Explain.

Professor Profile

Emmett Macfarlane

Constitutional law, Supreme Court of Canada, Charter of Rights and Freedoms
Author of *Governing from the Bench* (2013)

Emmett Macfarlane's research explores the relationships between rights, governance, and public policy. He is particularly interested in the Supreme Court of Canada's impact on public policy and political discourse under the Charter of Rights and Freedoms. He has provided non-partisan policy advice to the Government of Canada on the Senate appointments process and the Supreme Court appointments process, to the Senate on Senate reform, and appeared as an expert witness before the parliamentary committee on electoral reform.

Here is what Emmett Macfarlane told us about his career path from when he was an undergraduate student, why he is drawn to his area of specialization, what is challenging about studying Canadian politics, and what advice he has for students.

* * *

I completed my undergraduate degree at the University of Western Ontario as a combined honours degree in political science and media, information and technoculture. Western offered a full-year introduction to political science course that was taught by two professors covering everything from Canadian politics to international relations. I recall being particularly interested in the workings of Canada's democratic institutions, but one thing that became especially illuminating in hindsight was the focus of one professor on "The Four Asian Tigers" (Hong Kong, Singapore, South Korea, and Taiwan) as economic powerhouses and his prediction that East Asia would be the focal point for global politics for the next 20 years. This was in 1999–2000, and less than two years later the terror attack on 11 September 2001 occurred. So I learned early on that certain predictions in political science are perhaps unwise in the face of uncertainty and future events.

My work focuses on the intersection of constitutional rights and public policy, and I think this serves as a focal point for understanding the individual citizen's relationship with, liberty from, and obligations to the state and broader society. As a result, I believe the ways in which certain institutions and actors, including Supreme Court justices, are able to alter this relationship is innately political. I have found the myriad issues implicated by rights and the constitution both important and fascinating.

The most challenging part about what I study is interdisciplinarity. I am effectively a scholar of two disciplines: political science and the law. Many legal scholars question why a political scientist would be interested in courts and some political scientists do not pay much attention to law and courts as genuine forums of politics. It is also generally difficult to stay up to date on multiple areas of research, something that not all scholars attempt to do. What surprises me most about this area of study is the deference to and latitude enjoyed by courts, particularly the Supreme Court of Canada, in influencing public policy and the machinery of government in Canada. If politics is at least in part about power, how it is exercised, and who gets it, it might surprise some to learn how frequently elected actors defer important issues to courts for resolution and under which circumstances they are willing to delegate political power in that sense.

The one tip that I would offer students is to remain conscious of the distinction between "what is" and "what ought to be." It crucial to understand how politics, institutions, public policy, etc. all work (the empirical) before you can start to think about how they ought to work (the normative). This is not only important for those who want to advance reform arguments but also for analyzing proposals put forward by others; many arguments for reform can misidentify the problem or misrepresent how institutions or processes currently operate.

Up for Debate

Do mandatory minimum prison sentences go too far?

Yes: Argument Summary

Repeat and violent offenders should be kept behind bars. However, mandatory minimum sentences are in many cases arbitrary, discriminatory, and unconstitutional. They remove the ability of Crown attorneys and judges to apply their own constitutionally prescribed discretion when approaching criminal cases. This may result in cruel and unusual punishment for first-time, non-violent offenders. The judiciary and Crown attorneys—not elected politicians without a direct connection to the case—should have discretion to decide whether the circumstances behind a particular conviction warrant a lighter punishment.

Yes: Top 5 Considerations

1. The Canadian criminal justice system has always been built on a delicate balance between denunciation and deterrence, on one hand, and rehabilitation and restitution, on the other. Mandatory minimums disrupt this balance by removing the ability of Crown attorneys and judges to weigh the benefits of the latter.

2. Mandatory minimums don't work. There is no evidence that they deter crime or reduce recidivism rates. Research challenges the misconception that mandatory minimums reduce crime rates.

3. Not all people subject to mandatory minimums are violent or repeat offenders. Consider the case of a Canadian who posted a picture of himself on Facebook wielding a loaded handgun. The offence carried a mandatory minimum three-year sentence, which the superior court judge refused to impose on the grounds that the man was not using the gun in an intimidating manner.

4. Mandatory minimums are typically applied to crimes that are disproportionately committed by people of lower socioeconomic status, including Indigenous people and ethnic minority groups. They are not applied to white-collar crimes such as fraud and embezzlement, for instance.

5. Crown attorneys and judges may opt to drop some cases entirely when faced with the prospect of unfairly sentencing an individual to a lengthy prison term. This could result in more cases slipping through the cracks of the justice system.

Yes: Other Considerations

- Crown attorneys and judges are free to pursue lengthy prison terms for violent, repeat offenders regardless of the existence of mandatory minimums. The average sentence for some crimes now subject to mandatory minimums used to be longer. This could mean that sentences for these crimes became lighter than they were before mandatory minimums were imposed.

- Many US states are reviewing their approach to mandatory minimums. Decades of evidence demonstrates it is a failed policy leading to unequal treatment and overcrowded prisons. This leads to higher costs to taxpayers.

- Section 12 of the Charter of Rights and Freedoms states that "Everyone has the right not to be subjected to any cruel and unusual treatment or punishment." In 2015, the Supreme Court of Canada struck down a federal law containing mandatory minimum sentences for gun possession on the grounds that the penalties constituted cruel and unusual punishment.

THE COUNTERCLAIM: NO, THEY DON'T!

Mandatory minimum sentences are necessary to preserve community safety.

No: Argument Summary

People convicted of the most heinous offences—including violent crimes, drug offences, sexual assault, child abuse, gang activity, drinking and driving, and others—deserve to be sentenced to prison. They would pose a danger to society if judges were allowed to impose community-based sentences. It is in the best interest of the community at large if these criminals are placed behind bars. Mandatory minimums remove judges' discretion for community-based sentences and treat the worst offenders the same by ensuring they all serve the same amount of time behind bars.

No: Top 5 Considerations

1. Some people pose such a high level of danger to society that they should face mandatory prison sentences. The most dangerous among them may be held under preventive detention for an indefinite period if they are designated with the "dangerous offender" label.
2. Victims deserve to see their offenders duly punished for their crimes with prison time and a criminal record. Whether these convicted offenders are capable of rehabilitation is beside the point.
3. It is up to democratically elected governments to make laws. It is appropriate for the people's representatives, not judges, to dictate parameters for which sentences should be imposed for which crimes.
4. A common sentence for all crimes of a certain nature ensures that offenders are treated equally and according to standards developed by democratically elected representatives of the community. This eliminates the arbitrary treatment by judges for heinous crimes.
5. Mandatory minimum sentences punish the worst criminals more appropriately. They get placed behind bars instead of put under house arrest, probation, or community service.

No: Other Considerations

- Mandatory minimums are nothing new in Canada. Pierre Trudeau's Liberal government established them for gun-related crimes in 1977. These were stiffened under Jean Chrétien's Liberal government in 1997. Stephen Harper's Conservative government subsequently introduced many more in the 2000s as part of its "getting tough on crime" agenda. Justin Trudeau's Liberal government did not roll back these measures.
- There is no way of pinpointing whether any particular measure, including mandatory minimums, leads to a lower crime rate. Rates of crime are driven by a host of factors.
- Comparisons between mandatory minimums in Canada and the United States are misleading. Penalties south of the border are far harsher and are applied to far more offences.
- Mandatory minimums do not remove judicial or prosecutorial discretion entirely. Crown attorneys may still choose which offences to pursue. Judges may still determine whether or not to convict the individuals based on their assessment of the accused's guilt. In addition, governments have many alternative justice mechanisms to deal with cases outside the traditional criminal system. This includes drug treatment courts and restorative justice processes.
- Too often, the justice system favours the rights of criminals over the suffering of victims. Mandatory minimums take much-needed tough action against some of society's most heinous crimes.

Discussion Questions

- In your opinion, do mandatory prison sentences act as a deterrent to would-be criminals? Do mandatory minimums provide victims of heinous crimes with some measure of comfort and community safety?
- The federal government used to award two-for-one credit for time served while the accused awaits trial. Do you agree or disagree with the decision to end that policy? Why?
- What do you feel is a better use of public funds: creating longer incarceration sentences and spending more money on the penitentiaries that keep criminals off the streets, or reducing incarceration sentences

and spending more money on rehabilitation programs? Explain.

- Under what circumstances would it be appropriate to re-open the capital punishment debate?

- What would be the advantages and disadvantages of requiring that some judicial positions in the system be filled through a general election rather than by appointment?

Where to Learn More about Mandatory Minimum Sentences

Mary Allen, "Mandatory Minimum Penalties: An Analysis of Criminal Justice System Outcomes for Selected Offences," *Juristat: Canadian Centre for Justice Statistics* (2017): 3–37.

Anthony N. Doob and Carla Cesaroni, "The Political Attractiveness of Mandatory Minimum Sentences," *Osgoode Hall Law Journal* 39, no. 287 (2001): pp. 288–305.

Thomas Gabor, "Mandatory Minimum Penalties: Their Effects on Crime, Sentencing Disparities, and Justice System Expenditures" (Ottawa: Department of Justice Canada, 2002).

Jeffrey Mayer and Pat O'Malley, "Missing the Punitive Turn? Canadian Criminal Justice, 'Balance' and Penal Modernism," in *The New Punitiveness: Trends, Theories, Perspectives*, ed. John Pratt, David Brown, Mark Brown, Simon Hallsworth, and Wayne Morrison (Willan Publishing, 2005).

Anne-Marie Singh and Jane B. Sprott, "Race Matters: Public Views on Sentencing," *Canadian Journal of Criminology and Criminal Justice* 59, no. 3 (2017): pp. 285–312.

8

Public Policy and the Bureaucracy

Inside This Chapter

- How is public policy developed in Canada?
- How does the bureaucracy operate?
- What are the components of Canada's social safety net?
- How do governments pay for public-policy initiatives?

Inside Public Policy and the Bureaucracy

Most government decisions that affect citizens' daily lives are made outside the cabinet room or legislative assembly. Thousands of politicians and bureaucrats interact with each other through a series of complex networks, most of which remain behind closed doors.

This chapter offers an inside view of government bureaucracy. While reading, you should consider the following maxims about Canadian policymaking.

✔ **Unelected government employees play an important role in policy decisions.** It is tempting to imagine elected politicians single-handedly drafting legislation, or sitting around a boardroom brainstorming innovative policy ideas. In reality, much of the legwork is done by public servants and political staff. Policymaking involves a close interaction between these elected, appointed, and unelected officials.

✔ **Public policy is grounded in ideas and evidence.** Government leaders are elected to deliver policies to improve society. Public servants play a nonpartisan role in supporting government to make evidence-informed decisions. Politicians and government employees have perspectives that draw on varied experiences and information. Public policy is generated in the broad middle ground between ideology and fact.

✔ **Government bureaucracy is highly professionalized in Canada.** Patronage, corruption, and scandal sometimes erupt in Canadian politics. Yet, more than ever before, hiring and procurement practices insulate the public service from political interference. Increasing transparency and accountability through open government and e-government initiatives expose and deter dishonesty.

UP FOR DEBATE

Should all government jobs be awarded based on merit?

Keep this question in mind as you read through the chapter. Consult the end-of-chapter debate supplement for more material to help you engage in an informed discussion of the topic.

Public Policy and Government

Public policy is a broad concept that involves determining the kind of role a government will play in the lives of its citizens. At the simplest level, it is anything that a government "ought or ought not do, and does or does not do."[1] In essence, public policy is a set of principles, rules, and guidelines used to translate political direction into government action. Public policy therefore encompasses government laws, rules, regulations, and decisions. These are designed to define obligations, prohibitions, and rights belonging to Canadians. In this way, public policy sets the boundaries of acceptable conduct in society. These rules are enforced through an array of tools, including public education, financial incentives, guidelines or standards, and sanctions.

Public policy is often the outcome of an ideological competition among political actors who seek to influence the distribution of finite public resources. Political parties, the media, and special interests all seek to influence public policy by identifying problems and pitching solutions. Politicking results when there is disagreement about the urgency of the policy problem and/or the most appropriate policy solution.

Those who believe in a strong role for the state believe that government should devote more attention and resources to reducing the gap between the rich and the poor, for

public policy
A plan or course of action chosen by a government to respond to an identified problem.

instance. On the other side are those who worry about government overreach and over-spending, who dislike high taxes, and who believe that the social safety net discourages ingenuity. Should it be easier or more difficult for laid-off workers to access employment insurance (EI)? Should the government acquiesce to public servants' demands for more money, or should it hold the line on costs and risk a strike? Should taxpayers subsidize post-secondary tuition further, or should students have to pay their own way through college or university? If government intervention is appropriate, which actors should intervene—federal, provincial, territorial, municipal, Indigenous, or some combination of these? What role, if any, should the courts play in deciding what is proper government action or inaction? These are some of the many sources of debate about public policy and how government officials should manage public programs and the public purse.

The term "government" carries many meanings in Canada. In earlier chapters, we explained that **government** is the group of elected and nonelected officials charged with making executive decisions on behalf of Canadians. This conceptualization was narrowed to include the first minister and cabinet of the day. According to the constitution, these decision-makers must remain unified through cabinet solidarity, ensure accountability for the operation of their portfolios through ministerial responsibility, and maintain the confidence of the legislature.

In its broader sense, government is a system by which a state or community is ruled or controlled. It comprises institutions that make collective rules for society. Through the creation and enforcement of laws, the government attempts to regulate human behaviour to achieve a civilized society. Government maintains order and public security; supports economic development; conducts environmental stewardship; and implements public pro-grams and services. Revenues are raised largely through taxation. Resources are deployed in ways that policymakers deem appropriate. Consequently, there are many competing ideas and ways to run a government.

It can be difficult to keep track of the nuances of government. Below are some examples of the word's varied use, all of which capture proper uses of the concept:

- The exercise of authority: "Canadians expect good government from their politicians."
- All three branches: "Canada's system of government consists of the executive, legis-lature, and judiciary."
- A body of decision-makers: "The government chose to build three new hospitals."
- The political executive: "The government fell on a non-confidence vote."
- A partisan group: "NDP governments strive to spend more on social programs than PC governments do."
- A first minister's administration: "The Trudeau government prioritized policies that target middle-class families."
- A group of officials: "The government was quick to address the crisis."
- An organization: "Citizens demand more from their governments when it comes to the environment."
- A system of decision-making: "Government has become more transparent over time."
- An order: "The Government of Canada and Government of Nova Scotia signed an agreement to build a bridge."

The public servants who oversee and implement government business engage in **public administration**. As discussed in Chapter 5, these bureaucrats are obliged to follow

government
The people and systems that govern a society by designing, overseeing, and implementing laws and public policy. Can refer to the cabinet and/or the broader public sector.

public administration
The study and delivery of public policy by public servants.

the directives of their respective ministers, as long as the instructions are within the boundaries of the law. This does not mean that government employees are blind followers of the partisans who temporarily occupy seats at the cabinet table. Nor are they servants of those ministers' political staff. Rather, public servants are expected to live up to the mantra of "fearless advice and loyal implementation." This means that clerks, deputy ministers, and others provide prudent counsel to prime ministers, premiers, and ministers, and that whatever political decision is made by the government of the day will be acted upon faithfully. In other words, elected officials decide and direct, while bureaucrats advise and implement.

Government follows a chain of command whereby those with a higher rank issue directives to those with a lower rank. In this way, the government is organized very much like a military operation, with clearly defined roles and positions of authority. It has been this way for over a century. German sociologist Max Weber identified a number of characteristics of a functioning government that continue to apply to bureaucracy in Western societies, including Canada. For instance:

- Government must employ skilled experts.
- These experts must operate within an organized hierarchy.
- There must be employee training to encourage uniform performance.
- When bureaucrats take action, they must follow written rules and preserve their actions as files for others' reference.
- People must be treated equally, including through standardized hiring and firing.

These formalities are intended to ensure the smooth running of a non-partisan public service that will help develop and implement public policy on the direction of elected leaders.

A distinct feature of the Government of Canada is its commitment to official bilingualism. The commissioner of official languages is responsible for ensuring all federal institutions abide by the terms of the Official Languages Act. The commissioner promotes the use of English and French in the federal bureaucracy and as part of its hiring practices.

Connecting the Public to Policymaking

In representative democracies like Canada, governments often struggle to connect the public to the policymaking process. The Westminster traditions discussed in Chapter 2 offer Canadians indirect access. First ministers and their cabinets are accountable to legislatures, whose members, in turn, must answer to their constituents through elections held at least once every five years. Plebiscites, referendums, initiatives, and other forms of direct democracy are rarely used; in any event, they are technically non-binding on the government of the day, though public pressure may dictate otherwise. From time to time, governments launch public consultations on matters of particular interest, and designated officials visit communities to listen to local concerns. Day to day, however, most Canadians' interactions with government are with public servants.

Advances in communication technology offer ways for governments to engage with the public. Governments can gather information from polling citizens and monitoring social media. They can host policy discussions online and provide information to citizens

See the discussion of e-democracy on pages 384–5 of Chapter 11 for information on how governments are using information communication technologies (ICTs) to engage citizens.

green paper
A government document released to explore policy options, without any commitment to the outcome.

white paper
A document outlining a proposed policy commitment by government.

pluralism
The presence of diverse socioeconomic groups participating in public affairs.

through websites, email lists, and press releases. For their part, citizens and the media can obtain more information about government than at any point in history. They can do so faster than ever and at any time of day, from almost anywhere. This includes identifying what consultations are currently ongoing. The federal government's Consulting with Canadians website (www.canada.ca/consultingcanadians) maintains a chronology of past and ongoing consultations. This area of public administration involves myriad consultation tools, including draft documents, special reviews, consultation papers, invitations for public comment, updates on policy initiatives, and opinion surveys.

Occasionally, governments engage the public to review the effectiveness of public programs and services, or to solicit input on constitutional or intergovernmental positions. These sorts of public consultations are infrequent. When consultations occur, most citizens are unaware and/or do not participate. Those who offer opinions benefit from the opportunity to provide input without any sense of whether their participation makes a difference.

Sometimes, public engagement involves more formalized processes. A government may initiate a **green paper** to stimulate public discussion on a particular policy issue. These documents typically provide background on the issue at hand and a broad set of possible strategies to address it. Green papers are designed to inform a ministerial response. For example, the federal government issued a series of green papers on universal healthcare at the close of the Second World War. These proved to be the early formal stages of the Medical Care Act (1966) that was passed over two decades later. The federal government has sought public feedback on policy ideas expressed in green papers on topics as diverse as immigration, Internet piracy, voyeurism, same-sex marriage, official bilingualism, and national security. Green papers contain such a minutiae of policy details that they are foremost designed to collect input from a highly informed audience.

By contrast, **white papers** outline a government's proposed course of action. White papers are usually released prior to the drafting of legislation. They are direct and specific. They allow the government to adjust its planned approach after hearing from the public. For instance, the White Paper on Metric Conversion was initiated by a federal Liberal government in 1970, advocating that Canada abandon the imperial system of measurement (pounds, Fahrenheit, gallons, and so on). Fifteen years later, a Progressive Conservative government passed the legislation introducing metric as the national standard of measurement. The federal government issues roughly one white paper a year. Many of them deal with issues of national defence and private-sector regulation.

Engagement activities are designed to ensure a wide range of Canadians have input on the decisions that impact their day-to-day lives. **Pluralism** holds that the diversity of perspectives in a society should be reflected in the shaping of public policy. It is a belief that government power should not be concentrated in political elites, namely politicians, interest group leaders, business owners, and labour union bosses.[2] In Canada, pluralism is most vibrant at the federal level, where there is a vigorous struggle to influence government. Conversely, there is greater homogeneity within most provinces. Smaller places are more likely to have tighter government information control and weaker opposition parties; influential special interests operating without much competition; many reporters but few muckraking journalists; and a fear of sanctions for speaking out against government. Pluralistic societies are characterized by the engagement of various groups in policy decision-making as opposed to exclusion or even assimilation.

Democracy is theoretically stronger when decision-makers consider different points of view. However, there are major challenges with pluralism. The pressure of many competing voices does not necessarily result in good public policy. In fact, pluralism may even result in gridlock and policy paralysis. Governments must filter all available information and organize competing interests when crafting public policy. To do so, the political executive considers its election platform, public-opinion polls, news coverage, and the positions of special-interest groups. It often considers advice based on empirical evidence provided by the public service. Other sources of input include debate in the legislature and legal decisions. All of these come in addition to any public forums, petitions, and formal consultations.

The Public-Policy Cycle

The design of public policy may follow many different paths but generally proceeds through what is known as the **public-policy cycle** (see Figure 8.1). A number of variations of the policy cycle model exist. The stages are not always ordered and linear. They merely give shape to an often chaotic process involving a host of different actors.

The starting point in most public-policy cycles is **agenda setting**. This is the stage where a matter of public policy gains such prominence that it comes to the attention of decision-makers. Agenda setting involves defining the policy problem and identifying its root causes. The problem, itself, can enter the public-policy cycle in countless ways. It might originate as a resolution at a party convention and end up in an election campaign platform. It could come about as a result of a judicial ruling that forces the government to respond. It might be a solution proposed by an opposition party during Question Period. It might be put forward by an interest group, or the media jumping on a sensationalist issue. It might be a problem identified by public servants, or watchdogs like the auditor general. Whatever the details, people seeking to influence public policy during the agenda setting stage must achieve media coverage, influence public opinion, and apply public pressure.[3]

Officials must assess the most viable policy responses once the problem is identified. **Public-policy analysis** is typically the next stage in the cycle. Research specialists such as policy analysts examine the feasibility of potential policy responses and evaluate existing, revised, or new policies. They engage in objective analysis by using social science methods to collect and analyze data. This includes the use of statistics such as census data to inform cost–benefit analysis and risk assessment. Qualitative analysis includes formulating options in response to protests, media coverage, and inbound correspondence.

Policy analysis involves assessing the merits of the various courses of action. For instance, an analyst might attempt to anticipate the economic value of a possible policy, a common approach known as a cost–benefit analysis. Or the analyst might consider the benefits of the policy minus all of its possible financial implications. Many Canadian governments insist that policy analysis consider the differential impacts on each segment of the population, such as citizens living in remote rural areas. The shift away from one-size-fits-all approaches is embodied in gender-based analysis plus (GBA+), which encourages policy advisors to consider the impacts on women, gender-diverse people, persons with disabilities, and members of racial, ethnic, and religious minority groups. Many of these identity factors intersect, which makes a policy's overall impact even more challenging to anticipate.

public-policy cycle
The common stages in public decision-making, from conception to implementation and modification.

agenda setting
The use of strategies and tactics to generate public and government support for a proposed public policy.

public-policy analysis
The process of developing options to inform decision-makers.

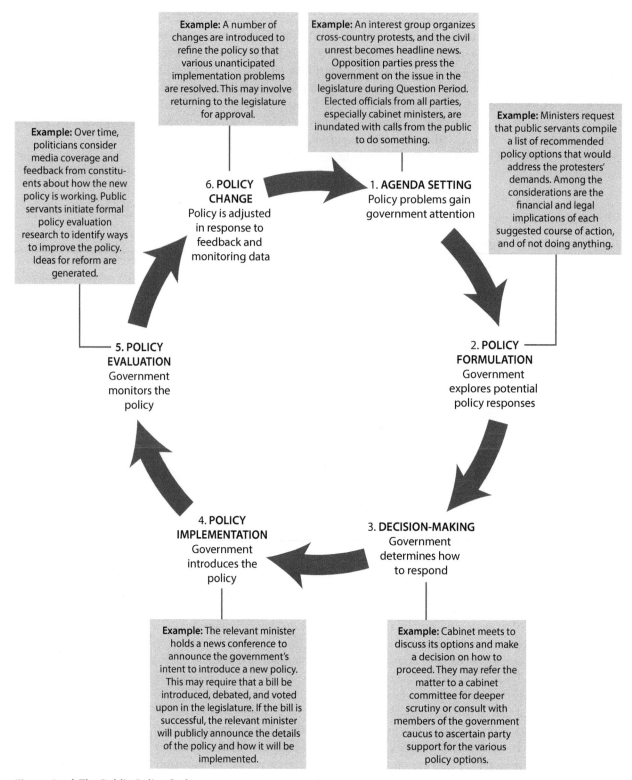

Example: A number of changes are introduced to refine the policy so that various unanticipated implementation problems are resolved. This may involve returning to the legislature for approval.

Example: An interest group organizes cross-country protests, and the civil unrest becomes headline news. Opposition parties press the government on the issue in the legislature during Question Period. Elected officials from all parties, especially cabinet ministers, are inundated with calls from the public to do something.

Example: Over time, politicians consider media coverage and feedback from constituents about how the new policy is working. Public servants initiate formal policy evaluation research to identify ways to improve the policy. Ideas for reform are generated.

Example: Ministers request that public servants compile a list of recommended policy options that would address the protesters' demands. Among the considerations are the financial and legal implications of each suggested course of action, and of not doing anything.

6. POLICY CHANGE
Policy is adjusted in response to feedback and monitoring data

1. AGENDA SETTING
Policy problems gain government attention

5. POLICY EVALUATION
Government monitors the policy

2. POLICY FORMULATION
Government explores potential policy responses

4. POLICY IMPLEMENTATION
Government introduces the policy

3. DECISION-MAKING
Government determines how to respond

Example: The relevant minister holds a news conference to announce the government's intent to introduce a new policy. This may require that a bill be introduced, debated, and voted upon in the legislature. If the bill is successful, the relevant minister will publicly announce the details of the policy and how it will be implemented.

Example: Cabinet meets to discuss its options and make a decision on how to proceed. They may refer the matter to a cabinet committee for deeper scrutiny or consult with members of the government caucus to ascertain party support for the various policy options.

Figure 8.1 | The Public-Policy Cycle

The research techniques used in policy analysis include media monitoring, literature and Internet searches, and public consultations. For large projects, the government requests data from Statistics Canada or purchases public-opinion research, including surveys and focus groups. Increasingly, policy analysts are expected to gather such data themselves, by designing and administering online polls, hosting group discussions, and conducting interviews. Policy advisors may engage in crowdsourcing, whereby online discussion forums are set up and different perspectives are compiled from contributors with little effort or expense. All of these sources of data help to make government more pluralistic.

While this sort of analysis can seem objective, public policy is created in an ideological environment. Politicians, interest groups, and other political voices practise agenda-setting to advocate for their preferred policy pathway. Policymakers—both elected and non-elected—are influenced by their own opinions and underlying value systems. Most policymakers assume that actors in a political system are rational thinkers who promote a course of action that aligns with their needs and wants. According to this **rational choice** approach, humans evaluate costs and benefits when making a decision, and seek to optimize their own situation. The theory can explain the behaviour of citizens and policymakers, and be used to inform action to address public issues. Take voter turnout, for instance. There are exceedingly low odds that a single vote will change the outcome of a national election. The costs of voting—such as the effort to research choices, the gasoline used to drive to the polling station, the time spent in line to vote—normally exceed the expected benefits. Through this lens, people who do not vote are more rational that those who do, a perspective that can help elections agencies figure out what, if anything, they can do to increase election turnout. This may involve highlighting additional incentives for voters, such as emphasizing the value of fulfilling one's civic duty, or creating disincentives for staying away from the polls such as fining people who do not vote. Policymakers could employ nudging (see Briefing Note) to increase turnout through small interventions. For instance, election signs could be required to mention the date of the election, and on Election Day social-media organizations could inform users whenever their friends post about voting. Policymakers are also rational actors, however. Based on the fact they were elected under the existing set of rules, some politicians may see little benefit in boosting turnout through measures like mandatory voting or electoral reform.

Rational choice is just one of many theoretical approaches. It is unsettling because it discounts the value of the broad social benefits of living in a vibrant participatory democracy. Public policy rarely, if ever, fits a single theoretical model. The application of many philosophical approaches by different participants tends to result in public policy that integrates the perspectives of a variety of competing interests—though that approach in itself describes pluralism theory.

The next stage of the public-policy cycle involves analysis of an array of information and considerations in order to make the best possible recommendation. Most models of policy innovation urge analysts to employ a variety of approaches. A policy advisor must draw on available data to determine, for example, how individuals and groups impacted by a particular policy are likely to react or how other jurisdictions have fared with similar policies. Consideration must be given to resource feasibility. A course of action is only implementable if government has enough time, funds, and employees to support it in the short and long terms. Political perspectives are a further factor. Prudent public servants take into account the timing of their recommendations and the government's agenda.

rational choice
A theory that citizens are self-interested actors whose decisions fulfill their own needs and wants.

Briefing Notes

Nudging

Policymakers are increasingly looking for ways to "nudge" citizens into complying with the government's direction.[4] Nudging involves designing policy tools that encourage the desired behaviour without providing direct incentives or disincentives to ensure compliance. In their book *Nudge: Improving Decisions about Health, Wealth, and Happiness*, Richard Thaler and Cass Sunstein cite the example of governments mandating grocery stores to display healthier foods at eye level to encourage people to shop and eat more responsibly. That particular policy helps the government move away from interventions such as subsidizing farmers or banning junk foods. In Canada, governments discourage tobacco use by requiring cigarette packages to feature graphic images and by requiring retailers to keep cigarettes out of sight. These nudges are cost-neutral for government compared with removing taxes from smoking cessation aids or increasing taxes on tobacco.

Bold new ideas are unlikely to be implemented in the months leading up to an election, for instance, as governments typically focus on fulfilling any remaining policy commitments made in the previous campaign.

The next stage of the public-policy cycle requires even more careful consideration of the inherent biases in public administration. Communicating policy advice gives rise to what is known as the **principal–agent problem**. For instance, ministers and political staff may interpret the viability of a policy option differently than nonpartisan public servants do. Political personnel may place different emphasis on certain parts of a proposed plan or on achieving the results. Only the principal decision-maker—normally the first minister or another member of cabinet—has the true authority to set public policy on behalf of the government. However, given the sheer volume of decisions confronting prime ministers, premiers, and ministers, some of these responsibilities must be delegated to employees. Political staff and the public service thus become agents for the principal decision-makers. This is a problem, because agents may arrive at different interpretations of policy than the principal might. Agents may have more information or expertise in the area, for instance, or simply misinterpret directives. These problems are exacerbated by the number of levels in the hierarchy through which a policy directive must pass. In this way the principal–agent problem is like the children's game of broken telephone. These different interpretations can blur the lines of accountability. The principles of responsible government are in jeopardy when public servants design and deliver policies contrary to their minister's wishes or when a minister delegates too much authority to subordinates.

Once developed and implemented, policies must be evaluated for their effectiveness, which is the next stage of the public-policy cycle. Most public servants use the input–output–outcome logic model to accomplish this evaluation. Program investments (inputs) are assembled to produce deliverables (outputs) that will have discernible short-, medium-, and long-term impacts on society (outcomes). For example, provincial and territorial governments maintain policies when it comes to immunizing their residents against the seasonal flu. The desired outcome of these policies is to produce a healthier population. To achieve this, policymakers must assemble resources, including vaccination supplies, sites,

principal–agent problem
A problem arising from the fact that someone (an agent) working on behalf of a decision-maker (the principal) may not take the course of action the principal intended.

and healthcare professionals to administer the vaccines, as well as public relations specialists to design promotional campaigns, and so on. These resources are used to produce concrete outputs, including a certain number of vaccinations per week or the launching of television and radio advertisements. Policymakers hope that these outputs will help to achieve the desired outcome of a healthier, flu-resistant population.

Policy inputs are relatively easy to measure, whether in terms of time, funding, or human resources. So, too, are policy outputs. When designed properly, goals are specific, measurable, agreed-upon, realistic, and time-oriented. Policy outcomes are far more difficult to measure. Assessing the longer-term impact of a policy change often requires qualitative analysis of subjective concepts, such as whether citizens in a community are happier. Analysis involves separating broad outcomes into measurable components. Discussed below, central agencies perform policy coordination and tracking functions to ensure outputs are being delivered. Furthermore, governments use business planning practices that prioritize the achievement of countable milestones over longer-term objectives. These shorter-term milestones help governments align the policy cycle with the election cycle (see Figure 8.2).

After an election, or if a new first minister is chosen by the party between elections, time is needed for the new government to orient itself to power. During this start-up phase, ministers receive direction from their prime minister or premier, and public servants brief

Globalmoments/iStock

Public-policy concepts can be used to predict how citizens might respond to a new policy. Suppose the government is concerned about a study showing that an alarming number of drivers admit that they text while driving. Among the policy options are (a) increasing the penalties for distracted driving, (b) placing more law-enforcement officers on the road to detect and arrest distracted drivers, (c) running a graphic online advertisement campaign to illustrate the deadly effects of distracted driving, and (d) imposing regulations on vehicle and phone manufacturers to install technology that disables handheld devices while a vehicle is moving. Assess each of these options from a rational choice perspective. Which would be most effective?

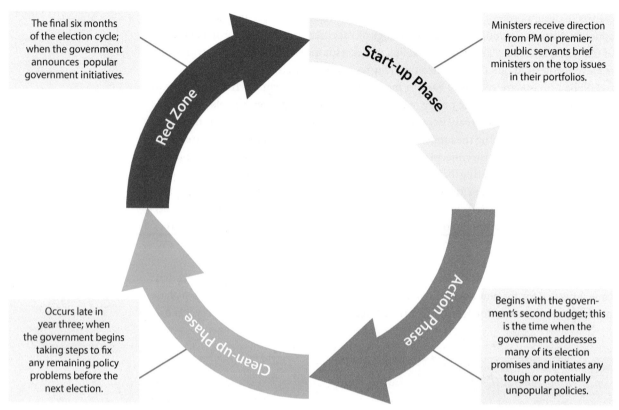

The final six months of the election cycle; when the government announces popular government initiatives.

Red Zone

Start-up Phase

Ministers receive direction from PM or premier; public servants brief ministers on the top issues in their portfolios.

Clean-up Phase

Action Phase

Occurs late in year three; when the government begins taking steps to fix any remaining policy problems before the next election.

Begins with the government's second budget; this is the time when the government addresses many of its election promises and initiates any tough or potentially unpopular policies.

Figure 8.2 | Public Policy and the Election Cycle

their respective ministers about the top issues in their portfolios. The action phase of the election cycle typically begins with the government's second budget. It is a period featuring an activist agenda designed to address many of the governing party's election promises and, if necessary, initiate any tough and potentially unpopular policy measures (e.g., increasing taxes or cutting programs). The action phase continues until late in year three, when the government begins taking steps to fix any remaining policy problems before the next election, during the clean-up phase. The final six months of the election cycle are the red zone—a period in which the government announces or re-publicizes popular government initiatives in an effort to gain momentum in the upcoming campaign.

The Machinery of Government

The capacity of governments to define, refine, and deliver on their policy goals depends heavily upon how they organize the bureaucracy. This structure is referred to as the machinery of government. The metaphor captures the interconnected nature of various organizations and individuals, all driven by a common engine. All federal, provincial, and territorial governments share a broadly similar framework consisting of central agencies that direct the work of line departments. This was discussed at length in Chapter 5. The role of other agencies, boards, and commissions (ABCs) requires some elaboration.

Central Agencies

Groups of elected and nonpartisan officials exert command and control other parts of the bureaucracy. This concentration of power in bodies like the Prime Minister's Office (PMO), Privy Council Office (PCO), Treasury Board, and the department of finance is worrisome to some critics. Centralization diminishes the role of individual cabinet ministers to shape policy within their respective portfolios. However, consolidating power has operational advantages, and is necessary due to the interconnected nature of public policy. The size and scope of government has increased markedly over time. Coordinating the work of dozens of ministers and thousands of public servants requires leadership from the centre to ensure all participants know the government's agenda and are committed and positioned to deliver on it. This coordination is driven by the PMO, which interacts with ministers' offices, and the PCO, which works with deputy ministers' offices. Premiers' offices and executive council offices perform similar functions at the provincial/territorial level.

See page 142 in Chapter 5 for discussion of how the centralization of power in the PMO gives rise to the notion of presidentialization.

Line Departments

Aside from central agencies at the top of the government hierarchy, the bureaucracy contains a host of **line departments**, each of which falls under the political direction of a minister of the Crown and the bureaucratic direction of a deputy minister. Department portfolios flow from the areas of jurisdiction spelled out in the constitution. There is a federal department of national defence; there are provincial departments of municipal affairs, of natural resources, and of education; and there are federal and provincial departments of agriculture and of environment. Each line department is overseen by a minister, who is accountable to the legislature for its performance. The minister receives counsel from a deputy minister who is the permanent department head. Deputy ministers work closely with ministers' chiefs of staff, who are political appointees. Together, they help connect the partisan side of government work with the non-partisan public service. Bureaucrats in the public service, including deputy ministers, are expected to provide fearless advice to elected officials and faithfully implement government directives.

line departments
Units responsible for the development and delivery of policy, programs, or services under a particular portfolio.

Agencies, Boards, and Commissions

The public service also consists of **agencies, boards, and commissions (ABCs)**. These advisory, operational, and regulatory organizations operate at a distance from the political or bureaucratic control that comes with the business of line departments. Their day-to-day business is not overseen or conducted by personnel in a central agency or by line department officials. Depending on the organization, the legislature, the cabinet, or an individual minister may be responsible for appointing an ABC's leaders, defining its mandate, approving its budget, reviewing its annual reports, or generally directing its business. Otherwise, however, the day-to-day functioning of an ABC is shielded from political interference and bureaucratic oversight. This may add a sense of non-partisanship, objectivity, and longer-term thinking to their work. ABCs are established by statute, regulation, or incorporation and have autonomy to make recommendations where necessary that the governing party might not like. Agencies, boards, and commissions include quasi-governmental bodies such as correctional systems, police forces, universities, hospitals, and school boards (see examples in Table 8.1). Some of them are permanent. Others are

ABC
An agency, board, or commission responsible for delivering a program or service, or producing goods, at arm's length from government. See also: government agency, government board, government commission.

See page 220 in Chapter 7 for more about the role of the judiciary.

Table 8.1   Examples of Government Departments and ABCs

Name (Government)	Mandate	Reports to
Departments		
Transport Canada (Canada)	Promotes a safe, efficient, and environmentally responsible transportation network in Canada	Federal minister of transport
Department of Agriculture, Fisheries and Food (Quebec)	Regulates and supports the province's food industry, with an emphasis on sustainable development	Quebec's minister of agriculture, fisheries and food
Agencies		
Canada Revenue Agency (Canada)	Administers tax, benefits, and related programs. Ensures compliance with such regulations on behalf of federal, provincial, and territorial governments across Canada	Federal minister of national revenue
Ontario Clean Water Agency (Ontario)	Responsible for water and sewer services, with an objective of delivering safe, reliable, and cost-effective clean water	Ontario's minister of the environment
Boards		
National Energy Board (Canada)	Regulates the international and interprovincial aspects of pipelines, energy development, and trade in the oil, gas, and electric utility industries	Federal minister of natural resources
Disaster Assistance Appeals Board (Manitoba)	Reviews appeals submitted by applicants for disaster financial assistance who were dissatisfied with their assessment	Manitoba's minister responsible for emergency measures
Commissions		
Canadian Human Rights Commission (Canada)	Promotes equal opportunity and protects human rights by administering the Canadian Human Rights Act and ensuring compliance with the Employment Equity Act, such as dealing with discrimination complaints	Speaker of the House of Commons
Financial and Consumer Services Commission (New Brunswick)	Crown corporation that protects consumer interests by administering and enforcing provincial legislation concerning co-operatives, credit unions, insurance, pensions, securities, trust and loan companies, and other consumer matters	New Brunswick's minister of justice

Source: © Privy Council Office, Orders in Council Division (2015)

discontinued when their original purpose is deemed to have run its course. In considering the function of ABCs we must bear in mind that the executive branch, which is accountable to the legislative branch, has ultimate authority to steer government policy and to set budgets.

Agencies, boards and commissions have a more direct daily impact on Canadians' lives than most other government actors.[5] As the Government of Manitoba explains it, ABCs are "entities established by government to carry out a range of functions and services, and include councils, authorities, advisory bodies, funding bodies, professional organizations, and quasi-judicial tribunals."[6] The Government of Nova Scotia differentiates between adjudicative and non-adjudicative ABCs. An adjudicative body performs quasi-judicial functions; it is expected to "consider evidence, make findings of fact and law, and issue decisions affecting a person's liberty, security, or legal rights."[7] Conversely, the function of a non-adjudicative ABC is to "make financial, regulatory, business, or policy decisions or recommendations to government that have far-reaching implications." To provide an idea of the scope of these bodies, consider that the Government of Ontario alone has over 500 agencies, boards, commissions, councils, authorities, and foundations.[8] They are distinct from agents of the legislature, such as the auditor general and chief electoral officer.

The first letter in ABC refers to an **agency** of government. An agency is a specialist organization that is tasked with overseeing the administration of specific legislation. The nature of an agency's scope of work is generally considered to require a depoliticized environment. Its operations are narrower and more autonomous than those of a government department. Whereas ministers steer the daily business of a department, their oversight of the agencies in their portfolio tends to be in an arm's-length, formal reporting capacity. Examples of federal government agencies include the Atlantic Canada Opportunities Agency, the Canadian Food Inspection Agency, and the Canadian Space Agency.

A **government board** is made up of appointed citizens who review potentially contentious issues, including decisions made by a government agency. This includes advisory councils and marketing boards. Members are appointed by the relevant minister or by the monarch's representative at the recommendation of cabinet. Examples of federal boards include the Copyright Board of Canada, the National Film Board, and the Parole Board of Canada.

Another type of ABC is a **government commission**. These are set up to provide detailed policy recommendations on a specific issue to government. A government commission's recommendations are not necessarily binding. Commissions, task forces, and tribunals conduct research to investigate an issue and may hold public hearings to ensure that the public has an opportunity to voice their concerns. Examples of federal commissions include the Canada Employment Insurance Commission, the Canadian Nuclear Safety Commission, and the Commission for Public Complaints Against the RCMP.

The highest-profile type of commission is a **royal commission**, also known as **a commission of inquiry**. Royal commissions are occasionally struck by cabinet to investigate an issue that is of significant public interest. They are equally a mechanism for the political executive to defer contentious policy decisions.[9] A commission is overseen by an appointed commissioner, usually someone who is distinguished in the field such as a judge or retired politician, and is commonly referred to by the commissioner's last name. For instance, the federal Royal Commission on the Future of Health Care in Canada became known as the Romanow Commission because it was headed by former Saskatchewan Premier Roy Romanow. The terms of reference establish a commission's scope of work. Its final report includes a variety of submissions, evidence, working papers, and other documents. The recommendations may or may not lead to significant policy changes, depending on the findings and the political will of the government.

Crown corporations are among the most well-known ABCs in Canada. A Crown corporation is set up by the government in an area of the economy that it feels is in the public interest but that the private sector has deemed unprofitable and/or fit only for the state's involvement. Unlike a profit-motivated business, the government offers services with a primary goal of serving the public interest. This includes ensuring fiscal sustainability. There is growing pressure on Crown corporations not to be a drain on the public purse and even to be profitable. They tend to be managed by a board of directors and report to the legislature through a minister. Examples of federal Crown corporations include the Canada Mortgage and Housing Corporation, the Canada Post Corporation, and the Canadian Broadcasting Corporation. Others include regulatory agencies with a sales component, like provincial liquor and cannabis control boards and gaming commissions. Periodically the government sells some or all of the assets, as the federal government did with Air Canada, Petro-Canada, and Atomic Energy of Canada.

Differentiating among ABCs can be difficult. Some commissions and agencies are Crown corporations, for instance. There is such a growing and "bewildering variety of

government agency
An arm's-length corporate body operating on behalf of a government.

government board
A public advisory committee made up of appointed citizens.

government commission
An agency of government that provides specialized policy expertise and oversight.

royal commission/ commission of inquiry
A special research investigation of a contentious area of public policy.

Crown corporations
Enterprises owned by a federal or provincial government.

By permission of of Egg Farmers of Canada.

Supply management was a contentious issue during Canada–US free-trade negotiations. The practice of setting minimum prices for dairy, poultry, and eggs originated from provincial marketing boards in the 1960s. In the 1970s, national boards such as the Canadian Dairy Commission began regulating a national supply management system. Control over production, pricing, and imports provides stability for Canadian farmers so they are less dependent on government subsidies, and they (farmers) continue to contribute to both rural and national economies. However, critics suggest this control may result in higher prices for Canadian consumers in some markets. The Canada–United States–Mexico Agreement (CUSMA) trade deal provides American farmers with slightly more access to the Canadian market while preserving supply management. In today's global economy, is supply management essential or outdated?

organizations and procedures, as well as names" that ABCs are often lumped together under the umbrella term "agencies."[10] One of many examples is the Canadian Dairy Commission, which is accountable to the federal minister of agriculture and agri-food. Its name indicates that it is a commission, but it is also a Crown corporation. Moreover, it chairs the Canadian Milk Supply Management Committee, which is a permanent board of provincial members of the National Milk Marketing Plan. Given that there can be such a variety of non-governmental organizations, the most prudent way to differentiate them is as either a department or an ABC.

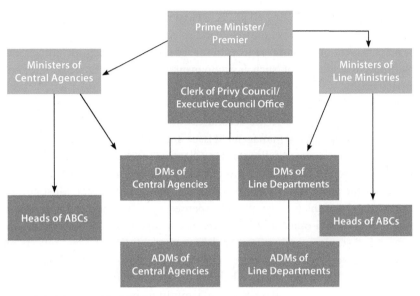

Figure 8.3 | Cabinet and Public-Service Managers in Canada

In working for ABCs, many civil service workers (professors, nurses, physicians, teachers, and so on) do not consider themselves public servants in the broader sense of the term. Nor do many government workers or citizens tend to view them as part of the formal public service. They sometimes belong to different unions, and often have different compensation and benefit plans. Most employment opportunities within ABCs appear on their own independent websites rather than on the main public-service job boards.

Financial Administration

The feasibility of any policy initiative hinges on whether the government can afford it. The fiscal capacity of a government is enormous and is as varied as its population. The federal government generates over $300 billion annually in revenues and a comparable amount in program expenses. To put this in perspective, the budget of the United States federal government is measured in trillions of dollars, while Prince Edward Island's entire budget is around $2 billion.

Two main bodies oversee the public purse in federal, provincial, and territorial governments across Canada. The **Treasury Board** presides over the government's fiscal decisions. It is a committee of ministers, including the president of the Treasury Board, who is often also the minister of finance. At the federal level, the Treasury Board is supported by the Treasury Board Secretariat, a bureaucratic central agency discussed in Chapter 5. The president of the Treasury Board submits estimated expenditures to the legislature and an annual report of the government's expenditures, revenues, assets, and liabilities. At the federal level, every three months, departments prepare fiscal statements and identify any significant changes to those plans found in the budget or estimates. Provincial governments operate their own treasury boards that generally follow the same processes as their federal counterpart.

The scope of the Treasury Board's authority is impressive. By law, the cabinet committee controls the following:

- general administrative policy in the federal bureaucracy;
- the organization of the federal bureaucracy and how it is controlled;

Treasury Board
The cabinet committee that is tasked with reviewing and authorizing government revenue and expenditure policies.

The role of the Treasury Board Secretariat is discussed in Chapter 5, on the executive: see page 158.

- fiscal management, including all projected and received revenues;
- determining the priorities of departmental spending and reviewing spending plans;
- the management of human resources in the federal bureaucracy, including terms and conditions of employment, such as group insurance and benefit programs; and
- internal audits.

The Ministry of Finance is the second major body charged with fiscal oversight within government. Any fiscal management issue not assigned to Treasury Board or other departments falls to Finance. As discussed in Chapter 6, each year the minister of finance delivers a **budget** to the legislature, in order to obtain approval from the people's representatives for the government's planned revenues and expenditures. Most government budgets contain the plans for operational expenses; spending on capital expenses such as roads, buildings, and other infrastructure; tax increases and/or reductions; changes in programs and services; and savings or debt repayment. Each budget reflects months of work by public servants and political staff who are guided by the throne speech and election promises. The budget strikes a balance between departmental and whole of government priorities. The process involves each minister and deputy minister acting as intermediaries with central agencies like the Treasury Board. A budget proposal submitted to the centre of government by a minister is most likely to be supported if it involves delivering on an election campaign commitment.

budget

A document containing the government's projected revenue, expenditures, and economic forecasts.

THE CANADIAN PRESS/Chris Young

A finance minister's purchase—or resoling—of shoes before budget day is a media tradition, with political commentators analyzing the symbolism of the minister's choice of footwear. In 2018, finance minister Bill Morneau took the unprecedented step of selecting shoes from the same retailer for a second consecutive year. The message that he sought to deliver was unchanged: Edmonton shoe manufacturer Poppy Barley was founded by women and the Trudeau government budgets sought to reduce the gender gap. Do we attach too much significance to a quirky Canadian tradition? Or is it a harmless photo-op that doesn't step on anyone's toes?

The budget is tabled in the legislature by the minister of finance amidst much secrecy and hoopla. Key representatives of the opposition parties, other governments, industry, civil society, and the media may be given advance copies on the day it is released, but only under the condition of secrecy, which might include signing a confidentiality agreement. These people are placed in what is known as a lock-up (sometimes called a lock-in) and herded behind closed doors with no ability to communicate with the outside world. This advance opportunity to review the budget allows them to ask government officials any questions and prepare to respond once the document is made public. It is essential that details not be leaked, as information contained in the budget can affect national security, personal livelihoods, stock markets, and other matters of high importance. The finance minister must be the one who announces the information. Members of the legislature must be informed first and speculators could profit from advance knowledge of the government's financial plans. Considerable effort is invested in preparing the finance minister's speech, briefing the media, and even selecting the minister's shoes.

Governments are sometimes incorrect in their budget projections. Economic circumstances may shift over the course of the year. For instance, a government that receives royalties from natural resources such as oil or minerals will experience changes in their projected revenues if the market price of those resources soars or plummets. Consequently, governments typically announce adjustments to their revenue and spending projections in a **fiscal update** later in the fiscal year. These tend to be humdrum affairs. Whereas a government's budget makes news for a week, and budget estimates may receive no media coverage, a fiscal update is often a single news story because the budget is staying the course. An acrimonious fiscal update occurred during the 2008 economic crisis, which led to the coalition crisis described in Chapter 6.

fiscal update
Announcement of the state of the government's economic, revenue, and spending projections since the budget was tabled earlier in the year.

Deficits and Debt

If the government is spending beyond its means and has to borrow money, this means it is running a **budget deficit**. The budget is said to be "in the red." Many view borrowing as sensible fiscal policy during an economic downturn. Society may benefit from government spending to stimulate job growth or to bolster social-support programs. Getting out of deficit and balancing the budget then becomes a major political challenge. A government that runs an annual deficit for many years will later be faced with repaying the accumulated borrowed funds. Paying down the **public debt**, which is the sum of money borrowed to finance the government's budget deficits plus any interest charges incurred, may move up the public agenda. Public debt mounts as budget deficits accumulate and as governments borrow to spend on things like roads, bridges, schools, and other infrastructure projects. Unlike countries with weaker economies, which borrow directly from international lenders and banks, Canadian governments borrow most of their money from domestic and foreign investors by issuing securities and selling government bonds through capital markets. Some of Canada's more prosperous provinces—including BC, Alberta, and Saskatchewan—have long-term savings and investment accounts. These funds may be counted as government assets and weighed against any debts the governments owe to lenders.

budget deficit
A situation in which spending exceeds revenues during a given period.

public debt
The accumulated amount borrowed by a government to finance budgets and considered owing.

A large public debt is a problem when the prospects of repayment diminish and when **interest rates** are high. Governments issue bonds as a means of borrowing money to cover budget deficits and must offer the purchasers a return on their investment. This interest

interest rate
The percentage rate of money charged by lenders to borrowers.

Briefing Notes

In the Black and in the Red

The expressions "in the black" and "in the red" originate in ages-old accounting practices, when operating expenses were recorded using red ink, and revenues in black. If revenues exceed expenditures once the ledger is tallied, the organization is running a surplus and is said to be in the black. If not, the organization is running a deficit and is in the red.

rate is determined largely by the government's credit rating. The credit rating is set by international bond credit-rating agencies like Moody's and Standard & Poor's (S&P). These global organizations use grading systems to assess a government's economic and fiscal strength to provide investors with a sense of how likely the government is to default on (fail to pay) their debts. In general, this rating includes a government's debt-to-GDP ratio, the state of its budget balance, and its fiscal and economic outlook. The riskier a government's finances, the lower its credit rating, and the higher the interest rate. The higher the interest rate, the more a government must pay to investors, which increases the overall debt load and makes it more difficult to pay off debt. Most Canadian governments rank in the top tier of credit ratings (e.g., AAA to A– on the S&P scale). Significant deficits or downturns can see agencies downgrade provinces within this tier, which often attracts negative attention.

Interest rates also affect private debts accumulated by corporations and individuals in Canada. The Bank of Canada is an independent federal Crown corporation that works closely with the federal department of finance. The Bank sets the minimum national interest rate that is followed by institutions like banks that loan money to Canadians and their businesses. The central bank's interest-rate policy is influenced by domestic and international economic considerations. A low rate encourages borrowing and spending. As a monetary policy tool, it contributes to devaluing the national currency in international markets, which increases the price of imports. A cheaper currency improves the attractiveness of goods and services offered by domestic manufacturers. This may stimulate economic growth. However, economic growth can cause inflation, which erodes Canadians' buying power and increases the risk of bankruptcies. A higher interest rate is then introduced by the Bank of Canada to cool the economy.

The toxicity of deficits, debt, and high interest rates can require difficult public-policy decisions. In the early 1990s, after nearly three decades of annual deficits combined with high interest rates, over a third of the Government of Canada's debt repayments were being used just to pay the interest. The cause was more than simply an underperforming economy. Even if the Canadian economy were operating at its full potential, government spending would have still outstripped its revenues. This is what is known as a structural deficit, as opposed to a cyclical one caused by short-term misfortunes. The government's financial situation was so bad that a *Wall Street Journal* editorial referred to Canada as "an honorary member of the Third World" and to the Canadian dollar as the "northern peso."[11] To get the debt under control, Prime Minister Chretien's government cut spending on the public service, the military, employment insurance, and other national departments and programs. Public servants were laid off and taxes were increased. Health and social transfer payments to the provinces were reduced by more than 25 per cent. By 1997, the deficit was gone and debt repayment began. However, a number of programs, in particular social programs administered by provincial governments, were operating with greatly reduced budgets. Citizens complained about the declining quality of healthcare services. Students were upset about rising tuition fees. Eventually, the government's situation improved and its spending increased. Today, the federal government is committed to ensuring moderate growth of federal transfers to provincial and territorial governments each year.

Sometimes a government finds itself with extra money. By the 2000s, the federal government's balance sheet was so strong that it was able to pay down debt, and was in a position to fund new policy initiatives. In such a scenario, the government operates a **budget surplus** and is "in the black." Surpluses often invite questions as to whether the government is over-taxing or under-spending, the answer to which depends on the ideological perspective of the observer (see Table 8.2). Those on the political left in Canada tend to believe that surpluses should be used to support or enhance public programs and services. Those on the political right believe that surpluses should be reduced through tax relief and debt repayment. Advocates for provincial governments often call for an increase in federal–provincial transfers to address the fiscal imbalances discussed in Chapter 3. These are general tendencies, of course, and not all governments live up to their ideological commitments. Some left-wing governments have proven more adept and dedicated to reducing budget deficits than their right-wing counterparts, just as some nominally conservative governments have been champions of increased government spending.

Economic downturns often bring an end to budget surpluses. These periods of contraction encourage governments to engage in deficit financing and borrow money to fund

budget surplus
A situation in which revenues exceed spending during a given period.

Table 8.2 General Ideological Approaches to Budgeting

Left-Wing Ideology	Right-Wing Ideology
In times of budget deficit	
Increase: • spending • borrowing • taxes Maintain: • programs and services Delay: • debt repayment • spending reductions	Maintain: • taxes Decrease: • spending • borrowing • programs and services Delay: • debt repayment • tax increases
In times of budget surplus	
Increase: • spending • programs and services Maintain: • revenues • taxes Delay: • debt repayment	Increase: • debt repayment Maintain: • programs and services Decrease: • revenues • taxes Delay: • spending increases

stimulus
Increased government spending to encourage job growth amid an economic downturn.

infrastructure projects in an attempt to create a **stimulus** for economic growth. This approach formed the foundation of the budget management approaches employed by governments led by Stephen Harper after a global recession and, to a lesser extent, by Justin Trudeau.

Some Canadian governments have passed balanced budget legislation in order to avoid public debt. Parliament and seven of ten provincial legislatures have, at one point, established these laws as a means of controlling their finances. Balanced budget laws are designed to require governments to balance their revenues with expenditures. Individually, each law includes its own provisions to regulate spending growth and the use of surpluses, restrict tax increases, and set aside funds for future downturns. Some laws have gone so far as to impose reductions on ministers' salaries in the event of a budget deficit. Most rely on transparency provisions to hold the government publicly accountable for failing to balance its books.

Balanced budget legislation can be amended or repealed at any time. Justin Trudeau scrapped the Harper government's balanced budget law, for instance, in favour of running deficits to stimulate the economy. At around the same time, the right-wing Saskatchewan Party government repealed its own balanced budget legislation to engage in the same sort of deficit spending. Proponents of balanced budget laws hold them up as tools to allow politicians to say no to special interests seeking increased public spending. Critics see them as tying governments' hands during economic downturns—the precise occasions when increased government spending is required to support the most vulnerable and stimulate

martinedoucet/iStock

Politicians and journalists are fond of comparing public finances with household budgets. Rhetoric during election campaigns encourages Canadians to think about public spending around the kitchen table, as opposed to around the boardroom tables of Canada's financial districts. Most economists and political scientists question the wisdom of comparing public and private finances. What are some of the major differences between the way Canadians handle their personal or family budgets and the way governments do? What lessons could governments take from the way households maintain their budgets?

the economy. Research is mixed when it comes to the effectiveness of balanced budget leg-islation in Canada.[12] Jurisdictions with balanced budget laws have nonetheless run deficits and amended or repealed their legislation to do so. It is impossible to determine whether those deficits would have been larger had the legislation not been in place.

Funding the Public Service

Few policy decisions are as fiscally and politically challenging as finding the right level of pay and benefits for public-sector employees. Doing so requires the government to negotiate with most public servants. Negotiations often occur in the limelight shone by interest groups on both sides of the ideological spectrum. The **collective bargain-ing** process is a source of considerable pressure on governments. They are tasked with controlling public spending, paying competitive wages to retain and attract public ser-vants, and ensuring that optimal levels of government services are offered with min-imal interruption. Conversely, a **labour union** seeks to optimize contract matters for its members, including wages and benefits, hours of work, workplace conditions, job classifications and duties, and human resource matters such as terms of hiring, promo-tion, and dismissal. When a labour agreement is reached, the terms of employment are detailed in a collective bargaining agreement that is in effect for a specified period, such as four years. A new deal must be negotiated upon its expiry. The collective bargaining process is partly funded by the union's membership. Union members have mandatory deductions on their paycheques that finance the salaries of union personnel, opera-tional costs, and strike funds that can be used to offset lost wages for those who walk out on the job.

Some of the most powerful unions in the country work on behalf of public servants. Unions representing public servants include the country's largest union, the Canadian Union of Public Employees (CUPE), and the Public Service Alliance of Canada (PSAC). In addition to collective bargaining, these interest groups engage in political activism to achieve their members' policy objectives. Labour union support for left-wing political par-ties, including formal alliances with the New Democratic Party, adds a pressure dynamic no matter which party is in power.

Provincial governments must navigate particularly challenging contract demands from public servants, doctors, nurses, homecare workers, police officers, teachers, profes-sors, road maintenance workers, administrative staff, and a variety of other public-sector employees. Those workers' unions often argue that their members are underpaid com-pared with workers in other jurisdictions. They may balk at the terms of employment being offered. To apply pressure, unions may urge their members to use work-to-rule tac-tics, that is, to refuse to perform any extra services beyond those that are required under the bargained agreement. Under rare circumstances, they may threaten to or go on strike. This can cause public unrest if services are interrupted, especially at peak demand, for example, if teachers or snowplow operators are off the job in January as opposed to July. In some cases, the government may have formally identified the sector as an essential ser-vice in order to remove the threat of job action. In other instances, the government may impose the terms of an agreement by introducing back-to-work legislation. These tensions often end in court action. The Supreme Court of Canada has ruled at various times in favour and against the notion that the Charter of Rights and Freedoms encompasses the right to strike.

collective bargaining
The formal negotiation of the terms of an employment contract between the representatives of a group of employees and their employer.

labour union
An organization of workers that represents its members' interests, especially in bargaining with their employer.

See page 59 in Chapter 2 for a discussion of the Alberta Labour reference, in which the Supreme Court determined the right to strike is not guaranteed under the Charter of Rights and Freedoms.

Because the government is interested in the smooth running of the state and the economy, it has an interest in ensuring labour peace in the private sector, as well. Unionized employees generally, but not always, enjoy better terms of employment than non-unionized workers do. Work disruptions and stoppages can grow from an internal matter to become a broader public-policy problem. Polarized negotiations and the breaking off of contract talks can lead to tense situations. Both sides may run advertising campaigns to generate public sympathy for their cause; picketers may attempt to prevent access to buildings; unions become irate when replacement workers (pejoratively known as "scabs") are brought in by employers; workers may be under financial duress as their strike pay dries up; and businesses may threaten to relocate or shut down permanently. Moreover, unionized employees in one sector may support their so-called union "brothers and sisters" by refusing to cross the picket line. All of this public unrest is fodder for media coverage. Calls grow for the government to intervene as the situation escalates or negotiations reach a standstill. To this end, most federal and provincial governments have ministries of labour that offer mediation and conciliation services, with provinces also enforcing employment standards and workplace safety.

In general, people and parties on the left side of Canada's political spectrum tend to support the rights of workers and the actions of unions. People and parties on the right tend to side with private- and public-sector employers. For example, in 2015 the federal Conservative government passed a bill requiring unions to take extraordinary measures to publicly report their expenditures.

Government Revenues

The federal (Figure 8.4) and provincial (Figure 8.5) governments raise money through a number of recurring revenue sources. The most universal method of generating government revenues is through taxes. **Taxation policy** details the requirements for citizens and corporate bodies to pay money to the public treasury. Individuals and businesses are taxed in a plethora of ways, including income tax, sales tax, property tax, licences and fees, and gas taxes, among others. This is in addition to payments citizens make into mandatory benefit programs, notably the Canada Pension Plan and employment insurance, and some dedicated levies, fees, or premiums for services like education and healthcare.

There are two broad ways of collecting taxes in Canada. **Direct taxation** occurs when the taxpayer pays the government without the involvement of any other body. Examples of direct taxation include health premiums, education levies, and property taxes. The provinces delegate property tax authority to municipalities, which collect funds from property owners, normally using a mill rate that calculates a percentage of the estimated value of the property. In some communities, local government is financed through a poll tax, which is a fixed amount paid by all residents regardless of whether or not they own property.

The second way of collecting taxes is through **indirect taxation**, whereby the taxpayer gives funds to an intermediary, who then transmits the funds to the government. This is more common than direct taxation. Examples of indirect taxation include income tax collected by an employer through paycheque deductions and sales tax collected by a retailer. The federal, provincial, and territorial governments all have income tax policies. To streamline the process, the Canada Revenue Agency collects personal income tax on behalf of all governments except for that of Quebec, which does so itself, and corporate income tax on behalf of all governments, except for those of Alberta and Quebec. The most recognizable form of indirect taxation is a **sales tax**, which is a levy applied to

taxation policy
The regulations, mechanisms, and rates set by government to generate revenues from people and businesses in its jurisdiction.

direct taxation
The collection of taxes by government without using an intermediary.

indirect taxation
The collection of taxes by an intermediate body on behalf of the government.

sales tax
A revenue-generating tax charged by a government on the sale of applicable goods and services.

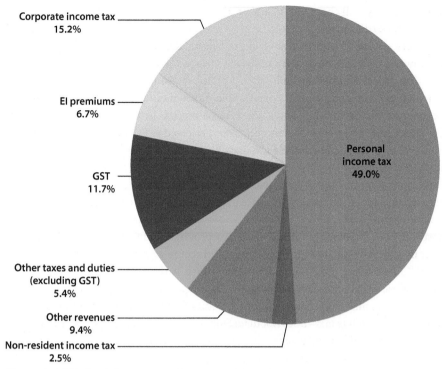

Figure 8.4 | Federal Government Revenues, 2017–18

Note: Numbers may not add up to 100% due to rounding.

Source: Public Accounts of Canada.

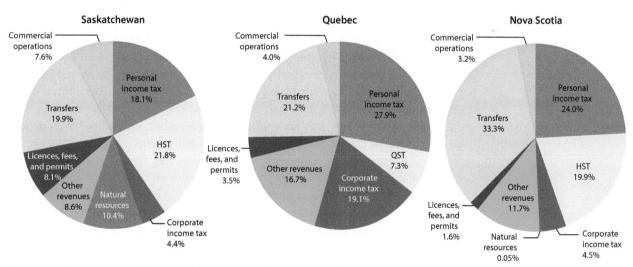

Figure 8.5 | Consolidated Provincial Government Revenues, for Three Provinces

Note: "Other revenues" includes other taxes, investments and other revenue. HST or QST includes other consumption taxes. Numbers may not add up to 100% due to rounding.

Source: Data from provincial ministries of finance budgets and economic plans, 2018–19.

the final sale of a good or service. The seller collects the tax from the buyer, and the seller transmits the money to the government on the buyer's behalf. For example, if the price of a can of pop is advertised at a convenience store as $1.00, and the sales tax is 8 per cent,

▷▷▷▷▷▷▷▷▷▷▷▷▷▷▷▷▷▷
See Inside Canadian
Politics: Why the Fuss over
the Government Putting a
Price or Tax on Carbon? on
page 499 of Chapter 14 for
the politics of hot air.

then by law the store will charge $1.08 and remit 8 cents to the government instead of the consumer doing so directly.

Canadians pay different direct and indirect taxes depending on where they engage in a sales transaction and where they ordinarily reside. Taxation policies reflect governments' philosophical approaches and fiscal capacity. Indeed, taxation is a tool of public policy, not simply a revenue source. For example, throughout Canada, governments levy sizeable taxes on liquor, tobacco, and cannabis as a mechanism to discourage consumption of products that bring social harm, sometimes referred to as "sin taxes." Likewise, the price of gasoline includes considerable tax costs, which are justified as a means for drivers to fund the building and maintenance of roads as well as an incentive for drivers to use public transportation or other alternatives to automobiles. In recent years, a new tax on gasoline has been added as a policy response to combating climate change and discouraging the use of fossil fuels.

Perspectives on income tax rates also vary by province and territory. A flat tax policy, as existed in Alberta from 1999 to 2015, taxes all income above a certain threshold at a single rate. Conversely, a progressive tax policy, which is the norm across Canada, is an incremental scale so that those with the highest incomes pay the highest tax rate. The proponents of a flat tax maintain that it is the most equitable approach, is easy to understand, and—unlike a progressive tax—does not deter upper-income earners from pursuing more work or investing locally. Conversely, the supporters of progressive tax rates argue that higher taxes on those who are better off means that there can be lower taxes on those who are less well off, and that society as a whole benefits from such a policy.

All Canadians may earn a basic personal amount of approximately $15,000 tax-free. This means that the least affluent members of society are not required to pay income tax. Parents of children under the age of 18, people over the age of 65, pensioners, people with disabilities, people supporting a spouse or other dependent relative, and caregivers are among those whom the federal government awards larger basic personal amounts to allow them more financial resources to deal with increased costs. Further deductions are available for Indigenous people living on reserves and residents of Northern areas. A proportion of charitable donations are tax-deductible, as are contributions to unions and political parties, though the latter receive a more generous rate. Canadians who contribute to these organizations are entitled to reduce their taxable income, and thus pay less tax.

tax credit
An income-tax provision that reduces a citizen's taxable income and thus reduces the tax payable.

Canadian governments offer **tax credits**, exempt amounts, and various other deductions as financial incentives that are designed to reward citizens' behaviour. Tax credits and deductions mean that governments give up revenues they would have otherwise collected, and individuals receive a tax break for engaging in certain types of activities. For example, New Brunswick is one of several jurisdictions that offers a small business investor tax credit and a venture capital tax credit, which are designed to encourage investment in provincial businesses and stimulate economic growth. Such tax incentives are a policy tool for encouraging or discouraging certain types of behaviour.

goods and services tax (GST)
A federal value-added tax applied to the sale of most goods and services in Canada.

Governments also tax Canadians as they consume goods and services. The federal government requires a 5 per cent sales tax, the **goods and services tax** (GST), throughout Canada. The GST is a sales tax added to the price of most products and services, with some exceptions, such as groceries and medical services. Because the intent is to apply the tax only to the finished product and not to any goods and services used in the manufacturing process, the GST is known as a value-added tax. This means businesses can claim a GST rebate on certain eligible expenses incurred in the creation of the final product or service.

As well, low-income Canadians can apply for a GST rebate, in recognition that higher proportions of their incomes are being used to pay for taxable goods and services. In 2006 and again in 2008, the Harper government cut the GST by a percentage point, reducing it from 7 per cent to 5 per cent, which led to some provinces correspondingly increasing their provincial sales tax rates. All provinces except Alberta add some form of a provincial sales tax (PST). There is no further sales tax required by the three territorial governments.

Half of the provincial governments combine their PST with the GST. The rationale is that streamlining operations generates cost savings for both orders of government and reduces the administrative burden on business. The federal government collects this **harmonized sales tax (HST)** revenue on the provinces' behalf and reimburses it to the participating governments. Harmonizing federal and provincial sales taxes involves melding together two sets of tax rules. Rates on certain goods and services may increase or decrease depending on the details of the federal–provincial agreement. For instance, the total sales tax might be lowered on some goods and services—in particular, on new homes—but go up on routine consumer purchases such as haircuts, magazines, dry cleaning, taxi rides, movie tickets, phone and cable bills, and restaurant meals. The choice of which products are exempt from sales tax is a politically charged one, as governments must determine which goods and services—like basic groceries, medical devices, houses, childcare fees, and feminine hygiene products—are necessities and thus non-taxable.

Government Spending

The mix of taxing and spending ensures all Canadians enjoy a baseline quality of life through the provision of public services. Above all else, government seeks to ensure that citizens are safe and have the basic necessities of life, namely access to water and food, clothing, and shelter. Public safety is a significant policy priority, but the bulk of government spending is focused on helping young families and seniors; those who fall on hard times when they lose their job, get sick, or experience some other type of crisis; and citizens who are perpetually homeless, unemployed, and/or poor. All levels of government offer many programs and services to improve the quality of life of Canadians and the vibrancy of Canadian society.

These examples make up only a tiny sample of government spending. Governments have many major recurring expenditure items (see Figure 8.6), the most expensive of which are the programs collectively referred to as the social safety net, or **welfare state**. Canada's welfare state is a defining characteristic of its political culture, particularly when it comes to the provision of universal healthcare (see Chapter 14). Given the country's ageing population and slow economic growth, sustaining these programs is one of the biggest public-policy challenges facing the next generation of Canadian public servants.

Over time, especially since the hardships of the Great Depression, governments have invested more into the expansion of the welfare state. These systems vary greatly from jurisdiction to jurisdiction, given each jurisdiction's unique authority over the policy area. The federal government supports the welfare state by managing income support programs like pensions and employment insurance, and transfers to other levels of government. Provinces and territories use those transfers to provide programs and services, such as healthcare and job training. There is no definitive list of government-funded programs that fit within the welfare state. We can broadly distinguish between entitlements and insurance programs.

See pages 175 and 203 in Chapter 6 for more discussion of the GST.

harmonized sales tax (HST): In Atlantic Canada and Ontario, a value-added consumption tax that combines both federal and provincial rates.

welfare state
A suite of government programs, services, and financial supports designed to assist the least fortunate in society.

For a discussion of the social safety net, see The Politics of Fiscal Federalism, beginning on page 78 of Chapter 3.

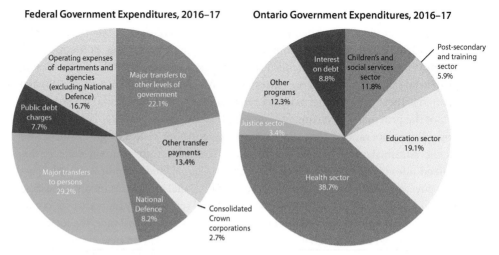

Figure 8.6 | **Federal and Ontario Government Expenditures**

1. Entitlement Programs

Entitlement programs represent part of the social contract between Canadians and their governments. Citizens can be reasonably confident that these supports will always be available as resources allow. The specific eligibility criteria and scope of services may be subject to change. The federal government has created policies that entitle eligible citizens to receive financial assistance. This is often in conjunction with provincial governments; alternatively, a federal program may supplement provincial policies. The most notable programs support citizens before their normal working years and after they exit the work-force. Entitlement programs are either universal (i.e., provided to all citizens, regardless of income) or means-tested (i.e., provided to citizens at varying levels, depending on their income).

A major federal government policy, initiated in 1944, is the family allowance, commonly referred to as the **baby bonus**. The financial needs of families with young children became acute as soldiers returned from war and the baby boom began. Initially a universal program, the family allowance provided monthly payments to parents for every child in their care who was up to 16 years of age. Since that time, federal child-benefit policies have changed from government to government. Most recently, Conservatives tend to favour universal approaches that promote nuclear family structures. Under the Harper Conservatives, each family was paid a fixed amount for every child in their household. This benefit was supplemented by a tax credit for two-parent families and an additional tax benefit per child per month for low-income families. Conversely, child benefits tend to be means-tested under recent Liberal governments, distributing funds based on income and without favour to two-parent households. The Justin Trudeau Liberals introduced the Canada Child Benefit. The amount each family receives is determined by their household income and the top 10 per cent of income-earning families are ineligible. Unlike previous versions, the Canada Child Benefit is tax free and indexed to inflation. The Trudeau government nixed the two-parent family tax credit and increased the amount of parental leave available to parents who choose to split it between partners. These reforms demonstrate the role of ideology in shaping governments' approaches to public policy.

baby bonus
A government policy that awards money to parents of young children.

Each provincial and territorial government operates a unique set of childcare programs and standards. These range from a heavily subsidized and regulated system in Quebec to a predominantly private and non-profit system in Alberta. The federal government funds provinces through the Canada Social Transfer and subsidizes parents through tax credits and benefit programs. What are the advantages of this decentralized form of policymaking? Why do you think politicians rarely question why government subsidizes the childcare costs of working parents who can afford to pay?

In addition to these family benefits, and those provided separately by provincial governments, most Canadian children attend publicly funded schooling from kindergarten to grade 12. Private schools and home schooling are available as alternatives. Provincial governments fund and maintain public school systems, with support from the federal government through the Canada Social Transfer. Canadian governments do not fully subsidize post-secondary education. Most of the costs of public college and university programming are paid for by provincial governments; nevertheless, tuition fees, textbooks, living costs, and other expenses are the responsibility of students. The expense of a post-secondary education is such that it could prevent students from lower-income households from enrolling. In 1964, the Government of Canada introduced the **Canada Student Loans** program to address this policy problem. The program provides, to eligible students, loans that begin incurring interest six months after graduation. Most provinces and territories supplement Canada Student Loans with their own student loan programs. These funds are intended to be supplemented with other funding, including non-repayable grants and savings. The idea is to subsidize the costs of studying at a public post-secondary school for those who demonstrate financial need, while simultaneously placing responsibility on students, who will gain a competitive edge in the job market, to fund their own education.

People in the workforce will experience different results regardless of their formal education. Those who are independent and not working may qualify for **social assistance**

Canada Student Loans
A federal program that helps qualifying students access post-secondary education by providing them access to loans that are interest free and do not need to be repaid while they study full-time.

social assistance
Financial support provided by government to citizens with no other recourse to income.

to provide them with a minimum level of income. Partially funded through the Canada Social Transfer, this government program is a provincial responsibility, and so it varies in nature across the country. Those who are eligible for social assistance may receive basic benefits for food, clothing, personal care, household maintenance, and utilities, as well as funding for rent or a mortgage.[13] If circumstances warrant, recipients may qualify for municipal tax payments, eye exams, prescription glasses, a prescription drug card, medical supplies, medical equipment, medical transportation, private childcare if it is related to employment or training, and/or funeral expenses. Social assistance is not without its critics. Those on the political right oppose aggrandizing social assistance programs, which they feel provide disincentives for recipients to find work and contribute to the economy. Those on the left seek to reduce the stigma of government handouts by recasting social assistance as "income support" or "income assistance." Proponents on both sides of the political spectrum have proposed that governments instead provide all citizens with a minimum level of money to support their basic needs. Cost savings would be found in the elimination of administering a complex suite of social services and subsidies. Governments in Manitoba and Ontario have fielded pilot programs to test this basic (or guaranteed) annual income model for broader use. No province has fully implemented the program.

Most Canadians will see their income levels decline when they exit the workforce. The financial pressures on senior citizens who have fixed incomes can be acute. This is

AJ Watt/iStock

Many Canadians rely on social programs despite having full-time jobs, or a series of part-time jobs, that pay minimum wage. Labelled the "working poor," these individuals and their families often struggle to meet basic needs including rent and groceries. Some provincial governments responded by raising their minimum wage rates to create what they call a "living wage." Opponents respond that raising the minimum wage forces employers to reduce the number of hours they provide to each worker in order to avoid raising prices. What are the advantages and disadvantages of raising the minimum wage? Why is it sometimes a contentious issue that makes news headlines?

especially true for those who did not contribute to a pension plan or amass personal savings, who do not own their own home, and who have medical expenses. People employed outside the public sector, contract workers, homemakers, widowers, renters, and those with health problems are particularly vulnerable. Moreover, as people live longer, their finances need to stretch further. For these reasons, women tend to be in greater need than men.

In 1927, the federal government consulted with provinces in creating a pension plan for retired Canadians, which provided funds to applicants if they could demonstrate financial need. It was the country's first non-contributory pension plan (i.e., funded completely by the government). This was replaced in 1952 with the Old Age Security (OAS) program, which was the country's first universal benefit for Canadians 65 years and older.[14] Today, recipients of OAS payments who have a low income also receive a Guaranteed Income Supplement (GIS) as a top-up. Seniors whose annual income exceeds a certain threshold have the OAS amount fully clawed back by the government. The OAS and GIS are funded out of the federal government's general revenues. They are designed to ensure that all seniors have a basic minimum income regardless of the extent to which they participated in the workforce.

Government needs people to save for their future expenses in order to maintain a solid social and economic foundation for society. Many workers would not save for retirement unless obligated by law. In 1966, the **Canada Pension Plan (CPP)** was created as a mandatory retirement savings program. It was designed to provide a modest income to citizens in their senior years, with the understanding that most would need to supplement this amount with workplace pensions, continued employment, and personal savings. Workers are required to pay into the CPP fund, up to an annual limit. Their employers supplement these contributions through additional payments into the CPP fund. Workers and employers in Quebec pay into the Quebec Pension Plan (QPP) instead. Governments periodically change the contribution rates required of both employees and employers to ensure the program remains sustainable. When they turn 65, pensioners are eligible to begin receiving monthly CPP payments as are their widows and widowers, if applicable. Alternatively, they may opt for early retirement at the age of 60, or earlier if they become disabled, but receive lower payments.

Canada Pension Plan
A mandatory federal retirement program funded by workers and employers.

There are concerns that the CPP and other pension plans are underfunded. Payments made by current employees are invested and are used to finance the pension cheques of current retirees. As the baby boomers exit the workforce, there is a growing number of retirees drawing on pension funds, and a smaller pool of workers contributing. Canadians are living longer and thus retirees are drawing more funds from their pension than anticipated. Moreover, as a defined benefit program, the CPP guarantees a minimum payout regardless of how much workers contributed or how successful the government's investments have been. This raises further questions about the CPP's sustainability at current contribution and payout rates. Similar challenges confront other public- and private-sector pension plans. Some provincial governments propose increasing CPP premiums for current workers or creating province-specific pension plans.

As retirement approaches, many Canadian workers begin to realize that the OAS, GIS, and CPP, which in some cases pay out less than $2000 per month, are unlikely to cover much beyond their normal living expenses. The solution proposed so far by the federal government has been to provide alternative savings options and encourage people to take responsibility to save for their own retirement. The federal government incentivizes citizens by offering to defer and forgo taxes. The federal government's Registered Retirement Savings Plan (RRSP) allows Canadians to defer taxes on a proportion of their saved income. Contributors reduce their taxable income and may qualify for a tax refund. They do not pay taxes on these funds or interest earned until the money is withdrawn from their account. Similarly, Canadians can save for a child's post-secondary education through a Registered Education Savings Plan and/or for a disabled dependant's needs through a Registered Disability Savings Plan. As well, Canadians may open a Tax-Free Savings Account (TFSA) and deposit up to $5500 a year without being taxed on any income that is earned on the investment. Many low- to middle-income Canadians struggle to set aside these savings. In this sense, the seniors' benefits system is a combination of mostly universal (OAS), means-tested (GIS), and contribution-based (CPP, RRSP, TFSA) components. The sustainability of retirement income policies will be a recurring issue as the Canadian population continues to age.

2. Insurance Programs

Publicly funded insurance programs are available to Canadians when an urgent need arises. As with any insurance program, a large number of people pay into it, but at any given time only a small proportion uses it. Moreover, the full cost of the insured service is not necessarily covered, and there may be a deductible that has to be paid by the user.

medicare
A publicly funded healthcare service administered by each province with the financial support of the federal government.

Public health services were offered by charities when Canada was formed. Today, **medicare** is the crown jewel in the country's welfare state. Since 1966, Canada's interconnected provincial healthcare insurance programs have existed as an area of provincial jurisdiction under broad national standards. Each jurisdiction has a public health insurance program that provides universal access to medical care regardless of a citizen's financial means. Provincial and territorial governments pay healthcare providers for delivering health services to Canadians. The Canada Health Act, 1984, identifies five main principles that provinces and territories must follow when delivering basic services if they wish to qualify for federal funds through the Canada Health Transfer. Healthcare must be:

The Canada Health Transfer is explained on pages 82–4 of Chapter 3, on federalism.

1. universal (i.e., everyone qualifies);
2. comprehensive (i.e., must cover all insured services);
3. accessible (i.e., must not impose financial barriers to essential services);
4. portable (i.e., citizens receive service in other provinces); and
5. publicly administered (i.e., not for profit).

Canada's healthcare system is both a source of pride to Canadians and a source of debate. In public-opinion surveys it is regularly cited as a point of differentiation from the United States and part of the Canadian identity. Yet there are constant complaints about timely access to family physicians; long wait times to see specialists; frustrations about costs and procedures that are not covered; and studies that show that public healthcare is of lower quality than private healthcare. Furthermore, the system is under increasing strain as the average age of the population increases, and as concerns persist over the federal government's obligation to provide health services to Indigenous communities, immigrants, and refugees. Political observers sometimes snidely remark that because of the growing expenses, we will one day see the provincial minister of health, not the minister of finance, deliver the provincial budget.

Debates abound: To what extent should the federal government be involved in an area of provincial jurisdiction? What can be done about wait times? How far should residents of rural communities be expected to travel to access care? Should a two-tier public/private system be allowed, where those Canadians who can afford more timely or sophisticated care should be allowed to pay out of pocket? Should a pharmacare program be established to subsidize the costs of medication? No matter what the policy options are, spending demands are increasing, which reduces the range of policy solutions that policymakers have at their disposal.

Employment insurance (EI) is the other major federal public insurance program in Canada. It provides temporary income to eligible workers who have been laid off. The Employment Insurance Act requires that many workers pay EI premiums through payroll deductions (i.e., money deducted from their paycheques). Approximately 2 per cent of Canadians' earnings fund this national insurance program. Workers who paid the premiums and who worked the minimum number of insurable hours may be eligible to receive EI benefits if their employer lays them off. Benefits are not available to people who are fired for cause. The number of workers who are eligible to draw EI benefits has also declined over time, forcing many to seek social assistance to make ends meet between jobs. Workers who leave work to care for a newborn child, who are ill, or who care for a sick family member have access to EI funds. After a brief unpaid waiting period, claimants receive roughly half of their insurable earnings, subject to a maximum amount. They receive payments for nearly a year. Resources are available through regional offices to help them find work and they may qualify to participate in job training programs. Once the EI benefits are used up, citizens may apply for other government programs, such as social assistance.

> **employment insurance**
> A mandatory government insurance program, funded by employees and employers, that provides temporary income to workers who lose their jobs.

The EI program is a source of as much controversy as publicly funded healthcare. Defenders point out that it supports seasonal economies in rural areas, such as those dependent upon agriculture, fishing, and tourism, which have recurring layoffs. The program can encourage employers to distribute finite work hours among available employees. For instance, instead of one person being employed year-round, the availability of EI provides an alternative of four people working for 13 weeks. In this way, defenders argue, EI creates an efficient economy that optimizes the availability of labour and supports rural communities. Others are unconvinced. The EI program creates a false economy, they say, and is a disincentive for repeat users to work year-round or to relocate to find work. Provincial governments are incentivized to offer so-called "make work projects" that involve workers doing menial tasks in order to qualify for EI instead of provincially funded social assistance. Defenders and critics alike do share one concern: that the employment insurance fund is too large. Contributions to the fund have outstripped the cost of benefits for a number of years. Whether the EI surplus signifies that premiums are too high or that benefits are too difficult for workers to access is a matter of debate.

Perhaps the biggest source of policy disagreement around employment insurance policy is its regional inequities. Workers in some areas of Canada who file an EI claim for the first time are frustrated to find out how difficult it is to access an insurance program they have paid into their entire working lives. Others are repeat users who routinely access EI and use it to supplement their income. The discrepancy can depend on where a laid-off worker lives and which of the dozens of regional rules apply. Some politicians want a single national standard or call for the categories reduced to just a few regions, such as urban, rural, and remote. Conservatives seek to place more responsibility on repeat claimants to travel for available work. Liberals and New Democrats tend to prefer multiple categories as a means of supporting people with unstable employment.

Two additional public insurance programs are worth mentioning. Federal, provincial, and municipal governments all have some form of disaster financial assistance programs. Disaster assistance is intended to assist people in greatest need after a calamity causes damage that is not covered by a private-sector insurance program. The other noteworthy program is public motor vehicle insurance, which is offered by Crown corporations in British Columbia, Manitoba, Quebec, and Saskatchewan. It is a rare example of government operating in a sector of the economy that is normally serviced by the private sector. In other provinces there is periodically public pressure, particularly from the NDP, to switch to a publicly owned insurance provider.

Toward Good Government

Patronage and the Merit Principle

Canadians require a competent public service to develop effective public policy and manage the multitude of public programs and services. It matters how that public service is assembled. Beyond the permanent bureaucracy, which consists of non-partisan employees, the prime minister and the premiers have thousands of contracts to dispense and thousands of political positions to fill. **Patronage** involves government contracts flowing to party supporters and government jobs going to partisans who are appointed to plum positions. Patronage is a reward for faithful service to the party in power. Partisan appointments often assume that individual will continue to be loyal, and patronage contracts are doled out in similar appreciation for supporting the party in power.

Patronage was the bastion of party politics in the early-twentieth century. Today, quid pro quo government contracts are becoming rare with government transparency and free trade. Over a minimum threshold, most governments post their contract opportunities online, and businesses are constantly monitoring government dealings to ensure they live up to open procurement rules. Patronage positions remain necessary when the primary criterion for the job is the executive's trust that the appointee will advance the government's agenda. This is particularly true for senior positions in ABCs, especially when the government is re-organizing or re-purposing an agency, or when the organization is a high-profile Crown corporation. In some cases, the appointment process is secretive. Some partisans receive appointments irrespective of their apparent qualifications. The practice may create a culture of entitlement within the governing party. In other cases, citizens may apply for positions in open competitions similar to those in the mainstream public service. In all scenarios, the choice of whom to appoint is left largely to cabinet or individual ministers, subject to final approval of the Crown.

Patronage often draws public criticism and rebuke. It runs counter to the **merit principle**, which holds that government contracts and jobs should be publicized and open to competition. The principle means that government work is awarded to the most competent applicants. All citizens should be eligible to apply for government positions, formal criteria should be consistently applied to evaluate candidates, and the most qualified person should be offered the job. There are standardized rules for disciplining employees and terminating their employment. The government cannot discriminate against applicants and employees on the basis of socio-demographic characteristics or their political

patronage
The awarding of government jobs, contracts, and/or other financial benefits to friends of the government party.

merit principle
The notion that the most qualified candidate should be awarded a position, contract, or other financial benefit.

activities outside work hours. Nevertheless, even with the existence of the merit principle, some demographic cohorts are disproportionately represented in the public service and some bureaucrats do face pressure to hide or curtail their spare-time political activities. The merit principle has limits. A highly competent individual is unlikely to be placed in a senior government position if that individual has close ties to an opposition party or is otherwise philosophically opposed to the governing party.

In the federal government, the Public Service Commission is responsible for the professionalism of staffing, and ensures that non-senior positions are free from political influence. Job vacancies are advertised, applications are screened by a committee, candidates are interviewed and tested, and the committee decides who should be offered the position. As well, employment equity programs exist to improve the representation of underrepresented groups in the public service. Similar processes are in place to govern the awarding of government contracts. Provincial and territorial equivalents exist to enforce the merit principle at those levels.

See Affirmative Action and Employment Equity, beginning on page 449 of Chapter 13, for an explanation of employment equity programs.

See Up for Debate: Should all government jobs be awarded based on merit? on pages 286–7 at the end of this chapter for a debate supplement that gives some of the arguments on both sides, and offers questions and resources to guide a discussion around this pressing topic.

Ethics and Scandal

It is inevitable that allegations of outdated practices in public administration and frustrations with policy blunders will arise. Canadian governments have had their fair share of scandal, ranging from tainted food cover-ups to high-profile infidelity; these incidents are memorable in part because of their rarity.

By far the greatest ethical challenges in Canadian politics concerns the dispensing of public funds. **Pork barrel politics** involves the cabinet's authorizing government spending in electoral districts where there is support for the governing party or where local projects may translate into votes and donations. "Pork" commonly refers to public funds being used for government programs or initiatives. Public infrastructure projects and grants for businesses promising to create local jobs are particularly susceptible to politicization. For example, under the Harper government, Conservative ridings in Ontario routinely received more funds than ridings held by other parties.[15] For its part, the Justin Trudeau government earned a reputation for extravagant spending in Quebec's aluminum industry, through its Atlantic Growth Strategy, and in ridings where a by-election was scheduled. Ministers fanned out across the country to make spending announcements in the months leading up to the 2019 federal election call. Pork barrel politics results from the activities of elected officials who want to "bring home the bacon" for their constituents. It is broader than patronage because even those who support a different political party, leader, and/or candidate(s) may benefit from the government spending. To some, pork barrel politics and patronage are unscrupulous; to others, they are smart politicking that operates within the law.

pork barrel politics
The partisan allocation of government spending to select constituencies, especially those districts held or sought by the governing party.

Anything that breaks or circumvents the rule of law is beyond the pale. Scandals periodically erupt involving isolated acts by individuals or behaviour by multiple public officials that in part can be attributed to the nature of the system itself. Arguably the worst kind of political scandal is mass collusion among people seeking to defraud the government for their own personal gain and/or their political party. For instance, one person in a position of power accessing government funds for personal benefit is a concern, whereas multiple people being reimbursed for fraudulent expense claims can expose a coordinated scheme. Major scandals in Canadian politics have implicated government parties in kickback schemes. Kickbacks involve someone within government receiving a secret payment

See page 335 in Chapter 10 for discussion of the in and out scandal, and page 392 in Chapter 11 for discussion of the sponsorship scandal.

Inside Canadian Politics

Was the Pacific Scandal the Biggest Political Scandal in Canadian History?

The Pacific Scandal remains perhaps the most egregious political scandal in Canadian history. Two business consortiums were bidding for a lucrative government contract to build the Canadian Pacific Railway. During the 1872 general election, a representative of one of the groups donated at least $350,000 (roughly $7.3 million in today's dollars) to the Conservative Party. That consortium was awarded the railway contract when the Conservatives were returned to power. Some Liberals broke into a government office and discovered a telegram from Prime Minister John A. Macdonald pleading for the funds. In the resulting kerfuffle, some Conservative MPs crossed the floor, the government fell on a non-confidence motion, and the governor general asked the Liberals to form the government. It is the only time in Canadian federal politics that power has switched hands without a general election preceding the switch. The Macdonald Conservatives lost the ensuing election; nevertheless, afterwards they went on to win four consecutive majority governments.

DISCUSSION ITEM

While governments may be held accountable by their legislatures and the Crown, and may be ousted for unethical behaviour, the electorate can be just as quick to forgive parties and politicians for their misdeeds.

VOX POP

What are the most effective public-policy tools when it comes to reducing the frequency or severity of scandals involving the public purse?

to help a firm to secure a government contract, as occurred with the Pacific Scandal (see box above) and the sponsorship scandal (see Chapter 11). In all cases, stronger accountability practices and increased transparency would have reduced the possibility of the misuse of public funds.

There are many ways that the government attempts to limit the possibility of financial mismanagement and unethical conduct. Government personnel, including members of cabinet, are subject to the rule of law. This includes possible sanctions under the Criminal Code of Canada and Conflict of Interest Act. The Financial Administration Act states that the federal government must take "appropriate measures to promote fairness, openness and transparency in the bidding process for contracts" (section 40.1). Strict campaign finance laws limit the amount of money Canadians can donate to federal political parties. Unions and corporations are prohibited from contributing. Most federal government contracts are put out for public tender and follow a rigorous evaluation process. Public-opinion research reports must be submitted to Library and Archives Canada within six months in order to limit the government's ability to hoard information. Government departments and agencies prepare annual reports on their spending and performance.

Lobbyists are required to register with most governments and basic information about lobbying is made public to ensure transparent dealings. Access to information laws provide Canadians with the ability to obtain certain government files and communication. These are just some of the many government policies that have been crafted in response to past problems. As well, legislatures employ a number of officers, including conflict of interest and ethics commissioners.

See Chapter 10 for a full account of Canada's campaign finance laws.

At the federal level, some of these policies were introduced as part of the Accountability Act, which was the most sweeping reform legislation in recent memory. The Act was introduced by the Harper government in 2006 in response to the sponsorship scandal and the report of the Gomery Commission. The Act's changes included increased scope of investigation for the auditor general; whistleblower protection to allow public servants who spot wrongdoing to speak out; and stricter rules for lobbyists, in particular requiring that five years lapse between the time government insiders may leave their positions and begin a lobbying career. Some politicians call for the government to go further. In 2015, the Liberal Party under Justin Trudeau campaigned on an "open Parliament plan" that would require parliamentarians to proactively disclose their travel and hospitality expenses and make meetings of the House of Commons' secretive Board of Internal Economy (BOIE) open to the public. Once in government, the Liberals backed away from reforms to expense disclosure, shaken by the prime minister's own ill-advised acceptance of gifts from a foreign donor. Tasked with overseeing the management of Parliament—including MPs' spending, building security, and human resources—the BOIE did open its doors to public hearings in 2017. According to the revised legislation, closed-door sessions will continue for particularly sensitive matters, including the harassment allegations that rocked Parliament Hill as part of the #MeToo movement.

See Chapter 12 for a discussion of lobbying rules in Canada.

Concluding Thoughts

Just about everything that Canadians do is governed by some aspect of public policy. This makes appreciating the scope and complexity of policymaking an integral part of understanding Canadian politics. As discussed in this chapter, problems and solutions are often structured by people selected through a merit-based system that values their ability to formulate recommendations to the government of the day. Yet, elected officials make policy choices based on a host of factors beyond the evidence provided by public servants. Partisanship plays a considerable role in this vein, which is where our attention turns next.

For More Information

Interested in learning more about the nuances of public administration in Canada? Take a look at the many topics covered in *The Handbook of Canadian Public Administration*, 3rd edition, edited by Christopher Dunn (Oxford University Press, 2018).

Want a deeper perspective into how public policy and public administration operate at the provincial level of government? See Michael M. Atkinson and colleagues' *Governance and Public Policy in Canada: A View from the Provinces* (University of Toronto Press, 2013).

Interested in learning about public administration in Indigenous governance? Take a look at Joanne Heritz's article "The Multiplying Nodes of Indigenous Self-Government and Public Administration" (*Canadian Public Administration* 60, no. 2 [2017]: pp. 289–90).

How do government budgets reflect partisan ideology and election promises? François Pétry and Dominic Duval examine two decades' worth of budgets in "Electoral Promises and Single Party Governments: The Role of Party Ideology and Budget Balance in Pledge Fulfillment" (*Canadian Journal of Political Science* [2018]).

Curious about policy analysis in Canada? Pierre-Olivier Bédard and Mathieu Ouimet outline some of the techniques used by ministerial policy analysts in "Awareness and Use of Systematic Literature Reviews and Meta-Analyses by Ministerial Policy Analysts" (*Canadian Public Administration* 60, no. 2 [2017]: pp. 173–91).

Is the non-partisan public service becoming politicized? The professional values of Canadian public administration are put to the test in Jill Anne Chouinard and Peter Milley's article "From New Public Management to New Political Governance: Implications for Evaluation" (*Canadian Journal of Program Evaluation* 30, no. 1 [2015]: pp. 1–22).

Doing some topical research about public policy in Canada? Visit the website of *Policy Options* magazine: https://policyoptions.irpp.org/.

Want help unpacking the ethics of public administration? Kenneth Kernahan and John Langford provide guidance in *The Responsible Public Servant*, 2nd edn (Institute of Public Administration of Canada, 2014).

Interested in building trust in government? The Public Policy Forum identifies how in "Time for a Reboot: Nine Ways to Restore Trust in Canada's Public Institutions" (October 2015).

Considering a career as a bureaucrat? We have written a guidebook for students and new professionals: *The Public Servant's Guide to Government in Canada* (University of Toronto Press, 2019).

Deeper Inside Canadian Politics

1. Some advocacy groups that advance the cause of political minorities receive government funding. However, they are some of the government's biggest critics. Do you agree that some interest groups should be given public funding? If so, how should governments decide which ones to fund?

2. Patronage tends to be decried by the public, attacked by political commentators and the opposition, and derided by editorial cartoonists. Yet no matter what political party is in power, it persists. Under what circumstances do you feel that patronage is acceptable and even necessary?

3. Budget deficits and public debt are common because politicians tend to be praised for making spending promises and criticized for spending cutbacks. For this reason, several governments have chosen to break, amend, or repeal balanced budget legislation in place in their jurisdictions. What other policies might be established to prevent governments from spending beyond their means?

Professor Profile

Jennifer Robson

Social policy, poverty and inequality, the governance of political staff

Author of *Spending on Political Staffers and the Revealed Preferences of Cabinet* (2015)

Courtesy Jennifer Robson

Jennifer Robson's research interests include social and tax policy, poverty in Canada, and public administration. Previously, she was a director of policy with a non-profit organization promoting financial empowerment, and held several political staff roles in the Jean Chrétien government. She regularly collaborates with community-based organizations and government.

Here is what Jennifer Robson told us about her career path from when she was an undergraduate student, why she is drawn to her area of specialization, what is challenging about studying Canadian politics, and what advice she has for students.

* * *

My undergraduate degree is actually an honours degree in psychology from the University of Ottawa. Until my fourth year, my plan was to complete my PhD and gain accreditation as a clinical psychologist. My graduate degrees are in political science and public policy, but I've ended up finding the psychology degree useful on more than one occasion. Even now, whenever I think about public-policy challenges, I think about the complexity of individual behavior and that comes from my undergrad training.

What I remember most about my first introduction to Canadian politics course is that I was working part-time for an MP at the time. I can recall feeling mild frustration in the class—both with what seemed to me like a disconnect between the course content and what I witnessed on Parliament Hill, and also with some fellow students who seemed to view the class as a partisan debate instead of a chance to learn. I never took another politics course in my undergrad, which is kind of funny given my career and teaching since then.

In the final year of my BA, I started to work in a junior role with the policy and research team of the Prime Minister's Office. I fell in love with public policy and Canadian social policy in particular. I came to see it as a better avenue for me to contribute to wellbeing in my community than pursuing a career in clinical psychology. My work continues to be very applied and I continue to feel a strong commitment to public service.

The biggest challenges in studying Canadian social policy are about how we, as a field, learn and figure out what is true. Unlike many other fields, issues of definition and methods of observation and measurement are always disputed in social policy. It means that it is very, very difficult to reach agreement on foundational knowledge and then collectively advance our understanding of what works (and doesn't). For example, it's much harder to reach agreement on how to reduce poverty if you can't even agree on how to measure poverty.

I continue to be surprised by how little is truly new in social policy. Different social problems and policy options move on and off the public agenda, cyclically but not predictably. I am now old enough that I can personally recall previous cycles of debates on current topics in Canadian social policy. We should all take more time to learn from history.

A tip for students is to read widely, thoughtfully, and outside your field. Take a course or pursue your own reading list. Don't just learn interesting facts from another field, learn how at least one other discipline sees the world. Develop your horizontal thinking by seeing what Canadian politics has in common, and in contrast, with another field. The ability to think horizontally—to see connections and identify patterns—is a very valuable and increasingly critical skill.

Up for Debate

Should all government jobs be awarded based on merit?

THE CLAIM: YES, THEY SHOULD!

Patronage is outdated, unethical, and outrageous.

Yes: Argument Summary

The blatant use of the executive power to reward party supporters is out of step with modern notions of democratic government. It is understandable that cabinet and members of the Prime Minister's Office or Premier's Office need to be appointed. However, the process of selecting chairs of government agencies and board positions needs reform. There is little reason why the process used by the political executive to fill public positions should not be open to more public scrutiny and participation.

Yes: Top 5 Considerations

1. Patronage in Canada is a holdover from the immediate post-Confederation era, when the governing party was expected to fill the public service with friends. It may encourage corruption and is at odds with the values of a modern liberal democracy. For example, party executives may promise a lucrative appointment to prevent a whistleblower from going public.

2. The modern public service strictly adheres to the merit principle and employment equity. Patronage is incompatible with the bureaucracy because it undermines the apolitical values of evidence-informed decision-making, its standards of professionalism, and its concern for demographic representation. It introduces fears of dismissal, the promotion of party interests over the public interest, constant suspicion, turmoil when there is a change of government, and the exploitation of the public service to prop up the governing party in election campaigns.[16]

3. Government plays an increasingly important role in Canadians' lives. This enhances the importance of appointing only the most highly skilled, trained, and experienced candidates to positions in the public service.

4. The clandestine nature of many patronage appointments is a telling indicator that political elites know that their decisions prioritize the interests of their party over those of the general public. Mindful that most media outlets will be unable to cover them, and that Canadians pay less attention to news on the weekends, politicians often make patronage appointments and pork barrel announcements at the end of the workday on Fridays. They purposely hide decisions that would otherwise attract negative publicity.

5. Each new head of government introduces experiments with reforms to operate a more ethical government. When these reforms complicate the ability to govern, they are abandoned in favour of the status quo.

Yes: Other Considerations

- Distributing the spoils of office among supporters may be legal, but by today's standards it is arguably unethical, and often out of touch with public expectations. Prominent Canadian journalist Jeffrey Simpson once wrote, "Patronage is the pornography of politics, enticing to some, repulsive to others, justified as inevitable, condemned as immoral, a practice seldom considered a fit subject for polite discussion."[17]

- When PC Party leader Brian Mulroney delivered his "you had an option, sir" knockout punch in the leaders' debate of the 1984 election, he was referring to the authority of the prime minister to put a stop to the practice of patronage appointments. At times, subsequent prime ministers have shown an interest in abandoning the tradition, such as Prime Minister Justin Trudeau installing a new Senate appointment process.

- Extensive rules may exist to prevent government contracts being awarded on the basis of partisanship, but the sponsorship scandal occurred nonetheless.

THE COUNTERCLAIM: NO, THEY SHOULDN'T!

Patronage is a tool used to bind political coalitions and is necessary for political executives to govern effectively.

No: Argument Summary

Clientelism—also known as patronage—has a longstanding place in democracies worldwide. Its persistence in Canada reflects the reality that often the most important criterion for a job in politics is a willingness to be loyal to the political executive. Alternatives such as using committees to decide on appointments, of opening positions up to the electorate, or of turning matters over to the Public Service Commission are romantic notions that ignore the mechanics of running government. It may be maligned, but patronage is popular among the political class, and it is deeply entrenched in Canadian politics.

No: Top 5 Considerations

1. The principles of responsible government dictate that executives have the power to develop and execute their political agendas. Abuses of power are judged by members of the legislature and then by voters in elections.
2. The appointment of friends of the party in power assures the governing party that its agenda will be implemented rather than stonewalled. The mandarins who adhere to the merit principle may not reflect the values of the broader public as expressed in a recent election or measured in opinion polls. Patronage ensures the smooth, accountable operation of the state, which is legitimately governed by people popularly elected by the citizenry.
3. Patronage glues political parties together and helps ensure that public officials are all on the same page.

The aspirations of parliamentarians and partisans to be appointed to a public position is a component of party discipline that is necessary for political parties' success and the stability of government.
4. Politics involves the brokering of competing demands. Patronage is a deal-making tool that can be leveraged to encourage opinion leaders to unite communities of competing interests and to promote their interests among party elites.
5. Patronage is more liberal than its critics suggest. The political executive's appointment power can be used as a tool of affirmative action to counterbalance the inequalities that result from democratically elected positions. Patronage allows positions such as governors general, lieutenant governors, ministers, senators, judges, and others to be filled by members of groups that are otherwise underrepresented such as Indigenous people, women, non-whites, non-anglophones, and people with disabilities.

No: Other Considerations

- Patronage is one of the few perks available to reward those who volunteer their time in politics. In some areas of the country it is part of the local political culture. Those attempting reforms have learned that it is exceedingly difficult to do so.
- All opposition parties criticize patronage. Yet once in government, all parties practise it. Likewise, Canadians who oppose patronage may view things differently if they are the ones who benefit from the spoils of office.
- Political appointees who make poor decisions can be quickly replaced; however, the public service has so many protections that the dismissal of incompetent bureaucrats may not be feasible. Furthermore, job security may create the very conditions that lead to underperformance.

Discussion Questions

- How realistic is it to expect members of the political executive to work with senior government personnel who were hired through the non-partisan merit system?
- Why do you think opposition parties criticize patronage, but once in power, they tend to maintain the status quo?
- How much weight do you place on the argument that when a political party forms the government,

it needs to hire its own friends as a counterbalance to all of the friends that were hired by the outgoing executive?
- Do you know anyone who has benefited from political patronage? In your opinion, should that position have been opened up to public competition, or not? Explain.

- The first minister's appointment power arguably hastens the number of political minorities holding top government positions. Does this change your opinion about patronage? Why or why not?

- To what extent does an independent advisory panel assuage critics' concerns with the prime minister's power to select senators for appointment?

Where to Learn More about Patronage in Canadian Politics

Matthew Flinders and Felicity Matthews, "Think Again: Patronage, Governance and the Smarter State," *Policy & Politics* 38, no. 4 (2010): pp. 639–56.

Alan Gordon, "Patronage, Etiquette, and the Science of Connection: Edmund Bristol and Political Management, 1911–1921," *Canadian Historical Review* 80, no. 1 (1999): pp. 1–33.

Jeffrey MacLeod, "Clientelism and John Savage," *Canadian Journal of Political Science* 39, no. 3 (2006): pp. 553–70.

Public Service Commission of Canada, "Public Service Impartiality: Taking Stock" (Ottawa: 2008). Available at www.psc-cfp.gc.ca/plcy-pltq/rprt/impart/impart-eng.pdf.

Steffen W. Schmidt, Laura Guasti, Carl H. Landé, and James C. Scott, eds., *Friends, Followers and Factions: A Reader in Political Patronage* (University of California Press, 1977).

Jeffrey Simpson, *Spoils of Power: The Politics of Patronage* (Toronto: HarperCollins, 1988).

David E. Smith, "Patronage in Britain and Canada: An Historical Perspective," *Journal of Canadian Studies* 22, no. 2 (1987): 34–54.

Reg Whitaker, "Politics versus Administration: Politicians and Bureaucrats" in *Canadian Politics in the 21st Century*, edited by Michael Whittington and Glen Williams (Thomson Nelson, 2007).

PART II
Politics and
Democracy

9

Political Parties

Inside This Chapter

- What is a political party?
- What types of political parties exist in Canada?
- Which political ideologies underpin party politics in Canada?
- What do party leaders do, and how are they selected?
- What is partisanship and party discipline?

Inside Political Parties

Political parties and their leaders are by far the most visible actors in Canadian democracy. They organize the executive and legislative branches and, controversially, play a role in the structure of the judiciary. Canadians are most familiar with the role of parties and leaders in elections.

A lot more goes on behind the scenes than most people realize. Normally, we expect that members of a political party will work together because they hope to win an election and form the government, but in fact parties have many other reasons for engaging in the public sphere. To understand their motivations we need to dissect their organizational apparatus and study their activities. The following maxims can help you interpret this chapter.

✔ **Parties play a formidable role in our political system.** Political parties are most visible when their candidates are campaigning for election. Yet, parties play a role in all corners of government and civil society. This is part of the reason they have become so deeply embedded in Canadian political culture.

✔ **Leaders have a lot of power over their parties.** The party leader and those in the leader's inner circle shape the party's political agenda. A leader is the public face of the party and has considerable control over its operations.

✔ **Political parties are continuously evolving.** Recent and historical reform movements demonstrate that political parties seldom stagnate. They have many functions in the electorate and in the halls of power. How they perform those roles, and the opponents they encounter, shift all the time.

UP FOR DEBATE

Should party leaders take bold steps to increase the presence of women and other Canadians underrepresented in legislatures?

Keep this question in mind as you read through the chapter. Consult the end-of-chapter debate supplement for more material to help you engage in an informed discussion of the topic.

Political Parties in Canada

The Nature and Role of Political Parties

A **political party** is a formal organization of citizens who unite under a common label and contest elections. Political parties bring together competing perspectives and unite like-minded people who seek to shape government decisions. They are political clubs that seek to influence and change public policy.

political party
A political entity that runs candidates in elections in an attempt to shape government policy and laws.

Political parties are arguably the most dominant political actors in the Canadian political system. They emerged in the nineteenth century out of a need to organize policy debate and representation in the legislature. Assembly votes without disciplined parties were highly unpredictable and legislative business often ground to a halt. Today, legislative affairs are far more orderly—to a fault, according to critics of party discipline. At the same time, parties have grown beyond the confines of the legislature to help organize elections. Their diversity reflects the vibrancy of pluralism, the public sphere, and political opinions.

Inside assemblies and among the electorate, political parties aggregate interests by acting as vessels that collect the many points of view on countless issues. They use varied mechanisms for identifying a common position and advocate the best way forward. A good deal of what political parties do involves identifying and connecting with potential voters.

In today's digital world, this involves sophisticated methods of data gathering and management. Political parties recruit and support leaders to champion these causes. Parties field candidates who will run under the party banner, often providing them with communications resources and a common policy platform with which they can connect with voters. This platform serves as the party's governing agenda, should voters entrust them with power. Governing and opposition parties organize legislative affairs, ensuring that there is political cohesion rather than instability. These are just some of the many ways that political parties organize politics in Canada.

Types of Political Parties

In Canada, political parties barely existed in 1867, and the first two parties that emerged were quite similar to each other. John A. Macdonald led the elites who comprised the Conservative Party into elections against a loosely organized Liberal Party. **Elite parties** such as these were closed cadres of the upper class.

elite party
A small political party run by people with ascribed social status.

Elite parties emerged out of the need to organize votes within the legislature. Elected representatives tended to make most decisions, including identifying who the party leader should be. Elite party leaders were the most experienced parliamentarians who commanded the respect of their caucuses. Many of them were more concerned with events in the capital city than with appealing to the then-narrow electorate. They performed little campaigning and they placed a high priority on their personal contacts. Those who ran the party controlled the distribution of resources and privileges.

Photo by Laura Politis

Volunteering on an election campaign is an excellent way for people to gain first-hand experience in politics. What are the advantages and disadvantages of becoming involved in partisan politics? What are other avenues for different types of people to influence the political system?

As the electorate grew beyond property-owning, white males, political parties gradually sought to reach across class divisions and empower their members. This gave rise to the **mass parties** that emerged in after World War I. A variety of forces helped to decentralize the major parties' power structure. Grassroots party members gained an increased role. Members selected delegates to party conventions where leaders were chosen and policies decided. Members became valuable campaign donors and volunteers. In the process, party objectives turned from organizing elites to reforming society. The party leadership became more accountable to the party membership as the size of the political party grew. A mass party's membership cares about the ideas that the leader espouses. Such a party may therefore have close ties with quasi-political organizations, such as labour unions, advocacy groups, or business groups.

Pure elite and pure mass parties no longer exist in Canadian politics—though a case could be made that they describe some of the weakest parties. In the mid–twentieth century, American political scientist Otto Kirchheimer identified a classification that remains applicable to the most successful Canadian political parties today.[1] The primary objective of what Kirchheimer labelled a **catch-all party** is to find ways to win elections in order to govern. This means appealing to voters with varying viewpoints and bringing them together to form as large an electoral coalition as possible. A catch-all party is said to have a big tent to accommodate many voters and diverse points of view. Compared to mass parties, the catch-all party places greater emphasis on the charisma of the party leader. Professional communication of broad messages supplants narrowly defined positions and policies. The role of individual party members is diminished, and made even less significant by the catch-all party's priority on raising funds from sources outside its membership, including government subsidies. This means that a catch-all party is not normally left-wing or right-wing, though an ideological party can shift to the centre without abandoning its core ideological values. For instance, at times the Conservative Party of Canada behaves as a catch-all party, because it downplays some of its conservative principles to appeal to voters outside its traditional base. This may mean, for example, choosing to run budget deficits in the face of an economic downturn, or opting not to appeal court decisions that result in more liberal social policies.

In Canada, the term **brokerage party** is often mistakenly used as a synonym for a catch-all party. Confusion stems from the commonality between brokering and mediating. Brokerage and catch-all parties are similar in that they aim to listen to citizens, identify policies that will appeal to competing viewpoints, and attract people who feel that the party embodies the public's values. Where a brokerage party differs, and why the terminology is used in Canada, is that it focuses more on geography and less on ideology. It refers to a party that explicitly attempts to reconcile the wide variety of regional interests found in Canadian society. In this way, brokerage parties are Canada's "shock absorbers," confining regional conflict within party organizations rather than promoting open disputes between parties.[2] At various points in time, the federal Liberals and (Progressive) Conservatives have been labelled brokerage parties. Their capacity to meet competing demands from different parts of the country has wavered, however. Brokerage parties are less common at the provincial level where regional conflict is less pronounced. With more homogeneous populations, provincial parties are able to appeal to a narrower set of interests, while still maintaining the level of popular support necessary to win seats and form governments. This said, in many provinces, parties do need to appeal to at least two or three different regions to win enough seats to form government.[3] In Manitoba, for

mass party
A grassroots political party characterized by its efforts to sign up members.

OBJECTIVES
- ELITE PARTIES → organize voters within legislature
- MASS PARTIES → reform society
- CATCH-ALL PARTIES → win elections to govern

catch-all party
A competitive political party that prioritizes appealing to the broadest base of electoral support possible.

brokerage party
The Canadian term for a catch-all party that brokers competing regional demands.

instance, parties need to cobble together support from at least half of the province's four main regions: the remote north, the rural south, north Winnipeg, and south Winnipeg.[4]

The brokerage party is arguably becoming obsolete due to technological and societal changes. Provinces compete in a global economy, news media no longer operate in a regional vacuum, opinion surveys have become affordable, and statistical modelling enables the targeting of voters in ways that reduce regional dimensions. Modern political parties have become professionalized: they know that in order to be competitive, they must work with political consultants—including media, marketing, opinion research, and social-media experts—to identify and win over floating and undecided voters. The consequences include an obsession with message control, an emphasis on images over

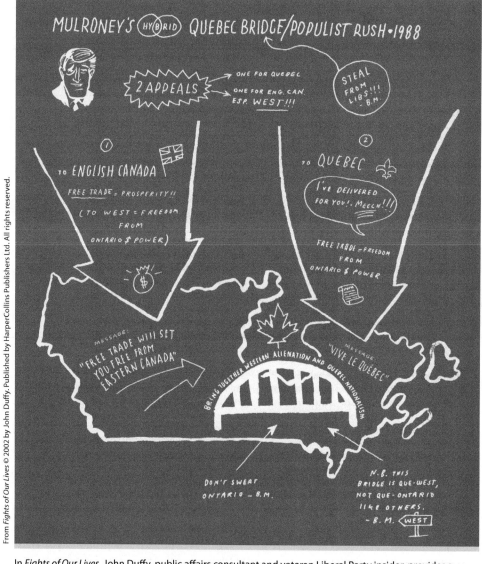

In *Fights of Our Lives*, John Duffy, public affairs consultant and veteran Liberal Party insider, provides a series of playbooks for party success over the ages. This one, from the 1988 federal election campaign, embraces the brokerage party ideal by mapping out a strategy to reconcile the competing interests of Quebec and Western Canada. What sort of brokerage strategies, if any, were used in the most recent federal election? What about in the most recent provincial election in your jurisdiction?

substance, the practice of permanent campaigning, and prioritizing the interests of the party centre over the grassroots. The integration of advanced research and communication techniques means that electors are targeted based on their shared interests that transcend provincial or regional boundaries. This has contributed to a shift in the regional fault lines of politics, where it matters less what province an elector lives in than whether the elector lives in a city, a suburb, or a rural area. The days of brokering provincial interests appear to have evolved into a landscape of retail politics, where ground-level salesmanship is used to peddle policies and promote brands of leadership at an individual level. This shift is reflected in the transformation of the Liberal Party of Canada under the leadership of Justin Trudeau. The Liberal Party used to be a brokerage party in order to champion national unity. Today, it constitutes a catch-all party that brands itself as the champion of mainstream, middle-class Canada, which necessarily transcends regional boundaries. However, Liberal values are less appealing in many rural areas and the Prairies, and consequently the party's support is heavily concentrated in urban centres such as Vancouver, Toronto, Ottawa and Montreal.

See pages 122–3 of Chapter 4, on regionalism, for a discussion of code politics and how political parties continue to exploit regional differences for political gain, despite the growth of retail politics.

Major and Minor Parties

We can distinguish between two types of political parties in Canada. Major parties are professional organizations with a significant daily presence. Minor parties are largely dormant until an election campaign is pending.

A **major party** is a political party that has significant public support and resources. Major parties typically feature leaders who see themselves as competing to become the head of government, or leader of the official opposition at the very least. A major party may alternatively be considered any party that has enough members in the legislature to be recognized by the speaker. According to one prominent definition, major parties have either governing or blackmail potential. That is, they are perceived to be strong enough to win elections or, if not, to exert such a threat as to be able to influence the policy positions of those in power.[5] Major parties in Canada tend to have a long history of being competitive in elections, of fielding candidates in all available electoral districts, and/or of having their leaders participate in mid-campaign leaders' debates.

Conversely, a **minor party** is typically a marginal organization with few, if any, elected members in the legislature. It operates with little public support on a shoestring budget.

major party
A political party that has many supporters and a large organizational infrastructure.

minor party
A small political party with much less support or infrastructure than a major party.

Table 9.1   Governing Party and Official Opposition in the 43rd Parliament of Canada

Party Name and Logo	Characteristics
Liberal Party of Canada	• Appeals to: Centre and centre-left voters • Objective: Form the government with a policy agenda that appeals to the median voter • Policies include: Stronger national programs; putting a price on carbon pollution; equality of opportunity
Conservative Party of Canada	• Appeals to: Right-wing and centre-right voters • Objective: Form the government with a conservative policy agenda • Policies include: Lower taxes; rein in government spending

Note: Intended to be illustrative only

Table 9.2   Other Parties in the 43rd Parliament of Canada

Party Name and Logo	Characteristics
Bloc Québécois	• Appeals to: Quebec sovereignists and left-wing voters • Objective: Advance Quebec's interests; advocate unique status within Canada; establish the conditions for a successful referendum on sovereignty-association • Policies include: Support for Quebec arts and culture; opposition to pipelines passing through Quebec; pressure on Ottawa to allow Quebec to keep more tax revenues
New Democratic Party	• Appeals to: Left-wing voters • Objective: Promote the cause of unions and the working class • Policies include: National pharmacare program; higher taxes on corporations and the super-wealthy; abolishing the Senate and changing the electoral system
Green Party of Canada*	• Appeals to: Environmentalists and protest voters • Objective: Advance an environmental agenda and some left-wing social policies • Policies include: Reduction of motor vehicle emissions; increased taxes on polluters; reforming the electoral system

*Although the Green Party was represented in the House of Commons after the 2019 federal general election, it did not elect the 12 MPs required to achieve official party status in the legislature.

A minor party's volunteers are frequently asked to run as candidates in ridings that they do not live in, and with almost no prospects of winning. Minor parties rely on inexpensive modes of communication such as the Internet. Their leaders are typically unknown to most citizens, and if they do manage to attract media attention, it is owing to public curiosity or a sense of fair play. Nevertheless, they are participants in the Canadian party system, and reflect the ideal that competing political viewpoints are welcome in a democracy.

Not long ago, a minor political party contesting the federal election was required to field a minimum of 50 candidates in order for its party name to be listed on the ballot. This rule, which was in effect from 1993 through 2000, effectively excluded tiny and poorly financed political organizations. It was designed to prevent the participation of nuisance or fringe parties that were disruptive to mainstream parties and those that used satire to mock the political system, such as the Rhinoceros Party. But the rule contravened the democratic principle of free and fair elections. One deregistered minor party, the Communist Party of Canada, took the matter to court. In a 2003 judgement, the Supreme Court of Canada struck down the 50-candidate rule, declaring that it contravened provisions in the Charter of Rights and Freedoms that protect the democratic rights of citizens. In particular, the Court upheld the primacy of section 3 of the Charter, which stipulates that every Canadian citizen has the right "to be qualified for membership in a legislative assembly." The ruling meant that the 50-candidate rule provisions in the Canada Elections Act could no longer be enforced.[6] Since the 2004 federal election there has been no candidate minimum to register a political party. The number of fringe political parties with no realistic chance of electing candidates has increased as a result.

Party Ideologies

Regardless of their reputation as amorphous, big-tent organizations, and their traditional focus on appealing to voters along regional lines, major political parties in Canada are by no means devoid of **ideology**. In fact, it is difficult to describe or explain Canadian party politics without reference to terms like "left," "right," and "centre," or mentioning political worldviews like socialism, libertarianism, liberalism, and conservatism.

ideology
A set of ideas that form a coherent political belief system.

Political ideologies are often differentiated by placing them on a spectrum. The left side represents one type of thinking, the right side another perspective, and the centre is middle ground between the two extremes. These viewpoints differ on a host of matters, from individual self-reliance and taxes, to the welfare state and government responses to climate change. The left–right line is useful, but simplistic. Ideologies are too complex to neatly compartmentalize this way. For instance, it is common for people to be situated on the political left on some issues, on the centre on some, and on the right end of the spectrum on yet other issue. This is also true of political parties. The Bloc Québécois and Greens often defy categorization on the traditional left–right spectrum. This is because their core values—be they Quebec nationalism or environmentalism—place them on different ideological planes compared to the New Democrats, Liberals, and Conservatives. This said, most Bloc and Green policies may be placed on the left side of the spectrum (e.g., support for a woman choosing whether to have an abortion), while other policies are on the right (e.g., more efficient government spending). Nevertheless left–right linear thinking is the typical way of differentiating between political points of view.

Generally speaking, **left-wing** parties believe in putting society first. They advocate increasing taxes on the incomes of the wealthy and big business, so that these revenues may be used to create and strengthen social programs. This fits with their progressive view of society, whereby those who are disadvantaged are provided with supports to achieve equality. In general the New Democratic Party is viewed as a left-wing party in Canada, as is the Liberal Party of Canada under Justin Trudeau. By comparison, **right-wing** parties like the Conservative Party of Canada advocate the merits of reducing taxes as a means of stimulating economic growth in the private sector. By reducing the size of government they can keep taxes low but at a cost of reduced government services. This fits with their objective of building a society that is more self-reliant and less dependent on the state. At the same time, many on the right believe in a role for the state in preserving traditional values.

It can be difficult to neatly differentiate between political parties or public policies as either left, centre, or right. In *Left and Right: The Small World of Political Ideas*, political scientist Christopher Cochrane argues that the terminology is useful, despite the problem that the meanings are difficult to precisely define. Many Canadians self-identify as left-wing or right-wing, even as the concepts differ across geography and over time, and they tend to prefer political parties that align with that positioning.[7]

Some other terms are used to account for this complexity. These ideologies are distinguished based on how they view the relationship between the individual as opposed to the community and state (see Figure 9.1). On the left, democratic socialists place greater faith in the institutions of the state whereas liberals tend to promote individualism and opportunity. On the right, conservatives value the social fabric that unites Canadians under common norms while libertarians prize individual autonomy.

Democratic Socialism

Democratic socialism is a left-wing, collectivist philosophy. It supports more state control over the economy, social justice, inclusiveness, and strong social programs delivered by government. Supporters of democratic socialism see government as a force for good, particularly for the most vulnerable members of society. Historically, countries governed by leaders with a socialist belief system, like Marxism or communism, do not necessarily uphold free and fair elections. Advocates of democratic socialism do.

left-wing
A political tendency that promotes a bigger role for government and proactive measures to achieve social and economic equality.

right-wing
A political tendency that promotes a smaller role for government and a greater emphasis on individual responsibility and market-based competition.

See page 10 in Chapter 1 for more on left-wing and right-wing thinking.

democratic socialism
An ideology that promotes more government intervention and assistance for those most in need.

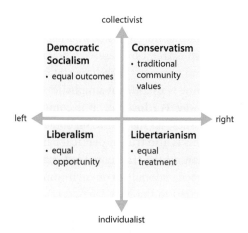

Figure 9.1 | Four Political Ideologies in Canada

There are two mainstream branches of democratic socialism in Canadian politics. The first is known as traditional social democracy. Adherents to that political worldview promote democratic reform. They advocate for the expansion of the welfare state. They want a more progressive system of taxation that imposes higher tax rates on large businesses and the wealthy. They strive toward a more inclusive society through the extension of rights. They argue against armed conflict in order to achieve peace on the international stage. Their dedication to replacing capitalism with a more co-operative economic system helps distinguish traditional social democrats (on the far left) from third-way social democrats (in the centre–left).

The other branch of Canadian socialism is third-way social democracy, which emerged in Canada in the 1990s. Moderates sought to take the radical edge off left-wing parties and advocacy groups. The decision by the New Democratic Party of Canada to remove the word "socialism" from the party constitution in 2013 marked its transition to this newer and more moderate approach to left-wing politics. Third-way social democrats do not believe in displacing capitalism. They seek to harness capitalism for the good of a greater number of people. They balance a commitment to social levelling of rights with promotion of individual and collective responsibility. Their focus has shifted from pacifism to human security in international relations.

Liberalism

liberalism
An ideology that promotes equality of opportunity.

In Canada, **liberalism** is a centre-left, individualist ideology. It is a belief system that seeks to ensure all Canadians have the freedom of equal opportunity to reach their full potential. This means using the levers of the state to ensure society's least advantaged have the chance to compete with those with greater privilege. Unlike right-wing ideologies, Canadian liberalism views social inequality as a remediable injustice. In advocating policies like affirmative action or employment insurance, liberalism falls short of the social levelling involved in democratic socialism, however. Liberalism affords people the opportunity to compete rather than guaranteeing equality of result.

There are two main branches of Canadian liberalism. Business liberalism stresses economic matters. Business liberals emphasize fiscal orthodoxy, promoting free trade within Canada and with other states, balanced budgets, debt reduction, and, when

Briefing Notes

Liberal and Conservative Ideologies in Canada and the United States

Ideology is often a critical element of a political party's brand. That is why many parties choose names that reflect their ideological orientations. There is a key difference between the two concepts, however, and it is captured by the use of upper- and lower-case letters. Small-l liberal thinkers are often big-L Liberal Party voters, but not always. The same goes for small-c conservatives who may or may not vote Conservative on election day.

American definitions of these terms differ from Canadian ones. A liberal in the United States might well be considered a socialist in Canada. A conservative in

Canada might get along better with an American liberal than with an American conservative. This is because politics south of the border is further to the right and more individualist than it is in Canada. For this reason, it is usually the case that Conservative prime ministers in Canada are more left-wing than American presidents, regardless of whether a president is a Democrat or a Republican. As well, a Republican president tends to get a rough ride in the Canadian media, whereas a Democratic president is portrayed as better aligned with Canadian political values.

necessary, government intervention in the economy to promote growth. The other main branch is welfare liberalism, which stresses social policy. Welfare liberals accept the market economy and seek to extend its benefits to create a more just society. They are less willing than democratic socialists to redistribute wealth in order to do so. Welfare liberals promote individual social rights, both in Canada and abroad. They support a strong social-welfare state, albeit less expansive than the one social democrats advocate. The differences between third-way social democrats and welfare liberals are more than a matter of degree. Their means may appear similar; however, their objectives are distinct. Social democrats aim to remake society into a more egalitarian one by engaging in social levelling. Small-l liberals aim to create a level playing field where everyone has an equal opportunity to compete (see Briefing Note above).

Conservatism

Compared to ideologies on the left, conservatism leans toward traditionalism and is resistant to change. Conservatives like to keep things the way they are or perhaps advocate for a return to the way things were in the past. Some of them are guided by religious values. The potential for divergent conservative worldviews makes conservatism the most complex political ideology in Canada.

As their name suggests, economic conservatives focus more on economic and fiscal matters. They seek freer markets and a smaller government. They support the elimination of some government programs, the deregulation of private industry activities, and the privatization of government services and assets. In turn, the streamlined operation of government means that taxes can be reduced.

Social conservatives are less reluctant to use the levers of the state—though not on economic matters. They value government intervention to safeguard public morality, often grounded in religious beliefs. Social conservatives favour government policies and programs that promote or protect traditional values. For instance, they support the defini-tion of marriage between one man and one woman, and oppose abortion in some if not all circumstances. These socially conservative views persist among some who see themselves as feminists.[8] Social conservatives are prone to support the expansion of anti-crime and pro-military measures.

A third brand of conservatism distinguishes the Canadian right from its counterpart in the United States. **Toryism** is defined by its reverence for the monarchy, hierarchy, and incrementalism. Underlying each of these principles is a collectivist belief in the social fabric of society.[9] Tories are communitarians, which is unlike liberals, but similar to dem-ocratic socialists. Tories believe that Canadian society is more than a sum of its individ-uals. Toryism's collectivist ties to social democracy have produced a political ideology unique to Canada: the red tory. Unlike other conservatives, red tories value the welfare state as a proven institution of the Canadian state. Thus red tories support programs like medicare and social security. Red tories tend to prioritize social issues ahead of economic ones, and may vehemently oppose the bottom-line views of economic conservatives and moral traditionalism espoused by social conservatives. Red tories support same-sex mar-riage and pro-choice policies on abortion, for example, as they seek to preserve Canada's inclusive social fabric. As political scientist Gad Horowitz once explained, "At the simplest level, [a red tory] is a Conservative who prefers the CCF–NDP to the Liberals, or a socialist who prefers the Conservatives to the Liberals, without really knowing why."[10]

Libertarianism

Libertarianism is right-wing philosophy that calls for more individual responsibility and less reliance on government. Libertarians prioritize the autonomy of each person to live their own lives as they see fit. They support laissez-faire capitalism, free trade, materialism, competition, and freedom from government interference. Libertarians want much smaller government and lower taxes than anyone else on the mainstream political spectrum. Lib-ertarians are more committed to reducing the scope of government than are business liberals or economic conservatives (for distinctions, see Figure 9.2). Whereas economic conservatives may see some room for business subsidies, bailouts, and systems like supply management, libertarians oppose these as "corporate welfare." Where welfare liberals see affirmative action as necessary to levelling the playing field, libertarians oppose any form of preferential treatment based on race, gender, and other group-based characteristics. In general, libertarianism tends to focus more on process than outcomes. Like red tories, this can make libertarians difficult to place on the left–right spectrum based purely on whether they support a particular policy outcome. Many libertarians support individuals' rights to choose same-sex marriage and abortion, for example, which puts them offside with social conservatives.

These ideological divisions often overlap with geographic and ethnic divisions. Western Canada is known to many as a bastion of libertarianism. Eastern Canada features a more receptive audience for greater state intervention in the economy and society. Different cultural groups, particularly those with devoutly religious members, often adhere more strongly to conservative principles than others. Combined or on its own, the ideological cleavage is a prominent feature of Canadian politics, shaping everything from the constitution to policy outcomes.

Canadian political parties are best considered amalgams of the various ideological groups, as depicted in Figure 9.2. In general, traditional and third-way social democrats

toryism
A collectivist branch of Canadian conservatism that promotes the preservation of government institutions.

libertarianism
An ideology that champions the least possible amount of state intervention in the lives of citizens.

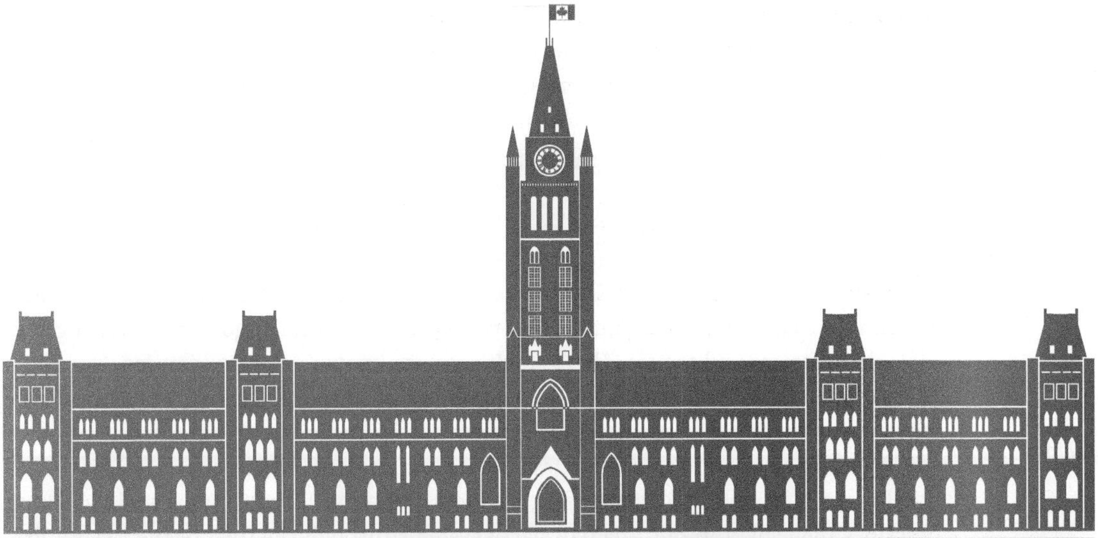

	LEFT-WING	RIGHT-WING
IDEOLOGY	• progressivism • communitarianism • feminism • support for unions and workers • bigger government: positive view of government role in the economy and society • peacekeeping doves	• conservatism • individualism • traditionalism • support for corporations and job-creators • smaller government: positive view of individual initiative and competition • military hawks
POLICY LEANINGS: economic/fiscal	• government planning and regulation • progressive taxation: higher on the wealthy and corporations, to redistribute to the poor • maintain/expand public services, particularly to improve the lives of the disadvantaged • environmental protection, even at the expense of economic growth	• privatization and deregulation • flatter taxation: lower and more equal tax rates for all • trickle-down economics: everyone benefits when the private sector thrives • economic growth, even at the expense of environmental protection
POLICY LEANINGS: social/moral	• pro-choice • support for alternative lifestyles and diversity • gun regulation • flexible sentencing with a focus on offenders' rights to rehabilitation	• pro-life • support for traditional lifestyles and conformity • gun ownership • strict sentencing with a focus on victims' rights and retribution

DEMOCRATIC SOCIALISM	LIBERALISM	CONSERVATISM	
traditional democratic socialists • egalitarianism • replacement of capitalism • group rights • challenge traditional institutions **third-way social democrats** • harness capitalism for public good • individual and collective responsibility • social levelling	**business liberals** • fiscal orthodoxy • free trade • government intervention where necessary **welfare liberals** • social justice • extend the benefits of the market economy to support a strong welfare state • seek a level playing field	**blue tories** • economic nationalism • state support of private business **red tories** • preserve the social fabric • support proven social programs like medicare • reverence for the monarchy	**neoliberals** • libertarian • free markets • fiscal austerity • smaller government through privatization **neoconservatives** • preservation of traditional values • use of military force to support moral objectives

Figure 9.2 | The Canadian Political Spectrum

Note: The colours used in this figure reflect traditional positioning but are not definitive. Political parties constantly refine their ideological positions. For instance, under Justin Trudeau the Liberal government purposely ran billion-dollar deficits, whereas in the 1990s Liberal governments led by Jean Chrétien made major spending cuts to eliminate the deficit. (Illustration credit: oleg7799/Shutterstock)

tend to support the New Democratic Party, just as welfare and business liberals tend to support the Liberal Party. The Conservative Party tends to combine the interests of libertarians, social conservatives, and tories.

Party Systems in Canada

Federal Party Systems

The history of party politics in Canada consists of long periods of stability. For decades at a time, a small set of dominant parties competes for control of government using predictable strategies and tactics. These stable eras are known as **party systems**. Once in a generation, the party system fractures. A combination of social, technological, economic, environmental, or political forces pushes new parties to the forefront. After a period of transition, a new party system emerges with its own, unique dynamics.

Research by political scientists R. Kenneth Carty, William Cross, and Lisa Young describes the evolution of Canadian party systems through the turn of the twenty-first century.[11] They and other political scientists generally agree that there have been three stable eras of Canadian party politics, as follows:

1. from Confederation to World War I (between 1867 and 1917);
2. from the inter-war period through to the late 1950s (between 1921 and 1957); and
3. from the 1960s through the early 1990s (between 1962 and 1993).

Each of these party systems was separated by a transition period. The inability of the major parties to represent the diverse and changing interests of Canadians led to electoral unrest. New political parties were born out of regional or ideological discontent. Minority governments occurred during these transitions, as voters shifted away from the more dominant parties, denying them a majority of seats in Parliament. Over time, the forces that propelled the new parties to prominence subsided. Some minor party supporters merged back into the major party fold. Others opted to stay the course with their own separate organizations. In rare instances, minor parties managed to take over major ones.

Since 1993, Canadian party politics has not followed a sustained pattern for political scientists to agree on the characteristics of the fourth or perhaps a fifth party system. Arguably, we are in such a long transition period that the instability constitutes a party system unto itself.[12] The dynamic nature of party competition from election to election during this period makes it difficult to label. The main players have been relatively fixed. Yet the post-1993 period has strongly resembled previous transitions: the volatility of individual party fortunes, a series of minority governments, and the prolonged presence of more extreme minor parties.

The results of each formative election that marked the beginning or end of a federal party system show how the fortunes of political parties change over time (see Table 9.3). The first party system, from 1867 to 1917, was characterized by power rotating between the Conservative and Liberal parties. They were the only two major parties of the period. They were so similar that in the early years of the Dominion of Canada they were known as the Liberal-Conservative party (which we now refer to as the Conservative Party) and the Liberal-Reform Party (which became the Liberal Party). Some historians note that the first nationwide party election did not occur until 1898 because elections were so

party system
A particular constellation of political parties guided by a unique framework of behaviour.

Table 9.3   Results of Pivotal Canadian Federal Elections

Party	Number of Seats Won (% vote)			
	1867	1921	1962	1993
Bloc Québécois	—	—	—	54 (13.5%)
Conservative*	101 (50.0)	50 (30.5)	116 (37.3)	2 (16.0)
Green	—	—	—	0 (0.2)
Labour	—	3 (2.7)	—	—
Liberal	80 (49.0)	116 (40.7)	99 (37.4)	177 (41.3)
NDP	—	—	19 (13.4)	9 (6.9)
Progressive	—	58 (21.1)	—	—
Reform Alliance	—	—	—	52 (18.7)
Social Credit	—	—	30 (11.7)	—
United Farmers	—	3 (0.8)	—	—
Other/independent	0 (1.0)	5 (5.1)	1 (0.2)	1 (3.6)
Total Seats	181	235	265	295

*Includes variants of party name

Note: Party affiliations were not formally recorded by Elections Canada until 1963.

Source: Elections Canada

localized. The dominant mode of campaigning involved these elite parties appealing to local notables whose financial resources and sway over their constituency's voters were crucial to a party's victory. Many party elites owned or controlled local newspapers, which served as organs for the party in favour, meaning the media was sharply partisan. Party leaders were usually proven politicians who were chosen by the party's MPs and senators.

The transition to the second party system saw several mass parties gain traction at the expense of elite parties. The independent press and radio allowed new parties to build regional followings. These new organizations, including the Progressives and their successors Social Credit and the Co-operative Commonwealth Federation (CCF), brought innovation to Canadian party politics. For instance, their success put pressure on the Conservative and Liberal parties to change their leadership selection processes from decisions made exclusively by MPs and senators to more open contests. Notwithstanding the regional focus of these mass parties, the overwhelming tenor of the second party system (from 1921 to 1957) was one of brokerage, with the Liberals and Conservatives building bridges across regional divides to form majority governments. For the Conservatives, this included a name change to appeal to regional interests, becoming known as the Progressive Conservative (PC) party in 1942. Between the second and third party systems, the CCF rebranded itself the New Democratic Party (NDP), becoming a permanent fixture in Canadian politics.

The brokerage of regional politics was easier during the third party system, from 1962 to 1993, with the advent of national media and broadcast television. The Liberals, PCs, and New Democrats used nationwide TV to build pan-Canadian agendas and support. The NDP become entrenched as the third major federal party. However, only the Liberals and PCs formed government, and the NDP never attained official opposition status in this era.

Canada became what political scientists dub a two-plus party system because it had two major parties and a third major competitor.

This period of relative stability was interrupted by the largest earthquake in Canadian electoral history. The reverberations of the 1993 federal election lasted the next two decades. There was significant regional instability and a long period of multipartyism during this transition. There were as many as five major parties competing in various regions of the country. The Liberal Party won a majority of seats and Jean Chrétien became prime minister. However, the Liberals relied heavily on near-sweeps of Ontario and Atlantic Canada to do so. Rival parties gained strength in different regions of the country. The Bloc Québécois became the official opposition by winning 54 ridings—all in Quebec. The Reform Party garnered most of its 52 seats in Saskatchewan, Alberta, and BC. The NDP likewise claimed all nine of its seats west of Ontario. The Progressive Conservatives, behind Prime Minister Kim Campbell, was reduced from government to just two seats, a historic low for the party. The two decades of Canadian party politics after that pivotal election were similar to the sort of regional tensions that marked earlier transitions. Just as the Progressives emerged in the 1920s and Social Credit became emboldened in the 1950s, so, too, did the Bloc Québécois and the Reform Party gather strength in the late 1980s and early 1990s.

The federal party system continued its metamorphosis in the early twenty-first century. The Reform Party rebranded itself as the Canadian Alliance in an effort to broaden its support base beyond Western Canada. This move was a precursor to merging with the PCs to form the Conservative Party of Canada. All three major parties transitioned from catch-all regional brokers into market-oriented organizations. Knitting together regional alliances was all but precluded given the persistence of minor regionalist parties like the Bloc. At the same time, broadcast television had given way to specialty cable TV and the Internet. These shifts encouraged parties to target new political groupings,

THE CANADIAN PRESS/Fred Chartrand

From left to right, Jean Chretien (Liberal), Kim Campbell (PC), Lucien Bouchard (Bloc Québécois), Audrey McLaughlin (NDP), and Preston Manning (Reform) take their places at a leaders' debate held during the 1993 federal election campaign. The 1993 election profoundly reshaped the Canadian party system and exposed deep regional cleavages. What factors do you think contributed most to the collapse of Canada's system of regional brokerage in that pivotal election?

with a particular focus on the urban/suburban/rural divides. Indeed, regionalism was replaced by divisive partisanship and gamesmanship during three successive minority governments in 2004, 2006, and 2008. The 2011 election was significant because the NDP became the official opposition for the first time, the Liberal Party earned the fewest number of seats in its history, the Bloc Québécois was nearly wiped out, and the Greens elected their first member of Parliament. By the time the Liberals regained their traditional place among the two major parties, winning a majority government in 2015, a fourth party system appeared to have taken shape. Yet 2019 marked a return to minority government. The resurgent Bloc Québécois displaced the NDP as the party with the third-most seats, while the Greens' three MPs was the most ever for that minor party. Once again, the relative stability that characterizes a party system was in flux, making it difficult to be definitive about classifying the current era of party politics.

Provincial Party Systems

Political parties operate in all 10 provinces and in Yukon (see Table 9.4). In most provinces, but not all of them, the most competitive parties are those that are affiliated with a federal counterpart. The nuances of provincial politics are such that it can be difficult for many people to recognize the extent to which a party has national ties. Just because two parties share the same label does not mean that they are like-minded or collaborative. Equally, just because two parties have different names does not necessarily mean they oppose each other, although it certainly increases the possibility.

Consensus government is discussed in Chapter 6, in the section on territorial legislatures: see page 205.

Table 9.4 Political Parties with Elected Members in Recent Canadian Provincial/Territorial Legislative Assemblies

Province/Territory	Left	Centre	Right	Other
British Columbia	NDP		Liberal	Green
Alberta	NDP		United Conservative Party	
Saskatchewan	NDP		Saskatchewan Party	
Manitoba	NDP	Liberal	PC	
Ontario	NDP	Liberal	PC	Green
Quebec	Parti Québécois Québec Solidaire	Liberal	Coalition Avenir Québec	
New Brunswick	NDP	Liberal	PC	Green People's Alliance
Newfoundland and Labrador	NDP	Liberal	PC	
Nova Scotia	NDP	Liberal	PC	
Prince Edward Island		Liberal	PC	Green
Yukon	NDP	Liberal	Yukon Party	
Northwest Territories		—does not have political parties—		
Nunavut		—does not have political parties—		

NDP: New Democratic Party; PC: Progressive Conservative Party

Historically, each province features its own set of party systems. Most generally follow the same left-centre-right dynamic found at the federal level. So, too, does Yukon—the only territory with partisan representation as opposed to consensus government. The premiers and governing parties for these various systems can be found in the appendix at the back of this book. In general, provincial party systems have come in the following main varieties:

- one-party dominant systems that feature long periods of rule by one party organization (as historically with the Progressive Conservatives and Social Credit in Alberta);
- two-party systems with close, but largely non-ideological, competition between the Liberals and PCs such that there is relatively little difference between them (as is often the case in the Atlantic provinces);
- polarized two-party systems that have close and pitched competition between two ideologically polarized parties (as with the NDP and Liberals in BC, and the NDP and Saskatchewan Party in Saskatchewan);
- two-and-a-half party systems that are comprised of two major competitors and a weak but still relevant third party (as in Manitoba, where the NDP and PCs lead the Liberals, and Nova Scotia and Newfoundland and Labrador, where the NDP serves as third party, after the Liberals and PCs); and
- three-party systems, where competition is tight among three relatively well-balanced parties (as in Ontario, where the Liberals, PCs, and New Democrats are relatively evenly matched, and Yukon, where the Yukon Party, Liberals, and New Democrats compete).

Jurisdictions move in and out of these categories as competitive dynamics change. For decades, Ontario featured a one-party dominant system governed by the PC's big blue machine, and Nova Scotia briefly saw the NDP rise to power. These transformations are often very slow. On occasion, party system realignment can be sudden. The rise of the NDP in Alberta transformed its party system into a two-party polarized model almost overnight when it formed government and spurred the merger of two right-wing parties. Likewise, the breakthrough victory by the right-wing Coalition Avenir Québec shifted the axis of that province's politics from debates over sovereignty to a more conventional left-right spectrum.

These party system changes may be influenced by each provincial party's relationship with its federal counterpart. Political scientist Rand Dyck described the linkages between federal and provincial parties in the following way.[13] **Integrated parties** are characterized by the teamwork, ideological similarities, and sharing of resources between federal and provincial units. The NDP is a classic case of an integrated party. So are the Liberal parties in the Atlantic provinces. In each case, the federal party organization is fully integrated with the provincial parties because they share fundraising apparatuses, lists of supporters, party workers, and policy objectives. For example, the top strategists who work on the NDP's federal campaign are dispatched to large provinces to run the party's provincial campaign. In general, Atlantic Canada features the most integrated political parties. Party ties between federal and provincial organizations are much weaker in the rest of Canada.

Unlike integrated parties, **confederal parties** share the same or a similar label but do not see eye to eye. Their leaders and parliamentarians may privately or publicly criticize each other, they may have different ideologies, and each side may see the other as getting in the way of an agenda. The federal Liberal Party and the BC Liberal Party are a good example of party units that have different ideologies and few formal ties. It may

integrated parties
Federal and provincial political parties whose behaviours and organization are interconnected.

confederal parties
Federal and provincial parties that operate autonomously from each other, even though they may have similar names.

The Coalition Avenir Québec (CAQ) won the 2018 Quebec provincial election, leaving the two traditional parties (the Liberals and Parti Québécois) in disarray. Premier François Legault, pictured above with Deputy Premier Geneviève Guilbault (left) and cabinet minister Andrée Laforest (right), co-founded the CAQ just a few years before, in 2011. Why do you suppose traditional parties dominate politics in some provinces? What do you think explains the success of a new political party like the CAQ?

surprise you to learn that the BC Liberals tend to have closer connections with the federal Conservatives than with the federal Liberals. Likewise, the provincial Quebec Liberal Party brings together federalists from all three major parties at the federal level, who work together for a united cause. There are confederal parties among big-C conservatives as well. The Conservative Party of Canada's constitution states that it shall not establish provincial parties. At various times, provincial Progressive Conservative parties have had strained, even icy, relations with their federal counterpart.

Lastly, there are many **truncated parties** that do not have namesakes at both levels. Organizations like the Yukon Party, Saskatchewan Party, and Coalition Avenir Québec do not run candidates at the federal level. These parties tend to ally themselves with the federal Conservatives. The Bloc Québécois and Parti Québécois are another example of sister organizations that share resources but not the same name.

Provincial elections, like federal elections, can feature a number of minor political parties that seek to advance an agenda but are not in contention to win any seats, let alone form the government. The number of political parties may be related to how difficult it is to register a party, the diversity of public opinions, and the ability to organize and fundraise; thus, the variety of political actors in one province is not necessarily indicative of party competition elsewhere. For instance, in some provinces there can be more than a dozen minor parties, each earning less than one per cent of the vote. In other provinces, only the three major parties and a handful of independents contest elections.

truncated party
A federal or provincial political party that does not have a similarly named party at the other level of government.

Political parties have a much smaller presence at the territorial and municipal levels of government in Canada. In Northwest Territories and Nunavut, candidates run as independents, and later participate in consensus government. During election campaigns, in some large cities and small towns there are electoral alliances of like-minded candidates who pool resources to campaign under a local banner. In most municipalities, candidates officially run as independents, though some may have an affiliation with a federal or provincial party that they may or may not communicate to electors.

The Evolution of Major Parties

Understanding the evolution of Canadian party politics can be challenging without reference to some sort of family tree (see Figure 9.3), whose components we discuss next.

At the federal level, the **Liberal Party of Canada** has been a constant. Nicknamed the Grits—a moniker that dates back to a pre-Confederation movement for democratic reform—the party began by promoting business liberalism and has evolved to promote welfare liberalism. Historically its key strength has been brokering the English–French divide, a role that has seen it currying the favour of Quebec, to the great frustration of Western Canada. The party's image of prioritizing Eastern Canadian interests, along with its reluctance to move more forcefully to implement free trade, prompted many Western and rural Liberals to form a splinter party in the period between the two world wars. The Progressives ran successfully under a variety of banners, forming provincial governments (under the banner United Farmers) in Ontario, Manitoba, and Alberta, and winning enough seats to become the official opposition in Ottawa in 1921. However, on principle, the Progressives handed the third-place Conservatives the official opposition

Liberal Party
A party that straddles the political centre and has governed Canada at the federal level longer than any other major party.

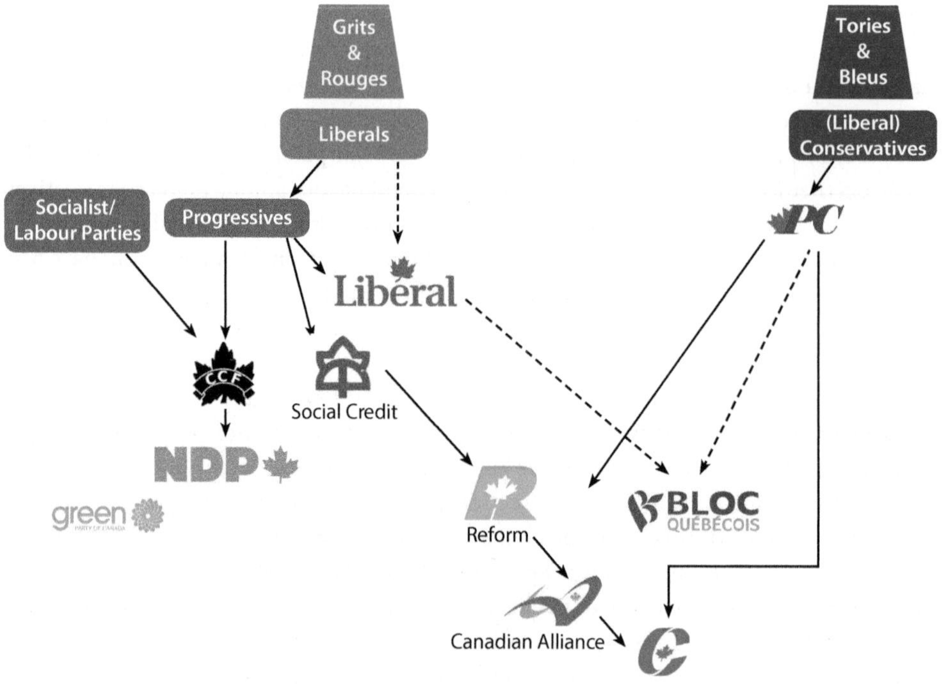

Figure 9.3 | The Canadian Federal Party Family Tree

title and function, seeing those as arcane relics of traditional party politics. Most Progressives returned to the Liberal fold by 1925, having convinced the party's establishment of the need to balance rural and Western interests with those of Central Canada and the cities. The Liberals went on to become a powerhouse from that point through 2006, controlling the federal government for long periods of uninterrupted rule, including 1935–57, 1963–79, and 1993–2006. Liberal prime ministers such as Wilfrid Laurier, Mackenzie King, Louis St Laurent, Lester Pearson, Pierre Trudeau, and Jean Chrétien governed during pivotal periods of Canadian history. King was in office for 22 years and is Canada's longest-serving prime minister.

This hegemony causes many observers to refer to the Liberals as Canada's **natural governing party**. The party's success is based, in part, on an appeal to the median voter by prioritizing a basket of policies that are likely to be supported by a majority of voters. Notably, the Liberals have been successful at cultivating support from the business community while maintaining a progressive public image on social issues.[14] From 1896 to 2006, every Liberal leader became prime minister, and the party never placed worse than second in a general election. In the ensuing decade, the party experienced more difficulty, and two Liberal leaders resigned after poor election results. It was amidst this backdrop that Justin Trudeau led his party to a surprise majority victory in 2015 and returned with a minority of seats in 2019. Under his leadership, the Liberal party's traditional brokerage party role of placating regions has been replaced with its emphasis on the middle class and defence of the Charter of Rights and Freedoms, the constitutional document championed by his father Pierre Trudeau.

The main alternative to the Liberal Party is the **Conservative Party of Canada**. Its ideology began as traditionalist tory conservatism and loyalty to Britain, particularly the monarchy. The party's principles have since evolved to attract libertarians, economic and social conservatives, and some median voters. This clustering of different points of view and political agendas has made for strange bedfellows. At times, the Conservative party has been held together most strongly by common frustration with Liberal governance, particularly among residents of Western and rural Canada. Some Conservative leaders have won the most lopsided election victories in Canadian history, with John A. Macdonald winning five majority governments in the late nineteenth century, John Diefenbaker winning the biggest federal landslide ever in 1958, and Brian Mulroney capturing the largest number of seats in Canadian history in 1984. Yet the party has seen these periods of success offset by precipitous failures, most notoriously in 1993, when it went from being the government to winning just two seats. The party is periodically unable to maintain its coalition of ideological factions. The instability is reflected in multiple instances of the party changing its name in an effort to broaden its appeal (see Table 9.5). The latest incarnation was formed in 2003, when the Canadian Alliance Party (previously known as the Reform Party) and the Progressive Conservative Party merged to become the Conservative Party of Canada. The new party's first leadership contest was won by former Reform MP and Canadian Alliance leader Stephen Harper, who went on to lead the Conservative Party in five federal elections, and was prime minister for nearly a decade. The other Conservative prime ministers who held office across multiple elections are Macdonald, Robert Borden, Diefenbaker, and Mulroney. Andrew Scheer, a former speaker of the House of Commons, became Conservative leader in 2017 and led the party in the 2019 federal general election.

natural governing party
A single party whose long-term dominance has become institutionalized.

Conservative Party
A centre–right major party that has periodically formed the Government of Canada.

The creation of the Bloc Québécois is discussed later in this chapter on pages 313–14.

Table 9.5 Name Changes of Major Political Parties in Canada	
Political Party	**Used to Be Known as . . .**
Conservative Party of Canada (since 2003)	Liberal–Conservative Party* (1867–73, 1920–30) Conservative Party (1873–1920, 1930–42) Progressive Conservative Party (1942–2003)**
Liberal Party of Canada (since 1878)	Liberal-Reform Party (1867–78)
New Democratic Party of Canada (since 1961)	Co-operative Commonwealth Federation (1932–61)

*Variations of this terminology were used at different times. The party presented itself as the Unionist Party in the 1917 federal election and headed the so-called Union government.

**In 2003 the PC Party merged with the Canadian Alliance Party to form the Conservative Party of Canada. The Canadian Alliance was created in 2000 as a rebranded version of its predecessor, the Reform Party of Canada.

Some nuances about the Conservative Party are noteworthy. Partisans and the party are commonly referred to as Tories. The nickname is a tradition dating back to seventeenth-century Britain. In addition, the federal Conservative Party is not officially affiliated with provincial Progressive Conservative parties. The federal Conservative Party changed its name to the Progressive Conservative (PC) Party in 1942, when Manitoba premier John Bracken became leader and sought to appeal to those who supported the Progressive Party of the era. Provincial parties followed suit, and to this day in all but four provinces (BC, Alberta, Saskatchewan, and Quebec) they are known as the provincial PC Party.

New Democratic Party
A left-wing major party that has formal ties with organized labour.

Unlike the Conservative and Liberal parties, the **New Democratic Party of Canada** does not trace its roots back to Confederation. Rather, its origins are in the post–World War I social gospel movement led by farmers and labour activists who championed the plight of frustrated workers and the unemployed. Socialist uprisings in Europe, notably in Russia, played a role in inspiring the Winnipeg General Strike of 1919. The implications of Canada's lack of a strong social safety net became clear during the Great Depression. Rising unemployment rates showed no signs of abatement, a drought devastated farms, and families were in need of food. Prominent members of fledgling left-wing protest parties including the United Farmers, the Progressive Party, and the Labour Party joined forces. The Co-operative Commonwealth Federation was formed, and at its 1933 convention, members adopted a policy statement known as the Regina Manifesto. That public declaration called for the free-market forces of capitalism to be replaced with government management of the economy through democratic socialism. The party advocated for nationalizing several sectors of the economy, which means to place them under state ownership.

A mass party, the Co-operative Commonwealth Federation experienced limited electoral success against rival catch-all parties at the federal level. This persisted, despite breakthroughs in some provincial elections, notably in Saskatchewan under Tommy Douglas. During the Cold War, critics decried the party's sympathies for communism, and in 1956 the CCF moved toward the political centre by passing the Winnipeg Declaration. That new policy plank continued to embrace socialism while adding the promotion of the Keynesian economics principle of government spending to stimulate economic growth. In the late 1950s, the party formed an alliance with the Canadian Labour Congress, a national trade union. In 1961, the CCF was dissolved and the New Democratic Party was formed. The preamble of its constitution pledged a belief in "the application of democratic socialist principles to government." This included championing the needs of individuals including

Briefing Notes

Names as Political Brands

The wide variety of names used to label political parties in Canada can be bewildering. The confusion is heightened when some of the names appear to be oxymorons, like Liberal-Conservative and Progressive Conservative. Others—like the Saskatchewan Party, Canadian Alliance, Parti Québécois, People's Party, and Confederation of Regions—avoid ideological references altogether. These names are part of a strategy taken up by party leaders and their advisers to build bridges between ideological camps. For this reason, it is best to consider some party names as brands and not as ideological labels.

the poor, supporting a sustainable environment, and seeking peace. The new party's formal alliance with labour unions fundamentally distinguishes it from opponents.

The New Democratic Party moved away from the outright rejection of capitalism. Yet, its founding constitution declared opposition to "the making of profit" and advocated "the principle of social ownership" and "economic and social planning." Federally, the NDP's achievements occur mostly when the Liberal Party forms a minority government and makes policy concessions in exchange for support on confidence votes in the legislature. In 2011, a surge of Quebec support helped the NDP win 59 seats in that province alone, and it formed official opposition at the federal level for the first time. The party by now embraced many third-way policies and political marketing techniques. However, the NDP's constitution still espoused socialist principles. At its 2013 convention, delegates voted to replace socialist passages with the progressive principle that "governments have the power to address the limitations of the market in addressing the common good."[15] The party continues to seek higher taxes on big business and the wealthy, stronger social programs, strict environmental protections, and a reduced role in military conflict. Despite the 2011 breakthrough, by 2019 the NDP held fewer seats than the Bloc Québécois. New Democrats have found more electoral success in provincial elections, where its affiliated units have formed the government in British Columbia, Alberta, Saskatchewan, Manitoba, Ontario, and Nova Scotia.

The 2011 election campaign that led to the NDP becoming the official opposition for the first time is described in Chapter 10 on page 356 (Inside Canadian Politics: What Was the Orange Wave?).

The Evolution of Minor Parties

Since the early twentieth century, a long series of protest parties have been outlets for voters to express their frustrations. Many began as inconsequential fringe parties but, unlike organizations such as the Rhinoceros Party of Canada, some protest parties eventually attract sufficient support in an election to influence the outcome. Organizations such as the CCF that grow to have a national focus tend not to elect many MPs. Parties whose support is concentrated in a region, such as the Bloc Québécois, can disrupt the party system.

In recent years, the Green Party of Canada has played a significant role in elections and party politics. Its core philosophy of environmentalism draws in elements of fiscal conservatism, social progressivism, and democratic idealism. For the first couple of decades after the party's founding in 1983, the Green Party was a fringe organization, earning less than 1 per cent of the vote in elections. Some significant political changes catapulted the Greens from the fringe to national attention. The Canada Elections Act was amended in 2003 to provide federal political parties with state funding. A formula awarded money for each vote received, up until it was discontinued in 2015. This per-vote subsidy incentivized the Green Party to get votes in every available electoral district across the country. It also gave voters an incentive to cast a ballot for the party, even if the local candidate did not have a reasonable chance of winning. In 2004 the Greens became only the fourth Canadian party ever to field a full slate of candidates in a federal election. This drive to field candidates combined with a surge of support in North America and Europe for the environmental movement. In 2008, Canada's national broadcast networks bent to popular demand to include Green Party leader Elizabeth May in the leaders' debates. Previously, only political parties with a seat in Parliament had been invited, and May was not yet an MP. The Greens reflect public concern about climate change, oil pipelines, energy efficiency, agriculture, sustainability, and democratic reform. The party is regularly cited as the preference of 5 to 8 per cent of respondents in public-opinion polls, but has difficulty translating this popular support into seats, due largely to its support being spread thinly across the entire country. Green parties have experienced bursts of success in provincial elections. The Greens held the balance of power after elections in British Columbia (2017) and New Brunswick (2018) resulted in minority governments. In the 2019 federal election, the first Green MP to be elected from outside British Columbia gained a seat in New Brunswick.

The flaring up of regional grievances has had the most significant implications for Canadian party politics. In Western Canada, several protest parties rose to prominence

>>>>>>>>>>>>>>>>
The election challenges facing the Greens are discussed in the context of PR electoral systems in Chapter 10, on elections and voting: see pages 341–2.

THE CANADIAN PRESS/Adrian Wyld

In recent years, the Green Party has made a number of electoral breakthroughs, including the election of three Green MPs in 2019. Pictured above, Green Party leader Elizabeth May celebrates with her new caucus colleague, Paul Manly, in spring 2019. What does it take for a fringe party to evolve to a minor party? Do issues-based parties still serve a role if their causes go mainstream? What about when their policies are adopted by major parties?

between World War I and World War II, and their appeal sometimes extended east of Manitoba. For instance, the Progressive Party (1914–30) was a vehicle for farmers who were upset about tariffs and rising train freight rates. They had alliances with the United Farmers parties that organized in provinces across Canada, particularly in Alberta, Manitoba, and Ontario. In those provinces, Progressives pressured the governing Liberals to implement democratic reforms, notably the right of non-Indigenous women to vote. The Progressives established a regional alternative to the two-party system dominated by the Liberal and Conservative parties, placing second in the 1921 election. That year, Canada's first woman MP, Agnes Macphail, was elected as a member of the upstart party. But supporters gradually gravitated back to the Liberal Party or on to other movements. On the left, the Progressives gave rise to the CCF, while those on the right launched Social Credit (1935–93). The Socreds were a band of libertarians and conservatives whose original goal of radical financial reform gave way to more mainstream forms of economic and social conservatism. The party formed the provincial government in Alberta from 1935 to 1971, found support as the Ralliement des créditistes in Quebec into the 1960s, and was successful in some BC provincial elections until the early 1990s, when it disbanded.

Another significant political force was the aforementioned Reform Party (1987–2000). This Western-based conservative protest party promoted an agenda captured in the slogan "The West wants in." Reform's familiar ideology of demanding smaller and more responsible government appealed to libertarians, conservatives, and disgruntled Westerners alike. To many people's surprise, 52 Reform MPs were elected in the 1993 election, and the party went on to form the official opposition in 1997. Leader Preston Manning led a rebranding of the party into the Canadian Alliance (2000–3). It was formed in an attempt to attract remaining supporters of the federal Progressive Conservative Party, as well as blue Liberals (Liberal partisans who are partial to fiscal conservatism) in voter-rich Ontario. The Alliance formed the official opposition after the 2000 general election; however, it had its sights on forming government. Stephen Harper, an original Reform MP who had left party politics, became leader of the Canadian Alliance. As leader, he pushed an agenda to merge the Alliance with the PC Party, which resulted in the creation of the Conservative Party of Canada in 2003.

Western alienation is discussed in the concept of sectionalism in Chapter 4, on regionalism: see pages 106–7.

Regional protest parties have been successful in Quebec. Unlike other protest parties operating at the federal level, these organizations field candidates exclusively in that province, and they have no aspirations of forming the government. The earliest such party was the Ligue Nationaliste Canadienne (1900–12), a fledgling organization created by disgruntled Liberals, who sought to bring together Quebecers who were fed up with British imperialism. The Bloc Populaire Canadien (1942–7) emerged in response to anger about the possibility of conscription in World War II and similarly attracted Quebec nationalists. But by far the most successful federal protest party in Quebec has been the **Bloc Québécois**. It was formed by nationalists who were frustrated by the defeat of the Meech Lake Accord in 1990. The Bloc attracted disaffected Liberals and Progressive Conservatives, in particular federal PC minister Lucien Bouchard, who became the party's leader. The BQ promoted sovereignty-association and shocked Canadians by forming the official opposition after the 1993 election. In the aftermath of the failed 1995 Quebec referendum, the Bloc began championing Quebec's concerns generally, particularly with respect to social democracy. It advocated on issues such as demanding tougher laws against biker gangs, stoking public anger about the sponsorship scandal, and advocating the need for more federal money for the province. Its raison d'être began to wane with the decline of

Bloc Québécois
A left-leaning protest party that promotes Quebec nationalism.

the sovereignist movement. By 2011, the party was devoid of new policy ideas, setting the stage for many Quebecers to turn to the NDP instead. The party experienced considerable in-fighting and churned through leaders. In 2018 many Bloc MPs temporarily left the party to sit in Parliament under the name Québec debout, an ultimately successful attempt to force their leader out. In the 2019 federal election the Bloc experienced a resurgence, widely attributed to the popularity of leader Yves-François Blanchet.

Structure of Political Parties

To further understand political parties, we must unpack their diverse parts, and the types of people who are affiliated with them. The extra-parliamentary wing is comprised of the many people who are formally involved with the internal machinery of the party. The small number of individuals who represent the party in a legislature comprise the parliamentary wing. All of them work to secure the support of the thousands if not millions of partisans who have some sort of attachment to the party.

The Extra-parliamentary Wing

Political parties have common organizational structures. The most formalized parties have their own constitution to establish basic matters such as the party's name, its hierarchy, its principles, and its objectives. A party constitution outlines eligibility criteria for joining the party, guidelines for maintaining a senior party council or board of directors, and requirements for controlling the party's finances. It ensures the party is ready for election campaigns by setting rules for member input on policies and selecting a leader; rules for running electoral district associations; and nomination rules for representing the party as an election candidate. There may be information about committees and commissions, as well as details about any official affiliation with other political organizations, such as unions or professional associations. Guidelines about the method for changing the constitution are identified, so that the party may evolve to reflect party members' priorities, and those of the leader. The components of party constitutions are therefore integral to how a political party takes shape.

The federal Conservative, Liberal, and New Democratic parties' constitutions share many commonalities, and yet each has distinctive elements. Each constitution identifies the party principles, namely the shared values, ideologies, and purposes. For the Conservative Party, this includes "A belief in a balance between fiscal accountability, progressive social policy and individual rights and responsibilities"; for the Liberal Party, the principles of "individual freedom, responsibility and human dignity in the framework of a just society, and political freedom in the framework of meaningful participation by all persons"; and for the NDP, the building of "sustainable prosperity and a society that shares its benefits more fairly."

Party constitutions also dictate who can become an official supporter of the organization. **Party members** are those people who formally applied to belong to a party, likely paid a membership fee, and are expected to help advance the party's objectives. All residents of Canada above a specified age may apply for membership. Party members are eligible to formally participate in party activities, normally in the riding where they live. For example, the Conservative Party constitution states that individual members may attend local party meetings, may seek election to the board of directors of their electoral

party member
A person who formally belongs to a political party, having joined by purchasing a membership.

district association, may stand for election to be a delegate at a national party convention, and may vote in internal party contests. In addition to individual membership, the NDP provides affiliated membership to "trade unions, farm groups, co-operatives, women's organizations and other groups" that share the party's values. That party designates formal roles and titles for members of organized labour within its organizational hierarchy, including a vice-president position and two positions on the party executive. It reserves up to 30 positions for representatives of national labour organizations on the party's national council.

The internal organizational structures of federal political parties vary somewhat but in general resemble the model shown in Figure 9.4. Provincial and territorial parties are supported by similar frameworks, albeit on a smaller scale, with fewer layers and internal bodies. In the figure, each party's extra-parliamentary wing is coloured in mauve, and consists largely of party members and their delegates, most of whom are volunteers.

Political parties attempt to maintain a presence in each electoral district through a local branch of the party. An **electoral district association (EDA)**, commonly referred to as a riding association or a constituency association, is a formal arm of the party that engages grassroots members in the electoral district where they live. These local associations are regional arms of each party that provide members with an opportunity to participate in public affairs, policy development, and election readiness. Members are eligible to attend meetings to discuss strategic matters, to select EDA executives and convention delegates, and to recruit people to seek the nomination to be the party's local election candidate. Electoral district associations are an organizational mechanism through which parties communicate with party activists, initiate local fundraising events, identify

electoral district association (EDA)
The local organization of a political party operating within the boundaries of an election riding.

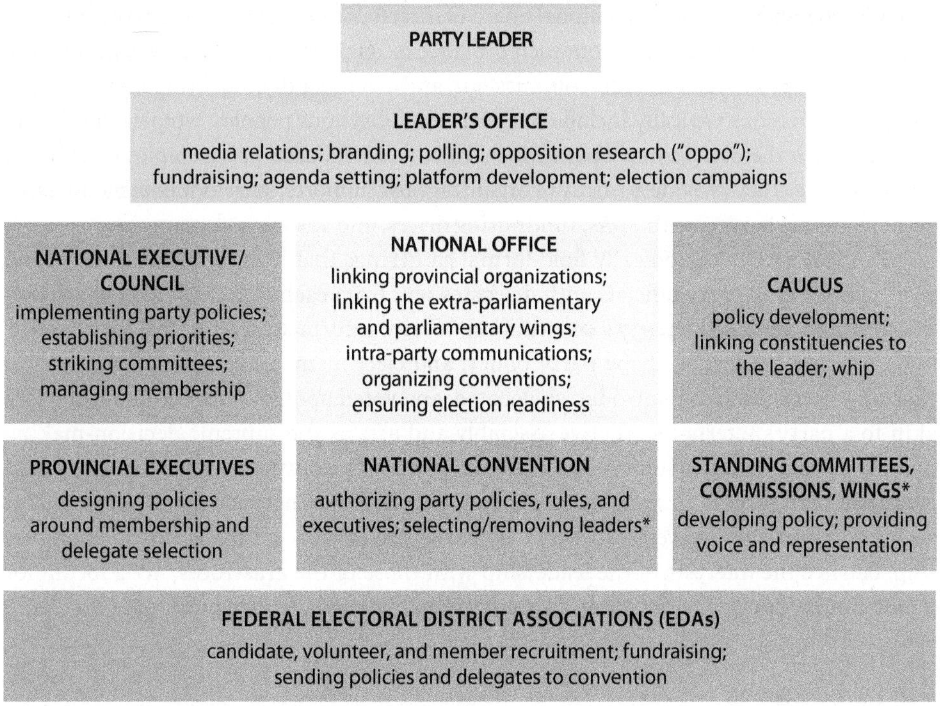

Figure 9.4 | Typical Structure of Federal Political Parties

* Not all parties have this component/role.

potential candidates, and stay in touch with local concerns.[16] In some cases, a national party may operate provincial associations as a means of coordinating local activity in the districts. In areas of the country where the party is popular, there tend to be vibrant district associations with intense competition for executive positions, and fierce nomination contests for the opportunity to represent the party in an election. The reverse is also true: in places where the party is unpopular, there may not even be an electoral district association, which inevitably results in the recruitment of a stopgap candidate at election time.

Each federal political party has some sort of organizational hierarchy to integrate members and EDAs while performing a central management function. Membership in national bodies normally comprises party members from across Canada. Politicians who hold public office at the federal or provincial level of government are typically ineligible for a high-ranking position within the extra-parliamentary wing by virtue of their position. The hierarchy ranges from people who are responsible for the party's day-to-day management to the participants in special-interest branches of the party, such as its youth wing. The latter may include commissions—which the NDP constitution defines as "a formal organization, internal to the party, which regroups members on a basis of identity, or around a specific political issue"[17]—in order to provide a forum for those members who have a shared interest. The Liberal and New Democrat constitutions expressly identify and formalize the role of youth in their parties. By comparison, the Conservative constitution remarks that the formalization of youth forums and post-secondary campus organizations will be addressed by the party's national council through bylaws.

The organizational structure to coordinate internal party affairs can be extensive. To illustrate, the Liberal Party designates executive officers, namely the national party president, English and French vice-presidents, a policy secretary, and a party secretary. These executive members belong to a national board of directors that includes the party leader, the past president, a representative from each province or territory, one Liberal MP, the chair of each of the party's special-interest commissions, and a number of non-voting members. The party's commissions typically include one each for Indigenous peoples, women, youth, and seniors, which themselves may operate local clubs. As well, each party employs staff in its national office. They provide an array of organizational supports, such as media monitoring, event planning, liaising with EDAs, fundraising drives, and ensuring election readiness.

Political parties periodically hold formal gatherings that bring together current and past high-ranking party officials with delegates sent from each EDA. A **party convention** is a forum to amend the party's constitution, receive information from the party executive including the leader, shape party policy, and elect members of the party's national executive. Resolutions are introduced, debated, and voted upon. A convention is therefore akin to a party's internal legislative assembly and acts as the supreme decision-making body over party affairs, subject to Canadian law. Party conventions are normally held every two years, unless circumstances warrant a special meeting, such as the need to select a new party leader. Conventions keep the party executive accountable to the membership, balance the interests of the leadership with those of the grassroots, are a forum for public-policy ideas, generate publicity, and generally stimulate team building.

party convention
An official gathering of party delegates to decide on matters of policy and/or leadership.

Party Leaders

party leader
The head of a political party's legislative wing.

The **party leader** is the chief public official for the party. That individual is the public face of the party and acts as its primary spokesperson. The leader embodies the party's principles, leads it in the legislature and during an election campaign, and is ultimately responsible for making decisions. Among the powers of a federal party leader is the authority to inform Elections Canada of the registration or deregistration of the party or its electoral district associations; to accept or overrule local nominations for a candidate to represent the party in a general election or by-election; and to act as a signatory on other official documents, such as the formal appointment of a registered agent of the party. The Liberal Party constitution enumerates the responsibilities and powers of its leader as follows:

(a) speak for the party concerning any political issue;
(b) take part in the development of the party policies and party platform;
(c) be guided by the party policies and the party platform;
(d) report to the party at every national convention; and
(e) appoint the campaign chairs.[18]

Given all of these responsibilities, leaders are often supported by a sizeable staff located in the leader's office. The prime minister's office (PMO) and premiers' offices often serve this purpose for parties in power. Political staff in the caucus research bureau provide further supports.

What does not appear in any party constitution is just how supreme the authority of the party leader is in practice. A federal party leader must have significant support within that party across the country to secure the position; likewise, a provincial party leader must have broad party support across the province. Once installed, that individual appoints supporters to key positions. In other parliamentary democracies there are mechanisms to remove an unpopular leader, even if that person is head of the government. For instance, in Australia the leadership review vote is conducted within caucus, rather than as an extra-parliamentary exercise.[19] Seeking to emulate that power for parliamentarians, a Conservative MP introduced a private member's bill in the House of Commons, resulting in the passage of the Reform Act in 2015. That legislation allows the caucus to decide if a leadership review vote is warranted.

In general, formal **leadership reviews** are held at party conventions. A leadership review vote typically occurs at the first convention after an unsuccessful general election campaign. Party delegates vote on whether they want the current leader to continue in the role; if they do not, a leadership contest will be required so that others may compete for the job. The mechanism is an opportunity for an opponent within the party to assume control of the internal party apparatus. Conversely, vote results showing that the leader is popular can convince disgruntled party members of the leader's supremacy. Technically, a party leader requires only a majority of votes to continue, but in practice the threshold is much higher. Ever since the Joe Clark episode, chronicled in the Inside Canadian Politics box on the next page, party leaders face pressure to resign if they receive less than a two-thirds endorsement in leadership review votes, even if the party constitution does not stipulate such a requirement.

A **leadership contest** occurs when a party leader vacates the position and a new leader needs to be selected. In between, the party may appoint an interim leader, who normally does not seek the leadership in the ensuing contest. If there is more than one applicant, then a leadership race is held, culminating in a party vote. Leadership hopefuls tour the country (or province), participate in debates, sign up members, are active on social media, and seek to attract news media attention. The stakes are especially high if contestants are vying to replace a sitting head of government. This sometimes results in a situation where

The role of the PMO is discussed throughout Chapter 5, on the executive: see especially pages 140–1.

leadership review
A vote held at a party convention on whether a leadership contest should be held.

leadership contest
An election within a political party to select a leader.

Inside Canadian Politics

Why Do Leaders Need Two-Thirds of the Party Membership to Support Them?

Party leaders seek to secure a strong endorsement from convention delegates in order to demonstrate their popularity within and control over the party. Leaders are generally held to an informal threshold of obtaining more than two-thirds of the votes in a leadership review. The origin of the two-thirds custom stems from a bizarre event involving Joe Clark, who became Canada's sixteenth prime minister in 1979, but lost the 1980 federal election. At the 1983 federal Progressive Conservative Party convention, Clark received 66.9 per cent support in a leadership review vote, signalling that a sizeable majority of party members wanted him to carry on. Clark shocked everyone by proclaiming that he would resign because he did not have enough support. Somewhat unusually, he stood as a contestant in

the ensuing leadership race to reclaim his vacated position, which he hoped would return him with a stronger mandate to lead the party. Instead, Brian Mulroney was crowned Tory leader, and went on to lead the party to majority governments in the 1984 and 1988 federal elections. In 1992, a public-opinion poll indicated that Mulroney's public support sat at just 11 per cent nationally, but there was no significant internal movement to replace him. Prime Minister Mulroney resigned on his own terms a year later, prompting a leadership contest, which resulted in Kim Campbell becoming Canada's first woman prime minister. Decades later, many pundits continue to cite the Clark episode as evidence that a leader needs to obtain more than two-thirds of the votes at a leadership review convention.

DISCUSSION ITEM

The threat of an internal putsch (overthrow) illustrates why a leader's first priority must be to keep party members, and chief rivals, happy. Moreover, a head of government who is unpopular in public-opinion polls may nevertheless have the party's support.

VOX POP

Is the informal two-thirds threshold appropriate in leadership review votes? What are the benefits and drawbacks of writing a vote threshold into a party's constitution?

party members, not the general public, choose the next prime minister or premier. Many, but not all, of these leaders go on to form governments in the subsequent general election.

Selecting Canadian Party Leaders

Canadian political parties have used a myriad of voting systems to select their leaders. In general, the leadership selection rules have become more inclusive over time, with a greater number and diversity of individuals participating than ever before. Various selection models are used, ranging from the decision being restricted to parliamentarians behind closed doors, through to opening the process to any eligible citizen who registers to participate. Some voting systems involve a heated and divisive struggle for the leadership of the party. This type of competition can allow dark-horse candidates to win when people endorse a least-hated alternative in order to prevent a presumed front-runner from winning.

The method of selecting a leader reflects evolutions in mass communication. The leader was selected by the party's parliamentarians during the newspaper era and the age of elite parties. In the radio and television era, as mass parties took shape, leaders were selected at special conventions by party delegates from electoral districts. Parties gradually broadened the eligibility of voting in leadership contests to include all party members in conjunction with technological advances in telecommunications and transportation. In the Internet era, leaders are increasingly selected by anyone recruited by leadership contestants, whether they are party members or not. Televoting and online voting sometimes involve limited scrutiny of a voter's eligibility. Moreover, the rules for leadership contests have evolved, with contestants to lead a federal party subject to the financial limits specified in the Canada Elections Act.

In the nineteenth and early twentieth centuries, party leaders were selected by and from the organization's elected representatives. This model began to disappear after the conclusion of the first party system. Today, most parties reserve caucus-only choice for the selection of interim leaders, who serve as the party's head following the resignation of a leader and until the official selection of a replacement. The interim leader holds the role indefinitely when an election campaign is imminent and there is no time to hold a more inclusive selection process.

Caucus selection processes were displaced by delegate conventions. Initially conventions were held in so-called smoke-filled rooms filled with party elites and were closed off from public view. Leadership conventions evolved into televised events involving party faithful numbering in the thousands. Depending on the party, these delegates include party notables (legislators, extra-parliamentary executives), leaders of affiliated organizations (such as unions), representatives of the party's special wings (youth, women's, Indigenous) if any, and envoys elected by the various electoral district associations. Collectively, these delegates—and not the grassroots party members themselves—vote to choose the leader. Some parties continue to use traditional delegate conventions. The events provide dramatic news coverage when they produce surprise outcomes.

The remaining forms of leadership selection allow party members a more direct role in leadership selection. First adopted by the Parti Québécois in 1985, the one member, one vote (OMOV) universal balloting process became one of the most common leadership selection processes among Canadian parties. As its name suggests, each party member receives one vote when it comes to selecting the leader. Most parties use multiple rounds of voting or rank-ordered ballots in contests featuring more than one contender. Many parties are experimenting with telephone and online voting to increase access to the voting process.

By comparison, in the weighted constituencies system, each electoral district is assigned an equal number of points. These points are then distributed to leadership candidates based on their share of the popular vote in that constituency. For instance, each electoral district might be allotted 100 points. A contestant who captures 48 per cent of party leadership votes in a given electoral district would be allotted 48 points. The remaining 52 points would be allocated to the other contestants proportionate to their percentage of the vote in that riding. Points are then totalled across all of the constituencies. This system ensures that leadership contestants must seek out support from the entire jurisdiction because they cannot rely on a large number of supporters clustered in a few regions.

The weighted constituency model combines the simplicity of the one-member, one-vote model with achieving geographic representation. Conversely, the hybrid model balances the advantages of OMOV with the participation of underrepresented groups. In hybrid systems, all party members cast a ballot for the leadership candidate of their choice. These votes are then weighted according to a specific set of rules. For instance, when the federal NDP selected Jack Layton in 2003, the votes of all party members were weighted at 75 per cent of the total, with the remaining 25 per cent of votes being reserved for unions. The party later used OMOV when it selected Jagmeet Singh.

The Parliamentary Wing

party caucus
All members of a political party who hold a seat in the legislature.

The **party caucus** is those members of the party who hold a seat in the legislature. The parliamentary wing of a party consists of its caucus and the partisan people who work directly for those public officials. Party caucuses at the federal level historically included both MPs and senators. However, the Conservative Party is now the only party whose caucus includes senators. At the provincial level, the party caucus comprises all of that party's members of the provincial legislative assembly. The caucus meets regularly in private. These meetings are not open to extra-parliamentary members of the party, nor are they accessible to the media or the general public. Caucus meetings provide an opportunity for members of the legislature to receive information from the party leadership. They are a private forum for parliamentarians to voice their concerns. At times, caucus discussions can be heated affairs, but once the meeting is over, any dissent is not disclosed, so that the party may present a unified front to the public. As discussed below, strict discipline means members risk being expelled from the party should they break ranks or speak about what happens during caucus meetings.

official party status
The minimum number of elected members a party needs to question the government in the legislature and qualify for other resources and privileges.

The number of people belonging to a party caucus varies considerably and reflects the party's performance in the most recent general election. A federal political party that has a majority government will have a caucus of at least 170 MPs, which swells if the party considers sensators as part of the caucus. Conversely, at the start of the 43rd Parliament, the Green Party caucus had just three MPs. The limited human resources of smaller parties are compounded when they have fewer than 12 MPs, which is the threshold for a party in the House of Commons to be granted **official party status**. This parliamentary designation brings with it extra financial resources and eligibility to participate in Question Period. The threshold for party status in provincial legislatures ranges from a dozen members in Quebec's National Assembly to at least one seat in the Legislative Assembly of Prince Edward Island. Official party status in the legislature should not be confused with whether a party has registered with an election agency, or the corresponding eligibility to include the party label on an election ballot next to a candidate's name. It foremost refers to the ability to qualify for additional supports and to play a greater role in legislative proceedings.

The government's cabinet and the opposition's shadow cabinets are discussed on pages 143–51 of Chapter 5, on the executive. The roles of different actors in Parliament are discussed on pages 182–6 of Chapter 6, on the legislature.

As discussed in great detail in Chapters 5 and 6, parties sit on either the government or opposition benches. Prominent parliamentarians are assigned ministerial or shadow ministerial roles.

Partisans

Not all people involved in party politics are card-carrying members, elected delegates, or members of a legislative assembly. Anyone who identifies strongly with a political party is known as a **partisan**. Some of the most ardent partisans are members who become deeply involved with the extra-parliamentary and/or parliamentary wings of a party. They choose to spend their time working to advance a political cause. Other partisans may give money to a party, volunteer in an election campaign to persuade others to vote for the party's candidate, promote the party in social-media forums or otherwise support the party. In short, they are loyal to the party and have a psychological attachment to it.

A person's partisan identification is not necessarily connected with how that individual votes. Not all Liberal partisans vote for Liberal candidates, for example, just as not all Liberal voters feel a strong attachment to the party. There is mixed evidence about whether the strength of partisanship in Canada has been waning. In the past, the connection that people had with a political party was more likely to be related to their dependency on patronage and pork barrel politics. Today, partisanship remains a prominent force, even though laws prohibit leaders from offering their supporters tangible rewards like government jobs or contracts. Indeed, even when party identification is in flux, at least a third of Canadians continue to support the same party consistently from election to election, and even those who vote for a different party still identify with their preferred party.[20]

While many Canadian citizens are open to switching their support for political parties, this is rare among politicians. The inducements of career advancement and bringing home the goods for constituents are used to ensure that party supporters voice their frustrations in private and never in public. Partisans exert control on each other to ensure that they do not deviate from the directives issued by the party centre, namely the members of the leader's inner circle. This stands in contrast with the members of various colonial, provincial, and federal assemblies of the nineteenth century who became known as loose fish because their voting behaviour was unpredictable. Today's apparent intensifying of party discipline is occurring in an environment where more than ever politicians have opportunities to publicly voice their opinions.

Nevertheless, partisans sometimes decide to switch parties. When a legislator does so, it is known as **crossing the floor**. The expression describes the action of a member of a legislature who leaves the party seated on one side of the chamber to join those on the other side. That individual's chair is literally moved across the aisle in the process. The decision to cross the floor is a personal one, and thus the motivations are not fully understood. The reasons tend to be philosophical differences with party leadership, frustration with the political system, and/or an opportunity for career advancement. Those who switch parties may do so to improve their own clout, as when a member of the opposition joins the government side in the hope of accessing the perks of office, or when a government backbencher leaves after accepting that upward mobility is impossible within that party. There is a lot of media attention when someone crosses the floor because it is a controversial action and is treated as a win or a loss for the corresponding parties. Although some constituents welcome such a decision, others criticize it as unethical, calling for the member to resign. A floor crosser may not necessarily be re-elected in a future general election because many of the partisans who previously voted for their party's candidate will choose to vote once again for the same party. Alternatively, those who are disaffected may choose to sit as an independent rather than join an opposing party. In that case, they face even greater constraints in terms of resources and prospects for re-election.

partisan
Someone who identifies with, and is a staunch supporter of, a political party.

Party discipline is defined and discussed at length in Chapter 6, on the legislature: see especially pages 186–7.

crossing the floor
A situation in which a member of the legislature leaves one political party to join another.

Inside Canadian Politics

Why Do High-Profile Partisans Cross the Floor?

A member of the legislature switching political parties is an episodic event. Two cases stand out in recent memory because of the unusual circumstances and intense public interest. In 2004, business mogul Belinda Stronach ran to be leader of the Conservative Party of Canada, and soon afterward was elected as a Conservative MP in Ontario. The next year, just as it appeared that the Liberal government headed by Prime Minister Paul Martin could fall on a budget vote, Stronach dramatically crossed the floor to the Liberals. Unusually, she was instantly made a cabinet minister, which drew controversy about the ethics of the Liberals leveraging public resources for their own political gain. Stronach was re-elected as a Liberal MP. However, the Martin Liberals were voted out of office, and Stronach was back on the opposition side.

The Conservatives were outraged. Yet, one of Stephen Harper's first acts as prime minister was to similarly leverage the perks of office. During the 2006 federal election, Liberal cabinet minister David Emerson publicly warned people not to vote for the Harper Conservatives, and was re-elected in his Vancouver riding. When the Conservatives formed the government, Harper invited Emerson into his first cabinet—an invitation Emerson crossed the floor to accept despite having just been elected as a Liberal. For days, protesters picketed in front of Emerson's constituency office, demanding that he resign. The media coverage was so negative and lasting that he did not seek re-election.

DISCUSSION ITEM

Even high-ranking partisans, like leadership contestants and former cabinet ministers, cross the floor.

VOX POP

Should floor crossers be required to resign their seats and seek re-election before serving in another party's caucus? How about parliamentarians who are expelled or who resign from caucus to serve as independents?

When someone crosses the floor, or resigns from the party caucus, there is discussion about whether that elected official should be required to resign and represent the new party in a by-election. Federal laws preclude that possibility: an elected member of a legislature is unlikely to be forced to vacate the seat until the next general election. British Columbia is the only jurisdiction in Canada to have recall legislation that allows people to petition to force a by-election.

Concluding Thoughts

Political parties play a dominant role in Canadian political society. They are the lifeblood of political debate, elections, and legislative activity. Canadian democracy is conceivable without political parties; indeed, it functions without them in two of the three territories and in many of Canada's largest cities. Yet, while many critics would like this sort of non-partisan politics to spread to other quarters, parties have become so entrenched in the electoral and legislative process that it is difficult to imagine Canadian politics without them. Indeed, despite their flaws, political parties are essential to differentiating conflicting political ideologies and organizing competition for political office, which is the subject of our next chapter on elections.

For More Information

How has the way that political parties recruit members, mobilize support, fundraise, and communicate changed in Canada over time? Find out in Dan Azoulay's article "The Evolution of Party Organization in Canada since 1900," *The Journal of Commonwealth & Comparative Politics* 33, no. 2 (1995): pp. 185–208.

Why does the electoral system reward regional protest parties and punish pan-Canadian parties? Find out in Alan C. Cairns's seminal article on the matter, "The Electoral System and the Party System in Canada, 1921–1965," *Canadian Journal of Political Science* 1, no. 1 (1968): pp. 55–80.

Want an insider's perspective on campaigning within a Canadian federal party? Read insights from party strategists like Tom Flanagan (*Harper's Team: Behind the Scenes in the Conservative Rise to Power*, McGill–Queen's University Press, 2007), and Brad Lavigne (*Building the Orange Wave: The Inside Story behind the Historic Rise of Jack Layton and the NDP*, Douglas & McIntyre, 2013).

How has floor crossing evolved over time in Canada? Look no further than Semra Sevi, Antoine Yoshinaka, and André Blais, "Legislative Party Switching and the Changing Nature of the Canadian Party System, 1867–2015," *Canadian Journal of Political Science* 51, no. 3 (2018): pp. 665–95.

To what extent do Canadian MPs follow party discipline? Cohesion in the parliamentary wing is the topic of study for David Chartash, Nicholas Caruana, Markus Dickinson, and Laura Stephenson in their article, "When the Team's Jersey Is What Matters: Network Analysis of Party Cohesion and Structure in the Canadian House of Commons," *Party Politics* (2018).

Has Canada entered a new party system? Is the era of brokering regional politics over? How did state funding of political parties contribute to the growth of the Green Party of Canada? These and other questions are examined in *Parties, Elections, and the Future of Canadian Politics*, a collection edited by Amanda Bittner and Royce Koop (UBC Press, 2013). See also Brad Walchuk, "A Whole New Ballgame: The Rise of Canada's Fifth Party System," *American Review of Canadian Studies* 42, no. 3 (2012): pp. 418–34.

There is no evidence that party leaders are growing in importance in Canadians' voting decisions—apparently, our attachment first and foremost to parties remains the strongest predictor of voting behaviour. Not convinced? Take a look at *Dominance and Decline: Making Sense of Recent Canadian Elections* by Elisabeth Gidengil, Neil Nevitte, André Blais, Joanna Everitt, and Patrick Fournier (University of Toronto Press, 2012).

Are the views of Canadian partisans becoming more entrenched? Anthony Kevins and Stuart Soroka provide the evidence in "Growing Apart? Partisan Sorting in Canada, 1992–2015," *Canadian Journal of Political Science* 51, no. 1 (2018): pp. 103–33.

What happens on the ground in local party activity? William Cross explains in "The Importance of Local Party Activity in Understanding Canadian Politics: Winning from the Ground Up in the 2015 Federal Election," *Canadian Journal of Political Science* 49, no. 4 (2016): pp. 601–20.

Are women still treated differently by the media when they seek to become a leader of a Canadian political party? Yes, they are. See Angelia Wagner, Linda Trimble, and Shannon

Sampert, "One Smart Politician: Gendered Media Discourses of Political Leadership in Canada," *Canadian Journal of Political Science* 52, no. 1 (2019): pp. 141–62.

Interested to see how well your views match with the policy programs of political parties in Canada (and beyond)? Take the quiz at http://votecompass.com.

Interested in learning more about the history of Canada's fringe parties? See the CBC's historical coverage of Libertarians, Marxist–Leninists, Rhinos, and others, archived in its video library under the title *Outside Looking In: Small Parties in Federal Politics*: http://www.cbc.ca/archives/topic/outside-looking-in-small-parties-in-federal-politics.

Can't get enough of party politics? Tune in to weekly and Sunday-only politics shows on CBC and CTV, or get your daily fix on CPAC. Monitor *The Hill Times* weekly newsmagazine. Subscribe to a political party listserv, like a politician or political journalist on Facebook, and follow your favourites on Twitter.

Deeper Inside Canadian Politics

1. Joseph Wearing (1996) lists what he considers to be five myths about Canadian party politics:
   - that the history of Canadian parties begins in 1867;
   - that the Conservative and Liberal parties are virtually indistinguishable brokerage, pro-business parties;
   - that third parties are constantly stifled by the two older parties, which steal all their progressive policies anyway;
   - that the two older parties keep alive antiquated conflicts between religious groups, regions, and French and English in order to prevent the emergence of a modern party system based on class divisions; and
   - that the resulting party system makes Canada an anomaly among modern nations.[21]

   Prepare your own evaluation of any two of these myths. Are they as misleading as Wearing argues—or is there more truth to some of them than he allows?

2. Throughout much of Canada, democracy is defined by party politics. This places a number of obstacles in the way of independents seeking office. Identify three main barriers confronting independent candidates, and ways in which each of these may be overcome.

3. Why do you suppose the views of partisans are solidifying into opposing camps? What does the research say? Explain.

Professor Profile

Anna Esselment

Canadian political parties, campaigns and elections, political marketing
Co-editor of *Permanent Campaigning in Canada* (2017)

Courtesy Anna Esselment

Anna Esselment's PhD work focused on the role of partisanship in intergovernmental relations in Canada. Her broader areas of research include political parties, campaigns and elections, political marketing, and Canadian institutions. Previously she worked at Queen's Park as a policy advisor to then opposition leader Dalton McGuinty.

Here is what Anna Esselment told us about her career path from when she was an undergraduate student, why she is drawn to her area of specialization, what is challenging about studying Canadian politics, and what advice she has for students.

* * *

I completed my undergraduate degree at McMaster University in Hamilton. I majored in political science, with a focus on Canadian and American politics, and completed an interdisciplinary minor in international justice and human rights. While I had always been interested in Canadian politics, my introduction to the topic occurred in second year. The course was taught by Dr Will Coleman, who later became my colleague at the University of Waterloo. Dr Coleman was an engaging and effective professor, and I distinctly remember him teaching the class about the Canadian bureaucracy by holding up a can of Campbell's soup and pointing out the various government regulations that affected the manufacturing of that one food product. I found it truly fascinating.

I have had a consistent interest in the institutions and processes of government, but I've focused my own research more narrowly on election campaigns. This has much to do with the three years I spent working at Queen's Park in Toronto, before I went back to school to pursue a PhD. My role as a policy analyst meant I did a lot of work on developing the campaign platform for the next election. I've since remained intrigued by how political parties fight elections, especially the strategies and tactics involved in executing a 45-day contest to win the hearts and minds of Canadian voters.

The most challenging part of studying campaigns is that the people you would most like to talk to—the campaign manager, the head of data analytics, the issues manager, the pollster—are all people who are difficult to reach, especially when the election is in full swing. They are kept busy by the demands of the campaign, and have little time to provide a researcher with context and details about their decisions. This is why research about campaigns mostly occurs in its aftermath, when key members of the campaign staff have more time available. But even then, election strategists can be choosy about who they talk to and about how much they are willing to reveal. Getting people to talk remains a perennial problem facing researchers in this field.

What I find most surprising about studying campaigns is that despite all the changes with technology, at their core very little has changed from campaigns that occurred decades ago. Parties still rely on volunteers to make phone calls and canvass neighbourhoods to identify their supporters; candidates still engage in local debates about the issues Canadians care about. Candidates and their teams still stand on street corners and wave to passing cars, hoping for an encouraging "honk." Campaigns still mobilize their vote the old-fashioned way, which is to call on their identified supporters and give them a lift to the polling station. The data science and accompanying algorithms are helpful, but they have not appeared to drastically alter campaign fundamentals.

If you ever get the opportunity, I encourage you to go out and volunteer for a political party during an election. The experience will give you great insight into the workings of Canadian democracy, and will go a long way to enhance your studies of politics in Canada.

Up for Debate

Should party leaders take bold steps to increase the presence of women and other Canadians underrepresented in legislatures?

THE CLAIM: YES, THEY SHOULD!

The best way to ensure that the views of women, visible minorities, Indigenous peoples, and other traditionally marginalized groups are reflected in government decision-making is for political parties to take significant steps to ensure that more of them are nominated and elected.

Yes: Argument Summary

A healthy democracy must be pluralistic—that is, it must include representatives with an array of socio-demographic characteristics to reflect the views of society as a whole. A legislature whose membership is consistently overrepresented by older white men, many of them drawn from the wealthiest socioeconomic class, cannot adequately speak for the people whose interests it is designed to represent. Canadian political parties are partly responsible for the noticeable lack of women, Indigenous peoples, members of visible minority communities, persons with disabilities, and other traditionally marginalized Canadians in our legislatures. The vast majority of candidates run under a party banner during election campaigns, meaning that inclusive legislatures require inclusive slates of candidates. Canadian party leaders hold a veto over who represents the party in elections, and they should be assertive in using this power to ensure their election slates are more representative of the Canadian population. This may mean rejecting a party nominee who was democratically selected by local party members so that someone else can be installed against the local membership's wishes. It requires special outreach and recruitment efforts. Bold action is needed in the form of target or quota-setting, mentorship, and financial assistance.

Yes: Top 5 Considerations

1. Section 3 of the Charter of Rights and Freedoms states that every Canadian citizen has a right to be a member of a legislative assembly. Section 15 states that every Canadian is legally equal and cannot be discriminated against on the basis of "race, national or ethnic origin, colour, religion, sex, age or mental or physical disability." Sometimes positive actions are required to overcome this sort of discrimination and achieve the democratic ideal of diversity enshrined in the Charter.

2. Parties are the gatekeepers to Canadian democracy. Unless parties take active steps to ensure people from traditionally disadvantaged groups have a fair chance of being nominated to become candidates, there is little chance that any will be elected to the legislature. Research demonstrates that many people from underrepresented groups have just as much chance of being selected by voters in a general election as those from mainstream political communities. The key is ensuring they are nominated in the first place, and that responsibility lies with parties.

3. Party leaders want party insiders, star candidates, and local notables to win nomination battles. Using this prerogative to ensure greater demographic diversity would be a more noble cause.

4. Countries around the world are taking steps to implement quotas and support systems to ensure that people from underrepresented groups, like women, are sufficiently represented. Canada ranks approximately sixtieth out of 193 countries worldwide for the percentage of women in its lower house, behind many developing countries including Rwanda, Cuba and Bolivia; the Nordic countries; and liberal democracies such as France, Italy, Portugal, Spain, New Zealand, and the United Kingdom.[22]

5. Political parties have the means to nurture the engagement of politically marginalized citizens through mentorship, targeted training opportunities, and recognition of special accommodation. Parties can make a difference by providing resources like fundraising assistance and childcare support for candidates, as well as ethnic outreach.

Yes: Other Considerations

- Getting candidates from traditionally underrepresented groups onto the ballot is more difficult than most people realize. Plenty of women, Indigenous peoples, allophones, LGBTQ2+ activists, and youth are involved in the political process in some manner. However, encouraging them to step forward as candidates for office requires help to overcome institutional barriers.

- Establishing quotas for a minimum number of women and others to be candidates can level the playing field. These quotas are needed in winnable ridings—otherwise, appointing people as candidates in unwinnable ridings is little more than token action.

- Beyond reform of internal party rules, legislative change is an option that party-dominated legislatures have been unwilling to debate. For instance, governing parties could pass legislation that reserves a number of seats in the legislature for traditionally underrepresented groups, or opposition parties could propose to create dual-member constituencies to ensure each district is represented by one man and one woman. Electoral reform and the adoption of proportional representation also have potential to improve the representativeness of our legislatures.

THE COUNTERCLAIM: NO, THEY SHOULDN'T!

A strong democracy must encourage unfettered political competition for seats in the legislative assembly.

No: Argument Summary

Free and fair elections are the embodiment of democracy. This involves the freedom to put one's name forward to seek election, the freedom of party members at the grassroots to select their preferred candidate, and the freedom of voters to choose who best represents them—as individuals or as communities. The special treatment of people from underrepresented groups is well-meaning, but it is anti-democratic. It is largely a symbolic effort that does little to meaningfully empower women, Indigenous peoples, ethnic minorities, and other politically underrepresented groups. Well-intentioned party elites with the power to intervene in the nomination process should not meddle in the democratic process. It is up to the general public to render their own judgement on which candidates should be elected.

No: Top 5 Considerations

1. In a free and fair election process, people must be able to compete in open nominations to represent the political party of their choice, rather than have that opportunity closed off by party elites. Anything else is an unhealthy practice that smacks of social engineering.

2. A party's success during a general election campaign does not result from nominating weaker candidates over stronger candidates solely on the basis of gender, ethnicity, or social characteristics. Research demonstrates that Canadians place little value on the local candidate when casting a ballot, meaning that there is little electoral incentive for party leaders to diversify their slates and little reason to expect Canadians would notice if they did.

3. Candidate quotas are problematic. They can become divisive for the party when the leadership's preferred candidate is imposed against the wishes of the grassroots who have followed proper democratic process to identify their own choice. Democratic dissatisfaction and backlash can occur against the same sense of inclusiveness quotas are designed to promote.

4. In order to meet artificial quotas, party elites are more likely to endorse people from traditionally marginalized groups in uncontested nominations in weak seats. As a result, these candidates often end up as cannon fodder during elections, further perpetuating the perception of discrimination and underrepresentation.

5. If inclusiveness were truly a top-of-mind concern for Canadians, they would vote with their feet, punishing or rewarding parties based on the candidates they nominate, or supporting efforts to reform the electoral system. As it stands, there is little evidence parties with the most diverse campaign slates tend to win more seats than those with less demographic balance. Canadians have repeatedly rejected electoral reform options that would create incentives for parties to run a more diverse field of candidates.

No: Other Considerations

- The idea that people can only be represented by people who look like them is mistaken. There are lots of people in the legislature who represent a variety of political viewpoints.

- People who champion more diversity in the legislature seem to ignore the ferocity of party discipline in Canada and the power of the party leader. Activists are so focused on the symbolism of descriptive representation that they overlook that individual parliamentarians must toe the party line.

- Those advocating the adoption of a quota system may attract narrow-minded righteous ideologues whose politics are an affront to those who have a more open-minded view of democracy and are satisfied with the status quo.

- There is a tenuous linkage between affirmative action and inclusive legislatures. It is possible to support employment-equity policies that introduce counter-discrimination hiring practices within the public service, and still be vehemently opposed to special status for traditionally marginalized people who run for election to a legislative assembly.

- Many women, Indigenous peoples, ethnic minorities, and other politically underrepresented groups are philosophically opposed to special treatment.

- A quota of one female and one male representative per district would discriminate against transgender persons.

Discussion Questions

- What are the advantages and disadvantages of giving a party leader final say over whether a candidate can represent the party in an election campaign?

- Why do you think that women might have a more difficult time getting a seat in a legislature than men? What about Indigenous peoples as compared with non-Indigenous peoples? Candidates with visible disabilities versus candidates without? Poor versus wealthy? Young versus old? Caucasian versus visible minority?

- To what extent do you think a candidate's sexual orientation affects someone's willingness to seek the party nomination and run for election? What about someone who does not identify with a binary gender?

- Would you support the government putting aside a pool of money for members of political minority groups to use in a bid to win their party's nomination? How would those funds be administered?

- Given that conservativism tends to cater to traditional values held disproportionately by white males, why is it that the Conservatives were the first party to appoint a woman to cabinet (Ellen Fairclough, in 1957); the first party to elect a black member of Parliament (Lincoln Alexander, in 1968) and to appoint him to cabinet (in 1979); and the only party to be led by a woman prime minister (Kim Campbell, in 1993)?

Where to Learn More about Canadian Political Parties' Recruitment of Traditionally Underrepresented Groups

Karen Bird, "The Political Representation of Visible Minorities in Electoral Democracies: A Comparison of France, Denmark, and Canada," *Nationalism and Ethnic Politics* 11, no. 4 (2005): pp. 425–65.

Sandra Breux, Jérôme Couture, and Royce Koop, "Influences on the Number and Gender of Candidates in Canadian Local Elections," *Canadian Journal of Political Science* 52, no. 1 (2019): pp. 163–81.

Miki Caul, "Political Parties and the Adoption of Candidate Gender Quotas: A Cross-National Analysis," *Journal of Politics* 63, no. 4 (2001): pp. 1214–29.

William Cross and Lisa Young, "Candidate Recruitment in Canada: The Role of Political Parties," in *Parties, Elections, and the Future of Canadian Politics*, eds. Amanda Bittner and Royce Koop (Vancouver: UBC Press, 2013): pp. 24–45.

Royce Koop and Amanda Bittner, "Parachuted into Parliament: Candidate Nomination, Appointed Candidates, and Legislative Roles in Canada," *Journal of Elections, Public Opinion and Parties* 21, no. 4 (2011): pp. 431–52.

Mona Lena Krook and Pippa Norris, "Beyond Quotas: Strategies to Promote Gender Equality in Elected Office," *Political Studies* 62, no. 1 (2014): pp. 2–20.

Semra Sevi, Vincent Arel-Bundock, and André Blais, "Do Women Get Fewer Votes? No," *Canadian Journal of Political Science* 52, no. 1 (2019): 201–10.

Melanee Thomas and Marc André Bodet, "Sacrificial Lambs, Women Candidates, and District Competitiveness in Canada," *Electoral Studies* 32, no. 1 (2013): pp. 153–66.

Manon Tremblay and Réjean Pelletier, "More Women Constituency Party Presidents: A Strategy for Increasing the Number of Women Candidates in Canada?" *Party Politics* 7 (2001): pp. 157–90.

Angelia Wagner, Linda Trimble, Shannon Sampert, and Bailey Gerrits, "Gender, Competitiveness, and Candidate Visibility in Newspaper Coverage of Canadian Party Leadership Contests," *The International Journal of Press/Politics* 22, no. 4 (2017): 471–89.

10 Elections and Voting

Inside This Chapter

- What are the rules and regulations governing Canadian elections?
- What kinds of activities occur during election campaigns?
- How have referendums been used in Canada?

Inside Elections and Voting

Canadian democracy is built on the premise of free and fair elections. The precise definitions of the terms "free" and "fair" are subject to debate. So, too, are the rules designed to ensure that all eligible voters have the opportunity to cast ballots and run for office. In tracing the evolution of elections in Canada, this chapter exposes the diversity of systems that exist in various parts of the country. While reading, you are encouraged to keep in mind the following maxims.

✔ **Canadians elect local representatives to the House of Commons and a provincial or territorial legislature.** Election ballots do not contain a list of people who are competing to become the prime minister or premier. The monarch's representatives appoint these heads of government, based primarily on the aggregate results of dozens of district races. Media coverage and political advertising focuses so much on party leaders that it is easy to overlook local representation.

✔ **Every system of electing representatives has benefits and flaws.** While recent efforts to transition away from the first-past-the-post system toward more proportional forms of representation have failed, provinces have experimented with alternative voting systems in the past. In addition, many jurisdictions have initiated other changes to their systems of elections, including improving the accessibility of the act of voting itself.

✔ **Canadians lack real tools of direct democracy.** Referendums and plebiscites are not common in Canada, although when they occur they tend to be viewed as defining moments that shape political outcomes. In reality, no referendum is binding on a Canadian government, as ultimate sovereignty rests with the Crown and not the people. This means that all public-policy outcomes are always contingent upon government support.

UP FOR DEBATE

Are election and referendum campaigns mostly a waste of time?

Keep this question in mind as you read through the chapter. Consult the end-of-chapter debate supplement for more material to help you engage in an informed discussion of the topic.

Democracy in Canada

Many societies throughout the world do not have free and fair elections—free from coercive influences and fair in terms of their impartiality. Canada, as presented in Chapter 2, is a liberal democracy, characterized by equality, rights, and freedoms preserved through free and fair elections and the rule of law. According to over a century of tradition, there must be regular, non-violent elections; the winner of elections assumes control of the government; the people are represented by elected officials in a general assembly; elections are contested by more than one societal faction; and power alternates over time.[1] As a liberal democracy, Canada should produce governments that reflect society's interests, and that raise and spend money in a manner that is approved by a majority of the public's elected representatives.

Canadian democracy is more complicated than this, however. It features a distinct blend of elements that distinguish it from other liberal democracies. Canada is first and foremost a representative democracy where citizens elect politicians to speak for them in an assembly. Under Westminster parliamentary traditions, the executive is accountable to the people's representatives in the legislature, not to citizens themselves. General elections are held at least every five years, allowing voters to pass regular judgement on their elected representatives. While fixed election dates exist in law across many jurisdictions, elections can be called on the spur of the moment. Canadians live in a federation, whereby they elect representatives to serve them at both the federal and at the provincial/territorial levels. These elections happen at different times, creating a complex campaign calendar. With very few exceptions, elections are contested by candidates representing various political parties. Independents do not fare well at the ballot box, if they choose to run at all. Save for the consensus-based systems that persist in Northwest Territories and Nunavut, the Canadian political system is unmistakably party-oriented. On occasion, governments put major decisions to referendum. These public votes are non-binding in a technical sense, but inform the government's final decision. Some provinces have employed other tools of direct democracy like recall and initiatives, allowing voters to remove sitting representatives and petition the government directly for legislation. But again: the foundations of the Canadian system lie in representative, not direct, democracy. In short, Canadian democracy is complex, and it is unique. Election rules, including who is entitled to cast a ballot, are likewise distinct from other countries.

The Franchise

The **franchise** is the right to vote. Section 3 of the Charter of Rights and Freedoms states that "Every citizen of Canada has the right to vote in an election of members of the House of Commons or of a legislative assembly and to be qualified for membership therein." Prior to 1982, Canadians' right to vote was not constitutionally protected. Governments initially restricted the franchise to a small segment of the population. Over time, citizens advocated for the right to vote, and gradually the franchise was broadly applied. Today, debate occurs over whether Canadians living abroad and people under 18 years of age should be eligible to vote. Debate about the franchise no longer revolves around a citizen's financial status, gender, Indigeneity, or race, as it once did.

> **franchise**
> The right to vote in an election.

The struggle to get the right to vote is known as **suffrage**. At Confederation, the provinces were in control of voting eligibility, until this became a federal power some years later. Provincial control recognized the local nature of the way elections were administered. The only citizens eligible to vote at that time were male British subjects at least 21 years of age or older.[2]

> **suffrage**
> The struggle to gain the right to vote in elections.

To vote, eligible men were typically required to own property worth between $100 to $300 dollars. The nature of financial qualifications varied across the Dominion of Canada in the first two decades after Confederation. Some provinces considered how much rent the voter paid and what their annual income was. In Prince Edward Island, if you were between 21 to 60 years old and wanted to vote, each year you had to donate four days' labour to the building of highways or else contribute the cash equivalent. In Nova Scotia, if you collected social assistance, you were ineligible. Conversely, while British Columbia had no property or income qualifications whatsoever, it did not allow Chinese immigrants to vote. Indigenous peoples living there or in Ontario or Manitoba did not have the franchise. Furthermore, all provinces prohibited a variety of public servants from voting. For instance, if you worked for the post office in Quebec, you were not allowed to cast a ballot. By the early 1900s, workers' groups succeeded in pressuring the removal of property qualifications to vote, but only among eligible men.

Greg Perry

Why do you think so many Canadians take their voting rights for granted? At what point does voter apathy pose a threat to Canadian democracy?

Things began to change during World War I. Suffragettes petitioned for all women to be able to vote on the same eligibility basis as men. Social activists such as Nellie McClung gave public lectures, met with politicians, and staged a play in Winnipeg to raise public awareness that the situation was both unfair and ridiculous. In 1916, Manitoba became the first province to allow women to vote, followed later that year by Saskatchewan and Alberta. The next year the laws were changed in Ontario and BC, and for the first time a woman, Louise McKinney in Alberta, was elected to a Canadian legislature. However, women were still not permitted to vote in federal elections.

The governing party in Ottawa responded to the political pressure by changing the election laws to its advantage. Prime Minister Robert Borden's Conservative government supported allocating more resources for the war effort. It passed the Military Voters Act and the Wartime Elections Act in advance of the 1917 Canadian election. The legislation gave the vote to women who were actively or previously a member of the Canadian Armed Forces, including military nurses. The Conservative government's two acts went further than this to obtain the votes of people sympathetic to Canada's commitment to its World War I allies. They stipulated that any woman directly related to someone serving in the Canadian forces, even if that relative had died, was now eligible: wives, sisters, mothers, grandmothers. Furthermore the laws took away the right to vote from thousands of Canadians, such as Mennonites, because they spoke German, as well as immigrants born in an enemy country. In other words, while some women were now allowed to vote in federal elections, other men and women were disenfranchised.

The move toward universal suffrage gathered momentum. Legislatures across the country changed laws to allow women to vote and be candidates for elected office on the same basis as men. The one exception was Quebec, where women were struggling for equality in other areas, such as the right to own property. Quebec women turned their attention to suffrage in the 1930s, finally gaining the right to vote at the outset of World War II (see Table 10.1).

The rules still favoured citizens of British origin. Certain Canadians did not yet have the right to vote. Others had that right taken away. Indigenous peoples were eligible only if they agreed to relinquish their status as a registered Indian. Racism figured prominently once again in World War II, when the intensity of battle carried over to Canadian voting rules. The biggest culprit was British Columbia, which revoked the vote from Indigenous peoples and Asian Canadians, notably those of Chinese, Japanese, and Indian descent. When Japan bombed Pearl Harbour, the Government of Canada disenfranchised many Japanese Canadians living elsewhere in the country, a law that existed for seven years. It was not until 1960 that Indigenous peoples living in Canada were given the franchise in federal elections.

Since then, the franchise has been extended to nearly every Canadian adult. In 1970, the voting age in federal elections was lowered from 21 to 18 years. In the late 1980s, the right to vote was given to federally appointed judges, and in the early 1990s it was extended to many prisoners and to Canadians with significant mental disabilities. Prisoners serving a sentence of two years or more continued to forfeit their right to vote until the Supreme Court of Canada ruled in the Sauvé v. Canada decisions (2002) that the prohibition violated sec. 3 of the Charter of Rights and Freedoms. Section 3 of the Charter was

Table 10.1   Democratic Firsts for Canadian Women

Jurisdiction	Right to Vote	Right to be a Candidate	First Woman to Win Office	First Woman in Cabinet	First Woman to Head a Government	First 50/50 Cabinet
Canada	1918*	1919	1921	1957	1993 (Kim Campbell, Progressive Conservative)	2015
BC	1917	1917	1918	1921	1991 (Rita Johnston, Social Credit)	—
AB	1916	1916	1917	1921	2011 (Alison Redford, Progressive Conservative)	2015
SK	1916	1916	1921	1982	—	—
MB	1916	1916	1920	1966	—	—
ON	1917	1919	1943	1972	2013 (Kathleen Wynne, Liberal)	—
QC	1940	1940	1961	1962	2012 (Pauline Marois, Parti Québécois)	2007
NB	1919	1934	1935	1970	—	—
PE	1922	1922	1970	1982	1993 (Catherine Callbeck, Liberal)	—
NS	1918	1918	1960	1985	—	—
NL	1925	1925	1930 (1975 as a province of Canada)	1979	2010 (Kathy Dunderdale, Progressive Conservative)	—

*Many Indigenous women and men did not gain the right to vote until 1960.

Source: Adapted from Elections Canada, *A History of the Vote in Canada*, 2nd edn (Ottawa: Office of the Chief Electoral Officer of Canada, 2007): p. 64, Table 2.4. Also Linda Trimble, Jane Arscott, and Manon Tremblay, eds, *Stalled: The Representation of Women in Canadian Governments* (Vancouver: UBC Press, 2013).

again at the fore in *Frank v. Canada* (2019) when the Supreme Court ruled that Canadians continue to be eligible to vote when they live abroad. As a result of these decisions, all adult Canadian citizens are eligible to vote in federal elections, save for the two highest-ranking officials at Elections Canada, namely the chief electoral officer and deputy chief electoral officer.

Today, some advocates suggest that the voting age should be lowered. After all, most 16-year-olds can obtain a driver's licence, they can join the Canadian Forces, and they can be tried as an adult in court. There are arguments on both sides of the issue. Those in favour of a lower voting age claim it would get young people involved in elections. Civic education in schools would increase and so would the total number of Canadian voters. Engaging young people would increase their likelihood of voting when they become adults. Politicians would pay more attention to young people's concerns. Those opposed to extending the franchise say that teenagers would be the least informed and most impressionable voters. Critics point out that the international standard for voting eligibility tends to be 18. The overall election turnout percentage would likely decrease because so many young citizens wouldn't vote. More legal rights apply to adults 18 years and older, who have more at stake in an election. Many young people themselves oppose the idea because they feel uninformed. Ultimately, there are partisan reasons why the change is so difficult to advance. Voting patterns suggest that left-wing parties would benefit because young people are more likely to support progressive politics. Conversely, right-wing parties would be disadvantaged because young people are less likely to support conservative politics.

Election Laws

Establishing who is eligible to vote is just one of many aspects of elections regulated by laws. Think of an election as a high-stakes game: there are written rules that govern the behaviour of the players, and there are unwritten ethical boundaries that are open to interpretation. Referees are tasked with organizing the competition and ensuring that the rules are followed.

At the federal level, detailed election rules are passed by Parliament, and the resulting legislation is known as the Canada Elections Act. These rules govern the behaviour of candidates and their supporters, and evolve over time (see Table 10.2). In Canada's early years, for instance, voters stood on a platform and publicly announced who they were voting for. This was a problem because voters could be intimidated and threatened. The introduction of the secret ballot reduced the ability for external actors to pressure individual voters. Today, among the many offences under the Canada Elections Act are casting more than one ballot, preventing candidates from accessing a public area to communicate with electors, and an employer not giving employees time to vote. Various types of rules exist across the country at the provincial and territorial levels.

Just how serious an offence is it to break an election law? It can be quite serious. Consider the following examples that occurred during Stephen Harper's tenure as leader of the Conservative Party—while bearing in mind that rules are broken by members of every political party at some point in time. A former Conservative staffer was sentenced to nine months in prison for his involvement in arranging a robocall—an automated phone call—designed to direct voters in Guelph, Ontario, to a nonexistent polling station on Election Day. A former Conservative MP was found guilty of exceeding campaign spending limits

Table 10.2   Examples of Rationale for Current Federal Election Rules

Old Rules	Problem	Current Rule
Electors stood up and publicly announced who they were voting for.	Electors could be threatened about how to vote.	Electors are given a secret ballot so that nobody can see how they have voted.
No limits existed on fundraising or spending.	Candidates with wealthy supporters had a big advantage.	Limitations on fundraising and spending level the playing field.
Electors were enumerated through door-to-door canvassing.	Collection of information by this means was labour-intensive.	Data for the list of electors are continuously updated through government records.
Election finance matters were secretive.	Candidates could feel pressured to return favours to donors.	Fundraising and spending details must be reported and publicly released after the election.
Businesses and unions could donate money and labour.	Organizations might seek favours from elected officials.	At the federal level, only citizens are allowed to donate to parties and candidates.
Political parties qualified for government funding, based on the number of votes received.	Parties could become dependent on the state, with little incentive to fundraise from supporters.	Per-vote funding subsidies have been eliminated.

Source: Adapted from Elections Canada, *A History of the Vote in Canada* (Ottawa: Minister of Public Works and Government Services Canada, 1997).

and trying to cover it up. He was sentenced to a month in jail, followed by four months of house arrest, and was banned from seeking elected office for five years. Such charges are exceedingly rare, however. Enforcement of election law is difficult, and the sanctions for anyone found guilty tend to be minimal, such as a fine rather than jail time. One of the reasons for the rarity of convictions is the significant likelihood that opponents will publicize any transgressions. In this sense, rule-breaking is limited less by fear of formal enforcement than by fear of public humiliation, the implications for the party as a whole, the likelihood of sanctions imposed by the offender's political party, and the consequences for the individual's political career and reputation.

Other times, voters seem unmoved by election misdeeds. The Conservative Party broke financing laws through some shifty accounting that came to be known as the "in and out" scandal. In 2008, the RCMP raided the party's national headquarters to collect evidence. The party pleaded guilty to exceeding the limit on advertising spending. It was fined $52,000 and repaid over $230,000 that it had received in government election subsidies.[3] Justice was served under the law, but by then the Conservatives had won two subsequent elections, and avoided facing their indiscretions as a significant topic of discussion during either campaign. The Bloc Québécois practised a similar form of "in and out" accounting in conjunction with the 2000 federal election. Since 2004, the Liberal and Conservative parties have received donations from employees of a number of Quebec-based companies which then reimbursed the donors, thereby circumventing rules that prohibit donations from corporations. Elections Canada accepted signed agreements from the companies promising to follow the rules in future, and the money was returned to the Receiver General.

The most common role for the courts in settling election controversies is a judicial recount. If the margin of victory in a constituency is very small (0.1 per cent or less, at the federal level), the law dictates there must be another count of the ballots. This process is overseen by a judge, who makes rulings on any questionable ballots. For instance, voters are instructed to mark a ballot with an X to identify their choice. Some voters, as a form of protest, intentionally ignore this instruction and instead write a message of complaint, resulting in a spoiled ballot. But many voters, ignorant of the rules, use a checkmark instead of an X, or they circle the name of their preferred candidate. Should a vote count if an elector draws a happy face next to a candidate's name? What if an elector crosses off all but one candidate's name? In a close race, these are the sorts of interpretations that can decide the outcome, and a judge is the final authority.

Election Administration

The Canada Elections Act provides for the independent administration of elections. It designates the chief electoral officer as the head of Elections Canada, the non-partisan organization that administers federal elections. Similar laws exist at the provincial/territorial level. To avoid the perception of political interference by the government of the day, the chief electoral officer reports to the legislature rather than to cabinet. Chief electoral officers are responsible for overseeing the smooth, non-partisan administration of elections and referendums. This includes providing direction to returning officers appointed by cabinet to serve in every electoral district, managing the registration of political parties, and maintaining a list of electors. The roles and components of election administration are outlined in Table 10.3.

Elections Canada coordinates information campaigns to increase public awareness of federal election rules. This includes mailing voting reminder cards so that citizens are informed about when and where they can vote. In addition to returning officers, temporary staff are hired to work at polling stations on Election Day to verify voters' eligibility to vote in the riding, to pass out paper ballots, and to count the votes for each candidate when the polls close. Electors such as those who are travelling or temporarily living out of the country can apply to Elections Canada to vote by special ballot so that they can receive a package to submit their vote by mail. Again, very similar arrangements exist at the provincial/territorial level.

Table 10.3   Key Terms and Officials in Election Administration

Term	Summary	Function
advance polls	Polling stations that are open roughly a week before Election Day to allow people to vote in advance	To ensure that everyone has the opportunity to vote, including election workers, political staffers, and party volunteers who will be busiest on Election Day
chief electoral officer	Responsible to the legislature, the independent person who bears responsibility for overseeing the entire election	To issue election writs, appoint returning officers, ensure that election workers are trained, officially recognize political parties, etc
list of electors	A central database of the name, gender, date of birth, and address of every Canadian who is eligible to vote	To allow election workers and election candidates to communicate directly with electors and process voters at the polls
polling stations	Accessible rooms in local buildings where booths are set up for people to vote	To organize voters into clusters, minimizing the likelihood of long lineups and wait times on Election Day
returning officer	A person in every electoral district who oversees the administration of the election in that area and who is supported by a team of workers, including the deputy returning officer and poll clerks	To ensure that someone is locally responsible for overseeing the election of a representative
scrutineer	Someone who observes the counting of the ballots; sometimes known as a candidate's representative	To ensure all of the candidate's votes are counted and that rules are followed
special ballot	A ballot that is submitted by mail rather than cast at a polling station	To allow people to vote who cannot do so in person, such as people travelling or temporarily living away, members of the Canadian Forces, and prisoners

A recurring question about election administration is whether Canadians should be able to vote online. If we can manage our bank accounts using smartphones and file our taxes over the Internet, then surely the technology exists for us to be able to vote online—doesn't it? This is becoming a burning question as voter turnout wavers and as mobile technology becomes indispensable to more Canadians. Online voting would be more convenient and could increase election participation among youth, people who are confined to their homes, people with special needs, people who have to commute a long way to vote, and people who are too busy to line up at a polling station. It would reduce the possibility of human error on handwritten ballots and the need for judicial recounts. Governments around the world are studying online voting. It is being tested in some localized elections, such as municipal and students' union elections, and is becoming the norm in party leadership contests. Indeed, section 18 of the Canada Elections Act states that the chief electoral officer may carry out studies on electronic voting, and that adopting such a process would need Parliament's approval.

The biggest concern with online voting is the possibility of election fraud and interference. The only way that an online system would be adopted is if the highest form of secure technology had the full confidence of elected officials, election administrators, and the public. There are significant set-up and maintenance costs to keep up with the latest

Briefing Notes

Recent Changes to Canadian Federal Election Rules

Election rules are constantly evolving. In 2018, the Elections Modernization Act changed the rules for federal elections in Canada. Some of the changes are as follows:

1. Reduced barriers to participation: There is a greater obligation to accommodate persons with a disability, expanded options for members of the Canadian Forces to vote, and all Canadians no longer living in Canada are eligible to vote.
2. Voter identification: Voter Information Cards may be used as valid ID, and voters may vouch for the identity of other voters who do not have identification.
3. Restrictions on pre-campaign spending: Spending by political parties and advocacy groups is restricted for approximately two months leading up to a general election. During that period, they must identify themselves in any partisan advertising they sponsor.
4. Ban on foreign funds: Advocacy groups engaging in the campaign are not permitted to use donations from sources based outside of Canada.

5. Registry of digital advertising: Any Internet platform, including Facebook and Google, that sells digital ads is required to publish a digital registry of all such ads, including the name of the person who purchased the advertisement.
6. Creation of a register of future electors: Canadian citizens 14 to 17 years old may opt to have their contact information added to a database for the purpose of reminding them to register to vote when they come of age.
7. Protection of personal information: Political parties are required to post on their websites a policy for the protection of Canadians' personal information.
8. Limit on the maximum campaign length: A federal election campaign period may not exceed 50 days.
9. Delay in calling a by-election: A by-election is not called if a seat is vacated within nine months of a scheduled general election.

technology. The system would need to be tested, electors would need to be informed about how to use it, and regular polling stations would still need to be staffed because not everyone would choose or be able to go online. There is a lack of evidence that an abundance of non-voters would suddenly become online voters. Many citizens refrain from participating in elections for reasons other than the inconvenience, meaning that online voting would simply make it easier for routine voters to cast a ballot. Lastly, public confidence in online voting technology in Canada remains hampered by the controversies surrounding some experiments by political parties who used online voting to select their leaders. Furthermore, confidence in digital technology's role in elections has been compromised by sinister political operatives seeking to influence voter behaviour, through actions such as the circulation via social media of so-called fake news. Defending Canadian elections from cyber-manipulation originating in foreign countries is a far greater priority.

This said, electronic voting continues to gain interest in some corners of the country, including Halifax, which held its first e-vote in 2008. A decade later, nearly half of Ontario's municipalities used online voting, although due to technical glitches dozens of them had to extend the voting deadline by an hour to 24 hours. Despite the municipal momentum, for now it seems that in most elections Canadians will be lining up for a paper ballot and using a pencil to mark an X.

The Electoral System

Translating votes into seats requires an electoral formula. Some electoral systems declare the winner based on whether the candidate captured a plurality (i.e., the most) of the votes cast, while others demand that the victor receive support from a majority (i.e., at least half) of electors. Still others assign seats proportionally, basing a party's representation in the legislature on its total share of the popular vote across the country, not on the number of geographic districts it wins. Other systems involve some mixture of these formulas. As its name suggests, Canada's **single-member plurality** (SMP) system belongs to the first of these main types. The others—majority, proportional, and mixed—exist elsewhere and at times have appeared at the provincial level throughout Canadian history.

single-member plurality (SMP)
An electoral system whereby the winner of a district needs just one vote more than the number amassed by the runner-up.

The rules of Canada's single-member plurality electoral system, also known as first past the post, are quite simple. Areas of the country are divided into electoral districts. These are alternatively known as ridings and constituencies. In each district, a variety of candidates appear on the ballot, including nominated representatives of different political parties, and sometimes independents who are not party representatives. After the votes are counted, the candidate with the most votes wins, even if the margin of victory is just one vote and regardless of whether most voters marked their ballot for other candidates. This is why the SMP system is known as first past the post—winning is comparable to how a horse wins a race by being the first to cross the finish line. The party that wins the most districts almost always forms the government because it will control the legislature. In this sense, each federal election consists of hundreds of simultaneous individual elections, all fought under the same rules, but each featuring its own unique campaign dynamics. The same SMP system governs elections in every province and territory, although some jurisdictions have experimented with other electoral systems in the past, and some have recently contemplated reforms.

Another element of an electoral system concerns the way in which the vote choice is framed. Ballots are structured according to two sets of considerations. First, are voters expected to cast only one ballot at one point in time, or are there multiple rounds of voting involved in each election? Is there a single Election Day, or do voters gradually narrow the field of candidates over a longer period of time? Second, does the voting process require voters to select only their top choice of candidates, or does it require them to rank the candidates in order of preference? Under SMP, Canadians cast a single ballot by placing a single mark next to their favoured candidate. The names of party leaders do not appear, unless a leader happens to be running as a candidate to represent that electoral district in the legislature.

District magnitude is a further element of an electoral system. Magnitude refers to the number of elected representatives awarded for a single district. The concept of having more than one representative is foreign to many Canadians. Most are accustomed to having a single politician represent their constituency. In the past some Canadian voters sent multiple representatives to the same legislative body. For instance, dual-member constituencies were used throughout Prince Edward Island history, where they were a mechanism to reflect different religious beliefs.[4] In that province, the practice ended in the mid-1990s following acceptance of a report that recommended single-member constituencies.

There are constant calls for jurisdictions across Canada to replace SMP with a different electoral system. One of the main complaints about SMP is that smaller political parties receive a lower share of the seats in a legislature than the percentage of votes received while larger parties receive a higher share. Consequently, champions of electoral reform tend to be opposition parties who are disadvantaged by the SMP system. For instance, entering the 2015 federal election campaign, the Liberals were a third-place party. The Liberal platform committed that election would "be the last federal election conducted under the first-past-the-post voting system." The Liberals promised that an all-party parliamentary committee would consider ranked ballots and proportional representation. Justin Trudeau pledged to introduce electoral reform within 18 months of forming a government. Once in power, the Liberals did indeed refer the matter to a special committee on electoral reform. The committee recommended a national referendum on retaining the SMP system or replacing it with a PR system. However, Liberal committee members issued a dissenting report recommending the status quo. After little more than a year in office, Prime Minister Justin Trudeau shuffled his cabinet, and his mandate letter to the new minister of democratic institutions stated that changing the electoral system would not be pursued. Many citizens were outraged, particularly supporters of the NDP and Greens, reflecting the reality that smaller parties are disadvantaged the most by the SMP system. In the aftermath of the 2019 federal election those parties once again called for a new electoral system.

Canada is one of the few countries to use a single-member plurality electoral system. Across the democratic world, there are over a dozen different types of systems to convert votes into representation in the legislature. Each electoral system is based on a different set of values and objectives. Some systems perform well in terms of representing different geographic regions, for instance, while others are better at representing different demographic groups. In parliamentary systems, some are likely to produce majority governments, whereby the governing party controls the legislature. Other systems are designed to produce minority or coalition governments, forcing political parties to co-operate, and prompting much bickering and gamesmanship. Some systems are more accessible and more easily administered. Other systems are more difficult to understand and expensive to operate.

Single-member plurality systems like Canada's have benefits. They tend to be easily understood by voters, generate decisive results, and produce a direct link between representatives and their constituents. Marking an X on a ballot is easy to comprehend, as is the notion that the candidate receiving the most votes—and the party winning the most seats—is the victor. This sort of first-past-the-post system often produces clear-cut winners, by virtue of translating pluralities in the popular vote into a majority of seats. By providing voters with a clear sense of which individual represents them in the legislature, constituents have less difficulty attributing blame or credit come Election Day. The manufacturing of majority governments provides more stability and improves the ability of the governing party to get things done.

The SMP system is designed to reflect geographic diversity. Each member of the legislature represents a territorially defined district. This geographic representation often comes at the expense of other types of communities. Francophones are geographically concentrated, both within the province of Quebec, and in several other ridings elsewhere in Canada. This clustering allows francophones considerable political clout. They have a set of collective interests and objectives. They can band together as a voting bloc to elect and influence a series of elected representatives to sit on their behalf in the legislature. To a lesser extent, the same may be true of members of other smaller socio-cultural communities who live in close proximity to one another, such as Filipinos in north Winnipeg or Italians in south Toronto. There is no perfect formula for defining these districts. In a seminal 1968 article in the first issue of the *Canadian Journal of Political Science*, Alan Cairns makes a persuasive case that SMP greatly exaggerates the seat counts of political parties whose support is geographically concentrated, to the disadvantage of parties that have broad-based appeal across Canada.[5] Equally, the party that wins the most seats is likely to gloss over sectoral cleavages.

This experience within the SMP system contrasts with that of groups that are not defined by territory, such as Canadian women and Indigenous peoples. Women do not have a substantial majority in any single riding. Therefore women do not have the same sort of collective power in Canada's geographically defined system of representation. Indigenous peoples are greatest in numbers in a handful of Northern ridings. Other electoral systems, particularly those based on proportional representation, tend to better reflect these groups. Systems such as PR combine votes across a larger geographical area and provide incentives for parties to appeal to non-territorial communities, including labourers, non-heterosexuals, and ideologues. In this sense, opponents of SMP often cite its lack of inclusiveness.

There are further trade-offs. While decisive, SMP systems often produce disproportional results in terms of how votes are translated into seats for political parties. Canadian federal elections consist of several hundred races. The percentage of seats won by a party can be quite different from the percentage of the total vote obtained. A party that goes on to form the government may have won a majority of these contests and thus at least half of the seats in the legislature; however, none of these individual victories needs to be based on a majority of the votes cast in each riding. In contests where three parties have candidates, for instance, it is possible for a candidate to win with just 34 per cent of the votes cast, even though 66 per cent of voters chose someone else. If a party wins enough of these close, multi-candidate races, it may win enough seats to form government without necessarily winning a majority of all of the votes cast across the country. It is common for governments to push forward a partisan agenda that much less than half of citizens voted for.

Indeed, in Canadian politics, winning a federal election seldom requires collecting a majority of support among all voters. Since the emergence of Canada's multiparty system following the First World War, only three Canadian governments have won a majority of the popular vote, known as earned majorities. The remaining elections resulted in either manufactured majorities or minority governments (Figure 10.1). Such a high number of hung parliaments, where no one party obtains a majority of seats, calls into question the ability of Canada's SMP system to produce the decisive results that its proponents tout.

Earned and manufactured majorities are defined and explained in the discussion of majority governments in Chapter 6, on the legislature.

First-past-the-post systems can produce disproportional, even counterintuitive, results. Frank McKenna's Liberal Party won the 1987 New Brunswick election with 60 per cent of all ballots cast—and yet won 100 per cent of the seats in the legislature. Without an opposition, McKenna's government chose to answer questions from journalists and opponents from the press gallery during Question Period, to maintain the veneer of responsible government. In other instances, as explained in Chapter 6, SMP rules contribute to "wrong" winners and losers. This occurs when a party wins the greatest share of the popular vote and yet fails to win the greatest share of seats in the legislature. Canadian elections that have produced wrong winners and losers are depicted in Table 10.4.

People who complain about the SMP system often find solace in advocating for proportional representation (PR). A PR system is designed so that the number of party representatives who are elected is proportionate to the party's share of the popular vote. Thus, in the example above, under a PR system the New Brunswick Liberals would have been awarded 60 per cent of the seats. Smaller parties like the Greens would have a greater chance to elect a larger number of representatives. Proponents argue that PR guarantees that every vote counts as equally as possible toward the eventual outcome. More citizens might participate in elections as a result. Arguably the most compelling feature of a PR system is that it tends to produce a legislative assembly that more accurately reflects a diversity of political viewpoints. However, there are downsides, including

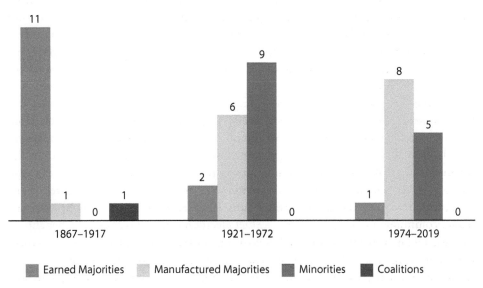

Figure 10.1 | Federal Government Compositions since 1867

Table 10.4	"Wrong" Winners and Losers in Canadian Elections, 1945-2019
Jurisdiction	**Election Years**
Federal	1957, 1979, 2019
British Columbia	1996
Saskatchewan	1986, 1999
Ontario	1985
Quebec	1966, 1998
New Brunswick	1974, 2006
Nova Scotia	1970
Newfoundland and Labrador	1989

the complexity of identifying a citizen's elected representative and the propensity for unstable governance. In his aforementioned article, Cairns briefly acknowledges the benefits of PR, but also observes that the system's supporters make idealistic arguments compared with the pragmatism of SMP.[6]

Experiments to consider alternatives to the first-past-the-post system occurred in western Canada in the first part of the twentieth century. Elections in British Columbia, Alberta, and Manitoba were conducted using a different electoral system in rural areas than in cities. In each case, the provincial government introduced the new systems out of a commitment to democratic reform, and in each case, it ended the experiment out of concern that its own grip on power was loosening under the new rules.

Electoral reformers have suffered similar setbacks elsewhere in Canada in the twenty-first century. Three referendums on a new electoral system were defeated in British Columbia between 2005 and 2018. The processes included a citizen's assembly and vote by mail. In PEI, a commission urged Islanders to adopt a mixed-member proportional (MMP) system. Under MMP, voters still elect a local member to the legislature. Another section of the ballot records the voter's party preference. These party votes are used to determine the overall partisan balance of the legislature, with extra members being added from party lists to achieve proportionality. Voters rejected the commission's recommendation in a plebiscite. Citizens later supported a mixed-member proportional system in a second plebiscite, this time including 16- and 17-year-old voters. The PEI premier rejected the result, however, arguing that turnout was too low. A third plebiscite was held in conjunction with the 2019 PEI provincial election, at which time a majority of Islanders voted against adopting the proposed new system. In New Brunswick, a commission similarly recommended a move to MMP. The premier pledged to hold a referendum; however, the government fell before the vote could be held. In Ontario, a citizens' assembly likewise recommended a move toward MMP, which voters rejected in a referendum. In Quebec, detailed study by committees, a commission, and the province's chief electoral officer suggested the benefits of a mixed-member formula. The Quebec government resisted implementing the recommendations. Thus, while many jurisdictions adopted or considered changes to their electoral system, these flirtations with reform have been fleeting. Voters and politicians seem to prefer the status quo.

Apportionment

Sorting out how to distribute seats in the House of Commons is one of the most politically charged and complex processes in all of Canadian politics. Deciding how many MPs are allocated to each province is a sensitive matter, given the nature of regional representation in federal institutions like Parliament. Attention must be paid to representing historical communities of interest and the terms of previous constitutional settlements. This must be balanced with consideration for the changing demographics of Canadian society.

The size and shape of federal ridings are calculated using two key elements:

- electoral formulas establish how many House of Commons seats each province is entitled to; and
- electoral boundary rules establish the means by which constituency maps are drawn.

Taken together, these rules guide appointed electoral commissioners who strive to ensure all Canadians receive effective representation in their elected assemblies.

The task of reapportioning seats is much more contentious in places where the number of districts is frozen, or even reduced, by law. This is not the case at the federal level. The number of seats in the House of Commons increases over time as Canada's total population increases. Section 51 of Canada's constitution states that the boundaries of federal electoral districts must be adjusted every decade. The current electoral formula is grounded in a standard of 111,166 people per riding. This quotient (average district size) is indexed to the average provincial population growth starting in 2021. This indexing will account for future shifts in population among the provinces. The formula includes a representation rule to prevent any provinces from losing seats because of future seat redistributions. Taken together, the steps produce the allocation of seats shown in Figure 10.2.

Redistribution (or redistricting) is the legal process by which governments redraw the boundaries between electoral districts. Population fluctuations require that electoral boundaries are revised to ensure effective and relatively equal representation for all voters. Generally speaking, over time the population in rural areas is shrinking whereas urban and suburban areas are becoming more densely populated. Governments must redraw electoral maps on a regular basis to ensure that people in these growth regions have as much voting power as their counterparts in other districts. Redistribution may occur in conjunction with reapportionment that results in a net increase or decrease in the total number of seats. The task is usually completed once per decade.

redistribution
The formal process used to periodically adjust electoral boundaries.

Population shifts are a primary consideration when redrawing boundaries. At the same time, provisions are put in place to protect communities of interest, whose representation may require special modifications to the standard one-person, one-vote ideal. Different formulas are used to address the challenges of representation in sparsely populated Northern communities. Special treatment must not veer too far from the average number of citizens per elected representative, however. At the federal level and in some provinces the redistribution process coincides with the decennial census that produces an official count of the number of citizens.

Left unchecked, the governing party could manipulate the boundaries of electoral districts for its own electoral advantage. Gerrymandering is the highly partisan redistribution practice of drawing boundaries to favour one political party over its opponents. A *Boston Gazette* reporter coined the term in reference to Massachusetts Governor

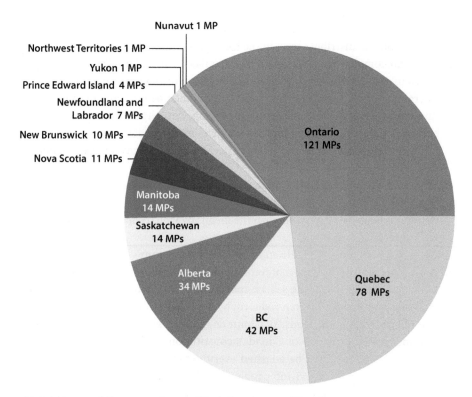

Figure 10.2 | House of Commons Seats of Each Province and Territory

Elbridge Gerry's redrawing of the state's senate map in the nineteenth century. Governor Gerry's partisanship led to certain Boston-area districts being so contorted that they resembled the shape of a salamander. This maximized his party's ability to win seats under the SMP electoral system by grouping together areas of Massachusetts that supported the other party. At each redistribution, pundits identify boundary changes that appear to lump known supporters of opposition parties together in an alleged attempt by the governing party to create so-called wasted votes.

boundaries commission
A body that recommends changes to election boundaries.

The appointment of a multi-partisan and/or non-partisan electoral **boundaries commission** is designed to prevent gerrymandering. Governments at the federal level periodically form boundaries commissions to examine redistribution for the House of Commons and at the provincial and territorial levels to do the same for those legislatures. Their work is reasonably transparent, and is supported by public servants who provide requested data. A commission conducts detailed analysis of population data, geographic sizes of districts, social aspects of specialized communities, and the history of boundaries. At the federal level, an independent commission is struck for each province to review the federal boundaries in that area of the country. Redistribution is not required in the House of Commons for the Northwest Territories, Nunavut, or Yukon because there is a single MP for each territory. A federal boundaries commission is required to consult with Canadians, to submit a preliminary report to obtain input from Members of Parliament in that province, and to submit a final report that establishes the boundaries.

Elected members of the legislature are typically barred from serving on these arms-length boundaries commissions. At the federal level, each commission is comprised of a judge and two people appointed by the Speaker of the House of Commons, such as academics or public servants with specialized expertise. At the subnational level, some commissions are made up of government or cabinet appointees, such as former politicians. Other commissions are comprised of people who hold a position in another organization. The terms and mandates granted to each commission vary.

Governments provide electoral boundaries commissions with guidance to inform how they should draw boundaries. When commissions create districts, some variation is allowed as long as it stays within permitted ranges. Commissions start by dividing the entire population by the total number of districts. Government directives permit the commissioners to vary from this average district size by a certain percentage, up or down, when drawing new boundaries around each constituency. Saskatchewan has Canada's strictest deviance formula. In that province commissioners have only 5 per cent leeway from the provincial norm. This means that when setting boundaries for representation in the Saskatchewan legislature, the most populous constituency cannot have more than 5 per cent more people than the average district, and the least populous district cannot have more than 5 per cent fewer people than the average district.

All Canadian jurisdictions allow for some exceptions to the normal deviance formula. Most exceptions involve Northern and remote communities. This preserves seats in the

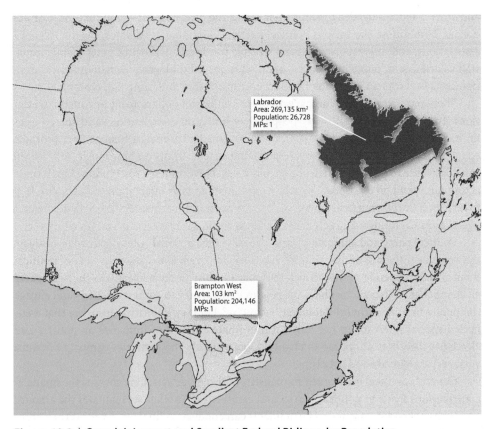

Labrador
Area: 269,135 km²
Population: 26,728
MPs: 1

Brampton West
Area: 103 km²
Population: 204,146
MPs: 1

Figure 10.3 | Canada's Largest and Smallest Federal Ridings, by Population

legislature for these traditionally marginalized groups. Manitoba, for instance, has a variance formula for the south (+/–10 per cent) and one for the north (+/–25 per cent). Other exceptions involve ethnic or cultural communities. Until recently, Nova Scotia allowed its electoral commissions the latitude to create a predominantly African-Canadian district, and three for Acadians. The ridings were phased out because their ethnic population became too small to justify deviating from the principle that all citizens should have reasonably equal representation in the legislature.

Ultimately, it is up to the executive and the legislature to sanction redistribution. Periodically a provincial government decides to set the number of seats for its own political purposes. This can include reducing the number of politicians in order to gain support for a wider cost-cutting agenda, increasing seats to satisfy a particular ethnic community, or rejecting a commission's recommendations due to backlash in the governing party's caucus.

Campaign Finance

Campaigning is one of the most resource-intensive activities in Canadian politics. It is an expensive undertaking for parties, candidates, organizers, journalists, election authorities, and other actors. It costs an immense amount of time and money to plan, conduct, deliver, oversee, and follow an election campaign. The direct costs of the election—including paying and training poll officials, printing ballots, renting space for offices and polling sites, mounting voter education campaigns, and acquiring information technology, supplies, and other resources needed to administer the voting process itself—amount to millions of dollars. In addition, the various political parties, individual candidates, electoral district associations, and interest groups spend sizeable funds on advertising, voter mobilization, staff salaries, rent, publicity, polling, and litigation. All told, each Canadian federal election costs well over $350 million in direct administration and campaign costs alone.

These numbers pale in comparison to the billions of dollars spent in American elections. In the United States, many people view limits on contributions and spending as limits on freedom of political expression. In Canada, campaign finance laws promote equality among parties and candidates, placing stricter limits on how much each citizen can contribute to political parties and candidates. Governments restrict how much these actors can spend on elections. Furthermore, Canadian laws often allocate public funding to help level the playing field among parties. As a result, Canadian elections do not feature nearly as much fundraising activity or lavish spending as is the case south of the border.

Political party and campaign finance regulations are legal rules designed to mitigate the negative influence of money in politics. The stringency of a state's system of political finance rules depends on the values that matter most to lawmakers. Do they prioritize ensuring that political actors have the resources necessary to contest elections and engage the public in a meaningful democratic exercise? Do they prioritize ensuring that well-heeled special interests do not have an inordinate amount of influence on politics and elections? Priorities are prone to change. Consequently the nature of campaign finance varies across Canada and over time.

Canada's political finance regime consists of three rule sets. One governs the financial contributions made to political parties and candidates. Another set regulates the amount and type of spending parties and candidates can conduct. A final set concerns the nature of public reporting required for donations and spending. Limits are usually placed on both revenue and expenditures. This prevents the most affluent citizens and most well-off parties from dominating the political competition. Public disclosure of campaign finance enables the identification of donors, how money was spent, and the eligibility of state-financed refunds. Generally speaking, rules about political finance are most strict in federal politics, and least rigorous in small provinces.

Party Revenues

Canadian political parties generate revenue from a wide range of sources. Money comes in from contributions from individual supporters and, to a much lesser extent, their membership dues. In addition to contributions initiated by supporters, political parties send out requests for donations, and organize fundraising events for donors to network with politicians. Governments supplement these donations with various types of subsidies.

At the federal level, the source and amount of political contributions are restricted. These restrictions apply to political parties, candidates, electoral district associations, and leadership contestants. Only individual Canadians can donate to federal parties, meaning that corporations, unions, interest groups, and other so-called third parties are not permitted to contribute funds. Likewise, at the federal level, individuals are restricted in the amount of money they can donate. As of 2019, Canadians were permitted to donate a maximum of $1600 in any calendar year to a registered federal political party's national organization, and $1600 to a candidate or constituency association. The same cap applies when donating to a contestant in a party leadership contest. The limits are per political party rather than per individual. The maximum amounts increase by $25 annually. The limits encompass both money and in-kind contributions. That is, non-monetary donations of services or goods (e.g., volunteering to set up a candidate's website, or loaning the party a campaign bus) must be counted against one's donation limit, based on the commercial value of the in-kind contribution. Candidates and leadership contestants can donate more to their own campaigns, both during the nomination and for the general election. Wealthier individuals are prevented from self-financing their own campaigns.

Political parties receive a variety of government subsidies. These public funds are used to support an individual, group, or cause. The federal government reimburses parties and candidates for a certain proportion of their election expenses. Federal political parties are reimbursed for 50 per cent of their election spending as long as they meet a minimum support threshold. Federal election candidates receive a refund of 60 per cent of their expenses if they receive 10 per cent of the vote.

Tax credits are the second form of government subsidy. Canadians who donate to political parties can deduct the allowable amount from their taxable income. These tax credits do not flow directly to the political parties per se, but they represent forgone revenue that the government would have otherwise collected, and would have spent on other priorities. In this sense, tax credits constitute a substantial subsidy to political parties, and are far more generous than the subsidies given to registered charities or other organizations. For federal-level contributions up to $400, for instance, Canadians are able to deduct 75 per cent of the amount from their tax payable. This rebate decreases proportionally as the contributions increase.

The most controversial form of subsidy involves governments directly funding political parties. As of 2015, federal parties no longer receive these sorts of government

tax credit
An income-tax provision that reduces a citizen's taxable income and thus reduces the tax payable.

payments. Up to then, a per-vote subsidy existed, paying eligible parties a dollar amount for every vote received in the previous general election. These allowances were initially designed to offset the introduction of bans on big donations and to level the playing field for smaller parties. The elimination of the per-vote subsidies increased the onus on political parties to fundraise themselves. Advocates in favour of the subsidy claim that it provides more resources for political parties to hold the government to account. It reduces the need to seek donations from people who might want political favours in return. Smaller political parties in particular benefit from the stability. Opponents argue that governments could make better use of the funds for more pressing public policy needs. Giving public money to political parties is particularly difficult to justify when the government is running a deficit and cutting spending in other areas. A further counterargument is that the funds exaggerate the public's support of small protest parties that disrupt the smooth operation of the state. Generally speaking, political parties on the left support per-vote subsidies, and parties on the right oppose them.

VOX POP

Which of the three subsidies most benefits larger parties, and which is most valuable to smaller parties? Why should political parties receive subsidies at all?

Party Spending Limits

spending limits
Legal restrictions on how much money can be spent in a campaign.

Canadian political parties and candidates are restricted in how they can spend money. At the federal level, **spending limits** are calculated based on the number of ridings a party contests and the number of voters in those ridings. Likewise, candidates' spending is constrained based on the number of voters in their constituencies, with a sliding scale allowing greater per capita spending in smaller, more sparsely populated districts. The strictest limits apply to the official campaign period, with slightly more lenient rules governing the months immediately before the fixed election date.

Political parties and their candidates spend money on an astounding array of things. Some of it is straightforward, such as political parties spending on advertising and the leader's tour. Less obvious is how local candidates spend money. Categories of expense declarations that they file with Elections Canada after the campaign offer a peek. These include advertising, voter contact, office, salaries/wages, campaign events, personal expenses, accessibility, travel/living, litigation, and other expenses. Even a casual examination of declarations quickly identifies the mundane nature of local politics: buying campaign signs from a local outdoor media company, mailing costs, campaign buttons, a list of staff who were paid for their time, babysitting, phone bills, renting a campaign headquarters, fees to maintain a bank account, and so forth. Closer scrutiny uncovers security alarm services, furniture rental, printer toner, food, mileage, language translators, computer repair, shredding services—all of these things are among the many facets of campaigning that cost money. Deeper inspection reveals surprising expenses, such as parking tickets, tire repair, helicopter rentals, PayPal fees, items declared stolen, flowers for funeral homes, haircuts, dry-cleaning, disc jockeys, and cleaning services after a victory party. Oddities range from hot-air balloons to denture repair.[7] These are among

Campaign signs from the 2019 provincial election in Prince Edward Island. Federal and provincial elections have strict rules regarding what constitutes an election expense, and what the spending limits are for candidates.

the many expenses incurred during elections and illustrates why money is the lifeblood of party politics. That we can learn about these expenditures is due to the practice of disclosure, discussed next.

Disclosure

The final component of Canada's campaign finance regime consists of the rules governing **disclosure**. National party organizations, local district associations, candidates, and leadership contestants are all required to report publicly on their various fundraising and spending activities. This is to ensure that the public is aware of precisely who is donating to whom in a given campaign and how the money is being spent. Candidates must file their audited electoral campaign returns within four months of Election Day. National party organizations must do so within six months. Among other details, these returns must include the names and addresses of all donors who contributed over $200, and the amount and type of expenditures incurred. Penalties for non-compliance range from the denial of election rebates to jail terms and fines.

disclosure
Revealing otherwise private information, such as campaign expenses.

As mentioned, federal rules bar corporations, unions, and interest groups from donating directly to federal political parties. Federal laws do not altogether prevent the participation of registered individuals and organizations who spend money on advocacy during the campaign. They are allowed to advertise during campaigns, subject to spending limits. The Supreme Court has upheld limits as constitutional despite arguments that the rules restrict Canadians' freedom of expression.

Every province has its own party and campaign finance rules, which are constantly evolving. For instance, some provinces have no limits whatsoever on how much individuals, corporations, unions or other organizations can donate. Per-vote subsidies are paid out by some provincial governments. Compared to the federal rules, most provinces have more lenient restrictions on third-party advertising.

Bob Englehart, PoliticalCartoons.com

Some people question the constitutionality of campaign finance laws and whether they improve or hinder democracy. The American Supreme Court ruled that "money is speech," meaning that to restrict an individual's right—or even a corporation's right—to spend money during a campaign is tantamount to infringing on freedom of speech. Conversely, the Supreme Court of Canada ruled that spending limits are a reasonable infringement of section 2b of the Charter of Rights and Freedoms, which protects the freedom of speech. Why do you suppose courts in Canada and the United States reached such a different view of democracy?

Campaigning

National Campaigns

Election campaigns are high-profile events that tend to occur roughly every two to four years and follow a common pattern. An official election campaign begins when the legislature is dissolved by the governor general or, at the provincial level, by the lieutenant governor. This can be prompted by a request by the prime minister or premier, a defeat of the governing party on a major vote in the legislature, or the end of the five-year period since the last election took place. Five years is the maximum term under the Canadian constitution. The only exception is if there is a war and less than a third of the members of the legislative assembly oppose delaying the election. The one instance that the Parliament of Canada went six years between elections was in World War I.

The authority of prime ministers and premiers to request elections has been restricted somewhat because most legislatures have fixed-date election legislation. The law states that elections be held on a designated day every four years, unless the legislature is dissolved before then. These laws must respect the constitutional authority of the monarch's representative to decide when to dissolve the legislature and the constitution's upper limit of five years. Thus, first ministers can still choose to seek an early election, and they can potentially come up with a reason to delay the campaign.

Once the monarch's representative agrees to dissolve the legislature, the cabinet directs the chief electoral officer to issue **writs of election** for every electoral district. The dropping of the writ officially sets in motion the nomination of candidates, the hiring of election workers, the setting up of polling stations, and a publicity campaign to inform electors where they can vote. Election Day usually occurs on a Monday or Tuesday.

writ of election
A legal document marking the official start of an election campaign.

Stages of an Election Campaign

Canadian elections tend to follow four unofficial stages:

1. the pre-writ period of political manoeuvring and candidate recruitment in the lead-up to the official start of the election;
2. the organizational period during the start of the campaign when citizens are just starting to pay attention;
3. the leaders' debate(s) which tend to attract considerable media coverage and galvanize public attention; and
4. the post-debate period when the campaigns tighten up and personnel get ready for Election Day.

The pre-writ period encompasses the days, weeks, or even months leading up to the start of the official election campaign. It has become increasingly common for political parties, as soon as an election is over, to behave as though the next Election Day is just around the corner. The non-stop politicking is known as a **permanent campaign**. This ongoing electioneering during the inter-election period involves political actors seizing all opportunities to outflank their opponents. Every political issue is treated with an urgency to appear as the victor. Under this outlook, preparations for the next campaign begin as soon as Election Day results are known, and tactics normally undertaken only during the official campaign become evident during governance. In the immediate lead-up to the campaign, the governing party prioritizes good news. The government's budget may be full of new spending initiatives and tax cuts, the details of which are announced many times to achieve the best possible news coverage. Opposition parties decry the government's use of public funds to campaign during this time, accusing the party of buying votes with taxpayers' own money.

permanent campaign
The practice of electioneering outside of an election period, especially by leveraging government resources.

Permanent campaigning is explained in greater detail in Chapter 11, on pages 391–2.

The official campaign period begins when the writs are issued. At the federal level, official campaigns last for a minimum of 37 days and (since 2019) a maximum of 50 days. During the period leading up to the first leaders' debate, the campaign begins to take shape. Electors are just starting to pay attention, the stakes are not as high, and most of the local campaign teams in electoral districts are starting to get organized.[8] Candidates are being nominated, signs and brochures are being ordered, and there are still opportunities to recover from a mistake—although, as discussed in Chapter 11, controversies involving social media can be fatal to a candidate's political career.

The national media designate reporters to follow the major party leaders around the country. The **leader's tour** begins immediately and features party leaders making campaign stops while surrounded by an entourage of party workers. The presence of journalists travelling with the leader gives party strategists the opportunity to arrange low-risk

leader's tour
A visit of various electoral districts by the party leader and an entourage of staffers and journalists.

THE CANADIAN PRESS/Lauren Kruge

Conservative Party leader Andrew Scheer flips pancakes at the Calgary Stampede in anticipation of the official start of the 2019 federal election. The Calgary Stampede is often the place where political leaders test public support ahead of an election. According to communication studies professor David Taras, "Coming to the Stampede also means, 'I'm one of you.'"[9] Is there an event in your community that is typically attended by political leaders during an election campaign? What impact do you think these campaign stops have on the leaders' overall success in the election?

visual events that will generate positive news coverage, such as a visit to a local candidate's headquarters for a rally, a speech to supporters in a friendly riding, or a photo op at a local landmark, restaurant, or market. The leaders are accompanied by a team of personnel who manage every detail of the appearance and handle media inquiries. The leader, party staffers, and the reporters travel across the country together on a chartered airplane or buses. Reporters are required to pay for their share of the travel. Many media outlets save money by pooling resources instead of each sending their own reporters.

election platform
A list of political pledges announced before or during an election campaign.

Party strategists finalize the details of their **election platforms** during the start of the campaign. The manifestos itemize each party's policy proposals, spending commitments, and general pledges if elected. The party that forms government later draws on the platform when preparing a throne speech and ministerial mandate letters. At the start of the campaign, each party sets up an information command centre known as the war room, where a team of strategists prepares news releases, monitors opponents' communications, issues rapid-response counterattacks, and handles special requests. Armed with opinion research data, the parties use political marketing strategies and communications tactics in an attempt to inform and persuade targeted segments of the electorate.

Traditionally, the leaders' debates fall at the midpoint of the campaign. These events are organized by major media organizations, and mark the point at which most electors begin paying attention. These forums are the only planned meetings of the major party leaders to deliberate each other's policies. The debates are designed to allow the leaders to make their pitches directly to voters while attempting to get the better of their opponents before an audience of citizen viewers, journalists, and opinion makers. At the federal level, televised debates in English and in French are held in the same week, organized by a consortium of broadcasters. In 2019, a government-appointed Debates Commission was struck to design and facilitate the debates. The ability to livestream debates means that major broadcasters such as the CBC, CTV, Global, Radio-Canada, and Télé-Québec no longer have a monopoly on debate coverage. Today, non-media organizations can organize additional debates, and leaders are faced with choices about which of these events to attend. Organizers tinker with the format and must consider demands made by political staff to determine whether, for example, the leaders should be standing at lecterns or sitting around a table. Journalists and sometimes carefully screened electors pitch questions that one or all leaders are expected to answer. The leader of the governing party and/or of the party that is ahead in opinion polls tends to go on the defensive. The opposition leaders seek to discredit the first minister and/or the frontrunner. At the local level, all-candidate debates are going through similar transformations, with some candidates choosing to knock on doors instead.

The 1984 leaders' debate is the standard for all others in Canada. In that debate's memorable exchange, Progressive Conservative leader Brian Mulroney delivered a stinging criticism of Liberal Prime Minister John Turner over a slew of party supporters who were appointed to government jobs, something that Turner could have overturned. "You had an option, sir," asserted Mulroney, to which the prime minister mustered only, "I had no option." Mulroney went on to lead his party to the biggest landslide in Canadian federal election history. That decisive episode became known as a knockout punch. Indeed, the question that everyone asks after a leader's debate is not what policies were discussed, but who won and who lost. A leader's performance in the debates can have an impact—favourable or unfavourable—on the image of the entire party.[10] However the debate winner does not necessarily go on to win the election.

Elections Canada no longer prohibits news outlets from releasing election night results until the last polls in BC and Yukon close. As a result, social media is rife with discussions of election outcomes in Eastern Canada while many citizens in Western Canada are still in line to cast a ballot. Why did the original ban make sense? How serious a problem is it that individual Canadians can go online to discuss election results in their region before polls have closed in the rest of the country? What can be done about it?

In the post-debate period, the stakes are high, as Canadians finalize their voting intentions. The parties intensify their campaigning, sharpen their messages, critique their opponents, and increase their advertising. The controversial tactic of running negative advertising intensifies during this period. Campaign organizers take additional measures to insulate their candidates from the sort of devastating mistake, or campaign gaffe, that could destabilize their messaging and their chances of winning. In the closing weeks, party strategists often urge local candidates to avoid public debates because the audience is stacked with committed partisans and there is a risk of bad media coverage that could undermine the campaign locally and possibly nationally. Party leaders stay focused on delivering scripted speeches. Leaders and candidates alike may limit or refuse reporters' questions.

In the final days of the campaign, the party leaders visit a handful of districts where they want to shore up support, before completing their tour in the electoral district where they are running as a candidate. On Election Day, the news media cover the leaders going to vote and report on how busy turnout has been at local polling stations. Election rules prohibit political advertising and the communication of previously unreleased opinion poll data. Party workers known as scrutineers observe the voting process throughout the day and during the vote count. That evening, after the last of the polls closes, journalists begin reporting the vote results as the ballots in each poll are counted. The media uses statistical analysis of early voting patterns to project the outcome. Their election decision desk dramatically proclaims a victor before the final results are tallied. These projections are typically reliable, although there are occasions where networks reverse their announcements. Leaders and candidates give victory or concession speeches; pundits begin to assess the reasons why parties and candidates won or lost; and some defeated leaders announce that they will no longer lead the party. The most organized of campaigns engage in a post-campaign evaluation. Organizers and strategists take stock of what worked and what failed so that they can learn for the next campaign.

Local Campaigns and Candidates

During an election campaign, the national party concerns itself with national communications such as advertising, media coverage of the leader's tour, and press releases. These are collectively known as the air campaign in reference to a desire to control the media airwaves. At the same time, candidates are competing to earn the right to represent an electoral district, such as Beauport–Côte-de-Beaupré–Île d'Orléans–Charlevoix or Parry Sound–Muskoka. This is where the ground campaign occurs. Candidates and local campaign workers interact directly with electors by knocking on doors, phoning electors, distributing brochures, and putting up lawn signs. Much of their focus is on identifying potential supporters. Increasingly, campaign volunteers enter information provided on doorsteps into an online party database. On advance polling days and Election Day, the data are used to rally favourable voters to the polls, a process known as getting out the vote, or **GOTV**. This involves phoning identified supporters to see if they have voted yet and offering to pick them up to drive them to their voting station.

The process of seeking election involves a lot of work.[11] In order to represent a party in an election, a person must first be nominated. When two or more people want to be the

---

Negativity—and whether it is good or bad for Canadian politics—is a theme that runs throughout Chapter 11, on communication.

GOTV
Get out the vote efforts to mobilize supporters to vote, such as telephone reminders.

party's candidate in an election, they must first apply to participate in a **party nomination** contest. This is a mini-election held among members of the party who live in the electoral district. They vote on which contestant should represent the party in the upcoming election. The internal contest is run by the party. In places where the party is popular, there are likely to be a number of contestants, and the race can be more vigorous than the election campaign itself. If only one person applies to represent the party in that riding, no nomination contest is held, and that individual is acclaimed to be the nominee. Becoming the candidate by acclamation is reasonably common when an **incumbent** seeks re-election or the party is unpopular in the district. Party leaders and/or their agents must endorse any candidates who wish to run under their party's banner in an election campaign. This can create tension between the local district association and the national party organization, as discussed below.

Not all candidates run under a party's banner. In each election there are candidates who run as **independents**. These people are not formally affiliated with any political party. Sometimes they simply wish to put their names forward in the election process. Other times they are former partisans, who severed their relationship with a party. Independents seldom contest, let alone win, general elections or by-elections in Canada. A member of Parliament who leaves a party for taking a stand on an issue of concern to constituents may have a chance at re-election. So, too, may a popular party insider who failed to secure the party nomination because the party leadership approved a different candidate. But there are no guarantees. Typically, even former MPs are unlikely to be elected as independents. As a consequence, parliamentarians who leave their party do so knowing that their chances of re-election are low unless they cross the floor to a popular party. This increases the power of political parties and party leaders over the legislative branch and political life in general.

Once the writ is dropped, an immediate priority of a candidate is completing the nomination papers for the election authorities. This includes obtaining the signatures of local electors to demonstrate that they endorse the candidate. Candidates must also submit a deposit that is returned if post-election financial reporting is completed. A candidate for election is required to appoint an official agent to authorize the campaign's election spending, which is later audited.

Many people erroneously think that local candidates are supported by a huge team of paid consultants and workers. That may be true in the case of celebrity candidates, but typically the campaigns of lower-profile candidates in Canada are managed by a small core of volunteers, many of whom may be the candidate's personal friends and family; sometimes the candidate doubles as the campaign manager. The trend, however, is to pay campaign workers, especially on Election Day, when fewer people are available or interested in committing to volunteering. In *Candidates and Constituency Campaigns in Canadian Elections*,[12] political scientist Anthony Sayers classifies Canadian parties' election candidates into star candidates, party insiders, local notables, and stopgaps. He differentiates them as follows:

- Star candidates are high-profile people hand-picked by the party centre to speak publicly on behalf of the party. In Canada, unlike the United States, it is rare for a star candidate to be a pop culture celebrity. Normally the star candidates in Canadian politics are people who held senior positions in business, advocacy groups, or not-for-profit organizations.

party nomination
An internal contest to decide who should represent a party locally in an upcoming election.

incumbent
An elected official who currently represents an electoral district.

independent
A candidate or parliamentarian who is not officially affiliated with a political party.

Inside Canadian Politics

What Was the Orange Wave?

Jack Layton led the federal New Democratic Party in four federal general election campaigns between 2004 and 2011. His party's seat count improved in each of the first three of those elections. Nevertheless each time the NDP placed fourth to the Conservatives, the Liberals, and the Bloc Québécois.

The NDP seemed destined for a similar finish in 2011. The characteristically robust Layton had hip surgery and needed a cane. He seemed physically frail and perhaps not up to the rigours of a drawn-out campaign. But around the time of the leaders' debates, Quebecers began to turn away from the Bloc Québécois, and support for the NDP began to spill over into other parts of Canada. The momentum seemed to energize Layton. The media began to scrutinize the party's platform and profiled some of its candidates, a number of whom were university students and other stopgaps parachuted into Quebec ridings with little hope—initially, at least—of winning. Nevertheless, on Election Day, the party won a majority of seats in Quebec and the second-most seats overall. Layton became the NDP's first-ever leader of the official opposition. The event became known as the Orange Wave in recognition of the party's official colour. However, the achievement was bittersweet: Layton passed away from cancer three months later. By the next election the party was relegated to its traditional status of the third-most seats in the House.

DISCUSSION ITEM

Campaigns can have a profound impact on improving a party's standing in the legislature.

VOX POP

What lessons can the New Democratic Party draw from the Orange Wave? To what extent is it a problem that some NDP candidates were elected in Quebec despite being names on a ballot who did not canvass for votes?

- Party insiders worked their way up through the party over the years and are extremely well connected internally, especially with the party leader.
- Local notables are well known in the electoral district in which they hope to run. Their candidacy tends to be more formidable than media coverage suggests. A local notable may be a mayor or a city councillor, or the leader of a community interest group.
- Stopgap candidates are more common than major political parties are willing to admit. Stopgaps are people whose candidacy goes uncontested, who run in a riding where there is no active electoral district association, who might live far away from the riding, and who operate a campaign on a shoestring budget. A stopgap is little more than a name on the ballot for the party because the prospects of winning are very weak; the candidate likely risks not even obtaining the minimum threshold

(currently 10 per cent of the vote) to qualify for a partial return of election expenses from Elections Canada. Stopgaps are often students, party volunteers, and idealists who want to help the party and who engage their families and friends for support. Although their electoral prospects are dim, once in a while they are elected amidst a sweeping electoral tide that favours one party's candidates above all others'.

Local campaigns are heavily influenced by the attention paid to them by the national party organization. Party strategists engage in a **seats triage** to identify which electoral districts they will retain with minimal effort, which ones they are unlikely to win, and which hotly contested **swing districts** (also known as marginal seats) will be close races.[13] They focus their resources on close races where they are competitive because a visit by the party leader and prominent candidates, some extra advertising, and additional workers may tip the scales. This typically leaves candidates in **safe seats**, incumbents seeking re-election, and stopgap candidates in unwinnable races to their own devices—though star candidates and assertive incumbents often manage to wrangle more resources from the party. But how much does the local campaign matter? Research suggests that the effects of the local ground campaign are minimal, usually accounting for less than 10 per cent of the vote, and that they matter only in extremely close races.[14]

seats triage
The identification of swing ridings where campaign resources should be concentrated.

swing district
A riding or constituency where the election outcome is uncertain.

safe seat
An electoral district in which the incumbent party is highly likely to be re-elected.

By-elections

Sometimes a special election, known as a **by-election**, is needed to fill a vacancy in an electoral district before the next general election is held. Seat vacancies arise when an elected official resigns or dies while in office. Resignations occur for a myriad of reasons: for example, a sitting politician may accept a different job; may run as a candidate for office in a different legislature; or may be forced to step down. Sometimes a politician will resign a safe seat to give an incoming party leader who is not currently a member of the legislature an opportunity to get elected. At other times the person simply retires owing to ill health or a change in career and family priorities. Within a number of months, the first minister, after seeking permission from the monarch's representative, announces that a by-election will be held for electors in that district to vote for a new representative.

by-election
A district-level election held between general elections.

Local issues and candidates matter more in a by-election because the question of which party will form the government isn't at stake. Even so, by-elections are usually treated as an opportunity for voters to send a message about their satisfaction with the governing party. For this reason, and because voter turnout in a by-election tends to be lower than in a general election, the winner is not necessarily re-elected in the general election when national media coverage intensifies.

Voter Turnout in Canadian Elections

Voter turnout is a common barometer of public engagement and the intensity of the election. Many people judge the health of a democracy by the proportion of registered electors who cast ballots. Turnout in Canada and other Western nations is in general decline. Non-voters give a variety of reasons for staying home. Too busy and uninterested top the list. Others cite a conscious decision not to vote, such as Indigenous people who

voter turnout
The proportion of eligible electors who cast ballots in an election.

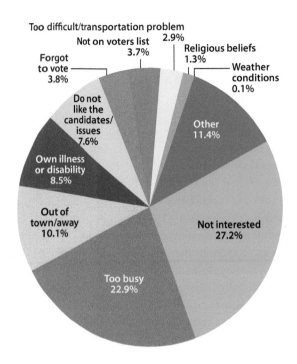

Figure 10.4 | Canadians' Reasons for Not Voting in a Federal Election

Source: Data from Statistics Canada, "Reasons for Not Voting in the Federal Election, October 19, 2015," *The Daily* (22 February 2016).

reject the settler colonial framework, would-be voters who are uninspired by the choices, and citizens who are prevented by their religious beliefs (e.g., Jehovah's Witnesses). Other reasons are unplanned, such as falling sick or having to face inclement weather. Being away, forgetting, not being on the voters list, and finding voting too difficult are among the other reasons that non-voters offer.[15] Studies indicate that, for as many as 6 in 10 non-voters, Canada's political system seems too complicated for them to engage in any meaningful way. Many voters feel like voting does not make a difference and the contest is not competitive. By comparison, people who vote tend to have a heightened sense of civic duty, which is a perceived obligation to participate in democracy.[16]

VOX POP

Figure 10.4 illustrates the results of Statistics Canada research on why people did not vote in federal elections. Given these reasons, what impact do you think online voting would have on voter turnout?

How serious a concern is low voter turnout? It suggests that Canadians are not engaged in elections, are ill-informed about public policy, and take democracy for granted. Or it may signify that people are reasonably content with the status quo and make a conscious decision that voting is not worth the effort. One explanation is the paradox of voting. Economists and rational-choice theorists have long argued that it is illogical to vote. The paradox of voting holds that a rational self-interested citizen will conclude that the personal costs of voting (investing time to become informed, travelling to the polling station, emotional upheaval, etc.) outweigh the potential benefits (the low probability of casting the deciding ballot, sense of community). One economist calculates that the expected benefit from voting must be over eight billion times the cost of voting.[17] Clearly, people vote for reasons other than to personally influence the outcome, such as the positive feelings they get from being part of a group and exercising their democratic right to participate in such a civic event.

Turnout fluctuates between elections. The percentage of citizens on the voter's list who cast a ballot varies widely across Canada at both the federal and provincial/territorial levels. Among the reasons for turnout variation are the density of population, the amount of time since a previous campaign, and the time of year that the election is held.[18] One constant is that residents of Prince Edward Island are more likely to vote than other Canadians. Complicating matters, it can be difficult to compare data over time given that the franchise has been extended, and not all Canadians appear on the government's list of electors. Nevertheless, the level of turnout raises questions about the representativeness of a party government in Canada, especially if we consider the

Figure 10.5 | Turnout in Canadian Federal Elections, 1945–2019

Note: 2019 turnout is a preliminary figure from Elections Canada and does not include revisions to the electors list after election day.

frequency of manufactured majorities. As it stands, a majority government tends to be formed on the basis of securing approximately 38 to 40 per cent of the votes cast. When only two-thirds of electors cast a ballot, this means that only about a quarter of eligible electors voted for the political party that forms a majority government—a calculation that assumes that everybody is accounted for on the official list of electors. Delving deeper, different socio-demographic clusters of electors disproportionately vote for or against the governing party, and the socio-demographic composition of elected officials does not align with that of the electorate. Political parties reach out to some voters more than others, especially older citizens over young voters. All of this suggests that the political executive is bound to be out of touch with the needs and wants of the general public and certain cohorts.

VOX POP

If an election were being held today, and a public-opinion poll indicated that one candidate in your riding was heading to a landslide victory, would you vote? Why or why not? What would have to change to make you more or less likely to vote?

Vote Choice in Canadian Elections

There are many factors involved in a vote decision.[19] Among the long-term influences are party identification, social class, social values, religion, ethnicity, gender, and regionalism. There are institutional effects, such as federal–provincial dynamics or the nature of the party

Most likely to vote   Least likely to vote

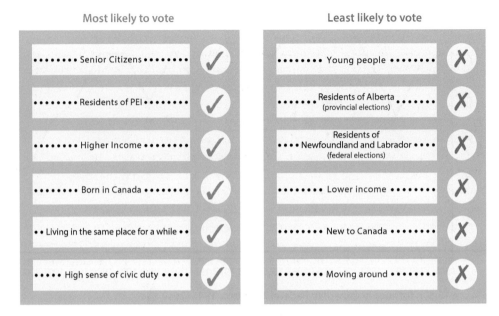

Figure 10.6 | Canadians Most and Least Likely to Vote

system. Then there are election-specific influences whereby the campaign itself makes a difference. This includes the perceived importance of issues and leader evaluations. Finally, there are strategic considerations, including whether to vote for a second choice in order to prevent another party or candidate from winning. Emotions, issues, candidate likeability, availability of political information—these are among the many influences on voter choice.

Canadian political scientists often draw on Canadian Election Study (CES) data to understand voter behaviour. In every federal election, academics conduct public-opinion surveys during the campaign and immediately afterwards. Thousands of Canadians participate, which enables researchers to conduct deep analysis of political attitudes. The CES datasets and codebooks are publicly available so that researchers, including students, may analyze Canadians' opinions and attitudes. Researchers also conduct surveys and experiments outside of elections to examine vote choice. One reasonably consistent finding is that political parties and party leadership are by far the most significant considerations for most voters.

Direct Democracy in Canada

referendum
A citizen vote whose outcome legislators are usually expected to follow.

plebiscite
A citizen vote held to inform a decision by a representative body.

Representative democracy entrusts elected representatives to make policy decisions. Yet there are moments when voters provide first-hand input into the policy-making process. Direct democracy provides an opportunity for voters to register their opinion on a specific policy question at the ballot box. In a **referendum**, governments ask voters for politically binding advice. Politicians almost always respect the results of referendums, although they can come up with reasons to disregard the results, such as saying that turnout was too low. In calling a referendum, governments typically decide whether a simple majority (50 per cent plus one) is sufficient or whether a higher standard must be imposed. A **plebiscite** is similar although usually non-binding. Politicians can simply treat the results of a plebiscite as advice. People commonly refer to any such vote as a referendum (see Briefing Notes). Neither form of direct democracy automatically produces law. As we have seen in Chapters 5 and 6, there are many other steps in the lawmaking process. While referendums may encourage legislators to act, it is ultimately up to the legislature to pass enabling legislation and for the Crown to provide assent before the changes become law.

Referendums and plebiscites are rare in Canada. They tend to be on divisive policy issues and risk disrupting the social order. The federal government has held two major national plebiscites, concerning the prohibition of alcohol (1898) and the desirability of military conscription (1942), and one national referendum on the Charlottetown Accord (1992). All three were relatively close and revealed regional cleavages. The prohibition plebiscite passed with 51 per cent, boosted by substantial support in English Canada. The conscription plebiscite produced similar regional results, albeit with a larger proportion (65 per cent) of Canadians voting in support of establishing a military draft. Quebec voters sided overwhelmingly against each proposal, making the province the only one to vote "no" to both prohibition (81.2 per cent) and conscription (72 per cent). For reasons explained in Chapter 2, the referendum on the Charlottetown Accord failed nationally (55 per cent opposed), and once again Quebec was opposed. In all three cases the proposed policy did not proceed, though in World War II the government wavered for two years before eventually establishing conscription. This latter point reveals the contingent nature of direct democracy in Canada: unlike the situation in the United States, where referendums may be binding and lead directly to new legislation, in Canada the choices made by the electorate still require the support of the government of the day in order to be implemented.

The provinces and territories are political laboratories for experiments with direct democracy. Province-wide referendums and plebiscites were most frequent in the early twentieth century. The prohibition, temperance, and sale of liquor was a heated topic in Alberta, Ontario, and Quebec, and especially in Prince Edward Island, whose government sought the opinion of voters seven times. In Alberta, voters weighed in on the continued private distribution of electricity, and the use of daylight saving time. In PEI, votes were held on automobiles, and on a Potato Marketing Board. Newfoundland and Labrador held two divisive referendums about whether to join Canada. Since the 1980 Quebec referendum on sovereignty-association, provincial and territorial governments have sought direct public input on weighty democratic and constitutional issues, including abortion, religious schooling, electoral systems, borders, and whether to join or leave Confederation

The debate surrounding conscription is discussed in Chapter 14, on Canada's place in the world.

Canada's regional cleavages are discussed in Chapter 4, on regionalism. See especially pages 109–17 on regionalism in Quebec.

Briefing Notes

Referendums and Plebiscites

For most intents and purposes, the terms "referendum" and "plebiscite" are synonymous in Canada. Strictly speaking, a plebiscite is a non-binding instrument to ascertain the public's opinion on an issue of public policy, while a referendum is a politically binding public vote on a concrete variety of policy alternatives. Many people use "referendum" to refer to any type of direct vote by citizens on a policy, without being aware that politicians have less obligation to act on the results of a plebiscite. Either way, a first minister will offer a public response to the vote outcome.

(Table 10.5). The James Bay Cree held a referendum surrounding the 1995 Quebec sovereignty vote, with 96 per cent of voters registering a desire to stay in Canada rather than join a sovereign Quebec. Moreover, every province except Nova Scotia, Ontario, and Manitoba has legislated requirements to hold a plebiscite prior to tabling any amendment to the Constitution of Canada in their respective legislatures. Manitoba has a requirement to hold public consultations before doing so.

In addition to direct votes on issues of public policy, several provinces have experimented with **recall** legislation—a formal process that allows the electorate to petition the government for the removal of a member of the legislature between elections. In jurisdictions where such legislation exists, a petition signed by a significant proportion (usually 40 per cent) of registered voters in the member's constituency is enough to have the elected official cease to hold office. That individual may, however, run in the by-election that is triggered by the successful recall. In this way, recall legislation is intended to ensure that members of the legislature remain accountable, responsive delegates of their constituents.

recall
Legislated process by which electors of a given district may petition for a by-election.

Table 10.5   Referendums and Plebiscites in the Canadian Provinces and Territories, since 1980

Province	Issue	Result
British Columbia	Initiative and recall plebiscite (1991)	approved introduction of legislation allowing initiatives and recall
	Treaty referendum (2002)	approved certain principles in treaty negotiations with First Nations
	Referendums on electoral reform (2005, 2009, 2018)	rejected single transferable vote electoral system
	Harmonized Sales Tax (HST) referendum (2011)	approved repeal of HST
Saskatchewan	Abortion plebiscite (1991)	rejected public funding of abortions
	Constitutional amendment plebiscite (1991)	approved mandatory referendums on constitutional amendments
	Balanced budget plebiscite (1991)	approved enacting balanced budget legislation
Ontario	Referendum on electoral reform (2007)	rejected mixed-member proportional system
Quebec	Referendum on sovereignty-association (1980)	rejected sovereignty-association
	Referendum on Quebec sovereignty (1995)	rejected sovereignty
New Brunswick	Video lottery terminal referendum (2001)	approved retaining video lottery terminals
Nova Scotia	Sunday shopping plebiscite (2004)	rejected establishing Sunday shopping
Prince Edward Island	Fixed-link crossing plebiscite (1988)	approved creation of bridge to NB
	Video lottery terminal referendum (1997)	approved removal of all video lottery terminals
	Plebiscites on electoral reform (2005, 2016, 2019)	rejected mixed-member proportional electoral reform; later approved it but the government rejected it; rejected mixed-member proportional reform in a third vote
Newfoundland and Labrador	Schools referendums (1995, 1997)	rejected then approved disbanding religious schools
Northwest Territories /Nunavut	Northwest Territories division plebiscite (1982)	approved dividing Northwest Territories
	Nunavut Creation Referendum (1992)	endorsed the Nunavut Land Claims
	Northwest Territories boundary plebiscite (1992)	approved the NWT–Nunavut boundary
	Nunavut capital plebiscite (1995)	approved Iqaluit as capital of Nunavut

Note: Excludes municipal plebiscites and referendums.

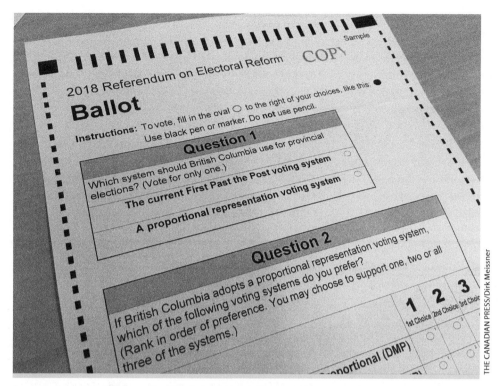

THE CANADIAN PRESS/Dirk Meissner

Sometimes governments go to the people more than once on the same issue, particularly if the first referendum was less than conclusive or if a new party comes to power. In 1980 and 1995, the Government of Quebec convened referendums on whether to separate from Canada. Alberta held plebiscites on whether to adopt daylight saving time in 1967 and 1971. British Columbia and PEI have each held three public votes on electoral reform. Should governments respect the results of referenda, or should the question remain open to future debate?

Recall legislation is common in the United States; however, it has not taken hold in Canada. Alberta's experience lasted only two years, when the premier repealed the legislation amid a threat posed by his own constituents to use the law against him. As it stands, British Columbia is the only province to have recall legislation. Since its introduction in 1995, the province's chief electoral officer has processed about one recall petition each year. While none was officially successful in removing a member of the Legislative Assembly, in that the petitions either did not receive enough signatures or else failed procedurally, one process did contribute to an MLA's resignation.

Concluding Thoughts

Elections and referendums are complex, fundamental events in Canadian democracy. They determine the course of public policy and governance. For this reason, considerable time and effort goes into ensuring elections are contested vigorously, reported objectively, studied rigorously, and conducted fairly. Given the stakes and resources involved, it has become increasingly difficult to determine when election campaigns end and governing begins. In this era of the permanent campaign, political organizations invest heavily ensuring that the right messages are delivered to the right audiences at the right time. This field of political communication forms the basis of the next chapter.

For More Information

Ever considered how much a single vote could mean in the course of Canadian history? In *Just One Vote* (University of Manitoba Press, 2009), Ian Stewart examines how one vote at a local Manitoba NDP nomination meeting contributed to the failure of the Meech Lake Accord.

Why do you suppose efforts and experiments with electoral reform have been so short-lived in Canada? Dennis Pilon explores the topic in his book *The Politics of Voting: Reforming Canada's Electoral System* (Emond Montgomery, 2007).

Does gerrymandering exist in Canada? Exactly how are electoral boundaries designed? Find out in Michael Pal and Sujit Choudhry's chapter "Constituency Boundaries in Canada" in *Election*, ed. Heather MacIvor (Emond Montgomery, 2009).

Do election rules in Canada seem strict? Should taxpayers subsidize political parties? Editors Lisa Young and Harold Jansen are among a variety of authors who examine political finance rules in their book *Money, Politics, and Democracy: Canada's Party Finance Reforms* (UBC Press, 2011).

Is there a political advantage in controlling the date of an election—and does that advantage vanish with fixed-date election legislation? Stephen White and Christopher Alcantara consider the evidence in "Do Constraints Limit Opportunism? Incumbent Electoral Performance Before and After (Partially) Fixed-Term Laws," *Political Behaviour* 41, no. 3 (2019): pp. 657–75.

How is "big data" used by party candidates? Dig into the data in Kaija Belfry Munroe and H.D. Munroe, "Constituency Campaigning in the Age of Data," *Canadian Journal of Political Science* 51, no. 1 (2018): pp. 135–54.

To what extent does the local candidate matter in vote choice? To find the answer, see Jason Roy and Christopher Alcantara, "The Candidate Effect: Does the Local Candidate Matter?" in *Journal of Elections, Public Opinion and Parties* 25, (2014): pp. 195–214.

Does Canada need more referendums? Richard Johnston, André Blais, Elisabeth Gidengil, and Neil Nevitte take a critical look at the topic in *The Challenge of Direct Democracy: The 1992 Canadian Referendum* (McGill–Queen's University Press, 1996).

Want to compare the laws, rules, and regulations that govern the various federal, provincial, and territorial elections? Elections Canada maintains an up-to-date Compendium of Election Administration in Canada. Search: Elections Canada compendium.

Interested in becoming a political citizen? Visit the Samara Centre for Democracy website to learn more about improving citizen engagement through research and education: https://www.samaracanada.com/

Deeper Inside Canadian Politics

1. Critics often accuse parties and governments of rigging the rules surrounding elections to ensure their own success. To what extent is there empirical evidence of this in Canadian history?
2. Businesses and unions cannot donate money in federal politics. Given this, should new rules be established to restrict how much money registered lobbyists can donate to political parties compared with other Canadians?
3. Imagine a friend of yours does not intend to vote in an upcoming election, saying, "It's not worth the hassle—what difference would it make anyway?" What arguments could you use to change your friend's mind?
4. Suppose you were going to run for office. What, if anything, could you do to differentiate yourself from the other candidates?
5. Think of a burning policy issue going on right now. What would be the advantages and disadvantages of the government announcing a referendum or a plebiscite on that issue?

Professor Profile

Mebs Kanji

Democratic governance, Canadian political culture, empirical research methods
Co-editor of *The Canadian Election Studies: Assessing Four Decades of Influence* (2013)

Courtesy of Mebs Kanji

Mebs Kanji uses public-opinion research to better understand democratic support, political culture, value diversity, and social cohesion. Some of his main areas of interest include public attitudes toward Canadian democracy and government, public orientations toward democratic performance, the causes and implications of variations in political support, and public support for political and policy reforms. His research focuses on finding ways to improve Canadians' perceptions of their political system and uncovering changing patterns in Canadian society, such as the expanding generational value divide which may have significant implications for the welfare state and democratic governance. He is also the founder and director of the Workshops on Social Science Research (WSSR), an innovative program which seeks to train future decision-makers, connecting theoretical understandings to practice through short, intensive learning experiences and networking opportunities with top-level practitioners and academics, all with years of experience in both the Canadian and international contexts.

Here is what Mebs Kanji told us about his career path from when he was an undergraduate student, why he is drawn to his area of specialization, what is challenging about studying Canadian politics, and what advice he has for students.

* * *

I completed a Bachelor of Commerce and a BA in political science at the University of Calgary. Coming from a business background, my first Canadian political science course was somewhat confusing to say the least. It was an entirely different way of thinking and every class revealed how little I really knew about my political system. I was sure that I would not do well. But then I started paying more attention to the politics section of the newspaper and gradually the connections between what I was learning and why it was relevant became exceedingly clear. The whole experience was immensely eye-opening and, looking back

now, it becomes monumentally apparent to me how significant this experience really was.

I now study Canadian politics on a daily basis, focusing specifically on Canadians' outlooks toward their political system. I feel that this is a worthwhile area of research where there is a pressing need and an incredibly challenging puzzle to figure out and resolve. Why are so many Canadians disillusioned with their political system? What do we need to focus on to better this? Where should we turn first? For me, this constitutes a wicked problem and the stakes are really high given that as shareholders in our democracy we value the robustness and legitimacy of our political process.

We have a very complex political system, one that appears to be genuinely suffering from a public perception problem, the core cause of which is neither immediately apparent nor likely simplistic. Worse, in order to get a handle on this problem we basically need to conduct in depth and systematic analyses of data that are not readily available. What surprises me the most so far is how much we have yet to learn about the true nature of this problem. It is clear to me, based on the more than 50 years of literature that I have covered and the data analyses that I have seen, that we still have an insufficient understanding of the symptoms and the probable causes and that there is a disconnect that exists between what some think we need to do to try and fix the problem and where the more in-depth data analyses are starting to suggest the problems truly lie.

My one piece of advice to Canadian political science students is: work hard and keep it real! Continuously try to connect what you learn in the classroom to what you read about in the daily news. This makes it all much more relevant, motivating, and worthwhile.

Up for Debate

Are election and referendum campaigns mostly a waste of time?

THE CLAIM: YES, THEY ARE!

Campaigns don't matter much and can even harm Canadian democracy.

Yes: Argument Summary

Electioneering and even voting don't matter as much as politicians and campaign workers suggest. Many Canadians know how they will vote regardless of an election campaign. The rest are tuned out from politics completely or turned off. Citizens appear to be figuring out that it is irrational to invest the time and effort in following a campaign when a single vote is so unlikely to change the outcome of the election. Moreover, whereas electioneering was once confined to a relatively short period leading up to an election, today there is a permanent campaign of relentless politicking. As a result, even without much of a formal campaign, Canadians have most of the information they need to make an informed vote on Election Day.

Yes: Top 5 Considerations

1. Canadians don't pay much attention to political campaigns. During the first half of an official campaign the parties and candidates are busy getting organized. They know that there is low awareness and interest at this stage.
2. Canadian campaigns do not feature the great debates one would expect from a fully functioning democratic system. Parties rarely present contrasting positions on major issues. Those voters who do pay attention to campaigns are exposed to relentless negativity and horse-race coverage. Political parties are so focused on identifying and mobilizing supporters that politicians rarely engage citizens in a genuine dialogue during campaigns.
3. "An election is no time to discuss serious issues" is a remark attributed to Prime Minister Kim Campbell. She was misquoted, but did say that discussing the overhaul of major policy cannot be accomplished during the confines of a campaign. Party leaders rarely get into detail about policies. Local candidates are told not to vocalize their own opinions. As a result, election campaigns hardly confer any sense of a democratic mandate for the winning party.
4. Roughly two-fifths of the Canadian electorate is made up of partisans. These voters will support the same political party regardless of election campaign dynamics. In fact, they are prone to be galvanized by controversy, creating a toxic political environment that divides society.
5. Political parties increasingly engage in permanent campaigning. The official campaign period leading up to the election is virtually indistinguishable from the rest of the time between elections.

Yes: Other Considerations

- Leaders' debates receive considerable media attention yet rarely make a difference to the final result.
- Individual candidates, paid workers, and volunteers campaign furiously—yet, local campaigning is thought to affect no more than 10 per cent of the vote.
- The media are guided by opinion polls that lead to horse-race coverage that ignores the parties and candidates that are likely to lose. For many parties and candidates, especially those considered minor and fringe, an election campaign is an unfair experience.
- Political parties elected to form the government rarely introduce radical changes. The adage "Liberal, Tory, same old story" exemplifies the public's frustration with opposition parties adopting the policies of the party that they replaced in government.
- Parties often campaign on vaguely defined policies designed to appeal widely to the electorate. A party's real legislative agenda becomes apparent only once it takes office.
- Campaigns used to be the best opportunity for voters to get to know their local representative. Today, at any time you can easily locate information online about local representatives and the issues at play in their riding.

- Referendum campaigns can be particularly divisive affairs based on misinformation and emotion. The result is a fractured society and questionable public policy.

THE COUNTERCLAIM: NO, THEY'RE NOT!

Campaigning for votes is vital to Canadian democracy.

No: Argument Summary

Cynics are misinformed about the fundamental purpose of election campaigns. These contests are not designed to present diametrically opposed viewpoints on major public-policy issues. Regular pitched battles of that sort would not only destabilize Canadian democracy, but would mask that—on most major issues—Canadians are in fundamental agreement. When parties present citizens with similar positions (in favour of public healthcare or opposed to military intervention, for instance), they are behaving rationally and responsibly by reflecting the interests of mainstream Canadians. Instead of placing voters in the position of having to decide which party or candidate is on the correct side of the issues, campaigns ask voters to choose who would be best at handling the issues in the years ahead, and whose priorities align best with their own. And voters often use the opportunity presented by a campaign to change their minds about whom they want to govern.

No: Top 5 Considerations

1. Election campaigns present voters with meaningful choices among competing agendas and competencies. Most election platforms contain the top five or six issues a party wants to address. The campaign is spent trying to convince voters that the party's leadership is the one best suited to managing those issues.
2. Heated ideological debates and detailed policy discussions occur as an act of election readiness. Citizens' input is collected, ideas are floated at leadership and policy conventions, and conversations occur in local constituency meetings and within caucus. These efforts contribute to the sort of practical, widely accepted positions we see in campaign platforms. Were it not for this pre-election work, Canadian elections would be fractious, divisive affairs, quite possibly threatening national unity.
3. Canadians do not identify as strongly or consistently with particular political parties the way voters in other countries do. Many Canadian voters are open to persuasion during election campaigns.
4. Electors often change their minds in the lead-up to Election Day. For instance, some public-opinion polls predict massive victories for one party, yet voters end up putting a different one in office. This suggests campaigns do matter in terms of changing people's minds.
5. Writ periods are often the only opportunity for otherwise occupied Canadians to assess their representatives. Many get to do so face to face, either through door-knocking or local debates.

No: Other Considerations

- Election campaigns are integral to free and fair elections—a core premise of Canadian democracy. Without them, we would live in an autocratic system of government.
- The fact that there is widespread agreement on major policy issues is not an indicator of the failure of Canadian democracy. It's a sign that political parties are fulfilling their duty to mediate varied interests to prevent them from tearing the country apart.
- Negative campaigns draw contrasts between the abilities of various leaders to govern in citizens' best interests.
- Some campaigns are focused on public policy. Some are akin to referendums on important issues, such as climate change.
- Referendum campaigns are formidable tools to get citizens to pay attention to a public-policy issue and pass judgement on what politicians should do about it.

Discussion Questions

- Could you imagine a system with longer terms of office, fewer federal elections, and more referendums?

What would be the advantages and disadvantages of such a system?

- Could a public-opinion poll based on a scientifically defined representative sample of eligible voters ever become a substitute for an election, plebiscite, or referendum?

- Have you ever worked in an election campaign? If so, how did you get involved? If not, what would it take to engage you?

Where to Learn More about Election Campaigns in Canada

R. Kenneth Carty and Munroe Eagles, *Politics Is Local: National Politics at the Grassroots* (Don Mills, ON: Oxford University Press, 2005).

Harold D. Clarke, Lawrence LeDuc, Jane Jenson, and Jon Pammett, *Absent Mandate: Interpreting Change in Canadian Elections*, 2nd edn (Toronto: Gage, 1991).

Anna Esselment, "The Governing Party and the Permanent Campaign," in *Political Communication in Canada: Meet the Press and Tweet the Rest*, eds. Alex Marland, Thierry Giasson, and Tamara A. Small (Vancouver: UBC Press, 2014).

Tom Flanagan, *Winning Power: Canadian Campaigning in the Twenty-First Century* (Montreal and Kingston: McGill-Queen's University Press, 2014).

Elisabeth Gidengil, Neil Nevitte, André Blais, Joanna Everitt, and Patrick Fournier, *Dominance and Decline: Making Sense of Recent Canadian Elections* (Toronto: University of Toronto Press, 2012).

Richard Johnston, André Blais, Henry E. Brady, and Jean Crête, *Letting the People Decide: Dynamics of a Canadian Election* (Montreal and Kingston: McGill-Queen's University Press, 1992).

Lawrence LeDuc, Jon H. Pammett, Judith I. McKenzi and André Turcotte, *Dynasties and Interludes: Past and Present in Canadian Electoral Politics* (Toronto: Dundurn Press, 2010).

Heather MacIvor, ed., *Election* (Toronto: Emond Montgomery, 2010).

R. Kenneth Carty and William Cross, "Political Parties and the Practice of Brokerage Politics," in *The Oxford Handbook of Canadian Politics*, eds. John C. Courtney and David E. Smith (Toronto: Oxford University Press, 2010).

11

Media and Communication

Inside This Chapter

- What are the characteristics and roles of Canadian news media?
- What are the major theories and practices of political communication?
- Why is access to information so complex?
- How is political marketing transforming Canadian democracy?

Inside Media and Communication

Canadian democracy is built on free speech. Section 2(b) of the Charter of Rights and Freedoms identifies the fundamental freedom of "thought, belief, opinion and expression, including freedom of the press and other media of communication." Understanding Canadian politics and government requires an appreciation for the ways that these thoughts, beliefs, and opinions are communicated. Astute citizens maintain a healthy skepticism of political information and avail of multiple sources. The following maxims apply to the evolving communication landscape.

✔ **Traditional political media is changing—and yet much remains the same.** Citizen journalists and activists rely heavily on accredited journalists for information. For their part, traditional media sources are experimenting with online delivery methods. An arsenal of online investigative techniques helps the media perform an essential role in Canadian democracy. Yet the nature of news coverage has much room for improvement.

✔ **To comprehend a political issue you need details from a variety of information sources.** Some citizens place too much trust in the media and believe everything they hear. Others distrust all conventional news sources and are partial to conspiracy theories. In between is a society where political actors, journalists, and citizens struggle to assess what is fact, what is rhetoric, and, most difficult of all, what is omitted from the public narrative.

✔ **Politicians are not required to answer journalists' questions.** Canadian political elites are not obliged to talk with journalists. The only requirement is that the government be held to account in the legislature, in elections and, in rare circumstances, in the courts. Most politicians are fond of communicating with the public. However their messages are seldom direct replies to questions posed by opponents and hostile reporters.

Political leaders and the press have a love–hate relationship. They need each other and their position is enhanced by controlling the other. This chapter delves into the constant jousting by political actors to manage and influence the media and communication.

UP FOR DEBATE

Does social media make Canadian democracy better or worse?

Keep this question in mind as you read through the chapter. Consult the end-of-chapter debate supplement for more material to help you engage in an informed discussion of the topic.

The Politics of Communication

In politics, nothing is as it seems.[1] Political information is filled with biases. Politicians, the media, pundits, advocates, interest groups, lobbyists, and others are selective when they release information to support their views. Consequently, citizens may form opposing impressions of public actors and government. Part of the reason is that public opinion is based on political ideologies and partisanship. More broadly, people often lack the information or ability to figure out what is real, and tend not to probe more deeply.

Politics is not always fair, either. Smart political communication, or even charisma and charm, can sometimes help politicians overcome bad political situations. An infamous tale involving Canada's first prime minister brings this to light. John A. Macdonald arrived in Northern Ontario feeling sick after drinking too much alcohol on a bumpy train ride. He mounted a platform where an opposing candidate was giving a thoughtful speech. Macdonald interrupted his opponent by vomiting on the stage. The audience was shocked. Even Macdonald's supporters expressed disgust. During the awkward pause, Macdonald collected himself, and said: "I don't know how it is, but every time I hear Mr Jones speak it turns my stomach!"[2] The audience burst into laughter and was impressed by such quick political wit. Through his choice of words Macdonald turned an embarrassing situation into a positive outcome. His opponent's arguments lost out to the spectacle and humour.

Communication is an essential if not primary activity of anyone involved in politics and government. In a democratic society like Canada's, where rights and freedoms are constitutionally protected, the free-flowing exchange of perspectives, ideas, and data is essential to a vibrant **public sphere**. Decades ago, German philosopher Jürgen Habermas articulated the need for reasoned public debate among the middle class, not just the political elite. He believed that good government is more likely if a society is made up of well-read citizens who freely discuss politics in coffee houses and other social settings. The general public must be informed and engaged in public affairs, Habermas reasoned, in order to constrain the power of government elites. However, not all political dialogue can occur face to face in small venues, and the quality and quantity of public debate is shaped by media technology. The influence of technology on communication is so profound that in the 1960s Canadian scholar Marshall McLuhan famously argued that "the medium is the message."[3] The catchphrase refers to how different mediums—print, radio, television, and now digital media—have such powerful effects that identical information is fundamentally changed.

> **public sphere**
> The venue for group and public discussion about social problems and government.

To get in front of an issue and advance a political cause in the public sphere, you need to do more than talk on stage or in line at Tim Hortons, however. Political actors push ideas, public problems, and policy solutions in a bid to attract news media coverage and penetrate the public consciousness. As discussed in Chapter 8, agenda setting refers to raising topics to the top of the public consciousness and pressuring political elites for action, while those issues that fall off the public agenda or never make it are more likely to be ignored. Every day that one issue dominates the news is a day that other issues go unnoticed. The prime minister—and, within a province or territory, a premier—can command the media's attention like no other politician. A first minister can set the agenda by announcing government policy, making a statement in the legislature, attending a meeting of community leaders, or perhaps hinting at an early election call. A prime minister has the added ability to convene a first ministers' conference, discuss initiatives at a summit of international leaders, and deliver a speech to the United Nations General Assembly. By comparison, opposition leaders and other political actors have much more difficulty attracting media attention. For everyone in politics, the media and communication are pivotal to setting the agenda and shaping public opinion.

Agenda setting is discussed in the context of the policy cycle in Chapter 8, on public policy: see page 253.

Canadians need not obtain information directly from politicians or government. In Canada's **mediated democracy**, citizens depend on the media to act as an intermediary between them and their political leaders. The news media circulate information between political elites and the people they represent. Politicians draw on news coverage to guide their decision-making, while for the attentive public, the news informs their knowledge of political happenings. The power of the media is such that the news production process influences the behaviour of creators and receivers of political information.

> **mediated democracy**
> A democratic society that relies on the media to provide citizens with information about politics and government.

The mediatization of Canadian democracy therefore alters how politics and government operate. In fact, the media's power is so significant that communications scholars refer to media logic, which is the idea that political actors must follow the unwritten codes and conventions of media routines.

Political journalists play a pivotal role within a mediated democracy. Investigative reporters keep politicians in check: they pose tough questions and filter elected leaders' responses and actions for their readers. Columnists and commentators critique politicians' choices and behaviour. Collectively, they perform an institutional function as the **fourth estate**, an expression that treats journalists on the same plane as the three branches of government (executive, legislative, and judicial). The term originated in eighteenth-century Europe to suggest that the news media constitutes a fourth layer of a power hierarchy, which at the time was comprised of the clergy, nobles, and commoners. The fourth estate consists foremost of professional journalists and media outlets. They are determined to obtain political information that they deem to be in the public interest. As we shall explain, many politicians are even more determined to prevent that from happening.

The ability of the fourth estate to uncover and report information about governments is strained in a fast-paced digital environment. Journalists can obtain more details about political actors and public administration more quickly than ever before by consulting information online. They can identify and connect with individuals through social media and email. However, all of that information is controlled. Moreover, journalists are under tremendous pressure to file stories multiple times a day and to participate in social media. They often lack the resources, time, and editorial commitment to conduct deeper research. These strains are worsened by staff reductions, particularly among those covering municipal and provincial politics. Furthermore, advertisers are drawn to stories that generate large view counts, shares, likes, and retweets.

Considerable technological change in recent decades introduces questions about the roles of traditional and digital media in covering Canadian politics. Citizens increasingly obtain their news from digital platforms, which provide them with up-to-the-second news on portable devices that display only small snippets. However, the speeding up of news cycles and sharing of information can have negative implications for democracy. As Prime Minister Justin Trudeau says, "Do we want our six o'clock news to turn into 'fail' videos and kittens tumbling down stairs? If that's what citizens actually want, well, there are consequences around the kind of governance we're going to get."[4] As well, the circulation of "fake news" (discussed in Chapter 12) is causing citizens to confuse trustworthy information with disinformation. The fourth estate is grappling with the media economics of funding trustworthy investigative journalism about public affairs.

fourth estate
An informal term for the media, implying that a free press is so vital to democracy that it is on par with the three branches of government (executive, legislature, judiciary).

Media Economics

Even a surface understanding of political communication and journalism requires some awareness of media economics. Generally speaking, the media is a competitive business characterized by a continual search for cost efficiencies and return on investment. Advertising revenues and profits go up when audience numbers are strong. News operations are thus pressured by market-oriented journalism that sensationalizes in order to generate attention. Given their resource constraints, journalists are drawn to using information packaged by political actors to fit the needs of news production, as well as to use social media as a source.

The digital environment has profound implications for news production. Reusing content across multiple platforms means that news operations can be merged or closed. Digital content is especially easy to repurpose, making it the cornerstone of modern reporting. There is a need to constantly update digital platforms with fresh content. Audiences might expect to access news for free online, which deprives news organizations of subscription fees. Furthermore, advertising dollars are flowing away from Canadian mainstream media toward American social media behemoths such as Facebook, Google, Twitter, and YouTube. The shift has been profound. The Government of Canada's own advertising placements bears this out (Figure 11.1). The federal government ranks among the country's largest advertisers. Its advertising has moved from print, radio, and especially television such that digital media now constitutes a sizeable majority of government advertising spending.

Many observers suggest that the ability of the news industry to fulfill its role as the fourth estate is compromised. A recent report about the future of Canadian news media suggests that "Canadian journalism finds itself at a crisis point—towns and cities continue to lose their local news sources, major city newspapers and TV stations are bleeding staff, and the industry is scrambling to find ways of securing revenue and holding the public's trust and interest."[5] The 2019 federal government budget contained a policy response. Eligible news organizations will qualify for a journalism tax credit to support employees. A new digital subscription tax credit provides incentives for citizens to pay for online journalism. As well, the government is awarding charitable status to eligible Canadian journalism organizations. The involvement of the government in the news media industry drew cheers from those concerned about journalism. It also drew jeers from those concerned that government intervention could constrain the freedom of the press. As we shall see in the next section, politics has always run through Canadian news production in some way or another.

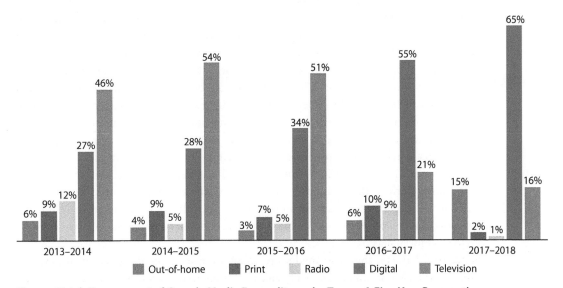

Figure 11.1 | Government of Canada Media Expenditures by Type—A Five-Year Perspective

Note: Due to rounding, percentages may not add up to 100%. In this graph, cinema is included in out-of-home.

Source: *The Annual Report on Government of Canada Advertising Activities.* Published by Public Services and Procurement Canada (PSPC) 2019.

The News Media Landscape in Canada

Evolution of Canadian Media

Political actors send and receive information in many ways. Outside of personal communication, the most prominent source is the mainstream news media, in particular newspaper, radio, and television outlets. Together, these media form a large network that enables information to be transmitted among political actors, individual media outlets, and the general public.

The media constantly evolve as a result of technological, economic and societal change. Media organizations obtain most of their revenues from advertising and/or subscription fees. The rates charged for advertising are related to audience readership, listenership, viewership, and web traffic. Intense competition means that publishers and editors seek ways to attract audiences in the most cost-efficient manner. They operate in a perpetual state of change as they adapt to new technologies, tastes, and trends.

In the early years of Confederation, innovations allowed large printing presses to mass-produce millions of pages in a single day, and small local presses could produce handbills. The **party press** consisted of partisan newspapers that gained income from printing government advertisements and official notices, or from ads run by corporations opposed to the party in power. These newspapers were operated by publishers who were sympathetic to a political party. The party press published speeches and good news about parliamentarians affiliated with their preferred party. The editorial content, sometimes authored by the printer, criticized political opponents. Prime Minister Macdonald was among those who arranged for friends to buy or launch newspapers that would support his party and slag his opponents. The readership was foremost society's elite.[6]

party press
Early newspapers that were blatantly partisan.

Demand for mass distribution of newspapers grew as literacy rates improved. The penny press gradually replaced the party press by earning revenues through low-cost subscriptions and business advertising. The reduced reliance on government advertising increased the expectation for non-partisan news, and by the early twentieth century, the party press was fading away. For a considerable time newspapers were the only source of information about legislative proceedings. Reports about happenings in the legislature were presented with an editorial slant. The role of newspapers in documenting debates was displaced when legislatures began assigning their own staff to create official records, known as Hansard. In some provinces Hansard was not instituted until the 1970s.

Ideological slants persist in newspapers in more subtle forms. For instance, the Toronto Star is historically a proponent of the welfare state, and continues to exhibit left-wing leanings. Conversely, the *National Post* and *Sun* newspapers espouse conservative views, particularly in their editorial content. *The Globe and Mail* is considered Canada's national newspaper and tends to be more centrist. Specialist publications such as *The Hill Times* and *Policy Options* publish detailed analysis of politics and public policy without an obvious editorial bias.

Across Canada, the print media are contending with the digitization of news by reducing the number and size of paper copies. Newspapers and magazines are struggling to adjust to a digital world where consumers can obtain information for free. Subscription-based national and city newspapers must also compete with dailies distributed for free to commuters, free community newspapers that serve specialized markets, and newspapers that cater to specific ethnic communities. The penny-press model that relied on business advertising is fizzling as advertisers turn to other medi-ums. Many community newspapers have closed. Some operations, such as *La Presse*, are now digital only.

Newspapers have survived technological disruption before. In the 1920s they adjusted to the onset of radio by becoming the authoritative source for news details. Radio was able to deliver news quickly and did so in a manner that resonated with audiences. Politicians gravitated toward the medium as they realized that their voices could be transmitted into citizens' living rooms without being filtered through journalists. Radio was particularly relevant in the early twentieth-century populist and progressive movements in the Canadian prairies. In 1935, Prime Minister R.B. Bennett copied the American president's practice of delivering radio addresses, which were known as fireside chats. Radio now tends to communicate political information through short news clips. Regional stations across the country operate call-in programs that constitute electronic public squares where participants discuss political issues of the day. Political news programs include CBC Radio's *As It Happens*, *The House*, and *Cross-Country Check-up*.

In spite of the immediacy of radio, and the analysis offered by print media, it was the emergence of television in the 1950s that fundamentally changed politics. Moving images enable the transmission of contextual information and resonate on an emotional level. Viewers form memorable impressions from a multitude of information points—a politician's personality, mannerisms, surroundings, and so forth. The transformative nature of television was most evident in the 1957 federal election. The Liberals had been in power for more than two decades and were expected to be returned to office. During the campaign Prime Minister Louis St Laurent largely stuck to newspapers and radio. On television he appeared scripted and flat. Conversely, Progressive Conservative leader John Diefenbaker's fiery speeches attracted crowds, and his animated delivery played well on the small screen. The PCs formed a minority government and the next year were re-elected in a landslide. Political parties learned to structure their campaign communications around the leader. From that point forward, the leader's power grew, and that of individual party candidates and parliamentarians diminished.

In 1977, proceedings in the House of Commons were first televised, which profoundly changed legislative debate. Long, unscripted speeches by MPs evolved into scripted soundbites. Party whips began providing the Speaker with lists of MPs scheduled to talk, a practice that makes for smoother television but that is a source of power for the whip over backbenchers. The Cable Public Affairs Channel (CPAC) broadcasts raw footage of proceedings in the Parliament of Canada and associated political programming. Proceedings of provincial and territorial legislatures are televised locally. All of this content is often available online.

Television is adjusting to the digital evolution. Production is expensive and less participatory than any other medium. Programming tends to treat viewers as passive participants who have no ability to shape what is covered. Large television networks are under stress as the multichannel universe expands, as consumers grow accustomed to obtaining content on demand, and as people cancel cable service in favour of online media streaming. Fewer Canadians get their news from the same national news broadcasts as they did a generation ago. Watching suppertime and evening news used to be appointment viewing around which people structured their weeknights. Now, citizens can time shift through satellite TV or a personal video recorder (PVR), or opt to stream video on their own schedule. Whereas the number of Canadians listening to news radio and talk radio is relatively stable, and newspaper websites are growing in popularity, declining numbers are turning to television for news.⁷ Nevertheless, Canadians place considerable trust in traditional mainstream media, and are least confident in other news they obtain from social media.

Digital communications irrevocably changed the fourth estate. In the early 1990s political parties began experimenting with email and basic websites, consisting of static information, low-resolution images, and hyperlinks. This started to erode the mainstream media's control over political information because the Web introduced a cost-efficient means of direct communication that party officials and volunteers could initiate. Even so, in the 2000 Canadian election, many candidates in Canada still did not have a website, nor did many members of Parliament.⁸

Interactivity and content collaboration among users gained steam in the early 2000s. Blogs with feedback forums, news sites with comments pages, file sharing, podcasts, video clips, and social networking were popularized. Today, email, texting, image-rich websites, and social media such as Facebook, Instagram, Twitter, and YouTube are major components of the permanent campaign discussed in Chapter 10. Political news and opinion can be obtained from online-only media such as *The Huffington Post* and *Rabble.ca* and through news aggregators such as *National Newswatch*. The rise of these outlets, and the emergence of citizen reporters, is redefining the fourth estate.

Digital media enable more efficient and more engaging ways of communicating. Political candidates and parliamentarians are expected to respond to issues faster than ever and to post on social media multiple times a day. Journalists must break news more frequently on more platforms. Small political parties, interest groups, and grassroots movements have a low-cost mechanism to stay in touch with their membership and to push their agenda. Citizens interested in politics have a forum for spontaneous and flexible debate. They can locate detailed information on matters ranging from parliamentarians' voting records to the minutiae of legislation. They can potentially attract mainstream

AP Photo/Tim Ireland

Prime Minister Justin Trudeau takes a selfie with spectators after making a speech at Canada House in London, England, in 2015. A politician's personality, mannerisms, and interactions are on display more than ever before now that many citizens have phone cameras and can upload photos and videos within seconds.

media attention by complaining online; mobilize supporters of a cause to an event; send, receive, and discuss breaking information; and quickly upload photos and video to a mass audience. Local and government happenings that otherwise might not attract public attention come to the fore.

The volume of information and compressed timelines affect the quality of political news and nature of public policy. Citizen journalists, bloggers, and other online contributors are typically not professionally trained. They are often ideological and partisan. Rumours, falsehoods, negativity, and hate speech can flourish online. In the past, a citizen who was unhappy with government would author a letter and would wait weeks to receive a well-researched reply; now, the moment something happens, an angry message is sent electronically by someone who expects an immediate response and solution. We live in a world where speed, emotion, visuals, and personal stories take precedence over reason and long-term thinking. Canadians may have access to more political information than ever, but they must be sterner judges of the sources, content, and tone of the messages communicated to them.

Canadian Content

The flood of information from other countries poses an added challenge for Canadian democracy. This is particularly true about news from the United States, which pushes aside Canadian content. Legitimate concern about the so-called Americanization of Canadian politics and culture is longstanding. Canadians rank second worldwide to Americans in how closely they follow American news.[9] Moreover, many Canadians are drawn to American content on entertainment television and streaming media services. They voice strong opinions on social media about the politics of places where they do not live and are not eligible to vote. When Canadian news outlets report on American political events, or run American programming, this reduces the attention paid to domestic public affairs and culture. Canada's Broadcasting Act requires that all domestic radio and television broadcasters—public and private—provide a minimum level of Canadian-produced programming. The challenge for broadcasters competing in a digital media system is to produce Canadian content (CanCon) that will attract enough viewers to justify the considerable costs. A predicament for the federal government is what to do about digital streaming services such as Netflix that, unlike Canadian media companies, avoid Canadian taxes and regulation.

Before Internet streaming, it was broadcast television that brought an influx of American news and entertainment programming to Canada. The federal government responded by implementing stringent new CanCon laws, mandating Canadian broadcasters to carry a proportion of Canadian-made shows. Canadian content is promoted through federal funding agencies including the National Film Board, Telefilm Canada, and the Canadian Television Fund that support Canadian artists and producers. There are foreign-ownership restrictions on Canadian media providers, including newspapers and magazines. Over time, the arrival of the Internet and global telecommunications has made such protectionist measures difficult to maintain, if not obsolete.

Canada's national public broadcaster is acutely aware of the need to evolve in response to changing consumer behaviour. The **Canadian Broadcasting Corporation** (CBC) and its French division, Société Radio-Canada, are funded by the federal government. Their mandate includes insulating Canadian audiences from the cultural influences of American

Canadian Broadcasting Corporation (CBC) A Crown corporation that is Canada's national public broadcaster.

media. The CBC was created based on a recommendation of the 1929 Royal Commission on Radio Broadcasting. The CBC has had a major presence in Canadian broadcasting and news. Its news divisions operate at arm's length from the government and have a duty to reflect perspectives from across Canada. The launch of its 24-hour news channel in 1989 both fed and intensified the demand for political information. Radio-Canada is a major source of information for francophones, especially in Quebec; however, in English Canada the CBC has ceased being a primary source of information or entertainment. *CTV News* long ago eclipsed *CBC News* as the most popular news program. Moreover, CTV and Global own the rights to top American programs, which command higher ratings and higher advertising revenues.

The amount of money allocated to the CBC and Radio-Canada for its Canadian programming is a constant source of debate. The so-called Mother Corp receives over $1 billion annually from the federal government. That public funding is supplemented by advertising revenues generated from the television network and CBC/Radio Canada websites. Its radio programming is commercial-free. Many of those who support the CBC believe the public broadcaster is more likely to investigate matters in the public interest than is a private-sector broadcaster that derives its revenues from commercial advertising. Critics argue that the public broadcaster appeals to a narrow segment of the body of taxpayers who keep it on the air. The government's funding of a competitor frustrates private-sector media organizations, especially those that are struggling financially. Many find it hard to compete with the expanding digital presence of CBC/Radio Canada. In recent years, Liberals have increased the funding amounts, whereas Conservatives have sought efficiencies. Generally speaking, the CBC's strongest advocates are found in the New Democratic Party, and its most vocal critics are affiliated with the Conservative Party.

JHVE Photo/Shutterstock

What do you think is the value of having a national public broadcaster? How well does the CBC deliver that value, particularly when it comes to coverage of Canadian politics? What are the implications for other media of the CBC putting more emphasis on competing in the digital space?

The **Canadian Radio-television and Telecommunications Commission** (CRTC) oversees broadcasting and telecommunications in Canada. It is the body that administers the Broadcasting Act. Its oversight roles include monitoring compliance of anti-spam legislation and defining what constitutes CanCon. The CRTC invites comments on broadcasting licence applications and holds public hearings on the practices of telecommunications carriers. Its regulatory policy requires that telecommunications and broadcasting services are available to Canadians who have hearing, visual, speech and other disabilities. The CRTC plays a special role in promoting the public interest during federal election campaigns. It ensures that broadcasters make an equal amount of airtime available for sale to political parties. Some of that time must be offered during prime viewing periods. Broadcasters that provide free airtime must do so for all parties and candidates. As well, the CRTC maintains the national voter contact registry. Political organizations planning to conduct robocalls during a federal election must inform the CRTC so that information can be added to the registry.

Among the CRTC's concerns is the merger and acquisition of media companies. Media conglomeration results in the same content being shown on multiple platforms and a decline in editorial independence. The narrowing of diverse points of view that results from concentrated ownership is a longstanding concern, dating to at least a 1970 Senate committee (the Davey report) and the 1981 Royal Commission on Newspapers (the Kent Commission). For example, Montreal-based Québecor operates the Sun Media newspaper chain, two major French-language newspapers, the TVA network, TVA publishing, Vidéotron cable and Internet services, and the Archambault music retailer. Other media giants include Bell Media, Postmedia, Rogers Communications, and Shaw Media. The associated disappearance of small media operations reduces the variety of local and ideological perspectives available to Canadians. Moreover, specialist reporters are replaced with multitaskers who are familiar with many topics but are intimately familiar with few. Given the global reach of the Internet, and the economic forces propelling media convergence, it is difficult to imagine how the CRTC can police media content as it has in the past.

It is worth bearing in mind that the recycling of news occurs irrespective of mergers and acquisitions. For instance, a CBC story airs on the radio, is broadcast on TV, is posted online, and is mentioned on social media. Other media outlets may pick up the story with little to no additional investigation. Canadians are exposed to more media stimuli than ever and yet must diversify their media consumption to become fully informed.

Canadian Radio-television and Telecommunications Commission (CRTC) An administrative tribunal that regulates television, radio, Internet, and telephone services.

Canadian Political Journalism

A strong, vibrant democratic system needs a formidable fourth estate. At its best, political journalism delivers factual information about government and politics, as free from bias as possible. The top journalists are relentless in gathering original information. They use all available tools to collect details and fact-check what they uncover. Their reports are presented in an even-handed manner that exhibit no signs of partisanship. High-quality Canadian political journalism tackles important public-policy issues that might otherwise not come to light. Some examples of journalistic excellence include:[10]

- the Canadian Press investigating the sexual trauma of children in Indigenous communities;
- CBC Edmonton disclosing how a wealthy businessman secured a multi-million-dollar government grant for his private alternative health foundation;

- CBC Nova Scotia finding that black people in Halifax were three times more likely than white people to be street checked by police;
- *Global News* exposing problems with the federal government rejecting residency applications from persons with disabilities;
- the *London Free Press* uncovering problems in the justice system after a man died in solitary confinement; and
- the *Toronto Star* questioning the health and safety practices of companies using temp agency workers.

These journalists and their editors are mindful that a single minor error can undermine an entire news report. They recognize the importance of accuracy and of independently choosing which topics to examine. Their stories may be raised by the Official Opposition during Question Period and generate reaction on social media. This in turn puts a policy issue on the public agenda and prompts a government response.

Many news media organizations designate personnel to monitor the daily activities of legislative assemblies. Each legislature has a **press gallery** comprising accredited journalists who are assigned to cover government business and legislative proceedings. They scrutinize government, filter political information, and report about election campaigns. Members have access to reserved seating in the viewing gallery and office space in the legislative precinct. They are granted special access to walk around some areas of the legislature so that they may interact with public officials. Journalists busily live-tweet about Question Period and seek comments from politicians afterwards. The dwindling number of members of Canada's press galleries (Figure 11.2) reflects broader trends of media conglomeration, digitization, diminished coverage of localized politics, and the shrinking presence of newspapers. The situation is acute in small provinces where there sometimes are not enough political reporters to cover government announcements.[11] In Nova Scotia, the premier's office sets up a microphone after some cabinet meetings so that journalists can call in to ask questions because so few of them are present. There are consequences for Canada's mediated democracy when the fourth estate has to do more with less.

Canadians place a remarkable level of trust in their news media. Public-opinion surveys indicate that a strong majority of them believe that the media does a good job with respect to treating political issues fairly, reporting news about government leaders and officials, presenting news accurately, and paying attention to the most important news events.[12] Canadians feel strongly that news organizations should never favour a political party. Their confidence in journalism is considerably higher than that of citizens in many other countries, including France, the United Kingdom, and the United States. As well, compared to other places, Canadians are not as fragmented into political media silos that lead to them having vastly different information or disagreeing about basic facts.[13] Nevertheless, Canadian news coverage could be better, and some aspects are worsening.

The media industry does not relay political information in a neutral manner with an emphasis on facts. The media sensationalizes the news in order to attract public interest and generate increased audience statistics. Political news is packaged with competing points of view, builds stories with dramatic arcs, and focuses on the personalities of political actors. The old adages that "if it bleeds, it leads" and that journalists should "comfort the afflicted and afflict the comfortable" influence how political information is reported. The negative tone of political reporting, combined with the intensity of partisan attacks, turns many people off politics altogether. This is believed to be a contributing factor to public disenchantment with politicians and lower voter turnout in elections.

press gallery
Political journalists who monitor government business and who personally observe proceedings in the legislature.

Reasons for the decline in voter turnout are discussed in Chapter 10, on elections: see the section Voter Turnout in Canadian Elections, beginning on page 359.

Figure 11.2 | Number of Press Gallery Members, Ottawa and the Provinces

Source: Data from http://j-source.ca/article/shrinking-press-galleries-leave-little-time-for-journalists-to-dig-deep/

The media's enduring quest to make politics interesting changes the style of news coverage. **Infotainment** is news and information delivered in an entertaining way. The news media blends opinion with facts in an effort to explain events and educate audiences in an engaging fashion. They make use of political pundits who draw on their own experiences with party politics and government to offer colour commentary. Members of the press gallery share their behind-the-scenes observations and impressions. Politicians respond to interest in personalities and everyday life by tweeting photos of their stylish clothing, Halloween costumes, selfies, family, pets, travel, and so forth. Other forms of infotainment

infotainment
The delivery of news about government and politics as a form of entertainment programming.

include political satire, such as *This Hour Has 22 Minutes,* and human interest conversations with politicians on *Tout le Monde en Parle* in Quebec. In his book *Breaking News? Politics, Journalism and Infotainment on Quebec Television*, political scientist Frédérick Bastien examines whether infotainment unduly simplifies serious political issues, and if it cheapens Canadian democratic discourse.[14] In fact, he finds that infotainment has underappreciated positive effects on democracy, most notably educating people about political news who would otherwise pay little attention. Nevertheless, the blending of humour with analysis of political affairs invariably contributes to the framing of political parties as combatants.

One example of a lack of impartiality and independent thinking is the tendency of media to all focus on the same issue. Pack journalism and groupthink are magnified when an issue is salacious or trending online. The homogeneity of coverage adds to problems of information convergence. Sometimes every media outlet on every platform seems to be obsessing with the same story. These episodes can be **focusing events** whereby everybody in society is paying attention to one dominant topic that demands a government response. Natural disasters, terrorism, health scares, and other forms of public crisis are so concerning that considerable media resources are devoted to covering these stories. Other times the public may disagree with the media's assessment of what warrants their attention. Many Canadians feel that the media's tendency to pile on is unfair when a leader makes a mistake or gaffe.[15] As we know from agenda-setting theory, this is a problem because it inhibits attention paid to other policy issues, and is especially troublesome when Canadian media is captivated by American politics.

A measure of independence is introduced by reporting on the results of scientific public-opinion surveys. These data assist journalists with understanding what issues matter to Canadians and which political parties or leaders are preferred. Unfortunately, polling data contributes to journalists approaching politics as a sporting contest. A strategic filter is applied by the media to political decisions and events with a view to declaring winners and losers. **Horse-race coverage** results when the media report on who is winning or losing in the latest polling data. They discuss which political party or leader is ahead or behind. They speculate on the reasons and whether that standing is likely to grow, shrink, or hold. Opinion polls guide editorial decisions about which issues to prioritize and which people to ignore. Horse-race coverage may be informed by anything that indicates the public mood, such as media straw polls, call-ins to talk radio, letters to the editor, social media conversation, and public protests. Other issues fall lower down the media agenda.

The horse-race frame reduces everything that political actors do to a conversation about who wins and who loses. So, rather than emphasizing the substance of public policy, media coverage might concentrate on declaring a victor. Every announcement and gaffe is interpreted as having implications for the party's popularity. The treatment of politics as a contest among opposing teams extends to incorporate the use of war and sports metaphors. Media proclaim that political parties are on an election war footing. Party caucuses are described as teams and the speaker in a legislature as a referee. Competitive ridings are known as battleground constituencies. Door-to-door campaigning and nationwide advertising campaigns may be referred to as the ground war and air war, respectively. After leaders' debates, the media ask who won and who lost, and which leader scored a knockout punch. Politicians and political operatives often join in the metaphor, as well, referring to their campaign headquarters as bunkers or war rooms. In fact, the word "campaign" is borrowed from military terminology, where it was originally used to describe a set of operations conducted over open land. Of course, political parties feed perceptions of an ongoing competition when they criticize each other, and are only too happy to exploit an opponent's mistakes.

focusing event
A public crisis that is so significant that it commands all news attention for an extended period of time.

horse-race coverage
Media attention focused on who is leading in public opinion.

The winners-and-losers narrative of the political horse race matters because media coverage informs public opinion and political power. The perspective that the media and political actors present about a subject is known as a frame. **Framing** is the manner in which a person, organization, or issue is publicly communicated. For instance, knowledge about past events informs the way that a current news event is covered, or a story is presented as conflict between political opponents rather than providing an analysis of the policy they are debating. Framing simplifies the presentation of information by packaging it in a manner that is familiar or relatable. It reflects the communicator's ideological bias and may be used unintentionally.[16] A typical framing practice is for the media to show images of a smiling politician when the accompanying story is positive and to depict the politician in an unflattering manner when the story is negative. Politicians who win an election, particularly leaders who form a government for the first time, enjoy a honeymoon period of positive press coverage for weeks and months afterwards. Negative frames are especially likely when the party is down in the polls.

Media framing can establish and reinforce an existing narrative about a politician or party. It can involve the skewed use of words, headlines, tone, information, still images, or video. Even an unflattering camera angle constitutes framing. Perhaps the most famous case of framing in Canada occurred during the 1974 federal election campaign. Progressive Conservative Party leader Robert Stanfield had a staid public image. One of Stanfield's handlers began tossing a football around with him on a North Bay airport tarmac. A Canadian Press photographer was present and took a roll of photos. Most of the photographs documented the PC leader throwing and catching the football. The next day, the photo that appeared in newspapers across Canada, including on the front page of *The Globe and Mail*, was of a distraught Stanfield at the one moment that he fumbled a catch. That iconic photo continues to be held up as the framing bias exhibited by the media and a reason why political handlers attempt to dissuade politicians from unscripted media opportunities. Framing is so common that every party and every leader can point to examples where an editorial decision led to their being portrayed in an unfair manner.

framing
The shaping of information so that communication recipients will interpret it in a manner that is advantageous to the sender.

THE CANADIAN PRESS/Doug Ball

PC leader Robert Stanfield drops the ball in this infamous photo (second from the right) that made *The Globe and Mail*'s front page during the 1974 election campaign. Other photos taken by the same photographer showed Stanfield catching the ball. Why would a newspaper editor have chosen to use this one? Would a photo of the more dashing Pierre Trudeau dropping a football have been treated the same way, or have the same impact? What is the lesson for today's politicians, given that citizens have cameras on their smartphones? What would happen if Justin Trudeau or an opposition leader were to fumble a football during a campaign?

Research suggests that certain segments of society are adversely affected by framing and how those citizens are represented in the media.[17] Indigenous people, women, racialized minorities, LGBTQ2+, youth, the elderly, persons with disabilities, some religions, some social classes, and others are treated differently. Their voices tend to receive less media attention and the media portrays them as outside the norm. Coverage is erratic and shallow. The media is drawn to extremists and protesters who do not accurately reflect the groups they are advocating for. The norm is that politics is framed by male characteristics; for instance, the use of sports and war metaphors apply masculinity to politics. This can limit the inclusiveness of the public sphere for women in particular. Yet in broader society young men are portrayed as troublemakers, particularly if they are not white. In Canadian politics, more attention is paid to metropolitan issues than rural ones, in part because most media centres are located in capital cities. The way that Canadians and political issues are framed matters to where their concerns are situated on the public agenda.

The topic of media injustices is a growing area of study. In her book *Ms Prime Minister: Gender, Media, and Leadership*, political scientist Linda Trimble finds that a woman leader's private life is more likely to be examined, and that the media is prone to mentioning gender when referring to women politicians.[18] Likewise, in *Framed: Media and the Coverage of Race in Canadian Politics*, Erin Tolley establishes that whiteness is treated as neutral in Canadian media coverage, whereas visible minorities' concerns are outside the mainstream.[19] Still, they and others believe that media treatment is improving, and is not as biased as some would have us believe. Diversity and representation are topics we explore in Chapter 13.

Digital Democracy and Transparency

Citizens connect with their elected officials in other ways, besides the mainstream media. The media is joined by governments and politicians in adapting to changes in digital communications. **E-democracy** holds the potential to democratize political decision-making and increase public engagement in politics. Existing political activities are enhanced by using the Internet to involve citizens in policy discussion and to share information. It connects citizens with candidates, elected officials, journalists, and interest-group leaders. E-democracy is a means of providing ready access to political platforms, of discussing political ideas, and of building social capital. But for all of its potential, in practice, e-democracy provides less social cohesion than optimists hoped. Arguably, it introduced unprecedented acrimony to political discourse, as parties, candidates, and interest groups use the technology to narrowcast their often divisive messages to specific segments of the population, a practice we will consider later in this chapter. In this way, digital media can bring together like-minded citizens who reinforce each other's views and denigrate opponents. Furthermore, e-democracy changed methods of journalism, as cultivating inside sources to obtain original information has been displaced by monitoring the social media feeds of political actors.

Digital communications technology enables members of diverse communities to connect with each other. An obvious mechanism is for activists to rally people to a protest in order to attract mainstream media attention for their cause (for more on this, see Chapter 12). Less visible is how digital communications brings together people regardless of the population size, geography, finances, or technological expertise. For instance, recent immigrants obtain information from online news sites, blogs, social media and email

e-democracy
The use of information communication technologies to get citizens involved in politics.

listserves that is not available through mainstream Canadian media.[20] This information need not originate locally. Politicians take notice and some of them expressly communicate in languages other than English or French. For that matter, all Canadians can obtain information from around the world, leading to some of them rethinking their identity and the nature of their citizenship.

Digital communication has transformed how government services are delivered. **E-government** involves the use of websites, email, videoconferencing, and social media to supplement the use of call centres and electronic kiosks. It expands the ability of government to be available around the clock and re-shapes the way that government bodies interact with each other. Citizens with access to a computer or mobile device can readily obtain accurate information from government bodies in any jurisdiction. They can pay taxes and fees online, obtain forms, and submit applications. The Government of Canada's main website (www.canada.ca) and its Service Canada site (www.servicecanada.gc.ca) are prominent examples. Among the top government website searches are information about the Canada Pension Plan, employment insurance, the GST/HST credit, jobs, old age security, tax documents, records of employment, social insurance numbers, and birth certificates.[21]

E-government encompasses the online availability of government information, services, announcements, employment opportunities, and other programs. Digital communications provide support services to businesses, are used to attract investment, and inform business operators about regulations, permits, and licensing and zoning matters. Governments use digital communications internally with employees to make information available about internal job competitions, human resources policies, and special initiatives, often through a password-protected intranet. As well, interactions occur among public servants in different jurisdictions, enabling policy coordination among bureaucrats in federal, provincial, and territorial departments. SharePoint sites and videoconferences allow governments to consult with each other, to gather information about laws and best practices, and to share data.

The Government of Canada is pushing forward e-government in ways that few Canadians are aware of. It is seeking to improve how business interacts with government, how Canadians access tax information, and how immigration processing works, for instance. The Canadian Digital Service (https://digital.canada.ca) is a public organization that helps the federal government design digital services. Projects have ranged from an online tool for military veterans to locate benefits to an e-briefing app that replaces traditional paper briefing binders used by ministers.

Even so, government's use of digital communications can be clunky. Social media is used in a bureaucratic manner that is sometimes misaligned with how Canadians engage online. Government communication is rarely spontaneous. Months and weeks ahead of a policy announcement, departments prepare social media plans that identify key messages and include draft tweets and posts. In the federal government, these plans can involve dozens of people proofing the draft content, and time is needed to translate it into the other official language to enable simultaneous release in English and French. Political staff in the minister's office are required to sign off on many messages before anything goes live. A similar level of preparation goes into photos and videos. A Canadian who sees a post on a minister's or a department's Facebook, Instagram, Twitter or other social media account may not realize how much planning went into it.

In contrast, Canadian politicians routinely use social media as part of everyday communication. Political parties require that their election candidates have a digital presence.

e-government
The interactive use of information communication technologies to deliver public programs and services.

Each party provides technical support such as webpage templates. Once elected, most members of a legislature carry on using social media, though sometimes their accounts are maintained by staff. Their posts are a mix of information about government announcements, photographs of events, social media shareables created by party personnel, interactions with the public, and peeks into their personal lives. Occasionally, controversy occurs about an inappropriate social media post. During election campaigns, political parties scrutinize candidates' digital footprint for anything offensive, and opponents call on candidates to resign over past remarks. Negativity on social media is a considerable problem, as we observe later in this chapter. The most significant downside of e-democracy and e-government is the security risk (see Chapter 14).

Generally speaking, the openness and accessibility that politicians portray on social media is largely a mirage. This is especially true for members of the governing party who hold appointed office. A safeguard against government secrecy and corruption is **access to information** legislation, also known as freedom of information. Access to information requires, by law, that the government make its internal documents available to the public upon request. The legislation improves government transparency by allowing citizens to obtain data that would otherwise be unavailable. To curtail nuisance inquiries, a nominal application charge (e.g., a $5 fee) normally must accompany each request, and further charges may be required if the request exceeds an internal research time limit. Applications are routinely filed by opposition parties, journalists, and public advocates seeking to understand government decisions and to exploit discrepancies with a minister's explanation of the matter. To ensure impartiality, the identity of the applicant is not widely disclosed within the public service, unless permission to do so is explicitly granted.

Public expectations of government transparency are increasing along with the volume of access to information requests. Many government bodies proactively post information online through e-government initiatives. The federal government's Open Data project makes hundreds of thousands of datasets publicly available online at http://open.canada.ca. Governments across Canada post online their responses to all completed access-to-information requests so that others may benefit from the disclosed data. Nevertheless, governments are criticized for not being sufficiently transparent, and for obstructing requests.

Access to information is an exceptional tool that has considerable room for improvement. Some internal files understandably cannot be publicly disclosed. For instance, the Department of Defence cannot release secret information about the Canadian military without sparking public-safety concerns, and many provincial governments cannot disclose information that may compromise their ability to conduct intergovernmental relations. The political executive needs to be free to deliberate a full range of policy options without fear of public sanction. Consequently, cabinet documents, draft briefing notes, and anything else that is prepared for ministers is often ruled off-limits. So, too, are many materials prepared for negotiations with other governments. This can be a problem, because released documents are heavily redacted, and requests can take months longer to complete than the legislation allows. As well, mindful that anything written might become public, some government personnel elect to transmit information via text message, private email accounts, peer-to-peer messaging or on USB sticks rather than via government email. They may also opt to deliver verbal briefings instead of written reports.

access to information
A legal requirement that governments release information upon request, subject to certain restrictions.

Briefing Notes

Access to Information Research

Opposition parties and interest groups draw on access-to-information research to obtain critical insights about government decision-making. Their formal requests generate internal materials such as briefing notes, draft legislation, working reports, PowerPoint decks, and email exchanges among public servants. Students can enhance their own research by drawing on completed requests that are posted on government websites. A student who is especially industrious can file an original request at minimal or no cost. Sometimes access-to-information coordinators will waive the filing fee when the research is for educational purposes. Some governments do not charge a fee at all. The biggest obstacle is often time: an original request takes weeks if not months to be fulfilled, with no guarantee that the generated information will be useful.

Despite the advent of e-government, there is a sense that the Canadian government is becoming more secretive, regardless of which party is in charge. International reports rank Canada poorly on its commitment to upholding access-to-information principles.[22] Despite the fundamental freedoms outlined in section 2(b) of the Charter, Canadian journalism fares poorly in international measures of press freedom, for reasons such as Quebec police spying on journalists to identify their confidential sources.[23] Furthermore, the Open Data project bombards people with quantitative data which do little to assist them with understanding the rationale for policy decisions.

The Open Data project illustrates the mixed success that e-government has in this country. While the project makes an abundance of information available, public servants may overlook that not everyone can readily access and navigate the Internet, including Canadians with certain disabilities. The reduction of personnel and the outsourcing of technical expertise can result in service disruptions. Technology exists for citizens to have greater interactivity with political elites and public servants. Yet, there is a general reluctance to invite feedback on public policy, and governments prefer to use digital communications for one-way transmission of information to target audiences.

Political Communication Tactics

Political journalism and communication are both exceptionally helpful and deeply flawed. There are millions of routine exchanges each day among people in the political, public, private, and non-profit sectors. Far more goes well in everyday communication exchanges than goes wrong. Nevertheless, an astute citizen ought to be mindful of some of the many ways that political actors in a mediated democracy seek to manipulate communication to their own advantage.

As mentioned, the fourth estate's dominant role as the purveyor of political information is under stress. The erosion of the newspaper industry, the conglomeration of media outlets, the rise of citizen journalists, and the availability of free information online create a perfect storm to reduce the mainstream media's clout. This is exacerbated by government elites who perceive media elites as opponents rather than partners in the dissemination of political messages. Prime Minister Stephen Harper's tussle with the Canadian parliamentary press gallery is a jarring example. In an effort to control the agenda, Harper and his ministers refused to participate in scrums organized by the press gallery unless their political staffers got to pick which journalists could ask questions. Many gallery members decried his demands and refused to attend the prime minister's news conferences. Those who acquiesced, including many local media outlets across the country, benefited from exclusive access. Upon taking office, Prime Minister Trudeau reinstated press conferences in the National Press Theatre and had better relations with the media. Yet many accessibility concerns persist. The prime minister's communications staff set up a microphone situated away from the cabinet room and choose which ministers exiting a cabinet meeting should be scrummed by journalists. Government personnel email statements in response to some interview requests. Journalists are not permitted to document the interactions between ministers and donors at party fundraising events. On international trips, the prime minister is not as accessible to Canadian media as they would like. It is a similar story across the country. It seems that no matter who is in power, first ministers seek to control information, while opposition leaders label the government as undemocratic.

Politicians are acutely aware of the declining relevance of professional journalism. Government officials no longer rely on the mainstream media to deliver the government message. Digital communication is used by political elites to bypass the filter of the mainstream media and provide information directly to citizens. This allows the elites to carry out a political agenda regardless of appropriate public scrutiny. Emails, texts, and tweets

THE CANADIAN PRESS/Fred Chartrand

Prime Minister Stephen Harper exiting the House of Commons after Question Period in February 2007. Harper and members of his government were known for refusing to hold news scrums organized by the press gallery unless their political staffers could choose which journalists could ask questions. As a result, many members of the press refused to attend the prime minister's news conferences. What obligations, if any, do first ministers and the members of their government have to the press gallery?

are sent to supporters and followers, selective information is posted on websites and social media, and a stream of government-produced photos and video present the leader in a positive light. Legislative debates and public remarks, including social media posts, are heavily scripted. Sometimes only photojournalists are permitted to attend events and thus no questions may be asked of politicians. Interviews are occasionally staged with a friendly moderator before an assembled audience to create the illusion that the leader is being scrutinized. Some academics label Canada a publicity state in reference to the government's emphasis on promotion and persuasion rather than information.[24]

The governing party, of course, would say that this criticism is overblown. Governments are far more transparent and information reaches far more citizens more frequently than at any other time in history. Journalists have unrealistic demands for speedy replies to their queries and represent a risk of torquing information. Government officials take longer to scrutinize what is publicly released because of the pressure of mistakes that reverberate around social media. The PMO's distribution of photographs and video of the prime minister responds to public interest. Finally, the media thrive on conflict and drama, so it makes sense for the government to seek to limit opportunities that stir criticism. Better to create the perception of a powerful leader in control than of a weak one presiding over instability, it is reasoned.

A number of public-relations (PR) tools are employed in the political arena. The communication activities of governments and political actors are largely designed to accommodate the media's needs. The media's appetite for fresh and interesting content while operating under tighter financial constraints leads to their accepting what are known as **information subsidies**. Content that is created and delivered by political actors free of charge is more likely to be reproduced. Information subsidies include news releases with prepared quotes, social media posts, and packaged text, still images, audio, and video distributed digitally. News conferences and other staged photo ops are among the other forms. All of these activities are a blurred version of reality. Repeating these pre-packaged messages without a filter can be tempting to media outlets facing time pressures and dwindling resources. The most skilled political communicators are able to design information subsidies that are brief and clear enough that the media will use them unaltered. Customizing information to fit the media's needs helps to ensure that the message gets across as intended.

information subsidy
Free packaged content provided to the media in a manner that is designed to meet their needs.

Briefing Notes

The Planning of Social Media Posts

The free-wheeling nature of social media does not align well with the measured and controlled culture of the public sector. Spur-of-the-moment posts from politicians can have unintended impacts on public policy, for instance, and sometimes their remarks have caused offence. That is why the social media posts from government officials and politicians often involve multiple stages of planning. In the Government of Canada, a single tweet can pass through layers of approvals processes and must also be translated so that it is posted in both official languages. The approved content is rolled out on a schedule to align with a larger government communications calendar. Political parties and caucus research staff participate in planning meetings to come up with ideas for infographics and memes that are then circulated to politicians for posting. What appear to be folksy and spontaneous posts by politicians are often well-orchestrated messages drafted by communications professionals and vetted by senior officials.

Another PR tool is to partner with a friendly journalist who gets to break a news story on the condition that the frame reflects the wishes of the person who provided the information. For instance, a senior political staffer may speak off the record with a sympathetic member of the press gallery, who in turn files a favourable story. The individual who provided the information is identified in the story only as an unnamed "source." This quid pro quo agreement is a preferred tactic to control the timing of news that was going to come out at an otherwise inopportune time. It is particularly helpful to gauge the public response to a potential policy decision. A **trial balloon** is an idea floated in the media by a high-ranking official, usually anonymously, who wants to understand how the idea will be publicly received. Examples could include relaying that the government is considering a study of electronic voting or that it is thinking about appointing a parliamentary secretary to head a new anti-racism initiative. The non-committal practice allows the organization to see which way the political winds are blowing and potentially adjust course. A trial balloon is different than a leak, which is the unauthorized release of potentially damaging information, and whose source is a concerned whistleblower or perhaps someone who is disgruntled.

A related PR tool is **spin**. When framing is practised by skilled political communicators, complex matters are simplified in a purposeful manner that fits the sender's position and obscures damaging information. The act of spinning a message is more complex than playing with words. It means researching what the public and media want, and how they want to hear it, in an effort to design the most effective strategies for winning elections, meeting public-policy goals, and achieving other objectives. Sometimes it involves providing key messages irrespective of what was asked in order to avoid addressing a difficult question. A sizeable industry of communication professionals is devoted to shaping public opinion through careful messaging and rhetoric. Spin doctors go further by manipulating words to deceive the public. Spin and avoidance are routinely practised during Question Period; an example of the prime minister doing this in an exchange with the leader of the opposition appears on page 197 of Chapter 6. All politicians practise spin in some manner. The fourth estate plays a significant role in deciphering and presenting the spin to Canadians.

Government communications are on the edge of being political **propaganda**. Propaganda is sinister, for it involves the intentional use of biased communications as part of a power struggle, and typically employs images intended to provoke an emotional response.[25] There are different types of propaganda ranging from provocative messages about public policies to psychological brainwashing. The mildest form of propaganda involves framing and counter-frames through word choices. For example, government personnel talk about investing instead of spending while critics refer to cuts rather than reductions. Environmentalists advocate putting a price on pollution that is denounced as a carbon tax by opponents. A similar war of words occurs over the world's oldest profession: referring to prostitutes as workers in the sex trade industry conveys a political statement about the practice's moral and legal legitimacy. Propaganda escalates into a grey territory when governments deliberately obscure or withhold information, such as intentionally omitting inconvenient facts from a news release, or liberally interpreting access-to-information legislation in order to redact most of the content in disclosed documents. Political parties practise grey propaganda when they make unsubstantiated claims about their opponents and run hard-hitting advertising campaigns that use powerful imagery and music. At the extreme, propagandist regimes operate a totalitarian state, whereby the messages of

trial balloon
A potential course of action that is reported by the media so that decision-makers can examine the reaction.

spin
The media relations tactic of providing information in a decidedly one-sided manner in order to persuade.

propaganda
One-sided persuasive communication that communicates falsehoods by virtue of its selective exclusion of truths.

Inside Canadian Politics

Are PMO Photos and Videos an Act of Transparency or of Propaganda?

The prime minister's website and social-media accounts reveal behind-the-scenes daily activities. Photographs and video clips are documentary footage compiled by the prime minister's photographer who is granted exclusive access. They provide information about the prime minister's busy itinerary that the mainstream media is not in the habit of reporting—at least, not in a cohesive manner: attending public events, meeting with cabinet ministers, announcing spending commitments, touring the country, shaking hands with citizens, backstage private moments with celebrities, personal moments with family members, and so on. The flattering images of the PM are unquestionably one-sided and are intended to facilitate sharing via social media. The exclusivity and visual appeal of the images make them tempting information subsidies for the fourth estate.

DISCUSSION ITEM

The prime minister's online presence is carefully managed to project a positive brand to the broader public.

VOX POP

What value do Canadians receive for public funds being used to finance the production of photos and video about the prime minister? What are the advantages and disadvantages of the media drawing upon this type of information subsidy?

party elites are omnipresent and free speech is a crime. In this context, the propaganda employed in Canada is routine politics, and sometimes a hallmark of free speech. Nevertheless, these actions do warrant scrutiny.

As mentioned in Chapter 10, these and other communications practices are components of what is commonly known as the **permanent campaign**. This is related to the game frame whereby political parties, knowing that the media is judging them, try to win every single legislative debate, social media tussle, fundraising campaign, and just about any other contest. Consequently, activities that were once restricted to the official campaign period are practised and honed between elections. Public resources are used to convince Canadians that the government's decisions are good ones and to prop up the governing party. Timeworn tactics include delivering good-news budgets in election years, re-announcing government spending initiatives, and using the free mailing privileges accorded to members of the legislature. This is in addition to image-management practices, such as placing an array of supporters behind the speaker at a media event, or using party colours on non-partisan government websites.

Advertising is a controversial aspect of permanent campaigning. In theory, government advertising should relay information about policies, programs, services, and public

permanent campaign
The practice of electioneering outside of an election period, especially by leveraging government resources.

advisories in a factual and non-partisan manner. In practice, government advertising often conveys information in a way that props up the governing party. Indeed, government advertising has a sordid history of being used for partisan purposes. There are checks in place to reduce the possibility of partisanship in the content of government-funded advertising. At the federal level, the planning process, from strategic conception to post-campaign evaluation, is designed to involve many organizations that are required to give their approval (see Figure 11.3). But since cabinet is responsible for the overall strategic direction of the government, and since senior political staffers are involved in both the initiation and approval of advertising programs, government advertising often appears to do little more than support a partisan agenda. Many governments have been accused of advertising to enhance their public standing on the pretext of educating the citizenry about new programs and policies. This leads to concerns that government advertising is a misuse of public resources. Some provinces have legislation to reduce the possibility of partisan government advertising and engage public servants to scrutinize advertisements before being released. Others have laws preventing governments from advertising in the lead up to an election campaign.

sponsorship scandal
An affair in which Liberal advertising agencies received public funds for work that was never performed.

One case of inappropriate government advertising stands out. The **sponsorship scandal** began in the wake of the 1995 Quebec sovereignty referendum. The federal government launched a sponsorship program to win back disaffected Quebecers. The program used advertising and other communications to raise awareness in Quebec of the benefits of federalism. *The Globe and Mail* filed access-to-information requests to obtain government contracts. In 2002 the newspaper reported that over $500,000 was spent on a report that could not be located. The finding prompted journalists, the opposition, and others to probe for more information. The auditor general determined that nearly $100 million in advertising contracts had been awarded to agencies that employed or were

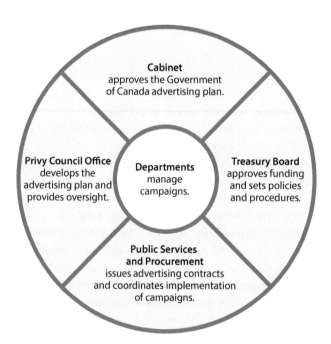

Figure 11.3 | Roles and Responsibilities of Federal Organizations in Government Advertising

Source: Adapted from *2016 to 2017 Annual Report on Government of Canada Advertising Activities*, Public Services and Procurement Canada (PSPC) 2018 - Catalogue Number: P100-2E-PDF, p. 21.

headed by Liberal Party members—often for little or no work. Public funds were being used to line the pockets of party supporters and the governing party itself. The controversy reached such a state that in 2004, the Liberal government, then led by Paul Martin, struck the Commission of Inquiry into the Sponsorship Program and Advertising Activities to investigate. Retired Justice John Gomery headed a team who called former prime minister Jean Chrétien and sitting prime minister Martin to testify. The Gomery report formed the basis of a number of policy and process changes, including the federal Accountability Act, and it sparked the criminal convictions of a senior public servant and the operators of some Quebec advertising agencies. The sponsorship scandal shows why accountability measures and transparency processes are needed. Without limitations, governing political parties may be tempted to exploit government resources for their own advantage, and engage in permanent campaigning behaviour that goes against the public interest.

In addition to government advertising, the public is exposed to advertising funded by political parties, which used to be confined to the official election campaign. Like so many other electioneering practices, party-sponsored advertising now occurs during the inter-election period, particularly after a new party leader is chosen and as an election approaches. Party advertising is more common during minority governments when the possibility of a snap election looms. Political advertising may increase citizen engagement and voter turnout by generating awareness among citizens about politics. It increases perceptions that more is at stake and gives partisans a reason to mobilize supporters to the polls. Furthermore, the considerable expense of advertising motivates political parties to connect directly with supporters, from whom they may request donations. The competitive nature of political advertising is evidence of the lengths that political parties will go to in order to promote their point of view and attract voter support.

Public-Opinion Research, Political Marketing, and Message Discipline

Political communication and public-policy decisions must take into account public opinion. Even a political party interested in catering only to its membership is concerned about how partisan opinions differ from those of the broader population. All political and governmental organizations monitor the news media and social media. This information can be collected with little effort or expense. However, what leads in the news or what is trending on social media is not an accurate reflection of public opinion, including when it is part of horse-race coverage.

Governments, well-funded political parties and interest groups, and some think tanks hire professional research companies to compile public-opinion data. Qualitative and quantitative **public-opinion research** helps them devise ways to improve the delivery of government programs and services. They avail of public-opinion polls to monitor issues that matter to Canadians. The media, as we have seen, tend to use polling data for horse-race coverage and to identify whether government and political parties are behaving in a manner that is in line with the general public's preferences. Political parties use opinion data as a form of strategic intelligence that can guide them to victory and avoid mistakes. This information helps with understanding where Canadians stand on issues and with assessing efforts to influence public opinion. The federal government in particular is a big consumer of public-opinion research. It uses focus groups to test policy ideas and communication concepts, and commissions opinion surveys to inform decisions (see Table 11.1).

public-opinion research
The systematic collection of people's views and attitudes.

Table 11.1   Quantitative and Qualitative Public-Opinion Research Tools

	Quantitative Research	**Qualitative Research**
Most common tool	Opinion surveys: the administration of a questionnaire to a representative sample of a population	Focus groups: the moderation of discussions with small meetings of 8–12 recruited people
Purpose	To obtain a statistically reliable snapshot of opinions	To obtain a deep understanding of attitudes from select cohorts
How data are used	To engage in a statistical analysis of a dataset and apply conclusions to the larger population	To consider the feelings, language, and ideas expressed by participants to inform generalizations
Limitations	Difficult to obtain a deep understanding of public attitudes; caller ID and mobile phones are resulting in lower response rates; online surveys may produce questionable results	Requires considerable advance planning; produces highly subjective data; is expensive; takes longer than surveys to administer; involves travel
Examples	• Client satisfaction survey • Online research panel • Survey assessing effectiveness of an advertising campaign	• Focus testing of radio and print ads prior to launch • Group reactions to political messaging, including speeches and terminology • Online group experiments to test brand adjustments

pollster

A senior employee of a research company who oversees the administration of public-opinion surveys.

The presidents and vice-presidents of polling firms are ubiquitous in Canadian public affairs. **Pollsters** are regularly in the news disclosing the results of their firm's latest opinion survey and privately may counsel the leaders of political parties and interest groups. Technological change, in particular computer-assisted interviewing and online panels, means that polls are affordable and commonplace. In addition to compiling quantitative (i.e., numerical) data, pollsters offer deeper insights obtained through qualitative research methods such as focus groups, which are used to test advertising and policy ideas (see Table 11.1). Examples of major public-opinion research firms in Canada include Abacus Data, EKOS, Environics, Forum, Ipsos, Léger, Nanos Research, and Pollara. Their training and use of social science research methods allow pollsters to speak with a detached credibility that distinguishes them from most political commentators. The validity of their horse-race polls are tested against final election results. Most of the time their survey forecasts are accurate within the stated margin of error. Occasionally, the pollsters get it wrong, for reasons that include difficulty surveying citizens who do not have landline telephones and the inability to predict how motivated a party's supporters are to show up to vote.

As with advertising, the potential exists for partisan use of government-funded opinion research and the awarding of contracts to party supporters. To curtail this possibility, departments that intend to invest in public-opinion research must observe standardized procedures, including subjecting the project to a competitive bidding process, and must consider the input of specialists within the public service. As well, according to the internal policies of some governments, commissioned research reports must be made publicly available online within a determined period. By comparison, the public-opinion research conducted by political parties and advocacy groups is under no such transparency obligation.

Public-opinion research plays a significant role in political campaigns. In *Shopping for Votes: How Politicians Choose Us and We Choose Them*, journalist Susan Delacourt describes the evolution of Canadian political parties' use of sales and marketing techniques.[26] She chronicles the history of Canadian consumerism and democracy and examines how, over time, business marketing practices entered the realm of Canadian politics.

These practices are founded on the principle that political parties must research the marketplace of political consumers and shape their products and communications to meet voters' needs and wants. In practice, however, political elites use research data to inform ways to promote what matters to themselves in a manner that is most likely to generate public support. As well, business marketing cannot be seamlessly transferred to politics. Among the limitations are that politicians are human beings who are not malleable like a product. Still, the application of marketing to politics is transformative.

Political marketing encompasses political actors drawing on market intelligence to adjust their product offering and communications to reflect public needs and wants. More commonly, political marketing is used to refer to a strategic mix of marketing-related and communications activities in politics. Whereas political parties once campaigned largely on a constituency basis in the early twentieth century, a regional basis in the mid-1900s, and a pan-Canadian basis at the close of the millennium, parties now target their appeals to specific groups of individuals scattered across Canada. Political actors communicate directly with citizens through specialty publications or television channels, email lists, and social media. **Narrowcasting** is used to maximize the efficiency of communicating with the slivers of the electorate who are likely to respond to a particular message. Opinion research is gathered to divide the population into groups and understand their attitudes, behaviours, interests, lifestyle, and media-consumption habits. Media planning data such as detailed audience ratings statistics, combined with internal party database information about supporters, are scrutinized to identify the most cost-effective advertising opportunities to reach the identified segments. This mainstream media data is supplemented, and increasingly replaced by, data analytics that draw on social media use. For instance, the federal Conservative Party identifies fans of hockey, football, and curling as potential supporters. Rather than advertising on programming that is watched by a broad cross-section of citizens, such as the evening news, they concentrate their advertising budget on programs and digital-media sites favoured by those sports fans. This is reinforced by other forms of narrowcasting such as direct mail, email blasts, online advertising, social media, and strategically selected photo ops that target those citizens. Other citizens, especially those who vehemently oppose the Conservatives, are ignored. Likewise the Liberals, New Democrats, and major political parties in the provinces conduct voter segmentation and target marketing with their own partisans and potential supporters.

Political parties compile information about Canadians and use it for direct voter contact. They populate their databases primarily with information obtained from election agencies that maintain the official list of electors. These data are then supplemented. When party volunteers knock on doors to promote their local candidate, they are also compiling information about each household, including whether its members are likely to vote for their party. Someone visiting a party website is urged to submit an email address to get updates. Social media posts urge people to electronically sign a petition and to add their name to take action on a public-policy issue. All of this information is instantly added to the party's database and the citizen soon receives emails asking for money. To a lesser extent, the messages encourage candidate recruitment and urge people to vote. Only rarely are the direct appeals a substantive information tool for citizens. Direct voter contact is a cost-effective way to bypass the filter of the mass media and control the message that is received by target audiences. Its practice will grow as businesses and political organizations harness so-called big data.

narrowcasting
A form of campaigning in which parties choose communications that will target narrowly defined groups of voters.

Narrowcasting is precise and efficient. It means that political parties purposely exclude communicating with voters who are likely to disagree with them. Consequently, because civil society is dividing into different media silos and social media echo chambers, citizens are prone to receive communication mostly from the political party that they already support. Many interest groups employ these same marketing techniques when targeting their audiences. So does the government when it purchases social media advertising that is intended to be seen by certain citizens only. A further source of concern is the unregulated nature of the party databases, which are not subject to privacy law. A 2018 scandal involving Cambridge Analytica brings this to light. The now-defunct data-mining company obtained personal information from millions of Facebook users without their knowledge or consent and used the data to target political campaigns in the United States. The Canadian whistle-blower who revealed the practices had previously assisted the Liberal Party of Canada with developing social media monitoring tools. These are among the reasons why the idealized notion of political marketing that enhances democracy does not exist in Canadian politics.

A related area of political marketing considers political parties as brands. A brand is a synthesis of all communication impressions that are absorbed by a consumer. That person may develop an emotional attachment to the brand as a result. The concept extends beyond symbols, such as a logo or slogan, to encompass core messages, media coverage, and personal interactions that collectively inform a mental image of the brand. The evoked image in an elector's mind becomes an information shortcut to pass judgement. This is why political strategists are relentless in their practice of media management to control the image of the party and the leader. Likewise, governments manage their corporate identity. Governments are rigorous about enforcing internal policies about the use of their logos, consistent colour palettes, and so forth.

The need to manage the party brand and control the message contributes to party discipline. Any public representative of a political party in Canada is expected to promote a consistent and authorized message. This guideline applies to members of the caucus, public spokespeople, party constituency officials, and even local volunteers. The importance of message discipline has increased with the reach of the media and speed of social media. Gone are the days when partisans could say one thing in one region of the country, while their fellow partisans said something different, even contradictory, in another. In Canada today, whatever is said or typed by a representative of a political party tends to align with what other representatives communicate, especially during an election campaign. This encompasses remarks made at public events, to the news media, via social media, on websites, in newsletters, through email, and by any other form of communication. In short, sameness is expected, regardless of one's personal opinions. Naturally, this has implications for representative democracy.

It can be frustrating for politicians to publicly support a party decision or policy that they vehemently oppose in private. They were elected to represent their constituents in a democratic country where free speech is protected both in the constitution and to an even greater degree within the legislature. But party leaders exert considerable power, leaving many representatives to complain of feeling reduced to little more than trained seals. Studies, pundits, political scientists, and some elected officials suggest that MPs should have more freedom to express themselves and the needs of their constituents. Conversely, many party members accept party and message discipline because they recognize that politics is not about getting one's own way all the time. They must choose issues on which

For a review of party discipline, see Chapter 6, on the legislature. See especially the section The Partisan Composition of Elected Assemblies and the end-of-chapter debate supplement.

to spend their political capital. A political party that operates as a cohesive whole presents itself as capable of governing and pushing forward its agenda. A party wrought with infighting projects the opposite image. For the government party, there is a heightened need to enforce party discipline because at all times the party must maintain the confidence of the legislature. There can be significant peer pressure to comply; going along with the party means that you remain part of the in-group, but operating as a free agent invites the risk of being socially and professionally ostracized. In short, the benefits of party discipline often outweigh the disadvantages to those involved. As a result, the message discipline expected of political parties turns MPs into representatives who publicly support their party even when they fiercely disagree in private.

Positive and Negative Messaging

Political strategists take all of this wisdom into account when engaging in election campaigns and the permanent campaign in general. Political actors seek out media coverage to set and control the public agenda; they attempt to frame issues and the image of opponents; and they campaign for the hearts and minds of electors. For instance, by drawing on public-opinion research, the New Democratic Party may call for action on affordable housing, better wages, and taxing the top one per cent of earners as a way of claiming ownership of socio-economic issues that other parties are less keen to address. The Conservative Party may want to talk about reducing budget deficits, because it is a topic that galvanizes its supporters and differentiates it from other parties. The Liberal Party seeks to put climate change on the public agenda and demonize the Conservatives in the hope of attracting support from New Democrats and Greens. Behind the scenes, many strategic calculations are involved with deciding which topics to raise and what messages to promote.

Some political leaders vow to stick to positive politics. They promote uplifting messages of the feel-good variety and may use inspirational messages or humour. This strategy captures the imagination of democratic romanticists who believe that politics should be about peaceful discussion in an honourable manner. Positivity tends to be somewhat ineffective because it fails to resonate on an emotional level and is seldom memorable. A more direct approach involves contrasting two choices. The strengths of a party or candidate are pitted against the weaknesses of an opponent. For instance, a political message may begin with negative information that creates concern about a problem (the opponent), and then transition to an uplifting tone when presenting a solution (the messenger sponsor) to resolve that anxiety. The audience sees the messenger as an antidote to partisan hostilities.

Broadly speaking, political parties, interest groups, and other actors employ either a confrontation strategy or articulation. Confrontation involves parties and organizations taking opposing positions on questions of policy or ideology. This competition results in great policy debates, such as whether to engage in war, whether to raise taxes, or whether to privatize certain public services. Confrontational debates are rare in Canadian politics because there are few issues on which Canadians are deeply divided. When political parties take the articulation approach, they talk past each other and do not assume divergent policy positions. They selectively emphasize issues that voters trust them to handle. Right-wing parties typically own issues such as taxation and debt relief. Left-wing parties own issues such as education and healthcare. Each party attempts to place its preferred issues on the public agenda. In doing so they are strategically ambiguous about issues that their opponents own.

wedge issue
A polarizing topic that divides electors, often in a manner that favours the party that is trying to put it on the public agenda.

Alternatively, parties may attempt to elevate **wedge issues** to the forefront of public debate. Wedge issues concern controversies about which there is not a unanimous opinion, such as crime, abortion, illegal immigration, transgender rights, war, religious symbols, and so on. They tend to differentiate one party from all the others. A political party that wants to draw attention to a wedge issue knows this will emotionally charge a campaign. The party may want to energize its supporters while dividing opponents among other parties. Alternatively, it may want to divide its opponents internally, creating dissension among their ranks and possibly demobilizing or converting their followers. If a party knows that an opponent's followers are deeply divided over a polarizing issue, it may seek to raise public awareness about its opponent's position in an attempt to drive a wedge into its opponent's base.

Relatedly, political parties may engage in dog-whistle politics. They highlight issues that are of particular interest to a small group of core supporters but that fail to resonate or even register with the general public. Parties will often use coded language when raising these issues and avoid drawing mass attention. Consider, for example, the use of "individual responsibility" by right-wing parties, or "working families" by left-wing parties. These expressions carry strong ideological connotations to each party's core base of supporters. Yet the significance of this language may escape the attention of most Canadians. The practice gets its name from how a dog whistle is heard only by dogs and not by humans. As a result of using these articulation strategies, political parties develop competing policy packages featuring distinct sets of priorities for the future, rather than specific, contrasting policy prescriptions.

political correctness
Social pressure to correct perceived injustices, typically by recasting or denouncing topics and language that is deemed offensive.

Political debate is influenced by words, expressions, and topics that cannot be vocalized because they are considered too obnoxious, insensitive, provocative, hurtful, and/or oppressive. **Political correctness** defines the boundaries of acceptable speech and behaviour in this sense. It involves the use of communication to confront biases, resolve inequalities, and change social norms. Much like ethics, the standards evolve over time to reflect current and emerging sensibilities. For instance, not long ago it was common to use only the male pronoun, because it was treated as universally encapsulating male and female. Then it became normal to use both female and male pronouns in order to be inclusive of both sexes. Today, Canadian law and governments no longer treat gender as binary, and increasingly Canadians avoid pronouns or use gender-neutral words such as "they." Disputes can occur over a person's desire to be referred to by new pronouns such as "hir" and "ze." Like many aspects of political correctness, the pronouns debate is divisive among its most fervent supporters of change, and the defenders of the status quo. Gender, Indigeneity, race, stereotyping, body size—these are just some of the many topics that require political sensitivity in order to avoid causing personal offence.

Political correctness is such a powerful phenomenon that a single errant remark can disrupt a political agenda and derail a political career. Social media is a graveyard of offensive comments that can be unearthed years later when someone enters politics and is forced to apologize, and possibly resign, over something flippant and inconsiderate. Advocates argue that this is necessary to create a more equal and equitable society. Calling out offenders is necessary to counter patriarchal, racist, colonialist, and privileged normative behaviour. Critics say that rather than encourage diversity and inclusivity, political correctness is a divisive force that stifles genuine debate over societal norms and values, and even threatens freedom of speech. They maintain that social-justice advocates become overly sensitive and perceive victimization at every turn. They argue that, instead of unifying Canada by treating everyone as Canadians, identity groups are pitted against each other. Some observers describe these divisions as a culture war in reference to the struggle over defining a community's political culture (or guiding ethos).

Premier Rachel Notley speaking to supporters in Edmonton during the 2019 Alberta election campaign. Notley and other female politicians in Canada have been targets of cyberbullying via email and social media to a much greater degree than their male counterparts. Why are men less likely to be targeted? What protections can be offered to women in public office?

Negative communication extends to all facets of political competition and is arguably damaging democracy worldwide. It is nothing new when it comes to Canadian politics, as a cursory review of early campaign literature attests. Negativity employs psychological techniques to generate an emotional response among audiences. Consequently, citizens become agitated, even outraged, about the message, the message sponsor, and the political realm as a whole. Negativity in politics contributes to critical media coverage, which in turn results in an electorate that dislikes and distrusts politics and government, and feels disenfranchised. The bad things that politicians say about each other undermine attempts to improve citizen engagement and increase election turnout. Pessimism and despondency do little to inspire intelligent debate on the issues. Negative communication distorts truths and lowers democratic discourse to name-calling and image framing rather than elevating democracy into a sophisticated debate about public policy. Being harshly critical about politicians has harmful effects on a politician's family and on that person directly.

Political communication that does nothing more than exploit the weaknesses of an opponent is arguably the most effective form. **Negative political advertising** denigrates an opponent—typically a leader or candidate—and the person's policy positions. The use of horror themes (e.g., black backgrounds with red text, grainy slow motion, grey colour tones, menacing music, unflattering photos, shocking headlines, judgemental narration) are designed to upset electors, causing them to become distressed about and suspicious of politicians, political parties, and politics. Negative political advertising is widely criticized when it is used. Yet, in spite of the outrage, audiences are thought to ultimately prioritize negative information over positive information. Another reason that negative ads are so effective is that the news media treat the latest controversial ads as news, increasing the advertisement's reach at no cost to the sponsor. Negative advertising often is not designed to win over new voters as much as it is meant to mobilize a party's base of committed supporters, to make them more likely to vote or to encourage them to increase their donations to the party. It is also effective in demoralizing the party's opponents, discouraging them from turning out to vote.

negative political advertising
Paid communication that criticizes an opponent's policy or record, and that may verge on attacking the person.

The worst type of political advertising takes negative advertising a step further. Attack advertising uses ad homimen arguments—it belittles someone's personal life or physical characteristics rather than the person's politics. Attack ads are widely considered to be beyond the pale and risk backfiring. In Canada, people often refer to the backlash against the so-called "Chrétien face ads" in the 1993 federal campaign as the limits

Inside Canadian Politics

Why Are the Jean Chrétien "Face Ads" Still Relevant Today?

The 1993 Canadian federal election was a watershed moment for negative advertising in Canadian politics. The positive bounce that an unpopular Progressive Conservative government received with the appointment of Kim Campbell as prime minister began to erode during the election campaign. PC Party strategists prepared television advertising that attacked Liberal leader Jean Chrétien. The ads used unflattering photographs of Chrétien that appeared to highlight his partial facial paralysis caused by Bell's palsy, while voiceovers made statements such as, "I would be very embarrassed if he became Prime Minister of Canada."

The PCs' internal polling found that the television ads weakened public impressions of Chrétien. However, the Liberal Party coordinated a cross-country phone-in campaign among its supporters, urging them to express outrage that the ads made fun of a disability. So acute was the public backlash—including within the PC Party—that Campbell immediately pulled the ads. On Election Day, the Liberals formed a majority government, and the PCs were reduced to only two seats. The

notorious case is widely cited as evidence of the risks of attacking an opponent's physical characteristics.

During the 1993 federal election campaign, the Progressive Conservatives ran negative advertisements highlighting what they saw as Liberal leader Jean Chrétien's lack of leadership qualities. One of these ads featured images like this one, which critics felt drew attention to Chrétien's slight facial deformity caused by Bell's palsy. What sorts of personal characteristics are off-limits when it comes to attack ads?

DISCUSSION ITEM

The line between negative advertising and personal attacks can be blurry for strategists in the midst of a heated campaign.

VOX POP

Given the disastrous election result for her party, do you think that Prime Minister Campbell was right to pull attack ads against the advice of some of her party's top strategists?

of public tolerance. Since then, political parties have exercised caution about criticizing opponents' looks or personal lives, which is not to say that it does not happen. This brings us back to the importance of framing, because it helps to explain why political advertising often attempts to exploit the weaknesses of individual politicians rather than philosophical ideas, party brands, or public policy.

Parties are not the only political actors to engage in negative politics. Combatants against sexism, homophobia, racism, xenophobia, cultural appropriation, hatred, and other offences are often the targets of nasty commentary on social media. This is especially true for people who are in the minority of elected representatives, including women. We explore this further in the Up for Debate section at the end of this chapter.

In Canada, denouncing negative politics is commonplace. Incivility undermines the democratic system itself by turning people off politics and politicians. Yet, negative political information is an important element of free speech. If used properly, negative communication promotes truthfulness in political discourse by using facts to dispel myths, information to confront media slants, and data to counter partisan falsehoods. Negative information draws public attention to weaknesses of opponents and holds governments accountable for their decisions. Even the threat of negative publicity may keep them from acting rashly. A combination of positive, comparative, and negative communication is an excellent way to inform people about their political choices. As with so much in politics, students of political science must bear in mind that what one elector may dismiss, another elector may perceive to be vital. Yet, negativity about personal characteristics remains politically incorrect in Canada. In an ideal world, Canadian political communication would present in a neutral manner a balance of factual information about policy ideas and the leadership qualities of candidates, thereby enabling citizens to arrive at informed judgements.

Concluding Thoughts

Political competition pits one set of ideas and people against others. Opponents struggle to convince the public that their interpretation of reality is the most accurate. In short, all political communication consists of a selection of information that is presented in a certain manner. The trick for citizens is to understand what the main facts are. This can be difficult when most information is projected in a slanted manner and when some information is not publicly disclosed. As journalists and political actors seek to outwit each other in the media game, the rest of us remain confronted with the age-old challenge of discerning what information is true, what is spin, and what is hidden from public view. As discussed in the next chapter, interest groups and social movements can help clarify or cloud our understanding of these matters.

For More Information

Interested in the history of the party press in Canada? Allan Levine provides a trove of detail about Canadian prime ministers' interactions with the media in *Scrum Wars: The Prime Ministers and the Media* (Dundurn Press 1996).

Want to learn about the history of the Canadian parliamentary press gallery? *Sharp Wits and Busy Pens: 150 Years of Canada's Parliamentary Press Gallery* (Hill Times Books 2016)

is a collection of contributions authored by members of the fourth estate.

Curious about understanding media bias in Canada? Try starting with "Rational Learners or Impervious Partisans? Economic News and Partisan Bias in Economic Perceptions," *Canadian Journal of Political Science* 52, no. 2 (2019): pp. 303–21 by Scott Matthews and Mark Pickup.

How does media framing work in practice? Brooks DeCillia delves into the matter in "But It Is Not Getting Any Safer! The Contested Dynamic of Framing Canada's Military Mission in Afghanistan," *Canadian Journal of Political Science* 51, no. 1 (2018): pp. 155–77.

What is permanent campaigning? Find out in *Permanent Campaigning in Canada*, edited by Alex Marland, Thierry Giasson, and Anna Lennox Esselment (UBC Press, 2017).

How should the government regulate advertising by interest groups, unions, and businesses? Tamara Small delves into how advocacy groups spend on digital advertising in her article "Digital Third Parties: Understanding the Technological Challenge to Canada's Third Party Advertising Regime," *Canadian Public Administration* 61, no. 2 (2018): pp. 266–83.

Should the government fund Canadian news? That question and others are explored in "What Do Canadians Want from Their News?" by Peter Loewen, Andrew Potter, Benjamin Allen Stevens, and Taylor Owen in *Policy Options* (October 30, 2018).

Interested in how the Government of Canada is turning to e-government? Take a look at *Opening the Government of Canada: The Federal Bureaucracy in the Digital Age* (UBC Press, 2019) by Amanda Clarke.

How are Canadian politicians and activists engaging in the digital sphere? The various contributions in *What's Trending in Canadian Politics: Understanding Transformations in Power, Media, and the Public Sphere* (UBC Press, 2019) provide some insights. Its editors are Mireille Lalancette, Vincent Raynauld, and Erin Crandall.

Concerned about the information that Canadian political parties have about you? If so, you may or may not want to read "Porting the Political Campaign: The NationBuilder Platform and the Global Flows of Political Technology" by Fenwick McKelvey and Jill Piebiak in *New Media & Society* 20, no. 3 (2018): pp. 901–18.

Want to monitor or participate in minute-by-minute conversations about Canadian politics? Twitter is an ideal venue for following topical discussions. For a list of top hashtags, visit PoliTwitter.ca.: http://politwitter.ca/page/canadian-politics-hash-tags.

Curious about the extent of Open Data in the federal government? Visit open.canada.ca/en to see what sort of information is on offer.

Want to view the latest direct messages from the prime minister of Canada? The prime minister's missives are available at pm.gc.ca.

Deeper Inside Canadian Politics

1. Much has been made of the rise of citizen journalists in Canadian politics. Which do you think is more effective at holding governments accountable in Canada: the mainstream media or digital media? Why?
2. Do politicians have an obligation to engage with the media on the media's terms? Why do you think conservatives are prone to be combative with the media whereas liberals have a cozier relationship with the press?
3. Compare the content and communication methods found in the Canadian prime minister's weekly online messages with those of the American president. What are the major similarities? What explains the major differences?
4. Why do you think so much attention is paid to the negative aspects of politics instead of the positive side?
5. How can lawmakers regulate advertising that appears online?

Professor Profile

Tamara A. Small

Digital politics, political communication, Canadian parties and elections
Co-editor of *Digital Politics in Canada: Promises and Realities* (2020)

Tamara Small researches various areas of digital politics in Canada, from parties to citizenship, to political memes. She is a leading voice on the use of digital technologies by Canadian political actors and frequent media commentator about political communications, especially during elections.

Here is what Tamara Small told us about her career path from when she was an undergraduate student, why she is drawn to her area of specialization, what is challenging about studying Canadian politics, and what advice she has for students.

* * *

I completed my undergraduate degree in political science at the University of Guelph, which means that I have the very great pleasure to be a professor in the same department where I once studied, and to teach the introduction to Canadian politics course that I once took. I remember a lot about that course—the professor (Ken Woodside) and the textbook (*Canadian Politics in Transition*)—which is currently sitting on the shelf in my office. The main focus on my research is digital campaigning: the use of digital technologies (e.g., websites, social media, mobile phones) by campaign organizations to inform, mobilize, interact and persuade voters. It was the topic of my MA thesis at the University of Calgary in communication studies. The choice of the topic came out of a conversation with my supervisor; he said that it would be the topic he'd pick.

The most challenging part about digital campaigning is that digital technologies are constantly changing.

I started studying websites, then social media; I am not sure what comes next. Every development of technology required a rethinking about how to access research materials and best approach to examine the topic. The thing that surprises you most about digital campaigning is that digital technologies change so much and so little about Canadian politics at the same time. It would be nearly impossible for a political party, government, or MP to not use some sort of digital technology, yet older technologies remain central. Despite the significance of digital technologies, it is still just one tool in the politics toolkit. If I had one tip for students studying Canadian politics, I would say to never listen to anyone that tells you Canadian politics is boring. It's not!

I am passionate about studying Canadian politics because I really think it is important for people to know their own country. I like teaching and contributing to students' awareness of their citizenship in Canada. The differences between American and Canadian political systems are significant. If Canadian citizens are unaware of how things work in Canada, it makes it harder to hold politicians to account. Knowing what federalism is, what parliamentary democracy is, how the electoral system impacts elections, where it is that citizens can have impact in the political system, Canadian political history (English, French, Indigenous, new immigrants), and lived experiences are so important.

Up for Debate

Does social media make Canadian democracy better?

THE CLAIM: YES, IT DOES!

Social media makes political elites more accountable to the public they serve.

Yes: Argument Summary

Social media has enhanced the amount of accessibility, accountability, and political knowledge in Canadian politics. Citizens have unprecedented access to their leaders, as well as to journalists and political scientists. The volume of political communication has grown exponentially as a result. This makes for a more vibrant public sphere, a more informed electorate, and a more responsive political elite.

Yes: Top 5 Considerations

1. Social media has made political information more accessible than ever before. Citizens can track political debates and events in real time. Live-tweeting journalists provide unprecedented access to important discussions taking place in courtrooms and boardrooms across the country. Television cameras aren't allowed in many of these venues, and it can take hours for the events to be published in print.
2. Politicians are more accessible than ever thanks to social media. Phone calls and letters to your representative have been replaced by open tweets or direct messages. Response time has declined immensely as a result, allowing citizens to gain information and support more urgently.
3. Social media holds governments, parties, and politicians accountable for their actions. Even the possibility of an online backlash is enough to encourage these actors to behave responsibly and in the public interest. Candidates have had their party memberships revoked and party leaders have been deposed on the basis of inappropriate behaviour or remarks on and off social media. There is almost nowhere to hide one's misdeeds. This helps to improve the quality of representatives across Canada.
4. Social media has reinvigorated the public sphere, creating a new digital forum for the exchange of information and ideas. Negativity and divisiveness are only natural in this environment. At its core, though, political conversation is the lifeblood of democracy.
5. Citizens have direct access to subject matter experts through social media. Some academics have larger followings than journalists and politicians, reflecting the thirst among many citizens to learn more about political topics. This knowledge is of tremendous benefit to democracy, as it helps dispel myths and encourage informed voting.

Yes: Other Considerations

- Previously marginalized groups are using social media to elevate important issues to the top of the political agenda. The Idle No More, Black Lives Matter, and Me Too movements are three poignant examples.
- Social media provides parties and candidates with direct access to citizens, not just vice versa. This allows them to connect more quickly and effectively than traditional routes through mainstream media.

THE COUNTERCLAIM: NO, IT DOESN'T!

Social media is tearing civil society apart.

No: Argument Summary

Social media was initially forecast as a panacea for democracy. Its democratic promise has not been achieved. Instead of connecting citizens to their representatives, social media has become a tool for party discipline and message control. Instead of facilitating meaningful debates among new and various voices, social media has devolved into fruitless discussions among like-minded tribespeople bent on demonizing their opponents. Worse yet, the rise of anonymous trolls (serial harassers) and the advent of bots (automated accounts) has lowered political debate even further into the gutter.

No: Top 5 Considerations

1. Political discussions on social media are not what idealists hold them out to be. So-called debates on Facebook and Twitter feature little more than ad hominem attacks. There is little genuine exchange of ideas or presentation of fact. Persuasion is even less frequent, as people seldom change their minds once locked in a social media exchange.

2. Political parties maintain tight control over their representatives' use of social media. Most often, citizens are not interacting with their local officials; they receive scripted responses that have been vetted by party communications gurus. For their part, most politicians treat social media as a one-way street, communicating information to their followers rather than soliciting their views.

3. Social media is subject to undemocratic manipulation. Bots are used to amplify negative, false, and divisive messages. This distorts the free flow of ideas and honest discussion. More ominously, this manipulation has the potential to affect election results by framing campaigns in a way that advantages certain parties, potentially influenced by foreign agents.

4. Very little productive democratic debate takes place on social media. Rather, citizens are divided into echo chambers where they interact only (and daily) with people who share the same political views. Some of this is due to self-selection, but a lot of it has to do with the algorithms built into the social media platforms themselves. In this way, social media is inherently detrimental to the democratic exchange of ideas.

5. Social media doesn't bring many new participants into the political arena. Studies demonstrate that people who engage in conventional forms of political activity (town halls, protests, voting, and so on) are the same people found engaging each other on social media. Social media has not been a democratizing force, in this sense.

No: Other Considerations

- Political parties treat backbenchers and candidates as cogs in their social media amplification network. This creates tensions about democratic representation.
- Social media is not a replacement for the traditional public square. Many social media actors are anonymous, giving them added confidence to troll public officials and people who do not share their views. Women, Indigenous people, and people of colour are among those who are targeted.
- Not everyone has equal power on social media. Public figures and opinion leaders are open about their reluctance to engage with anyone who has fewer than hundreds of followers. Newcomers to the medium and those with smaller networks tend to be ignored in this environment.
- For every fact an expert disseminates on social media, there are numerous lies and falsehoods that are propagated at a much faster rate. On the whole, social media is not making the electorate any more informed. If it were, we would see improved knowledge scores in surveys like the Canadian Election Study.

Discussion Questions

- Do you think it is appropriate for elected officials to block or mute people on social media?
- What are the keys to success in terms of political campaigns on social media?
- What would an average citizen need to do to raise awareness of a political issue and achieve reforms?

Where to Learn More about Social Media and Canadian Politics

Quinn Albaugh and Christopher Waddell, "Social Media and Political Inequality," in *Canadian Democracy from the Ground Up: Perceptions and Performance*, eds. Elisabeth Gidengil and Heather Bastedo (Vancouver: UBC Press, 2014): pp. 102–19.

Elizabeth Dubois and Devin Gaffney, "The Multiple Facets of Influence: Identifying Political Influentials and Opinion Leaders on Twitter," *American Behavioral Scientist* 58, no. 10 (2014): pp. 1260–77.

Thierry Giasson and Tamara A. Small, "Online All the Time: The Strategic Objectives of Canadian Opposition Parties," in *Permanent Campaigning in Canada*, eds. Alex Marland, Thierry Giasson, and Anna Lennox Esselment (Vancouver: UBC Press, 2017): 109–26.

Alex Marland, Thierry Giasson, and Andrea Lawlor, eds., *Political Elites in Canada: Power and Influence in Instantaneous Times* (Vancouver: UBC Press, 2018).

Kathleen McNutt, "Public Engagement in the Web 2.0 Era: Social Collaborative Technologies in a Public Sector Context," *Canadian Public Administration* 57, no. 1 (2014): pp. 49–70.

Vincent Raynauld, Mireille Lalancette, and Sofia Tourigny-Koné, "Political Protest 2.0: Social Media and the 2012 Student Strike in the Province of Quebec, Canada," *French Politics* 14, no. 1 (2016): pp. 1–29.

Tamara A. Small, "Parties, Leaders, and Online Personalization: Twitter in Canadian Electoral Politics," in *Twitter and Elections around the World*, eds. Richard Davis, Christina Holtz Bach, and Marion R. Just (New York: Routledge, 2016).

Tamara A. Small, "Online Negativity in Canada: Do Party Leaders Attack on Twitter?" *Journal of Language and Politics* 17, no. 2 (2018): pp. 324–42.

12

Interest Groups and Social Movements

Inside This Chapter

- What makes certain types of activism successful?
- What are interest groups and how do they contribute to Canadian democracy?
- How do social movements impact Canadian politics?

Inside Interest Groups and Social Movements

Canadian politics involves people and organizations representing a broad cross-section of societal interests. Political activists contribute ideas and voice interests that might not otherwise attract public attention. At times, they work alongside politicians in elections and co-operate with public servants in developing and implementing public policy. At others, they confront mainstream political elites on the campaign trail and in the courtroom.

Activists often operate behind the scenes or in non-traditional venues. Bear in mind the following maxims as you read through the chapter, which looks at the pressure exerted on government by interest groups and the influence of social movements in setting the public agenda.

✔ **Special interests play a significant, but restricted, role in shaping Canadian politics.** Activists are sometimes portrayed as powerful, well-financed individuals who hold disproportionate sway over politicians and political decision-making. In fact, most Canadian interest groups and social movements face resource challenges and institutional barriers in engaging governments and achieving their policy objectives.

✔ **Activism takes many forms beyond protests and public demonstrations.** Activists seek to raise public awareness and concern about their causes in a variety of ways. They advertise during elections, release research reports, campaign on social media, conduct backroom negotiations, and initiate courtroom litigation.

✔ **Lobbying in Canada is highly regulated to prevent undue influence.** The media and the entertainment industry cultivate an image of lobbyists as shady figures using secret meetings, bribes, and other discreditable means to coerce elected officials. In reality, lobbying is a means of connecting societal interests to government, and the practice has become increasingly regulated and professionalized over time.

UP FOR DEBATE

Should spending by interest groups be regulated in Canada?

Keep this question in mind as you read through the chapter. Consult the end-of-chapter debate supplement for more material to help you engage in an informed discussion of the topic.

Pluralism and the Balance of Power

Public policy is influenced by competing ideologies, interests, and pressures. According to the pluralist ideal, a vibrant civil society features different groups of active, like-minded citizens vying with each other to define and achieve the public good. This competition takes place among political parties, which are the most powerful purveyors of ideas and interests in Canadian democracy (see Chapter 9). Pluralism is also present in less conventional channels featuring lesser-known organizations and actors. Not all of these groups have the same impact on the political system. Some of the ideas they promote are more deeply embedded in the institutions of the state and the community's political culture. This makes them difficult to dislodge. Take liberalism and capitalism. Mounting a reform movement to transform Canada into a fascist state or socialist society would be immensely difficult. It would require taking control of the federal government and most provincial, territorial, and municipal governments, not to mention enacting hundreds of legislative changes and numerous amendments to the Canadian constitution. Nonetheless, there are fringe groups dedicated to those aims, and Canada's system of liberal democracy guarantees their right to organize peacefully. Like other advocacy organizations, they have the legal ability to voice their concerns and mobilize support.

The uneven distribution of resources in Canada's capitalist system gives some groups more influence over the policymaking process. Activists representing businesses and unions have more resources than most civil society organizations. They enjoy a formalized role in the government's budget-building and policymaking processes. This imbalance of power has led some to label Canada a neo-pluralist democracy, which recognizes the absence of level competition among equally powerful societal interests.

This power disparity complicates balancing the free flow of ideas and advocacy of varied interests with fair competition and equal influence among the groups that champion those ideas. To this end, governments face pressure to regulate the way these interests interact with the state and, on occasion, provide special access and resources to amplify traditionally marginalized voices. Governments also face criticism for limiting the competition of ideas to established elites, like elected officials and judges. The expectations of pluralism demand they make room for activists, most of whom operate in interest groups, think tanks, or broader social movements to advance their causes.

The topic of pluralism is taken up on page 252 of Chapter 8, on public policy.

Interest Groups

Canadian history is rife with examples of how supporters can be mobilized to pressure political parties and elected officials to weigh in on a public-policy issue. This is the trade of **interest groups**, a large collection of organizations that seek to advance a political agenda without fielding candidates during elections. Interest groups attempt to compel decision-makers to respond to their demands in a manner that is advantageous to their supporters. They are in a constant struggle to attract media attention and generate public sympathy for their cause. Occasionally, they bypass electoral politics entirely, and take their concerns to the courts in an effort to force governments to act.

interest group
A political organization that seeks to influence public policy without competing for election.

Interest groups are alternatively called advocacy or pressure groups, or special interests. Elections Canada refers to them as third parties, in the sense that they are actors outside the formal world of political parties and politicians. Their role in a pluralist democracy is an important one, for they attract attention to issues that courts, political parties, the media, and the voting public may otherwise ignore. Their political influence can at times undermine democratic principles if they become actively involved in secretive decision-making processes among political elites. Critics of the invisible role that interest groups have in political decision-making argue for greater regulation, but the courts have rejected many of these arguments in favour of free speech and freedom of association.

Canadians may feel represented by a variety of different interest groups. Table 12.1 presents a selection of interest groups, their goals, and their tactics. Some organizations are ideological, presenting themselves as the champions of liberal, progressive, conservative, libertarian, socialist, or other values. Others define themselves along the lines of gender, sexuality, ableness, ethnicity, culture, language, or region. Several interest groups exist to represent different business sectors, occupational groups, and workers in general. Still others are issue-oriented, advancing policies related to public health, climate change, taxation, Internet freedom, and other areas. There are competing interest groups within these various categories, including conservative and liberal women's groups, for example. As well, interest groups may be internally divided into factions, not unlike other political organizations.

Advocacy groups are a vital link between political decision-makers and the general public. Indeed, many Canadians have a more direct and substantive connection with

Table 12.1   Examples of Canadian Interest Groups and Their Tactics

Interest Group	Objective	Examples of Pressure Tactics
Canada Without Poverty CANADA WITHOUT POVERTY CANADA SANS PAUVRETÉ	Eliminate poverty in Canada	• policy education and development • promotion of human rights • deliver presentations and respond to media • conduct workshops and online courses
Canadian Association of Petroleum Producers	Ensure the economic sustainability of the Canadian oil and gas industry	• commission opinion polls • coordinate industry awards • deliver presentations • respond to government regulations
Canadian Federation of Students cfs fcéé	Achieve a high-quality, publicly funded, fully accessible system of post-secondary education	• engage in social media advocacy • organize direct actions (i.e., days of action, email blasts) • lobby governments through petitions, email blasts, and meetings with officials • educate the public and the media on issues related to post-secondary education
Canadian Taxpayers Federation Canadian Taxpayers FEDERATION	Promote lower taxes, monitor wasteful spending, keep politicians accountable	• conduct media interviews • encourage supporters to contact politicians • speak at events • publish *The Taxpayer* magazine
CARP (previously known as Canadian Association of Retired Persons) CARP	Promote retirement security, equitable access to health care and freedom from age discrimination for older Canadians	• inform government of position on legislation and policies • poll members on policy issues and government proposals • conduct media interviews, debates, and discussions
Egale Canada Human Rights Trust Egale	Improve the lives of LGBTQI2S people in Canada and to enhance the global response to LGBTQI2S issues by informing public policy, inspiring cultural change, and promoting human rights and inclusion	• conduct research • provide education, training, and resources • create awareness through campaigns and media • engage in legal advocacy
LifeCanada LIFECANADA VieCanada	Facilitate communication among educational pro-life groups across Canada	• provide anti-abortion educational resources • promote the activities of educational pro-life groups, including conferences, marches, national polling, and advertising campaigns
MADD Canada (Mothers Against Drunk Driving) madd* No alcohol. No drugs. No victims.	Stop impaired driving and support victims of this violent crime	• provide victim services • deliver youth programs across country • educate general public through awareness campaigns • promote legislative best practices in impaired driving
Physicians for a Smoke-Free Canada Physicians for a Smoke-Free Canada	Reduce illnesses caused by tobacco smoking and second-hand smoke	• research tobacco industry • work with departments of health • meet with groups in developing countries
Public Service Alliance of Canada PSAC AFPC	Representing federal public servants as a labour union	• negotiate labour issues • coordinate protests and strikes • testify at parliamentary committees

interest groups than with political parties. There are a handful of major political parties whereas there are over 20,000 interest groups in Canada. Anywhere between 10 and 25 per cent of Canadians consider themselves to be members of an interest group, depending on their own definition of the term. Fewer than one in ten Canadians belong to a professional political organization. At least twice as many participate in voluntary organizations, unions, professional associations, and religious bodies that have looser connections to the political system. These interest groups can be small, representing the interests of a few people or organizations, or they can be so large as to represent an entire industry or millions of citizens.

Some interest groups are internally more democratic than others. Those claiming to represent broad swaths of Canadian society tend to feature means of engaging the public, including forums and elections to choose members of their boards of directors. Interest groups with narrower objectives tend to lack the same connection with broader civil society and opt instead to represent the interests of their own members. Many of the strongest national interest groups are coalitions of smaller organizations united for a common purpose and do not have their own individual members. There can be opportunities for these peak organizations to represent the broader community indirectly.

In their 2004 democratic audit of Advocacy Groups, political scientists Lisa Young and Joanna Everitt found little evidence that interest groups in Canada are more inclusive than political parties when it comes to representing the broader population. Just like parties, interest-group membership tends to be older, whiter, wealthier, and more highly educated than Canadians as a whole. Women are just as likely to engage in interest group activity as men. The fact that many interest groups hold women's equality as a primary goal may help to explain the disappearance of the gender participation gap in this type of political activity. People who participate in interest groups are more likely to sign a petition, join a boycott, participate in a strike, vote, and join a political party. The same sorts of politically active people are often involved in both traditional politics and less conventional forms of activism.

Active participation is especially true at the tops of interest group organizations. The leadership of Canadian interest groups reflects John Porter's *Vertical Mosaic* in similar

Briefing Notes

The Vertical Mosaic

Imbalance of power is hardly new and involves more than wealth. John Porter was among the first academics to study the issue from a social-scientific perspective. His 1965 book *The Vertical Mosaic: An Analysis of Social Class and Power in Canada* pulled back the curtain on the Canadian business and political elite. The study revealed that, far from being an egalitarian system in which all cultures had equal opportunity and equal representation in the Canadian power structure, the country's fabled cultural mosaic was structured hierarchically (i.e., vertically). Certain cultures were dominant—namely, white, English-speaking men of British ancestry. Since then, strides have been made to include more women, Indigenous people, and people of colour in the bureaucracy (Chapter 8) and political parties (Chapter 9); however, disparities in representation remain an important area of focus for reformers (Chapter 13).

ways as that of political parties, legislatures, cabinets, judges' chambers, media offices, senior bureaucrats' boardrooms, and faculty clubs. Elites within all of these organizations tend to be drawn from a narrow segment of the population, as Porter found in the 1960s. By virtue of similar upbringings and common social circles, they tend to share many professional and personal connections. These networks insulate the centre of the policy-making process from outsider influence. Many of the most powerful interest groups hire lobbyists and secure leaders from the existing pool of political elites, helping to perpetuate the closed nature of the system.

Given this concentration of power, many interest groups struggle to maintain internal democratic processes. A large and inclusive membership base does not guarantee that an interest group's members have or seek meaningful input into the operations of the organization. Some interest groups are foremost chequebook organizations in that their members' main contributions are through monetary donations rather than volunteerism or substantive input. A few of these groups pretend to be more populist and popular than they really are. This is called **astroturfing**, so named because they fake a public image to look more like their grassroots counterparts, thereby exaggerating their support. Some interest groups feature more active members who mobilize on behalf of the organization and take part in collective decision-making. This engagement can result in competing visions and interests that make it challenging to define and accomplish the interest group's goals.

Interest groups perform a range of functions in Canadian democracy. They help define and highlight public-policy issues that might otherwise go unnoticed. This issue articulation is a formidable element of the agenda-setting stage of public-policy development discussed in Chapter 8. Governments must choose—or be compelled—to address a handful of issues at any given time. Interest groups identify concerns of importance to their own constituents and work to push those problems to the top of the political agenda. Many interest groups promote specific solutions to those challenges. Potential fixes might include proposing new legislation or amending existing laws, restructuring government, creating new government programs and services, launching commissions of inquiry, striking agreements with other governments or stakeholders, and so on. Calling on the government to allocate more resources is the most common demand.

astroturfing
The practice of masking an organization's elitist character to make it look like a grassroots organization.

Interest Group Tactics

Interest groups communicate problems and solutions to those in positions of authority who can do something about the issue. Most interest groups engage in campaigning, lobbying, litigation, and public demonstrations. Powerful interest groups may operate in several of these forums simultaneously.

Many interest groups participate in elections in an effort to persuade party leaders, candidates, and voters to commit to their cause. Television, radio, print, and online advertising are communications that get a controlled message out. Social media to organize protests is another popular tactic. Rules vary across Canada limiting how much money interest groups can contribute directly to political parties and candidates. Governments in Canada look to regulate interest group behaviour by constraining their ability to use resources to influence election outcomes. Interest groups face restrictions on how much they can spend during elections. At the federal level, interest group spending on political

See Up for Debate: Should spending by interest groups be regulated in Canada? on page 434 at the end of this chapter for some of the arguments on both sides of this issue, and for questions and resources to guide a discussion on this pressing topic.

activities is further restricted for a period of approximately two months leading up to the start of a fixed-date election.

Some interest groups send open letters to party leaders and to candidates asking them to respond publicly to a set of policy questions. Others cajole politicians to sign pledges committing them to take specific actions if elected. Based on these responses and other indications of candidates' support for their cause, interest groups may mobilize their supporters by encouraging them to donate money, volunteer time, or vote in their favour. In some cases, they make a determined effort to defeat certain candidates who stand in the way of their goals. The success of these pressure tactics depends heavily on the size and cohesiveness of the interest group's membership.

A wide range of interest groups engage in elections. Established, high-profile organizations such as the Canadian Labour Congress and the Canadian Taxpayers Federation are among the most visible on the national stage. Campaigns in local electoral districts offer smaller, localized interest groups an opportunity for influence. Some people register their own names as interest groups, as do organizations promoting democratic reforms. This occurs because, in a federal campaign, non-partisan organized interests (i.e., third parties) are required by law to register with Elections Canada if they spend a certain amount on advertising. Furthermore, their total spending is capped. These limits are intended to strike a balance between the constitutional protection of free speech and the deep pockets of some interest groups compared with others.

The presence of special interests in elections raises questions. Proponents cite the importance of including a wide variety of voices and ideas, many of which are filtered

THE CANADIAN PRESS/Justin Tang

The federal director of the Canadian Taxpayers Federation, and its event host pose with mascot "Porky the Waste Hater" at the organization's Teddy Awards for Government Waste in Ottawa in 2018. This annual mock awards gala attracts media focus by highlighting what this interest group views as the worst instances of government waste at all levels. Do you think events such as this one are an effective way to influence public opinion and ultimately government policy?

out of the democratic discourse. In building broad coalitions of voters, catch-all parties often avoid articulating controversial issues for fear of losing focus or support. Interest groups can hold political parties accountable by making them aware of public and members' concerns. Opponents cite the undue influence of well-heeled special interests during campaigns. Restrictions on how much interest groups can donate to politicians or spend on advertising might not go far enough. There is fear that corporations and unions drown out the voices of civil society groups and average citizens during campaigns.

Between elections, **lobbying** is a core activity carried out by some of Canada's largest interest groups. Lobbying involves communicating directly with public-office-holders and their staff, normally through in-person meetings, in order to advance policy objectives. This can include conversations about proposed or existing legislation, regulations, policies and programs, or efforts to secure grants, contracts, and other financial benefits. The term originated from the practice of waiting in the lobby of the legislature to intercept legislators and political staff in order to curry favours. Nowadays lobbying is a profession: a lobbyist is a professional who is paid to provide strategic advice to clients and to provide access to decision-makers in government. Lobbyists draw upon their professional connections with the political elite to act as intermediaries and advance their clients' policy objectives. They tend to be industry experts, political party insiders, and/or former senior political or government staffers.

Lobbyists may be employed exclusively by a corporation, they may work for an interest group, or they may be independent consultants hired for a fee. The latter tend to be the employees of government-relations and public-affairs firms, such as Earnscliffe Strategy Group, Summa Strategies, Hill+Knowlton Strategies, and Crestview Strategy. To some extent governments lobby each other, although practitioners of intergovernmental relations would view their profession otherwise. Several provincial and territorial governments maintain offices in Ottawa to build closer relationships with key federal decision-makers. A similar situation concerns the relationship between Indigenous organizations and governments. Organizations such as the Assembly of First Nations are considered by some to be interest groups who lobby the federal government on behalf of their members. The federal government reinforces this perception when it insists that Indigenous leaders meet with lower-ranking officials, rather than the prime minister or governor general. In contrast, National Indigenous Organization leaders view their relationship with the federal government as a full and equal partnership featuring government-to-government negotiations. They reject the notion that Indigenous groups operate on the same plane as interest groups that must lobby Ottawa for power or resources.

Lobbying is a legitimate activity with a poor public image. It is an essential means of ensuring that political elites are aware of the range of implications of public policy in a pluralistic society. By nature it occurs behind closed doors. The absence of transparency gives pause about whether its practice enhances or harms democratic discourse. Lobbying raises concerns that undue influence is for sale, and that those who stand to benefit from public policy engage in surreptitious behaviour. At its best, lobbying ensures that politicians and bureaucrats make informed decisions that take into account stakeholder perspectives. At the extreme, high-stakes influence campaigns lead to unethical activities such as bribery or graft, with lobbyists offering financial kickbacks to public officials in return for government contracts or specific legislative gains.

In some cases, interest groups find ways of organizing and regulating themselves. The Government Relations Institute of Canada, an interest group for government relations and

lobbying
Professional communication with public-office-holders initiated by advocacy groups as part of an effort to influence decisions.

National Indigenous Organizations are discussed beginning on page 460 of Chapter 13, on diversity and representation.

public affairs professionals, has a code of professional conduct. Members of the Institute are expected to comply with laws regarding lobbying, campaign finance, political activities, and business–government relations. In addition, they must not knowingly circulate falsehoods or misleading information, and must avoid conflicts of interest and other forms of professional impropriety.[1] Likewise, the federal Commissioner of Lobbying of Canada, who is an agent of Parliament, administers a code of conduct that is based on concepts identified in the Lobbying Act. The core principles of that act, which have been carried over into some provinces' legislation, are to uphold the importance of access to public officials and the transparency of lobbying activities. To encourage transparency, information about which lobbyists are working for whom, which government bodies they are lobbying, and which issues are discussed must be publicly disclosed. For a decade, the most lobbied federal government institutions have included the House of Commons and its members, the Prime Minister's Office, and various government departments related to the economy (namely Innovation, Science and Economic Development Canada; Global Affairs Canada; and Finance Canada). International trade, industry, and taxation are among the subjects most often discussed among lobbyists and government officials, alongside health and the environment. But the topics are prone to vary.

Engaging directly with elected officials in Canada is challenging for a variety of reasons. Federalism diffuses political power in Canada, meaning that interest groups who want to spark nationwide reforms must often operate in more than one jurisdiction. As discussed in the Inside Canadian Politics box on page 426–427, passing new legislation to make buildings more wheelchair accessible would require election and lobbying campaigns in all provinces and territories, as the policy area falls under their authority. Conversely, the combination of Westminster traditions and strong party discipline tend to concentrate power in each federal, provincial, and territorial cabinet (Chapter 3). This concentration of power simplifies the power structure. It also reinforces the culture of elite accommodation that gave rise to Canada's vertical mosaic and reduces the number of potential access points for lobbyists. This is why many national interest groups attempt to engage with politicians at federal–provincial/territorial meetings of ministers responsible for a particular policy area. Petroleum companies may offer to sponsor lunches or receptions at energy and mines ministers' meetings, just as unions may arrange side meetings at

Briefing Notes

Cooling Off before Lobbying Heats Up

As mentioned in Chapter 8, the federal Accountability Act bans people who have held senior positions in the federal government or public office from lobbying for five years after leaving their government post. This means that aspiring lobbyists with inside connections must wait at least one election cycle before they can leverage their contacts. The act encompasses such things as increasing the responsibility of deputy ministers, stipulating that the fraud of public funds is its own offence category in the Criminal Code, and tightening conflict-of-interest rules. More broadly, the act changed the culture around official Ottawa by curtailing many activities that were once common in government circles, such as lobbyists providing tickets to public servants to mingle in luxury boxes at entertainment events.

national meetings of labour ministers. Most interest groups find little value in pressuring individual legislators given the limited influence of a backbencher in the policymaking process. Notable exceptions are tight elections in swing districts or by-election campaigns, which are prime opportunities to extract policy promises from candidates. Those are rare circumstances and thus most interest groups apply pressure as close to the top of the political hierarchy as possible.

Many interest groups pursue less direct means of persuading elected officials. Some participate in public engagement processes launched by government departments. This provides them with a forum to join citizens and other interest groups in providing written or verbal submissions. If their support is integral to the legitimacy, completion, or success of a particular policy initiative, an interest group may be invited into the closer-knit policy community that supports government in the policy-development process. They may receive requests to attend legislative committee hearings or provide briefings to public servants on an area of expertise. This communication is a two-way street. Many interest groups help to advance, explain, or legitimize government actions to their members or the general public. Select interest groups may serve on behalf of the government, monitoring compliance with legislation or regulations, or even formally delivering programs and services on behalf of government. For instance, physicians' associations devise policies to police their own members on issues like assisted dying, and they are often called upon to make decisions as to how much each medical procedure should cost the healthcare system.

Not all interactions between government and interest groups are collegial. Many of Canada's largest lobbying firms employ lawyers who work on behalf of their clients in challenging governments and other interest groups in court. Some interest groups have their own lawyers on staff for this purpose. Litigation has long been a productive route for interest groups across the political spectrum. In the early days of Confederation, business groups allied themselves with provincial governments in mounting legal challenges to the centralized nature of Canadian federalism (see Chapter 3). They sought to empower local governments with whom they had closer connections, shifting authority away from Ottawa. Early court rulings transformed the constitution in their favour, helping to foster the decentralized mode of federalism we see in Canada today. Left-leaning groups have also enjoyed success. The Famous Five was one of the most successful early interest groups when five Alberta women successfully petitioned the courts to secure most women the right to vote in federal elections. Progressive interest groups have used the courts to expand these and other rights over time, particularly since the establishment of the Charter of Rights and Freedoms. In recent years, courtrooms have considered debates among interest groups, with governments often being drawn into the fray. Contests over the proper balance between environmental protections and economic development fall under this category.

The history of voting rights in Canada is discussed in Chapter 10, on elections: see the section titled "Democracy in Canada," on pages 330–46.

Taking issues out of the public square and into the courtroom raises the ire of populists and those who support the supremacy of the legislature over the judiciary. These critics feel that policy decisions should be made through the free exchange of ideas and popular support. They believe that people who are elected should be the ones creating laws as opposed to appointed judges who hear arguments from well-funded special interests. Supporters of interest-group litigation point out that election campaigns seldom feature the level of debate required to make progress against society's most vexing socioeconomic issues. They also point out the perils of pursuing majoritarian solutions on issues that affect minority communities.

Interest groups often plead their case in the court of public opinion. They work to raise public awareness and pressure decision-makers to join their cause through public demonstrations. Advocacy groups tend to employ a mix of public-relations activities, such as communicating via social media, issuing media advisories, putting up billboards, publicizing a website, and perhaps orchestrating acts of civil disobedience. However, unless they initiate something unusual, their efforts are unlikely to be deemed newsworthy and will fail to get on the public agenda. Consequently, interest groups often resort to publicity stunts to make the news.

See page 54 of Chapter 2 for more discussion of parliamentary supremacy.

In-person and online protests aim to attract the media's attention and move the group's concerns higher up the public's agenda. Their attempts to capture the public imagination face a considerable disadvantage compared to elected officials. Politicians command public attention by virtue of regular appearances in Question Period and by holding daily photo-ops as part of the permanent campaign. A government minister or opposition leader who wants to raise an issue often finds willing media outlets. Conversely, interest groups are faced with either paying to advertise, earning their media coverage by staging attention-grabbing events, or trying something provocative online that will generate public sympathy. Timing is crucial. Staging a strike or walk-out is a timeworn union tactic. Teachers who stage a protest during the school year, or postal workers who walk off the job at the height of the holiday season, are more likely to have an audience. So, too, are interest groups who capitalize on national or international events. Protests in conjunction

Fred Lum/The Globe and Mail via CP

Protesters at a Tim Hortons coffee shop in Toronto in 2018. That year, a rogue group of Tim Hortons restaurant franchise owners pushed back against the Ontario government's hiking the minimum wage by 20 per cent. These owners cited cost pressures as the reason for eliminating paid breaks and scaling back their staff's health and dental coverage. Unions rallied to the cause by encouraging consumers to #BoycottTimHortons and join "No Timmies Tuesdays." Some demonstrators prevented customers from entering the stores. The protests spread to the rest of the country and online petitions secured digital signatures from thousands of Canadians. The premier of Ontario publicly defended her government's minimum-wage policy whereas the leader of the official opposition was quiet. Why do you suppose these Ontario-centred protests grew to other parts of Canada?

with major international trade meetings like the G7 or sporting events like the Olympics garner markedly more media attention and, it is hoped, a swifter government response. Interest groups risk public backlash, however, if their demonstration disrupts a popular activity. On occasion, interest groups target specific governments, political parties, or politicians with protests. Sit-ins at the legislative assembly or at a local representative's office, and even occupying a government building, are rare tactics that can raise the profile of the group's concerns. Some interest groups organize boycotts of targeted companies or civil-society organizations in an effort to gain public support for their cause. Blaming and shaming those organizations for their political positions or leanings can be a proxy for critiquing their partisan allies.

Inside Canadian Politics

How Did Farmers Disrupt the Traditional Party System in Canada?

In the early twentieth century, farmers constituted one of the most influential groups in Canadian politics. Agriculture was a dominant industry and Canadian legislatures were heavily weighted toward rural representation; consequently, farmers' support was integral to federal parties wishing to form majority governments in Ottawa. Farmers formed their own political party when the Conservatives and Liberals balked at demands for free trade with the United States, for lower freight rates to transport grain and farm equipment, and for greater control by the Western provinces over their natural resources. The Progressives won the second-most seats in the 1921 federal election. Only after the Liberal Party made a concerted effort to address the farmers' grievances did the Progressives disband. Most became Liberals. Several went on to form new parties, including Social Credit and the Co-operative Commonwealth Federation.

Farmer support was also essential to any would-be premier seeking power at the provincial level. The United Farmers party formed a government in each of Alberta, Manitoba, and Ontario. In contrast, Saskatchewan farmers opted against creating their own party. In an effort to retain power, that province's Liberal Party courted the Saskatchewan Grain Growers' Association, and named several of its members to their executive committees and invited them into cabinet. Arguably, Saskatchewan farmers had as much power as their counterparts in Alberta, Manitoba, and Ontario, despite operating outside the traditional realm of party politics.

DISCUSSION ITEM

Organized interests have options when it comes to mobilizing politically. They may choose to become interest groups and ally themselves with existing parties, or form their own political parties to challenge old-line actors for control over the government. Parties can also co-opt activists by bringing them into leadership positions.

VOX POP

How much political power do farmers have in the twenty-first century? Which of today's most influential political groups do you think have the potential to disrupt the party system?

Some groups pursue radical tactics. At times these are unsanctioned and committed by fanatical fringes of the organization. In 2015, student groups in Quebec voted to boycott post-secondary classes to protest planned spending cuts by the provincial government. When some students attended class at l'Université du Québec à Montréal, masked intruders turned off the lights in classrooms, shut off computers, and chastised the students for disrespecting the boycott.[2] These actions frightened some of the very people that the student groups were purporting to represent. Interest groups must walk a fine line when designing their demonstration tactics.

Keys to Interest Group Success

Interest groups hold diverse objectives. For some, success entails raising public consciousness about an issue or set of concerns; for others, it involves directly influencing the development of public policy; for still others, it may involve a more partisan objective of shaming or defeating the party in power. To achieve any of these objectives, interest groups require a core set of tools and attributes, some of which are under their control and some of which rely upon outside forces. Successful interest groups often have sizeable amounts of popular support. Large and committed membership bases allow them to speak credibly when informing policymakers that they have the backing of a substantial portion of the electorate. CARP (formerly known as the Canadian Association of Retired Persons) boasts over 300,000 members, for instance, while Greenpeace Canada reports nearly 90,000 financial supporters. These followers are most effective when they are held together by a common set of beliefs and goals. Interest-group leaders behave much like party leaders in that they must define the organization's core values and objectives, nurture the relationships among followers, and promote synergy between the membership and the leadership. Promoting group cohesion has become a challenging task in a society where membership in community organizations and interest groups is less common. Joining membership-based organizations such as Rotary, Kinettes, or Lions clubs or being an active participant in a union or professional organization used to bring solidary from being part of a team. Social media and virtual communities mean that the demand for this form of communal experience is diminishing.

Interest groups require what have been called tangible and intangible resources.[3] Tangible resources involve money, access to funds, office space, staff, a functional and effective Web presence, and other types of hard assets. Intangible resources are of a softer variety and include experience and expertise in fields like public administration and marketing; a strong brand, track record, and reputation; and a broad network enhanced by deep relationships with key decision-makers. Tangible and intangible resources are mutually reinforcing, in that it takes hard assets to acquire soft ones, and soft assets can help to generate hard ones.

An interest group's prospects for success often rely on external factors beyond its direct control. The party in power might determine the group's access to policymakers and even funding. Interest groups that depend on public funding are in a precarious situation. Consequently, they may hesitate to publicly criticize the government and perhaps feel pressure to be seen as supportive of government policy initiatives. Interest groups enjoy more influence when a like-minded government is in office. For instance, certain business organizations are more influential when the Conservatives or Liberals are in power, whereas labour unions have more access when the New Democrats form a government.

Inside Canadian Politics

What Was the Manitoba Schools Question?

The Manitoba schools question ranks among Canada's most significant policy crises. It shows how a localized policy dispute can become a national issue that can fracture a political party and divide the country. The actors and activists involved resemble the societal interests that John Porter would go on to identify a century later in his study of Canadian political elites.

At the crux of the dispute was section 93 of the British North America Act, 1867, which stipulates that provinces have the exclusive authority to make laws about education. It also stipulates that the rights of denominational schools must be upheld, and that Protestant or Roman Catholic minorities can appeal to the federal cabinet if they feel that their rights have been affected by the province. The constitutional right of these aggrieved groups to plead directly with the federal political executive is what forced a series of prime ministers to get involved. Otherwise the dispute would likely have been foremost a provincial matter.

In 1870, the federal government's Manitoba Act created the province of Manitoba and included a clause to protect existing religious schooling. The growing English-speaking Protestant majority in Manitoba began demanding that the provincial government cease funding French schools for Roman Catholics. Bowing to public pressure, the Manitoba legislature passed the Public Schools Act (1890), ending the government's funding of religious schools. This left French-language Catholic schools to raise funds in order to continue to operate. Rather than interfere, Prime Minister John A. Macdonald left the matter to the courts. This upset his party's Quebec MPs, many of whom were Catholic and felt the religious and cultural protections outlined in section 93 were an important part of the constitutional bargain.

When Macdonald died in 1891, the governor general appointed Senator John Abbott as his successor. Prime Minister Abbott was in office when Britain's top court, the Judicial Committee of the Privy Council (JCPC), ruled that the Public Schools Act was legal. Consequently, Manitoba's French Catholic minorities proceeded to appeal to the federal cabinet to have the provincial law overturned. In the meantime, Abbott was replaced by John Thompson as prime minister. Thompson likewise stalled for time by asking the courts to verify that cabinet needed to respond to the Manitobans' appeal. Prime Minister Thompson died in office, too, leading the governor general to appoint Senator Mackenzie Bowell to the position. When the JCPC ruled in 1895 that the federal cabinet did indeed have

The salience and popularity of the group's cause is an obvious factor, as is the presence of supportive allies or unsupportive opponents. Unions on the left and business organizations on the right are excellent examples of how interest groups on each side of the political spectrum band together and oppose their political foes.

Taken together, these internal and external factors are necessary keys to most interest groups' success. Taken separately, none of them is sufficient to prevent the organization's failure. It takes more than a solid website and social-media campaign or a sizeable bank account and a supportive government to reach political goals.

institutionalized interest groups
Pressure groups that have become entrenched political organizations.

Types of Interest Groups

Many interest groups are institutionalized in that they are so well organized that they grow to become an enduring part of the state political system. **Institutionalized interest groups** are headed by political elites with experience in applying political pressure.

the duty to intervene, Prime Minister Bowell obfuscated. Instead of passing federal legislation to repeal the provincial government's law, he proposed that Manitoba should create and fund a Catholic school board. Internal party rancour led to the resignation of an astounding 11 federal ministers—both Catholic and Protestant—in an effort to get Bowell to resign. The federal government was in crisis.

The governor general resolved the situation by appointing MP Charles Tupper to be prime minister. Six ministers rejoined the cabinet. Tupper prepared legislation to repeal the province's Public Schools Act; however, the Conservatives had been in power for nearly five years, the constitutional limit. The Liberal party, led by Wilfrid Laurier, prolonged debate in the House of Commons until an election had to be called, and the remedial bill died on the order paper. During the 1896 election campaign, Laurier did not commit to a proposed solution, promising only "sunny ways and sunny days" to negotiate an amicable way forward. When Laurier assumed office as prime minister, he brokered a compromise that would require Manitoba to fund French Catholic education, but only if there were a minimum of 10 students per funded school. The principle that government will fund public education in English or French only where numbers warrant persists to this day.

The debate over religious education funding reappeared when Alberta and Saskatchewan were created (1905), during two contentious provincial referendums in Newfoundland (1990s), and in an Ontario election campaign (2007). In each of these cases, powerful interest group organizations exerted pressure on political parties in a bid to secure a favourable government decision. The topic continues to be a contentious issue when raised by provincial politicians.

DISCUSSION ITEM

On occasion, sustained pressure from interest groups can force politicians to address a sensitive issue that they would otherwise prefer to ignore.

VOX POP

What are some current examples of ways that religion and politics clash in Canadian politics? To what extent would the existence of the Charter of Rights and Freedoms have made a difference in the Manitoba schools question?

They typically feature a well-defined organizational structure and a stable membership, so continuity is assured even if there is turnover change in leadership. Their objectives tend to be well-defined and encompass a variety of connected issues and concerns. Examples of institutionalized interest groups include the Canadian Labour Congress, Equal Voice, Greenpeace Canada, and the Retail Council of Canada.

The success of an institutionalized interest group hinges on its inclusion of people who are very familiar with how government works and who the key players are. This group might include retired government officials and former high-ranking members of political parties. The institutionalized interest group focuses on the implications of specific legislation or financial decisions and negotiates concessions from government officials to meet the objectives of their supporters. The values and credibility of the organization are paramount, such that the group's leaders will prioritize winnable policy gains and accept defeat on unmovable issues.[4] Institutionalized interest groups are so entrenched in the political system that they are treated as credible participants in the policymaking process even while pushing their own values. They have evolved to become part of the mainstream political process.

By contrast, **issue-oriented interest groups** operate on the margins of mainstream political processes. They tend to lack internal cohesion and formal organization. They are the opposite of institutionalized in that they tend to have few resources, have small membership numbers, experience instability during leadership transitions, possess little insider experience in the processes of government, and have loose ties to the political elite. They might have a difficult time defining and accomplishing their objectives. Issue-oriented interest groups tend to prioritize one or two topics of concern, which limits the breadth of their appeal and popular support. Some of these organizations have a short lifespan, particularly those that come together for a single election campaign. Others maintain a stable presence for years, such as the Thalidomide Victims Association of Canada or the Monarchist League of Canada. Lack of institutionalization is somewhat offset by the ability to communicate via digital media. Even tiny organizations can mobilize, fundraise, share information, and apply public pressure in ways that were previously unimaginable.

Institutionalized and issue-oriented interest groups champion varied political issues. There is no definitive way to classify groups on the basis of their political concerns. One attempt identified a dozen typologies, including single-issue, trade association, labour union, intergovernmental, professional association, civil rights, religious, agricultural, public interest, corporation, think tank, and charity.[5] Another clustered the concerns of local interest groups into the categories of business, labour, moral, social services, non-economic interests, and environmental.[6] For simplicity's sake we can distinguish between the groups that act to advance the interests of their membership and those groups that are motivated to advance the broader public interest.[7] Self-interested groups include organizations representing businesses and labour unions such as the Canadian Bankers Association, the Canadian Labour Congress, and Canadian Manufacturers & Exporters. These operations tend to represent a large membership and are reasonably well financed. They are chiefly motivated by the pursuit of economic benefits for their members and supporters. The corporations and trade associations that finance these private interests tend to give institutionalized interests a financial and organizational advantage over other special interests. By contrast, public-interest groups promote policies that they argue will benefit broader society or a political minority. Examples of public interest groups include the Canadian Jewish Congress, Generation Squeeze, and the National Educational Association of Disabled Students. Such equality-seeking groups emphasize improved circumstances for particular people. By comparison, quality-of-life groups focus on change for the betterment of Canada as a whole. Examples include Greenpeace and Amnesty International whose Canadian chapters participate in a global network that promotes environmental and social justice throughout the world. In this vein, charities and non-profit organizations might be considered public-interest groups as well, and it may surprise some citizens to learn that such organizations lobby public officials.

Some interest groups receive financial grants and contributions from the federal government to sustain their activities. Government funding is a recognition that some public-interest groups play an important role in a pluralist society but lack the financial certainty of the larger groups with whom they compete. Take, for example, the now-defunct National Action Committee (NAC) on the Status of Women. Compared with men, women are less likely to seek election or become parliamentarians and may experience more difficulty with engaging in political activism. In recognition of these challenges, previous federal governments deemed that it was in the public interest to provide financial support to the Committee so that it could advocate on behalf of women on policy issues such as contraception, parental leave, child care, pay equity, family law, racism, and domestic violence. Federal government support included core operational funding, grants for research projects, and monies for special initiatives, among other things. Throughout the 1970s and 1980s, the NAC played a significant role on the national stage, particularly in terms of campaigning and lobbying. A series of cutbacks by PC and Liberal governments in the 1990s forced the NAC to close regional offices and curtail its operations. Attempts to replace government funding with private donations failed and the NAC dissolved in 2007. More than a decade later, the Liberal government under Prime Minister Trudeau increased funding to its own Status of Women agency and made it a full government department capable of issuing wider-ranging grants to interest groups. No countrywide interest group has emerged to replace NAC. A looser alliance of women's groups includes the Native Women's Association of Canada, the Women's Legal Education and Action Fund, Equal Voice, and others. To some, this new arrangement provides better representation for different types of women's interests, increased flexibility, and less reliance on a single organization to gain access to governments. To others, the lack of a peak organization means women's interests are splintered and receive less attention from political elites.

Governments and government agencies may have a significant impact on an interest group's resources. Gaining and retaining designation as a registered charity, for example, can have a real impact on an organization's ability to raise money. Canada Without Poverty found this out when the Canada Revenue Agency revoked its charitable status in 2016. Two years later, the group successfully challenged the revocation. In the process, an Ontario court overturned a law that prohibited charities from issuing tax rebates to supporters if the organizations spent more than 10 per cent of their resources on political activities. The court's decision is a good example of why some people get upset with judicial activism and argue that elected officials should be the ones setting public policy.

Think Tanks

Some forms of advocacy organizations seek media coverage of their research-based policy proposals. **Think tanks** generate revenue by selling consulting services, receiving financial gifts, and/or securing grants through their affiliation with government or a university. These quasi-academic operations conduct research on public-policy issues in order to stimulate public discussion about their ideas and proposed solutions. Most think tanks seek to advance an agenda that is based on an analysis of data on the economy and society. Their employees offer expert commentary in a manner that is projected as objective and non-partisan, even though their ideological slants are normally well known. Take, for example, the Manning Centre for Building Democracy, which is named after former Reform Party leader Preston Manning. Its mantra is "Strengthening conservatism in Canada." Conversely the Broadbent Institute's namesake is Ed Broadbent, the former leader of the New Democratic Party of Canada. Its slogan is "We fuel progress." Identifying ideological slants sometimes requires awareness of the party connections of employees, as with Canada2020, a Liberal think tank. Other think tanks have a clear ideological slant but no overt partisan ties.

think tank
An organization that performs research as a means of public advocacy.

Canadian think tanks focusing on economic policy and whose board members are foremost from the private sector include the Atlantic Institute for Market Studies, the C.D. Howe Institute, and the Fraser Institute. Think tanks that study social policy and promote social justice include the Canadian Centre for Policy Alternatives, the Council of Canadians, the David Suzuki Foundation, and the Pembina Institute. Those organizations' board members are more likely to be affiliated with labour unions, community activism, and the public sector. Other think tanks, such as the Canada West Foundation and the Frontier Centre, promote regionalist perspectives, attracting people from both the right and left of the political spectrum. So, too, do think tanks devoted to public policy, in general, like the Institute for Intergovernmental Relations and the Institute for Research on Public Policy. There are a plethora of other research institutes embedded in universities, as well, typically associated with faculty in political science and economics.

In many ways, think tanks in Canada fulfill a role played by political parties in European democracies, where public-policy research and development is contained within the formal party apparatus. Sometimes Canadian think tanks are commissioned to perform policy studies on behalf of governments. This type of policy work is illustrated by the Conference Board of Canada, which bills itself as "the foremost independent, evidence-based, not-for-profit applied research organization in Canada."[8] The organization disseminates data about economic trends, organizational performance, and public-policy issues, all in support of an agenda to achieve a more competitive economy for Canada. It employs experts in "conducting, publishing, and disseminating research; forecasting and economic analysis; helping people network; running conferences; developing individual leadership skills; and building organizational capacity." The Conference Board's activities are similar to those of an interest group, including issuing news releases, responding to media requests, coordinating a member database, hosting conferences, publishing reports, holding webinars, and testifying to legislative committees. The group is often commissioned by governments to produce independent reports, such as the Council of the Federation's studies into federal-provincial transfers. Like any interest group or think tank, it seeks to inform decision-makers and to influence public policy. For example, recommendations presented in the Conference Board's report about postal services in Canada contributed to Canada Post's initial decision to phase out door-to-door mail delivery in urban areas and to nearly double the price of postage stamps. Aside from the emphasis on research, a key difference between many think tanks and interest groups is the remark on the Conference Board's website that they "do not lobby for specific interests."

Whether a think tank, or an institutionalized or issue-oriented interest group, Canada's most successful interest operations are built to engage directly with key decision-makers. They often seek to affect specific types of political change or policy reforms. They have leaders, organizational hierarchies, rules of conduct, decision-making processes, budgets, vision statements, policy objectives, business plans, paid staff, and clear lines of accountability. There is little room for average citizens in the work of mos t interest groups and think tanks. Not unlike political parties, they are professional firms built to advocate on behalf of their members, followers, or donors. Some may welcome volunteers, but seldom does these supporters' involvement rise beyond a supporting role. This suggests that activism in pluralist societies like Canada tends to be organized, elitist, and exclusive. It may also lead you to believe that activism aims primarily to influence government. In fact there is much more to Canadian activism than interest groups, a subject to which we now turn.

Social Movements

The structure of interest groups differs dramatically from less embedded types of politics. **Social movements** are grassroots initiatives that gather momentum and inspire citizens to get involved. These shapeless mass movements emerge in Canada and around the world calling on people to demand government action, to reshape civil society, or to shift the political culture. Whereas interest groups are formal organizations with a hierarchy of roles, a social movement often emerges as a spontaneous reaction to political circumstances, and is characterized by its lack of formal structures. Sometimes they are the early formations of what may become an interest group; other times they fade away as enthusiasm recedes.

A social movement draws on a shared mindset that seeks to change the public's views about an issue and to alter their behaviour. Social movements lack the institutional structure of an interest group and hold societal transformation as the ultimate goal. People who are at the forefront of a social movement are not necessarily members of a political party or interest group. They likely do not interact directly with politicians. In some cases, social movements lack a definitive leadership altogether; rather, they are collectively an informal group of people who share a common concern, often on a topical issue. The concerns and goals of social movement activists may be wide-ranging, even within the same movement, perhaps drawing on such varied ideologies as feminism, environmentalism, anti-poverty, anti-racism, libertarianism, neo-conservatism, anti-colonialism, and anarchism, among others. Because of the lack of leadership and specific goals, it can be difficult for policymakers to immediately identify, let alone resolve, the policy problem at the heart of a social movement. Moreover, although the proponents may attract public sympathy, their demands may not be intelligible or palatable to broader society. This can lead politicians and citizens to dismiss movements as too unconventional to warrant a government response. Successful social movements are those that contribute to a groundswell of concern amongst members of the general public. This prompts attention and a different way of thinking among political elites. These movements often generate their own interest groups and think tanks to influence an array of policy decisions, such as the Council of Canadians with Disabilities' achievements (see Inside Canadian Politics box). Human-rights movements have achieved considerable success by creating strategic alliances with the leaders of other movements and seizing opportunities created by broader global forces.

Social movements are often an expression of the rejection of traditional politics and institutions.[9] They are a mechanism for frustrated citizens to express their political views and to participate in the political process in an unconventional manner. This gives rise to the idea that they are a form of "new" politics that is untarnished compared with the corruption and inequalities of "old" politics. Some social movements rail against a political establishment of traditional political elites in major political parties, institutionalized interest groups, the mainstream media, and even academics. They are motivated by notions of democratic idealism rather than necessarily personal gain. Many believe that change is more likely if society itself is transformed.

Social movements often consist of several interest groups who, while sharing common interests, may disagree over strategy and tactics. Consider the post-secondary student movement, which aims to improve the lives of university and college students. The Canadian Federation of Students (CFS) is the oldest and largest interest group of its kind in

social movement
An informal collection of people who share a public-policy concern and urge government action and changes to social values and behaviour.

Inside Canadian Politics

How Has the Disability Rights Movement Overcome Barriers?

Few social movements more clearly illustrate the challenges activists face in navigating the Canadian political system than the disability rights movement. Like many social forces, the movement is far from homogeneous. One in seven Canadian adults live with some form of disability; millions more family members and friends consider themselves allies. These numbers are growing as the population ages, as diagnostic capabilities improve, and as public perceptions around disabilities shift. The disabilities community tends to feature more seniors, women, and low-income Canadians than the general population. A vast majority of people with disabilities report more than one type of impairment. Each form of impairment creates a unique set of barriers to a higher quality of life. The most common disabilities are physical in nature, including challenges related to pain, dexterity, flexibility, and mobility. Accessing public and private spaces can be difficult for people with physical impairments as it is for those with sensory disabilities affecting their hearing and sight. People with cognitive disabilities confront challenges related to learning, development, and mental health. Most people with visible disabilities report facing discrimination and stigmatization, as well as difficulty accessing adequate supports to participate more fully in society, the economy, and democracy.

Public consciousness of physical and sensory disabilities rose with the return of injured veterans from the battlefields of World War I and World War II. Barrier-free homes, buildings, spaces, and transportation lagged behind advances in prosthetics and wheelchairs,

prompting many veterans groups to pressure governments to invest in community infrastructure and pass new laws to ensure accessibility. Early disability activists worked closely with veterans groups to expand the provision of supports to all people regardless of the source of their impairment. Progress to improve the lives of people with cognitive disabilities was much slower. Jurisdictional authority meant the movement needed to form separate groups to lobby all provincial governments to reform education systems across the country. Deinstitutionalization took decades. Activists formed non-profit organizations to replace residential hospitals and schools with community-based services. The groups eventually coalesced into the Coalition of Provincial Organizations of the Handicapped, which later rebranded itself the Council of Canadians with Disabilities (CCD).

Disability activists worked under the broader civil rights movement to achieve legal and constitutional freedoms. The Canadian movement benefited from international developments in the 1970s. The United Nations Declaration on the Rights of Disabled Persons provided CCD and other interest groups with traction and leverage to pressure governments for change. Agencies, advisory councils, and ministries were established across the country, with disability organizations serving as key members of the new policy community. Human rights codes were updated to bolster the rights of disabled people. Disability was included in the Charter of Rights and Freedoms. Disability activists could now use courts and tribunals to protect and expand disability rights across the country. The focus gradually shifted to integrating disabled people more

this country. It has long been known for its combative approach to advocacy; for organizing demonstrations, strikes and protests; and for taking hardline positions when negotiating with provincial and federal governments. By contrast, the newer Canadian Association of Student Associations (CASA) takes a more collaborative approach in its dealings with governments. Viewing themselves as stakeholders, they lobby elected officials for incremental gains on behalf of their members, which consist of student union organizations.

fully into the Canadian workforce. Several governments modelled the way by making their own hiring practices more inclusive and providing incentives to private-sector employers to do the same. Disability interest groups followed suit, with many seeking to transfer leadership roles from advocates and allies to people with disabilities.

Progress is sometimes interrupted by retrenchment. In the late 1980s and early 1990s, government priorities shifted toward the economy. Group rights were challenged; budgets were reduced for government-assistance programs, services, and grants; protective regulations were removed; and many points of access to government decision-making were closed. Several regional disabilities groups disbanded during this period. International forces once again buoyed the domestic movement when Canada signed on to the United Nations Convention on the Rights of Persons with Disabilities in 2010. This commitment requires the federal government to report publicly on its progress toward enhancing the rights of disabled people in Canada. It also represents an intention to improve the country's social and economic conditions for persons with disabilities. The public reporting includes contributions from all provincial and territorial governments. All Canadian governments now

have a level of accountability for global norms around the rights of disabled people.

The UN secretary-general Ban Ki-moon greets members of the Canadian delegation: foreign minister Lawrence Cannon (far left), Steven Estey of the Council of Canadians with Disabilities (second from left), Traci Walters of Independent Living Canada (centre), and Bendina Miller of the Canadian Association for Community Living (far right). This delegation was in New York in March 2010 for Canada's ratification of the UN Convention on the Rights of Persons with Disabilities, which is the first international treaty to comprehensively recognize the rights of persons with disabilities.

DISCUSSION ITEM

Social movement leaders must band together with other groups to overcome internal, constitutional, resource, and political barriers before they can remove the programmatic ones facing Canadians.

VOX POP

What are some of the most notable achievements of the disability rights movement? What challenges lie ahead for those working to remove barriers for Canadians with disabilities?

Unfortunately for many social movements, people who do nothing to support their cause can nevertheless benefit from the efforts of those working tirelessly to effect change. This conundrum of free riding is known as the **collective action problem**. In *The Logic of Collective Action: Public Goods and the Theory of Groups* (1965), American economist Mancur Olson theorized that people gain the most when a small group to which they belong achieves a favourable policy outcome. In larger groups, which have higher

collective action problem
The notion that people whose interests are promoted by a group will benefit from its efforts whether or not they actively participate.

expenses and broader objectives, there is a more diffuse commitment to the movement's core principles. To address this quandary, and to encourage people to participate in a large group or movement, it is essential that formal membership come with exclusive rewards. This is why interest groups promote members-only rates on consumer products (e.g., insurance, groceries, travel) and exclusive subscriptions to industry journals, magazines, or newsletters. Social movements seldom have formal membership lists, making these sorts of quid pro quo exchanges exceedingly difficult, resulting in many citizens getting a free ride on the backs of activists working to effect change.

In the case of social movements, the notion of offering special incentives is impractical, given that there is no formal organization that coordinates membership benefits. What benefits exist are often easy to clone and be appropriated by non-contributing members. Indeed, visible participation in a social movement can offer participants an improved social status. People who display a sticker or button with a political message, those who wear a colour of clothing in solidarity with a groundswell of support for a given topic, social media users who attach a temporary badge to their profile, people who grow moustaches as part of the "Movember" fundraiser for prostate cancer, and people who "like" a Facebook page devoted to a particular movement may be incentivized by the public attention they receive from communicating a cause.

Being motivated by social recognition, and fear of being left out, can be much different than what motivates people to put in the hard work necessary to cause change.

arindambanerjee/Shutterstock

Social media is an effective tool for drawing attention to social causes ranging from the reduction of sexual violence to the promotion of racial equality. Viral hashtags such as #IdleNoMore, #BlackLivesMatter, #MeToo, and others raise public awareness around key social issues like settler colonialism, racism, and sexual violence. People who participate in these online discussions can derive a sense of participation regardless of the extent to which their actions produce a tangible outcome. What do you think: does social media promote or diminish productive political activism?

Slacktivism involves people joining movements through social media but seldom engaging directly or meaningfully in promoting the cause. Slacktivism creates a false sense of action because there is none. Reposting comments, signing online petitions, and sharing or liking videos are ego-driven gestures that appeal to our sense of altruism. These vapid gestures are often timewasters that diminish rates of more productive engagement, like attending a political meeting, donating to a food bank, or volunteering at a homeless shelter. Defenders of slacktivism argue that one person with a smartphone can do more to raise civic engagement than a thousand people at a protest. Yet movements must spread beyond the virtual world and into the policy realm in order to effect political change. In this sense, interest groups, think tanks, and political parties play an important role in translating movement objectives into action.

slacktivism
Actions taken by individuals to appear part of a social movement, but that have no direct impact on the fulfilment of its objectives.

Hacktivism and Fake News

Like most elements of Canadian politics, activism has been transformed in the information age. Interest groups and social movements are using digital tools and platforms to organize and to reach larger audiences. On occasion, online activists can be motivated by more sinister motives. **Hacktivism** is a disruptive form of online political activity that exploits weaknesses in e-government. Its mildest form is electronic civil disobedience; at worst, it is highly unethical and criminal. Hacktivism ranges from political agitators defacing website content to political enemies engaging in electronic surveillance to the infiltration of election databases. International hacktivist organizations, such as Anonymous and WikiLeaks, destabilize social order as they promote a philosophy that government should be completely open and transparent. Consequently, they seek to expose government surveillance and intelligence-gathering operations (see Chapter 14). To their supporters, these organizations hold governments to account by exposing misdeeds. They act as a check on democratic societies becoming a police state and provide whistleblowers new avenues to share inside information. To their detractors, hacktivists jeopardize state secrets and may place undue pressure on duly elected officials to respond to their demands. The presence of hacktivists means that it is essential for government records and financial data to be protected from unauthorized access. This is one of the reasons so many Canadians and government officials are wary of moving to automated or online voting. A government department's loss of an external hard drive containing personal information for 500,000 Canadians who received student loans is just one example of the many serious concerns about governments' ability to protect personal information.

hacktivism
Politically motivated damage inflicted on government information communication technologies.

Local political actors engage in hacktivism as well. Their motivation is not to destabilize government but rather to inflict political harm on opponents. This includes a cyber-attack on the NDP electronic voting system during the party's 2012 federal leadership convention; a Liberal staffer's accessing a fake Twitter account from a House of Commons computer to tweet details about the minister of public safety's divorce; and a former Conservative supporter's unearthing embarrassing information about the party's election candidates. Periodically, there are media reports of government computers being used to change the content of a minister's Wikipedia entry, and party staffers may use fake names to post comments to online feedback forums as part of an astroturfing campaign.

Figure 12.1 | Spotting Fake News

Source: Developed by The International Federation of Library Associations and Institutions (IFLA). Licensed under Creative Commons Attribution 4.0 International (CC BY 4.0)

fake news
Fabricated stories designed to appear as authentic journalism and spread online to influence political attitudes through deception.

A serious public-policy issue confronting governments around the world, including in Canada, is guarding against the shady online practices of external actors seeking to influence elections. By spreading disinformation, they may seek to persuade some voters to abandon their preferred party or candidate, to generate support for their side, or to dissuade people from showing up to vote. This typically involves expanding on half-truths, rumours, or stereotypes to paint the activists' opponents in a negative light. It may involve spreading conspiracy theories to discredit reliable reporting that threatens the activists' interests. Disseminating **fake news** through social media can be an effective means of stirring mistrust and conflict among citizens. Memes and click-bait headlines can travel widely and quickly, particularly when activists employ bots to amplify their message. These falsehoods can affect elections in a number of ways. A strategically placed lie may drive a wedge between opponents or demotivate them from voting. An emerging trend involves the use of artificial intelligence to superimpose images of politicians, resulting in authentic-looking videos known as deepfakes. If plentiful enough, fake information can foster dissent among the broader electorate. Some of this activism is homegrown, but the global reach of social media has opened Canadian elections to potential interference by foreign actors. By exploiting social and political cleavages, bad actors may seek to divide citizens; by sowing distrust in the electoral process by challenging the legitimacy of the outcome, they can destabilize Canadian democracy.

Relatively little is known about the full impact of nefarious online activism on elections or citizens' faith in democracy. Governments are taking steps to limit the impact of fake news, chiefly through stiffer regulations on social-media giants like Twitter and Facebook, and local journalism has a vested interest in exposing mistruths that undermine the news industry. Ultimately, citizens' own knowledge and judgement provide the best protection against anti-democratic cyber-activism, and it is up to them to discern the difference between factual information and online falsehoods. This begins with awareness of system vulnerabilities. Breaking free of the online echo-chambers that divide Canadians into different political tribes would require overcoming steep technological and psychological barriers. Computer algorithms ensure most of what Canadians see in their newsfeeds reinforces their preferences. Individuals' confirmation bias tends to filter out any remaining information that conflicts with their belief systems. It takes extra effort to seek out multiple viewpoints on an issue. Even more effort is required to determine whether a source provides a valid and reliable account of an issue. As a starting point, dedicated citizens are wise to resist the temptation to take political information at face value or spread messages without reflecting on their authenticity and potentially negative impact on democratic discourse (Figure 12.1). However, as is the case with slacktivism, many people are unwilling or unable to invest the necessary time and effort.

Concluding Thoughts

The common objective of activists is to bring about political reform. Many interest groups and social movements do so by drawing attention to the shortcomings of existing political actors, organizations, and institutions in terms of representing the full spectrum of views in Canadian society. Addressed in the following chapter, this raises questions about the capacity of Canadian democracy to accommodate diversity within the various halls of power.

For More Information

Looking to trace the evolution of interest group and social movement influence in Canada? Note the similarities and trends among these seminal sources: Robert Presthus's *Elite Accommodation in Canadian Politics*, written in 1973 (Toronto: Macmillan); Paul Pross's *Group Politics and Public Policy*, the second edition of which was released in 1992 (Toronto: Oxford University Press); Lisa Young and Joanna Everitt's 2005 contribution to the UBC Press Democratic Audit series, *Advocacy Groups*; and the second edition

of Miriam Smith's *A Civil Society? Collective Actors in Canadian Political Life*, published in 2017 (Toronto: University of Toronto Press).

Want to learn about some of the modern pressure tactics used by interest groups grassroots activists? Consider Eric Shragge's 2013 examination of *Activism and Social Change: Lessons for Community Organizing*, 2nd edn (University of Toronto Press).

What type of influence can activists have as part of the policy community? Learn more in Marguerite Marlin's 2016 article, "Interest Groups and Parliamentary Committees: Leveling the Playing Field," *Canadian Parliamentary Review* 39, no. 1 (2016): pp. 24–8.

How did social media transform Idle No More into one of Canada's first successful online movements, and what became of the momentum? Candis Callison and Alfred Hermida explain the origins of the movement in their 2015 article, "Dissent and Resonance: #Idlenomore as an Emergent Middle Ground," *Canadian Journal of Communication* 40, no. 4 (2015): 695–716. Vincent Raynauld, Emmanuelle Richez, and Katie Boudreau Morris offer an updated account in "Canada Is #IdleNoMore: Exploring Dynamics of Indigenous Political and Civic Protest in the Twitterverse," *Information, Communication & Society* 21, no. 4: 626–42.

How have generational shifts influenced the identities and activist strategies of Canadian feminists? Brenda O'Neill discusses "Continuity and Change in the Contemporary Feminist Movement," *Canadian Journal of Political Science* 50, no. 2 (2017): pp. 443–59.

How did a shift in approach contribute to policy gains by the disabilities community? Ravi Malhotra and Benjamin Isitt edited a 2017 book that offers some explanations, and lessons for future reformers: *Disabling Barriers: Social Movements, Disability History, and the Law* (Vancouver: UBC Press).

Curious as to why Miriam Smith considers Canada's LGBTQ2+ community "one of the most successful social movements in the world"? Read her chapter in David Paternotte's 2011 edited volume, *The Lesbian and Gay Movement and the State* (London: Routledge).

Why do religious organizations continue to hold power over public policy? Clark Banack explores this question in "Understanding the Influence of Faith-Based Organizations on Education Policy in Alberta," *Canadian Journal of Political Science* 48 no. 4: 933–59.

Deeper Inside Canadian Politics

1. Interest groups often have limited resources and options when it comes to strategy. Public persuasion, litigation, and lobbying each carry their own risks, benefits, and costs. Imagine you are advising one of the following groups. Which strategy would you offer as your recommendation, and why?
   a) A pro-life group seeing to re-criminalize abortion
   b) A neighbourhood association seeking to block the building of a new professional sports stadium in your community
   c) A trade union opposed to a new free trade deal
2. Media coverage can give a false sense of public support for interest groups and social movements that engage in provocative activities to attract attention. Protestors tend to congregate in urban centres where journalists are based and only a segment of society participates in social media activism. Given this:
   a) How can governments and politicians ensure that activists' demands do not overwhelm public-policy issues that do not attract public attention and/or that matter to the silent majority?
   b) What can people in rural and remote communities do to combat attention paid to urbanites' concerns?
   c) What can citizens who are not savvy with social media activism do to attract attention to their concerns?
   d) What are some of the special challenges that persons with disabilities likely face when participating in political activism?

Professor Profile

Mireille Lalancette

Political actors' use of social media, gender mediatization
Lead editor of *What's Trending in Canadian Politics?* (2019)

Courtesy of Leïc Godbout

Mireille Lalancette publishes about mediatized images of politicians, gender, and representation. She studies the use and impact of social media by citizens, grassroots organizations, and Canadian political actors. Her work includes collaborations about digital politics with Canadian and American researchers and on mediatization of politics with European professors.

Here is what Mireille Lalancette told us about her career path from when she was an undergraduate student, why she is drawn to her area of specialization, what is challenging about studying Canadian politics, and what advice she has for students.

* * *

I completed my undergraduate degree at Laval University in Quebec with a major in communication and a minor in political science. I stayed at Laval for a master in political communication and went on to Université de Montréal for my PhD. My most salient memory is about studying the Canadian constitution. I did my BA in the 1990s when questions of federalism were pretty important. The Meech Lake Accord and the Charlottetown referendum occupied the attention of political science professors, students, media, and citizens. It was a busy and pretty exciting political time. I also remember professors' passion about their subject and willingness to share their knowledge with us. I was really amazed by students of all political allegiances eager to debate about the pros and cons of federalism.

As long as I can remember, I had an interest in politics, political actors, and discourses about them. Growing up in Ottawa sure fuels an interest in politics. I realized early on that, being a woman, my interest in politics was seen as peculiar and that there seem to be different standards when assessing the leadership of a woman. It was the case in school, but also in the media when discussing female politicians. They appeared to have different discourse in order to be able to reach out to citizens. Besides, I observed that there were few women in politics. Kim Campbell faced many criticisms as the first woman prime minister of Canada. Some of those criticisms looked to me as being related more to her gender and to gendered expectations. This interest stayed with me as I did my master's and PhD studies. I focused on personalization and spectacularization of politics in the media. Since these phenomena have a strong gendered component, I tried to unpack and understand what issues were at stake and how they affect women politicians in Quebec and in Canada.

The most challenging part about studying women and politics is to go beyond stereotypes. Researchers need to capture the nuances of both quantitative and qualitative analysis and offer a nuanced portrait of the situation. What surprises you most about this area of study is the incessant double standard that women have to face when they go into politics and the many obstacles and challenges they face when trying to make it into the political world.

The one tip that I would suggest to students is to read, read, read about what you study and also about what goes on in the world. Politics is all interconnected now, so we need to be able to understand the context as well as the transnational influences on politics.

Up for Debate

Should spending by interest groups be regulated in Canada?

THE CLAIM: YES, IT SHOULD!

Regulating spending by special interests is essential in a functioning pluralistic and democratic society.

Yes: Argument Summary

Interest groups perform an important function in Canadian politics. However, wealthy organizations have a greater capacity to pressure political elites and potentially influence government decisions. To equate freedom of speech with freedom to spend is to ignore this inequity of influence. It would mean drawing improper parallels between the American and Canadian systems of government. It is imperative that spending by interest groups be regulated, especially during election campaigns.

Yes: Top 5 Considerations

1. Allowing unlimited spending by special interests risks harming the very foundations of democracy by allowing people and groups with greater resources to have greater influence over the democratic process and government decision-making. Breaking up this concentration of funds creates the level playing field that is essential to a healthy, pluralistic democracy.

2. In 2004, the Supreme Court of Canada ruled that restricting spending by interest groups is justified under the Charter of Rights and Freedoms' provision that freedom of speech may be subject to "reasonable limits prescribed by law as can be demonstrably justified in a free and democratic society" (section 1). In this ruling, the court denied a petition brought by the National Citizens Coalition, a well-heeled interest group that was advocating the removal of such spending limits.

3. History shows that special interest money is often spent on the sort of negative advertising that turns people off the political process. Negative advertising sponsored by well-funded interest groups have played an influential role in a number of recent provincial election campaigns. This has been cited as a serious concern by chief election officers and has led to some provincial legislatures introducing stricter regulations.

4. Spending limits and regulations reduce the possibility of corruption. Under the Canada Elections Act, after a federal election the names of donors and a group's spending activities must be reported to Elections Canada. The information is then made available for public scrutiny.

5. There is little indication that interest groups are unable to operate in Canada within the existing regulations. Over 100 interest groups registered to spend money during the 2019 federal election campaign. This ranged from deep-pocketed institutionalized groups like the Canadian Union of Public Employees to tiny protests that communicated only through the Internet.

Yes: Other Considerations

- Most industrialized democratic nations impose some sort of limits on the influence of big money in political campaigns. Levelling the communication playing field for all political interests through regulation has been deemed to be the greater good over unregulated free speech.

- In the United States, the formidable influence of political action committees (PACs) and so-called super PACs that bundle money is a major public concern. Incidents have included the notorious Swift Boat Veterans for Truth group, which during the 2004 presidential campaign ran negative ads with claims that were so far-fetched that they spawned the term "swiftboating" to refer to political falsehoods.

- Given its level of income inequality and the persistence of what John Porter called the vertical mosaic, many critics already question Canada's status as a truly pluralist society. Without regulation, the perception of influence of big money in Canadian politics would only further reduce citizens' confidence that all democratic viewpoints are considered in the political process.

THE COUNTERCLAIM: NO, THEY SHOULDN'T!

Limiting what interest groups can spend represents a constraint on free speech and is undemocratic.

No: Argument Summary

In a democratic society, freedom of speech must be sacrosanct in political debates. Those in power should not be permitted to control or limit the messages expressed by special-interest groups during or between election campaigns; to do so is anti-democratic. Limits on the amount of advertising that third parties can buy are a mechanism to muzzle groups that could otherwise help determine the outcome of an election or policy debate. Should the country's political elites be the ones to decide what information or viewpoints Canadians are exposed to? If Canadians do not like the ideas they hear, they will choose to ignore such communication, and may even take action against the source. The ability to make that choice lies at the heart of our democracy.

No: Top 5 Considerations

1. Having access to money is essential for communicating with citizens. Therefore, limiting third-party spending is akin to limiting political communication. For democracy to function, it is imperative that the political elites who are in power do not limit the ability of others to hold them accountable, which includes the ability to provide information to Canadians about how the government is performing or how a prospective government would perform.
2. In Canadian federal politics as well as in several provinces, corporations and labour unions are not allowed to donate money to political parties or candidates. That they are also limited in their election spending

is an excessive restriction on their ability to advocate in their members' best interests.
3. In the United States, the Supreme Court ruled in 2010 that interest-group spending could not be restricted, because this would violate citizens' rights to free speech through their collective organizations. Canada has a long history of supporting similar collectivist rights. And Canada's Charter of Rights and Freedoms stipulates that Canadians must have "freedom of thought, belief, opinion and expression" (Section 2b).
4. The Supreme Court of Canada ruled that third-party spending limits are in the public interest. It has also ruled that legislation restricting the participation of small political parties is unconstitutional. This amounts to supporting free speech for small voices while denying it for those groups who enjoy more popular appeal. This moves beyond levelling the playing field to slanting the pitch in favour of fringe groups.
5. Restrictions on third-party ad spending creates a veneer of legitimacy. There is nothing to prevent wealthy organized interests from circumventing regulations by funding—instead of a single interest group—multiple interest groups united in a common policy objective. The challenges involved in closing these loopholes make attempts at regulation fruitless.

No: Other Considerations

- Restricting spending by third-party participants does a disservice to democracy if that money would have been used to provide positive information and add to constructive debate.
- Because the constitution does not distinguish between the freedom of speech for individuals and the freedom of speech for interest groups or other political organizations, we should infer that the freedom applies to all equally. This freedom should apply irrespective of financial capacity.
- The definition of what's reasonable in a "free and democratic society" should include the freedom to speak as loudly and as often as one is able, in advocating one's interests.

Discussion Questions

- To what extent should the government limit how much interest groups can spend during election campaigns?
- Should interest groups be treated differently than political parties when it comes to restricting their election activities? Why or why not?
- Why do you think that supreme courts in Canada and the US have arrived at different interpretations concerning the constitutional protection of free speech?
- Libertarian groups like the National Citizens Coalition have been especially critical of spending limits. What role does ideology play in the debate?
- In your opinion, should the government provide subsidies to poorly funded interest groups to help them communicate during election campaigns?

Where to Learn More about Interest Groups in Canada

Robert G. Boatright, *Interest Groups and Campaign Finance Reform in the United States and Canada* (Ann Arbor, MI: University of Michigan Press, 2011).

Nicole Goodman, "Private over Public: A Conservative Approach to Interest Advocacy," in *The Blueprint: Conservative Parties and their Impact on Canadian Politics*, eds. J.P. Lewis and Joanna Everitt (Toronto: University of Toronto Press, 2017).

Rachel Laforest, "Going Digital: Non-Profit Organizations in a Transformed Media Environment," in *Political Elites in Canada: Power and Influence in Instantaneous Times*, eds. Alex Marland, Thierry Giasson, and Andrea Lawlor (Vancouver: UBC Press, 2018).

David Langille, "Follow the Money: How Business and Politics Define our Health," in *Social Determinants of Health: Canadian Perspectives* 3rd edn, ed. Dennis Raphael (Toronto: Canadian Scholars Press, 2016).

Mario Levesque, "Vulnerable Populations and the Permanent Campaign: Disability Organizations as Policy Entrepreneurs," in *Permanent Campaigning in Canada*, eds. Alex Marland, Thierry Giasson, and Anna Lennox Esselment (Vancouver: UBC Press, 2017).

David Schneiderman, *Red, White, and Kind of Blue? The Conservatives and the Americanization of Canadian Constitutional Culture* (Toronto: University of Toronto Press, 2015).

Jacquetta Newman and A. Brian Tanguay, "Crashing the Party: The Politics of Interest Groups and Social Movements," in *Citizen Politics: Research and Theory in Canadian Political Behaviour*, eds. Joanna Everitt and Brenda O'Neill (Don Mills, ON: Oxford University Press, 2002).

Leslie F. Seidle, ed., *Interest Groups and Elections in Canada*, vol. 2 of the Research Studies of the Royal Commission on Electoral Reform and Party Financing (Toronto: Dundurn, 1991).

13

Diversity and Representation

Inside This Chapter

- What are the main types of representation?
- How is diversity defined and represented in Canadian democracy?
- Does Canada suffer from a democratic deficit?
- What lessons do the experiences of Indigenous peoples impart about representation in Canada?

Inside Diversity and Representation

Canada's political system has become more inclusive over the past two centuries. Nevertheless, various parts of the political system feature relatively low proportions of women, Indigenous peoples, visible minorities, persons with disabilities, young people, low-income citizens, and members of other traditionally marginalized groups. The extent to which you view this as a problem depends on your perspective on representation. Notions that women are underrepresented in legislatures, for instance, presume that female legislators are best positioned to defend women's interests or that having gender parity around decision-making tables results in better public policy. Critics take issue with this view by arguing that representativeness encompasses ideas, policy debates, local issues, and duty to the nation. Keep in mind the following aspects of representation in Canada as you read through this chapter.

✔ **Canada's self-image as a cultural mosaic can undermine efforts to advance equality.** The metaphor of a mosaic depicts Canada as differently coloured tiles that produce a rich and complex picture of multicultural harmony. The mosaic myth overlooks some of persistent ethnocultural inequalities in Canadian society as well as forms of discrimination based on non-ethnic identities.

✔ **Some of Canada's traditionally marginalized groups have overcome obstacles to political representation.** Politics in Canada is largely a white man's game. There are stories that buck this trend—of women, for instance, holding the highest positions of power, and of institutions featuring an overrepresentation of traditionally marginalized groups. Society must draw lessons from their achievements and consider ways to address impediments to further participation.

✔ **Indigenous peoples are not much better represented in Canadian politics today than they were decades ago.** New avenues of representation have opened up for Indigenous peoples living in Canada, but settler colonialism prevents further gains. Some Indigenous peoples do not seek representation in the Canadian political structure.

UP FOR DEBATE

Should Indigenous and non-Indigenous politics be considered as part of a common political system?

Keep this question in mind as you read through the chapter. Consult the end-of-chapter debate supplement for more material to help you engage in an informed discussion of the topic.

Glass Ceilings

Different types of diversity have been emphasized to varying extents throughout Canadian history. At the time of Confederation, Canada's constitutional framers prided themselves on reflecting the linguistic, religious, and cultural differences between English and French settlers within a single state. Federalism helped them to accommodate regional differences. Respect for Indigenous peoples' traditions, customs, and sovereignty factored little into their considerations. With the arrival of early immigrant waves from Britain, Western Europe, and Eastern Europe, diversity took on a heavier ethnic component. Racial differences added to the complexity when the immigrant pool was expanded to include Asia and Africa.

By the late twentieth century, Canadian governments began protecting diversity through law. Group rights were enumerated under the federal Multiculturalism Act and Official Languages Act. The Charter of Rights and Freedoms, provincial human rights codes, and judicial rulings went beyond ethno-cultural diversity to encompass gender, sexual orientation, Indigenous status, age, wealth, and ableness, among others. Furthermore, social progress has been realized through the Quiet Revolution in Quebec, advancements in women's equality, the success of ameliorative programs, and reduced discrimination.

Groups of people who experience difficulty reaching positions of political power due to invisible barriers are said to be constrained by a **glass ceiling**. The expression refers to the often invisible institutional and societal impediments that favour some members of society over others. Many of the obstacles faced by politically marginalized people are aspects of political life that seem normal—until it becomes evident that those norms are biased and need to change in order to make politics more inclusive.

Ellen Fairclough is among the many women who have broken glass ceilings (Table 13.1). In the late 1950s, she was the first woman to become a federal cabinet minister in Canada. Finding a washroom on Parliament Hill was a constant issue for women MPs because most of the facilities were built for men and the doors did not have locks. Fairclough was faced with walking long distances to another floor. Eventually she overcame the problem by asking an employee to stand watch outside while she used a male-only facility.[1] One day the cabinet was discussing a gruesome issue. The men worried that reviewing the details of a rape and murder during a deliberation about the death penalty would be too upsetting for a woman. The prime minister asked Fairclough to leave. Fairclough was initially puzzled about being treated in such a paternalistic manner. She later grew amused at the absurdity of high-ranking men grappling with a life-or-death decision who were fretting about using foul language in front of a woman.

Another poignant example of glass ceilings and political norms occurred half a century later in New Brunswick. Allison Brewer became the first openly LGBTQ2+ leader of a mainstream political party in Canada (also Table 13.1). The accomplishment is unquestionably newsworthy. However, the media was so fascinated by her sexual orientation and gender that the policies Brewer was championing often lost out to coverage of personal aspects of her life. As a lesbian, she confronted stereotypes that framed her leadership differently, and so she changed her behaviour to fit in. To align with heteronormative codes, Brewer brought her children to events, recruited an older conservative man to accompany her, and avoided wearing jeans.[2] Projecting how a politician was supposed to look improved her ability to advocate policy.

These are just some of countless examples of the ways that people throughout Canadian politics confront glass ceilings. These rules and practices extend advantages to those who have traditionally had the most success, namely people who are white, male, older, educated, wealthy, Christian, straight, English-speaking, Canadian-born, and/or without disabilities. Society's structures around European colonialist norms are so pervasive that some sociologists refer to the dominance of **whitestream Canadians**.[3] As Caucasians, Fairclough and Brewer were in a better position to be pathbreakers, and likely would not have reached such political heights had they also been Indigenous or disabled. The obstacles at that time would have been too large for them to climb the political ladder. When glass ceilings break, the political class becomes more diverse and new ways of practising politics emerge, which in turn opens opportunities for others.

Models of Representation

To say that Canada is a representative democracy means that its citizens are represented by elected officials who are granted the authority to make decisions on behalf of citizens. Free and fair elections and transparent appointment processes ensure that representatives

glass ceiling
Barriers that inhibit participation in politics by traditionally marginalized groups, particularly women.

whitestream Canadians
Caucasians who form the traditional mainstream of Canadian society.

Table 13.1   Women Who Have Broken Glass Ceilings in Canadian Politics

Year	First Woman to Be a . . .	Name (Party)
1902	Provincial candidate	Margaret Haile, Ontario (Canadian Socialist League)
1917	Member of a legislative assembly	Louise McKinney, Alberta (Non-Partisan League)
1917	Municipal councillor	Hannah Gale, Calgary
1920	Provincial cabinet minister	Mary Ellen Smith, British Columbia (Liberal)
1920	Mayor – appointed	Constance Hamilton, Toronto
1921	Federal candidate	Five women, including Agnes Macphail (Progressive)
1921	Member of Parliament	Agnes Macphail (Progressive)
1930	Senator	Carine Wilson (Liberal)
1936	Mayor – elected	Barbara Hanley, Webbwood
1951	Mayor of a major city	Charlotte Whitton, Ottawa
1951	Leader of a provincial party	Thérèse Casgrain, Quebec (Parti social démocratique)
1957	Federal minister	Ellen Fairclough (Progressive Conservative)
1974	Lieutenant governor	Pauline Mills McGibbon, Ontario
1977	Out LGBTQ2+ provincial candidate	Therese Faubert, Ontario (League for Socialist Action)
1982	Supreme Court of Canada justice	Bertha Wilson
1984	Governor general	Jeanne Sauvé
1984	Visible minority mayor	Daurene Lewis, Annapolis Royal
1988	Leader of a federal party	Kathryn Cholette (Green)
1988	Indigenous MP	Ethel Blondin-Andrew (Liberal)
1989	Leader of a major federal party	Audrey McLaughlin (New Democratic Party)
1991	Premier of a province	Rita Johnston, British Columbia (Social Credit)
1991	Premier of a territory	Nellie Cournoyea, Northwest Territories
1993	Prime minister	Kim Campbell (Progressive Conservative)
1993	Premier—elected	Catherine Callbeck, PEI (Liberal)
1997	Lieutenant governor using a wheelchair	Lise Thibault, Quebec
1999	Visible minority governor general	Adrienne Clarkson
2000	Chief Justice of the Supreme Court	Beverley McLachlin
2000	Leader of federal official opposition	Deborah Grey (Canadian Alliance)
2001	Out LGBTQ2+ MP	Libby Davies (NDP)
2005	Out LGBTQ2+ provincial party leader	Allison Brewer, New Brunswick (NDP)
2006	Out LGBTQ2+ senator	Nancy Ruth (Conservative)
2013	Out LGBTQ2+ premier	Kathleen Wynne, Ontario (Liberal)

Note: Not intended to be a definitive list.

‹‹‹‹‹‹‹‹‹‹‹‹‹‹‹‹‹‹‹
For more on what it means to say that Canada is a representative democracy, see page 33 in Chapter 2, on the constitution.

are chosen legitimately. Opinions will vary about the extent to which an elected official represents a community and whether that individual personifies what it means to be from that district. Standing up for local interests by securing infrastructure projects, being trusted to make decisions in the broader common good, looking physically like electors, coming from a common background or community—these are among the many variables of representation.

American political theorist Hanna Pitkin's seminal research suggests there are four main types of representation in Western democracies like Canada (see Table 13.2). A voter

Table 13.2   Pitkin's Types of Representation

Type	Example
Descriptive	A politician who looks most like you
Formalistic	A politician who holds your district's seat
Substantive	A politician who promotes your interests
Symbolic	A politician who reflects your sense of place in the political system

who is enthusiastic about any of these types must make trade-offs when weighing the available choices on the ballot. Even then, research finds that voters prioritize parties and party leaders in elections, meaning that relatively few voters are concerned with local candidate considerations when voting. In other cases voters have no say in who holds positions, such as appointed representatives of the monarch, senators, judges, and many others.

Citizens may sense **symbolic representation** when they feel a strong attachment to a particular political actor or entity. This symbolism involves a citizen identifying with a specific person to the extent that the person embodies the citizen's own sense of place in politics and government. Pitkin emphasizes this type of connection for religious communities. She argues, for example, that Christians may feel symbolically represented by Jesus. In Canada some citizens feel a symbolic attachment to the Queen, to a wartime prime minister, or to the first premier of their generation. Many women and people in the African-Canadian community celebrated Viola Desmond as a symbolic leader when her

symbolic representation
A political attachment to someone or something that is seen to epitomize what it means to be a part of one's political community.

THE CANADIAN PRESS/Darren Calabrese

Wanda Robson holds the $10 bank note featuring her sister, the human-rights icon Viola Desmond, in Halifax in 2018. Desmond was selected to be the first Canadian woman and person of colour to appear on Canadian currency following public consultations. Can you think of anyone else who should appear on a Canadian banknote? Is it a coincidence that a Liberal government removed Conservative PM John A. Macdonald from the $10 bill and kept Liberal PM Wilfrid Laurier on the $5 note?

image was placed on the 10-dollar bill. Symbolic leaders hold almost mythical status in the minds of their followers. The system is working well as long as they are in a position of power.

formalistic representation
A political attachment to someone by virtue of that person's status as a legitimately elected official.

Other Canadians may seek more **formalistic representation** from their elected officials. To them, members of the legislature are trustees of the public good, and should prioritize formal accountability. Once elected, politicians sit in the legislature as stewards of the public good, making collective decisions based on the needs of the entire population. Elections are pivotal events for citizens and elected officials who hold this formalistic view of representation. Voters pass judgement once every election cycle, which authorizes their representatives to conduct business with little interaction with their constituents. Canadians who value formal representation believe that whoever wins the most votes has a legitimate mandate as long as the election was free and fair. A voter who supports a representative's ability to craft policy has a formalistic view.

substantive representation
A political attachment to someone in a position to defend or promote one's own interests.

Other citizens believe that their own localized interests should prevail and that their representative should deliver specific services or programs to their community. Furthermore, ideas matter because elected officials are valued for their ideological principles. **Substantive representation** treats elected officials as delegates of their constituents. People who feel substantively represented do not perceive that their interests are subsumed by those of the larger community. Rather, they sense that their politicians are working directly for them, and expect their locally elected representative to prioritize their interests over broader ones. These citizens tend to follow their elected officials more closely. They attend town-hall forums and communicate frequently through letters, email, social media, or phone calls. Those who prize a substantive connection believe that the system works best when elected officials are rewarded for delivering the goods to local constituencies and punished for not doing so. Substantive representation can be encouraged through recall legislation, which allows constituents to petition the government to hold a by-election to oust elected representatives who are seen as delinquent in their duties to their constituents.

descriptive representation
A political attachment to someone viewed as sharing one's background or social profile.

When it comes to diversity and inclusion, we tend to think of representative democracy in the following way. **Descriptive representation** exists to the extent that Canadians feel that some of their elected officials look like them, come from a similar background, or otherwise are like them. Also known as mirror representation, this sentiment is common among citizens who value the presence of certain personal attributes among those they send to the legislature, and assume shared outlooks. People who prioritize gender, race, or other descriptive traits when voting view representation in descriptive terms. Supporters of descriptive representation can use statistics and visuals to persuade others to prioritize this form of representation. It is far more difficult to quantify or portray symbolic, formalistic, or substantive factors.

The level of democratic satisfaction that Canadians feel depends upon how well the system is performing relative to these four forms of representation. When it comes to measuring the inclusiveness of Canada's democratic institutions, most minds today turn to descriptive representation. Seeing someone who looks like you in elected office can send a powerful, positive message to would-be candidates. However, these politicians may identify with symbolic, formalistic, or substantive representation and have little desire to be a descriptive representative. In this regard, LGBTQ2+ politicians might choose not to publicly reveal that they are part of a marginalized group. Leaders in the LGBTQ2+ community call on these politicians to "come out" in order to serve as descriptive role models for others.[5]

Briefing Notes

Celebrating Pride in Canada

Each summer, cities and towns around the world including in Canada celebrate the LGBTQ2+ community and inclusivity by hosting a Pride parade. The annual festivals originated in 1970 in New York and are known for their use of a rainbow flag. News coverage of the events can report on political controversy, such as decisions by some Pride organizers to exclude uniformed police officers from marching. The events conflict conservatives in particular, with many leaders of right-wing parties declining to march, whereas many centrist and left-wing party leaders actively do so. In 2016, Justin Trudeau became the first Canadian prime minister to march in a Pride parade, in Toronto.

To what extent do legislatures, cabinet rooms, courtroom benches, and other seats of power feature people that look like the general population? There are plenty of ways to measure this diversity, as the following section attests.

The Canadian Mosaic

To appreciate the prominence of ethno-cultural diversity in Canada, try the following exercise. Assemble a small group of Canadians—classmates, roommates, family members, neighbours—and ask them to fill in the blanks of the following sentence aloud:

> When it comes to multiculturalism, Canada is a _____
> while the United States is a _____.

In unison, many will respond that Canada is a **mosaic**, a country whose makeup resembles a tapestry with patches of many different shapes, colours, and sizes. The salience of what John Murray Gibbon called the *Canadian Mosaic* (1938) is the product of socialization. Passed among generations and from residents to newcomers, Canada's association with multiculturalism has formed part of the Canadian identity. It is taught in schools, celebrated in pop culture and events, and championed by government departments and non-profit organizations across the country. It is a mindset where Canadians of all backgrounds promote their cultural heritage and traditions. Rather than be assimilated into Canadian society, they are encouraged to maintain ties to their ancestral homelands. By contrast, the US is typically viewed as a melting pot, a term most Americans embrace as a symbol of the country's willingness to subsume all cultures within a common American culture. This pair of symbols is often associated in Canada with the two countries' treatment of racial, ethnic, religious, and linguistic diversity.

Discussions of ethnic diversity tend to assume that individual citizens can be divided into discrete categories. For example, **visible minorities** have a skin colour other than white and do not have a Caucasian ethnicity. People in these communities are projected to make up 30 per cent of Canada's population by 2031. In Canada, the term "visible minority" does not include Indigenous peoples, who make up a separate category. It is noteworthy that census figures reveal over 4 in 10 Canadians report ancestors from more than one

mosaic
A metaphor used to depict Canada's multicultural character, which features and encourages many distinct yet interdependent ethnocultural communities.

visible minorities
Non-Indigenous Canadians who are non-white in colour or non-Caucasian in ethnicity.

ethnic group. The majority of these multiple-identifiers report geographically and cultur-ally similar backgrounds (e.g., both Scottish and English). This number also includes a sizeable proportion of inter-racial individuals with white ancestry. For those with lighter complexions, adopting the term "visible minority" can be a matter of internal conflict because they feel a deep connection to their non-Caucasian roots. They may pass as mem-bers of whitestream society, yet they are not of Caucasian, often British, English-speaking background. Even applying terminology is an act of racialization and otherness. Political scientists must keep these considerations in mind.

Overall, Canadian political culture has grown more inclusive of differences and more accepting of measures designed to ensure all citizens are able to participate meaningfully in society, the economy, and democracy. Challenges remain, however. A Senate committee has identified the following groups as either vulnerable or facing significant barriers to inclusion in Canada:[6]

- Recent immigrants typically are less fluent in Canada's official languages, encounter difficulty finding work in their fields of expertise, and earn less income than their non-immigrant peers.
- Lower rates of employment and income contribute to higher rates of poverty among visible minority Canadians. Discrimination and other forms of intolerance inhibit their full inclusion in various political institutions, including legislatures and the civil service.
- Religious minorities are those Canadians who identify as neither Protestant nor Catholic. They have grown substantially in number over the past two decades. Jews, Muslims, Hindus, Buddhists, and Sikhs, in particular, have been the targets of discrimination.
- Sexual minorities encompass lesbian, gay, bisexual, transsexual, transgender, two-spirit, intersex, queer, and questioning Canadians. Collectively, and unlike other traditionally disadvantaged groups, LGBTQ2+ individuals have suffered from being unrecognized in formal policies and programs that promote social inclusion. Sexual minorities are more likely to experience physical and sexual abuse, harassment, and discrimination.
- Urban Indigenous peoples face lower standards of living than their non-Indigenous counterparts. This is reflected in poorer levels of health, education, and income. Gang and criminal activities are more prevalent among urban Indigenous peoples. Indigenous peoples in rural and remote communities encounter many of the same challenges.
- Individuals with disabilities comprise one in every seven Canadians. On average, people with disabilities have income levels 20 per cent below the Canadian average.
- Youth and seniors face challenges in terms of employment and connections to the workforce.

Furthermore, the Senate report raised concerns about poverty in Canada, includ-ing people with low levels of formal education, the homeless, the working poor, and sin-gle parents. Advocates of descriptive representation look at power structures and the socio-demographic makeup of elected representatives to point to the failings of Canadian democracy that appear to leave some people behind. This concerns those who believe in an inclusive society.

Canada's Democratic Deficit

For these and other reasons, critics suggest that Canada suffers from a **democratic deficit**. The critique is that political institutions are failing to live up to the pluralist democratic standards of its citizens.[7] In this sense, the existence of a democratic deficit is in the eye of the beholder. The concept is defined by the gap between one's expectations and one's evaluation of the political system. For members of a legislature, the democratic deficit foremost concerns the power imbalance between the executive branch and the legislative branch, particularly the distance between the first minister's office and backbenchers. More broadly, it refers to power imbalances in society as a whole.

What one Canadian views as a problem with the democratic system may fail to resonate with others. Consider that most MPs are much older than 18-year-old and 19-year-old voters, and that no teenager has ever held a seat in the Canadian House of Commons. For younger voters who feel their representatives should look like them, or share their overall generational outlook, these disparities are alienating. Voters who feel that young MPs are more likely to represent their substantive interests, like creating entry-level job opportunities, may also perceive a problem. For those who value other elements of descriptive representation, like gender or ableness, these figures may not raise as much concern. The same would be true for people who prize formalistic representation; to them, the best candidate, regardless of age, should be selected to make decisions on behalf of the entire community.

There are many gaps in Canada's political institutions in terms of descriptive representation. Women typically make up approximately 25 per cent of legislatures despite constituting over half of the population. Visible minorities make up roughly 20 per cent of

democratic deficit
The gap between peoples' expectations for the performance of democratic institutions and the perceived performance of those institutions.

In 2018, the federal government selected Catherine Tait to lead the CBC. In becoming the first woman to fill the chief executive officer (CEO) role, Tait joined a small number of women in similar positions in government agencies across Canada. How do the impediments facing women in the public sector compare with those in the private sector?

THE CANADIAN PRESS/Frank Gunn

the population, yet occupy approximately 10 per cent of seats in the House of Commons, while Indigenous peoples, who comprise 4 per cent of Canadians, typically occupy 2 per cent of the seats. Similar patterns are found in municipal and provincial legislatures.[8] Statistics portray a comparable situation for minority-language communities. Francophones in predominantly anglophone regions are largely underrepresented and the reverse is true in francophone regions. Allophones—those whose first language is neither French nor English—are underrepresented throughout much of Canada.

Many public sector bodies fail on descriptive representation. Women are underrepresented on federal and provincial Crown corporation boards. Most Crown corporations and other government agencies are headed by men, particularly high-profile and economically focused organizations, such as provincial utilities. The inequality has prompted some governments to employ appointment quotas for public agencies, boards, and commissions.

Some counterevidence dispels claims that Canada suffers from a democratic deficit. Unelected democratic institutions often better reflect sociodemographic diversity. Some governors general have been women and members of visible minority communities. Some lieutenant governor positions have been held by people who use wheelchairs. At least three justices on the Supreme Court of Canada must be from Quebec in order to offer expertise in adjudicating cases involving the province's civil code. This ensures English and French linguistic representation because there is some need for non-Quebec appointees to be bilingual. In 2000, Beverley McLachlin became the first woman to serve as chief justice, and since then four of the nine justice positions have tended to be held by women. Some first ministers have made a point of maintaining 50/50 gender-balanced cabinets. Women typically comprise approximately half of all senators. Roughly one in ten senators are Indigenous, which is a larger proportion than found in the general population. Prime ministers have selected senators to represent minority communities of interest, including francophones outside Quebec and visible minorities. Descriptive representation is a key reason why some advocacy groups support an appointed Senate over an elected one.

See Table 10.1: Democratic Firsts for Canadian Women on page 333 in Chapter 10 for jurisdictions that have—and those that have not—formed 50/50 cabinets.

Diversity gaps vary across the country. Some provinces, like Quebec, perform better when it comes to representing women; others, like Manitoba, perform better at representing visible minorities. Certain provincial legislatures, such as Ontario and Newfoundland and Labrador, make special allowances to over-represent Northern regions. Some minority groups have achieved substantial overrepresentation in city halls, provincial assemblies, and Parliament. This trend is especially evident in urban and Western Canada, where there has been a gradual, but noticeable, increase in the number of politicians of non-British origin.[9] Nevertheless, gaps persist, and representational gains in one election can be erased in the next.

Barriers to Descriptive Representation

Assessing the representativeness of Canadian democracy usually begins with examining the composition of legislatures (Chapter 6). Many traditionally underrepresented people opt out of entering the electoral arena and refuse to put their names forward. When they do run for office, they often face steep resource disadvantages, as well as societal preconceptions about their suitability for politics. Factors contributing to their underrepresentation concern the supply of candidates and considerations affecting public demand for them.[10]

Supply-side factors are driven by deep public biases that impede political representation and social exclusion more generally. Members of marginalized groups are less likely to consider themselves suitable for public office. They have fewer role models in those positions and face societal assumptions of their subordinate place in politics. They are often less affluent and less well-connected to existing political networks. This limits their ability to raise the funds and build elite or grassroots-level support necessary to compete for office. It takes an immense amount of time to network and knock on doors. Many people cannot afford the expense of childcare or time away from work. Some feel uncomfortable engaging in glad-handing activities; perhaps it is outside the norms of their personality or culture, and perhaps out of fear for their personal safety.

For others, political life is unattractive. They may view Canadian politics as exclusionary and discriminatory. They have no interest in putting themselves or their friends and families through the intense, potentially prejudiced, rigours of modern campaigns. Travel, long periods away from home, and legislative schedules are difficult for people with family care responsibilities, which fall predominantly on women. Some individuals, particularly Indigenous peoples, may question the legitimacy of the Canadian political system entirely.

Canada's political institutions present imposing barriers to diverse representation. The single-member plurality (SMP) system fosters an intense form of competition that favours traditionally dominant candidates. Furthermore, it lacks incentives for political parties to nominate candidates from a variety of sociodemographic backgrounds. As discussed in Chapter 9, the Liberals and New Democrats have policies and institutions that ensure the representation of women and traditionally disadvantaged groups within the party apparatus. Right-leaning parties like the Conservatives are less likely to extend special treatment to members of traditionally disadvantaged groups. They promote equality by favouring free and open competition for office among individuals who are all subject to the same rules. Campaign finance laws apply to all parties and limit the material advantages of Canada's traditional political elite. The rules are most stringent at the federal level and exist in a growing number of provinces.

Canada's single-member plurality system, its advantages, and its disadvantages are discussed in Chapter 10, on elections and voting: see Electoral System, beginning on page 338.

The party nomination stage is among the most pivotal when it comes to determining elected representatives. Most federal and provincial political parties require that local constituency associations search for nominees from traditionally marginalized groups. This is in addition to special training or financing of candidates to support their name appearing on the party-level ballot. Some parties impose goals ranging from soft targets to hard quotas on the number of women or visible minorities in their overall slate of candidates. In the 1980s, the federal NDP set an ambitious goal to recruit women to contest 50 per cent of the seats, and in the 1990s the Liberal Party set a 25 per cent target. In the 2019 federal election, 49 per cent of NDP candidates were women, as were 39 per cent of the Liberal candidates, and 32 per cent of Conservatives.[11] These numbers mask the stubborn problem of women being disproportionately nominated to represent parties in unwinnable ridings.

The challenges of assembling cabinet are discussed in Chapter 5, on the executive: see page 144, on balancing geographic representation and socio-demographic considerations.

Traditionally marginalized candidates, particularly women, who win the party nomination are just as likely to win a seat as their traditionally dominant counterparts. Over the past decade, women have constituted around one-third of all legislators in British Columbia and Quebec—the highest proportions in Canada. Women make up closer to 20 per cent of legislators in Atlantic Canada, and roughly 25 per cent of MLAs and MPs in Ontario and the Prairies. Few provinces have achieved gender equality in cabinet.

Few women and fewer visible minorities have led Canada's major political parties. The premiers' table approached gender parity in 2013, when six of thirteen premiers were women, including those representing the four largest provinces. The first visible minority politician elected to the House of Commons was a Chinese-Canadian in 1957 (Douglas Jung); the first appointed to the Senate was a Lebanese-Canadian in 1951 (Michael Basha); and the first elected to a provincial legislature was a black Canadian in Ontario in 1963 (Leonard Braithwaite). Among many other visible minorities to break glass ceilings was Lincoln Alexander, who was the first black Canadian to become an MP and federal minister, in 1968 and 1979 respectively. Alexander embodied a sense of responsibility about descriptive representation when he delivered his first speech in the House of Commons:

> I am not the spokesman for the Negro; that honour has not been given to me. Do not let me ever give anyone that impression. However, I want the record to show that I accept the responsibility of speaking for [black Canadians] and all others in this great nation who feel that they are the subjects of discrimination because of race, creed or colour.[12]

Some ethnic minorities have experienced more success in Canadian politics than others, particularly Indian-Canadians and Chinese-Canadians. This includes Ujjal Dosanjh who became premier of British Columbia in 2000 and Jagmeet Singh who in 2017 became the first member of a visible minority group to win a major federal party's leadership contest. It is noteworthy that most political firsts by visible minorities have been accomplished by men rather than by women. Irrespective of gender, those who break new ground are trailblazers who make it easier for others to follow in their footsteps.

THE CANADIAN PRESS/Chris Young

Jagmeet Singh was elected leader of the New Democratic Party in 2017. A criminal defence lawyer, in 2011 Singh became an MPP in the Ontario legislature and built a reputation for his flamboyant style. He became an MP after winning a British Columbia by-election in early 2019 and was re-elected in the general election later that year. What other glass ceilings remain in Canadian party politics?

Periodically, public attention converges around an incident that reveals the types of embedded discrimination within society that constitute a barrier to political representation. One notable incident occurred during the 2019 Canadian federal election campaign when news outlets published images of Justin Trudeau wearing brownface and blackface on at least three occasions before he became an MP. The fact that Canada's prime minister had been hiding that he participated in racist behaviour was shocking, even more so given his Liberal government's record of promoting diversity and inclusiveness. Internationally, the photographs undercut Canada's genteel image on the global stage; domestically, the images prompted conversations about systemic racism in whitestream Canada. News stories suggested there was varied reaction across the country. One theme was that Quebec media reported less public concern in that province compared with other areas of the country; another was the diverging opinions about the degree of harm, including among racialized Canadians. Predictably, positions largely fell along partisan lines, with Liberals supporting their leader whereas the opposition parties were critical. The controversy faded as the campaign wore on. It is unclear to what extent the unsettling images played a role in the Liberals being reduced to a minority government and to what extent Trudeau's image was permanently tarnished.

Affirmative Action and Employment Equity

Proponents of descriptive representation and advocates of formalistic representation are often polarized on what, if anything, should be done to address the democratic deficit where the demographic characteristics of public officials are concerned. Some of those who are concerned about the makeup of public institutions advocate for special treatment on the basis of a person's demographic qualities or lived experience. Some policies fast-track people into public sector jobs by giving added consideration to these descriptive characteristics. Proponents refer to this as positive discrimination designed to address a wrong and to ensure that an organization reflects a variety of perspectives. Critics label it reverse discrimination.

Affirmative action policies impose artificial quotas to ensure that political institutions are well-balanced in terms of race, ethnicity, gender, and disability. Hiring managers are required to meet the quota, such as by hiring someone who is not the most skilled or experienced of applicants, or possibly even someone who does not meet the normal minimum standards expected for the position. Affirmative action is justified on the grounds that discrimination and social structures contribute to a greater proportion of marginalized groups experiencing difficulty achieving standardized qualifications. It is reasoned that privileged classes disproportionately have access to advanced education and opportunities to gain applicable work experience. Affirmative action is more prevalent in the United States. Canadian examples include police forces setting firm quotas to hire more Indigenous peoples and public-service commissions setting hard targets for the number of women in deputy minister positions.

affirmative action
A policy or policies consisting of proactive measures to guarantee the descriptive representation of traditionally underrepresented groups.

Employment equity differs from affirmative action in two significant ways. First, instead of quotas that must be met, there is an organizational ethos to eliminate systemic employment barriers. Employment-equity policies involve setting diversity goals for government managers. Departments must establish training programs aimed at educating human-resource personnel and managers about the merits of diversity and prevalence of unconscious bias. Development programs are established for employees from traditionally marginalized groups to ensure they are well-equipped for advancement. Second,

employment equity
A federal government policy requiring civil-service managers to proactively consider employing women, people with disabilities, Indigenous peoples, and visible minorities.

employment equity maintains minimum recruitment standards and merit-based hiring practices. This "equality of opportunity and treatment" approach is distinct from the "equality of result" expected from most affirmative action programs. Employment equity is widely practised in the Canadian public service.

The federal public service maintains a policy of employment equity to improve the representation of traditionally underrepresented groups in the civil service and in federally regulated industries. Co-administered by the Treasury Board Secretariat and Public Service Commission (PSC)—an independent agency reporting to Parliament—employment equity seeks to provide equitable access to federal government jobs for qualified women, Indigenous peoples, persons with disabilities, and members of visible minority communities, as identified under the Employment Equity Act. Francophones used to be considered a priority group under the employment equity framework. In pursuing employment equity, the PSC bases its hiring on the principles of non-discrimination and merit, which hold that every Canadian should have equal opportunity to compete for public sector employment, and that the sole criterion for selection should be fitness for the job. Similar employment-equity policies exist in other Canadian jurisdictions, but few (if any) have had as much success as the federal government's in terms of improving the representativeness of the bureaucracy. At the federal level, employment-equity policies have been so successful that of the four target groups, only people with disabilities tend to be underrepresented compared to their proportion of the general population. Bureaucracies throughout Canada are challenged to attain diversity among their highest ranks. The phrase "the higher, the fewer" captures the reality that junior ranks of the federal public service have become quite diverse; however, this is not the case in the upper ranks of government.

Affirmative action and employment equity are controversial—even those who stand to benefit from the policies may oppose the practice because they want to be treated equally. Some argue that politicians and other public officials ought not to be selected on the basis of their demographic characteristics. To them, merit is of utmost importance regardless of background. They prioritize the ability to deliberate and make decisions on behalf of the entire polity rather than representing one particular group or community.

Other critics believe that discrimination of any kind must never be condoned. They feel that these policies amount to reverse discrimination by purposely excluding otherwise qualified individuals from jobs. They cannot rationalize overriding the merit principle in order to advance the status of those who are underrepresented. To some, imposing hiring and appointment quotas favours descriptive representation over all other definitions, and treats whitestream Canadians especially harshly.

Employment equity is different from, yet complementary to, the concept of pay equity. The latter is a policy seeking to end gender-based discrimination standing in the way of "equal pay for work of equal value" as enshrined in section 11 of the Canadian Human Rights Act. Since 2018, the Pay Equity Act has required that federally regulated employers with at least 10 employees produce a pay-equity plan. Each organization's pay-equity plan must analyze job classes toward ensuring that men and women who engage in reasonably equal work are paid reasonably equally.

Reasonable Accommodation

Debates over the representativeness and inclusiveness of Canada's political system reach more deeply into civil society. In recent decades, these discussions have centred on the need for **reasonable accommodation** of diversity in Canadian laws and institutions.

See Up for Debate: Should all government jobs be awarded based on merit? on pages 286–7 in Chapter 8 for a deliberation about processes to fill public sector jobs.

reasonable accommodation Adjustments to policies that allow for the inclusion of traditionally disadvantaged groups without causing undue hardship to others.

The concept of reasonable accommodation means that governments must within reason, make appropriate adjustments to policies (i.e., accommodations) so that people can exercise their rights and freedoms on an equal basis. It ensures that these adjustments do not place a disproportionate resource burden on the state and civil society (i.e., that they be reasonable). Thus, reasonable accommodation requires governments to balance being inclusive and equitable with being practical and not placing undue hardship on the state or its citizens.

Debates over reasonable accommodation typically centre on what constitutes "reasonable." The issue of Canadian children being educated in English or French is a case in point. As history has shown, there are limits to how far governments will go to accommodate minority language education rights. These limitations are outlined in Table 13.3, and enshrined in section 23 of the Charter of Rights and Freedoms. In this example, francophone parents would not have legal grounds to compel the provincial government to deliver French schooling for their children in a rural or remote area of English Canada where there are no other francophone children. It would be far too expensive to allocate limited public resources. Conversely, the parents would have a case in a town or city where there are a number of other francophones, because there would be reasonable grounds to expect the government to offer education in an official language to a sizeable number of students. Charter protections exist for these official language communities. Allophones must rely on political pressure and government pragmatism to secure educational resources for their children to attend public schools in their mother tongues.

Ultimately, most questions of reasonable accommodation boil down to whether the rights and freedoms of members of a minority community outweigh those of the broader community, or whether the practices or beliefs of one community should be imposed on or integrated into the other. Section 15 of the Charter of Rights and Freedoms provides the legal foundation for those seeking reasonable accommodation in Canada, as do provincial human rights codes. Consider the following questions:

The Manitoba schools question is a seminal case about the state's obligations to accommodate citizens in a reasonable manner: see pages 420–1 in Chapter 12.

- Should Canadians whose religion requires the wearing of certain types of clothing have to conform to the uniform codes imposed by the Canadian military or RCMP? What about public-service codes established by provincial governments? Should Canadians be able to wear religious articles while playing organized sports, or should sports associations have the ability to ban their use?
- Should Indigenous peoples have the ability to conduct smudge ceremonies in public areas if doing so can result in smoke being spread in university or college classrooms?
- Should Canadians whose beliefs prohibit the unveiling of the face be required to produce photo ID to drive, vote, or secure a passport?

Table 13.3   Reasonable Accommodation of Minority Language Education

English Schools in Quebec	French Schools outside Quebec
There are large enough numbers of students to justify the accommodation. At least one of the following criteria are met: • A parent attended English primary and secondary schools in Canada. • A parent has a child in an English primary or secondary school in Canada.	There are large enough numbers of students to justify the accommodation. At least one of the following criteria are met: • A parent's mother tongue is French. • A parent attended French primary and secondary schools in Canada. • A parent has a child in a French primary or secondary school in Canada.

Source: 2018. Government of Canada. "The Rights and Freedoms the Charter Protects." Department of Justice. https://www.justice.gc.ca/eng/csj-sjc/rfc-dlc/ccrf-ccdl/rfcp-cdlp.html

- Should Canadian children whose religion involves carrying a weapon (like the Sikh ceremonial kirpan) be allowed to carry these items to school? How about adults on public transit or airplanes?
- Should small-budget community organizations be required to install wheelchair ramps on aging buildings?
- Should religious schools be allowed to prevent LGBTQ2+ teachers from working in their classrooms?
- Should governments be required to offer government services in all languages spoken by their citizens? New Brunswick is the only provincial government to offer bilingual services. Should all other provinces be required to do so?

These sorts of questions prompt debates across Canada, especially in Quebec. Given that its francophone majority constitutes a continent-wide minority, and given the province's long history of controversial policies designed to protect the dominant language and culture, it is not surprising that Quebec is the epicentre for debates over reasonable accommodation.

In the mid-twentieth century, for instance, the federal government struck a Royal Commission on Bilingualism and Biculturalism. The inquiry was launched in response to growing sentiment in Quebec that francophones should be afforded opportunities to participate meaningfully in political life and government decision-making across the country. Major changes to federal and provincial language policies followed, including the establishment of the federal Official Languages Act. The Bi and Bi Commission's public consultations unearthed a host of other cultural sentiments, however, including those opposed to the two founding nations view of the country (see Chapter 4). These voices included Indigenous, linguistic, and ethnic minorities in Quebec, who called for a more inclusive brand of multiculturalism within the province.

Interculturalism debates have dominated twenty-first-century Quebec politics in response to changing ethnic demographics. In 2007, the provincial Liberal government struck a commission to investigate the relationship between the province's white, francophone, predominantly secular majority and its minority cultural communities. The commissioners recommended that the provincial government establish Quebec as a formally secular state and actively address discrimination in society. In 2013, a Parti Québécois (PQ) government proposed a Charter of Quebec Values that would prohibit provincial

Briefing Notes

Interculturalism

In much of the rest of Canada, the mantra of multiculturalism is an integral part of the political culture. A slightly different concept has gained popularity among Quebec's intellectual and political elite. Multiculturalism is based on the concept that there is not, or ought not to be, a dominant cultural group in Canada. By contrast, Quebec's brand of interculturalism strives to integrate ethnic minorities into the dominant francophone culture. Proponents view it as a means of protecting minority rights within the province while preserving Quebec's unique character. Detractors view it as a means of assimilating minorities into the mainstream culture.

civil servants from wearing visible religious symbols, including burkas, hijabs, kirpans, turbans, and large crucifixes. All citizens would be required to leave their faces uncovered when providing or receiving a government service. The controversial bill never became law because the PQ government was defeated in the following general election. Subsequently, the Quebec Liberal government introduced a watered-down version of the PQ's cultural neutrality policy, preserving some room for accommodation of religious freedoms. When the Coalition Avenir Québec (CAQ) took office in 2018, it extended the religious garment ban. Bill 21, An Act Respecting the Laicity of the State, prohibits certain provincial government employees from wearing religious clothing or symbols while on the job. The act also establishes that inspectors will ensure compliance. The CAQ government used the notwithstanding clause to protect the law from legal challenges under the religious freedoms provisions of the Canadian Charter of Rights and Freedoms. Nevertheless, a number of civil-rights groups initiated legal action because they believe Bill 21 violates constitutional rights. During the 2019 federal election campaign, Liberal leader Justin Trudeau did not rule out joining in such lawsuits. The Quebec government also promised to reduce immigration levels and to impose language and values tests for new arrivals. All of these measures intend to protect the Québécois national identity and bring the debate about reasonable accommodation to the forefront.

Similar, smaller-scale debates over reasonable accommodation have occurred across Canada over the course of the past century. Hutterites whose religious beliefs forbid them

CBC licensing

Zunera Ishaq, a Sunni Muslim, took the oath of Canadian citizenship in October 2015 after winning court battles affirming her right to do so while wearing her niqab. The federal Conservative government had fought to ban the face-covering niqab during citizenship ceremonies. Some branded the niqab a symbol of Muslim oppression of women while others held it up as an important religious right. How would you set the limits of reasonable accommodation in a case such as this?

from being photographed launched an unsuccessful court challenge against Alberta's photo identification requirement for driver's licences, for instance. In Ontario, a seminal court case examined whether a major retailer was justified in firing an employee who was unavailable to work on Fridays and Saturdays. The employee claimed that working on those days would contravene her religious beliefs. In *Ontario (Human Rights Commission) v Simpsons-Sears Ltd* [1985], the Supreme Court of Canada ruled that the retailer's work schedule policy was discriminatory. The case established legal grounds for workplace accommodation in Canada. While ethnic and religious rights tend to dominate these discussions, reasonable accommodation involves addressing the needs of other minority groups. In many ways, then, conversations about reasonable accommodation tend to overlap with those concerning the calls for affirmative action in Canada.

Diversity and the Courts

Some advocates of inclusion seek redress and progress through the courts. They appeal to judges whose role is to be independent of the majoritarian influences found elsewhere in the political system. At times, the courts have been the greatest protectors of disadvantaged groups in Canada, as with the reasonable accommodation cases above. The judiciary promoted the political equality of women in the 1929 Persons case (*Edwards v Canada*), which established that women are equally entitled to serve in the Senate and, by extension, other political offices. The courts ruled on abortion rights in the 1988 *R v. Morgentaler* decision, which established that criminal sanctions placed on abortions violate women's rights. The inherent rights of Indigenous peoples were tested in the 1990 *R v. Sparrow* case, establishing that Indigenous rights predate the Charter and cannot be infringed. The rights of sexual minorities were upheld in the 1995 *Egan v. Canada* case in which gay, lesbian, bisexual, and transgender rights were read into the Charter of Rights and Freedoms. In 2013, the rights of sex-trade workers were considered in *Bedford v. Canada*, which deemed that anti-prostitution laws were unconstitutional on the basis that they exposed prostitutes to harmful situations by causing them to practise their trade in secret. These are just some of the many pivotal cases that have changed Canadian laws when a majority of legislators were not prepared to do so.

The rule of judicial impartiality is one of three core principles of Canada's justice system: see page 215 in Chapter 7.

In many of these instances, the courts acted in advance of political will and even public opinion. They struck down laws that were discriminatory and contrary to legislation or the constitution. Legal protections are found in the Charter of Rights and Freedoms, the federal Bill of Rights, and various federal, provincial, and territorial human rights codes. These codes are adjudicated by a series of human rights commissions and tribunals across Canada. Like the formal court system, these quasi-judicial bodies play a key role in protecting and promoting diversity in Canadian political life.

At the federal level, the Canadian Human Rights Act prohibits any federal government department or agency, or any federally regulated employer, from discriminating on the basis of race, national or ethnic origin, skin colour, religion, age, sex, marital or family status, sexual orientation, disability, or pardoned conviction. The Canadian Human Rights Commission handles complaints of discrimination against the federal government in terms of its employment practices and delivery of services to Canadians, including those under the Canadian Human Rights Act and the Employment Equity Act. If a complaint cannot be resolved, the commission may choose to investigate further, referring some cases to the Canadian Human Rights Tribunal. Much like a court of law, the tribunal holds hearings into those cases, and may order certain remedies including compensation or fines. The decisions of the tribunal may be reviewed by the Federal Court, with a range of further appeals reaching all the way to the Supreme Court of Canada. Similar human rights laws and codes, commissions, and tribunals exist throughout the provinces and territories, although specific grounds for discrimination, remedies, and processes differ from jurisdiction to jurisdiction.

Some of the most controversial cases appearing before these bodies surround the issue of **hate speech**. These cases often pit protections found in various human rights codes against provisions found in the Charter of Rights and Freedoms. The Charter both promotes multiculturalism and preserves Canadians' freedom of religion and expression.

hate speech
Messages that incite prejudice and promote harm toward an identifiable group of people.

Inside Canadian Politics

How Did the Courts Resolve the Marriage Equality Debate?

Canada was deeply divided over the issue of same-sex marriage at the turn of the twenty-first century. Courts had legally recognized it in half of the provinces and one territory. However, public-opinion polls showed that fewer than half of Canadians supported allowing two men or two women to marry. The federal governing party's caucus was divided.

In 2003, Liberal Prime Minister Jean Chrétien announced his government's intention to legalize same-sex marriage. Just four years earlier, the House of Commons had passed a resolution affirming the definition of marriage as "the union of one man and one woman to the exclusion of all others." Many Liberals had voted in favour of this traditional definition.

The prime minister referred the proposed Civil Marriage Act to the Supreme Court of Canada prior to introducing the bill to Parliament. In *Reference Re: Same-Sex Marriage* the Supreme Court ruled that the federal government has the authority to change the definition of marriage, that same-sex marriage does not violate the Charter, and that the legislation would not infringe upon the freedom of religion by compelling anyone to perform such marriages. Armed with this opinion, Chrétien's successor Prime Minister Paul Martin introduced the Civil Marriage Act to Parliament, which received Royal Assent in July 2005. Same-sex marriage became legal nationwide.

Public opinion in Canada quickly shifted to support same-sex marriage. The reason, in part, speaks to the weight that Canadians place in the legitimacy conferred by the courts.

DISCUSSION ITEM

Judges may be called upon to decide matters of public policy and human rights that politicians deem too controversial or divisive to handle.

VOX POP

What is the proper role of the courts when it comes to policymaking on deeply divisive issues? What other policy tools are available to the federal government, and how effective would they be at achieving the government's objectives?

The Criminal Code of Canada prohibits the spreading of "hate propaganda" and forbids "any writing, sign or visible representation that promotes genocide" or "incites hatred against any identifiable group." Tribunals and courts have been challenged to define what constitutes "hatred." They have sought to establish whether limitations on freedom of expression are justifiable and, if so, under what circumstances.

Alberta has been home to two such controversial cases. One involved a high school teacher charged under the Criminal Code in 1984 for instructing his students that the Holocaust had been fabricated to generate sympathy for Jews. The case went to the Supreme Court of Canada, which ruled that, while the teacher's right to freedom of expression had been violated, this violation was justified in order to prevent hatred against an identifiable group. A second case involved cartoons in a Danish newspaper that depicted the prophet Muhammad. The act was considered blasphemous among devout Muslims and caused an international furor in 2005. The editors of the Danish newspaper argued they wanted to spark a debate about Islam and censorship. Months later, Calgary-based Western Standard re-published the cartoons, prompting Muslim groups to file complaints with the Alberta Human Rights and Citizenship Commission. One of these complaints was eventually withdrawn and the commission dismissed the other.

The role of the courts and tribunals in promoting diversity raises the ire of critics. Some take issue with the judiciary's choice to favour group rights over individual ones, or positive entitlements over negative liberties. Others challenge the supremacy of appointed judges over elected legislatures, and arguing that judges are unaccountable, unelected lawmakers. Proponents of the judiciary's role look to the courts as an important, more impartial access point to policymaking. They view judges as independent, expert arbiters in disputes over minority rights, providing an essential check against the tyranny of the majority.

International Commitments to Human Rights

Canadian governments are bound to abide by a number of international human rights commitments. Many of these extend beyond the bounds of domestic law. Signatories are held to account through a combination of investigation and moral suasion.

Canada is a party to 8 of 10 core UN human rights declarations, including the International Bill of Rights, which encompasses the Universal Declaration of Human Rights (1948), the International Covenant on Civil and Political Rights (1976), and the International Covenant on Economic, Social and Cultural Rights (1976). Canada is also party to the following:

- the International Convention on the Elimination of All Forms of Racial Discrimination (1969);
- the Convention on the Elimination of All Forms of Discrimination against Women (1981);
- the Convention against Torture and Other Cruel, Inhuman or Degrading Treatment or Punishment (1987);
- the Convention on the Rights of the Child (1990); and
- the Convention on the Rights of Persons with Disabilities (2008).

Canada supports other UN conventions, including the Declaration on the Rights of Indigenous Peoples, though it may not officially sign, fully adopt, or implement them.

Canada is not a party to UN human rights conventions concerning migrant workers or the secret abduction or imprisonment of persons whose whereabouts are hidden from the public.

Upon request, the federal government has invited UN rapporteurs to tour the country; meet with government officials, civil society groups, and ordinary Canadians; and study and report on the state of human rights in Canada. UN agencies often make these requests after being approached by aggrieved interest groups and communities based in Canada. Previous UN reports have criticized Canada's treatment of First Nations peoples, its lack of progress in meeting the needs of persons with disabilities, and its use of religiously segregated schools. Often in collaboration with the provinces and territories, the federal government is obligated to respond publicly to these reports, detailing how it intends to address any shortcomings or explaining why it chooses not to do so. Ultimately, this form of public transparency, not any formal sanctions, ensures Canada meets its international human rights obligations.

Indigenous Representation in Canada

This brings us to one of the most critical and controversial aspects of representation in Canada: that of Indigenous peoples. Consider that many Indigenous peoples are represented by more people and organizations than most Canadian citizens. In addition to federal, provincial, and municipal politicians, Indigenous peoples are often represented by their local Band Council and chief; their tribal councils and treaty negotiators; or their regional or National Indigenous Organization leaders. Some Indigenous peoples reject some of these representatives as illegitimate. The quantity of these representatives should not be conflated with access to or influence in policymaking. Understanding these complex relationships helps us better understand the democratic perspectives of Indigenous peoples and of Canadians as a whole.

Definitions and Designations

Constitutionally, Indigenous peoples comprise four distinct groups: status Indians, non-status Indians, Métis, and Inuit. Approximately 1.7 million people in Canada, or roughly five per cent of the population, identify as belonging to one of these groups. Self-identification is only part of how Indigenous peoples are categorized in Canada. Through a colonial set of policies and labels, the federal government defines Indigenous peoples according to their eligibility for various government programs and services.

Approximately half of all Indigenous peoples in Canada are considered **status Indians**. The term derives from the Indian Act and applies to all First Nations individuals registered with the federal government, making them eligible for federal programs, services, and benefits. The term "status" is a legal definition that differs from "membership" in a particular Indigenous group. Membership in these groups is often defined internally; status is defined by the federal government. Prior to reforms in 1985, it was possible to lose one's status under the Indian Act for a variety of reasons, ranging from attending university or pursuing certain occupations to marrying a non-status man or opting to vote in federal elections. It is still possible to lose status through several generations of marriage and procreation among non-status individuals.

Many, but not all, status Indians are members of a **Band**. A Band is a group of status Indians for whom **reserve** land has been assigned, or who has been so designated by the Crown.[13] Some Bands are distributed over several reserves; some have no reserve

status Indian
A First Nations person registered and entitled to certain rights under the Indian Act.

Band
A group of status Indians defined by the federal government.

reserve
A tract of land owned by the federal government and set aside for First Nations peoples.

land whatsoever. About half of all status Indians live on-reserve. The remainder live in towns and cities, often retaining their membership in the Band. Complicating matters, not all people living on reserves are status Indians. Many non-status Indians, Métis, and non-Indigenous peoples do so, although they are not members of the Band. Many Bands were defined by the federal government with little or no regard for the history or cultural ancestry of the communities affected. As a result, some Bands consist of multiple First Nations, and several Bands may join together to form a more culturally succinct political group, operating under a single tribal council. Through the Band system, the federal government imposed British-style values and institutions without regard for traditional modes of governance. Democratic forms of representation replaced centuries-old communitarian, hereditary, matriarchal, elder-centric, or consensus-based systems, to which some Indigenous communities are now returning.

The governing body for all Band members, whether on- or off-reserve, is a **Band Council**. The council is chaired by a chief and elected by Band members. Chiefs and Band Councils are responsible for reporting to the federal government on the expenditure of certain funds. They serve as the primary liaison between Band members and the federal ministries responsible for Indigenous affairs. Band Councils often form corporations to administer some programs and services including healthcare, policing, and children's services. As well, they enter into formal agreements with federal, provincial, and territorial governments.

Indigenous peoples who are not registered under the Indian Act do not have an official status card. This includes the 15 per cent of First Nations people who are not defined by the federal government as falling under the Indian Act. They are formally known as **non-status Indians**.

Comprising 30 per cent of Canada's Indigenous population, **Métis** include those who self-identify as being of mixed First Nations and European ancestry, and who maintain some historical connection to and acceptance by a Métis community. There is considerable cultural and legal debate over the constitutional status of Métis peoples in Canada. There are conflicting views on whether they qualify for certain treaty rights or other forms of nationhood.

The **Inuit** are Indigenous peoples whose ancestral homeland lies in the northernmost lands of North America, mostly between Labrador and Northwest Territories, in close proximity to the Arctic Ocean. With just under 60,000 Inuit in Canada, the group makes up approximately 4.2 per cent of all Indigenous peoples but forms a majority of the population of Nunavut.

Status and treaty rights are distinct in Canada. Métis and Inuit peoples lack status under the Indian Act; however, they may still access treaty entitlements. Many Indigenous peoples have treaty cards that grant them distinct sets of benefits and rights. These treaty rights extend beyond the status Indian community; some non-status First Nations and Métis people claim treaty rights. Furthermore, many status Indians lack treaty rights. Large tracts of land fall outside the bounds of formal treaties and yet their First Nations inhabitants are still eligible to register for status under the Indian Act.

Band Council
Governing body elected by members of a Band.

non-status Indian
A First Nations person who is not registered under the Indian Act.

Métis
Indigenous peoples with mixed First Nations and European ancestry.

Inuit
Indigenous peoples with historic ties to the northernmost lands in Canada.

© Canada Post Corporation, 2017. Reproduced with Permission.

This Canada Post stamp, featuring Arctic Bay resident Leah Ejangiaq Kines (photographed by her spouse, Clare Kines), was created in 2017 to celebrate Canada's sesquicentennial and commemorates the creation of Nunavut in 1999. The stamp was unveiled at the legislature in Iqaluit in 2017 by Nunavut Premier Peter Taptuna; Commissioner of Nunavut Nellie Kusugak; and the Speaker of the Legislative Assembly of Nunavut George Qulaut.[14]

Demographics and Representation

Indigenous peoples make up some of the youngest and fastest-growing communities in Canada. Their numbers have been growing at a rate four times faster than the national average for reasons that include increased life expectancy, comparatively high fertility rates, and higher numbers of self-reported identification as First Nations, Métis, or Inuit.[15] However the portrait of Indigenous life in Canada is stark: there are sizeable gaps in socio-economic well-being between Indigenous and non-Indigenous peoples in Canada. Many but not all Indigenous communities tend to feature

See page 53 in Chapter 2 for more on the Nunavut Land Claims Agreement, which culminated in the creation of the new, Inuit-majority Northern territory in 1999.

- lower-than-average incomes and higher unemployment;
- lower graduation rates and education levels;
- lower standards of living, including housing, community services, public utilities, and food security;
- a higher proportion of children in foster care;
- higher rates of violent crime and incarceration; and
- poorer health outcomes, whether measured in terms of life expectancy, chronic disease, substance abuse, mental illness, suicide, or other terms.

Indigenous peoples are underrepresented in Canadian legislatures and appointed offices. Their participation rates in federal, provincial, and territorial elections are substantially lower than voter turnout rates among the non-Indigenous population. One reason is that Indigenous peoples tend to share the same socioeconomic characteristics of non-voters in the non-Indigenous population. Considering that Indigenous peoples in Canada are generally younger, have lower levels of education and income, have fewer political resources, have lower political knowledge and information, and have a weaker sense of civic duty than the general population, it should come as little surprise that they tend to vote in lower numbers. From this perspective, closing the political participation gap would require narrowing the socioeconomic gap that exists between Indigenous and non-Indigenous people in Canada.

A different school of thought holds that a unique combination of historical, sociocultural, institutional, and attitudinal impediments stand in the way of Indigenous engagement in Canadian elections. Many Indigenous peoples lack confidence in the institutions of the Canadian state and fail to see elections as producing legitimate, democratically representative results for themselves and their communities. More than a century's worth of policies and legislation have institutionalized settler colonialism against Indigenous peoples. This began with the Indian Act, 1876, which defined First Nations people as wards of the federal government, established the residential schools system, imposed a regressive reserve system and paternalistic form of Band governance, and stripped away most remnants of self-government. In the mid–twentieth century, cross-culture foster placement and adoption programs removed Indigenous children from their families and placed them in non-Indigenous homes. Forced relocation programs moved entire communities like the Innu of Davis Inlet to make way for economic development or to facilitate what governments viewed as more productive ways of life for the displaced residents.

The federal government's 1969 White Paper on Indian Policy marked a turning point in the relationship between Indigenous peoples and the Canadian state. It proposed to extinguish Indigenous rights and fully assimilate Indigenous peoples into whitestream society. The proposal prompted First Nations leaders to mobilize on a countrywide basis

The 1969 White Paper is discussed on pages 19–21 of Chapter 1.

Briefing Notes

Settlers and Colonialism

As discussed in Chapter 1, settler colonialism describes a system in which Indigenous people are disempowered relative to non-Indigenous people. Some see "settler" as a politically correct and pejorative term meant to de-legitimize the status of non-Indigenous people in Canada. Others view it as a dated reference to a bygone era of pioneers whose imperial conquest of Indigenous people is far removed from twenty-first-century life. Conversely, many believe that settler colonialism is the result of historical injustices (like residential schools), contemporary institutions (like the Indian Act), and present-day structures (like embedded racism). It is "settler" colonialism in that,

unlike other forms of colonization, non-Indigenous people settled the land and displaced or assimilated much of the Indigenous population. "Settlers," in this sense, include more than just English and French colonists, voyageurs, or homesteaders of centuries past. They include all non-Indigenous people who have settled what some Indigenous people call Turtle Island. Many settlers are active participants in reconciliation; a much smaller number are malicious in their intent to displace or assimilate Indigenous people. Ultimately, settler colonialism is a structure of which all people in Canada play a role, whether Indigenous or non-Indigenous.

National Indigenous Organizations (NIOs)
Five bodies formally recognized as representing the interests of different Indigenous groups across Canada.

and hastened the birth of the first **National Indigenous Organizations (NIOs)**. Prior to the 1960s, Indigenous political groups were almost entirely regional, based around individual tribes or Bands, or confined to specific provinces. The 1969 policy document convinced many Indigenous leaders of the importance of forming cross-country organizations to lobby, litigate, and engage in public persuasion. Indigenous communities across Canada gradually developed a greater number of increasingly specialized and sophisticated institutions to represent their interests on the national and international stages (see Figure 13.1). The evolution of NIOs coincided with various waves of constitutional negotiations.

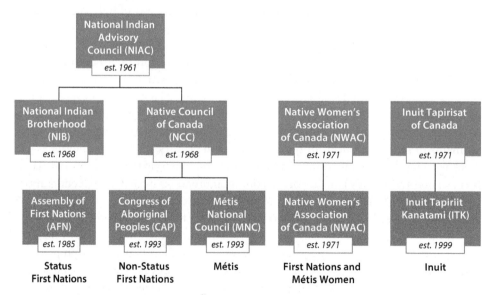

Figure 13.1 | The Evolution of National Indigenous Organizations

The first truly cross-country organization was the National Indian Advisory Council. A creation of the federal government, it was established to represent status and non-status Indians and Métis in their dealings with Ottawa; however, the council broke apart amid diverging interests among its members. First Nations groups founded the National Indian Brotherhood, which represented status Indians, and the Native Council of Canada, representing non-status Indians and Métis. The Brotherhood has since become the Assembly of First Nations. The groups represented by the Native Council developed into the Congress of Indigenous Peoples and the Métis National Council. Meanwhile, Indigenous women banded together to form the Native Women's Association of Canada, and Inuit Canadians founded the Inuit Tapirisat of Canada, which was later re-named the Inuit Tapiriit Kanatami. A series of regional and provincial Indigenous organizations developed, sometimes affiliated with the NIOs, sometimes at odds with them.

Federal, provincial, and territorial governments took notice as these NIOs formed. Growing unity across Canada helped force Indigenous rights closer to the forefront of megaconstitutional negotiations in the 1970s and 1980s. When first ministers drafted the terms of patriation, they were pushed by groups like the National Indian Brotherhood to enshrine the Royal Proclamation and treaty rights in the new Constitution Act, and promised future rounds of direct constitutional negotiations with Indigenous leaders. During the Charlottetown round of constitutional negotiations in the early 1990s, first ministers promised to recognize and take steps to fulfill the inherent right to Indigenous

THE CANADIAN PRESS/Sean Kilpatrick

Clément Chartier, the president of the Métis National Council, talks to the media after signing an agreement on post-secondary education on Parliament Hill in June 2019. This agreement with the Government of Canada is intended to close the education gap between members of the Métis Nation and non-Indigenous Canadians by allocating millions of dollars to support over 7000 Métis Nation post-secondary students. To what extent does this constitute a form of reconciliation?[16]

self-government, and furthermore to "safeguard and develop their languages, cultures, economies, identities, institutions, and traditions, and to develop, maintain and strengthen their relationship with their lands, waters and environment, so as to determine and control their development as peoples according to their own values and priorities and to ensure the integrity of their societies." While the Charlottetown Accord ultimately failed, the inclusion of Indigenous rights provisions was due, in no small part, to the success of NIO leaders and Indigenous community organizers in elevating such issues to the top of the political agenda.

The reasons for the failure of the Charlottetown Accord are discussed on pages 49–50 of Chapter 2, on the constitution.

National Indigenous Organizations are a more streamlined means for federal, provincial, and territorial governments to engage with Indigenous peoples on a Canada-wide basis. NIO leaders may meet with the prime minister on a regular basis. However, day-to-day relations between the federal government and the organizations are primarily of the principal–stakeholder variety. NIO and regional Indigenous leaders are invited to provide input into federal policymaking through ministerial and bureaucratic channels, just like many interest groups described in Chapter 12. Moreover, most of the key policy areas affecting Indigenous peoples fall under provincial jurisdiction. NIO leaders meet semi-annually with premiers to discuss issues and approve action plans to achieve and measure progress. Beyond theses summits, premiers work almost exclusively with regional Indigenous leaders on matters of mutual interest. Overall, the NIO model falls well short of a nation-to-nation approach featuring Indigenous self-government, which is what some feel is the most appropriate model for Indigenous representation in Canada.

Indigenous self-government is discussed in Chapter 2 on pages 52–4.

Concluding Thoughts

Canadian democracy has always featured tensions around the accommodation of difference. This chapter began by pointing to the glass ceiling and how deeply ingrained multiculturalism has become in the Canadian political ethos and national identity. It closed by highlighting the contested components of that mosaic and the work required to incorporate further diversity into Canada's democratic institutions. The country has come a long way in recognizing the value of acceptance, accommodation, and reconciliation. As we turn our attention to Canada's role on the world stage in the final chapter, it is worth bearing in mind that significant barriers exist to the full participation of traditionally marginalized groups in Canadian society.

For More Information

How inclusive are each of the major institutions of Canadian democracy? Led by William Cross, the Canadian Democratic Audit team compiled a series of 10 volumes on the subject, covering everything from political parties and legislatures to the courts and interest groups. Read *Auditing Canadian Democracy* (UBC Press, 2010) for a full synopsis of their findings.

Is identity politics a way of marginalizing Canadians? Nicole Bernhardt and Laura Pin think political scientists should be careful when referring to identity politics. Their 2018 analysis of its academic use was published in "Engaging with Identity Politics in Canadian Political Science," *Canadian Journal of Political Science* 51, 4: 771–94.

What explains the lack of women in positions of political power? Linda Trimble, Jane Arscott, and Manon Tremblay have assembled a comprehensive volume on the matter, entitled *Stalled: The Representation of Women in Canadian Governments* (UBC Press, 2013). Melanee Thomas and Amanda Bittner have edited a volume focusing on *Mothers and Others: The Role of Parenthood in Politics* (UBC Press, 2018).

Interested in the gender balance of Canada's legislatures today? Equal Voice Canada (www.equalvoice.ca) maintains a running tally of the number of women in Parliament and provincial assemblies.

Are there other perspectives on Indigenous self-government in Canada? For a rejoinder to Tom Flanagan's *First Nations: Second Thoughts* (McGill–Queen's University Press, 2000) and Alan Cairns's *Citizens Plus* (UBC Press, 2000), see Annis May Timpson's edited volume *First Nations, First Thoughts: The Impact of Indigenous Thought in Canada* (UBC Press, 2009). For an alternative to intergovernmental relations, see Christopher Alcantara and Jen Nulles's 2014 *Publius* article, "Indigenous Peoples and the State in Settler Society: Toward a More Robust Definition of Multilevel Governance" (44, 2: 183–204).

Confused about how the Indian Act operates, and how it has survived into the twenty-first century? Michael Morden provides guidelines for "Theorizing the Resilience of the Indian Act" (*Canadian Public Administration*, 2016).

Interested in the Truth and Reconciliation Commission? Visit the TRC website: www.trc.ca.

Want to learn more about the history of LGBTQ2+ rights in Canada? Miriam Smith's 2018 chapter on "Historical Institutionalism and Same-Sex Marriage: A Comparative Analysis of the USA and Canada" in *Global Perspectives on Same Sex Marriage* (Palgrave-Macmillan, pp. 61–79) is instructive.

Want to learn more about integration, diversity, and immigrant integration in Canada? Visit the Metropolis Project website: http://canada.metropolis.net/.

Looking for a debate on the merits of race-based affirmative action in other countries? *The Economist* hosted one. Search: Economist affirmative action debate.

Deeper Inside Canadian Politics

1. People from traditionally marginalized groups face many common challenges to their fair representation in Canadian democracy. They also face many barriers unique to their own respective groups. Consider the obstacles encountered by Indigenous women in Canada. Outline five challenges they face by virtue both of being members of an Indigenous community and of being women, comparing these to challenges faced by both Indigenous men and non-Indigenous women.

2. Are provincial and territorial governments more inclusive than the federal government when it comes to representing diversity? Why or why not?

3. In Chapter 4 we discussed the evolution of Quebec nationalism and the challenges facing its proponents. Compare and contrast these experiences with those of Canada's Indigenous people. Which group is more likely to achieve sovereignty (or self-government), and why?

Professor Profile

Cheryl Collier

Women and politics, social movements, federalism, public-policy analysis
Co-editor of *Handbook on Gender, Diversity and Federalism* (2020)

Courtesy of Cheryl Collier

Cheryl Collier's research ranges from feminism to comparative social policy. Her work looks at such topics as violence against women in politics, gender-neutral frames, childcare policies, and the National Action Committee on the Status of Women. In the area of Canadian parliamentary politics, she has published about sexism in Canadian legislatures, ministerial resignations, and the politics of Ontario.

Here is what Cheryl Collier told us about her career path from when she was an undergraduate student, why she is drawn to her area of specialization, what is challenging about studying Canadian politics, and what advice she has for students.

* * *

I completed my undergraduate degree in journalism at Carleton University in Ottawa. My area of expertise was political reporting. I didn't earn a degree in political science until my doctorate at the University of Toronto. My MA in Canadian studies, also completed at Carleton, focused heavily on political issues and included a large number of courses from the department of political science. My first intro to Canadian politics course was in my second year of my undergraduate degree. I took it with Miriam Smith and absolutely loved the class! I remember learning about the Hartz-Horowitz theory of Canadian political culture and how I thought it made so much sense in explaining how we were different from our neighbours to the south.

My teaching and research expertise is in the fields of Canadian and comparative women, gender, and politics. I was drawn to this area of study after one of my fourth-year journalism instructors informed me that a magazine piece I was writing on family and childcare responsibility leaves was "not newsworthy." This made me a bit annoyed to say the least and quickly illustrated how the gendered aspects of politics in this country were not obvious to many. Thus began my journey to learn why and to work to help change things for the better. I believe the latter part of this statement "changing things for the better" is the core of why I have made it the focus of my research.

Women, gender, and politics is still often (and sadly) seen as an add-on or side area of study inside of political science, as opposed to a central component of the discipline. Thus, I am not able to teach as many women, gender, and politics courses as I would like (I have many ideas!) and often have to settle for adding in a section on women and gender into courses whenever I can. Related to this is the ongoing challenge of having to convince some people that taking a gendered approach to research is good for all genders across the spectrum of society. This has changed somewhat over time, but there is still a long way to go in this respect.

Having said what I just did about the discipline writ large, I am constantly and pleasantly surprised by the number of young students and budding scholars who have a good, intrinsic understanding of the importance of gender and politics to their everyday lives. However, political examples and illustrations—in this country and beyond—of stubborn gendered stereotypes, myths, and misconceptions also continuously surprise many of my students.

It is important for students to recognize that there are many perspectives in Canada worth learning about. Contrary to popular belief, particularly to the uninitiated, Canadian politics is far more interesting and fun to study than most give it credit!

Up for Debate

Should Indigenous and non-Indigenous politics be considered as part of a common political system?

THE CLAIM: YES, THEY SHOULD!

Both Indigenous and non-Indigenous politics are integral to our understanding of the broader Canadian political system to which they belong.

Yes: Argument Summary

It is time to stop treating Indigenous politics as separate and apart from non-Indigenous politics in Canada. Far from assimilating Indigenous perspectives into the broader Canadian society, considering the two worldviews as part of a common political system helps foster a common understanding among both sides of the conventional cleavage. The segregation of Indigenous and non-Indigenous politics is counterintuitive given the extent to which both worlds have merged in recent decades. It is also politically counterproductive, because it perpetuates an ages-old division in Canadian society.

Yes: Top 5 Considerations

1. Indigenous politics is part of the mainstream discourse and a fundamental component of the institution of Canadian democracy. This is particularly true of the notion of treaty rights and the inherent right to self-government, which are entrenched in common government practice.
2. As evidenced in each chapter of this book, thanks to advances in scholarship and the progress achieved by Indigenous leaders, it is increasingly difficult to discuss the evolution and present state of Canadian politics without explicit and detailed discussion of the influence of Indigenous peoples. To leave Indigenous peoples out of core discussions about the constitution and core values of representation, or public policy and the courts, would be to miss the major trends and challenges that exist in the system as a whole.
3. Segregation risks a settler colonial approach to ghettoizing Indigenous politics by perpetuating a sense of difference or "otherness." Confining Indigenous politics to a separate chapter in a Canadian politics textbook, for instance, isolates the two sides of the traditional divide, thereby missing an opportunity to build conceptual and political bridges between them.
4. A realistic, pragmatic conceptualization of Indigenous self-government in the twenty-first century involves finding creative ways of integrating, not partitioning, Indigenous and non-Indigenous communities. Successes like the Nisga'a land claims settlement and the establishment of Nunavut are testament to this, as are the 94 calls to action by the Truth and Reconciliation Commission that investigated Canada's residential schools system. They are prime examples of how integrated discussions of Indigenous and non-Indigenous politics improve our understandings and expand the evolution of Canadian politics as a whole.
5. Considering Indigenous and non-Indigenous politics as part of the same political system does not have to mean assimilating the former into the latter. Nor does it mean papering over the disparities between Indigenous peoples and settlers. In fact, only by treating the two traditions as commensurable are we able to integrate Indigenous understandings of and approaches to power, sovereignty, territory, fairness, and diversity into the mainstream of Canadian politics.

Yes: Other Considerations

*   When it comes to the core issues of democracy and representation, Indigenous and non-Indigenous politics rest on a shared theoretical foundation. This is why people on both sides of the cleavage find common ground on notions like treaty-making and federalism. The latter owes its origins in large part to the Haudenosaunee Confederacy.

- In many ways, segregating the treatment of Indigenous peoples means taking the easy way out. Finding ways of integrating worldviews under a common political system is one of the most pressing political challenges in Canada today.

THE COUNTERCLAIM: NO, THEY SHOULDN'T!

Indigenous politics and governance are fundamentally distinct from non-Indigenous politics, and the two ought to be treated as separate political systems.

No: Argument Summary

Indigenous politics need not, and should not, be integrated into the settler colonial system of Canadian politics. Doing so risks downplaying, if not exacerbating, the unique and profound challenges facing Indigenous peoples. Only by recognizing and understanding the differences between the Indigenous and non-Indigenous worldviews can we hope to address the disparities between them and establish true partnerships based on mutual respect.

No: Top 5 Considerations

1. Considering the centrality of the settler colonial state to our understanding of Canadian politics, any treatment of Indigenous politics as part of this system would amount to academic assimilation. There are (at least) two broad worldviews on the nature of politics in Canada, and combining them into a single system further marginalizes and downplays these differences.

2. By its very definition, the ultimate achievement of Indigenous self-government would mean the creation of a separate—albeit likely co-operative—political system parallel to the Canadian one, not within it. Lip service may be paid to the concepts of treaty rights and the inherent right to self-government within settler colonial politics, but the true realization of these goals requires a separate political system.

3. Any parallels drawn between Indigenous and non-Indigenous approaches to politics are superficial and due largely to the fact that settler colonial institutions—Band elections, National Indigenous Organizations, land claims settlements, territorial governments, and so on—have been imposed on Indigenous peoples. These forms of representation are not based on Indigenous traditions and exist only to allow colonial governments a way to manage their relationships with Indigenous communities on colonial terms.

4. Indeed, the participation of Indigenous peoples in Canadian politics is limited, both in terms of Indigenous peoples' engagement in formal processes like elections, and in terms of the contingent nature of Indigenous leaders' relationship with colonial governments. National Indigenous Organizations and regional Indigenous organizations have a seat at the table only when invited by federal, provincial, or territorial governments. Even then, their participation depends on their ability to secure resources to engage meaningfully, and is confined to being consulted as a stakeholder (not an equal partner) in these governments' decisions.

5. The failure to treat Indigenous politics as fundamentally distinct from non-Indigenous politics risks subsuming the unique challenges faced by First Nations, Métis, and Inuit people under broader frameworks or policy approaches that apply solely to other traditionally marginalized groups. Using colonial approaches to addressing the relatively higher rates of poverty and domestic violence confronting Indigenous peoples, for example, perpetuates the same type of paternalistic treatment that contributed to these disparities in the first place.

No: Other Considerations

- The notion that there is one form of Indigenous politics—or one form of non-Indigenous politics, for that matter—dismisses the diversity that exists among and within the various First Nations, Métis, and Inuit communities.

- Indigenous peoples have different rights compared to the non-Indigenous population. Treaty rights are supposed to ensure the provision of educational and health services to Indigenous peoples, as well as the freedom to hunt and fish on ancestral lands. Indigenous communities have their own systems of justice and taxation, as well, making them distinct from the colonial state.

- By their very definition, settler colonialism and anti-colonialism are distinct paradigms, meaning that they cannot be combined under a single worldview or political system.

Discussion Questions

- How would you define the boundaries of the Canadian political system? Are they broad enough to encompass divergent worldviews, or are some perspectives so far outside the mainstream that they ought to be considered separately from the Canadian system?
- Would placing all content about Indigenous politics within a single chapter in this textbook enhance or hinder your understanding of Canadian politics? Why?
- Should political scientists and students devote resources to examining the full realization of Indigenous self-government? Or is it better for them to focus their efforts on finding realistic ways to advance causes like social justice?

Where to Learn More about the Traditional Divide between Indigenous and Non-Indigenous Politics

Naomi Adelson, "The Embodiment of Inequity: Health Disparities in Aboriginal Canada," *Canadian Journal of Public Health* 96 (2005): pp. S45–61.

Christopher Alcantara, *Negotiating the Deal: Comprehensive Land Claims Agreements in Canada* (University of Toronto Press, 2013).

Taiaiake Alfred, *Wasáse: Indigenous Pathways of Action and Freedom* (Peterborough: Broadview Press, 2005).

Marie Battiste, ed., *Reclaiming Indigenous Voice and Vision* (Vancouver: UBC Press, 2000).

Menno Boldt, *Surviving as Indians: The Challenge of Self-Government* (Toronto: University of Toronto Press, 1993).

Alan Cairns, *Citizens Plus: Aboriginal Peoples and the Canadian State* (Vancouver: UBC Press, 2000).

Canada, *Report of the Royal Commission on Aboriginal Peoples* (Ottawa, 1996).

Canada, *Truth and Reconciliation Commission of Canada: Calls to Action* (Ottawa, 2015).

Harold Cardinal, *The Unjust Society* (Vancouver: Douglas & McIntyre, 1969).

Glen Coulthard, *Red Skin, White Masks: Rejecting the Colonial Politics of Recognition* (Minneapolis: University of Minnesota Press, 2014).

Glen S. Coulthard, "Subjects of Empire: Indigenous Peoples and the 'Politics of Recognition' in Canada," *Contemporary Political Theory* 6, no. 4 (2007): pp. 437–60.

Michael Elliot, "Indigenous Resurgence: The Drive for Renewed Engagement and Reciprocity in the Turn Away from the State," *Canadian Journal of Political Science* 51, no. 1: pp. 61–81.

Tom Flanagan, *First Nations? Second Thoughts*, 2nd edn (Montreal and Kingston: McGill–Queen's University Press, 2008).

Kiera L. Ladner, "Taking the Field: 50 Years of Indigenous Politics in the CJPS," *Canadian Journal of Political Science* 50, no. 1: pp. 163–79.

Paul Nadasdy, "First Nations, Citizenship and Animals, or Why Northern Indigenous People Might Not Want to Live in Zoopolis," *Canadian Journal of Political Science* 49, no. 1: pp. 1–20.

Annis May Timpson, *First Nations, First Thoughts: The Impact of Indigenous Thought in Canada* (Vancouver: UBC Press, 2010).

Dale Turner, *This Is Not a Peace Pipe: Towards a Critical Indigenous Philosophy* (Toronto: University of Toronto Press, 2006).

14

Canada in the World

Inside This Chapter

- What is Canada's place in the global economy?
- What have Canada's military priorities been?
- How are Canadian national security organizations held to account?
- How does Canada participate in improving the global community?
- What are the politics of climate change in Canada?

Inside Canada in the World

Canada's limited role in international relations reflects its middle power status. Its positions on trade, foreign affairs, and climate change are driven by domestic concerns and interests. International affairs rarely factor into Canadian election campaigns.

Canada's participation in military missions, support for humanitarian aid and action on climate change usually take a back seat to local economic issues. Nonetheless, making sense of Canada's evolving place in the world is necessary to understand its economic performance, national security, and political sovereignty. As you read through this chapter, bear in mind the following maxims about Canada's role and position within the international community, as well as its own mission and identity.

✔ **Canada has freer trade with other countries than among its own provinces.** Divisive debates have occurred throughout Canadian history about whether foreign businesses should have free access to sell goods and services in the Canadian marketplace. Doing so may harm Canadian firms at home, but would give them reciprocal access to new markets abroad. The debate has largely settled on free-trade deals with other countries being a net positive for Canada. In contrast, provincial governments behave in a protectionist manner and maintain barriers to interprovincial trade within Canada. As one Western provincial trade minister put it, "It's easier to sell our beer in Tokyo than it is in Toronto."

✔ **Canada charts its own course on foreign policy.** Canada's economic and military dependency on the United States is beyond dispute. Many people believe that Canadian foreign policy is effectively American foreign policy. In fact, Canada's relationship with its American neighbour is far more nuanced than some observers suggest.

✔ **Canada's clout on the world stage fluctuates.** Canada tends to shy away from bold international action. When it does get involved, as with military operations, its contributions often stand out. Its status as a middle power allows it to periodically exert significant influence on issues like global trade and human rights.

UP FOR DEBATE

Should Canada give more money for foreign aid?

Keep this question in mind as you read through the chapter. Consult the end-of-chapter debate supplement for more material to help you engage in an informed discussion of the topic.

Staples Theory and Industrialization

Understanding Canada's place in the global economy begins with **staples theory**. Canadian political economist Harold Innis developed the thesis based on his review of Canada's historical economic, social, and technological development.[1] He argued that regions of the country evolved differently due to the types of natural resources in each area, principally fish, fur, lumber, agriculture, and minerals. Exporting raw materials, rather than manufacturing finished products, reduced the overall economic return. Goods shipped to Britain served to strengthen ties between the two countries. Business and mercantile structures grew in cities. Gradually, an economic and social divide differentiated the rural hinterland from the urban heartland.

staples theory
An idea that the Canadian economy is built on the natural resources that it exports to other countries.

Innis reasoned that regional economies emerged across Canada and revolved around local staples. The Atlantic region has deep economic and cultural ties to the fishery. Small settlements appeared along the coasts near the ocean. This required vast transportation networks and considerable co-operation among citizens living in harsh conditions. Political organizations found it difficult to organize such a diffuse populace and to centralize power structures. In Central Canada, the fur trade prompted exploration of remote areas by canoe and steamships, and definition of geographic boundaries. Economic, colonial relationships with Indigenous peoples were formed and corporate connections with European markets were nurtured. Forestry led to the building of canals when natural waterways could not be accessed to transport logs. In the West, the need to transport wheat and other agriculture helped spur the expansion of the railway. A political culture of independence emerged from farming the land whereas seeking government protections was normalized in other areas of the country. Thus, in Eastern Canada the belief that government is a force for good reflects a historical dependence on community, whereas in Western Canada perceptions of government interference and inefficiency are manifested in outbursts against the political establishment.

The twentieth century brought minerals exploration, oil extraction, and hydroelectricity infrastructure. New industries meant new opportunities, such as logs being refined into pulp and paper. Industrialization further strained differences between the heartland and hinterland. Raw materials were sent to industrial centres at a relatively low cost and manufactured goods were sold back to those in peripheral regions at a substantial markup. As well, foreign-owned corporations extracted profits to their home countries, principally Britain and the United States. Communities and regional economic centres emerged around this industry. All of these economies were subject to boom-and-bust cycles, with considerable price fluctuations, and difficulty aligning the supply of raw materials with demand. The emphasis placed on exporting raw materials meant that entrepreneurialism and technical skill sets were slow to develop. In this fragile environment, Canadian businesses wanted government protection from American competitors, setting up a debate over free trade that would endure for a century.

Canada and the Global Economy

As a trading nation, Canada has always had an interest in global markets. European settlers initially prioritized trading relationships with their homeland. Raw materials were sent back to Europe as trade was nurtured with other partners, such as the West Indies. Even prior to Confederation, businesses argued for the need for government protections to allow them to compete with their American counterparts. The economic, military, and cultural might of Canada's southern neighbour has coloured many heated political debates. Prime Minister Pierre Trudeau said when he visited the American president in 1969 that "Living next to you is in some ways like sleeping with an elephant. No matter how friendly and even-tempered is the beast, if I can call it that, one is affected by every twitch and grunt." Many Canadian politicians have discovered the necessity of a close working relationship with their American counterparts—at the peril of backlash among Canadians who do not like the relationship to be too cozy. Generally speaking, Conservatives and Republicans get along, as do Liberals and Democrats. Exchanges between the two countries are more likely to be testy otherwise.

Historically, federal governments in both Canada and the United States have used **tariffs** to nurture the growth of domestic businesses. A tariff is a government levy applied on imported goods and services. This makes the price of the imported item more expensive, thereby giving domestic businesses and workers a competitive edge locally, while raising money for the public purse. Tariffs were a key feature of the Macdonald Conservatives' National Policy, which was designed to protect local industry, labour, and agriculture from outsiders. In the 1878 election, the Conservatives promoted lower duties on raw materials but higher duties on finished goods. This was in addition to non-tariff barriers, such as the enforcement of strict regulations on importers and legal protections afforded to domestic companies. The National Policy measures angered Canadian farmers. Their livelihoods depended on open markets to sell their goods and import equipment, albeit with selective intervention from government.

tariff
A form of tax applied to imported goods and services.

Canadian businesses gradually developed a desire to negotiate the elimination of tariffs so that they could access the American marketplace, which was replacing Britain as Canada's biggest trading partner. **Free trade**, also known as reciprocity, is a binational or multinational policy whereby businesses can freely buy and sell goods and services in each other's jurisdiction. It provides domestic exporters with access to foreign markets and, owing to competition, the price of goods and services edges lower for consumers. Free trade can stimulate economic growth by encouraging sales and promote efficiency through a need to invest in productivity measures. Advocates of free trade argue that eliminating tariffs can benefit consumers by bringing them a greater range of products at lower prices overall. They believe that domestic businesses must prepare to compete with multinational corporations as free trade spreads to other parts of the world. However, the

free trade
The elimination of financial and regulatory barriers to allow unfettered market access.

THE CANADIAN PRESS/Tara Walton

A steel worker looks at rolls of coiled steel at a factory in Hamilton, Ontario. In 2018, the Trump administration put tariffs on Canada's steel and aluminum. Canada retaliated by placing tariffs on $16.6 billion worth of American imports. A year later, the standoff ended when the US removed these tariffs to help facilitate moving forward on ratifying the new Canada–United States–Mexico Agreement. What is the purpose of tariffs? How effective are they at protecting domestic economies when they also have significant consequences for relations with other countries?

elimination of tariff protections can devastate local industry and employment. Consumer demand may gravitate toward international competitors that offer more innovative and/or inexpensive goods and services. Countries that offer lower costs of production, typically through lower labour standards and corporate tax rates, tend to lure businesses from other parts of the world. Historically, free trade has met fierce opposition in Canada, invoking strong overtones of nationalism and anti-Americanism and forming deep cleavages in the political party system. Opponents have maintained that free trade puts Canadian jobs at risk and could lead to fewer Canadian-owned companies. Their warnings include the threats that Canada's trading partners would ignore a free-trade pact to protect their own businesses, that the Canadian economy would become Americanized, and that Canadian identity would erode if cultural industries were made to compete directly with their American counterparts.

In the 1988 Canadian federal election, Prime Minister Brian Mulroney, his Progressive Conservative Party, and big business interests promoted a free-trade agreement with the United States. The Liberals, the New Democratic Party, and labour unions resisted with passionate opposition. They portrayed themselves as defenders of Canadian jobs, Canadian industry, Canadian culture, and the Canadian way of life. The partisan positions were the polar opposite of the century before, when the Liberals were proponents of free trade, and the Conservatives and business were protectionists. The Liberals and New Democrats combined to win more votes than Mulroney's PCs; however, the latter won a majority of seats, and Prime Minister Mulroney forged ahead with free trade. The following year, the Canada–US Free Trade Agreement took effect and, in 1994, Mexico joined on when the North American Free Trade Agreement (NAFTA) was implemented. The deal eliminated tariffs on most goods and services moved among the three countries. NAFTA created the world's largest free-trade zone. It benefited Canadian businesses that accessed the American and Mexican markets, which raised the standard of living for Canadians. Trade between Canada and Mexico now far exceeds trade between Canada and Britain (see Figure 14.1 and Figure 14.2). Today, both the Conservative and Liberal parties support free trade, with the NDP more skeptical of breaking down protectionist barriers.

Trade disputes have periodically erupted under the agreement, with most harming Canadian exporters. In the early 2000s, the US government responded to concerns that its softwood lumber and cattle industries were disadvantaged by duty-free trade with

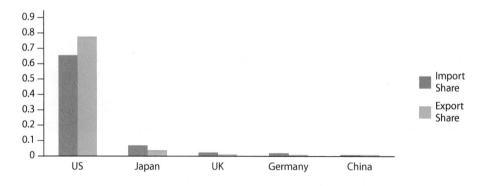

Figure 14.1 | Canada's Top Five Merchandise Trade Partners in 1992

Source: Industry Canada North American Industry Classification System (NAICS) Trade Statistics.

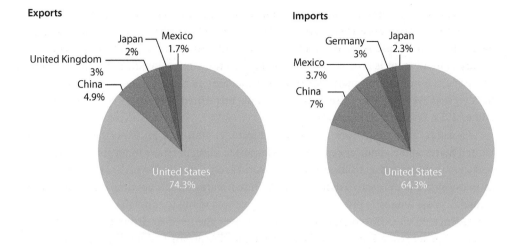

Figure 14.2 | Canada's Top Five Merchandise Trade Partners in 2018

Source: Data from Statistics Canada, 2018. Table 1: Merchandise Trade: Canada's Top 10 Principal Trading Partners.

Canada, and introduced subsidies and import tariffs to support American businesses and workers. After the 2008 recession, the US government included "buy American" provisions in its stimulus-spending initiatives, shutting out Canadian businesses as suppliers for lucrative American public-sector contracts. These measures reflected rhetoric from politicians in both major American parties about how their country was disadvantaged by the trade agreement. Many US politicians' biggest grievances lay in American jobs migrating south to Mexico. Concern about Canadian industry included rules for automobile manufacturing and the export of raw materials. The discontent culminated in President Donald Trump demanding to renegotiate the deal.

The result of a flurry of trilateral trade negotiations was the announcement in 2018 of the proposed **Canada–United States–Mexico Agreement** (CUSMA), which is subject to approval by the Parliament of Canada. It retains many aspects of NAFTA, including the same dispute settlement processes. A cultural exception continues to allow the Canadian government to support local artistic content such as books, broadcasting, film, and music. Likewise, preferential treatment for Indigenous businesses may continue. Among the new provisions are more North American–sourced content in automobile production; protection of workers' rights, such as collective bargaining; a new chapter on the environment; and elimination of gender-based employment discrimination. The revised agreement standardizes and modernizes customs procedures. Some aspects of CUSMA are less encouraging from a Canadian perspective. A preferred partner clause requires the US, Mexico, or Canada to provide each other three months' notice before entering into free-trade negotiations with a non-market economy, like China. Of the three countries, Canada is most enthusiastic about building new free-trade relationships, and this could have a chilling effect on efforts to build new markets for Canadian exports. A two-year increase in how long drug companies retain exclusivity over patented formulas will delay the availability of lower-cost generic pharmaceutical products. Rising drug costs remain a major cost driver in Canada's public healthcare system. The most controversial aspect of the CUSMA is the reduction of tariff quotas on Canadian dairy, eggs, and poultry. The increased access for American dairy and

Canada–United States–Mexico Agreement (CUSMA)
A free-trade agreement that provides tariff-free market access among the three participating countries, with some restrictions.

chicken farmers to Canadian markets should reduce prices for consumers. This will disrupt the supply management system in place to provide stability to Canadian farming businesses (see infographic in Chapter 8). Time will tell to what extent the debate over supply management is an echo of historical protectionism or constitutes a special case. The issue is bound to re-emerge given that the CUSMA is a 16-year agreement that must be reviewed every six years. The agreement must be ratified by all three countries. By the end of 2019, only Mexico had done so.

Canada's benefiting from free trade reflects its status as an exporter nation. The United States and Canada are each other's largest trading partners in terms of goods and services. Their economic relationship is the world's most lucrative, worth over $600 billion in two-way trade per year. Trade with the United States makes up almost two-thirds of Canada's gross domestic product (GDP). This prompts many to raise alarm over Canada's dependence on the US economy and concerns over the need to diversify its trade with other countries, especially China, India, and the European Union. That said, Canada maintains a trade surplus in goods and services with the US. It exports more to the United States, largely in the form of energy and natural resources, than it imports in return, which largely involves manufactured goods. By contrast, Canada maintains a trade deficit with all of its remaining partners.

Canada is a signatory to free-trade deals with a number of other countries (Table 14.1). The most significant is a huge international pact with the European Union known as the Comprehensive and Economic Trade Agreement (CETA). Canada is part of an agreement involving Pacific Rim countries known as the Comprehensive and Progressive Agreement for Trans-Pacific Partnership. Country-to-country agreements exist with a variety of countries around the world. Further agreements are being negotiated with blocs of Central and South American countries. Today, free-trade agreements tend to be broadly supported in Canada. Some opposition is voiced by the New Democratic Party, organized labour, and some industry groups.

After decades of debate, free trade is now generally believed to benefit Canadian businesses and workers. Business relationships may nevertheless thrive in the absence of free trade. Global communication and transportation systems mean that there can be viable opportunities to sell goods and services around the world even where tariffs apply. Of note, Canadian trade with China has increased substantially even without a free-trade deal, and despite the hesitation of some Canadians to engage with that country due to its poor human rights record.

Briefing Notes

Different Names for the Successor to the North American Free Trade Agreement

Each signatory uses a different name for the renegotiated North American Free Trade Agreement (NAFTA). Americans refer to the United States–Mexico–Canada Agreement (USMCA); Mexicans to the Tratado entre México, Estados Unidos y Canadá (T-MEC); and Canadians to both the Canada–United States–Mexico Agreement (CUSMA) and the Accord Canada–États-Unis–Mexique (ACEUM). The competing monikers reveal the protectionist tone of negotiations.

Table 14.1   Canada's Free-Trade Agreements (FTAs) as of 2019

Free-Trade Agreements (FTAs) in Force	Country Grouping
Comprehensive and Progressive Agreement for Trans-Pacific Partnership (CPTPP) Entered into force on 30 December 2018	Australia, Brunei, Chile, Japan, Malaysia, Mexico, New Zealand, Peru, Singapore, Vietnam
Canada–Chile FTA Entered into force on 5 July 1997	Chile
Canada–Colombia FTA Entered into force on 15 August 2011	Colombia
Canada–Costa Rica FTA Entered into force on 1 November 2001	Costa Rica
Canada–European Free Trade Association (EFTA) FTA Entered into force on 1 July 2009	EFTA: Iceland, Liechtenstein, Norway, Switzerland
Canada–European Union Comprehensive Economic and Trade Agreement (CETA) Entered into force on 21 September 2017	European Union (EU): Austria, Belgium, Bulgaria, Croatia, Cyprus, Czech Republic, Denmark, Estonia, Finland, France, Germany, Greece, Hungary, Ireland, Italy, Latvia, Lithuania, Luxembourg, Malta, Netherlands, Poland, Portugal, Romania, Slovak Republic, Slovenia, Spain, Sweden, United Kingdom* *The United Kingdom will no longer be part of CETA when it exits the European Union.
Canada–Honduras FTA Entered into force on 1 October 2014	Honduras
Canada–Israel FTA (CIFTA) Entered into force on 1 January 1997	Israel
Canada–Jordan FTA Entered into force on 1 October 2012	Jordan
Canada–Korea FTA (CKFTA) Entered into force on 1 January 2015	South Korea
North American Free Trade Agreement (NAFTA)* Entered into force on 1 January 1994 *Will be replaced by the Canada–United States–Mexico Agreement (CUSMA)	North America (Mexico, United States of America)
Canada–Panama FTA Entered into force on 1 April 2013	Panama
Canada–Peru FTA Entered into force on 1 August 2009	Peru
Canada–Ukraine FTA (CUFTA) Entered into force on 1 August 2017	Ukraine

Note: Negotiations are currently in progress for approximately 15 more free-trade agreements.

Source: Government of Canada, Trade and Investment Agreements. Retrieved from https://www.international.gc.ca/trade-commerce/trade-agreements-accords-commerciaux/agr-acc/index.aspx?lang=eng

Related to issues surrounding free trade are debates over the appropriate level of foreign direct investment in Canadian industries. This involves the influx of capital into a company in one country by way of investors from another country. As an exporting nation, and with higher demand for capital than domestic sources can provide, the Canadian economy relies heavily on investment from companies—and often governments—from other countries. Well over three-quarters of foreign direct investment flows into Canada from the United States, although an increasing proportion is being derived from other sources, including Chinese investors and state-owned enterprises. This influx of foreign capital, which is most prevalent in the energy sector, poses serious challenges for the federal government.

The federal government regulates foreign spending in Canada and determines whether high-level investments are in the best public interest of Canadians. Foreign direct investment is necessary to stimulate economic growth, create jobs, and spur innovation. However, it can create a culture of dependency on foreign sources of capital, expose the Canadian economy to foreign influence or control, and result in the outflow of profits to investors outside the country. Critics feel the rules surrounding this national-interest determination are unnecessarily opaque and subject to change. Provincial governments and foreign investors seek clarity to allow for a more predictable investment environment.

trade mission
A networking opportunity led by politicians hoping to sign bilateral relations agreements and for businesspeople who are looking to strike deals.

Canadian politicians periodically embark on **trade missions** to drum up foreign investment and business deals. The head of government leads a group of government officials and members of the business community to prearranged meetings with foreign counterparts. There is much media fanfare as the participants are celebrated for promoting international awareness of economic opportunities and for stimulating economic growth. Liberal Prime Minister Jean Chrétien led annual forays known as Team Canada missions. The minister of international trade and a number of premiers accompanied the prime minister to distant locales. Provinces initiate their own trade missions as well. They participate in annual junkets organized through the Council of the Federation and set up their own meetings. Larger provinces seek to advance their policy interests by funding official offices in foreign cities, often national capitals. The economic and political value of trade missions and international offices is lauded by the participants. Critics tend to question the value for money. They allege that the international travel is a sightseeing trip financed by the public purse and that the existence of international offices is largely symbolic.

Under the mantra "open trade for the benefit of all," Canada and the other 163 members of the World Trade Organization (WTO) follow voluntary rules that promote the free flow of goods, services, and people across borders. Through the WTO, member states negotiate the reduction of tariffs and other barriers to international trade and create mechanisms for settling trade disputes. Canada is also a member of the Asia–Pacific Economic Cooperation (APEC) forum. APEC brings together 21 Pacific Rim countries—including Australia, China, Indonesia, Japan, Mexico, Russia, Thailand, and the United States—to promote economic integration throughout the region. As with the WTO, it advocates economic growth through reducing trade barriers, encouraging private-sector business investment, simplifying rules, and reducing administrative burdens. APEC holds an annual summit to encourage dialogue among international leaders. Canada participates in a number of other multinational economic initiatives, such as the Organisation for Economic Co-operation and Development, the World Bank, and the International Monetary Fund.

Compared with the free flow of goods and services among Canada and many foreign states, internal trade within Canada faces many constraints. While actual tariffs are unconstitutional, the scope of interprovincial non-tariff barriers is extensive. Many provincial governments have different business registration requirements, for example, and apply them differentially to firms with headquarters outside their borders. Whether building roads or purchasing office supplies, provincial government procurement policies often favour local contractors. Different standards for worker qualifications or food safety can discourage outsiders from competing for jobs and business. Some provincial governments offer grants, tax credits, or other forms of subsidy to encourage the development of local industries. Provincial laws prohibit residents from bringing high amounts of alcohol and tobacco across provincial borders, and provincial governments regulate which types of beer, wine, and spirits are sold on liquor-store shelves. Some provinces prevent Canadians from purchasing recreational cannabis from online retailers in another province. These and other restrictions are established to achieve economic, social, and political ends. Ultimately, they add complexity and tension to Canada's economic union.

The federal government has orchestrated efforts to lower these sorts of obstacles. In 1995, the Government of Canada and all provinces and territories signed the Agreement on Internal Trade (AIT). The deal outlined a list of areas in which governments wanted to collaborate. These governments also formed the Committee on Internal Trade, which is made up of federal, provincial, and territorial ministers who meet annually to negotiate the reduction of interprovincial trade barriers. Western provinces remained unsatisfied with the scope and pace of reform, however. They felt that too many products and industries were exempted from the AIT and that it was hindering their economic growth. Beginning with British Columbia and Alberta, and gradually expanding to include Saskatchewan and Manitoba, these provinces formed the New West Partnership, which they billed as Canada's freest internal trade zone. By expanding the terms to include things like government procurement, and by creating provisions that would allow businesses to sue governments for infringements, the New West Partnership Trade Agreement more strongly resembled international free-trade agreements than the AIT. It gradually became a model for the rest of the country. In 2017, federal, provincial, and territorial governments signed an expanded **Canadian Free Trade Agreement (CFTA)** to replace the AIT. Unlike the previous deal, CFTA was struck on an exclusion basis. This means that every part of Canada's economic union is covered by default unless governments can all agree to exclude certain elements. Alcohol, cannabis, and financial services were carved out of the new deal, but many sectors like energy, the sharing economy, and service sector were added. As with its New West prototype, the CFTA allows governments to take each other to a tribunal over breaches of the agreement, and an investor–state dispute settlement system allows private businesses to seek damages if governments break the terms of the agreement. This adds another layer of accountability. The CFTA still leaves governments latitude to pursue their own economic and social objectives, including public health preservation, consumer protection, environmental sustainability, and workers' rights.

Canadian Free Trade Agreement (CFTA) Federal–provincial–territorial agreement to lower internal trade barriers within Canada.

The stubborn interprovincial trade protections that linger in Canada prove that domestic politics can sometimes be pricklier than international relations. The federalist system and provincial interests create incentives for provincial governments to protect their own economies from each other. Section 121 of the constitution states "All articles of the growth, produce, or manufacture of any one of the provinces shall, from and after the union, be admitted free into each of the other provinces." On the surface this suggests that free trade has always existed among the provinces. In fact, the courts interpret the constitution to decree that the provinces are only restricted from applying tariffs. Provinces have the constitutional authority to impose legal restrictions, such as imposing packaging standards on goods and services, or limiting the quantity of goods that may be imported from another province. A good example is that provinces protect their own trucking industries by imposing rules on the size of tires and the number of consecutive hours that drivers may work. To get around the restrictions, some Canadian trucking firms travel through the United States to get to a Canadian destination, and some Canadian organizations elect to do business with American markets instead. In this respect, the AIT leaves much to be desired, and runs counter to globalization and trade liberation.

The Supreme Court of Canada has ruled that a constitutional amendment would be required to eliminate the provinces' autonomy to impose restrictions. In *R v. Comeau* (2018), the court rendered an opinion on the constitutionality of a $292 fine imposed on a New Brunswick man who purchased 14 cases of beer and 3 bottles of liquor in Quebec and who brought it across the provincial border. The New Brunswick government restricts interprovincial imports to a maximum of a dozen bottles of beer or one bottle of liquor. The matter wound its way through the legal system and escalated into a bigger issue because of the implications for interprovincial movement of other goods and services across the country. The Supreme Court ruled that New Brunswick was within its rights to apply the fine. The court reasoned that federalism and the autonomy of provincial governments to develop their own regional economies and societies trumps interprovincial free trade.

The existing patchwork of laws, regulations, rules, and policies are estimated to cost the Canadian economy between $50 billion to $130 billion annually.[2] A Senate committee has called for the prime minister to lead the renegotiation on the Agreement on Internal Trade with an objective of the provinces agreeing to reduce trade barriers; however, there appears to be little political interest among first ministers to engage in such a significant undertaking. Instead, some regions have negotiated their own freer trade zones. In addition to the

RADIO-CANADA/SERGE BOUCHARD

Gérard Comeau, a resident of New Brunswick, buying beer in Quebec in 2016. In 2018, the Supreme Court of Canada upheld a fine of $292 against Comeau for buying beer and liquor from Quebec and bringing it into New Brunswick. The amount of alcohol that he brought over the border exceeded the amount allowed by the New Brunswick government. What is the purpose of interprovincial trade protections within Canada? Do you agree with the Supreme Court's decision?

New West Partnership, Ontario and Quebec have collaborated on economic issues, and Atlantic provinces are pursuing greater harmonization of their economies. Even so, when interprovincial disputes flare up, politicians are prone to urge citizens to buy local. The existence of trade barriers and regionalism, combined with the anxieties of some businesses and workers, mean that Canada is far from operating a free market within its borders.

Canada participates in various international forums and organizations where the foremost objective is to advance economic interests. The **G7 (Group of Seven)** brings together the leaders of some of the world's most advanced economies in an annual summit. It originated in 1975 as a meeting of the leaders of France, Germany, Italy, Japan, the United Kingdom, and the United States. The next year, Canada joined the group, making it the G7. Today, these seven countries account for roughly half of all global economic activity. For a period Russia was included, expanding the network to become the G8; however, its membership was suspended due to the West's dispute over Russia's incursions into Ukraine. Representatives from the European Union also attend the summits although they do not have official member status. The G7 annual summits attract global media attention because some of the world's most powerful heads of government promote their economic and foreign policy agendas, while also discussing topical world issues. Canada is the only member of the G7 to have free-trade agreements with all other members of the group. This reflects the priority it places on free trade as an export-dominated economy.

A parallel Group of Twenty (G20) includes representatives of 19 major countries plus the European Union. The idea was advanced by Paul Martin while he was Canada's finance minister in the Chrétien government. Martin and his American counterpart saw a

G7 (Group of Seven)
Annual meeting of the leaders of seven of the world's most industrialized economies.

Michael Kappeler/picture-alliance/dpa/AP Images

Canada hosted the G7 summit in 2018 in Charlevoix, Quebec. The organization has a rotating presidency, with each country taking turns holding the presidency for a one-year term. The country holding the presidency sets the agenda for the year and hosts the leadership summit. The themes of Canada's presidency included preparing for jobs of the future, advancing gender equality and women's empowerment, and climate change. Why are G7 summits a flashpoint for activists?

need for an annual forum to bring together finance ministers and central bank governors from the world's major economies to discuss financial markets, financial stability, and economic co-operation. Other participants include representatives of the International Monetary Fund and the World Bank. The G20 has evolved to feature leaders' summits. When the global economic crisis of 2008 occurred, the G20 convened to identify the causes of the problem, to discuss possible policy responses, and to establish ways to reform financial markets. Recent topics have included tariff disputes and policies to encourage low-carbon economies. Like the G7, hosting responsibilities for the G20 rotate among the members, with the chair inviting a select group of developing countries to join parts of the discussions. Unlike the G7, the Group of Twenty features non-democratic countries like China, Russia, and Saudi Arabia, which establishes unique dynamics.

The G7 and G20 summits are an opportunity for interest groups and social movements to coordinate protests in an attempt to attract world attention to their concerns. When Canada hosted the summits in Ontario in 2010, there was considerable criticism of the federal government's spending on security, infrastructure, and media events. Controversy emerged when peaceful protests turned violent. Four police cars were burned, storefront and bank windows were smashed, and masked protesters threw projectiles at police. Over 1000 people were arrested and, for the first time in Toronto's history, the police deployed tear gas. It was a scene reminiscent of the 1997 APEC summit in Vancouver, where police deployed pepper spray. Circumstances were far more peaceful when Canada hosted the G7 in the more remote location of Charlevoix, Quebec, in 2018. Every international forum attracts anarchists and brings the possibility of coordinated attacks, putting international security agencies on high alert.

See Chapter 12 for a comprehensive introduction to political activism.

National Security and Defence

middle power
Canada's status as an intermediary, rather than a leader, in international affairs.

As it has shifted out of the British economic and political orbit, Canada's approach to foreign policy has been defined by its position as a so-called **middle power**. It has a cautious international presence and benefits from sharing a continent with the world's leading superpower. Canada's role in world affairs involves striking a balance between asserting its own sovereignty and the geo-political necessity of aligning defence policy with its American ally. This sometimes results in disagreements with its neighbour.

As a middle power, Canada leans toward diplomacy and peace-building, instead of military force and intervention. Canadian foreign policy exhibits a preference for preserving human security of individuals abroad rather than intervening to preserve its own state security or advance its own interests. Canada has a penchant for multilateralism (the use of international alliances) over unilateralism (going it alone). In general, the federal government tends to cautiously support Canada's allies in major international disputes; to derive a sense of security that is afforded by international alliances; and above all, to recognize that Canadians prioritize domestic policy matters over global affairs. To some, Canada's rise to middle-power status in the postwar period was a mark of self-reliance and self-determination. Being a middle power also signals that the country is becoming more independent as growing numbers of Canadians, particularly those in large urban centres, see themselves as global citizens. To others, middle-power status is emblematic of a country whose citizens like to think that they are global leaders, but who tend to leave it to more powerful allies to be on the front lines of global conflicts in their shared interests.

Conscription and Peacekeeping

Canada's military, much like the country's economy, has evolved with the maturation of Canada itself. Worries about American territorial expansionism above the forty-ninth parallel were long ago replaced by a sense of security that comes from sharing the longest unprotected border in the world with the globe's mightiest military force. A major factor driving Ontario, Quebec, New Brunswick, and Nova Scotia toward Confederation was the threat of America's territorial ambitions.

Without a standing army of paid soldiers, the young dominion relied heavily on British military protection. Concerns grew, especially in French Canada, that Canadian troops would be used for the advancement of British interests. These worries crystallized during the South African Boer War (1899–1902). That far-away military conflict had nothing to do with Canadian security. Yet all members of the British Empire, including the Dominion of Canada, were required to participate. The Boer War spurred Canadian political leaders to develop a homegrown military that would not be subservient to Britain. Prime Minister Wilfrid Laurier accepted that Canada would fulfill its obligation to support Britain in the South African conflict. He did so by offering only volunteers whose participation was funded by the British government. Even the outbreak of the Great War (World War I) was not enough to convince Canadian leaders of the need to move beyond sending volunteers. Heated political discussions over **conscription** were inevitable and risked fracturing Canada's tender political union. The notion of forcing able-bodied citizens to serve in the military during a war is highly contentious and divisive. As the war dragged on, and as the casualties mounted, it became clear that Canada would need to provide troops beyond those who had volunteered.

conscription
A compulsory war draft by the government to recruit soldiers.

In World War I, the government of Prime Minister Robert Borden faced pressing demands for a permanent army, military equipment, and war funds under Canadian control. The rationing of limited supplies was a further challenge. When the war broke out, Borden pledged that "there will not be compulsion or conscription," but within a couple of years he privately resigned himself to the inevitability of a military draft. The prime minister understood that such a controversial policy would provoke a rift between English and French Canada. Nevertheless, the gravity of the war led him to propose the need for conscription. As he anticipated, the topic was a heated issue, especially in Quebec, where many were opposed to fighting under the command of the British Empire. In 1917, his government passed the Conscription Act and the Military Service Act, requiring most able-bodied men aged 20–45 to enroll in military service. Canada's most divisive general election ensued later that year, with pro-conscription English Canadians aligning with Borden's (renamed) Union Government Party, and anti-conscription French Canadians supporting the Liberal Party. The next year, anti-conscription protest marches and rioting in Quebec resulted in the deaths of four civilians. World War I ended before conscription was fully implemented.

In World War II, Prime Minister King likewise faced the urgency of limited soldiers and resources. King was among the few anglophones during in World War I who publicly expressed opposition to conscription. Like Laurier, he pushed back against the automatic deployment of Canadians—who were British subjects in that time—when Britain became embroiled in an international conflict. In 1922, Britain threatened war over a dispute involving the Turkish seaport of Chanak, and the call came for Canadians to participate. King delayed sending troops by first consulting Parliament. The matter was still being debated when the Chanak crisis passed and the point was made: Canada would no longer automatically be involved in British military conflicts.

As prime minister, King's style of politics was strategically ambivalent and is captured in a pledge he made to the House of Commons: "Not necessarily conscription, but conscription if necessary." This famous statement illustrates the brokerage approach to Canadian politics—the need to deal with contentious political issues, usually running along regional fault lines, by appearing to satisfy opposing sides in a debate without capitulating to either. Aware of the political strife associated with conscription, and the fragile nature of Canadian unity, the prime minister urged Canadians to have their say at the ballot box in a national plebiscite. A clear majority of 63 per cent of voters supported conscription in the 1942 non-binding referendum. This masked the lingering regional divide and ethnic cleavage: 83 per cent of anglophones voted in favour of the compulsory draft while 76 per cent of francophones voted against it. As he had done in the Chanak crisis, King succeeded in delaying a decision, and once again the war ended before conscription recruits were compelled to be sent into battle.

‹‹‹‹‹‹‹‹‹‹‹‹‹‹‹‹‹‹
For an explanation of brokerage parties, see Types of Political Parties, beginning on page 292 of Chapter 9.

The scope of devastation wrought by the world wars is indescribable. Tens of millions of people were killed and injured. Among them, over 65,000 Canadians died in World War I

Canadian Governor General Alexander Cambridge (front right) hosts World War II Allied leaders Canadian Prime Minister Mackenzie King (back left), US President Franklin Roosevelt (front left), and British Prime Minister Winston Churchill (back right) at the Citadelle of Quebec, 1943. King's style was to avoid controversial decisions. In 1942, Canada held a plebiscite on conscription while other Allied countries sent troops. When Canada hosted two wartime conferences, here in 1943 and again in 1944, its prime minister was not invited to the table with Churchill and Roosevelt. To what extent do you think this was a result of King's indecisive approach to conscription?

battles, and more than 45,000 were killed during World War II. Over 1.5 million Canadians served over the course of the two wars and almost 200,000 of them were wounded in battle. The sacrifices of Newfoundland—not yet a Canadian province—during World War I included a strategic advance at Beaumont Hamel that killed 324 men and wounded 386, with only 68 of the soldiers answering roll call the next morning.

It is a gross understatement to say that the human costs and political repercussions of the wars are too extensive to discuss here. Suffice it to say that Canada was granted greater say in British war planning and its own place at international conferences. Moreover, the wars prompted a crystallization of the Canadian identity as a self-visualization that is indelibly linked to Britain and yet is fundamentally distinct. The emblems worn on Canadian war patches—the maple leaf, in particular—would become national symbols in the decades to come.

Today, the Canadian Armed Forces employs officers and non-commissioned members located in Canada and around the world. The Royal Canadian Air Force defends Canadian airspace and, in conjunction with the United States, defends North American airspace. The Canadian Army consists of land-based full-time soldiers, as well as part-time reservists across the country and the Canadian Rangers in remote areas of Canada. The Royal Canadian Navy operates frigates, coastal defence vessels, and submarines to defend Canadian coastline. Traditionally a male-dominated occupation, the Canadian military has been increasing the number of women in all ranks and trades.

Unlike many other countries, Canada has avoided forced conscription in the postwar period. Its permanent, paid military consists of approximately 68,000 active personnel and 27,000 reservists. This places Canada among the least militarized countries in the developed world. Just over 2 in every 1000 citizens are employed in the Armed Forces. At any given time, thousands of these personnel are deployed across Canada and overseas. Canada has a distinguished record in international peacekeeping, which involves defusing dangerous situations. In 1956, Lester Pearson was Canada's minister of external affairs when the Suez Canal crisis erupted. Egypt had proclaimed its desire to control the shipping link and was invaded by Britain, France, and Israel. Canada's position as a middle power allowed Pearson to take a lead role in achieving a diplomatic solution. He proposed that an international peacekeeping force should be created. Military resources provided by countries from around the world, including Canada, coalesced to form the United Nations Emergency Force and contributed to defusing the crisis. The next year, Pearson was awarded the Nobel Peace Prize for his efforts, and later he went on to become prime minister.

The United Nations is discussed later in this chapter, on pages 492–3.

Recognized by their blue berets, international peacekeepers today include military and police personnel from countries around the world and provide on-the-ground support to foster peace and security. This includes attempting to stabilize conflicts, supporting the fortification of stable law enforcement, and assisting with the repatriation of refugees. Canadian peacekeeping missions have tended to avoid frontline conflict and have prioritized distributing humanitarian aid, providing emergency shelter, clearing landmines, and supervising elections. For instance, between 2018 and 2019 the Canadian Armed Forces participated in a United Nations stabilization mission in Mali. Canada contributed air transport to medically evacuate UN personnel, as well as transporting troops, supplies, and equipment.

In other examples of Canada's role as a middle power and interest in brokering peace, Canada was the proponent of an international agreement to ban landmines, signed by over 160 nation-states, which became known as the Ottawa Treaty (1997). Canadians chaired working groups and helped fund the involvement of non-governmental organizations in a negotiation process that led to the creation of the International Criminal Court, the world's first permanent international court to consider charges of genocide, crimes against humanity, and crimes of war. Prime Minister Chrétien's announcement in 2003 that Canada would not join the American-led coalition to invade Iraq—a mission that was not sanctioned by the UN—was consistent with a peacekeeping image and with many of his predecessors' approach to military conflict. The decision was especially popular in Quebec. Canada's role as a middle power explains, in part, why the government's decision to send Canadian troops to participate in combat roles in Afghanistan was initially kept quiet.

Not all military personnel are directly engaged in armed combat. Canadian forces personnel are deployed to assist Canadians in times of domestic natural disasters, like floods and wildfires. Those on the front lines are supported by other members of the Canadian Armed Forces, including engineers, healthcare specialists, technicians, sensor and radar operators, administrators, and emergency responders.

Terrorism

All of the wars and peacekeeping operations discussed above occurred on other continents. Diligence at home is essential because foreign combatants and homegrown radicals can bring armed conflict to North American soil. The catastrophic acts of coordinated terrorism on 11 September 2001 in New York City and Washington had far-reaching implications worldwide. American airspace was shut down, and airplanes from around the world—some of which might have been carrying other terrorists—were diverted to Canadian airports. Under Canada's Aeronautics Act, only the minister of transport has the authority to issue emergency orders related to Canadian airspace. Canadian-bound airplanes were permitted to proceed to their destinations, flights with sufficient fuel were ordered to return to their points of departure, and remaining flights were allowed to land in Canada. In an effort to minimize potential casualties, the transport minister ordered redirected flights to attempt to land in less populated regions of the country, resulting in airports across the country accepting thousands of displaced passengers. In Newfoundland, the town of Gander's population of less than 10,000 nearly doubled with the unexpected arrival of 7000 guests needing food, accommodation, and basic necessities. Local residents donated bedding; the Canadian Forces provided cots; temporary beds were set up in churches, schools, and community centres; and volunteers and community organizations coordinated meals. After five days, the last of the diverted flights left Canadian soil. The Gander story was later made into a Broadway musical.

After the immediate crisis of 9/11 passed, the Parliament of Canada approved sweeping policy changes, beginning with the Anti-terrorism Act in 2001. The original act's full title identified its purpose, namely to "amend the Criminal Code, the Official Secrets Act, the Canada Evidence Act, the Proceeds of Crime (Money Laundering) Act and other Acts, and to enact measures respecting the registration of charities, in order to combat terrorism." The Canada Border Services Agency was established in the aftermath of 9/11. It oversees the movement of goods and people into and out of Canada alongside the Canadian Air Transport Security Authority, which is responsible for screening air passengers and baggage. A number of government bodies were granted more authority to share information with police. The Canada Revenue Agency, responsible for collecting taxes, now provides data about charities that may have connections with terrorist organizations, and border services share data about travellers and goods arriving in Canada. While many of the increased security measures operate behind the scenes, anyone travelling at a Canadian airport, marine port, or train station is affected by more rigorous passenger screening.

The provisions of the Anti-terrorism Act are subject to regular review. Changes introduced in 2015 further expanded the powers of Canadian security agencies. Courts were granted the authority to order the removal of terrorism propaganda from Canadian websites; security agencies were empowered to share more information with each other to coordinate investigations. The revised act features provisions for a no-fly list for air travel and fewer restrictions on preventative arrest to stop a crime from occurring. Most of these changes were widely seen as a reasonable compromise on constitutionally protected rights and freedoms. Others drew criticisms related to government overreach. Opponents decried the infringement on civil liberties and argued that Canada was becoming a police state. They challenged the authority of the government to treat protesters as terrorists who warranted surveillance and whose activism should be prevented. In 2019, Prime Minister Justin Trudeau's government passed Bill C-59, An Act Respecting National Security Matters, to address some of these concerns.

The justifications for anti-terrorism legislation have mounted as Canada has been affected by homegrown terrorism. The longest reign of terror involved bombings carried out by a Marxist–nationalist terrorist organization in Quebec. The Front de Libération du Québec (FLQ) advocated the use of violent tactics against wealthy anglophones and English businesses in Quebec to advance the separatist cause. As mentioned in Chapter 7, over 150 violent crimes were attributed to the organization in the 1960s, including bank robberies and the detonation of bombs set in Canada Post mailboxes and within the Montreal stock exchange, leading to five deaths. Their campaign of fear culminated in the October Crisis of 1970 and the murder of Quebec's minister of labour.

In 1985, Canada experienced its worst act of mass murder when bombs hidden in luggage were checked in for two flights departing Vancouver International Airport. One bomb detonated at a Tokyo airport, killing two baggage handlers. The other bomb exploded on board Air India Flight 182, downing the jumbo jet into the Atlantic Ocean and killing 329 people, of whom 280 were Canadian citizens. The bomb maker, one of multiple suspects belonging to a Sikh separatist group residing in British Columbia, was the only person convicted. Two alleged co-conspirators were found not guilty due to lack of evidence after a lengthy trial. Twenty-five years after the tragedy, the Commission of Inquiry into the Investigation of the Bombing of Air India Flight 182 identified errors by Canadian security organizations, including the failure of agents to recognize the sound of a test bomb being detonated while spying on suspects. In the words of the Commission, "Government agencies were in possession of significant pieces of information that, taken together, would have led a competent analyst to conclude that Flight 182 was at high risk of being bombed by known Sikh terrorists."[3] Within days of the report's release, Prime Minister Harper issued a public apology on behalf of the Government of Canada.

Intelligence forces have foiled some terrorism plots. In 1999, two members of al-Qaeda hid explosives in the trunk of a car, and one of them drove it onto a ferry in Victoria, BC, which was headed for the state of Washington. American customs agents found the explosives, thwarting a plot to bomb the Los Angeles International Airport. In 2006, hundreds of police officers raided homes in Toronto and Mississauga, Ontario, to make arrests and

The FLQ was discussed on pages 105 and 110 in Chapter 4, and on pages 216–17 in Chapter 7.

collect evidence concerning terrorist plots developed by al-Qaeda sympathizers. Members of the so-called "Toronto 18" (18 people were arrested) had been monitored for months as they made plans to bomb the Toronto Stock Exchange and other public and government buildings. A number were charged under the Anti-terrorism Act for planning what a judge called an act of terrorism that "would have resulted in the most horrific crime Canada has ever seen."[4]

There is political disagreement about the motivations of the more numerous sporadic acts of terror by individual actors. Those on the political right tend to connect such events to larger terrorism networks and a threat to domestic security. Those on the left see deplorable actions by a deranged person in need of mental health supports and/or a manifestation of social prejudices and injustices. Politicians in urban areas call for gun control, which upsets their counterparts in rural areas. In the 2019 federal election campaign, the Liberals promised to prohibit semi-automatic assault rifles. They also pledged to negotiate with provincial and territorial governments to authorize municipalities to restrict or ban handguns. The promises played to the Liberals' support base in urban Canada and sought to appeal to suburban voters.

Some lone-actor events are noteworthy for their political ramifications. The most significant of these occurred on 6 December 1989, when a gunman killed 14 women at the École Polytechnique in Montreal. The anti-feminist entered a classroom, separated the men and women, and shot only the women. He then targeted women in other areas of the building before killing himself. Across Canada, the Montreal massacre is remembered every 6 December, which is designated a National Day of Remembrance and Action on Violence Against Women.

Other episodes have led to increasing levels of security at Canadian legislatures. In 1984, a man used a submachine gun to kill three employees at the Quebec legislature in a failed attempt to attack Parti Québécois MNAs. In 1989, a man who was angry about the Lebanese Civil War hijacked a Montreal bus and ordered it driven to Parliament Hill, where it became stuck in mud, and, after a standoff with police, the hostages were released. In 2014, an armed attacker shot and killed a soldier standing guard at the National War Memorial in Ottawa. The attacker then entered the Centre Block at Parliament Hill. Prime Minister Harper was addressing the Conservative caucus when gunfire erupted. He was whisked into a closet while MPs snapped flag poles and stood at the ready with spears.[5] The attacker was fatally shot by the sergeant-at-arms. Before these episodes and 9/11, it was possible

THE CANADIAN PRESS/Ryan Remiorz

Fourteen lights shine into the night sky at a 2018 vigil in Montreal to honour the 14 women killed in the 1989 massacre at the École Polytechnique. Issues persist today regarding gendered violence and calls for more gun control. Why is restricting access to firearms such a divisive issue?

for visitors to enter some legislative precincts after little more than signing an entry log, without security even checking identification. Nowadays, many legislatures restrict vehicle access to the area, and entering the legislature can be as rigorous as the security processing at an airport.

At the centre of the counter-terrorism efforts that thwarted the Toronto 18 was the **Canadian Security Intelligence Service (CSIS)**. Its agents are engaged in espionage, counter-intelligence, and counter-terrorism to manage the risk of domestic and foreign security threats. The spy agency's routine duties include administering security checks on incoming new Canadians and assessing clearance for senior government jobs. Its agents undertake such extraordinary tasks as entering private buildings, engaging in eavesdropping, and reviewing government data on suspects. CSIS (pronounced SEE-sis) can seek further special powers with the authorization of the relevant minister or warrants from a judge. After the 11 September terrorist attacks, CSIS commanded more resources. Its annual budget is threefold what it received in the late 1990s. Part of the agency's budget allocation is used to pay informants: in the case of the Toronto 18, for example, its agents paid informants millions of dollars to obtain intelligence that helped put an end to the plot. Periodically CSIS suspects complain about the organization's tactics, such as phoning them at home to ask questions and agents showing up unannounced at workplaces. The scope of CSIS's ability to collect and retain electronic data about Canadians has led to the federal privacy commissioner and others, including the courts, to express concerns about the methods employed by the secretive organization.

The Canadian Security Intelligence Service reports to a federal minister and cabinet. Unlike most other government agencies, its activities are exempt from scrutiny by Parliament. Even the instructions from the minister of public safety to CSIS outlining the parameters of using tools permitted under the Anti-terrorism Act are not publicly revealed.

The five civilians who make up the independent Security Intelligence Review Committee (SIRC) monitor CSIS on the public's behalf. The prime minister, after consulting with leaders of the opposition parties, recommends to the governor general who should be appointed. The committee meets throughout the year to consider complaints about CSIS and to review situations where the agency has denied security clearance to Canadians. The civilians' recommendations to cabinet are secret. The committee does file an annual report with Parliament about reviews and complaints that the SIRC has investigated. We know, for example, that in recent years it has examined how the spy agency used new warrant powers and has considered allegations of racial profiling. Recent reviews include CSIS top-secret security issues such as cyber threats, foreign fighters, government security screening, terrorist financing, and the use of warrants to collect information. That Canadians appear to trust that the SIRC acts in the public interest—or that they remain blissfully unaware of its existence—is the epitome of the country's political culture of "peace, order, and good government."

Operating through the Department of National Defence is an elite spy agency even more secretive than CSIS —so secretive, in fact, that it existed for over three decades without the public's knowledge. The **Communications Security Establishment (CSE)** engages in high-level monitoring and sharing of international intelligence. Whereas CSIS prioritizes human sleuthing, the CSE is concerned with foreign security threats that are communicated via social media, websites, email, text, radio, telephone, and other electronic means. The organization saw its yearly budget decline when its Cold War raison d'être of

Canadian Security Intelligence Service (CSIS) Canada's spy agency.

The doctrine of peace, order, and good government, or POGG, is discussed throughout Chapters 2 and 3; see especially the section Centralization and Decentralization, beginning on page 71 of Chapter 3.

Communications Security Establishment (CSE) Canada's electronic communications spy agency.

monitoring communists was rendered defunct. Since the 9/11 terrorist attacks and with the growth of digital media, the profile and importance of this covert organization have increased. Its budget today is approximately five times what it was at the end of the 1990s and its workforce has more than doubled. The cyberspy agency uses the latest technologies to test the vulnerabilities of government computer systems to guard against hacktivism. It monitors foreign communications to identify potential threats against Canadians including terrorism, espionage, kidnappings, attacks on Canadian embassies, and cyber attempts to influence elections. As well, the CSE collects intelligence about international events and crises. However, the agency has compiled data from public Wi-Fi at Canadian airports to track the movements of Canadian travellers—even though the CSE mandate precludes the authority from monitoring the private communication of Canadian citizens.[6]

Hacktivism is discussed on page 429 of Chapter 12, on political activism.

Today, the Communications Security Establishment no longer operates in the shadows and engages in public outreach, including social media. Among the many clients of its intelligence services are CSIS, the RCMP, the Privy Council Office, the Departments of National Defence and Global Affairs, and the federal Treasury Board Secretariat.[7] In 2019, Bill C-59 was passed, which granted the organization new powers. With cabinet-level authorization, the CSE can now launch cyberattacks and maintain electronic datasets. The bill also set the groundwork to create the National Security and Intelligence Review Agency to provide oversight of national security activities by the CSE, CSIS, the RCMP, and the Canada Border Services Agency. Otherwise, only a retired judge is authorized to scrutinize the activities of the CSE and must submit a report to Parliament.

The Communications Security Establishment and CSIS are members of a covert international partnership known as the Five Eyes. They exchange intelligence with counterpart agencies in Australia, New Zealand, the United Kingdom, and the United States. This arrangement dates to the Cold War. The special relationship between these countries, combined with the similarities of their security standards, means that more intelligence is shared between them than occurs within other multilateral agreements. The network expands to include other countries when circumstances arise. For instance, select data are shared with a trustworthy ally if a terrorist attack occurs. Currently, the Five Eyes spy network is working with German and Japan intelligence agencies to combat foreign influence by states like China and Russia.

The Five Eyes has drawn the ire of Canada's Security Intelligence Review Committee. The oversight committee has warned that information gathered by a Canadian agency and shared with other countries could be used against Canadians when they travel abroad.[8] Concerns have been raised that, as part of the Five Eyes partnership, the CSE co-operates with its American counterpart, the National Security Agency, which has spied on world leaders at international summits including ones held in Canada.

Canada belongs to a number of international security alliances that are much better known than the highly secretive Five Eyes network. After World War II, international relations were characterized by the dominance of two superpowers and competing ideologies, with Canada and Western European nations aligning with the liberal democracy of the United States, and Eastern European nations formalizing alliances with the communist Soviet Union. In 1949, the **North Atlantic Treaty Organization (NATO)** was formed to unite the defence of a dozen Western nations, including Canada. The organization exists to defend and advance the security objectives of its members through political and military means. Its political objectives are the promotion of democratic values, consensus decision-making, and collaboration on defence issues. NATO's crisis-management activities range from protecting people from natural disasters to initiating military strikes

North Atlantic Treaty Organization (NATO) International military alliance of Western nations.

Inside Canadian Politics

Should the Government of Canada Monitor Internet Use by Canadians?

Whenever Canadians use the Internet on a personal computer, and every time their mobile phones connect with a cell tower, they are transmitting data. The degree to which these processes fall short of privacy may not occur to them. In order to carry out surveillance, it is essential that the online surveillance methods used by government agents not become public knowledge. This raises philosophical questions. Most people would want the authorities to catch those involved with a cyber-crime, such as distributing child pornography, cyberbullying, promoting hate speech, and conspiring to commit acts of terrorism or anti-government fraud. But how can security intelligence officers and the police distinguish between law-abiding citizens and online criminals? What type of information should be shared with foreign governments? Is it appropriate for public servants in government departments to actively monitor the social media communications of critics and activists? How do we keep government monitoring accountable?

Canada's privacy laws were not designed to address such fundamental questions. In a democratic system, there is a need for public oversight of such clandestine activities by the state. This is a challenge with respect to matters that cannot, by their nature, be publicly disclosed due to the potential harm to the very citizens the state is trying to protect.

DISCUSSION ITEM

Privacy laws lag behind changes in the norms and behaviour of Canadians online.

VOX POP

To what extent should the Canadian government police online behaviour? When is it appropriate for information to be exchanged with foreign governments? What checks should be in place to ensure agents are using the information responsibly?

against hostile regimes. It is foremost an instrument of mutual security and collective deterrence. Article 5 of the North Atlantic Treaty states that:

> The Parties agree that an armed attack against one or more of them in Europe or North America shall be considered an attack against them all. Consequently they agree that, if such an armed attack occurs, each of them, in exercise of the right of individual or collective self-defence recognised by Article 51 of the Charter of the United Nations, will assist the Party or Parties so attacked by taking forthwith, individually and in concert with the other Parties, such action as it deems necessary, including the use of armed force, to restore and maintain the security of the North Atlantic area.[9]

When the Cold War ended in 1992, and as armament reduction pacts were signed, communism and the Soviet bloc no longer challenged the supremacy of the United States and its Western European allies. The relevance of NATO appeared to be waning. However, the terrorist attacks in the United States that brought down the World Trade Centre, as well as subsequent episodes, demonstrated the continued need for protection against security threats. A number of nation-states subsequently joined NATO, including many former Soviet allies. Currently, membership stands at 29 states.

North Atlantic Treaty Organization military operations have included bombing in Bosnia and Herzegovina, Kosovo, and Libya, and the deployment of troops to Afghanistan. Canadian soldiers were engaged in combat operations in the Afghanistan War between 2002 and 2011—158 of them lost their lives. As with Canada's past military conflicts, support for the Afghanistan operation was highest in Western Canada, and opposition was most pronounced in Quebec. As well, Conservative partisans and men tended to favour the mission; women, young people, and supporters of the NDP, Green Party, and Bloc Québécois tended to be opposed.[10] Among the differences compared with the Boer War, the Chanak crisis, or the world wars is that concerns about British imperialism were replaced by opposition to American interventionism.

Membership in NATO affords Canada the security of alliances with some of the world's most formidable military forces. Canada further leverages the deterrence strategy and its role as a middle power through a separate alliance with the United States. In 1958 the two countries signed the **North American Air Defense Command (NORAD)** to create a joint air defence system. Its monitoring of air and water activity warns of a possible attack on North America by aircraft, missile, space, or waterways. As with NATO, objectives shifted after the Cold War, and once again after 9/11. NORAD has intensified its air patrols and provides air defence for potential terrorism targets when major events are held in either of the two countries, including international leaders' summits, the Olympic Games, and the NFL Super Bowl. The bi-national organization coordinates a security response to emerging situations, as when a Thunder Bay flight school student stole a small airplane and flew into US airspace, prompting a sortie interception by two F-16 fighter aircrafts. On a lighter note, many Canadians hear about NORAD every Christmas Eve, when it issues news bulletins about its tracking of Santa Claus's progress through airspace around the world.

Canada's Northern presence is expressed through an international organization that advances the interests of Canada's Arctic Indigenous peoples. In 1996, representatives of Canada, Denmark, Finland, Iceland, Norway, Russia, Sweden, and the United States met in Ottawa and issued a declaration to create the **Arctic Council**. The high-level forum fosters co-operation and interaction among Arctic states. Among its objectives are promoting sustainable development, environmental protection, and awareness of Arctic-related issues. A number of international organizations, such as the Inuit Circumpolar Council, are formally engaged as permanent participants. The Arctic Council's objectives include improving the lives of Arctic residents, preparing for environmental emergencies, addressing pollution in the Arctic, and conserving Arctic flora and fauna. Its activities are allocated to a series of working groups and task forces that seek to advance a reduction in pollution, support biodiversity, improve connectivity, and generally protect the marine environment.

Canada's Arctic is patrolled by the Canadian Rangers, a sub-component of the Armed Forces Reserve, who carry out national security and public safety missions in remote and sparsely settled regions. A military presence in the North allows Canada to compete with other countries for the right to the land at the top of the world—and the prized reserves of subsea oil beneath. The Ottawa declaration that created the Artic Council expressly states that the organization should not be involved with military security matters.

North American Air Defense (NORAD)
A Canada–US air defence agreement.

Arctic Council
An international forum that brings together eight Arctic states and Arctic Indigenous peoples.

What considerations should be applied when deciding which countries have sovereignty over Arctic lands, ice, and waterways? What role should Canada's military play in promoting its claims to sovereignty in the Arctic?

Global Affairs

In addition to furthering its own economic and security interests through interactions with other nations, Canada is involved in a number of international organizations that promote democracy, human rights, the rule of law, the socioeconomic development of emerging economies, and action on climate change.

Diplomacy

Canada maintains an official presence in other countries. **Ambassadors** have executive, diplomatic, intergovernmental, and international experience, though connections with the party in power are normally required to get the job. Canadian ambassadors are recognized by the host nation as state diplomats, as are the foreign representatives of some provincial governments. Together, they operate out of a government office known as an embassy or out of smaller offices known as consulates. Ambassadors perform a variety of ceremonial and bureaucratic roles. They maintain formal relations between the two countries, such as by representing Canada at official events. They promote local awareness of Canada, such as by sponsoring Canada Day festivities. As well, they act as service points for Canadian citizens travelling abroad by providing assistance with passport problems and other issues. Periodically, governments formally express dissatisfaction with policies in a host nation by recalling their ambassador. From time to time, Canadian ambassadors have played an intermediary role, characteristic of their position as a middle power. The Academy Award–winning movie *Argo* depicted just such an incident, when

ambassador
An official state representative to another country.

Briefing Notes

Ambassadors and High Commissioners

The highest-ranking Canadian diplomats serving in Commonwealth nations are referred to as high commissioners rather than ambassadors. Their diplomatic building is a high commission instead of an embassy.

United Nations (UN)
The world's primary international political body.

the Canadian ambassador to Iran and his officials aided in the exfiltration of six American embassy staff following the siege of the American embassy.

The foremost political forum for international diplomacy is the **United Nations (UN)**. Canada was one of the original signatories of the League of Nations, an intergovernmental organization formed after World War I with an objective of achieving world peace through disarmament and other policies. It was the precursor to the UN, which was formed in 1945 at the conclusion of World War II. The Charter of the United Nations and Statute of the International Court of Justice was signed by 51 member nations, including Canada, and took effect after it was endorsed by the world's five great powers as the UN Security Council's permanent members (China, France, Russia, United Kingdom, and United States). That document identifies the purposes and principles of the UN, namely:

- to maintain international peace and security;
- to promote equal rights and self-determination;
- to pursue international co-operation on socioeconomic issues with an objective of upholding human rights; and
- to attempt to unify nations to achieve these objectives.

Collectively, the United Nations' work ranges "from sustainable development, environment and refugees protection, disaster relief, counter terrorism, disarmament and non-proliferation, to promoting democracy, human rights, gender equality and the advancement of women, governance, economic and social development and international health, clearing landmines, expanding food production, and more" in a bid to create "a safer world for this and future generations."[11] At the United Nations headquarters in New York, representatives from 193 member nations attend meetings of the General Assembly and may participate in a variety of councils, committees, specialized agencies, funds, and programs.

The UN Security Council is among the most prominent intergovernmental bodies in the world. It comprises the five aforementioned permanent members, who have veto power, and ten rotating members elected by members of the General Assembly for two-year terms. The Security Council has the power to issue binding resolutions on matters that include initiating peacekeeping missions, authorizing diplomatic and economic sanctions, and approving the use of international military force. It has authorized a number of peacekeeping operations and military interventions. Canada was elected as a non-permanent member to the UN Security Council once per decade during the twentieth century. It was a source of consternation to some in 2010 when Canada experienced its first failed bid. For critics, this affirmed Canada's diminished international status, and was a consequence of the Conservative government's interventionist foreign affairs policies. To others, Canada was a victim of the mysteries of closed-door bargaining for votes, and the outcome should be contextualized by the fact that dozens of countries have never been a member of the Security Council.

Beyond the UN, Canada also belongs to the Organization of American States (OAS; not to be confused with the same acronym for Old Age Security). The OAS is a regional political association of all independent states in the Americas. It brings together 35 nations in North, Central, and South America to advance democracy, development, human rights, and security in the hemispheres. Given that its original objective was to restrict European influence in the Americas, and to expand the influence of the United States, Canada opted not to join the Organization of American States until 1990. Canada has since become one of the organization's largest financial contributors, and provides supports such as election observation, legal assistance, and humanitarian aid.

The Commonwealth and the Francophonie

Canada is part of the post-colonial British and French communities. The relationship between Britain and Canada has deep partisan, ethnic, and ideological undertones. Canada has many significant formal and cultural ties to Britain, including the same head of state. Conservatives are traditionally attached to the mother country; Liberals tend to advance Canadian independence and English–French dualism. Conservative prime ministers have exhibited their loyalty by brokering a British-style constitution (Macdonald), pledging support to Britain during wartime (Borden), becoming a British Lord after leaving office (Bennett), proclaiming allegiance to the Union Jack (Diefenbaker), and reinstituting Royal into the name of the Canadian military (Harper). This reverence for the Crown and accompanying traditions is a key element of toryism discussed in Chapter 4. Conversely, Liberal prime ministers have refused a British knighthood (Mackenzie) and have avoided engagement in British military conflict (Laurier, King, Pearson and, to some extent, Chrétien). Liberals presided over the creation of distinct Canadian citizenship (King), the Canadian flag (Pearson), the Order of Canada (Pearson), official bilingualism (Pierre Trudeau), and the patriation of the constitution (Pierre Trudeau). This political divide continued under Justin Trudeau. One of the first acts of his government was to remove the portrait of the Queen from the foyer of the Global Affairs headquarters, which had been put there by the Conservatives (see page 136 in Chapter 5).

Regardless of which party is in power, Canadian government representatives participate in the Commonwealth of Nations (or, simply, the **Commonwealth**), which brings together nation-states that have a constitutional relationship with Britain. The group of 53 countries includes Australia, Bangladesh, India, Nigeria, Pakistan, South Africa, and, of course, the United Kingdom. A small number of members, such as Mozambique and Rwanda, have no historical connection to Britain. The Commonwealth's organizational values are to promote democracy, human rights, and the rule

Commonwealth
An association of nation-states with ties to the United Kingdom.

THE CANADIAN PRESS/Jacques Boissinot

The premier of Quebec greets the secretary general of La Francophonie in Quebec City in 2019. Should provincial premiers have direct access to the leaders of international organizations, or should the federal government be involved in these interactions? What are the risks and benefits involved with giving Quebec a seat at international tables, like La Francophonie?

of law. Every two years it holds a meeting of heads of government, where recent priorities have been discussions aimed at the strengthening of "development and democracy . . . good governance, human rights, gender equality, and a more equitable sharing of the benefits of globalization."[12] From time to time, Canada assumes a leadership role in the Commonwealth. For three decades beginning in the early 1960s, successive Canadian prime ministers applied international pressure, particularly through the Commonwealth, to end apartheid in South Africa. Periodically, prime ministers attempt to assert this moral suasion by refusing to meet with foreign dignitaries in protest of a government's violations of human rights. Other functions are more harmonious. The Commonwealth Games combine a variety of Olympic sports with non-Olympic sports such as lawn bowls.

Canada also participates in the Organisation internationale de la Francophonie (or simply **La Francophonie**). It comprises a network of countries where the French language and/or culture flourishes such as Belgium, France, Switzerland, and a number of former Belgian and French colonies in Africa. In this way the organization resembles the Commonwealth of Nations by bringing together countries or regions with ties to a linguistic tradition or colonial power. La Francophonie's activities centre on promoting the French language, culture, and education. As well, the organization seeks to advance peace, democracy, human rights, sustainable development, digital technologies, and sport. The organization holds biennial summits where members' heads of state and/or heads of

La Francophonie
Association of nation-states and regions with French language and cultural connections.

Briefing Notes

Quebec and Paradiplomacy

In international relations, the global engagement of regional governments is called paradiplomacy.[13] Quebec is Canada's dominant paradiplomacy actor. Its intergovernmental presence improves the attention paid to Quebec's interests and helps to exert Quebec independence. Quebec maintains over a dozen government offices abroad to promote its economy, education, culture, immigration, and public affairs in international cities such as Brussels, London, Mexico City, Paris, Rome, and Tokyo, as well as in American cities such as Los Angeles and New York.[14] Quebec also has bureaus and trade offices in more than a dozen other cities around the world that provide more limited services, such as recruiting local support staff. Quebec is represented in multilateral affairs as part of the francophone and multilateral affairs delegation that interacts with the Organization internationale de la Francophonie. A 2006 agreement with the Government of Canada allows Quebec to include a government representative on Canada's permanent delegation to the United Nations Education, Science and Culture Organization (UNESCO). Finally, the province has a historic relationship with France such that the Quebec premier is accorded special treatment normally reserved for heads of state. Quebec paradiplomacy is of particular importance to Quebec nationalists. Its voice in international diplomacy has implications for Canadian international relations, which must consider Quebec's demands and perspectives.

governments convene to discuss topical issues and to celebrate their shared culture. In addition, ministerial conferences are held on a focused policy matter, such as Internet access or human security. The Francophonie Games feature cultural events including poetry, song, and traditional dance. The Francophonie is the only multilateral government organization where Canadian provinces—in this case Quebec and New Brunswick—hold full membership alongside nation-states. Traditionally, the Canadian cabinet includes a minister responsible for La Francophonie who meets annually with provincial and territorial minsters responsible for francophone affairs. As well, Quebec has a special presence on the international stage (see Briefing Note).

International Development

As a member of the G7 and regular member of the UN Security Council, Canada is among the world's richest, most democratic, and well-respected countries. Worldwide, UN reports show that the quality of life of humans has been getting better as people live longer, fewer of them live in extreme poverty, and there is less famine. Yet many people are faced with deprivations, inequities, and violent extremism. Some of the most marginalized human beings on Earth are ethnic minorities, Indigenous peoples, refugees, and migrants.[15] Many feel Canada's privileged status carries with it an obligation to ensure people within and outside its borders receive the benefit of its relative wealth.

Canada's primary foreign investment body operates through Global Affairs Canada, whose legal name is the Department of Foreign Affairs, Trade and Development. The department is involved with diplomatic relations, promoting international trade, and coordinating humanitarian assistance to foreign countries, foreign non-profit groups, and international organizations. Overall values promoted by the Government of Canada include environmental sustainability, gender equity, and democratic governance. Funds for international aid programs are prioritized for local food sustainability (e.g., agriculture), children and youth (e.g., education), and economic growth (e.g., local business development). Funding programs must meet certain criteria, including an established need for aid, a likelihood of benefiting from Canadian support, and overall alignment with Canadian foreign-policy objectives. Promoting democratic values such as transparency and accountability are a component of this international assistance. Some policy objectives change depending on which government is in power in Ottawa. A key policy mandate under the Harper Conservatives was to improve the efficiency, focus, and accountability of international aid programs that assist people living in poverty. The focus shifted under Justin Trudeau's Liberals toward advancing gender equity. This includes work to address experiences of women and girls in conflicts and post-conflict, promote sexual health, end forced marriage, eliminate gender-based violence, and improve the health and rights of women and girls.

The amount of foreign aid a country gives is typically measured as proportion of its gross national income, or GNI. Figure 14.3 shows Canada's level of international development assistance compared with that of other G7 countries. Canada falls in the middle of the pack. The United Kingdom, Germany, and France commit more than Canada does, the United States offers proportionately less, and Italy and Japan's assistance is relatively proportionate to Canada's. Each country has its own reasons for its commitments. For instance, the United States might argue that in dollar terms it offers more than any other country, and that this is in addition to its considerable investments in global security.

In Canada, as elsewhere, the desire to allocate limited resources to other countries must be weighed against domestic pressures to allocate those resources at home. Canadian politicians are incentivized to respond to local interests, media pressure, and party members' priorities. If we believe that most elected officials want to be re-elected, then it is natural that they will consider that public-opinion polls show that Canadians prioritize healthcare, job creation, taxation, climate change, accountability, and other matters within Canada. Few national surveys indicate Canadians view foreign aid as a major concern. Moreover, when government budgets operate in a deficit situation, it is difficult for finance ministers to defend foreign spending at a cost of cuts to domestic spending

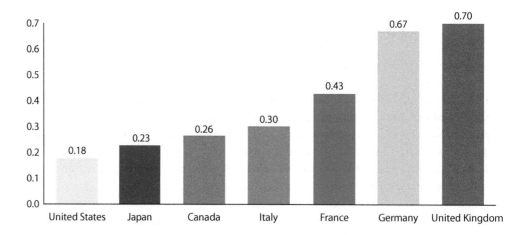

Figure 14.3 | Official Development Assistance (ODA) as a Percentage of Gross National Income (GNI) in G7 Countries

Source: Based on data from OECD (2019), Net ODA (indicator). doi: 10.1787/33346549-en (Accessed on 03 September 2019).

initiatives. The exception is when an international humanitarian crisis rises to the top of the public consciousness, which in turn results in public expectations that government will help. In such situations, the Government of Canada commits special financial support to the affected nation and may deploy human resources expertise such as the Canadian Forces' Disaster Assistance Response Team (DART).

Canada's privileged status in the global community gives rise to calls for it to open its borders to people from other countries. People seek to come to Canada and other parts of the developed world for a host of reasons. Most enter Canada as economic immigrants (i.e., skilled workers) or as family class immigrants (i.e., relatives of people living in Canada). Others are economic migrants, who may be granted work visas or permanent resident status if they are able to secure and maintain employment. Still others are fleeing civil war, crime, or other forms of persecution in developing countries around the world. Those who apply for refuge are referred to as asylum seekers; once accepted by the federal government to enter Canada, they become refugees. As a result of political, economic, and military instability in the developed world, these various types of migration have risen to the top of the political and media agenda in many advanced countries. The issue rarely receives much attention in Canada, however. Canada is generally welcoming to economic immigrants, as they are viewed as contributing meaningfully to industries in need of workers. Over one in five Canadians is an immigrant, making the population more empathetic to family class immigration as well. Compared to Europe and the United States, Canadian borders are relatively insulated from asylum seekers and unconventional border crossers because the country is geographically difficult to access.

That said, Canada is not immune to migration politics. The widely published photograph of Syrian toddler Alan Kurdi's lifeless body on a Mediterranean beach caused migration to be an issue during the 2015 Canadian federal election, because the child's family was reportedly headed for this country. Subsequently, travel bans and immigration crackdowns by US President Donald Trump's administration resulted in a manifold increase in asylum seekers to Canada from the United States. Prime Minister Justin Trudeau's government's open-door policy prompted fiscal concern among provincial and municipal leaders along the border and among conservatives. Under the Trudeau Liberals, the number of refugees granted legal permission to enter the country increased, with over 50,000 refugees of the Syrian civil war settling in Canada. A 2017 tweet from Trudeau stating "To those fleeing persecution, terror & war, Canadians will welcome you, regardless of your faith. Diversity is our strength. #WelcomeToCanada" was widely shared and was celebrated for its contrast with Trump. The tweet immediately caused problems within the Canadian bureaucracy as immigration officials struggled to scale up screening procedures and government supports to meet the increased targets. Critics raise concerns about the vetting of asylum seekers, their integration into Canadian society, their employment prospects, and their potential dependency on government financial assistance. Politicians and public servants strive to find an acceptable balance between accepting new residents and implementing screening protocols that ensure migrants selected to enter Canada are best-suited to succeed.

Each year, the United Nations releases its Human Development Report, which assesses human freedoms in countries around the world. The index encompasses life expectancy at birth, the number of years of schooling, and gross national income per capita. Canada often placed near the top of the ranking at the close of the last century. Since that time, Canadians' overall quality of life has been improving and Canada continues to be judged as having very high human development, although it has slipped out of the top 10 countries. Canada performs well on health, education, standard of living, gender gaps, and

See Up for Debate: Should Canada give more money for foreign aid? on page 502 at the end of this chapter for some of the arguments on both sides of this issue, and questions and resources to guide a discussion around this topic.

women's empowerment. It performs poorly compared with many countries in terms of socioeconomic sustainability, measured by such things as how much interest is being paid on government debt, how skilled the labour force is, the diversity of exports, spending on social programs compared with military spending, and income inequality between men and women. Canada is one of the world's largest exporters of natural resources and consequently performs worst on its environmental sustainability. This encompasses energy consumption, carbon dioxide emissions, and changes in forest areas and fresh water.[16]

Climate Change

climate change
A long-term shift in weather brought about by greenhouse gas emissions caused predominantly by human activity.

Climate change has become a policy issue of international concern. Carbon dioxide emitted from industry and machines is damaging the ozone layer that filters the sun's energy. Forests that absorb carbon dioxide are being cleared for farmland to feed a growing global population. Temperatures are rising, which causes considerable change to the world's ecosystems and can increase the potential for natural disasters. For Canada, the impacts are mostly water-related, including decreased marine biodiversity, drier conditions leading to increased risks of wildfires in some areas, and increased flooding in others.[17] There is political disagreement about the pace and extent of climate change, but the scientific consensus is that human behaviour is a contributing factor. Politicians are under growing public pressure to take action on climate change and to find ways to reduce society's use of fossil fuels.

In 2019, the Trudeau government implemented a levy on fossil fuels that emit greenhouse gas, which opponents decry as a carbon tax. (See Inside Canadian Politics: Why the Fuss over the Government Putting a Price or Tax on Carbon?) Companies that produce and distribute the fuels pay the levy to the government. Provinces such as Ontario and New Brunswick experienced immediate price increases on gasoline, propane, and home heating fuel. Prices are scheduled to rise through 2022 as the levy escalates. The federal government provides a household rebate of roughly a few hundred dollars to eligible Canadians who file tax returns in order to offset those added costs. Provinces such as British Columbia and Quebec were exempt from the federal levy because they already had carbon pricing policies in place. Some provinces led by conservative governments mounted constitutional challenges because they believed the Greenhouse Gas Pollution Pricing Act infringes on provincial jurisdiction. Climate change was a significant issue in the 2019 federal election campaign. It attracted considerable media attention and was a top concern in public-opinion polls. All parties had policies on combatting climate change. At one point, the Green Party was more popular than the New Democratic Party. The topic exposes regional divides given that many in Western Canada want the Trans Mountain pipeline built whereas the Bloc Québécois, NDP, and Greens oppose pipeline development.

Figuring out ways to protect the natural environment promises to be at the forefront of many government agendas irrespective of which political party has the most seats in the legislature. Generally, right-wing political parties are more likely to promote industry self-regulation and offer economic incentives through tax reductions, whereas left-wing political parties tend to urge government regulation and financial penalties. Increasingly, governments of all political stripes consider providing incentives for companies to create so-called green jobs. In response to evolving public and political pressure, and motivated by a search for cost efficiencies, many private, non-profit, and public-sector organizations are initiating their own energy-reduction measures. Whether Canada is doing enough to combat climate change is a matter of debate.

Canada is often cited by global environmentalists as a major culprit because of high emissions from its agriculture, buildings, oil industry, and transportation. The Chrétien

Inside Canadian Politics

Why the Fuss over the Government Putting a Price or Tax on Carbon?

Opinion polls indicate that most Canadians believe climate change poses a significant danger to the environment and economy. Some politicians advocate for a so-called "price" on carbon dioxide (CO_2). Carbon pricing places a tax on products and services that produce carbon emissions. The resulting increased sale price is an economic incentive for companies to produce more environmentally friendly goods and services. The government uses the revenues to pay for rebates and subsidies for low-income households. As well, governments spend the proceeds on green technology, research, and on mitigation against natural disasters caused by climate change. Other politicians prefer a cap-and-trade system that provides industrial emitters with a declining allotment of pollution credits. Corporations that reduce their emissions below the allotment can sell their unused credits to other companies.

Opponents decry these policies as a carbon "tax" and as a "tax on everything." They observe that all Canadians will have to pay more for goods and services such as gasoline, motor vehicles, plastic products, and home heat. They warn of a less competitive economy and oppose any policies that align with a high-tax, big-government agenda. While the carbon tax is permanent, the promised rebates are not. Alternative solutions include carbon capture and storage, and shifting our economies to renewable forms of energy. Others question the extent to which human activity is responsible for the globe's changing climate.

DISCUSSION ITEM

While the effects of climate change become increasingly evident, Canadian governments continue to debate a range of approaches to address it.

VOX POP

What would it take to bring all federal, provincial, and territorial governments onside with a common national strategy to address climate change?

government signed on to the Kyoto Accord to reduce greenhouse gases. The Harper government later withdrew from that pact. In 2015, the Trudeau government endorsed the Paris Agreement, within a broader United Nations Framework Convention on Climate Change. The pledge means Canadian politicians intend to find ways to limit the global temperature increase, such as by placing a price on carbon pollution. Canada emits nearly three times as much CO_2 per capita as the other signatories. The Paris Agreement is non-binding, but signatories must publicly account for their progress toward meeting the assigned targets.

Concluding Thoughts

Canada's place in the world has shifted considerably since Confederation. In recent years, age-old debates have emerged about the role of advanced industrialized nations such as Canada in the global community, and the relationships that should exist among states.

Some countries, including Canada, push for cautious loosening of borders when it comes to trade, immigration, peacekeeping, and foreign aid. Others, including Britain and the United States, have turned inward by thickening their borders against these global forces. While these differences can become exaggerated, Canada's economic, moral, and strategic place in the world continues to depend on its ability to navigate these tensions.

For More Information

Interested in how trade barriers between provinces measure up to other countries? See Jörg Broschek and Patricia Goff, 2018, "Federalism and International Trade Policy: The Canadian Provinces in Comparative Perspective," *Policy Options*, October 24.

How does Canada's role as a middle power square with its economic and military relationship with the United States? John Stewart provides a primer about the convergence between Canada's economy and borders with those of its American neighbours in *Strangers with Memories: The United States and Canada from Free Trade to Baghdad* (McGill–Queen's University Press, 2017).

Want a quick summary about ways to improve trade among Canada's provinces? A Fraser Institute research bulletin makes the case. See "Toward Free Trade in Canada: Five Things the Federal Government Can Do to Open our Internal Market," by Laura Dawson (2015).

Should Canada's spy agency expand overseas? Richard Geoffrey St John argues that a more global CSIS would reduce reliance on other countries' intelligence gathering and sharing. See "Should Canada Have a Foreign Espionage Service?" *Canadian Military Journal* 17, No. 4 (2017): pp. 56–6.

Gain an appreciation for the government's response to the Air India disaster. See the summary of the commission of inquiry into the disaster by searching "Air India report."

Expand your awareness of multinational organizations and international forums. Plenty of information about the United Nations (www.un.org/en), the World Trade Organization (www.wto.org), the Commonwealth (thecommonwealth.org), and La Francophonie (www.francophonie.org) is available online.

How is Canadian foreign aid spent? Contributors to *Struggling for Effectiveness: CIDA and Canadian Foreign Aid*, edited by Stephen Brown (McGill–Queen's University Press, 2012), explore such matters as the scope of Canadian donations to developing countries, the federal government's food security policies, and the challenges associated with reforming foreign aid practices.

What happens when staples theory, federalism, and climate change collide? Angela Carter explains in "Policy Pathways to Carbon Entrenchment: Responses to the Climate Crisis in Canada's Petro-Provinces," *Studies in Political Economy: A Socialist Review* 99, No. 2 (2018): pp. 151–74.

Deeper Inside Canadian Politics

1. What is it about Canadian politics that makes it easier to negotiate international trade deals than to encourage freer trade among Canadian provinces?
2. Consider the most recent case of terrorism that you're aware of. What role do you think Canadian security forces played behind the scenes?
3. There are many misconceptions around how asylum seekers become refugees. Review the Global Affairs Canada website to determine precisely how Canada selects and admits refugees.

Professor Profile

Miriam Anderson

International relations, war and peace, women and politics
Author of *Windows of Opportunity: How Women Seize Peace Negotiations for Political Change* (2016)

Miriam Anderson researches international security. She specializes in the study of women's participation in peace processes and transnational actors in war and peace. For instance, some of her research examines the impact of gender-inclusive peace negotiations on women's political influence in post-conflict politics. Originally from Creston, British Columbia, and now based in Toronto, she has spent time working, conducting research, and studying in countries such as Belgium, Burundi, Bosnia-Herzegovina, Croatia, El Salvador, Kenya, Nicaragua, Rwanda, the United Kingdom, and the United States.

Here is what Miriam Anderson told us about her career path from when she was an undergraduate student, why she is drawn to her area of specialization, what is challenging about studying Canadian politics, and what advice she has for students.

* * *

I completed my BA in international relations at the University of British Columbia. I didn't take any Canadian politics courses during my undergraduate studies because I was more interested in global politics. That said, a number of the international relations courses considered Canadian foreign policy, particularly Canada's role in peacekeeping and its work in international organizations. I was particularly interested in how Canada differentiates itself from the United States on the world stage.

I was drawn to better understand peace processes and post-conflict reconstruction after spending time in Nicaragua and El Salvador and working as a Human Rights Monitor for the Organization for Security and Co-operation in Europe Mission to the Republic of Croatia. Through those experiences, I became interested in the transnational and international dynamics of armed conflict and peacebuilding. War is destructive and disruptive and, in its wake, major social and political changes often follow. My research focuses on the changes to gender roles that occur, especially the increases in women's engagement in politics. Researching women's participation in peace processes and their representation in contemporary post-conflict institutions can be tricky because of the potential for political instability in countries emerging from war. Sometimes it's necessary to conduct interviews in third countries that are more secure for the interviewers and interviewees. It takes quite some effort to identify who the key players are in contemporary activist groups since there is very little—if anything—already published about them. Locating them requires some detective work, such as searching through NGO reports and combing through LinkedIn, Facebook, and Twitter accounts. The resilience of political activists who survive great hardship, and reach some of the highest levels of national politics, is impressive.

In our increasingly interconnected world, I suggest that students consider the extent to which Canadian politics is influenced by various transnational and international forces. Global social movements, such as #MeToo, are part of our political and social discourse and have led to high-profile resignations at all levels of government. Although women face discrimination worldwide, women's rights are sufficiently strong, making it possible for over 100 countries to have various forms of women's electoral quotas and for countries such as Canada and Sweden to officially declare their foreign policy "feminist." Another Canadian politics example is debating how to deal with its citizens who went abroad to join ISIS—a self-declared state comprised of foreign fighters drawn from countries across the globe—who now wish to return. Canadian politics cannot be fully understood without examining the international and transnational dynamics in which it is embedded.

Up for Debate

Should Canada give more money for foreign aid?

THE CLAIM: YES, IT SHOULD!

Canada should increase its foreign aid to help combat poverty in developing countries.

Yes: Argument Summary

The global need for foreign aid is steep. Malnourishment, disease, sexual violence, inadequate environmental standards, and a lack of basic education are some of the many acute and chronic problems facing people in developing countries. The United Nations target for foreign aid is 0.7 per cent of an industrialized nation's gross domestic product; Canada commits roughly half of this objective. Western nations can minimize human suffering if they choose to prioritize humanitarian aid over domestic politics. There is moral imperative for privileged countries like Canada to allocate more funds to combat global poverty.

Yes: Top 5 Considerations

1. Reducing global poverty has been, and should be, the primary purpose of Canadian foreign aid. The Government of Canada, whose citizens enjoy some of the best living standards in the free world, has a moral obligation to help those in greater need living in impoverished societies. As with domestic social assistance programs, relying on corporations and citizens to donate to their preferred causes is not enough.

2. Canada's position as a middle power means that it can leverage the political value of funds that would have otherwise been committed to its military. Through foreign aid, Canada can reward foreign governments that prioritize improving the quality of life of their citizens, form alliances with like-minded leaders, and redirect support from regimes with poor human rights records. This can inspire other developing countries to follow suit, while reducing the conditions that lead to terrorists targeting Canada.

3. It is imperative that countries like Canada commit their resources in order to advance the objectives of multinational organizations like the United Nations (UN) and the Organisation for Economic Co-operation and Development (OECD). Advancing human rights, promoting democracy, achieving the equality of girls and women, encouraging sustainable economic development, and distributing medicine to those in need are noble values. Without concrete, government-sponsored action, those in need are left only with unfulfilled promises.

4. So-called "economic diplomacy," whereby industrialized nations prioritize trade and economic investment in emerging economies, is a capitalist approach to solving a problem that requires a communitarian mindset. Trade liberalization may serve the interests of businesses in large economies while exploiting smaller ones, thereby worsening the plight of the poor rather than helping them.

5. Countless organizations in Canada, including the Canadian offices of global advocacy groups such as Amnesty International and Doctors Without Borders, seek to fill the foreign aid policy vacuum. Political parties should listen to these perspectives and show leadership by advancing an international development agenda.

Yes: Other Considerations

- By engaging Canadian businesses in public aid programs as opposed to using public funds, the government legitimizes attempts by profit-motivated commercial interests to present themselves as corporate citizens. This may increase the influence of the private sector over public policy, divest the government of its own responsibilities, and harm Canada's international image.

- Canada's determination to address gender equality cannot be confined to its own borders—it must be a global leader to eliminate discrimination against women and girls around the world. This requires additional spending in order not to undermine existing foreign aid commitments.

THE COUNTERCLAIM: NO, IT SHOULDN'T!

Canada's priority should be ensuring that its foreign aid commitments deliver excellent value for money.

No: Argument Summary

On behalf of all Canadians, the federal government spends approximately $6 billion annually on international assistance benefiting more than 100 countries, and many Canadians choose to make individual donations. Idealists who romanticize Canada's international role and believe that its foreign-aid budgets should be increased have little appreciation for the complexity of the task. In reality, to meet the interests of transparency and public accountability while remaining viable, any foreign aid dedicated to eradicating global poverty and related foreign development initiatives must generate some benefits to Canada.

No: Top 5 Considerations

1. The top priority for politicians and governments in Canada is to improve the quality of life of Canadian citizens. It is naive to think that political elites can maintain power if they are criticized for diverting public funds toward citizens in other countries. As long as Canadians pressure their government to spend more locally, or to cut their taxes, then their elected representatives will be incentivized to respond in kind.

2. The amount of foreign aid distributed by the federal government doesn't tell the whole story. Canadian citizens, corporations, religious organizations, and other groups have the option of giving their own money to charities that dispense foreign aid. Charitable donations are subsidized through tax-deductible status, and in the event of an episodic crisis (e.g., a natural disaster) the federal government tends to match the donations of Canadian citizens and corporations.

3. The public often thinks that political leaders make foreign aid decisions. In truth, the complexity of international relations and offering assistance to developing countries means that it is largely, and necessarily, a bureaucratic process led by international aid organizations. Achieving transparency, value,

and accountability for Canadian taxpayer dollars spent on foreign aid is challenging in this context.

4. Money given to developing countries needs to be spent in an efficient manner to optimize its impact. Public-policy operations within Canada are subject to transparency and regular program evaluation to ensure that money is being spent appropriately. The same standard of care is needed for foreign aid programs.

5. News media coverage of foreign aid polices can be moralistic, simplistic, and judgemental without comprehending the complexity of the policy problems. This introduces all sorts of biases into decisions about where to allocate limited assistance. For instance, the government may respond to pressure to direct aid to geographic areas that the media pays attention to, but the media has difficulty generating coverage of remote locations where help may be needed most.

No: Other Considerations

- Public-opinion surveys routinely indicate that foreign aid is not a top priority of Canadians. Accordingly, it tends to be a minor element of political parties' campaign platforms.

- Canadians who want to donate to international causes are welcome to do so. Countless organizations accept donations to assist with natural disasters, poverty, health epidemics, famine, population displacement, and more. Given this, there is a reduced need for politicians and bureaucrats to decide where to send their money outside the country.

- Whether under a Conservative or Liberal government, Canada simply has other priorities. It was 1970 when the United Nations established its target of 0.7 per cent of wealthy nations' GDP for foreign aid spending. Canada has never met that target, even though it claims to be committed to doing so.

- Canada should be more selective with its foreign assistance. Some Canadians are concerned that government funds are used by anti-Semitic organizations. They also observe that Canada gives money to foreign dictatorships, such as Iran and North Korea.

- Critics question why Canada provides financial assistance to relatively well-developed countries, such as Argentina and Mexico.

Discussion Questions

- How can the Canadian government ensure that money given to foreign organizations is used in an appropriate manner?
- Why do you think Canadian politicians spend so little time advocating for foreign aid?
- What are the strengths and weaknesses of a policy where the Canadian government offers to match what Canadian corporations and individuals donate?

- Should Canadian provinces, territories, and municipalities get involved in foreign aid programs?
- Is it right that the government attaches criteria to foreign aid, such as requiring that Canadian businesses benefit from any spending?

Where to Learn More about Canada and Foreign Aid

David R. Black and Rebecca Tiessen, "The Canadian International Development Agency: New Policies, Old Problems," *Canadian Journal of Development Studies* 28, no. 2 (2007): pp. 191–212.

Stephen Brown, "All About That Base? Branding and the Domestic Politics of Canadian Foreign Aid," *Canadian Foreign Policy Journal* 24, no. 2 (2018): pp. 145–64.

Stephen Brown, Molly den Heyer and David R. Black, eds., *Rethinking Canadian Aid*, 2nd edn (Ottawa: University of Ottawa Press, 2016).

Jeffrey Monaghan, "Security Development and the Palestinian Authority: An Examination of the 'Canadian Factor,'" *Conflict, Security & Development* 16, no. 2 (2016): pp. 125–43.

Stephanie Nixon et al., "Canada's Global Health Role: Supporting Equity and Global Citizenship as a Middle Power," *The Lancet* 391, no. 10131 (2018): pp. 1736–48.

Ian Smillie, "Institutional Corruption and Canadian Foreign Aid," *Canadian Foreign Policy Journal* 23, no. 1 (2017): pp. 47–59.

Rebecca Tiessen, "Gender Essentialism in Canadian Foreign Aid Commitments to Women, Peace, and Security," *International Journal: Canada's Journal of Global Policy Analysis* 70, no. 1 (2015): pp. 84–100.

First Ministers of Canada

Prime Ministers since 1867 and Premiers since 1945

CANADA

YEARS	PRIME MINISTER	PARTY*
1867–73, 1878–91	John A. Macdonald	Conservative
1873–8	Alexander Mackenzie	Liberal
1891–2	John Abbott	Conservative
1892–4	John Thompson	Conservative
1894–6	Mackenzie Bowell	Conservative
1896	Charles Tupper	Conservative
1896–1911	Wilfrid Laurier	Liberal
1911–20	Robert Borden	Conservative/Unionist
1920–1, 1926	Arthur Meighen	Unionist/Conservative
1921–6, 1926–30, 1935–48	Mackenzie King	Liberal
1930–5	Richard Bennett	Conservative
1948–57	Louis St Laurent	Liberal
1957–63	John Diefenbaker	Progressive Conservative
1963–8	Lester Pearson	Liberal
1968–79, 1980–4	Pierre Trudeau	Liberal
1979	Joe Clark	Progressive Conservative
1984	John Turner	Liberal
1984–93	Brian Mulroney	Progressive Conservative
1993	Kim Campbell	Progressive Conservative
1993–2003	Jean Chrétien	Liberal
2003–6	Paul Martin, Jr	Liberal
2006–15	Stephen Harper	Conservative
2015–	Justin Trudeau	Liberal

*The federal Conservative party has experienced name changes over time; see Chapter 9.

PROVINCES

British Columbia

YEARS	PREMIER	PARTY
1941–7	John Hart	Liberal–Conservative coalition
1947–52	Byron (Boss) Johnson	Liberal–Conservative coalition
1952–72	W.A.C. Bennett	Social Credit
1972–5	Dave Barrett	New Democratic Party
1975–86	Bill Bennett	Social Credit
1986–91	Bill Vander Zalm	Social Credit
1991	Rita Johnston	Social Credit
1991–6	Mike Harcourt	New Democratic Party
1996–9	Glen Clark	New Democratic Party
1999–2000	Dan Miller	New Democratic Party
2000–1	Ujjal Dosanjh	New Democratic Party
2001–11	Gordon Campbell	Liberal
2011–17	Christy Clark	Liberal
2017–	John Horgan	New Democratic Party

Alberta

YEARS	PREMIER	PARTY
1943–68	Ernest Manning	Social Credit
1968–71	Harry Strom	Social Credit
1971–85	Peter Lougheed	Progressive Conservative
1985–92	Don Getty	Progressive Conservative
1992–2006	Ralph Klein	Progressive Conservative
2006–11	Ed Stelmach	Progressive Conservative
2011–14	Alison Redford	Progressive Conservative
2014	Dave Hancock	Progressive Conservative
2014–15	Jim Prentice	Progressive Conservative
2015–19	Rachel Notley	New Democratic Party
2019–	Jason Kenney	United Conservative

Saskatchewan

YEARS	PREMIER	PARTY
1944–61	Tommy Douglas	Co-operative Commonwealth Federation
1961–4	Woodrow Lloyd	CCF/New Democratic Party
1964–71	Ross Thatcher	Liberal
1971–82	Allan Blakeney	New Democratic Party
1982–91	Grant Devine	Progressive Conservative
1991–2001	Roy Romanow	New Democratic Party
2001–7	Lorne Calvert	New Democratic Party

| 2007–18 | Brad Wall | Saskatchewan Party |
| 2018– | Scott Moe | Saskatchewan Party |

Manitoba

YEARS	PREMIER	PARTY
1943–8	Stuart Garson	Liberal–Progressive coalition
1948–58	Douglas Campbell	Liberal–Progressive coalition / Liberal–Progressive majority
1958–67	Duff Roblin	Progressive Conservative
1967–9	Walter Weir	Progressive Conservative
1969–77	Edward Schreyer	New Democratic Party
1977–81	Sterling Lyon	Progressive Conservative
1981–8	Howard Pawley	New Democratic Party
1988–99	Gary Filmon	Progressive Conservative
1999–2009	Gary Doer	New Democratic Party
2009–16	Greg Selinger	New Democratic Party
2016–	Brian Pallister	Progressive Conservative

Ontario

YEARS	PREMIER	PARTY
1943–8	George Drew	Progressive Conservative
1948–9	Thomas L. Kennedy	Progressive Conservative
1949–61	Leslie Frost	Progressive Conservative
1961–71	John Robarts	Progressive Conservative
1971–85	Bill Davis	Progressive Conservative
1985	Frank Miller	Progressive Conservative
1985–90	David Peterson	Liberal
1990–5	Bob Rae	New Democratic Party
1995–2002	Mike Harris	Progressive Conservative
2002–3	Ernie Eves	Progressive Conservative
2003–13	Dalton McGuinty	Liberal
2013–18	Kathleen Wynne	Liberal
2018–	Doug Ford	Progressive Conservative

Quebec

YEARS	PREMIER	PARTY
1944–59	Maurice Duplessis	Union Nationale
1959–60	Paul Sauvé	Union Nationale
1960	Antonio Barrette	Union Nationale
1960–6	Jean Lesage	Libéral
1966–8	Daniel Johnson, Sr	Union Nationale
1968–70	Jean-Jacques Bertrand	Union Nationale

1970–6	Robert Bourassa	Libéral
1976–85	René Lévesque	Parti Québécois
1985	Pierre-Marc Johnson	Parti Québécois
1985–94	Robert Bourassa	Libéral
1994	Daniel Johnson, Jr	Libéral
1994–6	Jacques Parizeau	Parti Québécois
1996–2001	Lucien Bouchard	Parti Québécois
2001–3	Bernard Landry	Parti Québécois
2003–12	Jean Charest	Libéral
2012–14	Pauline Marois	Parti Québécois
2014–18	Philippe Couillard	Libéral
2018–	François Legault	Coalition Avenir Québec

New Brunswick

YEARS	PREMIER	PARTY
1940–52	John B. McNair	Liberal
1952–60	Hugh John Flemming	Progressive Conservative
1960–70	Louis Robichaud	Liberal
1970–87	Richard Hatfield	Progressive Conservative
1987–97	Frank McKenna	Liberal
1997–8	Ray Frenette	Liberal
1998–9	Camille Thériault	Liberal
1999–2006	Bernard Lord	Progressive Conservative
2006–10	Shawn Graham	Liberal
2010–14	David Alward	Progressive Conservative
2014–18	Brian Gallant	Liberal
2018–	Blaine Higgs	Progressive Conservative

Nova Scotia

YEARS	PREMIER	PARTY
1945–54	Angus Macdonald	Liberal
1954	Harold Connolly	Liberal
1954–6	Henry Hicks	Liberal
1956–67	Robert Stanfield	Progressive Conservative
1967–70	G.I. Smith	Progressive Conservative
1970–8	Gerald Regan	Liberal
1978–90	John Buchanan	Progressive Conservative
1990–1	Roger Bacon	Progressive Conservative
1991–3	Donald Cameron	Progressive Conservative
1993–7	John Savage	Liberal
1997–9	Russell MacLellan	Liberal

1999–2006	John Hamm	Progressive Conservative
2006–9	Rodney MacDonald	Progressive Conservative
2009–13	Darrell Dexter	New Democratic Party
2013–	Stephen McNeil	Liberal

Prince Edward Island

YEARS	PREMIER	PARTY
1943–53	Walter Jones	Liberal
1953–9	Alex Matheson	Liberal
1959–66	Walter Shaw	Progressive Conservative
1966–78	Alexander Campbell	Liberal
1978–9	Bennett Campbell	Liberal
1979–81	Angus MacLean	Progressive Conservative
1981–6	James Lee	Progressive Conservative
1986–93	Joe Ghiz	Liberal
1993–6	Catherine Callbeck	Liberal
1996	Keith Milligan	Liberal
1996–2007	Pat Binns	Progressive Conservative
2007–2015	Robert Ghiz	Liberal
2015–2019	Wade MacLauchlan	Liberal
2019–	Dennis King	Progressive Conservative

Newfoundland and Labrador*

YEARS	PREMIER	PARTY
1949–72	Joey Smallwood	Liberal
1972–9	Frank Moores	Progressive Conservative
1979–89	Brian Peckford	Progressive Conservative
1989	Tom Rideout	Progressive Conservative
1989–96	Clyde Wells	Liberal
1996–2000	Brian Tobin	Liberal
2000–1	Beaton Tulk	Liberal
2001–3	Roger Grimes	Liberal
2003–10	Danny Williams	Progressive Conservative
2010–14	Kathy Dunderdale	Progressive Conservative
2014	Tom Marshall	Progressive Conservative
2014–15	Paul Davis	Progressive Conservative
2015–	Dwight Ball	Liberal

*Joined Canada in 1949.

TERRITORIES
Yukon*

YEARS	PREMIER	PARTY
1978–85	Chris Pearson	Progressive Conservative
1985	Willard Phelps	Progressive Conservative
1985–92	Tony Penikett	New Democratic Party
1992–6	John Ostashek	Yukon Party
1996–2000	Piers McDonald	New Democratic Party
2000–2	Pat Duncan	Liberal
2002–11	Dennis Fentie	Yukon Party
2011–16	Darrell Pasloski	Yukon Party
2016–	Sandy Silver	Liberal

Commissioners served as heads of government in Yukon until 1978.

Northwest Territories*

YEARS	PREMIER	PARTY
1980–4	George Braden	No party system
1984–5	Richard Nerysoo	No party system
1985–7	Nick Sibbeston	No party system
1987–91	Dennis Patterson	No party system
1991–5	Nellie Cournoyea	No party system
1995–8	Don Morin	No party system
1998	Goo Arlooktoo	No party system
1998–2000	Jim Antoine	No party system
2000–3	Stephen Kakfwi	No party system
2003–7	Joe Handley	No party system
2007–11	Floyd Roland	No party system
2011–19	Bob McLeod	No party system
2019–	Caroline Cochrane	No party system

Commissioners served as heads of government in Northwest Territories until 1980.

Nunavut*

YEARS	PREMIER	PARTY
1999–2008	Paul Okalik	No party system
2008–13	Eva Aariak	No party system
2013–17	Peter Taptuna	No party system
2017–18	Paul Quassa	No party system
2018–	Joe Savikataaq	No party system

* *The territory was created in 1999 from land under the jurisdiction of Northwest Territories.*

Glossary

ABC An agency, board, or commission responsible for delivering a program or service, or producing goods, at arm's length from government. *See also* government agency, government board, government commission.

access to information A legal requirement that governments release information upon request, subject to certain restrictions.

adjournment The temporary suspension of a legislative sitting until it reconvenes.

administrative law The branch of public law involving the review of government decisions and disputes between citizens and state agencies.

administrative tribunals Quasi-judicial bodies empowered to decide administrative law cases, and whose decisions may be appealed to the court system.

affirmative action A policy or policies consisting of proactive measures to guarantee the descriptive representation of traditionally under-represented groups.

agenda setting The use of strategies and tactics to generate public and government support for a proposed public policy.

allophones Canadians whose dominant language is neither French nor English.

ambassador An official state representative to another country.

amending formula A set of rules governing how the constitution can be changed.

appointment power The authority to decide who should be selected to fill a government position.

Arctic Council An international forum that brings together eight Arctic states and Arctic Indigenous peoples.

astroturfing The practice of masking an organization's elitist character to make it look like a grassroots organization.

asymmetrical federalism A model of federalism in which jurisdictional powers are distributed unequally among provinces.

attorney general A cabinet member and the highest-ranking elected legal officer in a jurisdiction.

auditor general An independent officer responsible for auditing and reporting to the legislature regarding a government's spending and operations.

baby bonus A government policy that awards money to parents of young children.

backbencher A rank-and-file member of the legislative assembly without cabinet responsibilities or other special legislative titles or duties.

Band A group of status Indians defined by the federal government.

Band Council Governing body elected by members of a Band.

bicameral legislature A legislative body consisting of two chambers (or "houses").

bill A piece of draft legislation tabled in the legislature.

Bill of Rights, 1960 A federal law detailing Canadians' rights and freedoms vis-à-vis the federal government.

Bloc Québécois A left-leaning protest party that promotes Quebec nationalism.

boundaries commission A body that recommends changes to election boundaries.

brokerage party The Canadian term for a catch-all party that brokers competing regional demands.

budget A document containing the government's projected revenue, expenditures, and economic forecasts.

budget deficit A situation in which spending exceeds revenues during a given period.

budget estimates The detailed, line-by-line statements of how each department will treat revenues and expenditures.

budget surplus A situation in which revenues exceed spending during a given period.

by-election A district-level election held between general elections.

cabinet The leaders of the political executive, consisting of the sitting prime minister and federal ministers, or the premier and provincial ministers.

cabinet committee A subgroup of cabinet members assigned to scrutinize a particular set of executive actions.

cabinet shuffle A change in the composition of a government's political executive between elections.

cabinet solidarity The understanding that members of the executive remain cohesive and jointly responsible for the government's undertakings.

Canada Health Act Federal legislation imposing conditions on provincial governments for the expenditure of funds from health transfers.

Canada Pension Plan A mandatory federal retirement program funded by workers and employers.

Canada Student Loans A federal program that helps qualifying students access post-secondary education by providing them access to loans that are interest free and do not need to be repaid while they study full-time.

Canada–United States–Mexico Agreement (CUSMA) A free-trade agreement that provides tariff-free market access among the three participating countries, with some restrictions.

Canadian Broadcasting Corporation (CBC) A Crown corporation that is Canada's national public broadcaster.

Canadian Free Trade Agreement (CFTA) Federal–provincial–territorial agreement to lower internal trade barriers within Canada.

Canadian Radio-television and Telecommunications Commission (CRTC) An administrative tribunal that regulates television, radio and telephone services.

Canadian Security Intelligence Service (CSIS) Canada's spy agency.

catch-all party A competitive political party that prioritizes appealing to the broadest base of electoral support possible.

central agencies Coordinating bodies that steer government business across all departments.

centralized federalism A federal system of government where the national government has considerable power.

Charlottetown Accord An accord in the early 1990s that proposed to renew the constitution, but was defeated in a national referendum in 1992.

Charter of Rights and Freedoms A portion of the Constitution Act, 1982, enshrining Canadians' core liberties and entitlements vis-à-vis their governments.

Charterphiles Supporters of the enhanced role of judges in the Canadian rights regime.

Charterphobes Opponents and skeptics of the enhanced role of judges in the Canadian rights regime.

chief of staff The most senior, non-elected partisan employee in the government.

citizen A member of a state who is under the authority and protection of its government.

citizens plus The notion that Indigenous peoples (ought to) hold a special set of rights in addition to those conferred by Canadian citizenship.

civil law The body of rules governing disputes between or among private parties.

civil-law system A legal order used in Quebec that is based on a written code.

Clarity Act Federal legislation passed in 2000 that sets out the terms for the federal government to deal with a province proposing to secede.

classical federalism A model of federalism in which federal and provincial governments operate independently of each other in their own respective areas of jurisdiction.

cleavage A division that separates opposing political communities.

clerk of the Privy (or Executive) Council The highest-ranking public servant in the federal (or provincial/territorial) bureaucracy.

climate change A long-term shift in weather brought about by greenhouse gas emissions caused predominantly by human activity.

closure A procedure requiring that debate conclude so that the question may be addressed by the end of the sitting.

co-operative federalism A model of federalism in which federal and provincial governments work together to solve public-policy problems.

coalition government A hung parliament in which the cabinet consists of members from more than one political party, a rarity in Canada.

collaborative federalism A model of federalism in which provincial governments take the lead to solve common public-policy problems together.

collective action problem The notion that people whose interests are promoted by a group will benefit from its efforts whether or not they actively participate.

collective bargaining The formal negotiation of the terms of an employment contract between the representatives of a group of employees and their employer.

commission of inquiry An independent body of experts created by a government to investigate an issue of great importance.

committee of the whole Another name for the body of all legislators meeting as a committee, minus the speaker.

common-law system A legal order based on customs, usage, and precedent.

Commonwealth An association of nation-states with ties to the United Kingdom.

Communications Security Establishment (CSE) Canada's electronic communications spy agency.

conditional grants Federal transfers to the provinces that may only be used for a specific purpose, and are subject to federal government restrictions or standards.

confederal parties Federal and provincial parties that operate autonomously from each other, even though they may have similar names.

Confederation The federal union of provinces and territories forming Canada, originally comprised of Ontario, Quebec, New Brunswick, and Nova Scotia.

confidence convention The practice under which a government must relinquish power when it loses a critical legislative vote.

conscription A compulsory war draft by the government to recruit soldiers.

consensus government A system of governance that operates without political parties.

Conservative Party A centre–right major party that has periodically formed the Government of Canada.

constitutional convention An unwritten rule that binds political actors to adhere to the traditions of the constitutional order.

constitutional monarchy A system in which the sovereignty of the Crown is maintained, but exercised by elected officials according to prescribed rules.

constitutional law The branch of public law dealing with the authority of the state.

constitutional order The body of written and unwritten rules that govern all laws in Canada.

contempt A formal denunciation of a member's or government's unparliamentary behaviour by the speaker.

correctional system The network of community-based and institutional programs designed to detain, rehabilitate, and deter those involved in illegal activity.

Council of the Federation An organization that supports regular meetings among provincial and territorial premiers.

criminal law Body of legal rules governing misconduct affecting both victims and society as a whole.

critic An opposition party member assigned to scrutinize the activities of a particular minister of the Crown.

crossing the floor A situation in which a member of the legislature leaves one political party to join another party.

Crown The legal concept dictating the supremacy of the monarch over the executive, legislative, and judicial branches of government.

Crown attorney A lawyer who acts on behalf of the government when deciding how to pursue criminal cases.

Crown corporations Enterprises owned by a federal or provincial government.

decentralized federalism A federal system of government where the regional units have considerable power.

declaratory power The authority of the federal government to decide that an issue falls within its jurisdiction.

democracy A system of government featuring primary decision-makers chosen by citizens through free and fair elections.

democratic deficit The gap between peoples' expectations for the performance of democratic institutions and the perceived performance of those institutions.

democratic socialism An ideology that promotes more government intervention and assistance for those most in need.

Department of Finance The central agency responsible for setting and monitoring the government's fiscal and economic policy, including overseeing the budget process.

deputy minister Reporting to the minister, the highest-ranking public servant in a given government department.

descriptive representation A political attachment to someone viewed as sharing one's background or social profile.

devolution The act of transferring (devolving) powers from a central government to regional or local governments that remain under its constitutional purview.

dialogue model The notion that the definition of rights and freedoms is reached through the interaction of judges, legislatures, and executives.

direct democracy A system in which citizens make political decisions by voting on individual issues, such as through a referendum.

direct taxation The collection of taxes by government without using an intermediary.

disallowance The constitutional power of the federal government to veto provincial legislation and cause its termination.

disclosure Revealing otherwise private information, such as campaign expenses.

dissolution The process by which a Parliament or legislature is closed, resulting in a general election of new members.

distinct society A proposed designation for the province of Quebec, recognizing that it features a French-speaking majority, a unique culture, and a civil-law tradition.

divided Crown A monarchy whose sovereignty is split among different orders of government.

e-democracy The use of information communication technologies to get citizens involved in politics.

e-government The interactive use of information communication technologies to deliver public programs and services.

earned majority A majority government in which the governing party's share of the popular vote is at least 50 per cent.

election platform A list of political pledges announced before or during an election campaign.

electoral district association (EDA) The local organization of a political party operating within the boundaries of an election riding.

elite party A small political party run by people with ascribed social status.

emergency federalism A model of federalism in which the federal government assumes control in a national crisis.

employment equity A federal government policy requiring civil-service managers to proactively consider employing women, people with disabilities, Indigenous peoples, and visible minorities.

employment insurance A mandatory government insurance program, funded by employees and employers, that provides temporary income to workers who lose their jobs.

equalization A federal transfer program that is designed to lessen the fiscal disparities among provinces.

executive federalism A system in which the elected leaders of federal and provincial governments make public-policy decisions.

fake news Fabricated stories designed to appear as authentic journalism and spread online to influence political attitudes through deception.

federal spending power The capacity of the federal government to spend its available funds, even on areas that fall outside its constitutional jurisdiction.

federalism A constitution-based division of powers between two or more orders of government.

feminism A political ideology and social movement that seeks to advance women's rights and achieve gender equality.

filibuster The extension of parliamentary debate, typically by opposition members, to delay the passage of a bill.

first minister diplomacy The characterization of Canadian premiers and prime ministers as the primary spokesperson of their government's interests.

first ministers The heads of government in Canada, namely the prime minister and the premiers.

first ministers' meetings Formal gatherings of the premiers, sometimes hosted by the prime minister.

First Nations Indigenous groups descended from a variety of historical Indigenous nations; collectively, the earliest inhabitants of North America and their descendants, other than Métis and Inuit.

fiscal federalism The manner in which revenues and responsibilities are distributed among various orders and governments.

fiscal update Announcement of the state of the government's economic, revenue, and spending projections since the budget was tabled earlier in the year.

fixed-date election law Legislation prescribing that general elections be held on a particular date, or range of dates, typically every four years.

focusing event A public crisis that is so significant that it commands all news attention for an extended period of time.

formalistic representation A political attachment to someone by virtue of that person's status as a legitimately elected official.

fourth estate An informal term for the media, implying that a free press is so vital to democracy that it is on par with the three branches of government (executive, legislature, judiciary).

framing The shaping of information so that communication recipients will interpret it in a manner that is advantageous to the sender.

franchise The right to vote in an election.

Francophonie, La Association of nation-states and regions with French language and cultural connections.

free trade The elimination of financial and regulatory barriers to allow unfettered market access.

free vote A bill or motion in the legislature on which party members, except members of cabinet, are allowed to vote however they choose without sanction.

freedoms The autonomy to live and act without external restraint.

functional federalism A system in which civil servants conduct the bulk of intergovernmental activity.

glass ceiling Barriers that inhibit participation in politics by traditionally marginalized groups, particularly women.

GOTV Get out the vote efforts to mobilize supporters to vote, such as telephone reminders.

government The people and systems that govern a society by designing, overseeing, and implementing laws and public policy. Can refer to the cabinet and/or the broader public sector.

government agency An arm's-length corporate body operating on behalf of a government.

government board A public advisory committee made up of appointed citizens.

government commission An agency of government that provides specialized policy expertise and oversight.

governor general The monarch's representative at the federal level in Canada.

green paper A government document released to explore policy options, without any commitment to the outcome.

G7 Annual meeting of the leaders of seven of the world's most industrialized economies.

goods and services tax (GST) A federal value-added tax applied to the sale of most goods and services in Canada.

habeas corpus The right not to be detained without cause or due process.

hacktivism Politically motivated damage inflicted on government information communication technologies.

harmonized sales tax (HST) In Atlantic Canada and Ontario, a value-added consumption tax that combines both federal and provincial rates.

hate speech Messages that incite prejudice and promote harm toward an identifiable group of people.

head of government The highest-ranking elected official in a jurisdiction, namely the prime minister or premier who is appointed by the Crown to lead the executive.

head of state The highest-ranking figure in a sovereign state, serving as its foremost ceremonial representative.

horizontal fiscal imbalance A situation in which some provinces have greater capacity to fund their constitutional responsibilities than others.

horse-race coverage Media attention focused on who is leading in public opinion.

House of Commons The lower house of the Canadian Parliament, consisting of elected members from across the country.

house leader A member of the legislature responsible for the overall performance of a political party in the legislative process.

ideology A set of ideas that form a coherent political belief system.

incumbent An elected official who currently represents an electoral district.

independent A candidate or parliamentarian who is not officially affiliated with a political party.

Indigenous people First Nations, Métis, and Inuit living in Canada.

indirect taxation The collection of taxes by an intermediate body on behalf of the government.

information subsidy Free packaged content provided to the media in a manner that is designed to meet their needs.

infotainment The delivery of news about government and politics as a form of entertainment programming.

inner cabinet Members of the political executive who hold its most important portfolios, including finance, treasury board, and justice (among others).

institution A structure that defines, constrains, or encourages behaviour within a political system.

institutionalized interest groups Pressure groups that have become entrenched political organizations.

integrated parties Federal and provincial political parties whose behaviours and organization are interconnected.

inter-state federalism A system of formal interactions among government officials and leaders.

interest group A political organization that seeks to influence public policy without competing for election.

interest rate The percentage rate of money charged by lenders to borrowers.

intra-state federalism A system in which regional interests are represented within the institutions of the central government.

Inuit Indigenous peoples with historic ties to the northernmost lands in Canada.

issue-oriented interest groups Loosely organized political organizations that focus on a core issue (*see* interest group).

judicial impartiality The principle by which judges decide cases based on evidence and an objective interpretation of the law.

judicial independence The principle by which judges are free from political interference when deciding cases.

judicial review The authority of the courts to adjudicate matters of constitutional law.

jurisdiction The ultimate authority to make legal decisions, or the seat of power for such decision-making.

justice of the peace An individual appointed to provide routine, administrative judicial services.

King–Byng affair A 1926 constitutional crisis when the governor general refused the prime minister's request for a general election.

labour union An organization of workers that represents its members' interests, especially in bargaining with their employer.

land claims Statements of Indigenous entitlement to territory within Canada.

Laurentian thesis A theory that historic perceptions of Central-Canadian dominance have spawned regionalist resentment in peripheral parts of the country.

leader of the official opposition Typically, the leader of the party with the second-most seats in the legislature.

leader's tour A visit of various electoral districts by the party leader and an entourage of staffers and journalists.

leadership contest An election within a political party to select a leader.

leadership review A vote held at a party convention on whether a leadership contest should be held.

left-wing A political tendency that promotes a bigger role for government and proactive measures to achieve social and economic equality.

legislative committee A small group of legislators assigned to deliberate and report back to the legislature.

liberal democracy A system in which equality, rights, and freedoms are preserved through public debate and free and fair elections.

Liberal Party A party that straddles the political centre and has governed Canada at the federal level longer than any other major party.

liberalism An ideology that promotes equality of opportunity.

libertarianism An ideology that champions the least possible amount of state intervention in the lives of citizens.

lieutenant governor The monarch's representative in each province.

line departments Units responsible for the development and delivery of policy, programs, or services under a particular portfolio.

lobbying Professional communication with public-office-holders initiated by advocacy groups as part of an effort to influence decisions.

major party A political party that has many supporters and a large organizational infrastructure.

majority government A government in which the governing party controls more than half of the seats in the legislature.

mandatory minimum sentence The shortest allowable prison term a judge may impose upon a person convicted of certain crimes, such as firearms and drug offences, or under certain conditions (e.g., a repeat offence).

manufactured majority A majority government in which the governing party's share of the popular vote is less than 50 per cent.

Maritimes The provinces of New Brunswick, Prince Edward Island, and Nova Scotia. When Newfoundland and Labrador is added, the four provinces constitute the Atlantic region.

mass party A grassroots political party characterized by its efforts to sign up members.

mediated democracy A democratic society that relies on the media to provide citizens with information about politics and government.

medicare A publicly funded healthcare service administered by each province with the financial support of the federal government.

Meech Lake Accord A failed constitutional amendment package in the late 1980s that would have recognized Quebec as a distinct society.

member of Parliament (MP) One of the 338 representatives elected by Canadians to serve in the House of Commons.

merit principle The notion that the most qualified candidate should be awarded a position, contract, or other financial benefit.

Métis Indigenous peoples with mixed First Nations and European ancestry.

middle power Canada's status as an intermediary, rather than a leader, in international affairs.

minister of justice The member of the government responsible for the administration of the justice system within a given jurisdiction.

minister of the Crown The political head of a government ministry, responsible for directing and overseeing the activities of its departments and agencies, boards, and commissions.

ministerial responsibility The understanding that ministers remain individually responsible for the activities of staff in their respective departments.

minor party A small political party with much less support or infrastructure than a major party.

minority government A government in which the governing party controls less than half of the seats in the legislature.

monarch The absolute head of a monarchy, whose power is typically derived by birth.

mosaic A metaphor used to depict Canada's multicultural character, which features many distinct yet interdependent ethnocultural communities.

motion A proposed parliamentary action.

narrowcasting A form of campaigning in which parties choose communications that will target narrowly defined groups of voters.

National Indigenous Organizations (NIOs) Five bodies formally recognized as representing the interests of different Indigenous groups across Canada.

nationalism A unifying ideology among people who share a common homeland, ancestry, and language or culture.

natural governing party A single party whose long-term dominance has become institutionalized.

negative political advertising Paid communication that criticizes an opponent's policy or record, and that may verge on attacking the person.

New Democratic Party (NDP) A left-wing major party that has formal ties with organized labour.

Night of the Long Knives An incident in November 1981 in which the federal government and 9 of 10 provincial governments reached a deal to patriate the constitution, without the presence of Quebec government officials.

non-status Indian A First Nations person who is not registered under the Indian Act.

North American Air Defense (NORAD) A Canada–US air defence agreement.

North Atlantic Treaty Organization (NATO) International military alliance of Western nations.

notwithstanding clause Section 33 of the Constitution Act, 1982, which permits legislatures to pass laws that breach certain rights and freedoms.

Oakes test A model employed by the court to weigh the democratic benefits and assess the constitutionality of a law that breaches certain Charter rights.

official party status The minimum number of elected members a party needs to question the government in the legislature and qualify for other resources and privileges.

omnibus bills Bills or laws that address a wide variety of public-policy issues in a single document.

opposition days Time allotted to opposition parties to raise their own motions and legislation.

parliamentary democracy A democratic system in which government executives must be supported by a majority of elected representatives in a legislature.

parliamentary privilege The extraordinary rights and immunities enjoyed by members of a legislature to ensure they can carry out their duties without interference from the executive or the courts.

parliamentary supremacy A doctrine under which legislatures and executives, not courts, define key elements of public policy.

partisan Someone who identifies with, and is a staunch supporter of, a political party.

party caucus All the members of a political party who hold a seat in the legislature.

party convention An official gathering of party delegates to decide on matters of policy and/or leadership.

party discipline Legislators' strict adherence to the directives of their party leadership.

party leader The head of a political party's legislative wing.

party member A person who formally belongs to a political party, having joined by purchasing a membership.

party nomination An internal contest to decide who should represent a party locally in an upcoming election.

party press Early newspapers that were blatantly partisan.

party system A particular constellation of political parties guided by a unique framework of behaviour.

party whip Individual member of the legislature responsible for ensuring that caucus members toe the party line.

patriation The process through which Canadian governments gained the authority to amend the country's main constitutional documents.

patronage The awarding of government jobs, contracts, and/or other financial benefits to friends of the government party.

peace officer A specially trained individual granted government authority to enforce laws.

per capita transfers Federal funds distributed to provinces based on how many people live in their jurisdictions.

permanent campaign The practice of electioneering outside of an election period, especially by leveraging government resources.

plebiscite A citizen vote held to inform a decision by a representative body.

pluralism The presence of diverse socioeconomic groups participating in public affairs.

POGG The acronym for the constitutional objective of "peace, order, and good government."

political correctness Social pressure to correct perceived injustices, typically by recasting or denouncing topics and language that is deemed offensive.

political culture A society's innate political characteristics, embodied in the structure of its institutions and the beliefs of its members.

political party A political entity that runs candidates in elections in an attempt to shape government policy and laws.

politics Activities involving the pursuit and exercise of decision-making over the collectivity.

pollster A senior employee of a research company who oversees the administration of public-opinion surveys.

populism A political movement that seeks to reduce elite authority over ordinary people, and that is often led by a charismatic figure.

pork barrel politics The partisan allocation of government spending to select constituencies, especially those districts held or sought by the governing party.

portfolio An office or area of responsibility for a minister of the Crown.

power The ability to control or influence other members of a political community.

Prairies The provinces of Alberta, Saskatchewan, and Manitoba.

premier The head of government in a provincial or territorial government.

premier's office Partisan staff appointed who advance the political interests of the provincial cabinet, in particular those of the premier.

prerogative authority Powers that are not explicitly granted to the political executives, and that remain vested in the Crown.

presidentialization The concentration of executive power in the office of the prime minister or premier, at the expense of broader cabinet authority.

press gallery Political journalists who monitor government business and who personally observe proceedings in the legislature.

prime minister (PM) The head of government at the federal level.

Prime Minister's Office (PMO) Partisan staff who advance the political interests of the federal cabinet, in particular those of the prime minister.

principal–agent problem A problem arising from the fact that someone (an agent) working on behalf of a decision-maker (the principal) may not take the course of action the principal intended.

private laws Rules governing the relationships among citizens and organizations.

Privy Council The formal body of prominent federal politicians and officials that typically advise the governor general. Not to be confused with the Privy Council Office (PCO).

Privy Council Office (PCO) The central agency responsible for coordinating the federal government's overall implementation of policy. The PCO is not to be confused with the Privy Council.

propaganda One-sided persuasive communication that communicates falsehoods by virtue of its selective exclusion of truths.

prorogation The process by which a legislative session is closed in anticipation of a new speech from the throne being delivered.

public administration The study and delivery of public policy by public servants.

public debt The accumulated amount borrowed by a government to finance budgets and considered owing.

public laws Rules governing individuals' relationships to the state and society.

public-opinion research The systematic collection of people's views and attitudes.

public policy A plan or course of action chosen by a government to respond to an identified problem.

public-policy analysis The process of developing options to inform decision-makers.

public-policy cycle The common stages in public decision-making, from conception to implementation and modification.

public-service management Non-partisan bureaucratic officials serving at the pleasure of the Crown and the first minister.

public sphere The venue for group and public discussion about social problems and government.

Quebec nation motion A non-binding federal motion passed in 2006 that recognized the unique character of the Québécois.

Question Period The time allotted for members to ask oral questions of the government in the legislature.

Quiet Revolution An early 1960s modernizing movement in Quebec, geared toward a stronger provincial government and outward nationalism.

rational choice A theory that citizens are self-interested actors whose decisions fulfill their own needs and wants.

RCMP Royal Canadian Mounted Police; pan-Canadian police force commissioned by the federal government.

reasonable accommodation Adjustments to policies that allow for the inclusion of traditionally disadvantaged groups without causing undue hardship to others.

reasonable limits clause Section 1 of the Charter, which allows governments to pass laws that would otherwise contravene rights and freedoms but that are deemed necessary to protect other democratic norms.

recall Legislated process by which electors of a given district may petition for a by-election.

reconciliation The process of establishing respectful relationships among Indigenous people and non-Indigenous people.

redistribution The formal process used to periodically adjust electoral boundaries.

reference cases Proceedings initiated by governments asking for the court's opinion on the constitutionality of legislation.

referendum A citizen vote whose outcome legislators are usually expected to follow.

regionalism An allegiance or psychological connection to a territory with its own unique political characteristics.

regional minister A minister whose portfolio includes additional responsibility for government in a broad geographic area.

regulation A directive passed by the executive specifying how the primary legislation is to be administered.

remand Court-ordered, temporary detention for accused offenders awaiting trial.

representative democracy A system in which citizens elect officials to make political decisions on their behalf.

republic A system of government in which sovereignty is vested in the people, not the Crown.

reservation The constitutional power of the federal government to withhold the passage of provincial legislation, so as to cause short-term or permanent delay.

reserve A tract of land owned by the federal government and set aside for First Nations peoples.

residential schools system A program of state- and church-run schools designed to assimilate Indigenous children into whitestream Canadian society.

residual powers Any powers not specifically identified in the constitution, which default to the federal government.

responsible government The constitutional principle whereby the executive (cabinet) must be supported by a majority of elected members of the legislature.

restorative justice Drawn from Indigenous traditions, a set of principles that emphasizes repairing relationships among criminal offenders, their victims, and the community.

right-wing A political tendency that promotes a smaller role for government and a greater emphasis on individual responsibility and market-based competition.

rights Legal claims or entitlements to have something or to act in a particular manner.

royal assent The final stage of legislation being approved, involving the monarch's representative signing the bill into law.

royal commission/commission of inquiry A special research investigation of a contentious area of public policy.

Royal Commission on Indigenous Peoples (RCAP) An investigation launched to study the relationship between Indigenous and non-Indigenous peoples in Canada.

Royal Proclamation of 1763 A British document setting out the terms of European settlement in North America following the Seven Years' War.

rule of law The principle that no one is above the law, and that any powers granted to elected or non-elected officials must be conferred by legislation.

safe seat An electoral district in which the incumbent party is highly likely to be re-elected.

sales tax A revenue-generating tax charged by a government on the sale of applicable goods and services.

seats triage The identification of swing ridings where campaign resources should be concentrated.

secessionism A widely held sentiment that a province or territory should leave the Canadian federation.

sectionalism An emotional connection with one's regional homeland, more than with one's country.

self-government The inherent right of a people to sovereignty (or self-determination) over their own affairs.

Senate The upper house of the Canadian Parliament, consisting of members chosen by the executive.

senator One of the appointed members of the upper house of the Canadian Parliament.

settler colonialism Belief in the supremacy of European settler institutions over those of Indigenous groups, and policies and practices that impose this belief.

7/50 amending formula A rule for passing most amendments to the constitution, requiring the consent of Parliament and the legislatures of seven provinces representing 50 per cent of Canada's population.

shadow cabinet A group of opposition party members responsible for holding ministers of the Crown to account for their actions.

single-member plurality (SMP) An electoral system whereby the winner of a district needs just one vote more than the number amassed by the runner-up.

slacktivism Actions taken by individuals to appear part of a social movement, but that have no direct impact on the fulfilment of its objectives.

social assistance Financial support provided by government to citizens with no other recourse to income.

social movement An informal collection of people who share a public-policy concern and urge government action and changes to social values and behaviour.

social safety net Government-funded social-welfare programs designed to assist citizens in their time of need.

solicitor general A cabinet member typically responsible for the penal and policing aspects of the justice system.

sovereignty The power to exercise government authority over a polity within a defined geographical area.

sovereignty-association A legal arrangement whereby Quebec would be politically independent but maintain economic ties with Canada.

speaker The member of the legislature responsible for presiding over its rules and general decorum.

speech from the throne Document read by the governor general, lieutenant governor, or commissioner officially opening a new session of the legislature and detailing the government's plans.

spending limits Legal restrictions on how much money can be spent in a campaign.

spin The media relations tactic of providing information in a decidedly one-sided manner in order to persuade.

sponsorship scandal An affair in which Liberal advertising agencies received public funds for work that was never performed.

standing committee Also known as a permanent legislative committee, whose existence is defined by standing orders.

standing orders The body of rules governing the conduct of the legislature.

staples theory An idea that the Canadian economy is built on the natural resources that it exports to other countries.

state A structured political community with a single source of ultimate authority over its territory.

status Indian A First Nations person registered and entitled to certain rights under the Indian Act.

Statute of Westminster A British law that permitted its Dominions to opt out of future legislation passed by the British Parliament.

stimulus Increased government spending to encourage job growth amid an economic downturn.

substantive representation A political attachment to someone in a position to defend or promote one's own interests.

suffrage The struggle to gain the right to vote in elections.

Supreme Court of Canada Canada's final court of appeal.

swing district A riding or constituency where the election outcome is uncertain.

symbolic representation A political attachment to someone or something that is seen to epitomize what it means to be a part of one's political community.

symmetrical federalism A model of federalism in which provincial governments are entitled to equal powers.

tariff A form of tax applied to imported goods and services.

tax credit An income-tax provision that reduces a citizen's taxable income and thus reduces the tax payable.

taxation policy The regulations, mechanisms, and rates set by government to generate revenues from people and businesses in its jurisdiction.

think tank An organization that performs research as a means of public advocacy.

toryism A collectivist branch of Canadian conservatism that promotes the preservation of government institutions.

trade mission A networking opportunity led by politicians hoping to sign bilateral relations agreements and for businesspeople who are looking to strike deals.

Treasury Board The cabinet committee that is tasked with reviewing and authorizing government revenue and expenditure policies.

Treasury Board Secretariat The central agency responsible for coordinating government spending, as well as human and technical resources.

treaty federalism A system of governance recognizing the equal-order relationship between First Nations and the Crown.

trial balloon A potential course of action that is reported by the media so that decision-makers can examine the reaction.

truncated party A federal or provincial political party that does not have a similarly named party at the other level of government.

Turtle Island The name used by many Indigenous communities for what is now called North America.

two-row wampum A ceremonial beaded belt symbolizing the parallel paths and equal-order relationship between the Crown and First Nations people.

unicameral legislature A legislative body consisting of one chamber (or "house").

unitary system A political system featuring a central government that chooses what powers to devolve to regional bodies.

United Nations (UN) The world's primary international political body.

vertical fiscal imbalance The federal government has an excess of revenue, and the provinces an excess of responsibilities, with respect to their constitutional obligations and fiscal capacities.

visible minorities Non-Indigenous Canadians who are non-white in colour or non-Caucasian in ethnicity.

voter turnout The proportion of eligible electors who cast ballots in an election.

wedge issue A polarizing topic that divides electors, often in a manner that favours the party that is trying to put it on the public agenda.

welfare state A suite of government programs, services, and financial supports designed to assist the least fortunate in society.

Western alienation Political discontent in areas west of Ontario, normally encompassing frustration with perceived political favouritism to areas east of Manitoba.

white paper A document outlining a proposed policy commitment by government.

whitestream Canadians Caucasians who form the traditional mainstream of Canadian society.

writ of election A legal document marking the official start of an election campaign.

Notes

CHAPTER 1

1. Richard Simeon and David J. Elkins, eds., *Small Worlds: Provinces and Parties in Canadian Political Life* (Toronto: Methuen Publications, 1980).
2. Spain continued to control lands west of the Mississippi River.
3. The cartoon was titled "Notre drapeau national"; see Charles Hou and Cynthia Hou, *Great Canadian Political Cartoons, 1820 to 1914* (Vancouver: Moody's Lookout Press, 1997).
4. Harold D. Lasswell, *Politics: Who Gets What, When, and How* (Gloucester, MA: Peter Smith Publisher Inc., 1911).

CHAPTER 2

1. Janet Ajzenstat and Peter Smith, *Canada's Origins: Liberal, Tory or Republican?* (Ottawa: Carleton University Press, 1995).
2. David E. Smith, *The Invisible Crown: The First Principle of Canadian Government* (Toronto: University of Toronto Press, 2013).
3. Peter Aucoin, Jennifer Smith, and Geoff Dinsdale, *Responsible Government: Clarifying Essentials, Dispelling Myths and Exploring Change* (Ottawa: Canadian Centre for Management Development, 2004).
4. Huron Miller, "Record of the Two-Row Wampum Belt," *Turtle Quarterly* (Native American Center for the Living Arts: Niagara Falls, NY, Winter 1980).
5. Andrew Heard, *Canadian Constitutional Conventions: The Marriage of Law and Politics*, 2nd edn (Don Mills, ON: Oxford University Press, 2014).
6. Peter Aucoin, Mark D. Jarvis, and Lori Turnbull, *Democratizing the Constitution: Reforming Responsible Government* (Toronto: Emond Montgomery, 2011).
7. Edwards v Canada (Attorney General) (1929), [1930] A.C. 124.
8. Christopher Moore, *1867: How the Fathers Made a Deal* (Toronto: McClelland & Stewart, 1997).
9. Roy Romanow, John Whyte, and Howard Leeson, *Canada . . . Notwithstanding: The Making of the Constitution 1976–1982* (Agincourt: Carswell/Methuen, 1984).
10. Patrick Monahan, *Meech Lake: The Inside Story* (Toronto: University of Toronto Press, 1991).
11. Kenneth McRoberts and Patrick Monahan, *The Charlottetown Accord, The Referendum, and the Future of Canada* (Toronto: University of Toronto Press, 1993).
12. Richard Johnston, *The Challenge of Direct Democracy: The 1992 Canadian Referendum* (Montreal and Kingston: McGill–Queen's University Press, 1996).
13. See Kiera Ladner, "Treaty Federalism: An Indigenous Vision of Canadian Federalisms," in *New Trends in Canadian Federalism*, 2nd edn, ed. Francois Rocher and Miriam Smith (Peterborough, ON: Broadview Press, 2003).
14. Tom Flanagan, *First Nations: Second Thoughts* (Montreal and Kingston: McGill–Queen's University Press, 2000): p. 195.
15. David S. Law and Mila Versteeg, "The Declining Influence of the United States Constitution," *New York University Law Review* 87, no. 3 (2012): pp. 762–858.
16. Richard Sigurdson, "Left and Right-wing Charterphobia in Canada: A Critique of the Critics," *International Journal of Canadian Studies* 7–8 (1993): pp. 95–115.

CHAPTER 3

1. See, for example, Bruce E. Johansen, *Forgotten Founders: How the American Indian Helped Shape Democracy* (Boston: Harvard Common Press, 1982).
2. Peter John Boyce, *The Queen's Other Realms: The Crown and Its Legacy in Australia, Canada, and New Zealand* (Riverwood, New South Wales: Federation Press, 2008): p. 93.
3. Barry L. Strayer, *Canada's Constitutional Revolution* (Edmonton: University of Alberta Press, 2013).
4. David Cameron and Richard Simeon, "Intergovernmental Relations in Canada: The Emergence of Collaborative Federalism," *Publius: The Journal of Federalism* 32, no. 2 (2002): pp. 49–71.
5. Kathy L. Brock, "The Politics of Asymmetrical Federalism: Reconsidering the Role and Responsibilities of Ottawa," *Canadian Public Policy* 34, no. 2 (2008): pp. 143–61.
6. John Richards, "Cracks in the Country's Foundation: The Importance of Repairing Equalization," *Canadian Political Science Review* 2, no. 3 (2008): pp. 68–83.

CHAPTER 4

1. Janine Brodie, "The Political Economy of Regionalism," in *The Canadian Political Economy*, ed. Wallace Clement and Glen Williams (Montreal and Kingston: McGill–Queen's University Press, 1989): p. 139.
2. Michael D. Ornstein, H. Michael Stevenson, and A. Paul Williams, "Region, Class and Political Culture in Canada," *Canadian Journal of Political Science* 13, no. 2 (1980): pp. 227–71.
3. Allan Kornberg and Marianne C. Stewart, "National Identification and Political Support," in *Political Support in Canada: The Crisis Years*, eds. Allan Kornberg and Harold D. Clarke (Durham, NC: Duke University Press, 1983): p. 83.
4. Harold D. Clarke, Jane Jenson, Lawrence LeDuc, and Jon H. Pammett, *Political Choice in Canada* (Toronto: McGraw–Hill Ryerson, 1979): p. 404.
5. Brodie, "Political Economy of Regionalism," p. 141.
6. Richard Simeon, "Regionalism and Canadian Political Institutions," in *Canadian Federalism: Myth or Reality?* ed. J. Meekinson (Toronto: Methuen, 1977): p. 293.
7. Tracy Summerville, "British Columbia" in *Big Worlds: Politics and Elections in the Canadian Provinces and Territories*, ed. Jared J. Wesley (University of Toronto Press, 2016), p. 171.
8. Anthony M. Sayers and David Stewart, "Alberta" in *Big Worlds: Politics and Elections in the Canadian Provinces and Territories*, ed. Jared J. Wesley (University of Toronto Press, 2016), p. 154.
9. Ken Rasmussen, "Saskatchewan" in *Big Worlds: Politics and Elections in the Canadian Provinces and Territories*, ed. Jared J. Wesley (University of Toronto Press, 2016), p. 137.
10. Jared J. Wesley, "Manitoba" in *Big Worlds: Politics and Elections in the Canadian Provinces and Territories*, ed. Jared J. Wesley (University of Toronto Press, 2016), p. 122.
11. Cameron D. Anderson, "Ontario" in *Big Worlds: Politics and Elections in the Canadian Provinces and Territories*, ed. Jared J. Wesley (University of Toronto Press, 2016), pp. 103–5.
12. Kerry Tannahill and Mebs Kanji, "Quebec" in *Big Worlds: Politics and Elections in the Canadian Provinces and Territories*, ed. Jared J. Wesley (University of Toronto Press, 2016), p. 82.

13. Mario Levesque, "New Brunswick" in *Big Worlds: Politics and Elections in the Canadian Provinces and Territories*, ed. Jared J. Wesley (University of Toronto Press, 2016), p. 60.

14. Louise Carbert, "Nova Scotia" in *Big Worlds: Politics and Elections in the Canadian Provinces and Territories*, ed. Jared J. Wesley (University of Toronto Press, 2016), p. 36.

15. Don Desserud, "Prince Edward Island" in *Big Worlds: Politics and Elections in the Canadian Provinces and Territories*, ed. Jared J. Wesley (University of Toronto Press, 2016), p. 19.

16. Luke Flanagan and Alex Marland, "Newfoundland and Labrador" in *Big Worlds: Politics and Elections in the Canadian Provinces and Territories*, ed. Jared J. Wesley (University of Toronto Press, 2016), p. 1.

17. Graham White, "The North" in *Big Worlds: Politics and Elections in the Canadian Provinces and Territories*, ed. Jared J. Wesley (University of Toronto Press, 2016), p. 190.

18. Margaret Canovan, "Trust the People! Populism and the Two Faces of Democracy," *Political Studies* 47, no. 1 (1999): pp. 2–16.

19. Valérie Vezina and Karlo Basta, "Nationalism in Newfoundland and Labrador," in *First among Unequals: The Premier, Politics and Public Policy in Newfoundland and Labrador*, eds. Alex Marland and Matthew Kerby (Montreal and Kingston: McGill–Queen's University Press, 2014).

20. George Radwanski, *Trudeau* (Toronto: Macmillan, 1978): p. 316.

21. *CBC News*, "Tory Minister Quits Post over Motion" (27 November 2006), https://www.cbc.ca/news/canada/tory-cabinet-minister-quits-post-over-motion-1.585951

22. *CBC News*, "Majority of Quebecers Believe Question of Independence Is Settled: Poll" (3 October 2016), https://www.cbc.ca/news/canada/montreal/quebec-angus-reid-canada-indepdence-1.3788110

23. Melville H. Watkins, "The Innis Tradition in Canadian Political Economy," *Canadian Journal of Political and Social Theory* 6, no. 1/2 (1982): pp. 12–34.

24. Janine Brodie, *The Political Economy of Canadian Regionalism* (Toronto: Harcourt Brace Jovanovich, 1990).

25. Harry Eckstein, "A Culturalist Theory of Political Change," *American Political Science Review* 82, no. 3 (1998): pp. 789–804.

26. Michael McDevitt, "The Partisan Child: Developmental Provocation as a Model of Political Socialization," *International Journal of Public Opinion Research* 18, no. 1 (2005): p. 69.

27. Richard E. Dawson and Kenneth Prewitt, *Political Socialization* (Boston: Little, Brown, 1969): p. 152.

28. Harry Hiller, "Regionalism as a Social Construction," in *Regionalism and Party Politics in Canada*, eds. Keith Archer and Lisa Young (Don Mills, ON: Oxford University Press, 2000): pp. 24–40.

29. Jared Wesley, *Code Politics: Campaigns and Cultures on the Canadian Prairies* (Vancouver: UBC Press, 2011).

30. James Feehan and Melvin Baker, "The Churchill Falls Contract and Why Newfoundlanders Can't Get Over It," *Policy Options* (Sept. 2010): pp. 65–70.

31. *CBC News*, "Elections Quebec Doesn't Recognize the Official Labrador-Quebec Boundary Line." (2 October 2018), https://www.cbc.ca/news/canada/newfoundland-labrador/quebec-labrador-border-1.4847624

32. Roger Gibbins, "Federalism and Regional Alienation" in *Challenges to Canadian Federalism*, eds. Martin Westmacott and Hugh Mellon (Toronto: Prentice Hall, 1998), pp. 40–52.

CHAPTER 5

1. Angus Reid Public Opinion, "Canadians Lukewarm on Monarchy, Would Pick William as Next King" (30 April 2013), www.angus-reid.com/wp-content/uploads/2013/04/2013.04.30_Monarchy_CAN.pdf.

2. Kathleen Harris, "Queen's Portrait Pulled Down, Alfred Pellan Paintings Back Up in Foreign Affairs Building," *CBC News* (9 November 2015), https://www.cbc.ca/news/politics/canada-foreign-affairs-art-queen-1.3310633

3. Susan Delacourt, *Juggernaut: Paul Martin's Campaign for Chrétien's Crown* (Toronto: McClelland & Stewart, 2013): p. 230.

4. Ashley Martin, "Chiefs of Staff for Trudeau, Harper Lift Veil on Behind-the-Scenes Roles," *Regina Leader-Post* (1 June 2018), https://www.pressreader.com/canada/regina-leader-post/20180601/281633895919911

5. Jeffrey Simpson, *The Friendly Dictatorship* (Toronto: McClelland & Stewart, 2001); Lawrence Martin, *Harperland: The Politics of Control* (Toronto: Viking, 2010).

6. Samantha Wright Allen, "Trudeau PMO Tightening Control over Ministerial Staffing, 'Identical' to Harper Approach, Says ex-Liberal MP," *The Hill Times* (25 October 2017), https://www.hilltimes.com/2017/10/25/trudeau-pmo-centralizes-power-just-like-harper-critics/123427

7. For instance, Donald J. Savoie, *Governing from the Centre: The Concentration of Power in Canadian Politics* (Toronto: University of Toronto Press, 1999).

8. In the US, members of cabinet do not hold seats in the legislature, which has more independent clout, whereas in Canada the presence of cabinet members in the legislature leads to a so-called "fusion of powers," because the people's elected representatives are meant to hold the executive to account.

9. Savoie, *Governing from the Centre*, p. 8.

10. Herman Bakvis and Steven B. Wolinetz, "Canada: Executive Dominance and Presidentialization," in *The Presidentialization of Politics: A Comparative Study of Modern Democracies*, eds. Thomas Poguntke and Paul Webb (Oxford: Oxford University Press, 2005).

11. Thomas Poguntke and Paul Webb, eds., *The Presidentialization of Politics: A Comparative Study of Modern Democracies* (Oxford: Oxford University Press, 2005).

12. Herman Bakvis, "Regional Politics and Policy in the Mulroney Cabinet, 1984–88: Towards a Theory of the Regional Minister System in Canada," *Canadian Public Policy* 15, no. 2 (1989): pp. 121–34.

13. Things are different in the consensus government model of Northwest Territories and Nunavut. The absence of political parties means that cabinet is chosen by a secret ballot process. See Graham White, *Cabinets and First Ministers* (Vancouver: UBC Press, 2005).

14. Matthew Kerby, "Worth the Wait: Determinants of Ministerial Appointment in Canada, 1935–2008," *Canadian Journal of Political Science* 42, no. 3 (2009): p. 594.

15. Linda Trimble and Manon Tremblay, "Representation of Canadian Women at the Cabinet Table," *Atlantis* 30, no. 1 (2005): p. 32.

16. Paul Martin, "The Democratic Deficit," *Policy Options* (1 December 2002).

17. Sharon Sutherland, "Responsible Government and Ministerial Responsibility: Every Reform Is Its Own Problem," *Canadian Journal of Political Science* 24, no. 1 (1991): pp. 91–120.

18. Savoie, *Governing from the Centre*.

19. Michael Chong, "Reform Act, 2014, Passes Senate, 38–14," News release (23 June 2014), http://michaelchong.ca/2015/06/23/reform-act-2014-passes-senate-38-14/.

CHAPTER 6

1. Independent Advisory Board for Senate Appointments, "Questions and Answers" (2018), https://www.canada.ca/en/campaign/independent-advisory-board-for-senate-appointments/frequently-asked-questions.html#q2

2. Heather Hughson, "Senate Reform: The First 125 Years," *Policy Options* (21 September 2015), http://policyoptions.irpp.org/magazines/september-2015/the-future-of-the-senate/senate-reform-thefirst-125-years/.

3. Alan Siaroff, "Seat Imbalance in Provincial Elections since 1900: A Quantitative Explanation," *Canadian Political Science Review* 3, no. 1 (2009): pp. 77–92.

4. Peter Regenstreif, *The Appeal of Majority Government* (Toronto: Longmans, 1965); Peter H. Russell, *Two Cheers for Minority Government: The Evolution of Canadian Parliamentary Democracy* (Toronto: Emond Montgomery, 2008).

5. Eugene Forsey, "The Problem of 'Minority' Government in Canada," *Canadian Journal of Economics and Political Science* 30 (1964): pp. 1–11; Howard Cody, "Minority Government in Canada: The Stephen Harper Experience," *American Review of Canadian Studies* 38 (2008): pp. 27–42.

6. Regenstreif, *The Appeal of Majority Government*; Russell, *Two Cheers for Minority Government: The Evolution of Canadian Parliamentary Democracy*.

7. Alison Loat and Michael MacMillan, *Tragedy in the Commons: Former Members of Parliament Speak Out about Canada's Failing Democracy* (Toronto: Random House, 2014).

8. Hansard, "Canada, House of Commons Debates," 41st Parliament, 2nd Session (19 Nov. 2013), www.parl.gc.ca/HousePublications/Publication.aspx?Language=E&Mode=1&Parl=41&Ses=2&DocId=6307745.

9. Hansard, "Canada, House of Commons Debates," 41st Parliament, 1st Session (9 Feb. 2012), www.parl.gc.ca/HousePublications/Publication.aspx?DocId=5373230&Mode=1&Language=E.

10. Royce Koop, Heather Bastedo, and Kelly Blidook, *Representation in Action: Canadian MPs in the Constituencies* (Vancouver: UBC Press, 2018).

11. Éric Grenier, "Liberal Backbenchers, Tory Leadership Hopefuls among Parliament's Biggest Dissentersm" *CBC News* (21 February 2017), https://www.cbc.ca/news/politics/grenier-party-line-voting-1.3984516

12. Loat and MacMillan, *Tragedy in the Commons: Former Members of Parliament Speak Out About Canada's Failing Democracy.*

13. Hansard, "Canada, House of Commons Debates," 42nd Parliament, 1st session (20 June 2018), http://www.ourcommons.ca/DocumentViewer/en/42-1/house/sitting-318/hansard

14. Paul E.J. Thomas and J.P. Lewis, "Executive Creep in Canadian Legislatures," *Canadian Journal of Political Science* (October 2018): pp. 1–21.

15. Ailsa Henderson, *Nunavut: Rethinking Political Culture* (Vancouver: UBC Press, 2007).

CHAPTER 7

1. CBC Digital Archives, "1970: Pierre Trudeau Says 'Just Watch Me' during October Crisis," www.cbc.ca/archives/categories/politics/civil-unrest/the-october-crisis-civil-liberties-suspended/just-watch-me.html.

2. Details outlined here are drawn from a summary of the trial evidence by Guy Quenneville, "What Happened on Gerald Stanley's Farm the Day Colten Boushie Was Shot, as Told by Witnesses," *CBC News*, 6 February 2018, https://www.cbc.ca/news/canada/saskatoon/what-happened-stanley-farm-boushie-shot-witnesses-colten-gerald-1.4520214.

3. Office of the Commissioner for Federal Judicial Affairs Canada, "Number of Federally Appointed Judges as of July 1, 2014," www.fja.gc.ca/appointments-nominations/judges-juges-eng.html.

4. Jacob Greenland and Sarah Alam, "Police Resources in Canada, 2016," Statistics Canada, 29 March 2017, https://www150.statcan.gc.ca/n1/pub/85-002-x/2017001/article/14777-eng.htm.

5. Steven Hayle, Scot Wortley, and Julian Tanner, "Race, Street Life, and Policing: Implications for Racial Profiling," *Canadian Journal of Criminology and Criminal Justice* 58, no. 3 (2016): pp. 322–53.

6. Sean Fine, "Mandatory-Minimum Sentencing Rules Unravelling into Patchwork," *The Globe and Mail*, 4 March 2018, https://www.theglobeandmail.com/news/national/mandatory-minimum-sentencing-rules-unravelling-into-patchwork/article38205652/.

7. International Centre for Prison Studies, World Prison Brief (2012), www.prisonstudies.org/info/worldbrief.

CHAPTER 8

1. Christopher A. Simon, *Public Policy: Preferences and Outcomes* (New York: Pearson, 2007): p. 1.

2. William Kelso, *American Democratic Theory: Pluralism and Its Critics* (Westport, CT: Greenwood, 1978).

3. Stuart N. Soroka, *Agenda-Setting Dynamics in Canada* (Vancouver: UBC Press, 2002).

4. Richard H. Thaler and Cass R. Sunstein, *Nudge: Improving Decisions about Health, Wealth, and Happiness* (New Haven, CT: Yale University Press, 2008).

5. Donald C. MacDonald, "Ontario's Agencies, Boards, and Commissions Come of Age," *Canadian Public Administration* 36, no. 3 (2013): p. 350.

6. Government of Manitoba, "Agencies, Boards, and Commissions" (2013), www.manitoba.ca/government/abc/index.html.

7. Government of Nova Scotia, "Agencies, Boards, and Commissions" (2013), www.novascotia.ca/exec_council/abc/.

8. Government of Ontario, "Government" (2014), www.ontario.ca/government/government.

9. John C. Courtney, "In Defence of Royal Commissions," *Canadian Public Administration* 12, no. 2 (1969): pp. 198–212.

10. MacDonald, "Ontario's Agencies, Boards, and Commissions," p. 351.

11. Michael Babad, "'Honorary' Third World Then: How WSJ Describes Canada Now," *The Globe and Mail* (8 Feb. 2012).

12. Wayne Simpson and Jared J. Wesley, "Effective Tool or Effectively Hollow? Balanced Budget Legislation in Western Canada," *Canadian Public Policy* 38, no. 3 (2012): pp. 291–313.

13. Department of Advanced Education and Skills, Newfoundland and Labrador, "Program Overview," www.aes.gov.nl.ca/income-support/overview.html.

14. The earlier example of constitutional responsibilities did not identify whether, as per section 94A, there is a federal department of old age pensions and benefits. There is not. Rather, the Department of Employment and Social Development Canada is responsible for administering the Old Age Security program.

15. Steven Chase, Erin Anderssen, and Bill Curry, "Stimulus Program Favours Tory Ridings," *The Globe and Mail*, 21 October 2009.

16. Public Service Commission of Canada, "Public Service Impartiality: Taking Stock" (Ottawa: 2008): p. 7. Available at www.psc-cfp.gc.ca/plcy-pltq/rprt/impart/impart-eng.pdf.

17. Jeffrey Simpson, *Spoils of Power: The Politics of Patronage* (Toronto: HarperCollins, 1988): p. 6.

CHAPTER 9

1. Otto Kirchheimer, "The Transformation of the Western European Party Systems," in *Political Parties and Political Development*, eds. Joseph LaPalombara and Myron Weiner (Princeton, NJ: Princeton University Press, 1966).

2. Jack McLeod, "Explanations of Our Party System," in *Politics: Canada*, 4th edn. ed. Paul Fox (Toronto: McGraw-Hill Ryerson, 1977).

3. Jared J. Wesley, ed., *Big Worlds: Politics and Elections in the Canadian Provinces and Territories* (Toronto: University of Toronto Press, 2015).

4. Christopher Adams, *Politics in Manitoba: Parties, Leaders, and Voters* (Winnipeg: University of Manitoba Press, 2008).

5. Maurice Duverger, *Political Parties: Their Organization and Activity in the Modern State* (New York: Wiley, 1954).

6. *Figueroa v. Canada (Attorney General)*, 2003, http://scc-csc .lexum.com/scc-csc/scc-csc/en/item/2069/index.do.

7. Christopher Cochrane, *Left and Right: The Small World of Political Ideas* (Montreal and Kingston: McGill-Queen's University Press, 2015).

8. See for example Elise von Scheel, "Cabinet Ministers, MPs Spar over Who Gets to Call Themselves a Feminist," *CBC News*, 7 July 2018, https://www.cbc.ca/news/politics/ministers-mp-feminism-twitter-1.4737965.

9. Jack McLeod, "Explanations of Our Party System," in *Politics: Canada*, 4th edn. ed. Paul Fox (Toronto: McGraw-Hill Ryerson, 1977).

10. Gad Horowitz, "Conservatism, Liberalism and Socialism in Canada: An Interpretation," *Canadian Journal of Political Science* 32 (1966): p. 158.

11. R. Kenneth Carty, "Three Canadian Party Systems: An Interpretation of the Development of National Politics," in *Party Democracy in Canada*, ed. G.C. Perlin (Scarborough, ON: Prentice-Hall, 1988): pp. 15–30; R. Kenneth Carty, William Cross, and Lisa Young, *Rebuilding Canadian Party Politics* (Vancouver: UBC Press, 2000).

12. Royce Koop and Amanda Bittner, "Parties and Elections after 2011: The Fifth Canadian Party System?" in *Parties, Elections, and the Future of Canadian Politics*, eds. Amanda Bittner and Royce Koope (Vancouver: UBC Press, 2013): pp. 308–31.

13. Rand Dyck, "Links between Federal and Provincial Parties and Party Systems," in *Representation, Integration and Political Parties in Canada*, ed. Herman Bakvis (vol. 14 of the Research Studies for the Royal Commission on Electoral Reform and Party Financing): pp. 129–77.

14. Joseph Wearing, *The L-Shaped Party: The Liberal Party of Canada 1958–1980* (Toronto: McGraw-Hill Ryerson, 1981); Reginald Whitaker, *The Government Party: Organizing and Financing the Liberal Party of Canada 1930–58* (Toronto: University of Toronto Press, 1977).

15. Laura Payton, "NDP Votes to Take 'Socialism' out of Party Constitution," *CBC News*, 14 April 2013, www.cbc.ca/news/politics/ndp-votes-to-take-socialism-out-of-party-constitution-1.1385171.

16. Royce Koop, *Grassroots Liberals: Organizing for Local and National Politics* (Vancouver: UBC Press, 2011).

17. New Democratic Party of Canada, "Constitution of the New Democratic Party of Canada" (2013), http://xfer.ndp.ca/2013/constitution/2013_CONSTITUTION_E.pdf.

18. Liberal Party of Canada, "Constitution" (2016), https://www.liberal.ca/wp-content/uploads/2016/07/constitution-en.pdf.

19. A notable case of leadership change saw Kevin Rudd lead the Australian Labour Party to victory in 2007, but within three years his public approval ratings had plummeted. In 2010, his colleague Julia Gillard announced that she would seek the leadership, prompting Rudd to immediately resign. Gillard led Labour to another election victory in 2012, and in 2013 Rudd attempted to coordinate a caucus vote against her. He was successful on the second attempt and once again became leader and prime minister. However, this time Rudd held the job for less than three months, as Labour was defeated in the 2013 election and was replaced by Liberal leader Tony Abbott.

20. Joanna Everitt, Elisabeth Gidengil, Patrick Fournier, and Neil Nevitte, "Patterns of Party Identification in Canada," in *Election*, ed. Heather MacIvor (Toronto: Emond Montgomery, 2009).

21. Joseph Wearing, "Finding Our Parties' Roots," in *Canadian Parties in Transition*, 2nd edn. eds. Brian Tanguay and Alain-G. Gagnon (Toronto: Nelson Canada, 2009): pp. 14–31.

22. Inter-Parliamentary Union, "Women in National Parliaments," (2018), http://archive.ipu.org/wmn-e/classif.htm.

CHAPTER 10

1. José Antonio Cheibub, Jennifer Gandhi, and James Raymond Vreeland, "Democracy and Dictatorship Revisited," *Public Choice* 143 (April 2010): pp. 67–101.

2. Elections Canada, *A History of the Right to Vote in Canada*, 2nd edn. (Ottawa: Office of the Chief Electoral Officer of Canada, 2007): p. 46.

3. Postmedia News, "Conservatives Drop Appeal of 'In and Out' Ruling," *National Post* (6 March 2012).

4. John Andrew Cousins, "Electoral Reform for Prince Edward Island," *Canadian Parliamentary Review* 25, no. 4 (2002): pp. 22–31.

5. Alan C. Cairns, "The Electoral System and the Party System in Canada, 1921–1965," *Canadian Journal of Political Science* 1, no. 1 (1968): pp. 55–80.

6. Cairns (1968): p. 55.

7. Alex Marland, "Promotional and Other Spending by Party Candidates in the 2006 Canadian Federal Election Campaign," *Canadian Journal of Media Studies* 3, no. 1 (2008): pp. 57–89.

8. For instance, see Lawrence LeDuc, "The Leaders' Debates: (. . . and the winner is . . .)," in *The Canadian General Election of 1997*, eds. Alan Frizzell and Jon H. Pammett (Toronto: Dundurn, 1997): p. 207.

9. Madeline Smith, "Trudeau Faces Treacherous Political Territory at Calgary Stampede ahead of Fall Federal Election," *Toronto Star*, 11 July 2019, https://www.thestar.com/calgary/2019/07/11/trudeau-faces-treacherous-political-territory-at-calgary-stampede-ahead-of-fall-federal-election.html.

10. André Blais, Elisabeth Gidengil, Richard Nadeau, and Neil Nevitte, "Campaign Dynamics in the 2000 Canadian Election: How the Leader Debates Salvaged the Conservative Party," *Political Science and Politics* 36 (2003): pp. 45–50.

11. Tom Brook, *Getting Elected in Canada* (Stanford, ON: Mercury Press, 1991).

12. Anthony M. Sayers, *Candidates and Constituency Campaigns in Canadian Elections* (Vancouver: UBC Press, 1999).

13. Tom Flanagan, "Campaign Strategy: Triage and the Concentration of Resources," in *Election*, ed. Heather MacIvor (Toronto: Emond Montgomery, 2010).

14. R. Kenneth Carty and Munroe Eagles, "Do Local Campaigns Matter? Campaign Spending, the Local Canvass and Party Support in Canada," *Electoral Studies* 18 (1999): pp. 69–87.

15. Statistics Canada, "Reasons for Not Voting in the May 2, 2011, Federal Election," *The Daily*, 5 July 2011, www.statcan.gc.ca/daily-quotidien/110705/dq110705a-eng.htm.

16. Jon H. Pammett and Lawrence LeDuc, "Explaining the Turnout Decline in Canadian Federal Elections: A New Survey of

Non-Voters," Elections Canada (2003), www.elections.ca/res/rec/part/tud/TurnoutDecline.pdf.

17.   Timothy J. Feddersen, "Rational Choice Theory and the Paradox of Not Voting," *The Journal of Economic Perspectives* 18 (2004): pp. 99–112.

18.   Donley T. Studlar, "Canadian Exceptionalism: Explaining Differences over Time in Provincial and Federal Voter Turnout," *Canadian Journal of Political Science* 34 (2001): pp. 299–319.

19.   Content here is drawn from James Farney and Renan Levine, "Canadian Voting Behaviour in Comparative Perspective," in *The Comparative Turn in Canadian Political Science*, eds. Linda A. White, Richard Simeon, Robert Vipond, and Jennifer Wallner (Vancouver: UBC Press, 2008): pp. 194–204. Also, Andrea Perrella, "Overview of Voting Behaviour Theories," in *Election*, ed. Heather MacIvor (Toronto: Emond Montgomery, 2010): pp. 221–49.

CHAPTER 11

1.   Hugh Heclo and Lester M. Salamon, *The Illusion of Presidential Government* (Boulder, CO: Westview, 1981).

2.   Quoted in Jack McLeod, ed., *The Oxford Book of Canadian Political Anecdotes* (Toronto: Oxford University Press, 1988): p. 28.

3.   Marshall McLuhan, *Understanding Media: The Extensions of Man* (New York: New American Library, 1964).

4.   Quoted in Susan Delacourt, "Justin Trudeau's Twist on Helping Out the Media: Delacourt." *Toronto Star*, 28 April 2017, https://www.thestar.com/news/insight/2017/04/28/justin-trudeaus-twist-on-helping-out-the-media-delacourt.html.

5.   "The Future of Canadian Journalism," *Policy Options*, 23 January 2017, http://policyoptions.irpp.org/magazines/january-2017/the-future-of-canadian-journalism/.

6.   Allan Levine, *Scrum Wars: The Prime Ministers and the Media* (Toronto: Dundurn Press, 1993).

7.   Rebecca Joseph, "Trust in the Media Fell 4% in Past Year: Ipsos Poll," *Global News*, 25 May 2018.

8.   Paul Attallah and Angela Burton, "Television, the Internet, and the Canadian Federal Election of 2000," in *The Canadian General Election of 2000*, eds. Jon H. Pammett and Christopher Dornan (Toronto: Dundurn, 2001): pp. 215–41.

9.   Pew Research Center, "Publics Globally Want Unbiased News Coverage, but Are Divided on Whether Their News Media Deliver," 11 January 2018, www.pewglobal.org.

10.   All profiled examples won or were finalists for Canadian Journalism Foundation awards. See http://cjf-fjc.ca/awards/cjf-awards.

11.   Beatrice Britneff, "Parliamentary Press Gallery Now the Smallest It's Been in 22 Years," *iPolitics*, 8 December 2016, https://ipolitics.ca/2016/12/08/parliamentary-press-gallery-now-the-smallest-its-been-in-22-years/.

12.   Pew Research Center, "Publics Globally Want Unbiased News Coverage, but Are Divided on Whether Their News Media Deliver," 11 January 2018, www.pewglobal.org.

13.   Peter Loewen, Andrew Potter, Benjamin Allen Stevens, and Taylor Owen, "What Do Canadians Want From Their News?" *Policy Options*, 30 October 2018, http://policyoptions.irpp.org/magazines/october-2018/what-do-canadians-want-from-their-news/.

14.   Frédérick Bastien, *Breaking News? Politics, Journalism and Infotainment on Quebec Television* (Vancouver: UBC Press, 2018).

15.   Rebecca Joseph, "Trust in the Media Fell 4% in Past Year: Ipsos poll," *Global News*, 25 May 2018.

16.   Robert Entman, "Framing Bias: Media in the Distribution of Power," *Journal of Communication* 57 (2007): pp. 163–73.

17.   Augie Fleras, *The Media Gaze: Representations of Diversities in Canada* (Vancouver: UBC Press, 2011).

18.   Linda Trimble, *Ms. Prime Minister: Gender, Media, and Leadership* (Toronto: University of Toronto Press, 2017).

19.   Erin Tolley, *Framed: Media and the Coverage of Race in Canadian Politics* (Vancouver: UBC Press, 2015).

20.   See Karim H. Karim, "Are Ethnic Media Alternative?" in *Alternative Media in Canada*, eds. Kirsten Kozolanka, Patricia Mazepam and David Skinner (Vancouver: UBC Press, 2012): pp. 165–83.

21.   Service Canada, "Service Canada: People Serving People" (2014), www.serviceCanada.gc.ca/eng/home.shtml.

22.   "Canada Ranked 51st in Access to Information List," *Toronto Star*, 22 June 2012.

23.   Reporters Without Borders, "2018 World Press Freedom Index," 2018, https://rsf.org/en/ranking.

24.   Kirsten Kozolanka, ed., *Publicity and the Canadian State: Critical Communications Perspectives* (Toronto: University of Toronto Press, 2014).

25.   L. Fraser, *Propaganda* (Oxford: Oxford University Press, 1957).

26.   Susan Delacourt, *Shopping for Votes: How Politicians Choose Us and We Choose Them* (Toronto: Douglas & McIntyre, 2013).

CHAPTER 12

1.   Government Relations Institute of Canada, "Code of Professional Conduct" (2014), http://gric-irgc.ca/about/code-of-professional-conduct-2.

2.   Robert M. Alexander, *The Classics of Interest Group Behaviour* (Belmont, CA: Thompson Wadsworth, 2006).

3.   Rand Dyck, *Canadian Politics: Critical Approaches*, 5th edn (Toronto: Nelson, 2008): p. 392.

4.   A. Paul Pross, "Pressure Groups: Adaptive Instruments of Political Communication," in *Pressure Group Behaviour in Canadian Politics*, ed. A. Paul Pross (Toronto: McGraw-Hill Ryerson, 1975): p. 1.

5.   Alexander, *The Classics of Interest Group Behaviour*.

6.   Brian A. Tanguay and Barry J. Kay, "Political Activity of Local Interest Groups," in *Interest Groups and Elections in Canada*, vol. 2 of the Research Studies of the Royal Commission on Electoral Reform and Party Financing, ed. F. Leslie Seidle (Toronto: Dundurn, 1991).

7.   Lisa Young and Joanna Marie Everitt, *Advocacy Groups* (Vancouver: UBC Press, 2004): p. 6. See also Fraser Valentine, "Public Interest Groups: Some Important Facts" (2013), www.ilCanada.ca/article/public-interest-groups-251.asp.

8.   Conference Board of Canada, "About Us" (2014), www.conferenceboard.ca/about-cboc/default.aspx.

9.   Jacquetta Newman and A. Brian Tanguay, "Crashing the Party: The Politics of Interest Groups and Social Movements," in *Citizen Politics: Research and Theory in Canadian Political Behaviour*, ed. Joanna Everitt and Brenda O'Neill (Don Mills, ON: Oxford University Press, 2002).

CHAPTER 13

1.   Peter Stursberg, *Diefenbaker: Leadership Gained, 1956–62* (Toronto: University of Toronto Press, 1975): pp. 185–6.

2.   Joanna M. Everitt and Michael Camp, "Changing the Game Changes the Frame: The Media's Use of Lesbian Stereotypes in Leadership versus Election Campaigns," *Canadian Political Science Review* 3, no. 3 (2009): pp. 24–39.

3.   See Claude Denis, *We Are Not You: First Nations and Canadian Modernity* (Toronto: Broadview Press, 1997).

4.   Globe Staff and Wire Services, "A Viola Desmond Primer: Who's the Woman on Today's New Canadian $10 Bill?" *The Globe and*

Mail, 19 November 2018, https://www.theglobeandmail.com/canada/article-viola-desmond-10-bill-explainer/.

5. Rick Mercer, "Rant: Teen Suicide," CBCtv YouTube Channel, 18 December 2013, www.youtube.com/watch?v=J1OvtBa2FK8.

6. Standing Senate Committee on Social Affairs, Science and Technology, *In from the Margins* (2013).

7. The term is also commonly used to refer to the limited influence of backbenchers compared with the growing clout of the Prime Minister's Office. However, here we refer to it in the context of population diversity and the representation of that diversity.

8. Karen Bird, "Obstacles to Ethnic Minority Representation in Local Government in Canada," in *Our Diverse Cities*, ed. Caroline Andrew (Ottawa: Metropolis and the Federation of Canadian Municipalities, 2004): pp. 182–6.

9. Nelson Wiseman, "The Pattern of Prairie Politics," in *Party Politics in Canada*, 8th edn, eds. Hugh Thorburn and Alan Whitehorn (Toronto: Prentice Hall, 2001); R. Kalin and J.W. Berry, "Ethnic and Multicultural Attitudes," in *Ethnicity and Culture in Canada: The Research Landscape*, eds. J.W. Berry and J. Laponce (Toronto: University of Toronto Press, 1994): pp. 308–9.

10. Joanna Everitt, "Gender and Sexual Diversity in Provincial Election Campaigns," *Canadian Political Science Review* 9, no. 1 (2015): 177–92.

11. Equal Voice, *Power in Parity*, https://www.equalvoice.ca/power_in_parity (Accessed: 28 October 2019).

12. Sandra Martin, "Former Lieutenant-Governor Took Discrimination as Personal Challenge," *The Globe and Mail*, 20 October 2012, http://v1.theglobeandmail.com/servlet/story/LAC.20121020.OBALEXANDER1019PRINTATL/BDAStory/BDA/deaths.

13. All Band members must be status Indians, but not all status Indians are Band members. Prior to Bill C-31, Band membership was automatically assigned with status. Since 1985, individual Bands have the ability to define their own membership rules (or to remain under the old system of automatic designation).

14. "'Our Land': Nunavut Becoming a Territory Celebrated in Seventh Stamp Marking Canada 150," Canada Post News Release, 30 May 2017, https://www.canadapost.ca/web/en/blogs/announcements/details.page?article=2017/05/30/our_land_nunavut_bec&cat-type=announcements&cat=newsreleases.

15. See Statistics Canada, "First Nations People, Métis and Inuit in Canada: Diverse and Growing Populations" (2018), https://www150.statcan.gc.ca/n1/pub/89-659-x/89-659-x2018001-eng.htm.

16. "Canada Signs Historic Post-Secondary Education Agreement with Métis Nation," Métis Nation, 10 June 2019, http://www.metisnation.ca/index.php/news/canada-signs-historic-post-secondary-education-agreement-with-metis-nation.

CHAPTER 14

1. See for example Brendan Haley, "From Staples Trap to Carbon Trap: Canada's Peculiar Form of Carbon Lock-in," *Studies in Political Economy* 88, no. 1 (2011): pp. 97–132.

2. Report of the Standing Senate Committee on Banking, Trade and Commerce, "Tear Down These Walls: Dismantling Canada's Internal Trade Barriers," June 2016, https://sencanada.ca/content/sen/committee/421/BANC/Reports/2016-06-13_BANC_FifthReport_SS-2_tradebarriers(FINAL)_E.pdf.

3. Canada, "Key Findings of the Commission," Commission of Inquiry into the Investigation of the Bombing of Air India Flight 182 (2010), http://epe.lac-bac.gc.ca/100/206/301/pco-bcp/commissions/air_india/2010-07-23/www.majorcomm.ca/en/reports/finalreport/key-findings.pdf.

4. Michael Friscolanti, "The Merciless and Meticulous Toronto 18 Ringleader Goes to Prison for Life," *Maclean's* (18 January 2010).

5. Steven Chase, "Ottawa Attack: MPs Fashioned Spears while Harper Whisked into a Closet," *The Globe and Mail* (24 October 2014), https://www.theglobeandmail.com/news/politics/ottawa-attack-mps-fashioned-spears-while-harper-hid-in-closet/article21278580/.

6. "CSEC's Collection of Metadata Shows Ability to 'Track Everyone'," *CBC News* (4 February 2014), www.cbc.ca/news/technology/csec-s-collection-of-metadata-shows-ability-to-track-everyone-1.2522916.

7. Colin Freeze, "How CSEC Became an Electronic Spying Giant," *The Globe and Mail* (30 November 2013).

8. Colin Freeze, "'Five Eyes' Intelligence-Sharing Program Threatens Canadians Abroad, Watchdog Warns," *The Globe and Mail* (31 October 2013).

9. North Atlantic Treaty Organization, "The North Atlantic Treaty," (4 April 1949), www.nato.int/cps/en/natolive/official_texts_17120.htm.

10. Ekos, "Decisive Opposition to Canada's Afghanistan Mission," 16 July 2009, http://ekos.com/admin/articles/cbc-2009-07-16.pdf.

11. United Nations, "UN at a Glance," 14 February 2014, www.un.org/en/aboutun/index.shtml.

12. The Commonwealth, "Aso Rock Declaration on Development and Democracy" (2003), http://thecommonwealth.org/sites/default/files/history-items/documents/AsoRockDeclaration2003.pdf.

13. André Lecours, "Paradiplomacy: Reflections on the Foreign Policy and International Relations of Regions," *International Negotiation* 7, no. 1 (2002): pp. 91–114.

14. "Offices abroad," Quebec: Relations internationals et Francophonie, modified on 18 April 2019, http://www.mrif.gouv.qc.ca/en/ministere/representation-etranger.

15. United Nations Development Programme, "Human Development Report 2016" (2016), http://hdr.undp.org/en/2016-report

16. United Nations Development Programme, "Human Development Indices and Indicators: 2018 Statistical Update, Canada" (2018), http://hdr.undp.org/sites/all/themes/hdr_theme/country-notes/CAN.pdf.

17. Climate Transparency, "Brown to Green: The G20 Transition to a Low-Carbon Economy, Canada" (2018), https://www.climate-transparency.org/wp-content/uploads/2018/11/BROWN-TO-GREEN_2018_Canada.pdf.

Index

Note: Tables are indicated by a *t*, Figures are indicated by a *f*, and Photos are in *italics*

elite parties, 292

Elizabeth II, 20, 34, 46, *46*, 132–33

emergency federalism, 76*t*, 77, 87

Emerson, David, 322

employment equity, 449–50

employment insurance (EI), 250, 279

Employment Insurance Act, 279

English Canada, 78

entitlement programs, 274–78

equalization payments, 23, 80–82, 82*f*

Equal Voice, 421, 423, 463

Esselment, Anna, 325

Essential Readings in Canadian Government and Politics (Russell, Rocher, Thompson, D., and Bittner), 26

ethics, government and, 281–83

ethics commissioner, 188

ethnicity, 6, 9–10; as cleavage, 23; glass ceilings and, 439; in political parties, 448; visible minorities and, 443–46

ethnic nationalism, 109

EU (European Union), 68, 474

eugenics, *55*

European Union (EU), 68, 474

Everitt, Joanna, 323, 411, 431

executive: accountability of, 130–31, 151–55; BNA Act and, 136; central agencies and, 158–59, 259; formal, 131–36, 132*f*, 137*f*; political, 131–32, 132*f*, 136–37, 137*f*; power, 131, 155; presidentialization and, 142; provincial legislatures and dominance of, 199; public-service management and, 155–59, 157*f*; size of, 131; structure of, 138*t*. *See also* cabinet

executive federalism, 85–86

Eyolfson, Brian, *228*

Facebook, 376, 431; Cambridge Analytica scandal and, 396

Fairclough, Ellen, 439

"fake news," 372, 430–31, 430*f*

Famous Five, 416

farmers, as interest group, 418

federal courts, 231

federal government: central agencies of, 158–59, 259; elections and compositions of, 341, 341*f*; line departments of, 259; provincial law and, 73; regions defined by, 103–4; revenues of, 270–73, 271*f*; social safety net and, 79

federalism, 3*t*, 66; Alberta and, 79; asymmetrical, 76*t*, 78; BNA and, 71–73; Canadian history of, 69; centralized, 71–73, 77–78, 88*f*; classical, 76, 76*t*, 89; collaborative, 76*t*, 77; confederations compared to, 68, 68*f*; Constitution Act of 1982 and, 73; in constitutional monarchy, 69–71; constitution and, 34; co-operative, 76, 76*t*; courts and, 224; debates on success of, 92–93; decentralized, 71–73, 77–78, 88*f*; definition of, 68; emergency, 76*t*, 77, 87; evolution

of, 87–89; executive, 85–86; fiscal, 78–85; fiscal gaps and, 79–80; functional, 86; healthcare and, 83; imbalances and, 79–84; interest groups and, 415, 416; inter-state and intra-state, 85–87; jurisdiction and, 70, 70*t*; limits of, 75; models of, 76–78, 76*t*; municipalities and, 71; Newfoundland and Labrador and, 79–80; oil pipeline debates and, 74; regionalism and, 120–21; Senate and, 86–87; sovereignty and, 70; symmetrical, 76*t*, 78, 89; territories and, 70–71; tools of, 73–74; treaty, 52, 76*t*, 78; unitary system compared to, 67–68, 68*f*; in US, 67, 68*f*

Federalism (Smith, J.), 89

Federalism: An Introduction (Anderson, G.), 89

federal paramountcy, 72

federal party systems, 302–5, 303*t*

federal ridings, 343, 345*f*, 346

federal spending power, 73

feminism, 10

Fête Nationale du Québec, 99

Fights of Our Lives (Duffy), 124

filibuster, 203

financial administration, public policy and, 263–80

Financial Administration Act, 282

Financial and Consumer Services Commission, New Brunswick, 260*t*

first minister diplomacy, 143

First Minister Diplomacy (Simeon), 159

first ministers, 3*t*, 136, 139; advisors to, 148–49; constraints on, 142–43; meetings of, 86; patronage and, 140; power of, 141–42

First Nations, 4, 7, 24, 45, 238–39, 457–58, 461. *See also* Indigenous peoples

First Nations (Flanagan), 463

first past the post system, 338–42

fiscal federalism, 78–85

Fiscal Federalism (Anderson, G.), 90

fiscal gaps, federalism and, 79–80

fiscal update, 265

Five Eyes, 488

fixed-date elections, 167, 194, 331, 350

flag, creation of national, 20–21, 21*f*

Flag Act of 1965, 21

Flanagan, Tom, 52, 323, 463

flat tax, 272

fleur-de-lis, 21, 21*f*

FLQ (Front de Libération du Québec), 110, 485

flu vaccines, 256–57

focusing events, 382

Ford, Doug, 106, 107, *148*

Ford case, 57

foreign aid, 496–97, 496*f*, 502–3

formal executive, 131–36, 132*f*, 137*f*

formalistic representation, 441*t*, 442

Forsey, Eugene, 26

Fournier, Patrick, 323

fourth estate, 372

Framed (Tolley), 384

framing, media, 383–84

franchise, 331–34, 333*t*

francophones, 17, 18; employment equity and, 450; interculturalism in Quebec and, 452–53; Quiet Revolution and, 19, 87, 110; reasonable accommodation for, 451–52, 451*t*; representation of, 340, 446; rights of, 54

La Francophonie, 494–95, 500

Francophonie Games, 495

Frank v. Canada, 334

freedoms: democratic, 56; fundamental, 55–56; types of, 54. *See also* Charter of Rights and Freedoms

free trade, 22, 471–80, 475*t*

free votes, 187–89

French Canada, 78. *See also* francophones

Front de Libération du Québec (FLQ), 110, 485

Fulton-Favreau formula, 47

functional federalism, 86

G7 (Group of Seven), 479, *479*

G20 (Group of Twenty), 479–80

Gallant, Brian, 152

Gang of Eight, 45

gas prices, *7*

Gazette, 203

GBA⁺ (gender-based analysis plus), 253

gender, 6; in cabinets, 147, *149*; Supreme Court appointments and, 235. *See also* diversity; pluralism; women

gender-based analysis plus (GBA⁺), 253

The Genetic Imaginary (Gerlach), 242

geography: as cleavage, 7–9; culture and, 8, 8*f*; SMP system and, 339–40

Gerlach, Neil, 242

Gerry, Elbridge, 344

gerrymandering, 343–44

getting out the vote (GOTV), 354

GGs (governor generals), 133–35, 151

Gibbins, Roger, 124

Gibbon, John Murray, 443

GIC (Governor in Council), 150–51

Gidengil, Elisabeth, 323, 364

GIS (Guaranteed Income Supplement), 277–78

glass ceilings, 439, 440*t*, 446

Global News, 380

The Globe and Mail, 374, 383, *383*, 392

Goff, Patricia, 500

Gomery, John, 227, 393

Gomery Commission, 283

Goods and Services Tax (GST), 22, 203, 272–73

GOTV (getting out the vote), 354

Governance and Public Policy in Canada (Atkinson), 283

Governing from the Bench (Macfarlane), 242

Governing from the Centre (Savoie), 159

government, 4; advertising, 391–93, 392*f*; agencies of, 261; boards of, 261; chain of command in, 251; coalition, 177*t*, 178*f*,